T0392478

Storyteller

Storyteller

THE LIFE OF
ROBERT LOUIS STEVENSON

Leo Damrosch

Yale UNIVERSITY PRESS

New Haven & London

Published with assistance from the Kingsley Trust Association Publication Fund established by the Scroll and Key Society of Yale College. Published with support from the Fund established in memory of Oliver Baty Cunningham, a distinguished graduate of the Class of 1917, Yale College, Captain, 15th United States Field Artillery, born in Chicago September 17, 1894, and killed while on active duty near Thiaucourt, France, September 17, 1918, the twenty-fourth anniversary of his birth.

Copyright © 2025 by Leo Damrosch. All rights reserved. This book may not be reproduced, in whole or in part, including illustrations, in any form (beyond that copying permitted by Sections 107 and 108 of the U.S. Copyright Law and except by reviewers for the public press), without written permission from the publishers.

Yale University Press books may be purchased in quantity for educational, business, or promotional use. For information, please e-mail sales.press@yale.edu (U.S. office) or sales@yaleup.co.uk (U.K. office).

Set in Adobe Garamond type by Integrated Publishing Solutions.
Printed in the United States of America.

Library of Congress Control Number: 2024950785
ISBN 978-0-300-26862-1 (hardcover)

A catalogue record for this book is available from the British Library.

Authorized Representative in the EU: Easy Access System Europe, Mustamäe tee 50, 10621 Tallinn, Estonia, gpsr.requests@easproject.com

10 9 8 7 6 5 4 3 2 1

Contents

Acknowledgments, vii

Introduction: The Man and the Artist, 1
1 The Early Years, 11
2 Schooling and Travels, 38
3 Happiness in the Countryside, 46
4 The Master Builders, 60
5 A New Life at the University, 68
6 "I Want Pleasure," 83
7 A "Horrible Atheist," 98
8 A Mentor and a Madonna, 107
9 "Ordered South," 121
10 First Steps as a Writer, 132
11 Artists and Boats, 143
12 Enter Fanny, 156
13 The Donkey Book, 173

14 From Glasgow to San Francisco, 187

15 A Year in California, 201

16 Edinburgh and Davos, 225

17 A Breakthrough in the Highlands, 236

18 Alpine Cold, and *Treasure Island*, 256

19 Two Years on the Riviera, 269

20 A Home in England, 279

21 A Torrent of Writing, 297

22 Creating a Myth: *Jekyll and Hyde*, 305

23 *Kidnapped*, 315

24 Farewell to Europe, 327

25 An Adirondack Winter, 331

26 Sailing the High Seas, 351

27 Hawaii, 365

28 The Cruise of the *Equator*, 374

29 Interlude, 387

30 Life at Vailima, 398

31 Missionaries, Chiefs, and Bureaucrats, 422

32 The End of Paradise, 433

33 The Last Novels, 446

34 "I Was Not Born for Age," 461

Epilogue, 469

Chronology, 477

Notes, 483

Illustration Credits, 527

Index, 533

Color Plates follow Page 278

Acknowledgments

As with my four previous Yale University Press books, I owe particular thanks to three people. Tina Bennett, my agent, has provided advice and encouragement throughout. Jennifer Banks, my peerless editor, managed the development and publication process with wisdom and skill. And my wife, Joyce van Dyke, who brings a fellow writer's insight, inspired the idea of this book, gave crucial advice throughout, and improved every page and every chapter with a keen critical eye. I'm grateful as well for valuable comments by David Damrosch, Norman Etherington, and Robert Friedman. Robin DuBlanc contributed superb copy editing, and Margaret Otzel oversaw the final stages of production.

Storyteller

Introduction

THE MAN AND THE ARTIST

Robert Louis Stevenson spent the last day of his life working on his latest novel in his mountainside home in Samoa. That evening he poured wine for his wife Fanny and himself, and was mixing mayonnaise for a salad when he suddenly said, "Do I look strange?" and fell over backwards. It was a cerebral hemorrhage, and the doctor who was called to his side could do nothing to help. Three weeks previously, at a feast attended by his many Samoan friends, he had celebrated his forty-fourth birthday.

All his life Stevenson suffered from a dangerous lung condition that may or may not have been tuberculosis, and he drove himself hard because he expected to die young. Yet everyone who knew him was impressed by his intense vitality. Andrew Lang said, "He ran forth to embrace life like a lover." Sidney Colvin, recalling "fourteen years of close intimacy" with Stevenson, complained indignantly that because he was thin and often ill, people described him as "shadowy" and "anemic."

> He was indeed all his life a bag of bones, a very lath for leanness. Nevertheless when he was in the room it was the other people, and not he, who seemed the shadows. The most robust of ordinary men seemed to turn dim and null in the presence of the vitality that glowed in the steadfast, penetrating fire of the lean man's eyes, the rich, compelling charm of his smile, the lissome swiftness of his movements and lively expressiveness of

his gestures, above all in the irresistible sympathetic play and abundance of his talk. Anemic!

Colvin added, "He was a fellow of infinite and unrestrained jest and yet of infinite earnest, the one very often a mask for the other; a poet, an artist, an adventurer." In a poem about Stevenson, his friend William Ernest Henley said he had "much Antony, of Hamlet most of all." Colvin liked the description but said it left out "the one essential, never-failing and ever-endearing thing under all that play and diversity of being. This was the infinitely kind and tender, devotedly generous, brave and loving heart of the man."[1]

Numerous photographs of Stevenson exist, but few of them capture these qualities. They are in black and white, of course, and often dim. The long exposures that photographers required encouraged a fixed expression, and as Stevenson commented himself, the sitters were expected to adopt "a fitting solemnity of visage."[2]

A fine exception is a portrait made near the end of his life, which has been enhanced in a superbly colorized adaptation by Grant Kemp (color plate 1). An old school friend wrote after his death, "The eyes were always genial, however gaily the lights danced in them, but about the mouth there was something a little tricksy and mocking." And a comment by someone who had been a child when his family used to entertain Stevenson remembered "the fun, vivacity, courteousness, and daring curiously blended, with a smile that was enchanting, the more so perhaps because the corners of his mouth turned down, as I recollect it, and his eyes smiled even more than his mouth. Of what the talk was about I have no idea, no doubt I was too young to understand, but I know I sat enchanted watching the play of expression in his face."[3]

His eyes were unusually far apart and struck everyone as compelling. Mark Twain, who spent an afternoon chatting with him in Washington Square in New York, called them "Stevenson's special distinction and commanding feature," burning with "a smouldering rich fire."[4]

MASTER STORYTELLER

After her husband's death, Fanny wrote, "There have been few lives of such absorbing interest as Louis's—even leaving literature out of the question." This biography will relate the events of that life in full, including a remarkable amount of travel, but of course literature cannot be left out of the question; I aim to celebrate what is great in his writing, and to inspire new readers to enjoy it. Indeed, art and life were inseparable for him. He didn't just write about adventure, he lived it, as he said himself in a playful self-portrait not long before his death: "He loved but three things, women, adventure, art—and art the least of these three, and, as men whispered, adventure the most."[5]

The biographer Richard Holmes has said, "I started out writing, some thirty years ago, largely because of Stevenson. He was the man who opened the magic door. His wit, his style, his courage, his wanderlust, all enchanted me; and they still do. He made England seem small, and the world look big. He made the dreams of childhood sing with adult possibilities."[6]

By the time of his death Stevenson had a high reputation, not just for his novels but for his essays and poems as well. But the modernists of the twentieth century soon repudiated him, as they did "Victorianism" in general—though he was hardly a typical Victorian. The Bloomsbury group held him in contempt, and by 1947 the Scottish critic David Daiches acknowledged, "The works of Robert Louis Stevenson are not widely read today." Four years after that, the author of the first major biography, J. C. Furnas, commented that when he was working on it people would say, "'How interesting that you are doing a life of Stevenson! I hadn't thought of him since my children read him,' as if the subject were Beatrix Potter."[7]

It's true that by then *Treasure Island* was his only work that most people had heard of, apart from the novella *Strange Case of Dr. Jekyll and Mr. Hyde,* which is far from typical of his writing and was known mainly in film adaptations. The widely used *Norton Anthology of English Literature* omitted him completely from seven successive editions, from 1962 to 2000, and when he was finally included in 2006 it was only with *Dr. Jekyll and Mr. Hyde.*

Yet many of the world's greatest writers continued to honor Stevenson as a master, which is all the more impressive since their own work was very different from his. He is a writer's writer, appreciated by fellow artists who understand how brilliantly his fictions are constructed. In Proust's *Le temps retrouvé,* the aesthete Swann hears Stevenson dismissed as a children's writer and protests, "But he is *tout à fait* a great writer, I assure you, Monsieur de Goncourt, equal to the very greatest." Vladimir Nabokov, in lectures at Cornell in 1940, analyzed him acutely and at length as a master of narrative; Italo Calvino called himself "a Stevenson worshipper" and praised his "marvelous lightness."[8]

Stevenson would have agreed wholeheartedly with something else Calvino said: "I belong to that portion of humanity that spends a large part of its waking hours in a special world, a world made up of horizontal lines where the words follow one another one at a time, where every sentence and every paragraph occupies its set place: a world that can be very rich, maybe even richer than the nonwritten one." Yet true though that is in its way, it's only partially true for Stevenson. It was always life, not art, that he put first.⁹

Jorge Luis Borges, who was fluent in English and read Stevenson in the original, once listed things he especially liked: *Me gustan los relojes de arena, los mapas, la tipografía del siglo XVIII, las etimologías, el sabor del café, y la prosa de Stevenson*—"I like hourglasses, maps, eighteenth-century typography, etymologies, the flavor of coffee, and the prose of Stevenson." And introducing a Stevenson story for Italian readers, Borges wrote, *Fin dall'infanzia Robert Louis Stevenson è stato per me una delle forme della felicità*—"Ever since childhood Stevenson has been for me one of the forms of happiness."[10]

Stevenson's novels and stories combine two different kinds of excellence that aren't often found together: he is at once an exacting craftsman and a spellbinding narrator. Gerard Manley Hopkins, whose own poems are so knotty, said that "Stevenson is master of a consummate style, and each phrase is finished as in poetry." There are no wasted words. "He hated dilution," G. K. Chesterton said, "and loved to take language neat, like a liqueur."[11]

Stevenson cared so much about style in order to achieve clarity and intensity. He disliked the "realism" of his era that sought to reproduce reality with exhaustive descriptions. Balzac, he wrote, was an egregious example: "He would leave nothing undeveloped, and thus drowned out of sight of land amid the multitude of crying and incongruous details. Jesus, there is but one art: to omit! O if I knew how to omit, I would ask no other knowledge." In our own time George Saunders, writing about Chekhov, likewise praises "the wisdom of omission" that gives the reader more to guess at and wonder about. "The most artful and truthful thing is sometimes simply that which allows us to avoid being false: the swerving away, the deletion, the declining to decide, the falling silent, the waiting to see, the knowing when to quit."[12]

Flaubert insisted on the *mot juste*, and Stevenson cared about it just as much. In *Treasure Island* Long John Silver is described thus at a critical moment: "his eye a mere pin-point in his big face, but gleaming like a crumb of glass." An early reviewer commented, "An ordinary writer would have said a bead of glass." Conan Doyle said that at every turn the reader of Stevenson finds "some new combination of words which just fits the sense as a cap fits a nipple." We learn from the *Oxford English Dictionary* that Doyle must have been thinking of "a short perforated piece constructed on, or screwed into, the breech of a muzzle-loading gun, on which the percussion cap is fixed and exploded." Stevenson's tales are indeed often explosive.[13]

Style is also crucial in giving pleasure to the reader. Stevenson praised in Dumas, whom he loved, "the particular crown and triumph of the artist—not to be true merely, but to be lovable; not simply to convince, but to enchant." At another time he wrote, "In anything fit to be called by the name of reading, the process itself should be absorbing and voluptuous; we should gloat over a book, be rapt clean out of ourselves, and rise from the perusal, our mind filled with the busiest, kaleidoscopic dance of images, incapable of sleep or of continuous thought. The words, if the book be eloquent, should run thenceforward in our ears like the noise of breakers."[14]

When Stevenson talked about the process of reading he didn't mean conscious attention to stylistic art, but very much the opposite. When we are "rapt clean out of ourselves" we are swept along by spellbinding narration, anxious for the characters when danger threatens, sharing their relief when they win through. And although the Bloomsbury group denigrated Stevenson, the novelist E. M. Forster said that "story" is the one fundamental element in fiction. Considered as story, a work "can only have one merit: that of making the audience want to know what happens next. And conversely it can only have one fault: that of making the audience not want to know what happens next."[15]

Again and again in Stevenson's fiction, there are knife-edge moments where we don't know which way the story is going to go. "No other writer," a reviewer of *Treasure Island* said, "possesses such an extraordinary power of filling the reader with a sense of coming danger." His Samoan friends gave him the name Tusitala, "Storyteller," from which I have drawn the title of this biography.[16]

Stevenson's published output was remarkable: eleven novels (the last of which, the unfinished *Weir of Hermiston,* might well have been his masterpiece), over a hundred essays, and several hundred poems. Impressive though that is, there could have been more. Roger Swearingen's indispensable *Prose Writings of Robert Louis Stevenson* lists a staggering number of stories and essays that he projected, sometimes began, but never finished. With some writers that might suggest a failure of discipline. With Stevenson it was usually perfectionism, unwillingness to keep on with a piece of writing that didn't promise to turn out well. It was certainly not due to lack of ideas. He told a friend, "I have a whole world in my head."[17]

In his final decade Stevenson became immensely popular, in America as well as in Britain, and was increasingly translated into foreign languages. Reporters hounded him for interviews—which he greatly disliked, wanting to be known for his writing, not as a celebrity. Publishers competed to sign him up with generous contracts. Yet at some level he always felt he was a failure, since he had refused to pursue the career that was originally intended for him. His family was celebrated in Scotland for designing and building the first lighthouses ever constructed on its rocky, perilous coast, often on reefs that were submerged at every high tide. When he was thirty-five he told his publisher, "All the sea lights in Scotland are signed with our name, and my father's services to lighthouse optics have been distinguished indeed. I might write books till 1900 and not serve humanity so well; and it moves me to a certain impatience to see the little, frothy bubble that attends the author his son, and compare it with the obscurity in which that better man finds his reward." To some extent this was just filial piety, but he did always feel guilty for being a mere writer.[18]

THE LETTERS

Stevenson once claimed, "I am a d——d bad correspondent, and hate the writing of letters," but over three thousand have survived, and they have been well described as " the autobiography that he was always writing." He said when he was twenty, "What one wants to know is not what people did, but why they did it—or rather, why they *thought* they did it." And the letters are remarkably personal. His stepson Lloyd commented, "They reflect with an astonishing sensitiveness the person whom he is addressing, and whose regard he is tacitly courting."[19]

Five years after his death, the first collection of Stevenson's letters was published by his friend and sometime mentor Sidney Colvin. In his introduction Colvin commented, "He does not care a fig for order or logical sequence or congruity, or for striking a key of expression and keeping it, but becomes simply the most spontaneous and unstudied of human beings." Actually he was never really that; there was always a deliberate quality to his self-presentation. Still, it's true that the letters were crafted to feel spontaneous. After reading this collection Henry James, also a friend, said that Stevenson "never fails of the thing that we most love letters for, the full expression of the moment and the mood." James noted especially "the play of his shades of feeling, the way his spirits are set off by his melancholy, and his brave conclusions by his rueful doubts."[20]

One challenge that faced Colvin was Stevenson's crabbed handwriting; he himself admitted that "calligraphy is horrid to me." Careful inspection of the originals reveals that in one letter Colvin printed "weather lovely" when it should have been "weather beastly," and in another the baffling expression "wappus"— Stevenson had written "appears."[21]

A bigger challenge for Colvin was deciding which of the letters then available should be included, and of those that were, which parts should be silently deleted. He had the usual Victorian concern for proprieties, and a determination not to embarrass living persons. Most significantly, he omitted many of the letters to his own companion (and future wife) Frances Sitwell, whom Stevenson as a young man virtually worshiped, and those that he did include were drastically abridged.

In 1978, when many more letters had been discovered but were scattered in libraries throughout the world, the critic Robert Kiely wrote, "In an effort to protect Stevenson's literary and personal reputation as a cross between Peter Pan and St. Anthony of the Desert, Colvin not only omitted from publication but literally pasted over references to sex, religion, money, and family that he thought might put Stevenson in even the palest light of controversy."[22]

For many years a definitive edition of the letters was expected from Yale University Press, to be edited by Bradford Booth, but at Booth's death it was very far from complete. Fortunately, the work was resumed by Ernest Mehew, a lifelong civil servant whose passion was to learn all that he could about Stevenson, which made him the world's leading Stevenson authority at the time of his death in 2011 at the age of eighty-eight. After the Yale edition was published in 1995, Mehew left his collection to Edinburgh Napier University, whose website has this appreciation of his achievement: "Working only with his wife, Joyce, and never using a computer, he located, sorted, transcribed, dated, annotated and linked some 2,800 letters, the majority of which had never been published before." Although they were written over just thirty years, they fill more than three thousand pages in eight volumes. Roger Swearingen, the dean of Stevenson studies today, describes it as "among the most distinguished works of literary scholarship in this or any other generation."[23]

Richard Holmes, reviewing the Yale edition, said that it "establishes Stevenson as our greatest nineteenth-century letter-writer after Byron." He went on to characterize the way the letters give depth to our understanding of Stevenson: "The well-known voice—tender, facetious, bawdy, reckless, teasing, extravagant, admirably descriptive, and self-dramatizing—continually modulates and drops into this inner world of passion, myths, and dreams. It is essentially a writer's world, compact of tales and memories. And it is—the central revelation perhaps—a world of conflict and hauntings."[24]

BIOGRAPHIES

In a letter to a friend Stevenson once mentioned "my biographer, if ever I have one." He has had at least a dozen, starting with his cousin Graham Balfour, who lived with the family in Samoa for a time, and preserved much that would otherwise have been lost. The next significant one was *Voyage to Windward: The Life of Robert Louis Stevenson* by J. C. Furnas in 1951. Since then there have been many more, most notably by James Pope Hennessy (1974), Jenni Calder (1980), Nicholas Rankin (1987), Ian Bell (1992), Frank McLynn (1993), Philip Callow (2001), Claire Harman (2005), and Jefferson Singer (2017). Every one of them adds much of value to the understanding of Stevenson, and I acknowledge frequently what I have learned from them; their own voices will be heard often in this book, in an ongoing conversation with others who have spent much time with Stevenson. It should be added that all except Harman and Singer wrote before the Yale edition of the letters was available.[25]

It used to be assumed that an ideal biography would be "definitive" and make all others unnecessary. Hermione Lee says, "There is a lingering idea of biography as the complete true story of a human being, the last word on a life. But if it is, rather, a mixed, unstable genre, whose rules keep coming undone, then perhaps the only rule that holds good is that there is no such thing as a definitive biography." And we should keep in mind a historian's reminder that on any subject "what has been published is only a fraction of what was written, and what was written was only a fraction of what was thought and said." It's essential to avoid what has been called the archive fallacy—the assumption that there is always written evidence for everything that happened in the past, with the corollary that if there isn't written evidence, then it never happened.[26]

My own emphases in this biography differ from those of my predecessors in a number of ways. I try to illuminate Stevenson's achievement as a writer more fully than others have done; they seem often to assume that his works are already familiar to readers, which is generally not the case. For each of the major works, including essays and poems as well as novels, I hope to show what makes them remarkable, in an exceptionally inventive writing career. These will usually be discussed at the time in his life when they were being written, rather than by publication dates, which often came later.

It needs to be added that Stevenson's literary production was uneven, as he often acknowledged. Sometimes from lack of inspiration, more often from an urgent need to make money, he turned out a number of novels that disappointed readers then and later. Stevenson specialists have sought to rehabilitate these, but in such cases I will offer my own judgment, subjective though it is.

Many biographers have taken a critical view of Stevenson's wife Fanny, but their relationship was one of deep and lasting love, and I have attempted to demonstrate that in depth. A wealth of surviving material confirms that he was surely right when he said that marrying her was the best thing he ever did. According to an old friend of his, "It had on both sides the elements of what we call a grand passion. It was, in a word, an attachment in which the whole nature of each participant was wholly engaged."[27]

Just as this book was going to press, a dual biography was published by Camille Peri: *A Wilder Shore: The Romantic Odyssey of Fanny and Robert Louis Stevenson*. It was too late to incorporate anything from it here, but I am glad that Fanny's role in Louis's life and career is sympathetically traced. My book also tells that story, but ranges more widely in the historical, cultural, religious, and literary contexts that give it depth, as well as drawing on the rich resources of Stevenson scholarship.[28]

Scores of people who knew Stevenson well left insightful reminiscences, and I will quote from these—and from his immediate family—much more liberally than previous biographers have done. Likewise, his own words deserve to be quoted much more generously than they have been, for their eloquence, imagination, and playful wit. And I quote also from commentators and critics who have given us valuable insights into his writings.

Finally, biographers have tended to recycle the same set of contemporary photographs. Throughout the time of working on this book I have searched for compelling illustrations, most of which have never appeared in modern studies of Stevenson. I am especially grateful to Adrienne Sharpe-Weseman and Moira Fitzgerald of the Beinecke Library at Yale, who tracked down hard to locate materials in their great Stevenson collection, and also to Gabrielle Van Amburg at the Robert Louis Stevenson Silverado Museum in St. Helena, California.

A NOTE ON REFERENCES

There is no complete modern edition of Stevenson's works (a new one is currently appearing in installments from Edinburgh University Press), an indication of neglect over the years. Between 1894 and 1924, however, no fewer than six editions were published—successively the Edinburgh, Pentland, Swanston, Vailima, Tusitala, and Waverly Editions—but since they have been out of print for a century, they are hard to find even in major libraries (my own, at Harvard, lacks most of them). When writers give page references to one or another of those editions, therefore, they are useless to readers. Even in those days it was highly unusual for multiple competing editions to appear. The explanation is that

Stevenson's various publishers banded together for mutual profit and issued a series of limited editions, each with minor differences intended to attract collectors, along with more inexpensive editions for the general public.[29]

In every case, I have tried to cite quotations in the way that will be most helpful. For the novels, which exist in editions from numerous publishers, I give chapter numbers rather than page numbers. Short stories are cited from Barry Menikoff's *Complete Stories of Robert Louis Stevenson*. Stevenson's essays are cited by title only, with dates of first publication, except that page numbers are given as well for those included in Jeremy Treglown's excellent selection, *The Lantern-Bearers*. Poems are cited from Janet Adam Smith's *Collected Poems* or, when not included there, in the recent edition of Roger C. Lewis.[30]

It should be added that many early books about Stevenson were published in Britain and the United States with different pagination. In the notes I indicate which version I'm citing.

CHAPTER 1

The Early Years

AN ONLY CHILD

At the midpoint of the nineteenth century, on November 13, 1850, Robert Louis Stevenson was born in Edinburgh. He always identified profoundly with his native city, though he disliked its bleak architecture and chilly climate. "The Scotch dialect," he wrote, "is singularly rich in terms of reproach against the winter wind. *Snell, blae, nirly,* and *scowthering,* are four of these significant vocables; they are all words that carry a shiver with them."[1]

Louis (in this book he will generally be called Louis, not Stevenson, since the story will be heavily populated by other Stevensons as well) always felt that he was a Scot to the core, and never lost the accent. Although most of his adult life would be spent elsewhere, his stories and novels were often set in Scotland. He was fascinated by his country's past—and especially by its lost causes. The greatest of those was its failure to break free from English domination, in what he called "the brawl that makes Scottish history." In this he was going against the attitude of his family and social class, for whom union with England was altogether a good thing.[2]

From both sides of the family he received profound influences. One was religious, the dark and sin-haunted Scottish version of Presbyterianism; though he would become an agnostic, a gnawing sense of conscience never left him. James Joyce's friends used to say that even though he had lost his faith, he never ceased to be a Jesuit. Something similar might be said of Louis, and a comment of his on Robert Burns could apply equally well to himself: "He was not perhaps devoted to religion, but haunted by it." His mother Margaret was a clergyman's daughter, and he was christened by her father, the Reverend Lewis Balfour. In fact he was given both of those names at birth, Robert Lewis Balfour Stevenson (he later changed the spelling to Louis, which he thought of as the French version, but everyone pronounced it the old way and not as "Louie"). Staying often at his grandfather's house in a village near Edinburgh, he was exposed not only to a stern faith, but also to tragic tales of local rebels who died in its defense.[3]

The other grandfather, Robert Stevenson, had died just months before Louis was born. A brilliant civil engineer, he designed and supervised construction of the very first lighthouses on the perilous Scottish coast. Louis's father Thomas, along with two brothers, was carrying on the work, and when Louis was growing up it was taken for granted that he would one day join the firm. During visits to his father's construction projects he developed a passion for the sea. "I loved a ship," he would write later, "as a man loves burgundy or daybreak." (A friend confirmed that he had "a peculiar passion for burgundy.")[4]

Margaret was nineteen when she married Thomas, who was eleven years her senior. "A wife and mother at barely twenty," one biographer comments, "Maggie was delightfully spoiled by her devoted husband, and together they worshiped at the cradle of their only son." But Margaret was not what has been called "the weak, coddled Victorian wife of cliché." In her late fifties, shortly after her husband's death, she would travel with Louis and his wife to America and then onward into the Pacific, settling with them in Samoa. A missionary who met her there commented, "It was pleasant to see the attention of R.L.S. to his mother, and her passionate devotion to him; and as we listened to the conversation of this gracious lady it was easy to divine from whom he received the heritage of brilliant fancy and quaint thought which made him great."[5]

A portrait made at the time of her marriage (fig. 1) remains the best image of Margaret that we have, although one of her nieces said, "None of Mrs. Stevenson's photographs do her justice, for she was very pretty, graceful, and refined-looking." According to Louis's cousin and first biographer Graham Balfour, "In person she was tall, slender, and graceful, and her face and fair complexion retained their beauty, as her figure and walk preserved their elasticity, to the last. Her vivacity and brightness were most attractive. As a hostess she had great social tact, and her hospitality was but the expression of her true kindliness of heart."[6]

When Louis was twenty-four he filled out a questionnaire in Francis Galton's *Record of Family Faculties* and described his mother as "tall, slim, aquiline,

1. Margaret Stevenson at nineteen

handsome," with a temperament that was "sanguine, cheerful, very fond of amusement, very easily amused." One of his friends commented, "It was easy to see that much of the character, much of the courage, and much of the cheerfulness of Louis came from his mother."[7]

Louis's father Thomas (fig. 2) had a lively sense of humor too; a friend remembered him as "a dear, lovable old man, very amusing and also amusable." Another friend said that during conversations at dinner, "the father's face at certain moments was a study—an indescribable mixture of vexation, fatherly pride and admiration, and sheer bewilderment at [his son's] brilliant flippancies, and the quick young thrusts of his wit and criticism."[8]

There was a darker side to Thomas's temperament, though. After his death in 1887 Louis published a moving obituary, paying tribute to his work in engineer-

2. Thomas Stevenson at sixty-two

ing and declaring that "few men were more beloved in Edinburgh," but also speaking frankly about his moods.

> He was a man of a somewhat antique strain: with a blended sternness and softness that was wholly Scottish and at first somewhat bewildering; with a profound essential melancholy of disposition and (what often accompanies it) the most humorous geniality in company; shrewd and childish; passionately attached, passionately prejudiced; a man of many extremes, many faults of temper, and no very stable foothold for himself among life's troubles.... His sense of his own unworthiness I have called morbid; morbid, too, were his sense of the fleetingness of life and his concern for death. He had never accepted the conditions of man's life or

his own character; and his inmost thoughts were ever tinged with the Celtic melancholy.

In an unpublished memoir Louis wrote, "A profound underlying pessimism appears to be the last word of the Stevensons; their sense of the tragedy of life is acute and unbroken."[9]

Soon after Louis's birth, his mother began making entries in a "Baby Book" (fig. 3), recording that his eyes were blue at first, as is common with newborns, but turned to hazel later on, and that he had fair hair, though that too would darken. Two locks of it are preserved (color plate 2) in the Stevenson collection at Yale. At the bottom of the page in the Baby Book a series of "pet names" appears: "Boulihasker—Smoutie—Baron Broadnose—Signor Sprucki otherwise Maister Sprook and many others but Smoutie stuck to him till he was about 15." It's not clear who wrote the note about the curls, or typed the note pasted at the top; "Aunt Maggie" was the family name for Margaret, and "Auntie" was her sister Jane. Incidentally, his name is spelled "Louis" here, not the original "Lewis," but that's because whoever filled in the blanks did it after he himself began insisting on the change.[10]

Actually, as photographs confirm, Louis inherited his mother's nose, which was not broad at all. Smoutie was a diminutive of Smout (rhyming with "shout"), a Scottish word meaning "small fry." He was called that because when his father saw him for the first time he declared that "he had never seen such a wee thing—he's just a smout." Louis grew to hate the name, and got his parents to drop it by fining them a penny each time they used it.[11]

In a photograph with his mother when he was three years old (fig. 4), Louis's vacuous expression may be due to the requirement to remain perfectly still for the long exposure. Dressing little boys as girls may look odd today but was not uncommon at the time. A portrait sketch of him (fig. 5) captures the androgynous appearance that was apparently preferred.

The house on Howard Place where Louis was born was close to a river polluted with sewage, so in 1853 they moved to higher ground. That house too turned out to be damp and unhealthy, and in 1857 they settled at 17 Heriot Row, where Louis would grow up and his parents would live until his father's death. In the picture (fig. 6) it's the house in light-colored stone, to the right of the lamppost. Someone who visited there frequently said, "It was wisely chosen, for Heriot Row is sunny and open, faces the south, and looks on to the lawns and trees of the gardens that fill the sloping space between it and Queen Street above it." Close by was a private garden to which only the neighboring tenants had a key.[12]

BIRTH.

Place of Birth *8 Howard Place Edinburgh*

Time of Birth *Wednesday 13th Nov. 1850 at 1.30 P.M.*

Weight..................

Length..................

Breadth..................

Colour of Eyes *blue at pres.t turning to hazel*

Colour of Hair *very fair – almost none at pres.t*

Nurse's Name *Mrs Sayers*

Doctor's Name *Dr Malcolm*

NAMES.

Surname *Stevenson*

Christian Names *Robert Lewis Balfour*

Pet Names *Baulibaster – Smoutie – Baron Broadnose – Signor Sprucki otherwise Maister Sprook & many others but Smoutie stuck to him till he was about 15.*

3. First page of the "Baby Book"

4. Margaret and Louis

That was in the fashionable New Town, but in compact Edinburgh the disreputable and slummy Old Town was just a short distance away. In his college years Louis would get to know its pubs and its prostitutes intimately.

In a formal portrait with his father taken when he was ten (fig. 7), Louis still has the vacuous expression. He was always restless, and it must have been exasperating to pose, especially in such fancy clothes. The family was partial to Skye terriers, and one of them, whose name was Coolin, is dozing beside the chair.

When Louis was young the family's arrangements revolved around illness,

5. Louis at four

and especially his mother's poor health. She was said to have a "weak chest" that provoked coughing and fevers, and most days she stayed in bed until noon. She had inherited a lung condition from her father; her brother George Balfour, who became the family physician, said that she was diagnosed with "a patch of fibroid pneumonia in her left lung, with slight haemoptysis." That meant coughing up blood from the bronchial arteries, exactly as would happen to Louis in later life. As is often the case with someone who lived over a century ago, however, modern specialists aren't certain what diagnosis would be reached today.[13]

Even privileged Victorian children were subject to numerous ailments, and Louis suffered more than most. He was often confined to bed, and at various times endured mumps, chicken pox, croup, whooping cough, scarlet fever, "gastric fever," influenza, bronchitis, and pneumonia. Very possibly he had diphtheria as well. The author of some reminiscences of Edinburgh wrote, "When he grew

6. 17 Heriot Row

big enough to make daily walks abroad, a neighbour recollects watching him as he was led along on the sunniest side of the pavement, firmly gripping his nurse's hand, his face flanked with flannel, for he suffered continually from earache." Agonizing ear infections were a bane of childhood in the days before antibiotics.[14]

In addition, he had an exceptionally scrawny physique. His father was sturdily built, and his mother was graceful in youth and rather heavy later on. Louis's extreme gauntness and odd bone structure may well have been due to some kind of endocrine problem, perhaps thyroid abnormality. At any rate he looked strik-

7. Thomas Stevenson and Louis, aged ten

ingly different from almost everybody else. For a young child that was a serious disadvantage.

CUMMY—AND RELIGION

The most important person in Louis's early life, however, was neither his mother nor his father but Alison Cunningham, always called Cummy (sometimes spelled Cummie), who arrived when he was eighteen months old to be his nanny or nurse. She was twenty-nine—seven years older than Margaret—and experienced with children. Margaret was not, and happy to leave Louis to Cummy most of the time; also, she was monopolized by her demanding husband. Louis once told a friend, "My mother is my father's wife; the children of lovers are orphans."[15]

The jurist Charles Guthrie, an old friend from Louis's student days, thought highly of Cummy: "She had brilliant eyes, a bright smile, and a hearty, contagious laugh. She gesticulated, as the Scots seldom do, and would seize you by the arm to tell you something specially intimate.... She had an inquisitive mind, a vivid imagination, and a retentive memory." Guthrie mentioned that she had grown up in a fisherman's family and had several brothers, "so she knew all about boys' ways."[16]

A portrait at this time (fig. 8) shows Cummy posing with books, very appropriately since she loved to read, much to Louis's benefit. Someone who knew her said, "Cummy had enjoyed a solid education such as falls to most of their kind [i.e., social class] if they have the good fortune to be born Scots. Her family sent her regularly to school."[17]

Cummy also appears in a group portrait (fig. 9) in which Thomas dominates, gazing sternly into the camera, while the normally lively Margaret stands quietly at his side. Louis appears as a sullen teenager; beside him is an attractive and rather diminutive Cummy. At the left are a pair of housemaids, and in the foreground, clearly finding it difficult to stay still, is Coolin.

As a child Louis was often overtaken by nightmares, and when that happened Cummy was an essential source of comfort. Perhaps she slept in the same room, though that isn't clear.

> I remember with particular distinctness how she would lift me out of bed and take me, rolled in blankets, to the window, whence I might look forth into the blue night starred with street lamps, and see where the gas still burned behind the windows of other sickrooms.... The sight of the outer world refreshed and cheered me, and the whole sorrow and burden of the night was at an end with the arrival of the first of that long string of country carts that, in the dark hours of the morning with the neighing of horses, the cracking of whips, the shouts of the drivers, and a hundred other wholesome noises, creaked, rolled, and pounded past my window.[18]

But if Cummy was a source of comfort against the nightmares, she was also their principal source. Scottish Presbyterianism took various forms. For the upper

8. Alison Cunningham ("Cummy")

class it was an expression of proper behavior and social conformity, not altogether different from the Church of England from which it had split in 1560; when Queen Victoria spent her holidays in Scotland she worshiped in a Presbyterian church. The main distinction between the two denominations had to do with church government: elders in the Presbyterian Church, bishops in the Anglican. In England, bishops appointed parish vicars, while in Scotland each parish elected its own minister.

9. Stevenson family group

Among the lower classes and in rural areas, however, faith was more fervent, and more preoccupied with sin and damnation. Cummy had a vivid conception of sin, and deplored worldly temptations such as card playing and theatergoing, both of which Louis's parents enjoyed. More ominously, she filled the boy's mind with fears, and at night he was tormented by them.

To inculcate doctrine, Scottish children were required to memorize the Shorter Catechism, which is actually not very short, and Cummy drilled Louis in it. This is a typical entry: "Question. What is the misery of that estate whereinto man fell? Answer. All mankind by their fall lost communion with God, are under his wrath and curse, and so made liable to all the miseries in this life, to death itself, and to the pains of hell forever."[19]

A favorite book of Cummy's that she would read to Louis was *The Biography of Robert Murray McCheyne,* which begins, "The Holy Spirit carried on his work in the subject of this memoir by continuing to deepen in him the conviction of his ungodliness, and the pollution of his whole nature." In his diary McCheyne called himself "a mass of corruption," and although he became a charismatic preacher, he never ceased to revile himself in the approved manner. "I am helpless in respect of every lust that ever was, or ever will be, in the human heart. I am a worm—a beast—before God."[20]

Louis was highly impressionable, and the imprint of Cummy's indoctrination was deep. To the extent that Margaret was aware at all of her son's precocious religiosity, she seems to have regarded it as cute. When he was three she noted in her Baby Book, "Smout's favourite occupation is 'making a Church.' He makes a pulpit with a chair and stool and reads sitting and then stands up and sings by turns." He was just pretending to read, of course. Other entries are more disturbing. "Smout's sermon verbatim, 'Whoever entereth into a field on the Sunday and repeath or picketh sticks is not of God and shall not go to Heaven, but if he does anything more on the Sunday he must go to Hell. Everyone must do nothing that's wrong.' Then a psalm was sung."

In 1858, just before she stopped making entries, Margaret noted without comment that when Louis would talk about his future, he was careful to add "If I'm spared." For example, when he had just turned seven:

> Smout: "The Churches are much to blame for not sending missionaries to convert the Arabs." Mama: "But if people won't go what can the Churches do? Will you go when you're big?" Smout: "I think you've forgotten one word that was needful." Mama: "What is that?" Smout: "If I'm spared."

Not surprisingly, in social situations the smarmy piety tended to backfire. Louis told a friend that "as a little boy with curls and a velvet tunic, he read *Ministering Children* and yearned to be a ministering child himself. An opportunity seemed to present itself: the class of boys called 'keelies' [street urchins] by the more comfortable boys in Edinburgh used to play in the street under the windows of his father's house. One lame boy, a baker's son, could only look on. Here was a chance to minister! Louis, with a beating heart, walked out on his angelic mission. 'Little boy, would you like to play with me?' he asked. 'You go to——!' was the answer."[21]

As an adult Louis recalled with disgust how sanctimonious he had been in those days. "I piped and sniveled over the Bible, with an earnestness that had been talked into me. I would say nothing without adding 'If I am spared' . . . I was sentimental, sniveling, goody, morbidly religious. I hope and do believe I am a better man than I was a child."[22]

The worst result of this training was the terrifying nightmares. In an essay entitled "A Chapter on Dreams" Louis referred to himself in the third person, but then acknowledged that the dreamer "is no less a person than myself."

When he had a touch of fever at night, and the room swelled and shrank, and his clothes, hanging on a nail, now loomed up [in an] instant to the bigness of a church, and now drew away into a horror of infinite distance and infinite littleness, the poor soul was very well aware of what must follow, and struggled hard against the approaches of that slumber which was the beginning of sorrows. But his struggles were in vain; sooner or later the night-hag would have him by the throat, and pluck him strangling and screaming, from his sleep. . . . He seemed to himself to stand before the Great White Throne; he was called on, poor little devil, to recite some form of words, on which his destiny depended; his tongue stuck, his memory was blank, Hell gaped for him; and he would awake, clinging to the curtain-rod with his knees to his chin.

The Book of Revelation was alarming material to feed to a small child: "I saw a great white throne, and him that sat on it, from whose face the earth and the heaven fled away; and there was found no place for them. And I saw the dead, small and great, stand before God; and the books were opened: and another book was opened, which is the book of life: and the dead were judged out of those things which were written in the books, according to their works."

As he got older the nightmares moderated, but only somewhat. "The cries and physical contortions passed away, seemingly for ever; his visions were still for the most part miserable, but they were more constantly supported; and he would awake with no more extreme symptom than a flying heart, a freezing scalp, cold sweats, and the speechless midnight fear."[23]

His mother was shocked, Louis recalled, "when in days long after she heard what I had suffered." That she never suspected it at the time suggests how much closer he was to Cummy than to her.[24]

In his notes for a memoir, describing the "dark and vehement religion" he'd been taught, he wrote: "All the rose-water theology in the world cannot quench the great fire of horror and terror that Christianity has kindled in the hearts of the Scottish people." Under Cummy's supervision he internalized that terror early, and she never did understand how damaging her influence had been. "She would tell you proudly," according to someone who met her much later, "that Louis, in his childhood, was a very religious boy. 'He got that from me, you know,' she added, with a friendly little nudge." As an adult he would leave the grim theology behind, and even be accused of atheism, but he never lost the Calvinist sense of inner dividedness, and phrases from the Bible would show up constantly in his conversation and letters.[25]

If Cummy had been cold and severe, Louis might have been more able to resist the indoctrination, but she was quite the reverse. According to Graham Balfour,

> In spite of her restrictions, Cummie was full of life and merriment. She danced and sang to her boy, and read to him most dramatically. She herself tells how, the last time she ever saw him [in his mid-thirties], he said to her before a room full of people, "It's *you* that gave me a passion for the drama, Cummie." "Me, Master Lou," I said, "I never put foot inside a playhouse in my life." "Ay, woman," said he, "but it was the grand dramatic way ye had of reciting the hymns."[26]

Early familiarity with the Bible stimulated Louis's first attempt at writing, or rather dictating, at the age of six. An uncle had offered a prize to the family children for the best essay on Moses, and as a friend remembered it, "Louis was all agog to compete. 'But I can't write,' he cried in sudden despair. 'You can dictate, and I will write,' said his mother, 'and not one word will be put down but what you say.'" He proceeded enthusiastically, and drew a picture of the Israelites crossing the Red Sea with heavy suitcases and smoking huge cigars. He didn't win, but "from that time forward," his mother said later, "it was the desire of his heart to be an author."[27]

Predictably, Cummy's harping on sin produced the opposite result from what she intended. "The worst consequence," Louis wrote, "is the romance conferred on doubtful actions, until the child grows to think nothing more glorious than to be struck dead in the very act of some surprising wickedness. I can never again take so much interest in anything as I took, in childhood, in doing for its own sake what I believed to be sinful. And generally, the principal effect of this false, common doctrine of sin is to put a point on lust." An undated poem recalls how in the night "my spirit beat / The cage of its compulsive purity," longing for wickedness that his training "had made an itching mystery."[28]

The best thing Louis got from his early religion was deep appreciation of the language of the King James Bible, which Cummy read straight through with him three or four times. He remembered her "gloating on the rhythm, dwelling with delight on assonances and alliterations." From Psalm 47 he recalled the verse "The Lord is gone up with a shout, and God with the sound of a trumpet," and said that "it rings still in my ear from my first childhood, and perhaps with something of my nurse's accent. There was possibly some sort of image written in my mind by these loud words, but I believe the words themselves were what I cherished."

He also remembered associating phrases in the Scottish metrical version of the twenty-third Psalm with particular scenes in Edinburgh. "The 'pastures green' were represented by a certain suburban stubble field where I had once walked with my nurse, under an autumnal sunset, on the banks of the Water of Leith.... 'Death's dark vale' was a certain archway in the Warriston Cemetery: a formidable yet beloved spot, for children love to be afraid." And he imagined "thy rod and thy staff they comfort me" in familiar images—"on one side of me a rude, knobby, shepherd's staff, such as cheers the heart of the Cockney tourist, on the other a rod like a billiard cue appeared to accompany my progress; the staff sturdily upright, the billiard cue inclined confidentially, like one whispering, towards my ear."[29]

A fable that Louis wrote in his twenties dramatizes the effects of religious indoctrination. It's entitled "The House of Eld," a word meaning age as opposed to youth. In English it survives only in "elder" and "elderly," but in Scots dialect it lasted into Stevenson's time. The fable begins when a fetter is fastened to a child's right leg, so that he and his fellows "limp about in their play like convicts"; as adults they have painfully ulcerated legs. The boy naturally complains, but is reproved. "'My dear boy,' said his uncle, the catechist, 'do not complain about your fetter, for it is the only thing that makes life worth living. None are happy, none are good, none are respectable, that are not gyved like us. And I must tell you, besides, it is very dangerous talk. If you grumble of your iron, you will have no luck; if ever you take it off, you will be instantly smitten by a thunderbolt.'" The uncle adds that heathens should not be envied, since they are deprived of "the joys of being fettered." As a result they are "not truly human—for what is man without a fetter?"

The youth goes on a journey during which his uncle, mother, and father successively appear to him as scary apparitions; he smites each one with a sword, and as they shrivel away they are revealed to be evil sorcerers. After he returns home he finds that everyone is now wearing a fetter on the left leg instead of the right, because "the old was found to be a superstition." And that's not all—"There lay his uncle smitten on the head, and his father pierced through the heart, and his mother cloven through the midst. And he sat in the lone house and wept beside the bodies." By defying religious repression he has murdered them.

The fable ends with a "Moral":

> Woodman, is your courage stout?
> Beware! the root is wrapped about
> Your mother's heart, your father's bones;
> And like the mandrake comes with groans.

This sounds so Blakean that one wonders if it was inspired by Blake, whose poems we know Louis read at some point. Were his mother and father well-meaning but unwitting sorcerers?[30]

However damaging the religious indoctrination may have been, Louis always felt deep affection for Cummy, and an appreciation of how much she must have sacrificed in her own life. In his early twenties he wrote an essay (never published) entitled "Nurses," in which he imagined the nurse's sorrow after a child has grown up, "gradually forgetting and forsaking her, fostered in disrespect and neglect on the plea of growing manliness, and at last beginning to treat her as a servant whom he had treated a few years before as a mother."

What follows can perhaps be read as a tacit reproach to his mother and also to himself. "I believe that in a better state of things there will be no more nurses, and that every mother will nurse her own offspring; for what can be more hardening and demoralising than to call forth the tenderest feelings of a woman's heart and cherish them yourself as long as you need them, as long as your children require a nurse to love them, and then to blight and thwart and destroy them, whenever your own use for them is at an end."[31]

Louis said much the same thing in a letter to Cummy herself.

> Do not suppose I shall ever forget those long, bitter nights, when I coughed and coughed and was so unhappy, and you were so patient and loving with a poor, sick child. Indeed, Cummy, I wish I might become a man worth talking of, if it were only that you should not have thrown away your pains. . . . If you should happen to think that you might have had a child of your own, and that it was hard you should have spent so many years taking care of someone else's prodigal, just you think this: you have been for a great deal in my life; you have made much that there is in me, just as surely as if you had conceived me; and there are sons who are more ungrateful to their own mothers than I am to you. For I am not ungrateful, my dear Cummy, and it is with a very sincere emotion that I write myself Your little boy. Louis.

As it would turn out, he would have no children of his own, for at least two reasons. His wife, ten years older than himself, already had two children (who became close to him as stepchildren), had lost a third to a tragically early death, and was reluctant to start again. Also, he was convinced that his serious health condition was hereditary and likely to be passed on.[32]

If Cummy did experience feelings of loss, she left no sign of it. She remained with the family until Louis reached adulthood (living by herself after that), and corresponded warmly with him over the years. She always had a high opinion of Margaret, too. When someone commented that Margaret's portrait showed a beautiful face, "'Yes, Mum,' said old Cummy, 'but she had a beautiful soul.'"[33]

A CHILD'S GARDEN OF IMAGINATION

When he was thirty-five Louis published a collection of poems that re-create what those early years had felt like, *A Child's Garden of Verses,* that became an instant classic. For generations they were read to and by children throughout the English-speaking world. What makes the poems wonderful is the immediacy with which they relive childhood; a family friend said they were written "not so much for the child as by the child." Henry James commented, "A child might have written it if a child could see childhood from the outside." That comment was very acute. Louis had an extraordinary gift for making a young person's experience real—a boy in *Treasure Island,* a teenager in *Kidnapped* and *Catriona*—while embedding the story in a full context that only an adult could grasp.[34]

By the time he wrote *A Child's Garden,* Louis was struck by the way in which certain memories, far from fading, acquire a sharpened focus over time. "What is lately past is too much loaded with detail to be distinct, and the canvas of the picture is too large for the eye to encompass. But this is no more the case when our recollections have been strained long enough through the hourglass of time. All that is worthless has been sieved and sifted out of them."[35]

The immediate impetus for the *Child's Garden* was *Kate Greenaway's Birthday Book for Children,* published in 1880, in which Greenaway's illustrations were accompanied by four-line poems by Lucy Sayle Barker, one for each day of the year. In these poems children are seen from above by complacent adults.

>Baby ran to meet me, she had a sash all blue,
>A bran new gown,
>Just come from town,
>A cap so crisp and new.

"Baby girls" love to look pretty; boys are noisy and need to go outside to work off their energy.

>Come and play at cricket now,
>Come along, you boys;
>Mind how you come, and quickly come,
>And do not make a noise.

Louis, disgusted by the patronizing sentimentality of the Greenaway poems, was inspired to write some of his own. In the *Child's Garden* adults are seen from below, and most of the time not seen at all. Although he wrote the poems in his thirties, he did it when illness confined him to bed, just as it had when he was little and needed diversions to stay happy. They are about a world of imagination more capacious and more satisfying than the everyday one.

One of the finest poems is "The Land of Counterpane," which re-creates the way a simple bedspread can become a populous landscape in a child's imagination.

> When I was sick and lay a-bed,
> I had two pillows at my head,
> And all my toys beside me lay
> To keep me happy all the day.
>
> And sometimes for an hour or so
> I watched my leaden soldiers go,
> With different uniforms and drills,
> Among the bed-clothes, through the hills;
>
> And sometimes sent my ships in fleets
> All up and down among the sheets;
> Or brought my trees and houses out,
> And planted cities all about.
>
> I was the giant great and still
> That sits upon the pillow-hill,
> And sees before him, dale and plain,
> The pleasant land of counterpane.[36]

At first the toys lie motionless beside the child; then he becomes a pleased spectator as they march among the hills and valleys of the bedclothes. Or suddenly the sheets can be an ocean on which fleets set sail, or the landscape can swell until it accommodates whole cities. In Lucy Barker's poems children were tiny; here "I was the giant great and still / That sits upon the pillow-hill." He isn't even pushing the toy people about, but lying in repose as they lead lives of their own.

Louis never lost his sense of the strangeness of adults as they appear to children, as he showed in an essay called "Child's Play," written when he was twenty-eight. "Surely [children] dwell in a mythological epoch, and are not the contemporaries of their parents. What can they think of them? what can they make of these bearded or petticoated giants who look down upon their games?"[37]

In "Little Land" in *A Child's Garden,* an ordinary lawn becomes a forest filled with inhabitants, and then with a jolt we're back in the land of the giants.

> In that forest to and fro
> I can wander, I can go;
> See the spider and the fly
> And the ants go marching by,
> Carrying parcels with their feet
> Down the green and grassy street. . . .
>
> When my eyes I once again
> Open, and see all things plain:
> High bare walls, great bare floor;
> Great big knobs on drawer and door;
> Great big people perched on chairs,
> Stitching tucks and mending tears,
> Each a hill that I could climb,
> And talking nonsense all the time.

Even poems of personal affection retain the child's perspective. Jane Balfour was Margaret's unmarried sister, much loved by her nephews and nieces. A few years after finishing *A Child's Garden* Louis wrote to her, "You are Auntie, and all that is kind and pretty and gay in my childhood finds in you one of its darling centres; and I cannot think of you seriously today but I must smile with my mouth, and the tears come into my eye: my pretty, clever, daft, delightful Auntie." But in a little four-line poem, "Auntie's Skirts," what the child registers is the strangeness of a Victorian lady's costume.

> Whenever Auntie moves around,
> Her dresses make a curious sound,
> They trail behind her up the floor,
> And trundle after through the door.

It's a child's view, from much closer to the floor than Auntie herself is. "Trailing" and "trundling" are neat visual perceptions, and "curious sound" is still more striking—very much the kind of thing a child would notice and an adult would ignore.[38]

Many illustrators have tried their hand at the *Child's Garden* over the years. One of the best, because fully in sympathy with the poems, was Jessie Wilcox Smith in 1905. Auntie (fig. 10) is appropriately slim and elegant, but it's her vo-

10. "Auntie's Skirts"

luminous skirts that are seen at child's-eye level while she glances down from her adult height.

One poem, "The Lamplighter," captures a familiar experience at Heriot Row, the lighting of gas lamps as evening comes on.

> My tea is nearly ready and the sun has left the sky;
> It's time to take the window to see Leerie going by;
> For every night at teatime and before you take your seat,
> With lantern and with ladder he comes posting up the street.

> Now Tom would be a driver and Maria go to sea,
> And my papa's a banker and as rich as he can be;
> But I, when I am stronger and can choose what I'm to do,
> O Leerie, I'll go round at night and light the lamps with you!
>
> For we are very lucky, with a lamp before the door,
> And Leerie stops to light it as he lights so many more;
> And O! before you hurry by with ladder and with light,
> O Leerie, see a little child and nod to him tonight!

The child can't imagine being a banker, or for that matter a civil engineer, but he enjoys the idea of accompanying Leerie on his rounds. The actual street lamp at Heriot Row can be seen in the photograph above (fig. 6).

In 1910 the artist Norman Wilkinson made an evocative illustration (color plate 3) to accompany an 1878 essay by Louis called "A Plea for Gas Lamps." Electric lights, which were replacing them, turned on unromantically when a "sedate electrician somewhere in a back office" casually threw a switch. In the picture Leerie is looking up as he carefully ignites the lamp, with lit windows in the house across the street and stars glowing in the darkening sky. He is making, Louis says in the essay, "another luminous hole into the dusk."[39]

A sequence of poems about fantasy play is entitled "The Child Alone," and to introduce it Jessie Wilcox Smith evokes the child's dream of a vast world beyond (fig. 11). The little poem "Happy Thought" expresses wonder at that vastness:

> The world is so full of a number of things,
> I'm sure we should all be as happy as kings.

The point is not sentimental. Astonished by the richness of the world, a child is amazed that people are *not* happy. Among Louis's papers was another version of the poem:

> The world is so great and I am so small,
> I do not like it at all, at all.

The illustration captures that too—what it's like to *be* small.[40]

The final poem, "To Any Reader," is an acknowledgment that the actual child of the poems is long gone.

> He does not hear; he will not look,
> Nor yet be lured out of this book.
> For, long ago, the truth to say,

11. "The Child Alone"

> He has grown up and gone away,
> And it is but a child of air
> That lingers in the garden there.

When *A Child's Garden of Verses* was published in 1885—the same year as *Dr. Jekyll and Mr. Hyde*!—Margaret was pained to find that it was dedicated to Cummy and not herself. In the dedication Louis wrote:

> For the long nights you lay awake
> And watched for my unworthy sake:
> For your most comfortable hand
> That led me through the uneven land:

> For all the story-books you read:
> For all the pains you comforted:
> For all you pitied, all you bore,
> In sad and happy days of yore—
> My second Mother, my first Wife,
> The angel of my infant life—
> From the sick child, now well and old,
> Take, nurse, the little book you hold!

Louis had written to Cummy personally, "I have just seen that the book must be dedicated to Alison Cunningham, the only person who will really understand it."[41]

The volume was well received, but one reviewer complained that it was too cheery. "Mr. Stevenson knows nothing of the fierce rebellions, the agonized doubts as to the existence of justice, human or divine, which mar the music of childhood; or if he realizes their existence, he relegates them to that other life, the life of pain, and terror, and weariness, into which it is part of his philosophy to look as seldom as possible." After reading this Stevenson wrote to thank the reviewer for "the best criticism I ever had," and confirmed that "my childhood was in reality a very mixed experience, full of fever, nightmare, insomnia, painful days and interminable nights; and I can speak with less authority of Gardens than of that other 'land of counterpane.' But to what end should we renew these sorrows?"[42]

THE INTOXICATION OF STORIES

Cummy told a visitor that when Louis was five, he had done "something naughty" and was told to stand in a corner for ten minutes. When she returned and said it was time to come out, he didn't answer. "'That's enough; time's up,' repeated Cummy. And then the child mystically raised his hand, and with a strange light in his eyes, 'Hush,' he said, 'I'm telling myself a story.'"[43]

He liked to sing himself to sleep with a kind of incantation. "After I was in bed, I used to be heard lying awake and repeating to myself—crooning over to myself in the dark—certain curious rambling effusions, which I called my 'songstries.'" Sometimes his father would come to his room and entertain him with made-up tales of heroism and adventure, which reflected his own imaginative life. Many years later Thomas would enthusiastically contribute suggestions when *Treasure Island* was being conceived.[44]

Louis's own fantasy life followed his father's example.

> To confess plainly, I intended to spend my life (or any leisure I might have from piracy upon the high seas) as the leader of a great horde of irregular cavalry, devastating whole valleys. I can still, looking back, see myself in many favourite attitudes: signaling for a boat from a pirate ship with a pocket handkerchief, I at the jetty end, and one or two of my bold blades keeping the crowd at bay; or else turning in the saddle to look back at my whole command (some five thousand strong) following me at the hand-gallop up the road out of the burning valley—this last by moonlight.

These imaginary adventures were soothing as well as exciting, facilitating escape into sleep, much as "magic lantern" images do for the young Marcel in Proust's *Combray*.[45]

Louis assumed that such fantasies must be universal. Before he had met Henry James he encountered an essay in which James praised *Treasure Island* but said he wasn't qualified to criticize it—"I have been a child, but I have never been on a quest for buried treasure." That provoked Louis to retort, also in print, "Here is indeed a willful paradox; for if he has never been on a quest for buried treasure, it can be demonstrated that he has never been a child."[46]

Another source of imaginative pleasure was a toy theater in which little cardboard characters could be made to act out plays. The characters were published in a series known as Skelt's Juvenile Drama, and could be purchased for a penny apiece, or two if already colored—"A Penny Plain and Twopence Coloured," as Louis called them in an essay on Skelt. The plain versions might even be preferable, since you got to color them yourself. "With crimson lake (hark to the sound of it—crimson lake!—the horns of elf-land are not richer on the ear)—with crimson lake and Prussian blue a certain purple is to be compounded which, for cloaks especially, Titian could not equal."

When he wrote this essay Louis was living far away from Edinburgh, but added, "There stands, I fancy, to this day (but now how fallen!) a certain stationer's shop at a corner of the wide thoroughfare that joins the city of my childhood with the sea." The shop was indeed there for many years after his time (fig. 12). Gazing into its window, he would yearn to possess such titles as *The Smuggler* and *Three-Finger Jack, the Terror of Jamaica*, evoking a world drastically different from his own. He says in this essay, "What am I? what are life, art, letters, the world, but what my Skelt has made them? He stamped himself upon

12. The shop in Leith Walk

my immaturity. The world was plain before I knew him, a poor penny world, but soon it was all coloured with romance."⁴⁷

A typical example (color plate 4) illustrates Skelt's appeal. The fearless tar wields a cutlass while wearing a sword and a brace of pistols, and bravely displays the Union Jack. The caption identifies him as Newton Foster, hero of an 1832 novel of that name by Captain Frederick Marryat, whose nautical tales enchanted Louis in his youth. "Fiction is to the grown man," he wrote in "A Gossip on Romance," "what play is to the child."⁴⁸

CHAPTER 2

Schooling and Travels

AN ERRATIC EDUCATION

Louis's early education was casual and intermittent. The main thing he learned was that he couldn't stand schools. At the age of seven he entered his first, a little establishment down the hill in the Cannonmills district, where he was unhappy and stayed only briefly. Someone who had been there at the time remembered him as "the butt of the school from the oddity of his appearance." He was never the kind of boy who fit in easily, and when he got older he would make a point of dressing eccentrically.[1]

That was followed by Mr. Henderson's little school in India Street, right around the corner from his home, where his tenure was likewise brief. Beatings were routine in schools in those days, for misbehavior but also for slacking in the work, and the boys had a song that an acquaintance remembered hearing Louis sing "with great gusto" ("in fact he may have been the author of it"):

> Here we suffer grief and pain
> Under Mr. Hendie's cane.
> If you don't obey his laws
> He will punish with his tawse.

The first line was borrowed from a popular hymn:

> Here we suffer grief and pain,
> Here we meet to part again;
> In Heaven we part no more.

The tawse or taws was a leather strap with two or three tails, a juvenile version of the cat-o'-nine-tails. Those were common in Scotland and also Ireland; in a poem by Yeats, Aristotle "played the taws" on the rear end of Alexander the Great.[2]

After Henderson's, Louis was enrolled in the prestigious Edinburgh Academy. He disliked that too, and stayed for less than two years. A schoolmate recalled, "I vividly recollect him one day in the Academy Yards in a towering rage; some of the other kiddies were ragging him, and the rim of his straw hat was torn down and hanging in rings round his face and shoulders."[3]

When he was twelve a boarding school in England was tried, Burlington Lodge Academy at Spring Grove, Isleworth, not far from London. It was chosen because an aunt of his lived close by and had two sons there. A letter survives: "My dear Papa you told me to tell you whenever I was miserable. I do not feel well and I wish to get home. Do take me with you." He was indeed taken away, and never went back.[4]

One thing Louis did carry away from Isleworth: a deep sense of the difference between the Scots and the English, who struck him then and later as emotionally repressed.

> John Bull's is a domineering nature, steady in fight, imperious to command, but neither curious nor quick about the life of others.... England and Scotland differ, indeed, in law, in history, in religion, in education, and in the very look of nature and men's faces.... The speech of Englishmen is too often lacking in generous ardour, the better part of the man too often withheld from the social commerce, and the contact of mind with mind evaded as with terror.[5]

Fortunately, Thomas Stevenson, a self-made man, had contempt for conventional education, which made him tolerant of his son's erratic progress. In some unpublished notes Louis wrote,

> There seems to have been nothing more rooted in him than his contempt for all the ends, processes, and ministers of education. "Tutor" was ever a by-word with him; "positively tutorial," he would say of people or manners he despised; and with rare consistency, he bravely encouraged me to neglect my lessons, and never so much as asked me my place [i.e., rank]

in school. What a boy should learn in school, he used to say, is "to sit upon his bum."

A family friend confirmed that this was Thomas's fixed attitude.

> He would stop schoolboys in the street, look at their burden of books, shake his head over such trash, and advise them with earnestness to pay no heed to the rubbish which was being crammed into them. He begged them to look about them, play to their heart's content, but to read or study only what their inclination dictated. The schoolboys would gaze open-mouthed at the firm-faced man who seriously propounded such palatable views.[6]

When Louis was fourteen one more school in Edinburgh was tried, with better success; he stayed there for three years. Known simply as Thomson's school, its sole instructor was Robert Thomson, who had the merit of being easygoing. A classmate of Louis's, Bellyse Baildon, recalled, "I do not think there were at this little seminary more than a dozen boys, ranging in ages from nine or ten to fourteen or fifteen, and our intellectual calibre varied fully as much as our years. Some of us were sent there for reasons of health, and others because they had not made that progress with their studies which their fond parents had hoped." Another former classmate said that Louis's father "thought the system suitable for a boy not in strong health, of curious individual habits and tastes and fancies, that made him unfit for the rough-and-tumble of a schoolboy's life."[7]

For the first time Louis was relatively happy at a school—but only relatively. Long afterward Baildon wrote in a memoir of his friend, "The gentle, rather girlish boy who, I am sure, was never responsible for a black eye or bloody nose among his schoolfellows, and whose one attempt to play the 'big boy' and bully at school was, to my knowledge, one of his failures, seems in private to have sated himself with theatrical and imaginary carnage."[8]

As in earlier days, imagination was a defense and a liberation. For the first time since his history of Moses with the cigars and suitcases, Louis was inspired to write. He and Baildon collaborated on a magazine called the *Jack o' Lantern*. Two decades later Baildon dedicated a volume of poems to him: "I can only send you from my stripped vineyard raisins for grapes, and when you 'pree' [sample] them, as we say in Scotland, you must bethink you of Frederick Street and the Gardens and the short-lived *Jack o' Lantern,* and let the glow of old fellowship renew the bloom and plump the skin of these wizened berries." Baildon had become a scholar, earning a PhD at the University of Freiburg in Germany (the degree was not offered in British universities until the twentieth century). Louis wrote back that Frederick Street and the magazine "are again with me—and the note of the east wind and Froebel's voice, and the smell of soup in Thomson's stair."⁹

The sole copy of the magazine that has survived includes a story called "The Wrecker," which shows Louis savoring the clichés of thriller fiction.

> On the shore at North Berwick were two men. The older and stronger of the two was a tall, ill-looking man with grizzled hair and a red nose. He was dressed in a tarnished gold-laced blue coat, a red waistcoat, and leggings. The other might have been a fisherman except for the fact that from each of the pockets of his pea-jacket there projected a pistol. He was a more villainous-looking fellow than the other. "Dan," said the first, "what is that clinging to that mast?" "I think," said the other, "it is a sailor. You had better go and secure him."

In another story, "Adventures in the South Seas," a pair of shipwrecked sailors fall into the hands of savages who decide to burn them alive.

> We shuddered to think of being killed so soon. But I forgot to tell you that I had made love to a beautiful girl even in one day, and from all I knew she loved me. The next thing they did was to build round us sticks and rubbish of all kinds till we could hardly see what they were doing. At last they finished. They then set fire to it, and after it had got hold well, they began to dance, which is called a war-dance. (To be continued.)¹⁰

In Louis's early teens there was an encounter with romantic fiction when he and Katharine Stevenson, his favorite female cousin, were exploring a ruined castle south of Edinburgh. "The place stood open to incursive urchins; and there, in a deserted chamber, we found some half-a-dozen numbers of *Black Bess, or the Knight of the Road,* a work by EDWARD VILES." The highwayman-hero was the celebrated Dick Turpin, and Black Bess was his horse. Due to their sensational nature and cheap price, romances of this kind were known as penny dreadfuls.

Carrying their prize outside, Louis and Katharine read *Black Bess* "in the shade of a contiguous fir wood, lying on blaeberries" (Scots for the European bilberry).

> A horrifying sight met his gaze. Cowering on the floor, and divested of almost every article of attire, was a young girl of about seventeen years of

age. She was dark, and had long glossy hair hanging disorderly about her.... "Save you, my poor girl!" he said, in his deep, manly tones, which thrilled through every nerve of the girl's body with a feeling of exquisite delight which she had never before experienced. "Of course I will!"

Louis and Katharine would remain close for many years, though there would eventually be a painful falling-out.[11]

All of this reading and writing was extracurricular, of course. Another schoolmate from Thomson's recalled, "An hour every Friday afternoon was devoted to the writing of essays on some given subject. In after years I asked Mr. Thomson if he had ever noticed in those written by Stevenson anything calling for special remark. 'No,' he replied. 'Except for an occasional striking phrase, they never showed much grasp of, or interest in, their subject, or of a distinctive literary turn of mind.'" Set topics never interested Louis. It would no doubt have astonished Thomson to know that one day his pupil would be a world-famous writer.[12]

One point is worth mentioning: Louis learned to read unusually late, and all his life he was an uncertain speller and ruefully aware of it. He could never even remember the "I before E except after C" rule; in one of his manuscripts we find *wiegh, niether, nieghbour,* and *siezed.* Might there have been some dyslexia, which wasn't understood at all at that time? In his edition of the letters Sidney Colvin said he felt free to correct misspellings. "As all his friends are aware, to spell in a quite accurate and grown-up manner was a thing which this master of English letters was never able to learn."[13]

EARLY TRAVELS

A life of constant traveling began in Louis's teens, when Margaret's poor health prompted extended residence in places that were thought to be therapeutic. Two stays in Torquay on the south coast of England were boring, of interest today only for Louis's letters home, playfully addressed to "Dear Papa" or "Mein guter Väter." He must have liked the look of the German umlaut, but "Vater" doesn't actually have one—though "güter" does.

The first of these letters, in the spring of 1865, gives an unenthusiastic picture of life there: "We spent a rather miserable day Mama on the sofa myself on a chair both reading. The stillness only broken by the noise of turning the pages, or a sigh from Mama.... The sky is a fine, dull, gloomy, leaden grey." In another letter he demands payment of one shilling, which by now was the penalty if his parents forgot themselves and still addressed him as "Smout."

A year later they were back in Torquay and Louis wrote again, "Respected paternal relative, I write to make a request of the most moderate nature.... I appeal to your charity, I appeal to your generosity, I appeal to your justice, I appeal to your accounts, I appeal, in fine, to your purse. My sense of generosity forbids the receipt of more—my sense of justice forbids the receipt of less— than half-a-crown. Greeting, from, sir, your most affectionate and needy son R. Stevenson." He was still using his first name, and at school he was indeed known as Robert. A half crown was equivalent to two shillings and sixpence, or one-eighth of a pound. To be sure, money went a lot further then than it does today, and the half crown would now be worth £7.[14]

More exciting was a two-month stay in 1863 with both parents on the Riviera, undertaken (as usual) for his mother's health. They rented an apartment in Menton, within walking distance of the Italian border, and it made a profound impression. Years later Louis would live there with his wife. Menton had only recently become French, and was still known to British tourists by the old spelling Mentone, which is how he heard it. When he was pleading to be liberated from the Isleworth school he said, "I long so to see dear old Mentoni again with the olives and the oranges."[15]

The stay in Menton was the beginning of a lifelong love affair with France. A writer introducing a collection of his essays and stories about France comments on the contrast between foggy Scotland and *la torpeur lumineuse de la baie des Anges,* the luminous torpor of the Bay of Angels. Stretching from Nice to Cap d'Antibes, it was favored by English people seeking sun and health. To this day the avenue that borders the sea at Nice is known as the *promenade des Anglais.*[16]

Neither Louis nor his parents left much in writing about this episode, but Cummy accompanied them—the photograph of her above (fig. 8 in chapter 1) was taken at that time—and she kept a diary. It took the form of letters to Catherine ("Cashie"), a nanny in the family of Thomas Stevenson's brother David. "My dear Cashie, O woman, I like fine to write in this Journal of yours, but I would like better if I could speak to you."[17]

Predictably, Cummy's entries are permeated with religiosity. In London she was horrified to see boats busy on the Thames on Sunday, when no work should ever be done. "How sad it makes one to see such things! How God's holy day is dishonoured! Oh Cash, when will the time come that this world will really become like the garden of the Lord, and bloom and blossom as the rose?" Journeying through France she was struck by the earnestness of monks and nuns, but in Marseilles she exclaimed," It is awful to think that people in this beautiful country, and very nice people too, are under the reign of the man of sin [the

Antichrist—i.e., the pope]; the Roman Catholics seem to have the sway." At another time, "The people here seem to live in a perfect round of pleasure. Everything is done to please the natural heart of man. The things of eternity seem banished, and what is worse, carnal man appears to love and have it so." Young Louis, we may guess, was having a very different reaction; he would grow up to be a very carnal man.

Biblical allusions occurred to Cummy constantly. "We are really like the wayfaring man mentioned in the Song of Solomon, we turn aside to tarry for a night and are gone in the morning." "How strange, as the horses go along, to hear the bells at their head! It reminds one of that verse in Scripture, I forget where to look for it at present, but shall do so after." No doubt she located it in Zechariah 14: "This shall be the punishment of Egypt, and the punishment of all nations that come not up to keep the feast of tabernacles. In that day shall there be upon the bells of the horses, HOLINESS UNTO THE LORD." In Nice she commented on "a palm tree, flourishing it was though in a very unfavourable situation. Thought of the words, 'So like the palm tree flourishing shall be the righteous one.'" That was the ninety-second Psalm. She was delighted to discover that "there is scarcely a plant mentioned in Scripture which is not found here."

More disturbingly, she evinced the puritanical repression with which she had indoctrinated Louis. A Sunday in Nice was horrifying—the family happened to be there during Mardi Gras. "The people here have been going on at a fearful rate today, men and boys dressed in all conceivable costumes, having false faces on and playing some kind of music. How sweet it was to leave this foolery and great rabble of people, and go into the [Protestant] House of Jesus! ... It is awful to see the dozens of priests going about and allowing such wickedness to go unchecked."

Though Cummy knew no French when they arrived, she studied the language and practiced conversing with local people, even though they might laugh at her attempts. "Here comes *souper,* so *bonne nuit,* which means good night, and *bon jour* is good day. *Je suis* is I am." She was amused by the multiple languages she was hearing. "Sugar is in Deutsch *der Zucker,* in French *sucre.* Spoon is *Löffel* in Deutsch, *cuiller* in French. Isn't it so funny?" She must have had a dictionary, since she knew that German nouns are capitalized.

In the diary there are frequent references to Margaret's cough, symptoms of the illness that had prompted the trip. "Mrs. Stevenson has been coughing a good deal; O, I wish it would leave her! O Cashie, woman, I think I love her more than ever now when I am with her in a foreign land." The cough did get better once they reached the Riviera.

Perhaps surprisingly, the only references to "Lewis" are casual and infrequent, though positive. "My dear Lew has got a tutor into the house. Lew is a very good bit boy, no trouble indeed."

When the party moved on to Italy, Cummy was impressed by the church music and "lovely oil paintings," but baffled when a young woman in Genoa spent ten minutes in a confessional and still wasn't finished. "I wonder what she could be saying to him, the priest, a poor wretched sinner like herself. How could he pretend to give her absolution? I cannot understand the Church of Rome at all. It is all a mystery to me."

At Pisa she was surprised to see "a tower which looks as if it were going to topple over." After that they went by sea to Naples and made an excursion to Pompeii, where Cummy found the amphitheater affecting. "I thought of the thousands who sat, looking down to that great arena, feasting their eyes with that cruel sport—wild beasts fighting together, sometimes men also, but all their bodies are now hushed in death, and we were walking over their graves."

She was disgusted to see that "men and even boys seem to be inveterate smokers all over the Continent; it is a filthy habit." Louis had not yet acquired the filthy habit.

After that they went by railway to Rome, then Florence and Venice, and onward through Austria, Germany, Belgium, and France. On May 22 they arrived in London, and soon after that were home. All of that sightseeing was something of a whirlwind, and it seems to have left little impression on Louis. In later life he seldom referred to Italy, and never with enthusiasm; for him the Continent would always mean France. Besides, they had spent much of their time tramping through churches and museums. When he traveled as an adult he preferred to go at his own pace and as the spirit moved him. Best of all would be to settle down in one place for an extended stay.

CHAPTER 3

Happiness in the Countryside

THE SPIRIT OF PLACE

All his life Louis experienced a deep emotional response to landscape, not as picturesque views but as worlds to immerse himself in. Just south of Edinburgh lay the rolling Pentland Hills, and from his earliest days he relished frequent stays there in the village of Colinton, where his grandfather was minister of the Presbyterian church and lived in the "manse" next door. Lewis Balfour was the only grandparent Louis ever knew, "the noblest looking old man I have ever seen." The photograph (fig. 13) shows him wearing the "clerical bands" that identified a clergyman.[1]

Louis acknowledged that although the old man was a striking figure, he seemed so alien and distant that it was hard to grasp their connection. "Try as I please, I cannot join myself on with the reverend doctor; and all the while, no doubt, and even as I write the phrase, he moves in my blood, and whispers words to me, and sits efficient in the very knot and centre of my being."[2]

More welcoming at Colinton was Margaret's unmarried sister Jane, the "Auntie" of *A Child's Garden of Verses,* who kept house for their widowed father. In his draft of a memoir Louis wrote, "There were thirteen of the Balfours, as (oddly enough) there were of the Stevensons also, and the children of the family came home to her to be nursed, to be educated, to be mothered.... There must sometimes have been half a score of us children about the Manse, and all were born a second time from Aunt Jane's tenderness."[3]

Colinton Manse was a paradise for Louis. "I have been happier since," he

13. The Reverend Lewis Balfour

wrote, "for I think most people exaggerate the capacity for happiness of a child; but I have never again been happy in the same way. For indeed, it was scarce a happiness of this world, as we conceive it when we are grown up, and was more akin to that of an animal than to that of a man. The sense of sunshine, of green leaves, and of the singing of birds, seems never to have been so strong in me as in that place." A cousin remembered an old yew tree "under which R.L.S. used to love to hide and put his ear against the wall which divided the garden from the graveyard, declaring he heard 'the spirits of the departed' speaking to him."[4]

In the picture (fig. 14), the Water of Leith tumbles below the house, on its way northward to the Firth of Forth. A bit further along the stream turned the

14. Colinton Manse

wheel of a flour mill, which could be reached by transgressing a boundary, as he recalled in *A Child's Garden of Verses*:

> Over the borders, a sin without pardon,
> Breaking the branches and crawling below,
> Out through the breach in the wall of the garden,
> Down by the banks of the river we go.
>
> Here is the mill with the humming of thunder,
> Here is the weir with the wonder of foam,

> Here is the sluice with the race running under—
> Marvellous places, though handy to home!

By the end of the century the mill and weir (a little dam) had both been demolished.[5]

Lonely and bullied in Edinburgh, here Louis was in his element. With the gang of cousins he could truly belong, and even take the lead in games. Incidentally, no fewer than five of the cousins were also named Lewis after their grandfather, and among themselves they had to use nicknames.

The cousin he was closest to was Bob—Robert Alan Mowbray Stevenson, son of Thomas's brother Alan. Bob was three years older than Louis and also had artistic inclinations; he would become a painter and art critic.

In an essay called "Child's Play" Louis talked about the roots of fiction in childhood imaginings, and recalled how he and Bob created little worlds with their morning porridge. "He ate his with sugar, and explained it to be a country continually buried under snow. I took mine with milk, and explained it to be a country suffering gradual inundation. You can imagine us exchanging bulletins; how here was an island still unsubmerged, here a valley not yet covered with snow; what inventions were made; how his population lived in cabins on perches and travelled on stilts, and how mine was always in boats; how the interest grew furious as the last corner of safe ground was cut off on all sides and grew smaller every moment; and how in fine the food was of altogether secondary importance."[6]

Bob's father had been a partner in the family engineering firm, but when Bob was five he had a breakdown and was forced to give up work. When he died thirteen years later an obituary in the *Scotsman* said tactfully, "The mental tension caused by the responsibilities and difficulties of this work, acting upon his sensitive, chivalrous, and unsparing nature, was the main cause of the sudden shattering of his nervous system which, in 1852, made it necessary for him to withdraw absolutely from his profession and the world."[7]

Alan shared with his brother Thomas a grim religious faith. When their father died Alan wrote, "A high sense of duty pervaded his whole life, and he died calmly in the blessed hope and peace which only an indwelling and personal belief in the merits of the Redeemer can impart to any son of our guilty race." That conclusion, "our guilty race," is a classic Calvinist reflection. At the time of Alan's retirement he gave Bob a Bible with this inscription:

> Read in this blessed Book, my gentle boy;
> Learn that thy heart is utterly defiled. . . .

> Seek thy Creator in thine early youth;
> Value thy soul above the world, and shun
> The sinner's way; oh! seek the way of truth.

But Bob was never gentle, and would grow up to be even more transgressive than Louis.[8]

Louis deeply cherished the opportunities for play with his cousins. At the end of *A Child's Garden of Verses* is a poem addressed to his cousin Minnie, who by then was living in India:

> The river, on from mill to mill,
> Flows past our childhood's garden still;
> But ah! we children never more
> Shall watch it from the water-door!
> Below the yew—it still is there—
> Our phantom voices haunt the air
> As we were still at play,
> And I can hear them call and say:
> "How far is it to Babylon?"
> Ah, far enough, my dear,
> Far, far enough from here.

He was remembering an old nursery rhyme:

> How many miles to Babylon?
> Three score miles and ten.
> Can I get there by candle-light?
> Yes, and back again.[9]

Nearby, to the south of Colinton, rose the Pentland Hills (fig. 15). "At close quarters," the biographer Jenni Calder says, "one sees and feels their starkness. There are few trees. Their slopes seem to have been stripped and scrubbed bare by the wind." Louis enjoyed that spareness, and he wrote later, "A crying hill-bird, the bleat of a sheep, a wind singing in the dry grass, seem not so much to interrupt as to accompany the stillness."[10]

The Colinton idyll came to an abrupt end when Louis was nine; his grandfather died and a successor moved into the manse. Stevenson fans who visited Colinton years later found that a few old-timers still remembered the boy lying against a stone wall with a book. "He wasna thocht verra muckle of," they would say, or "It wasna jaloosed [suspected] that he wad ever come to muckle [much]."[11]

15. The Pentland Hills

THE SEASIDE, SWANSTON, AND THE HILLS

For a time the family took its holidays in various seaside places. Louis particularly enjoyed their repeated stays at North Berwick, thirty miles east of Edinburgh, where he organized his playmates in the games that he describes in his essay "The Lantern-Bearers." The title refers to tin "bulls-eye" lanterns concealed beneath tightly buttoned coats. Also known as dark lanterns, as in the Sherlock Holmes stories, they gave off light only when their covers were slid open. "As it was the rule to keep our glory contained, none could recognise a lantern-bearer, unless (like the polecat) by the smell."

To adults the game might have seemed trivial, but it didn't to Louis and his playmates. "The essence of this bliss was to walk by yourself in the black night, the slide shut, the topcoat buttoned; not a ray escaping, whether to conduct your footsteps or to make your glory public—a mere pillar of darkness in the dark; and all the while, deep down in the privacy of your fool's heart, to know you had a bull's-eye at your belt, and to exult and sing over the knowledge." This is a recreation of childhood, but more than that as well: it's a metaphor for an imaginative power that survives deep down in even the most stolid adult.[12]

North Berwick was memorable for something else: a mile offshore loomed a towering volcanic plug called the Bass Rock. Louis mentions "the surf ringing it with white, the solan geese [gannets] hanging around its summit like a great and glittering smoke." In later life he acquired a spectacular print of the Bass, after a painting by J.M.W. Turner, and the rock would make an important appearance in his novel *Catriona.*

Another favorite place in the country was the town of Cramond, a few miles west of Edinburgh. One of Louis's uncles, Dr. George Balfour, lived there, and as a boy he often explored the neighborhood with his cousin Lewis (nicknamed "Cramond" to distinguish him from the several other Lewises). The inn at nearby Queensferry, where ferries connected with the northern shore of the Firth of Forth, likewise appealed to him. Years later he wrote: "Some places speak distinctly. Certain dank gardens cry aloud for a murder; certain old houses demand to be haunted; certain coasts are set apart for shipwreck. The old Hawes Inn at the Queen's Ferry makes a similar call upon my fancy.... The man or the hour had not yet come, but some day, I think, a boat shall put off from the Queen's Ferry, fraught with a dear cargo, and some frosty night a horseman, on a tragic errand, rattle with his whip upon the green shutters of the inn at Burford." Five years later he added in a footnote that he had launched the boat in *Kidnapped.*[13]

When Louis was sixteen the family found a new haven at the foot of the Pentlands, a couple of miles from Colinton. They took a lease on Swanston Cottage, and from then on spent as much time there as they could. As the picture shows (fig. 16), it was actually a considerable house, built of carefully fitted stone and with a handsome bay window. It was a "cottage" only by virtue of being a country retreat.

At Swanston Louis especially enjoyed the Lowland or "Lallans" dialect that the country people spoke. It was common in Edinburgh too, but standard English was usual in his social class and at 17 Heriot Row. Robert Burns, who grew up speaking Lallans in the west of Scotland, mastered the art of using just enough of it in a poem to bring out its flavor without bewildering Anglophone readers. For example,

> There's ae wee faut they whiles lay to me,
> I like the lasses—Gude forgie me!
> For mony a plack they wheedle frae me
> At dance or fair;
> Maybe some ither thing they gie me,
> They weel can spare....

16. Swanston Cottage

>But, to conclude my lang epistle,
>As my auld pen's worn to the gristle,
>Twa lines frae you wad gar me fissle,
>   Who am, most fervent,
>While I can either sing or whistle,
>   Your friend and servant.

A *plack* is fourpence; *fissle* means "tingle."[14]

By now Louis was old enough to roam freely on the hills, and he enjoyed describing what they were like in Lallans, using the same stanza form that Burns did.

>Frae nirly, nippin', Eas'lan' breeze,
>Frae Norlan' snaw, an' haar o' seas,
>Weel happit in your gairden trees,
>   A bonny bit,
>Atween the muckle Pentland's knees,
>   Secure ye sit....

> Frae the high hills the curlew ca's;
> The sheep gang baaing by the wa's;
> Or whiles a clan o' roosty craws
> 	Cangle thegether;
> The wild bees seek the gairden raws,
> 	Weariet wi' heather.

The poem moves from summer to winter: "In the mirk nicht, the winter rain / Dribbles an' blads"—"in the dark night the winter rain dribbles and blows." Whatever the season, this was a landscape that Louis loved. The poem's title, "Ille Terrarum," comes from an ode of Horace: *Ille terrarum mihi praeter omnes angulus ridet,* "This corner of the earth smiles for me more than any other."[15]

Louis picked up much of his Lallans from a shepherd named John Todd, known as "Lang John" for his height, with whom he would tramp for hours in the hills while the sheep were grazing. "My friend the shepherd," he said later, "speaks broad Scotch of the broadest, and often enough employs words that I do not understand myself." Louis recalled Todd in an essay entitled "Pastoral": "He laughed not very often, and when he did, with a sudden, loud haw-haw, hearty but somehow joyless, like an echo from a rock. His face was permanently set and coloured; ruddy and stiff with weathering; more like a picture than a face."

But it was Todd's eloquence that captivated Louis. "He spoke in the richest dialect of Scotch I ever heard, and this vocabulary he would handle like a master. I might count him with the best talkers, only that talking Scotch and talking English seem incomparable acts. He touched on nothing, at least, but he adorned it; when he narrated, the scene was before you." Many of Louis's original readers would have recognized a famous phrase that Samuel Johnson composed in Latin for his friend Oliver Goldsmith, *Nihil tetegit quod non ornavit:* "He touched nothing that he did not adorn." The allusion is a beautiful tribute to the old shepherd, ranking his skill in language on a level with a writer of great distinction.[16]

It was Todd, Louis said, who taught him to appreciate the spirit of the hills.

> He it was that made it live for me, as the artist can make all things live. It was through him the simple strategy of massing sheep upon a snowy evening, with its attendant scampering of earnest, shaggy aides-de-camp, was an affair that I never wearied of seeing, and that I never weary of recalling to mind: the shadow of the night darkening on the hills, inscrutable black blots of snow shower moving here and there like night already come, huddles of yellow sheep and dartings of black dogs upon the

snow, a bitter air that took you by the throat, unearthly harpings of the wind along the moors; and for centerpiece to all these features and influences, John winding up the brae [slope], keeping his captain's eye upon all sides, and breaking, ever and again, into a spasm of bellowing that seemed to make the evening bleaker. It is thus that I still see him in my mind's eye, perched on a hump of the declivity not far from Halkerside, his staff in airy flourish, his great voice taking hold upon the hills and echoing terror to the lowlands; I, meanwhile, standing somewhat back, until the fit should be over, and, with a pinch of snuff, my friend relapse into his easy, even conversation.

Though the shepherd's casual talk might be "easy," it was direct and to the point. In another essay Louis contrasted it with the conversational style in England, where "the contact of mind with mind [is] evaded as with terror. A Scottish peasant will talk more liberally out of his own experience. He will not put you by with conversational counters and small jests; he will give you the best of himself, like one interested in life and man's chief end."[17]

Swanston people remembered that Todd used to say of Louis, "He is an awfu' laddie for speirin' questions about a' thing, an' whenever you turn your back, awa' he gangs an' writes it a' doon." A "speirin" questioner is prying and inquisitive. Years later some old-timers told a visitor the same thing. "Stevenson would dae naething but lie aboot the dykes. He wouldna wark. He was aye rinnin' aboot wi' lang Todd, amang the hills, getting him to tell a' the stories he kent." "Lang Todd" prompts one to wonder if John passed his nickname on to Long John Silver in *Treasure Island*.[18]

As at Colinton, the locals were surprised that Robert Louis Stevenson ever amounted to anything. One old lady summed up the general feeling: "He was just naething."[19]

Louis's cousin Henrietta kept a fragment of fiction that he wrote at this time. As her husband described it, "It is a very weird tale of the time of the plague in Edinburgh—thoroughly Stevensonian. He must have been about fourteen when he wrote it, and tossed it to my wife, who was a favorite cousin. She always kept it among her treasures." This was the beginning: "It was freezing pretty hard, and all the streets were slippery; and the more sheltered corners of the Loch had curdled into watery ice, in spite of the gale. There was good promise of snow before the dawn." That is remarkable writing for a fourteen-year-old! After this it turns into standard blood-and-thunder stuff. "In front of the fire stood a tall thin sallow man, of some seven and twenty years of age. His face was worn and haggard; his brow was tied up in a bloodstained napkin, and his eyes gleamed with a cold, fierce, feverish light." When the story ends a few pages later, "The mystery of the Plague Cellar was never solved."[20]

In Samoa a year before his death, Louis heard that his cousin still had this piece and wanted to publish it. He told his mother, "I would rather perish tomorrow than allow 'The Plague Cellar' to appear under any form or under any pretense. You can break this to Henrietta as tenderly as you can; but it must be final."[21]

There must have been other literary attempts in these years, but nearly all are lost. We do know that at fourteen Louis composed a rhyming libretto for a comic opera with a title worthy of Edward Gorey—*The Baneful Potato.* The heroine was to sing an aria that began "My own dear casement window."[22]

READING, AND A PRECOCIOUS PUBLICATION

People who remembered Louis lying against a stone wall reading a book were describing what he would later acknowledge himself. "All through my boyhood and youth," he wrote in his thirties, "I was known and pointed out for the pattern of an idler; and yet I was always busy on my own private end, which was to learn to write. I kept always two books in my pocket, one to read, one to write in. As I walked, my mind was busy fitting what I saw with appropriate words; when I sat by the roadside, I would either read, or a pencil and a penny version-book would be in my hand, to note down the features of the scene or commemorate some halting stanzas. Thus I lived with words."[23]

When he was forty he told a correspondent, "I read now, yes, and with pleasure, but years ago I read with the greed and gusto of a pig, sucking up some of the very paper (you would think) into my brain."[24]

To call him a voracious reader would be putting it mildly. The number of books he mentions in his essays and letters is staggering, as is his almost total recall of passages in them. And he didn't just read, he reread. A particular favorite was Dumas's *Le Vicomte de Bragelonne,* the third and last of the Three Musketeers novels. He recalled the pleasure it gave him in his teens when he was staying by himself at Swanston:

> I would return in the early night from one of my patrols with the shepherd; a friendly face would meet me in the door, a friendly retriever scurry upstairs to fetch my slippers; and I would sit down with the *Vicomte* for a long, silent, solitary lamp-light evening by the fire. And yet I know not

why I call it silent, when it was enlivened with such a clatter of horseshoes, and such a rattle of musketry, and such a stir of talk; or why I call those evenings solitary in which I gained so many friends. I would rise from my book and pull the blind aside, and see the snow and the glittering hollies chequer a Scotch garden, and the winter moonlight brighten the white hills. Thence I would turn again to that crowded and sunny field of life in which it was so easy to forget myself, my cares, and my surroundings: a place busy as a city, bright as a theatre, thronged with memorable faces, and sounding with delightful speech. I carried the thread of that epic into my slumbers, I woke with it unbroken, I rejoiced to plunge into the book again at breakfast, it was with a pang that I must lay it down and turn to my own labours; for no part of the world has ever seemed to me so charming as these pages, and not even my friends are quite so real, perhaps quite so dear, as d'Artagnan.

By the time he wrote this, Louis had read the *Vicomte* "either five or six times."[25]

It's not actually easy to see why he loved this book so much. It's prolix, hundreds of pages long, and dense with confusing details from seventeenth-century French history; it hasn't been translated into English since 1857. What appealed to him must have been what a critic calls "the power of the irresistible personality that lies behind Dumas' tales, the generous spirit of the man with his contagious lust for life, his verve and perennial good humour." Also, the *Vicomte* follows the Musketeers when they have reached middle age and are swashbuckling no more: "The superman heroes are all too vulnerable: they cannot defeat time, nor can they halt the erosion of the musketeering spirit." Louis's mature fiction would be much like that.[26]

Scotland too had a past full of compelling stories, some very close to home. A friend, Eve Simpson, wrote, "The lonely hills for the lonely Louis were peopled with the makers of history." As a child he had been deeply moved by stories of the doomed Covenanters, upholders of the National Covenant of 1638 that sought to preserve Presbyterian practices when the London government was attempting to impose Episcopalianism. In 1666 a failed rebellion at Rullion Green, eight miles south of Edinburgh, became known as the Pentland Rising, and in 1680 a final attempt led by Richard Cameron was brutally put down. His followers were known as Cameronians.[27]

Cummy used to read a poem to Louis entitled "Cameronian Dream," which he said long afterward awakened in him "the sentiment of romantic Scottish history." Though he never sympathized with the old theology, its lost cause moved him deeply, and "Cameronian Dream" was a celebration of just such a cause:

> In a dream of the night I was wafted away
> To the moorland of mist where the martyrs lay;
> Where Cameron's sword and his Bible are seen
> Engraved on the stone where the heather grows green....
>
> Their faces grew pale and their swords were unsheathed,
> But the vengeance that darkened their brows was unbreathed;
> With eyes raised to Heaven, in meek resignation,
> They sang their last song to the God of salvation.

Commenting on the tragic sense of history that would pervade Stevenson's mature fiction, Mary Lascelles says that any Scot at that time would grow up knowing about the Covenanters, but not with "the terrible consciousness of their history which Stevenson suffered under the dominion of his devoted nurse."[28]

The Pentland Rising, led by the militant Cameron, got its name from the hills that Louis knew so well, and he was inspired to write a brief history that his father had privately printed, *The Pentland Rising: A Page of History, 1666*. It was an impressive piece of work for a sixteen-year-old: "Two hundred years ago a tragedy was enacted in Scotland, the memory whereof has been in great measure lost or obscured by the deep tragedies which followed it. It is, as it were, the evening of the night of persecution—a sort of twilight, dark indeed to us, but light as the noonday when compared with the midnight gloom which followed."

Louis depicts the Covenanters as heroes, giving their lives for faith and liberty. His storytelling gift is already apparent: "The wind howled fiercely over the moorland; a close, thick, wetting rain descended. Chilled to the bone, worn out with long fatigue, sinking to the knees in mire, onward they marched to destruction, onward to their defeat at Pentland and their scaffold at Edinburgh."

The rebels pause to rest at Colinton and then climb into the hills.

> The sun, going down behind the Pentlands, cast golden lights and blue shadows on their snow-clad summits, slanted obliquely into the rich plain before them, bathing with rosy splendour the leafless, snow-sprinkled trees, and fading gradually into shadow in the distance.... It was while waiting on this spot that the fear-inspiring cry was raised: "The enemy! Here come the enemy!"... When they fell there was none to sing their coronach [keening at a funeral] or wail the death-wail over them. Those who sacrificed themselves for the peace, the liberty, and the religion of

their fellow countrymen lay bleaching in the field of death for long, and when at last they were buried by charity, the peasants dug up their bodies, desecrated their graves, and cast them once more upon the open heath for the sorry value of their winding-sheets!

Thirty rebels who survived were executed in Edinburgh, and their heads and limbs were distributed around the country for display.

Louis's narrative concludes, "Perhaps the storm of harsh and fiercely jubilant noises, the clanging of trumpets, the rattling of drums, and the hootings and jeerings of an unfeeling mob, which were the last they heard on earth, might, when the mortal fight was over, when the river of death was passed, add tenfold sweetness to the hymning of the angels, tenfold peacefulness to the shores which they had reached."[29]

Thomas Stevenson had second thoughts, however, after having this little work printed, and quickly bought back all of the hundred copies (one does survive in the National Library of Scotland). He wouldn't even show *The Pentland Rising* to members of the family. Graham Balfour thought it might have been because it was too novelistic: "[Louis] had made a story of it, and by so doing had, in his father's opinion, spoiled it." But Thomas loved the novels of Walter Scott, and that explanation seems improbable. More likely he disapproved of celebrating rebellion against authority. The future author of *Kidnapped* and *Catriona* would always sympathize with rebels.[30]

In later years Louis himself didn't think much of this youthful effort. Shortly before he died he wrote to a friend who was planning a complete edition of his works, "I heartily abominate and reject the idea of reprinting *The Pentland Rising*." To another friend he said it was "an absurdity written by a schoolboy," and when he was asked for an account of his career, he called it "a bulky historical romance without a spark of merit, and now deleted from the world." Still, it was valuable apprenticeship for his mature writing. *Kidnapped*, *Catriona*, and *The Master of Ballantrae* are all its direct descendants.[31]

CHAPTER 4

The Master Builders

When Louis was in his teens it was taken for granted that he would study engineering and then take his place in the family firm. Its achievements had been extraordinary. Thomas Stevenson's father Robert constructed his first lighthouse in 1811 on the notorious Bell or Inchcape Rock off the eastern Scottish coast. The Bell Rock's name came from a legend that the Romantic poet Robert Southey dramatized in a ballad: a medieval abbot hung a warning bell on the rock, but a pirate removed it to encourage shipwrecks, and later perished there himself:

> But even in his dying fear
> One dreadful sound could the Rover hear;
> A sound as if with the Inchcape Bell
> The Devil below was ringing his knell.[1]

Louis grew up hearing stories of the heroic planning and labor that went into constructing the Bell Rock lighthouse. It took four years because the work could only be carried on at low tide and in good weather, which didn't occur often. He also read his grandfather's own account of the achievement, published in 1824 and dedicated to King George IV. He relished his forebear's problem-solving ability and courage in the face of danger, and commented, "His whole relation to the [lighthouse] service was, in fact, patriarchal; and I believe I may say that throughout its ranks he was adored." He added, "The joy of my grand-

17. Bell Rock Lighthouse under construction

father in this career was strong as the love of woman." For Louis that meant it was very strong indeed.[2]

An illustration in Robert Stevenson's book (fig. 17) gives a good sense of the accomplishment. It's low tide, and the reef is partially exposed. The smaller tower at the left is a temporary beacon that also housed workmen during the night. Between the two structures can be seen three blocks of granite, pre-cut in accordance with diagrams made by Robert Stevenson, that are being lifted by cranes.

A print after a painting by Turner (fig. 18) shows the lighthouse in a storm, its foundation covered by waves, with lightning flashing in the sky and a sailboat steering away to safety. In later life Louis mounted a copy of this print over his fireplace.

The Bell Rock was only the second lighthouse ever constructed in the entire British Isles, after the Eddystone Light in the southwest of England (best remembered for the song "My father was the keeper of the Eddystone Light, slept with a mermaid one fine night"). Robert continued steadily on with the work, joined in due course by his sons Alan, David, and Thomas. By 1877 the firm was responsible for designing and building fifty-seven more. Most are still standing and working to this day, including the Bell Rock, though it no longer has a resident keeper; it was automated in 1998.

18. Bell Rock Lighthouse, by Turner

A modern photograph (color plate 5) gives an effective sense of another lighthouse, Skerryvore, which was built by Alan Stevenson in 1844 off the west coast of Scotland and is often described as the most beautiful lighthouse in Britain. In the picture the circle marked with an "H" is a helicopter landing pad. During Louis's final years in Britain in the late 1880s, he and Fanny named the first house they ever owned Skerryvore.

Thomas Stevenson is credited with a major invention, a revolving intermittent light. Apertures in a turning screen made the light, instead of projecting an unchanging beam, blink at a specific and unique rate that allowed mariners to identify which particular lighthouse they were seeing. Regarding this as a contribution to human safety and not a money-making proposition, he refused to patent it. In any case he didn't really need the income from that; the firm prospered with its government contracts, and the Stevenson brothers were comfortably well-to-do.

Though largely self-taught as an engineer, Thomas had a keen intuitive sense of natural forces, and an active imagination as well, anticipating how tides and storms might threaten a particular structure. When Louis was still a boy, his father began trying to initiate him into this art, but without apparent success.

On Tweedside, or by Lyne or Manor, we have spent together whole afternoons; to me, at the time, extremely wearisome; to him, as I am now sorry to think, bitterly mortifying. The river was to me a pretty and various spectacle; I could not see—I could not be made to see—it otherwise. To my father it was a chequerboard of lively forces, which he traced from pool to shallow with minute appreciation and enduring interest. "That bank was being undercut," he might say. "Why? Suppose you were to put a groin out here, would not the *filum fluminis* [the course of the stream, a legal term] be cast abruptly off across the channel? and where would it impinge upon the other shore? and what would be the result? Or suppose you were to blast that boulder, what would happen? Follow it—use the eyes God has given you—can you not see that a great deal of land would be reclaimed upon this side?" It was to me like school in holidays; but to him, until I had worn him out with my invincible triviality, a delight.

It's notable, though, that in Louis's fiction the various qualities of water in motion are frequently described.[3]

During his teens Louis made three trips along the Scottish coast to see the work at first hand. At Wick, on the northern tip of Scotland, the Stevenson firm was supervising construction of a breakwater to protect an extremely dangerous harbor. The actual work didn't interest Louis much, but the people there did. It was the first time he had heard Gaelic spoken. Writing to his mother, he described an accident in which a worker fell into the sea and was rescued with some difficulty, after which Louis asked how he was, "but he was a Highlander and—need I add it?—dickens a word could I understand of his answer. What is still worse, I find the people here about—that is to say the Highlanders, not the northmen—don't understand *me*." The northmen were descendants of the Vikings; *vik* was a Norse word for a bay.[4]

The next day he reported that a drunk had kept everyone awake in the boarding house by preaching loudly on the stairs in the dark. "At last I opened my door. 'Are we to have no sleep at all for that drunken brute?' I said. As I hoped, it had the desired effect. 'Drunken brute!' he howled, in much indignation; then after a pause, in a voice of some contrition, 'Well, if I am a drunken brute, it's only once in the twelvemonth.'" Margaret showed this to Thomas, who wrote back, "Do not interfere with that drunk man. You may get into trouble. I never should have acted as you have done. You may get your head broken before you know where you are."[5]

The rocky coast itself excited no romantic thoughts in Louis. A few years later he recalled this stay in an essay, "On the Enjoyment of Unpleasant Places," suggesting that discomfort and ugliness can force one to appreciate moments of relief all the more. "The country to which I refer was a level and treeless plateau, over which the winds cut like a whip. For miles and miles it was the same. The earth seemed to know that it was naked, and was ashamed and cold" (Adam and Eve were ashamed of their nakedness when they were expelled from Eden). The high point, if it can be called that, came in taking refuge from the gale. "This was the sort of pleasure I found in the country of which I write. The pleasure was to be out of the wind, and to keep it in memory all the time, and hug oneself upon the shelter."[6]

At a place closer to Edinburgh called Anstruther, he wrote to his mother, "I am utterly sick of this grey, grim, sea-beaten hole. I have a little cold in my head which makes my eyes sore; and you can't tell how utterly sick I am and how anxious to get back among trees and flowers and something less meaningless than this bleak fertility." Fertile, yet bleak; not "more meaningful," but at least "less meaningless."[7]

One excursion did bear imaginative fruit, a stay on the little island of Earraid (pronounced "Errid") off the western Isle of Mull, where stone was being quarried for the Dhu Heartach lighthouse that the Stevenson firm was constructing on an offshore reef. Earraid would appear twice in Louis's fiction, in "The Merry Men," one of his best stories, and in *Kidnapped*, when David Balfour believes he's stranded there and doesn't realize that at low tide it's possible to walk to the nearby mainland.

To survive on Earraid, David eats raw shellfish. Louis may have been thinking of an occasion in his boyhood at North Berwick that a former playmate recalled: "Louis and I were wading, he with very skinny legs well displayed by much rolled-up thin trousers. 'Were you ever marooned?' he said suddenly, with the strange look in his eyes that always indicated with him 'an idea.' 'Well, look here, suppose you were on a desert island with nothing to eat, what would you do?'" He pointed out that they would have no way to catch fish, but could certainly eat shrimps from the tide pools, and suggested the proper procedure: "The head would be best; it would die at once—bite quick!"[8]

On one occasion Louis had an opportunity to go down in a diving suit. As Nicholas Rankin remarks, he was the only Victorian novelist who ever did that. He described the experience later in "The Education of an Engineer"—ironically titled, since he never became one. He descended slowly in a cumbersome diving suit, accompanied by a workman named Bob Bain in a similar suit, while air was pumped down through hoses. What struck him most was a sensation of weightlessness.

> As I began to go forward with the hand of my estranged companion, a world of tumbled stones was visible, pillared with the weedy uprights of the staging: overhead, a flat roof of green; a little in front, the sea-wall, like an unfinished rampart. And presently in our upward progress, Bob motioned me to leap upon a stone; I looked to see if he were possibly in earnest, and he only signed to me the more imperiously. Now the block stood six feet high. It would have been quite a leap to me unencumbered; with the breast and back weights, and the twenty pounds upon each foot, and the staggering load of the helmet, the thing was out of reason. I laughed aloud in my tomb; and to prove to Bob how far he was astray, I gave a little impulse from my toes. Up I soared like a bird, my companion soaring at my side. As high as to the stone, and then higher, I pursued my impotent and empty flight. Even when the strong arm of Bob had checked my shoulders, my heels continued their ascent, so that I blew out sideways like an autumn leaf, and must be hauled in, hand over hand, as sailors haul in the slack of a sail, and propped upon my feet again like an intoxicated sparrow.

He was overwhelmed by the strangeness of this world just below the everyday one, and returning to the surface was a powerful experience too.

> Although I had a fine, dizzy, muddle-headed joy in my surroundings, and longed, and tried, and always failed, to lay hands on the fish that darted here and there about me, swift as humming-birds—yet I fancy I was rather relieved than otherwise when Bain brought me back to the ladder and signed to me to mount. And there was one more experience before me even then. Of a sudden, my ascending head passed into the trough of a swell. Out of the green, I shot at once into a glory of rosy, almost of sanguine light—the multitudinous seas incarnadined, the heaven above a vault of crimson. And then the glory faded into the hard, ugly daylight of a Caithness autumn, with a low sky, a grey sea, and a whistling wind.

Louis had fallen in love with Shakespeare's phrase when he and other children were taken to a performance of *Macbeth*. A girl who happened to sit next to him remembered his murmuring to himself, "The multitudinous seas incarnadine."[9]

Thomas Stevenson was a gifted mathematician who used his ability constantly in his professional work, and he was shocked to discover that his son had no head for mathematics at all. After arriving at Wick, Louis wrote to him, "What is the weight of a square foot of salt water? how many pounds are there to a ton?" Salt water does weigh more than fresh, but asking the weight of a square foot is meaningless—it would have to be a cubic foot. And it's almost incredible that Louis didn't know the British ton is 2,240 pounds.[10]

It was clear to Louis that this career was not for him. The construction of lighthouses and breakwaters was interesting, but he knew he could never be reconciled to the laborious work of design. Two decades later he recalled those excursions to the construction sites:

> [The work] takes a man into the open air; it keeps him hanging about harbour-sides, which is the richest form of idling; it carries him to wild islands; it gives him a taste of the genial dangers of the sea; it supplies him with dexterities to exercise; it makes demands upon his ingenuity; it will go far to cure him of any taste (if ever he had one) for the miserable life of cities. And when it has done so, it carries him back and shuts him in an office! From the roaring skerry [rocky islet] and the wet thwart of the tossing boat, he passes to the stool and desk, and with a memory full of ships, and seas, and perilous headlands, and the shining pharos [lighthouse], he must apply his long-sighted eyes to the pretty niceties of drawing, or measure his inaccurate mind with several pages of consecutive figures. He is a wise youth, to be sure, who can balance one part of genuine life against two parts of drudgery between four walls, and for the sake of the one, manfully accept the other.[11]

Louis didn't have romantic thoughts about the life of a lighthouse keeper, either. During one of these trips he wrote a poem about it.

> Poetry cunningly gilds
> The life of the light-keeper,
> Held on high in the blackness
> In the burning kernel of night.
> The seaman sees and blesses him,
> The poet, deep in a sonnet,
> Numbers his inky fingers
> Fitly to praise him.
> Only we behold him,
> Sitting, patient and stolid
> Martyr to a salary.

Louis didn't mind numbering his inky fingers to get the poetic meter right, but he would never incur martyrdom to a salary.[12]

Sadly, the breakwater project at Wick turned out to be a terrible disappointment for his father. It had to be repeatedly rebuilt, and each time huge waves dislodged even the heaviest stones, which weighed as much as 2,600 tons. Thomas was deeply distressed by this failure. A historian says it was the only unfinished task in the 150-year history of the Stevenson firm, and another adds, "Dhu Heartach was his monument and Wick his epitaph."[13]

CHAPTER 5

A New Life at the University

"ORGANIZED BOREDOM"

In November 1867, just as he was turning seventeen, Louis entered the University of Edinburgh as the first step toward a professional career, and his life changed dramatically. It was the same year in which the Stevensons took their lease on Swanston Cottage. Something else happened at that time that has only recently been realized by specialists: Margaret probably suffered a stroke. There is a five-month gap in her diary, after which she noted in it that she often talked "nonsense" and couldn't remember the words she wanted. Though diagnoses of people in the past are always conjectural, it's possible that she suffered from a rare condition known as hereditary hemorrhagic telangiectasia, which affects blood vessels throughout the body and causes lung damage, recurring hemorrhages, and susceptibility to stroke. Louis had those symptoms all his life and would indeed die of a stroke.[1]

As an undergraduate Louis continued to live at home; there was no residential housing at the university, and students from out of town had to rent lodgings. All the same, he enjoyed plenty of freedom, unlike students at Oxford and Cambridge, who had compulsory chapel and lectures, wore caps and gowns, and were punished if they stayed out after curfew. It's notable that those were the only two universities in all of England. In Scotland, in addition to Edinburgh, which was the most recently founded, there were also St Andrews, Glasgow, and Aberdeen.

In an essay some years later Louis celebrated his university's freedom and urban energy.

The English lad goes to Oxford or Cambridge; there, in an ideal world of gardens, to lead a semi-scenic life, costumed, disciplined and drilled by proctors. Nor is this to be regarded merely as a stage of education; it is a piece of privilege besides, and a step that separates him further from the bulk of his compatriots. At an earlier age the Scottish lad begins his greatly different experience of crowded class-rooms, of a gaunt quadrangle, of a bell hourly booming over the traffic of the city to recall him from the public-house where he has been lunching, or the streets where he has been wandering fancy-free. His college life has little of restraint, and nothing of necessary gentility. . . . Our tasks ended, we of the North go forth as freemen into the humming, lamplit city. At five o'clock you may see the last of us hiving from the college gates, in the glare of the shop windows, under the green glimmer of the winter sunset. The frost tingles in our blood; no proctor lies in wait to intercept us; till the bell sounds again we are the masters of the world.[2]

As a master of the world, Louis declined to do much studying. He found the teaching formal and tedious, and was already accustomed to self-education. Besides, he was supposedly there to learn engineering, which he already knew he disliked. That engineering was taught at all made Edinburgh very different from the English universities, where the curriculum was heavily classical and mathematical. At Cambridge Isaac Newton, one of the greatest physicists of all time, had been a professor of mathematics, not physics.

Louis did attend lectures in various subjects, but only sometimes, and then he would sit at the back of the room reading, writing, and sketching. He wrote later of "shiverings on wet, east-windy morning journeys up to class, infinite yawnings during lecture, and unquenchable gusto in the delights of truantry."[3]

His opinion of academics is evident in a poem he wrote about one of his professors:

> Here he comes, big with Statistics,
>   Troubled and sharp about fac's.
> He has heaps of the *Form* that is thinkable—
>   The *stuff* that is feeling, he lacks.
>
> Do you envy this whiskered absurdity,
>   With pince-nez and clerical tie?
> Poor fellow, he's blind of a sympathy!
>   I'd rather be blind of an eye.[4]

Louis did take his degree, but was proud of having avoided as much formal education as he could. He told Graham Balfour that at his final exam on ethical and metaphysical philosophy, "the examiner asked me a question, and I had to say to him, 'I beg your pardon, but I do not understand your phraseology.' 'It's in the textbook,' he said. 'Yes, but you couldn't possibly expect me to read so poor a book as that.' He laughed like a hunchback." It's not clear how a hunchback was supposed to laugh.[5]

At a later time Louis had occasion to write to his former professor of history, Aeneas Mackay, asking for a reference. Mackay responded courteously but with a pointed comment on his absentee behavior as a student. Louis replied frankly if undiplomatically, "You are not the only one who has regretted my absence from your lectures; but you were to me, then, only a part of a mangle through which I was being slowly and unwillingly dragged—part of a course which I had not chosen—part, in a word, of an organized boredom." Throughout his life he would never settle for boredom. It has to be added, however, that as his friends were well aware, family money made it possible for him never to hold a conventional job.[6]

Though he read French with ease, thanks to stays in France with his parents, his command of the language was colloquial rather than formal. A Balfour cousin remembered hearing that the night before he was examined in French, he asked his mother if she had a grammar in the house, because he had never studied one. "As it turned out, the examiner said it was a most extraordinary case, as Lou spoke French exactly like a Frenchman, and yet acknowledged plainly when the questions came to grammar that he had not learnt any; but under these unusual circumstances he could not help passing him."[7]

Even lectures on literature by the distinguished David Masson attracted him only occasionally. Masson's daughter Rosaline, who wrote one of the early Stevenson biographies, said that in her father's roll book, "in which so many now great names are written, his name has been searched for in vain. The class enjoyed the distinction of being the one that Stevenson did not take, but did sometimes attend. He used to 'slip in and listen.'" She added, "He willfully selected, sought out, and went about with companions of habits and characters that made him appear unsuited for the society in homes where he might otherwise have found sympathy and inspiration"—including, clearly, her own. Since she was seventeen years younger than Louis, this was hearsay.[8]

Louis was never a snob in the ordinary sense, but he failed to understand how his casual behavior might offend fellow students as well as professors. "The mass of students," one of them wrote much later, "knew very well that we should have to earn our own living by the sweat of our brows, that our course at the university was the highest privilege we were ever likely to enjoy before buckling to life's work, and necessity was laid upon us to improve such talents that we might possess. For the most part we could not afford to mix ourselves up with apparent idlers." That writer did live to see that Louis hadn't been idle in every respect; his remarks were delivered to the Robert Louis Stevenson Club in Edinburgh in 1921.[9]

Many students came from farming or working-class backgrounds. For them education was a crucial avenue to a better life, and they naturally resented the privileged layabout who constantly cut classes or walked out shortly after they began. After Louis's death William Ernest Henley, whose friendship with him had ended in a bitter falling-out, recalled cuttingly that when he did show up classmates were likely to call out, "Here comes the Gifted Boy!" They evidently meant that he behaved as if his gifts excused him from ordinary obligations.[10]

Given that he did have financial security, he felt no shame in refusing the rat race. A few years later he published "An Apology for Idlers":

> Idleness so called, which does not consist in doing nothing, but in doing a great deal not recognized in the dogmatic formularies of the ruling class, has as good a right to state its position as industry itself. . . . Extreme busyness, whether at school or college, kirk [church] or market, is a symptom of deficient vitality; and a faculty for idleness implies a catholic appetite and a strong sense of personal identity. There is a sort of dead-alive, hackneyed people about, who are scarcely conscious of living except in the exercise of some conventional occupation.

His own family, of course, was securely established in what he called "the ruling class."[11]

READER AND WRITER

Meanwhile, Louis's self-education was proceeding energetically, and as he commented on Burns, "Schools and colleges, for one great man whom they complete, perhaps unmake a dozen." If he wasn't studying much, he was thinking a lot, and aware that most people don't. He was a voracious reader of recent literature, which was not taught at all in universities in those days. He kept up to date on the latest French fiction, which he read in the original, and he had a passion for American writing. He loved Hawthorne and Poe at a time when they weren't fashionable in Britain, and found the poetry of Whitman absolutely life-changing. He somehow discovered *Leaves of Grass* soon after it was published in 1867—apparently keeping his copy hidden from his parents—and twenty years later called it "a book which tumbled the world upside down for me, blew into space a thousand cobwebs of genteel and ethical illusion, and having thus shaken my tabernacle of lies, set me back again upon a strong foundation of all the original and manly virtues."[12]

Leaves of Grass remained a favorite book for the rest of Louis's life, and his stepdaughter said that he reread "The Song of the Open Road" so often that his copy of the book fell open at those pages. "He put infinite fire and vibrancy" into it, she said, when he would read the poem aloud:

> Afoot and light-hearted I take to the open road,
> Healthy, free, the world before me,
> The long brown path before me leading wherever I choose.

That was the path that Louis would take.[13]

He also read extensively in English literature from all periods, with a goal of learning from great writers how to form his own style. Whenever he encountered a passage that struck him as especially effective, he set himself to imitate it. "I was unsuccessful, and I knew it; and tried again, and was again unsuccessful and always unsuccessful; but at least in these vain bouts I got some practice in rhythm, and harmony, in construction, and the coordination of parts. I have thus played the sedulous ape to Hazlitt, to Lamb, to Wordsworth, to Sir Thomas Browne, to Defoe, to Hawthorne, to Montaigne, to Baudelaire and to Obermann."

In later years the expression "sedulous ape" came in for derision, as if he had been a mere copyist. On the contrary, he was doing what every successful artist does—striving to understand how the masters created their effects. Chesterton commented, "In the very act of claiming to have copied other styles, Stevenson writes most unmistakably in his own style. I think I could have guessed amid a hundred authors which one had used the expression 'played the sedulous ape.'"[14]

Something else is worth emphasizing: the list of writers is remarkably eclectic, and most were no longer fashionable when Louis was young. They range widely: the solemn stylist Thomas Browne, the ingratiating essayists Montaigne and Hazlitt, and the melancholic Romantic Étienne de Sénancourt, whose 1804 novel *Obermann* featured a sensitive and tormented young man.

The "sedulous ape" description appeared in a self-deprecatory essay "A College Magazine," recalling that he and a classmate had founded the *Edinburgh University Magazine,* which "ran four months in undisturbed obscurity, and died without a gasp." He contributed six essays of facetious commentary on university life, and complained that most students didn't know how to have fun. "Wherever you seek it, you will find a dearth of merriment, and absence of real youthful enjoyment." Of course, unlike himself, few students could count on family money to support them for as long as they might need it while they were pursuing enjoyment.[15]

It's worth noting that although he admired the poetry of Robert Burns, he thought of an earlier Scottish poet as his spiritual forebear. That was Robert Fergusson, who led the kind of bohemian life in the eighteenth century that Louis aspired to in the nineteenth, and who died at the age of twenty-four after hitting his head falling downstairs. A few months before his own death Louis wrote, "I had always a great sense of kinship with poor Robert Fergusson—so clever a boy, so wild, of such a mixed strain, so unfortunate, born in the same town with me, and, as I always felt rather by express intimation than from evidence, so like myself."[16]

NEW FRIENDS, AND TWO CLUBS

At Colinton and Swanston Louis had had playmates; now he formed several friendships that would endure for many years. In addition to his cousin Bob, to whom he had been close since they were boys, these now included his fellow students Charles Baxter, Walter Ferrier, and Walter Simpson. This was important, since most of the other students made him feel like an outsider or even a misfit.

There's an obvious self-portrait in the unfinished novel *Weir of Hermiston,* in which Archie Weir is desperately lonely at the University of Edinburgh. In the novel another student is asked if he's a friend and replies, "I know Weir [the father], but I never met Archie." The narrator continues, "No one had met Archie, a malady most incident to only sons. He flew his private signal, and none heeded it. It seemed he was abroad in a world from which the very hope of intimacy was banished; and he looked round about him on the concourse of his fellow-students, and forward to the trivial days and acquaintances that were to come, without hope or interest." Louis loved slipping in Shakespeare allusions, and there's one of them here. In *A Winter's Tale* Perdita says that pale primroses die unmarried, "a malady most incident to maids."[17]

Bob Stevenson went to Cambridge, but since he was three years older than Louis he had graduated and returned to Edinburgh by now. He aspired to be a painter, and a few years later the two of them would live together in an artists' colony in France. Bob did have artistic talent, but what most impressed everyone was his brilliant conversation. Years later Louis described his style:

> He had the most indefatigable, feverish mind I have ever known; he had acquired a smattering of almost every knowledge and art. There was an insane lucidity in his conclusions; a singular, humorous eloquence in his language, and a power of method bringing the whole of life into the focus of the subject under hand; none of which I ever heard equaled or even approached by any other talker. In sheer trenchancy of mind, I have ever been his humble and distant follower. The multiplicity and swiftness of his apprehensions, if they do not bewilder, at least paralyze his mind.

Though a compelling conversationalist himself, Louis was in awe of Bob, and in these years very much looked up to him.[18]

Conversation wasn't just entertaining, it was virtually life itself. A decade later Louis wrote in "Talk and Talkers," "There can be no fairer ambition than to excel in talk; to be affable, gay, ready, clear and welcome.... There are always two to a talk, giving and taking, comparing experience and according conclusions. Talk is fluid, tentative, continually 'in further search and progress,' while written words remain fixed."

Louis acknowledged that such talk was often competitive. "The spice of life is battle; the friendliest relations are still a kind of contest; and if we would not forgo all that is valuable in our lot, we must continually face some other person, eye to eye, and wrestle a fall whether in love or enmity. Every durable bond between human beings is founded in or heightened by some element of competition." Yet the whole point was shared pleasure. "Talkers, once launched, begin to overflow the limits of their ordinary selves." Socrates used to say very much the same thing.[19]

Louis's parents distrusted his bond with the mercurial Bob, fearing that his influence would deflect their son from the paths of virtue, professional and otherwise. They were not wrong, but their reaction suggests how little, in important ways, they understood Louis. "The mere return of Bob [from Cambridge]," he wrote in an autobiographical fragment, "changed at once and forever the course of my life; I can give you an idea of my relief by saying that I was at last able to breathe. The miserable isolation in which I had languished was no more in season, and I began to be happy."[20]

When they were both in Edinburgh there was no reason to correspond, but some letters survive that Louis wrote when Bob was out of town, and they show how deeply he revealed his feelings to his cousin. When he was seventeen he wrote, "Strange how my mind runs on this idea. Becoming great, becoming great, becoming great. A heart burned out with the lust of this world's approbation: a hideous disease to have." And a few days after he turned eighteen, "What an egotistical brute I am! self! self! self! That is the tune, the burthen, the fable, the moral. Self! self!" He added, "My daily life is one repression from beginning to end, and my letters to you are the safety valve."[21]

One of Louis's new friends was Charles Baxter, two years ahead at the university and preparing for a legal career. In later life Baxter would become his faithful lawyer and business agent, and portraits of him make him look stolid (fig. 19), but in his youth he was no such thing. The poet Richard Le Gallienne said he was "a preposterously vital and imaginative talker, ample of frame, with a voice like a column of cavalry, and what a swashbuckler he would have made in the heroic days his friend loved to write of! With what an air of braggadocio he would have gone clanking into a tavern, with his long sword and high boots and feathered hat!"[22]

Baxter drank a lot, and eventually that would catch up with him. Louis had weaknesses, but not that one; he enjoyed wine and occasionally whisky but never to excess. Concern for his precarious health probably encouraged moderation. Several of his friends would drink themselves to death, and he once commented, "There is, in our drunken land, a certain privilege extended to drunkenness. In Scotland it is almost respectable."[23]

Reviewing the Yale edition of the letters, Richard Holmes calls Baxter "a steadfast rock in every crisis; this continuity, which stretches across twenty years and half the globe, itself says a great deal about Stevenson's astonishing gift for friendship and loyalty." Holmes adds that Louis's letters to Baxter have "a range of tone—from ribald to bleakly philosophical—which I can only compare with Byron's."[24]

An example of the ribaldry is a letter from 1874, written when Louis was in France and heard about revival meetings back home. "Simpson tells me MacGill has stopped liquoring; he will take to buggery very likely. I bless God I am an infidel when I read of such nervous fiddle-de-dee; and these people are down upon the spiritualists! Why I saw that bald-headed bummer J. Balfour [a cousin]

19. Charles Baxter

had been describing a meeting he was at. He said, 'They then enjoyed very precious and manifest tokens of the Lord's Presence.' If I had hold of James B. by the testicles I would knock his bald cranium against the wall until I was sick." The letter is signed *"baisez mon cul"*—"kiss my ass." At another time Louis wrote, after asking Baxter to do him a favor, "Do you twig, my lovely friend? if not, you may retire up your own fundament."[25]

A fellow student remembered Louis and Baxter ("one always thought and spoke of him as Charlie") as something of an odd couple, "a slim and graceful spaniel with a big bulldog, jowled and popeyed, trotting in its wake." In correspondence Louis often called his friend "Jokester" or "Jinkster," referring to impromptu hoaxes they liked to carry out, such as inventing someone called John Libbel and distributing "Mr. Libbel" calling cards all over town. "Set down in cold blood," Rosaline Masson says, "these jinks seem dull, and not redeemed by any spark of real cleverness," but they enjoyed themselves greatly. "Jinks" may sound odd, but was in regular use in Scotland; elsewhere it survives in "high jinks," and in rugby a jink is a sudden swerve to make a tackler miss.[26]

For the rest of Louis's life he and Baxter often addressed each other in the personas of a pair of dissolute church elders named Thomson and Johnstone (Baxter said he could never be sure which one was which). As a private joke, Louis made the fictional editor of *The Master of Ballantrae* say that he got a manuscript account of the story from a lawyer named Mr. Johnstone Thomson.

Louis's other two close friends were Walter Ferrier, son of a professor of philosophy at the University of St Andrews, and Walter Grindlay Simpson. Simpson's father, Professor Sir James Young Simpson, gained fame for establishing the use of chloroform in operations. That achievement was preceded by some memorable experimentation. We are told that "he handed out tumblers of chloral at home until he and his guests were insensible upon the floor."[27]

Like Louis himself, Bob, Charles, and the two Walters came from highly respectable families, and were engaging in mildly transgressive rebellion. Their drinking took place in howffs and shebeens. J. C. Furnas explains: "In Scots 'howff' means 'haunt'; the American equivalent would be somewhere between 'dump' and 'joint.' A 'shebeen' is a tavern depending principally on after-hours, illegal business." An earlier writer described these more diplomatically as places "where the convivially inclined of Edinburgh citizens could obtain drink after licensed hours." Louis and his friends especially frequented Rutherford's in Drummond Street, which remained in business as Rutherford's Public House until 2008; at that time it was merged with an Italian restaurant and renamed Hispaniola, after the ship in *Treasure Island*.[28]

Though Louis never learned to read Greek, he described a typical evening in a parody of translations of Greek tragedies, particularly Euripides' *The Bacchae:*

> My dear Baxter, Like one full of new wine—and so indeed I was, for I had a cab at my disposal this lovely evening—I went and called on you. I learned you were out at dinner, and then indeed, O person well known unto R. L. Stevenson, then indeed did I remember the tale known to men, how that on this night of all nights you should tread the Thessalian measure, being girt with the skin of leopards and your temples girt with ivy leaves and shining as to your face with ruddy Bacchus. Then in-

deed, then indeed did I recollect that you should deftly move forth your patent-leather footsteps, swaying as to your auburn head in the measure of them that touched the reed, and your left arm curved about the slender waist of one fair among the virgins.

Quite possibly not a virgin, of course. The biblical allusion may not be obvious: when the disciples were touched by tongues of fire and empowered to speak in all languages, "Others mocking said, These men are full of new wine."[29]

When he was thirty Louis wrote a series of sonnets called *Brasheana* that he dedicated to Baxter. Peter Brash, lately deceased, had kept a tavern that they often frequented. There were eleven poems in all, only five of which appear in Janet Adam Smith's *Collected Poems*. Her selection is a good one, but she might have found space for another poem with the playful title "Ode by Ben Jonson, Edgar Allan Poe, and a Bungler."

> In a flash
> Immortal Brash
> Burst, like Elijah, upward and was gone!
>
> Yet fear not—we shall follow; for wherever
> Great Brash his way made plain, the common herd
> May follow that extraordinary turd.[30]

By now Louis was a confirmed smoker, though at this stage he generally preferred pipes. When he was nineteen he told Bob, "I am smoking just now at the mean [i.e., average] rate of twelve pipes a day." A couple of months after that he reported that pipes alone weren't enough to battle depression: "Today I was in the depths again ... I tried to find out where I could get hashish, half-determined to get drunk, and ended (as usual) by going to a graveyard. I stayed about two hours in Greyfriars Churchyard in the depths of wretchedness." At this period in his life he often hung out in graveyards, the better to indulge melancholy. He added, "I am better now, but it leaves me in a state of intellectual prostration, fit for nothing but smoking and reading Charles Baudelaire. By the bye, I hope your sisters don't read him: he would have corrupted St. Paul."[31]

Not all of the graveyard visits were morbid. Sometimes, he recalled later, "a beautiful housemaid flirted with me from a window and kept my wild heart flying. Once—she possibly remembers—the wise Eugenia followed me to that austere enclosure. Her hair came down, and in the shelter of the tomb my trembling fingers helped her to repair the braid."[32]

More dignified was election to the Speculative Society, founded a century

20. The Speculative Society

earlier during the Scottish Enlightenment to promote "Improvement in Literary Composition and Public Speaking." Many of Edinburgh's most prominent citizens had been members, including Walter Scott, who was a lawyer and judge by profession. The "Spec," as it was known, had the unusual privilege of occupying university premises with no supervision or interference.

The picture (fig. 20) shows the Spec's Inner Hall, with a desk on a raised dais from which the evening's speaker would hold forth. Scott's portrait dominates the wall; the marble bust at upper right is of Francis Jeffrey, jurist and journalist, who was notorious for damning the poetry of Wordsworth. After Louis's death the ensign of the yacht *Casco,* in which he had sailed the Pacific, would be framed and likewise mounted on that wall.

The first paper he read there, not surprisingly, was "The Influence of the Covenanting Persecution on the Scotch Mind." In 1873, president of the society by then, he prepared a valedictory address: "Who knows, gentlemen, with what Scotts or Jeffreys we may have been sharing this meeting hall? About what great man we shall have curious anecdotes to tell over dining tables, and write to their biographers in a fine, shaky, octogenarian hand?"[33]

He was supposed to deliver this address on March 25, 1873, but when the time came he was bedridden and sent it to Baxter to read in his place, with this note: "I am strictly on my back—have not turned on either side since yesterday morning. Very jolly, however. R.L.S." Episodes of stress would often provoke the symptoms of illness.[34]

There was also a different kind of club. Proposed by Bob, it was called the L.J.R., which stood for "Liberty, Justice, Reverence." There were just three other members: Louis, Baxter, and Ferrier. They met in a pub in Advocate's Close in High Street.

The club's name sounds uplifting, though Louis wrote to Baxter later that he never got around to writing an essay that was supposed to describe Liberty, and Baxter likewise failed to produce one on Reverence—"so I never knew what Reverence was." The L.J.R. constitution began with the rule "Disregard everything our parents have taught us." That may sound like routine adolescent bravado, but what Louis meant by it is suggested by a passage he admired in Whitman: "Re-examine all you have been told at school or church, or in any book, and dismiss whatever insults your own soul."[35]

During this period he was much taken with socialism, which meant the artist and socialist prophet William Morris, not Marx, whose *Kapital* had not yet appeared in English. Before long he would decide that this moderately radical attitude had been only a phase, but when he was twenty-seven he wrote,

> I am no more abashed at having been a red-hot socialist with a panacea of my own than at having been a sucking infant. I look back to the time when I was a socialist with something like regret. I have convinced myself (for the moment) that we had better leave these great changes to what we call great blind forces: their blindness being so much more perspicacious than the little, peering, partial eyesight of men. I seem to see that my own scheme would not answer; and all the other schemes I ever heard propounded would depress some elements of goodness just as much as they encouraged others. Now I know that in thus turning Conservative with years, I am going through the normal cycle of change and travelling in the common orbit of men's opinions. I submit to this, as I would submit to gout or grey hair, as a concomitant of growing age or else of failing animal heat; but I do not acknowledge that it is necessarily a change for the better—I daresay it is deplorably for the worse.

Still later Louis praised Hugo's *Les Misérables* for awakening readers "to the great cost of the society that we enjoy and profit by, to the labour and sweat of those who support the litter, civilization, in which we ourselves are so smoothly carried forward. People are all glad to shut their eyes." The word *litter* recalls an old usage: a curtained couch resting on shafts with which four men carry its privileged passenger through the streets.[36]

PREPARING FOR THE LAW

Well before it was time to graduate, it was obvious that Louis not only disliked engineering but had no aptitude for it. "I never was good at figures," he remarked a few years later, "although an amateur of the female figure in all its branches." A fellow student once introduced him as "son and successor of Thomas Stevenson, the well-known lighthouse engineer." Louis objected, "Son, certainly, but not successor, if I can help it."[37]

Thomas Stevenson identified deeply with the family firm, and could well have felt betrayed when his only son refused to carry it on (Bob likewise refused). There was a strong element of Protestant ethic in the Stevensons, for whom their work was literally a vocation, a calling. Henry James once described Louis as a "recusant engineer"—a recusant dissents from the received religion and refuses to attend its services.[38]

However, Thomas had a generous spirit, and when Louis insisted on quitting engineering, Graham Balfour says that "he met the request with calm." In her diary Margaret noted that he was "wonderfully resigned." They knew Louis wanted to become a writer, but the chances of earning a living that way were remote. So they came to an agreement: he would study law in order to have a profession to support him.[39]

Louis took the commitment seriously, passed preliminary examinations in 1872, and for the first time actually worked at his studies. To become an advocate he had to pass examinations in civil law, Scots law (very different from English), conveyancing (complex regulations concerning deeds), constitutional law, constitutional history, and medical jurisprudence. That he succeeded in all of this, Barry Menikoff says, "is a testament both to his powers of concentration and to his ability to absorb an enormous amount of technical as well as historical information." Legal issues, and the psychology of lawyers and judges, would play a role in both *Catriona* and *Weir of Hermiston*.[40]

Still, his contemporary Charles Guthrie, who went on to become a distinguished judge as Lord Guthrie, said that "he had no natural taste for law" and was a casual student at best. "At college we did not look for Louis at law lectures, except when the weather was bad." They became good friends, though Guthrie was rather overwhelmed by his unconventional posturing. When asked for his opinion of Louis in later years he would answer, "Which Louis Stevenson? I knew several! The Bohemian, or the Puritan? The Scotsman, or the Frenchman? Nobody would ever have taken him for an Englishman."

In his memoir of his friend Guthrie recalled "his indiscriminating thirst for novelty; his fondness, in season and out of season, for the bizarre and the gruesome, the grotesque and the uncanny; his childish inquisitiveness ('insatiably curious in the aspects of life,' as he phrased it); his strange relish of rough jests; his toleration of Rabelaisian and so-called strong language; and his curious liking for queer company—all marked his Bohemian instinct."[41]

The temperamental difference between these friends speaks well for the qualities that each was able to value in the other. Someone who knew them both at the Spec said, "Charles Guthrie was scrupulously correct in appearance and behavior, a respecter of conventions and social distinctions. Stevenson hated conventions, whether in dress, manners, morals, or beliefs. He admitted no authority but his own conscience, and cared little or nothing for general opinion. That Guthrie was not constantly shocked and horrified by him always astonished me."[42]

Having made a respectable start with his legal studies, Louis was in no hurry to make progress, and there would be frequent interruptions during the next three years. Not until 1875 would he be admitted to the bar, and by then he had a fixed determination that he would never practice law. The psychobiographer Erik Erikson popularized the idea of a moratorium, in which a person of genius seems to be just marking time while his contemporaries get on with their careers. Louis's moratorium was now underway.

CHAPTER 6

"I Want Pleasure"

RECREATIONS

The university was only part of Louis's life, and not the most important part. In 1874, before his legal studies were finished, he exclaimed in a letter, "O I do hate this damned life that I lead. Work—work—work; that's all right, it's amusing, but I want women and I want pleasure." He may have had some brief and tentative love affairs, though if so he covered his tracks successfully. He certainly had experiences with prostitutes. He was taken up by an Edinburgh artistic circle that put on theatrical performances. And he enjoyed skating and boating.[1]

In the winter the Stevenson family and friends joined skating parties on Duddingston Loch, which was located, as Louis mentions in *Edinburgh: Picturesque Notes,* "under the abrupt southern side of Arthur's Seat; in summer a shield of blue, with swans sailing from the reeds; in winter, a field of ringing ice." Bonnie Prince Charlie's soldiers had camped there during the 1745 rebellion, as mentioned in Walter Scott's *Waverley.* Flora Masson remembered Louis moving in and out of the group, "skating alone, a slender, dark figure with a muffler about his neck, darting in and out among the crowd, and disappearing and reappearing like a melancholy minnow among the tall reeds that fringe the loch."[2]

Other people were less complimentary. A former schoolmate remembered that "his skating was the reverse of graceful, his one object being to perfect himself in what he called the 'Canadian Vine.' I completely fail to remember its intricacies, but I can never forget the ungainly way he carried himself: bent knees, twisted legs, feet continually crossing and uncrossing, head on a level with his chest as he tried to trace an imaginary figure on the ice." Better known from clog dancing, the Canadian Vine does require crossing and uncrossing the feet. Still, "although he always skated with the utmost vigor and what the French would call 'abandon,' I never saw him come to grief," and fifteen years later his landlord in upstate New York called him "one of the best skaters I ever saw."[3]

Samuel Bough's painting *Snowballing outside Edinburgh University* catches the atmosphere of the student days (color plate 6). In his college magazine Louis mentioned just such a snowball fight, but with a note of disappointment at his fellows' lack of commitment.

> At present we are not a united body, but a loose gathering of individuals, whose inherent attraction is allowed to condense them into little knots and coteries. Our last snowball riot read us a plain lesson on our condition. There was no party spirit—no unity of interests. A few, who were mischievously inclined, marched off to the College of Surgeons in a pretentious file, but even before they reached their destination the feeble inspiration had died out in many, and their numbers were sadly thinned. Some followed strange gods in the direction of Drummond Street, and others slunk back to meek good-boyism at the feet of the Professors.

In the painting a sign indicates the corner of Drummond Street.[4]

In summertime Louis often went canoeing on the Firth of Forth, though what he and his friends called canoes would now be called kayaks. When he invented Jim Hawkins's adventure in a crude homemade boat in *Treasure Island,* he drew upon "some recollections of canoeing on the high seas."[5]

One of his boyhood companions at North Berwick remembered that he "ruled autocratically" over their games, but "so far as games such as golf and football were concerned, he was 'out of it.' Golf, of course, was our principal game, but I never saw Stevenson even try to play." An old-fashioned golf ball was once dug up in a Swanston park with the initials "R.L.S." cut into it, so perhaps he did give the game a try, but he told his friend Walter Simpson's sister Eve that it seemed "very poor amusement to interrupt meditation or talk to hit a ball." She commented that golf "was then a Calvinistic sport, stern and hardy."[6]

Walter, a gifted golfer, went on to publish the much-admired *Art of Golf,* notable for illustrating the swing with stop-action photographs, and also acknowledging the fiendish difficulty of the game. Though Walter was generally quiet and reserved, his book reflects the playful humor that Louis appreciated. "The mere appearance of a niblick suggests doubts and fears. Other clubs are graceful, smiling, elegant things. The niblick is an angry-looking little cad, coarse, bullet-headed, underbred. Its face looks up as if to say, 'I will raise the ball into the air.' Its smile is treacherous. It does fulfill its promise sometimes, but just as often it smothers its laughter in the sand, leaving you and the ball nonplussed. No one is ever proud of his bunker play." It was to address this issue that the sand wedge was invented half a century later.[7]

A page in Margaret's "Baby Book" was titled "Boys' Amusements," and offered as examples Cricket Match, Foot-Ball Match, Lawn Tennis, Racquets, Fives (a form of handball played in boarding schools), and Rowing Match. Margaret left the page blank.[8]

LOVE AFFAIRS?

After Louis's death there was much speculation about his early romantic relationships, but no firm evidence. One poem, written in 1871, evokes a heady moment while skating:

> You leaned to me, I leaned to you,
> Our course was smooth as flight—
> We steered—a heel-touch to the left,
> A heel-touch to the right. . . .
>
> I swear by yon swan-travelled lake,
> By yon calm hill above,
> I swear had we been drowned that day
> We had been drowned in love.

Jenni Calder thinks this partner may have been Eve Simpson, but she doesn't say why.[9]

Another poem describes a flirtation in church.

> You looked so tempting in the pew,
> You looked so sly and calm—
> My trembling fingers played with yours
> As both looked out the Psalm.
>
> Your heart beat hard against my arm,
> My foot to yours was set,
> Your loosened ringlet burned my cheek
> Whenever they two met.

> O little, little we hearkened, dear,
> And little, little cared,
> Although the parson sermonized,
> The congregation stared.

This might have been in Swanston, not Edinburgh; there is a scene like it in a village church in *Weir of Hermiston.* But again we have no idea who his companion might have been.[10]

There is a passing remark in an essay Louis wrote about his college magazine: he sent a copy of it "to the lady with whom my heart was at that time somewhat engaged, and who did all that lay in her to break it. She, with some tact, passed over the gift and my cherished contributions in silence."[11]

One startling document has survived. In 1880 Louis wrote to William Ernest Henley, "I received from an enchanting young lady whom you have seen, or rather from her inspiration, threatening letters, exposure etc." The fact that it's impossible to identify this person is hardly proof, as some writers assert, that she never existed. Louis's own words refute that, and he takes it for granted that Henley will know exactly who she is. "From her inspiration" may suggest that some male companion was writing on her behalf.[12]

Years later there was a rumor that this person, with the weirdly coincidental name of Margaret Stevenson, was the daughter of a servant in the household of Anne and Fleeming Jenkin, and a young man claimed long afterwards to be Louis's illegitimate son, but this was decisively refuted.[13]

In 1924 an Edinburgh writer named J. A. Steuart published a biography entitled *Robert Louis Stevenson: Man and Writer,* in which he related stories that he had picked up from old-timers who remembered Louis's youth. This gave immediate scandal, since Steuart declared that there had been one or more love affairs with servant girls, and in particular someone named Kate Drummond. Foreseeing hostile reactions, he prefaced his book with a quotation from Stevenson on Burns: "If you are so sensibly pained by the misconduct of your subject, and so paternally delighted with his virtues, you will always be an excellent gentleman, but a somewhat questionable biographer."[14]

One of Steuart's conjectures has been refuted, that there was a tragic relationship with someone called Claire. It's now known that Claire was a name he sometimes used for a woman he was infatuated with in England later on, but it doesn't follow that since an Edinburgh Claire never existed, Kate didn't either.[15]

An early poem takes its title from Horace, "Ne Sit Ancillae Tibi Amor Pudori"—"Do not be ashamed of your passion for a servant girl":

> There's just a twinkle in your eye
> That seems to say I *might,* if I
> Were only bold enough to try
> An arm about your waist.
>
> I hear, too, as you come and go,
> That pretty nervous laugh, you know;
> And then your cap is always so
> Coquettishly displaced....
>
> O graceful housemaid, tall and fair,
> I love your shy imperial air,
> And always loiter on the stair
> When you are going by.
>
> A strict reserve the fates demand;
> But, when to let you pass I stand,
> Sometimes by chance I touch your hand
> And sometimes catch your eye.

A group of poems from the same period begins with this dedication:

> I write the *finis* here against my love.
> This is my love's last epitaph and tomb.
> Here the road forks, and I
> Go my way, far from yours.

Taken as a whole, though, these read like exercises and not love poems.[16]
Whatever relationships there may have been, Louis's Whitmanesque poems from this time are filled with erotic longing.

> I walk the streets smoking my pipe
> And I love the dallying shop-girl
> That leans with rounded stern to look at the fashions....
> I love night in the city,
> The lighted streets and the swinging gait of harlots.
> I love cool pale morning
> In the empty bye-streets,

> With only here and there a female figure,
> A slavey with lifted dress and the key in her hand,
> A girl or two at play in a corner of a waste-land
> Tumbling and showing their legs and crying out to me loosely.

"Slavey" was the Victorian term for a housemaid.[17]

Leaves of Grass undoubtedly inspired Louis with stronger language than that, for example in "I Sing the Body Electric":

> This is the female form,
> A divine nimbus exhales from it from head to foot,
> It attracts with fierce undeniable attraction....
> Hair, bosom, hips, bend of legs, negligent falling hands all diffused, mine too diffused,
> Ebb stung by the flow and flow stung by the ebb, love-flesh swelling and deliciously aching,
> Limitless limpid jets of love hot and enormous, quivering jelly of love, white-blow and delirious juice....[18]

LOUIS IN NIGHTTOWN

In these years Louis was leading a life of privilege but not really of freedom. Rosaline Masson, who was familiar with his family's social circle, brings out what that means.

> His parents, probably with anxious intentions for good, kept their son on very short allowance of pocket money. He was treated as many a man treats a dependent wife, and as many parents treat grown-up dependent children. He was allowed to share, and even to command, what money can buy, but he was not allowed to handle money. The town house and the country cottage were both at his disposal; dinners his parents were delighted to give for him and his friends; foreign tours were undertaken lavishly; he might, had he wished, have run up many accounts for clothes and harmless luxuries, and his parents would have paid them; but his sense of freedom and his individual tastes in spending had to be restricted to a pound a month of pocket money.

That was a modest allowance. When he turned twenty-three he was deemed ready for a raise to a more generous £7 a month, equivalent to £400 today. It should be added that although these figures represent adjustment for inflation, they don't take into account the low incomes that greatly limited actual purchasing power. The usual wage of a Scottish farm worker at that time was £1 per month, and even a skilled artisan would earn just £4—little more than half of Louis's allowance.[19]

If Louis's parents thought they were keeping him on a short leash, it didn't work; he made small sums go a long way. "I was the companion," he wrote in an autobiographical fragment, "of seamen, chimney sweeps, and thieves; my circle was being continually changed by the action of the police magistrate." A fellow student remembered that "he loved to plunge into vagrancy, into the lower strata of society, where he could purge himself of that middle class respectability that so stank in his nostrils." Sidney Colvin, with whom he would soon be close, said admiringly, "All such as feel the daily pinch and stress of life, down to the cadger, the chimney sweep, thief, vagrant, and prostitute—these, and the variegated company with which he peopled in imagination the historic past, were all more real and more significant to him than were the majority among the comfortable classes of his contemporaries." Louis's sympathies were much like George Orwell's.[20]

Edinburgh was a compact city, and as its population grew within a confined area, the solution was high buildings known as "lands." They were the skyscrapers of their time, and in the days before elevators it was the poorest tenants who lived high up. "From their smoky beehives, ten stories high," Louis wrote in *Edinburgh: Picturesque Notes,* "the unwashed look down upon the open squares and gardens of the wealthy." As many as forty people might be "herded together" in a single land.

An illustration in his book shows Planestones Close (fig. 21), which no longer exists today. He described what it was like to enter such a warren: "You go under dark arches, and down dark stairs and alleys. The way is so narrow that you can lay a hand on either wall; so steep that in greasy winter weather the pavement is almost as treacherous as ice. Washing dangles above washing from the windows; the houses bulge outwards upon flimsy brackets."[21]

A few years earlier the American traveler Isabella Bird described exploring these tenements, which were invariably dark, cramped, and infested with vermin. "It was not possible to believe that the most grinding greed could extort money from human beings for the tenancy of such dens as those to which this passage led. They were lairs into which a starving dog might creep to die, but nothing more." Bird mentioned Planestones Close in particular as "considered good property, and fit for the stowage of human beings."

The people she met were fully aware of their plight. "Coming down a long

21. Planestones Close

dark stair late at night from an overcrowded land, a frightful hag clutched my arm with her skinny hand, and hissed into my ear, 'Is it God's elect you are seeking here? It's the devil's elect you'll find,' laughing fiendishly at her own wit. 'So this is Blackfriars Wynd,' remarked one of our party, as we passed down the crowded alley. 'No, it's hell's mouth,' exclaimed a forlorn woman, who was dragging a drunken man to his joyless home." Wynds were narrow lanes between houses.[22]

A historian says, "The age of great industrial triumphs was an age of appalling social deprivation. I am astounded by the tolerance, in a country boasting of its high moral standards, of unspeakable urban squalor, compounded of drink abuse, bad housing, low wages, long hours and sham education." Louis saw all of that at first hand, and it's no wonder that he was attracted to socialism in his youth.[23]

Sordid though the Old Town was, it held a special attraction. "Youth," Louis once wrote, "is a hot season with all." It had become obvious that "nice" girls were severely repressed if not actually uninterested in sex, and whether or not he got involved with servants, he definitely did with prostitutes. Heriot Row was in the heart of the posh New Town; the Old Town, just a short walk away, was Edinburgh's city of the night.[24]

A poem from this time begins "Hail! childish slaves of social rules," and goes on to declare,

> O fine, religious, decent folk,
> In Virtue's flaunting gold and scarlet,
> I sneer between two puffs of smoke,
> Give me the publican and harlot.

In British usage a publican is the keeper of a pub, but Louis was remembering the Gospel of Matthew in which Jesus tells the chief priests, "Verily I say unto you, that the publicans and the harlots go into the kingdom of God before you."[25]

Late in life Louis told Graham Balfour,

> You know I very easily might have gone to the devil; I don't understand why I didn't. Even when I was almost grown up I was kept so short of money that I had to make the most of every penny. The result was that I had my dissipation all the same but I had it in the worst possible surroundings. At the time I used to have my headquarters in an old public house frequented by the lowest order of prostitutes—threepenny whores—where there was a room in which I used to go to write. I saw a good deal of the girls; they were really singularly decent creatures, not a bit worse than anybody else. But it wasn't a good beginning for a young man.

Balfour recorded this in his papers, but made no allusion to it in his biography.[26]

At some point Louis wrote in his notebook, "The harm of prostitution lies not in itself, but in the disastrous moral influence of ostracism. You may make many a prostitute cry by merely naming her trade to her. If you think seriously of all the depressing, demoralising, decivilising influences brought to bear upon her, I think you will find it matter for wonder not that she is so fallen, but that she is still (and that in so many instances) as honest, kind, and decent as she is."²⁷

In an autobiographical fragment he described one of them, Mary H., as "a robust, great-haunched, blue-eyed young woman, of admirable temper and, if you will let me say so of a prostitute, extraordinary modesty." In hindsight he believed that she had been genuinely attracted to him, but he was too naïve to realize it. Years later they happened to run into each other when she was about to emigrate to America. "We had much to talk about, and she cried bitterly, and so did I. We found in that interview that we had been dear friends without knowing it; I can still hear her recalling the past in her sober, Scotch voice; and I can still feel her good honest loving hand as we said goodbye."²⁸

Another reminiscence is much sadder.

> I see now the little sanded kitchen where Velvet Coat (for such was the name I went by) has spent days together, generally in silence and making sonnets in a penny version-book. I was distinctly petted and respected; the women were most gentle and kind to me. Such indeed was my celebrity that when the proprietor and his mistress came to inspect the establishment I was invited to tea with them; and it is still a grisly thought to me that I have since seen that mistress, then gorgeous in velvet and gold chains, an old, toothless, ragged woman with hardly voice enough to welcome me by my old name of Velvet Coat.

He was well known in Edinburgh as "the lang, lean chiel who wore the velvet jacket."²⁹

After Louis's death his stepson Lloyd wrote, "His early life had been tempestuously intermixed with those of many women, and I have never heard him express a wish that it might have been otherwise." In fact, Lloyd said, "He was emphatically what we would call today a feminist. Women seemed to him the victims alike of man and nature. He often spoke of the chastity enforced on them under pain of starvation; he often said there would be no children had men been destined to bear them and that marriage itself would disappear. What man, he asked besides, would ever have the courage of a woman of the streets?"³⁰

Some biographers describe these experiences condescendingly as slumming, but Jenni Calder makes the crucial point: "He retained a sensitive and generous attitude toward women that was far from typical of his time. He learned to ignore the barriers of class and sex, a lesson of the greatest importance."³¹

In his thirties Louis read Augustine's *Confessions* and was overwhelmed by the account of the saint's youth when, as in the passage Eliot adapted in *The*

Waste Land, "to Carthage then I came, a cauldron of fleshly lusts." In a letter to Colvin Louis said (with his quotations in Latin translated here), "See his splendid passage about 'the brightly lit pathway of friendship' and the 'clouds of muddy carnal concupiscence,' going on 'confusion of the two things boiled within me; it seized hold of my youthful weakness, sweeping me through the precipitous rocks of desire.' That is damn knowing for a father of the Kirk."[32]

A SOCIAL AND ARTISTIC HAVEN

Although Louis rejected a career in engineering, it was with his professor in that subject, Fleeming Jenkin, and Jenkin's wife that he found what Rosaline Masson called "a haven, an oasis in a desert of convention and prejudice, whither he might bring his unrest, his self-doubts, his dreams."[33]

Fleeming Jenkin (the name was pronounced "Fleming"), Regius Professor of Engineering at the university, was a man of great distinction who had invented the cable car, was a leading specialist in electricity, supervised the laying of undersea cables to communicate between continents, and was an important mathematical economist. In his portrait (fig. 22) he is appropriately solemn, but he was anything but a stereotypical engineer. Louis found his style of conversation irresistible. In the essay "Talk and Talkers" he appears under the name of Cockshot:

> The point about him is his extraordinary readiness and spirit. You can propound nothing but he has either a theory about it ready-made, or will have one instantly on the stocks, and proceed to lay its timbers and launch it in your presence. "Let me see," he will say. "Give me a moment. I *should* have some theory for that." He is possessed by a demoniac energy, welding the elements for his life, and bending ideas as an athlete bends a horseshoe, with a visible and lively effort.... Cockshot is bottled effervescency, the sworn foe of sleep. Three-in-the-morning Cockshot, says a victim. His talk is like the driest of all imaginable dry champagnes. Sleight of hand and inimitable quickness are the qualities by which he lives.

Jenkin was like a more mature and accomplished Bob Stevenson, exactly the kind of person Louis would have liked to be.[34]

At the Jenkin social occasions Louis's bohemian style was accepted as natural, not affected. Eve Simpson remembered how he struck most people in sober Edinburgh: "Louis's outlandishness of dress, his mannerisms, his frenchified

22. Fleeming Jenkin

flourishing of his hands, and his transparent modes of attracting attention, used to come in for derisive condemnation." She added, "Many think he was careless in regard to dress. That was not so. He gave much thought and time towards the getting together of his ill-assorted wardrobe." But as for the frenchified flourishing, she understood it as many did not. "The mercurial movements of his hands were part of his speech; they were emphasis, interrogation marks, italics to his phrases."[35]

When he embraced a bohemian style of life, David Daiches says, "it was not a fad but a profession of faith." Even his parents reconciled themselves to his self-dramatizing. Rosaline Masson remembered an occasion when Margaret and her sister Jane—the "Auntie" of *A Child's Garden of Verses*—were riding along the fashionable High Street in a carriage and noticed "a queer-looking ragamuffin walking along the pavement with a bag of bones over his shoulder." Margaret sighed and said, "Oh, Louis! Louis! What will you do next?" Scruffy rag-and-bone men were a familiar sight in Victorian towns, scavenging for discarded items that they could sell to merchants.[36]

Just as important as Fleeming Jenkin was his wife Anne, who has been described as the first woman of Louis's own class to understand him. After Fleeming's death Louis wrote a memoir in which he paid tribute to the couple's relationship: "Jenkin's marriage was the one decisive incident of his career; from that moment until the day of his death he had one thought to which all the rest were tributary, the thought of his wife." Rosaline Masson's sister Flora, six years younger than Louis, remembered them at the Duddingston Loch skating parties. When Anne got tired easily and paused to rest, her husband "described wonderful figures round about his kneeling wife, circling and pirouetting by himself till she seemed to be rested, when they took hands again."[37]

Anne Jenkin was a gifted amateur actress, and since her husband also loved the theater, putting on plays was a regular event at their house. Rehearsals directed by Fleeming went on for weeks, and there were five complete performances of each play.

Sidney Colvin thought that Anne's theatrical gifts were equal to any professional's. "Her features were not beautiful, but had a signal range and thrilling power of expression. In tragic and poetic parts, especially in those translated or adapted from the Greek, she showed what must, had it been publicly displayed, have been recognized as genius." She was highly versatile too, successfully playing Cleopatra, Kate in *The Taming of the Shrew,* Viola in *Twelfth Night,* and Sheridan's Mrs. Malaprop.[38]

The spell Anne Jenkin cast was recalled by Alfred Ewing, a young student at that time who went on to become principal of the University of Edinburgh. "Fleeming worshiped his wife, and those who had the happiness to know her could well understand the worship. Her humor was as graceful as it was gay; I have never known talk that equaled hers in well-bred brilliance, in distinction of feeling, expression, and thought. To hear her read verse or prose aloud was to enjoy a revelation of its meaning and music." This tribute came not from an aesthete but from an engineering student; Professor Jenkin had complimented him on his essay "Relative Merits of the Wet and Dry Systems of Sewerage." Into this firmament, Ewing said, "Stevenson from time to time would flash, erratic, luminous, arresting—a comet with no calculable orbit or recognizable period."[39]

Louis took part in the plays at the Jenkins' house, but although a compelling reader of prose and verse, he was too self-conscious to excel as an actor and always had subordinate roles. He especially enjoyed fancy costumes such as the elegant robes worn by Duke Orsino in *Twelfth Night,* and Flora Masson remembered "the satisfied languor" with which he delivered the duke's opening speech:

> If music be the food of love, play on.
> Give me excess of it, that, surfeiting,
> The appetite may sicken, and so die.
> That strain again! It had a dying fall.

After the first performance of that play,

> When the audience was thronging into the hall, and the carriages were being called at the front door in stentorian tones, we saw Louis Stevenson's mother making her way out alone, her pretty face still radiant with maternal pride. Louis, one of a little group of the performers who were waiting, I suppose, "to sup afterwards with those clothes on," was looking down over the balustrade, halfway up the staircase. But in a moment he was down among the departing guests, wrapped his mother's cloak with an infinite tenderness about her, and then, escaping from the crowd's admiring eyes, fled up the staircase again. I can still see the upward look of adoration his mother gave him as she went on her way among the departing guests, triumphant.

It was offstage, Ewing said, that Louis's talents blossomed. "In the merry nightly gathering that followed rehearsal or performance, he took a recognized lead, bubbling over with inspired nonsense."[40]

Stimulating though these experiences were, they were only interludes, and Edinburgh was always where Louis didn't want to be. *Edinburgh: Picturesque Notes*—written when he was living in France—begins like this:

> Edinburgh pays cruelly for her high seat in one of the vilest climates under heaven. She is liable to be beaten upon by all the winds that blow, to be drenched with rain, to be buried in cold sea fogs out of the east, and powdered with the snow as it comes flying southward from the Highland hills. The weather is raw and boisterous in winter, shifty and ungenial in summer, and a downright meteorological purgatory in the spring. Many aspire angrily after that Somewhere Else of the imagination, where all troubles are supposed to end. They lean over the great bridge which joins the New Town with the Old—that windiest spot, or high altar, in this northern temple of the winds—and watch the trains smoking out from

under them and vanishing into the tunnel on a voyage to brighter skies. Happy the passengers who shake off the dust of Edinburgh, and have heard for the last time the cry of the east wind among her chimney-tops!

Louis himself often leaned over that bridge to dream of escape on one of the trains. But after this introduction he admits, "Yet the place establishes an interest in people's hearts; go where they will, they find no city of the same distinction; go where they will, they take a pride in their old home."[41]

CHAPTER 7

A "Horrible Atheist"

"THE THUNDERBOLT HAS FALLEN"

In 1873, when Louis was twenty-two and a year before he qualified for the bar, there was a crisis at 17 Heriot Row. He realized that he was losing his religious faith and told his parents so. What was at stake was not just belief; they felt it as an attack on everything they stood for. He had rejected the profession that gave Thomas Stevenson his very identity, and now he was rejecting the religion that was an important element in their status in Edinburgh.

Conventional churchgoing had always bored Louis, though he dutifully accompanied his parents on Sundays. Just after turning twenty-one he called Scotland "the country of Pharisees and whisky," and much later wrote to Baxter, "Youth cannot endure tedium; middle age is quite at peace in the focus of boredom. Think how we *suffered* in church—physical suffering, I remember, actual pangs."[1]

After he escaped from Cummy's repressive moralism, he always deplored ostentatious religiosity, which in his opinion had nothing in common with the teachings and example of Jesus.

> Ye dainty-spoken, stiff, severe
> Seed of the migrated Philistian,
> One whispered question in your ear—
> Pray, what was Christ, if you be Christian?
>
> If Christ were only here just now
> Among the city's wynds and gables,

> Leading the life he taught us, how
> Would he be welcome to your tables?
>
> I go and leave your logic-straws,
> Your former friends with face averted,
> Your petty ways and narrow laws,
> Your Grundy and your God deserted.

These conventional people aren't believers in any spiritual sense. Philistines (Louis used the less common "Philistian" for the sake of the rhyme) worship a false God whom he has rightly deserted, as well as their Mrs. Grundy, a fictitious character personifying propriety and conformity.[2]

As Louis got older, there were intellectual exchanges with his father that presaged the crisis of faith, especially when the subject was evolution, anathema to orthodox believers. In the essay "Books Which Have Influenced Me" he would remember, "Close upon the back of my discovery of Whitman, I came under the influence of Herbert Spencer." It was Spencer who coined the phrase "survival of the fittest" and originated the concept of Social Darwinism, with faith in the progress of humanity as a substitute for religion. "No more persuasive rabbi exists," Louis continued, "and few better. His words, if dry, are always manly and honest; there dwells in his pages a spirit of highly abstract joy, plucked naked like an algebraic symbol but still joyful."[3]

For a while Thomas Stevenson assumed that his son's interest in evolution was a passing fad. A fellow student remembered taking a walk with them while Louis grew impassioned on the subject, invoking Spencer for support. "At length his father said, 'I think, Louis, you've got evolution on the brain. I wish you would define what the word means.' 'Well, here it is verbatim' [Louis replied]. 'Evolution is a continuous change from indefinite, incoherent homogeneity to definite, coherent heterogeneity of structure and function through successive differentiations and integrations.' 'I think,' said his father, with a merry twinkle in his eyes, 'your friend Mr. Herbert Spencer must be a very skillful writer of polysyllabic nonsense.'"[4]

For Louis, the strain of his religious skepticism provoked a paralyzing depression. In early 1873, on a holiday in England with his mother, he wrote to Baxter,

> I am demoralized. There is no use attempting to deny it. I am unstrung, undone, mind and body. . . . My brain is just like a wet sponge: soft, pulpy, and lying spread out, flat and flaccid, over my eyes. . . . O Lord, old

man, I'm getting tired of this whole life business.... O fie, fie upon the whole foolish, violent, and wearisome game, say I. Let me get into a corner with a brandy bottle, or down on the hearthrug, full of laudanum grog; or as easily as may be, into a nice, wormy grave.

He was remembering Hamlet's first soliloquy:

> How weary, stale, flat, and unprofitable
> Seem to me all the uses of this world!
> Fie on't! Oh fie! 'tis an unweeded garden
> That grows to seed; things rank and gross in nature
> Possess it merely.

"Laudanum grog" was opium dissolved in alcohol, easily available in those days; Coleridge wrote "Kubla Khan" under the influence of laudanum.[5]

Two weeks later he was back in Edinburgh and the disaster struck. To Baxter again:

> The thunderbolt has fallen with a vengeance now.... In the course of conversation my father put me one or two questions as to beliefs, which I candidly answered. I really hate all lying so much now—a new-found honesty that has somehow come out of my late illness—that I could not so much as hesitate at the time; but if I had foreseen the real Hell of everything since, I think I should have lied as I have done so often before.... I do not think I am thus justly to be called a "horrible atheist" and I confess I cannot exactly swallow my father's purpose of praying down continuous afflictions on my head.
>
> Now, what is to take place? What a damned curse I am to my parents! As my father said, "You have rendered my whole life a failure." As my mother said, "This is the heaviest affliction that has ever befallen me." And, O Lord, what a pleasant thing it is to have just *damned* the happiness of (probably) the only two people who care a damn about you in the world.

The letter is signed "Ever your affectionate and horrible Atheist. R. L. Stevenson, C.I., H.A., S.B., etc." In his edition of the letters Ernest Mehew guesses that the initials may represent Careless Infidel, Horrible Atheist, and Son of Belial. That may sound jocular, and no doubt Louis wanted Baxter to hear it that way, but it was black humor at best. His parents were not just being critical, they were rejecting him for who he was.[6]

Louis was recalling this crisis when he asked Baxter some years later, "Do you remember the night I lay on the pavement in misery?" And he told Bob's sister Katharine, who was suffering through a marriage going bad, "You must not despond; however bad things are, you know they do come straight. When I think of the time when I wished to kill myself, for instance, and see the pleasure I should have missed, I am humbled at my own precipitate folly."[7]

This conflict was never just about dogma, though his parents chose to understand it that way. Margaret, the daughter of a preacher, was conventionally religious, but not in the intense way that Cummy was. (Cummy herself was no longer living with the family, and if she heard of this crisis there is no record of it.) As for Thomas the engineer, his religion was intellectual and social rather than spiritual. We have seen that he ignored the taboos that meant so much to Cummy, cheerfully going to the theater and playing cards. What wounded Louis's parents in his apostasy, though they didn't articulate it that way, was the betrayal of themselves.

The storm abated, but there were recurrences. One evening Louis's cousin Bob came into his room "with his hands over his face and sank down on a chair and began to sob." It turned out that another cousin had informed Thomas Stevenson that Bob was a "blight" and "mildew" who was perverting Louis's mind. Bob undoubtedly shared Louis's feelings about religion, but he insisted that he wasn't personally to blame. At that point, he reported, "the conversation went off into emotion and never touched shore again." In recording this Louis added that to complete the drama, "my mother had hysterics privately last night over it all."[8]

Thomas was given to overdramatizing his feelings. Just three days later he and Louis took a peaceful walk along the seashore. As Louis described it, "When the tide is out, there are great, gleaming flats of wet sand, over which the gulls go flying and crying; and every cape runs down into them with its little spit of wall and trees. We lay together a long time on the beach; the sea just babbled among the stones."[9]

Even when things calmed down for a while, the rupture persisted. "It was really pathetic to hear my father praying pointedly for me today at family worship, and to think that the poor man's supplications were addressed to nothing better able to hear and answer than the chandelier." And soon enough there would be another storm of denunciation and despair.

> I am killing my father—he told me tonight (by the way) that I alienated utterly my mother—and this is the result of my attempt to start fresh

and fair to do my best for all of them. . . . He said tonight "he wished he had never married," and I could only echo what he said. "A poor end," he said, "for all my tenderness." And what was there to answer? "I have made all my life to suit you—I have worked for you and gone out of my way for you—and the end of it is that I find you in opposition to the Lord Jesus Christ—I find everything gone—I would ten times sooner have seen you lying in your grave than that you should be shaking the faith of other young men and bringing such ruin on other houses as you have brought already upon this."[10]

It's altogether shocking that even though Louis strove to be a good person and a loving son, his father could declare that he would have been better off dead or never born. As for Margaret, it's hard to know how she really felt. What provoked her hysteria may not have been Louis's unbelief so much as the breach between her husband and her son. And with her determined optimism, she avoided knowing how deeply Louis was wounded. Two years after Louis's death Colvin told her that during this crisis "I think his cousin Bob, Baxter, Mrs. Sitwell [Colvin's partner] and myself were the only people in the world who knew what Louis was inwardly suffering." We don't know whether Margaret responded to this reproach.[11]

THE FATHER-SON DYNAMIC

It has recently been noticed that this crisis happened just one month after the disastrous failure of Thomas Stevenson's harbor works at Wick. With his professional reputation in danger, he now found himself under threat from his only son.[12]

Rosaline Masson evoked the anguish that pervaded 17 Heriot Row. "All those first months of 1873 there must have been hours of much wretchedness and misunderstanding—Louis dashing off his almost illegible letters, hot from his seared heart, in the study upstairs; Thomas Stevenson with his head bent and his great broad forehead in his hands, downstairs; Mrs. Stevenson, not intellectually strong enough to cope with the situation, pitifully anxious to see the two men she loved good and happy." Rosaline was a child of the same culture as Louis, and when she wrote his biography half a century later she said that it was still common for a daughter or son "to remain economically dependent under the parents' roof, compelled to live their life and think their thoughts."[13]

Even after the conflict subsided, Louis was finding life at home increasingly difficult to bear. "I have discovered why I get on always so ill, am always so nasty, so much worse than myself, with my parents. It is because they always take me at my worst, seek out my faults, and never give me any credit." Henry James, who became one of his closest friends and got to know his parents, said that "the filial relation" was "quite classically troubled."[14]

In historical hindsight, this was an era of cultural change during which many young people experienced conflict like Louis's. If religion was often the focal point, still deeper was rebellion against traditional hierarchy. Edmund Gosse's *Father and Son* is a classic version of that story, as is Samuel Butler's *The Way of All Flesh,* whose narrator exclaims, "There are orphanages for children who have lost their parents—oh! why, why, why, are there no harbours of refuge for grown men who have not yet lost them?"[15]

Steven Mintz's *A Prison of Expectations: The Family in Victorian Culture* is a study of the psychological burdens imposed by the patriarchal family at this time, and Louis is one of his examples. "Religion," Mintz says, "provided the Stevensons with a common language and a common set of symbols by which they could give tangible expression to their central concerns with authority, self-discipline, independence, dependence, and self-denial. The entire family dispute embodied larger cultural tensions and contradictions."[16]

Louis was clearly thinking of this conflict in "Truth of Intercourse" six years later, by which time he had achieved independence and would soon be married.

> To speak truth there must be moral equality or else no respect; and hence between parent and child intercourse is apt to degenerate into a verbal fencing bout, and misapprehensions to become ingrained. And there is another side to this, for the parent begins with an imperfect notion of the child's character, formed in early years or during the equinoctial gales of youth; to this he adheres, noting only the facts which suit with his preconception; and wherever a person fancies himself unjustly judged, he at once and finally gives up the effort to speak truth.[17]

At some point Louis wrote in a notebook a critique of the biblical story of Abraham and Isaac, in which the father confirms his absolute faith by accepting God's command to execute his son (though God then rewards him by providing a sacrificial ram instead). Louis focused not on the father but on the son.

> Nothing so thoroughly brings back to us the unthinkable moralities of the past as the story of Abraham and Isaac. It is strange enough that this grown man should have consented to follow his father on such a fool's

errand, and when he learned at last the object of the journey, should have meekly suffered himself to be bound for the sacrifice; but it is far stranger to think that while we have plenty of praise of Abraham's faith, we hear not a syllable of comment on Isaac's obedience, that the whole course of his conduct in the matter was too much *matter of course* for commendation.

Artists often depicted Isaac as a child, but whether or not he was a "grown man" as Louis thought, he was old enough to say, according to the Book of Genesis, "The fire and the wood are here, but where is the lamb for the burnt offering?" In the same notebook Louis commented, "Faith means holding the same opinions as the person employing the word."[18]

In an essay entitled "A Chapter on Dreams," written fourteen years after the crisis, Louis described the origin in dreams of a number of his stories, notably *Dr. Jekyll and Mr. Hyde*. One that didn't get turned into a story is a vision of patricide so startling that one wonders how fully he understood what it might reveal.

The dreamer—he confirms that this was himself—is the son of a very rich man with "a most damnable temper." To avoid his father the son lives abroad for years, and when he returns he finds that his father has married again, to a young wife. Father and son avoid each other for a while, but finally,

> Meet they did, in a desolate, sandy country by the sea; and there they quarreled, and the son, stung by some intolerable insult, struck down the father dead. No suspicion was aroused; the dead man was found and buried, and the dreamer succeeded to the broad estates, and found himself installed under the same roof with his father's widow, for whom no provision had been made. These two lived very much alone, as people may after a bereavement, sat down to table together, shared the long evenings, and grew daily better friends; until it seemed to him of a sudden that she was prying about dangerous matters, that she had conceived a notion of his guilt, that she watched him and tried him with questions. He drew back from her company as men draw back from a precipice suddenly discovered; and yet so strong was the attraction that he would drift again and again into the old intimacy, and again and again be startled back by some suggestive question or some inexplicable meaning in her eye.

After some time the dreamer spies his stepmother searching in the very place where the murder took place, and realizes that she must have found proof of his guilt. Yet she never accuses him, and finally he can stand it no longer.

With a pale face, she heard him as he raved out his complaint: Why did she torture him so? she knew all, she knew he was no enemy to her; why did she not denounce him at once? what signified her whole behaviour? why did she torture him? and yet again, why did she torture him? And when he had done, she fell upon her knees, and with outstretched hands: "Do you not understand?" she cried. "I love you!"

It would be another decade before Freud would begin to develop his concept of the Oedipus complex, and it's impossible to know how, or even whether, Louis applied the symbolism of this dream to his own relationship with his parents. Perhaps he didn't. If he had, would he have been willing to put it in print?[19]

A particular affinity between Thomas and Louis was that both were notable for ebullient good humor but also for episodes of depression. In *Exuberance: The Passion for Life,* Kay Redfield Jamison presents Louis as one of her examples of elation that can all too easily tip over into depression. She quotes Edmund Gosse's description of him: "A childlike mirth leaped and danced in him; he seemed to skip upon the hills of life. He was simply bubbling with quips and jests; his inherent earnestness or passion about abstract things was incessantly relieved by jocosity; and when he had built one of his intellectual castles in the sand, a wave of humour was certain to sweep in and destroy it." But sometimes the exuberance would spin out of control and he would burst into tears, doubting that he could ever be happy again. Thomas Stevenson had similar changes of mood, and his brother Alan had suffered a psychotic breakdown. Louis often feared that he shared their temperament, which today might be called bipolar.[20]

Writing to a psychologist about fever-induced hallucinations during a night of extreme pain, he once said, "I believe it must have been well on in the morning before the fever (or *the other fellow*) triumphed. . . . I have called the one person *myself,* and the other *the other fellow.* It was myself who spoke and acted; the other fellow seemed to have no control of the body or the tongue; he could only act through myself, on whom he brought to bear a heavy strain, resisted in one case, triumphant in the two others."[21]

Claire Harman has taken this statement as the key to Louis's personality, titling her biography *Myself and the Other Fellow,* but he was describing an atypical experience of dissociation, not a fundamental insight into himself. What he did retain from his early religious training was awareness of what St. Paul called "war in the members," irrational impulses that lurk within every human being, not just the mentally ill. "The Calvinism in which he had been born and nurtured," Rosaline Masson said, "made him take himself in deadly earnest, and rack himself on the wheel of conscience."[22]

As for orthodox belief, he never regretted his rejection of it—especially its distortion of the teaching of Christ. Years later he published an essay entitled "A Christmas Sermon," in which he said,

> It is certain we all think too much of sin. We are not damned for doing wrong, but for not doing right. Christ would never hear of negative morality; *Thou shalt* was ever his word, with which he superseded *Thou shalt not*. To make our idea of morality centre on forbidden acts is to defile the imagination and to introduce into our judgments of our fellow men a secret element of gusto. If a thing is wrong for us, we should not dwell upon the thought of it; or we shall soon dwell upon it with inverted pleasure.

He added that condemning the alleged sins of others "is the playground of inverted lusts."[23]

These feelings are very similar to William Blake's. Louis must have admired "The Garden of Love" when he read Blake's *Songs of Experience*, as we know he did:

> I went to the Garden of Love
> And saw what I never had seen:
> A chapel was built in the midst
> Where I used to play on the green.
>
> And the gates of this chapel were shut,
> And "Thou shalt not" writ over the door;
> So I turned to the Garden of Love
> That so many sweet flowers bore.
>
> And I saw it was filled with graves,
> And tombstones where flowers should be,
> And priests in black gowns were walking their rounds,
> And binding with briars my joys and desires.

Like Blake, Louis thought that it was St. Paul and his successors, not Jesus, who turned Christianity into a forbidding institution and made it preach "Thou shalt not."

CHAPTER 8

A Mentor and a Madonna

A FATEFUL ENCOUNTER

At one stage in the spring of 1873 there was a lull in the tension at Heriot Row and Louis jotted down a hope that his life would "run stiller year by year." This note has survived (fig. 23). "As I am glad to say that I do now recognise that I shall never be a great man, I may set myself peacefully on a smaller journey; not without hope of coming to the inn before nightfall. O dass mein Leben Nach diesem Ziel ein ewig Wandeln sey! DESIDERATA: I. Good Health II. 2 to 3 hundred a year. III. O du lieber Gott, *friends!* AMEN, Robert Louis Stevenson." The quotation from Goethe means "O that my life may be eternal progress toward this goal." He would seldom enjoy good health, and it would be years before he could earn £200.

That summer his parents thought it would do him good to get away, and suggested a stay with Margaret's niece Maud at Cockfield in Sussex, forty miles east of Cambridge. He had visited there in 1870 and had gotten on well with Maud's husband, an Anglican clergyman named Churchill Babington, who was professor of archaeology at Cambridge as well as rector of Cockfield. After meeting him Louis reported, "He is really very kind, very merry, and incredibly innocent; he knows about as much of the world as a child." If the elder Stevensons hoped that this gentle character might bring the infidel back to the fold, that was never likely to happen.[1]

Staying with the Babingtons when Louis arrived in July was Maud's close as I am glad to say that I do now recognise that I shall never be a great man, I may set myself peacefully on a smaller journey; not without hope of coming to the inn before nightfull Odass mein leben nach diesem ziel ein ewig wandeln sey!

Desiderata.

I good-Health
II 2 to 3 hundred a year.
III «O du lieber Gott, friends!

A M E N

Robert Louis Stevenson

23. "Desiderata"

friend Frances Sitwell, thirty-four at the time and twelve years older than Louis. Frances recalled long afterward that he made an immediate impression.

> The hours began to fly by as they had never flown before in that dear, quiet old rectory. Laughter, and tears too, followed hard upon each other until late into the night, and his talk was like nothing I had ever heard before, though I knew some of our best talkers and writers. Before three days were over I wrote to Sidney Colvin, who was then Slade Professor [of Fine Art] at Cambridge, and begged him not to delay his promised visit to Cockfield if he wanted to meet a brilliant, and to my mind unmistakable, young genius called Robert Louis Stevenson.

Frances's eight-year-old son Albert ("Bertie") was with her and made friends with Louis immediately.

"For nearly three years after this," Frances continued, "Louis wrote me long letters almost daily, pouring out in them all the many difficulties and troubles of that time of his life. A number of these letters have been published, or part-published, in the volumes of letters edited by Sir Sidney Colvin, and a great many more, too sacred and intimate to publish, are still in my possession." Although many have survived—some were quoted in the preceding chapter—it's likely that others were destroyed. At Frances's request Louis did destroy all of her letters to him; Jenni Calder suggests that they may have seemed compromising.[2]

Frances had married the Reverend Albert Sitwell when she was just sixteen, and went to live with him in India, where he had a chaplaincy, until a cholera epidemic drove them back to England. "All might have gone well," E. V. Lucas says in *The Colvins and Their Friends,* "had Mr. Sitwell not been a man of unfortunate temperament and uncongenial habits." Another writer puts it less diplomatically: "Whether these habits involved drink or choirboys is no longer known."[3]

A couple of years before Louis's visit, Frances had met Colvin and was now his acknowledged companion, though they maintained separate residences. She wanted a divorce, but her husband refused it. Just five years older than Louis, Colvin was already a success in the world. He had recently been appointed to the professorship at Cambridge, and to that would soon be added directorship of the Fitzwilliam Museum there. Ten years later he would become keeper of prints and drawings at the British Museum.

He and Frances were something of an odd couple. She was animated, charming, and a beauty; a pencil sketch by Edward Burne-Jones made just three years after Louis met her (fig. 24) captures the Madonna quality that moved him—in

24. Frances Sitwell

his letters he sometimes called her by that name. It's true that most of the Pre-Raphaelites' women look like Madonnas, but in this case Burne-Jones actually used his drawing of Frances as the model for the Virgin Mary in his painting *The Annunciation*.

The photograph of Colvin reproduced here (fig. 25) was taken much later, but it's clear that he never seemed young. Oscar Wilde's quip about Max Beerbohm might well be applied to Colvin: that the gods bestowed on him the gift of perpetual old age. A. C. Benson, a fellow academic and author of the patriotic song "Land of Hope and Glory," called him "a pompous fool, in whose veins runs the blood of a fish," and the poet Austin Dobson said there was no need to add ice to a drink "if Colvin puts the beverages against his person." But neither man knew Colvin well. A colleague at the British Museum said, "Under a manner that often seemed stiff and shy, he concealed an emotional and excitable

25. Sidney Colvin

temperament, capable of occasional explosions. He had deep feelings, strong affections and antipathies."[4]

Colvin took to Louis just as Frances and Bertie did. He said much later of their initial acquaintance, "He was at that time a lad of twenty-two, with his powers not yet set nor his way of life determined. But to know him was to recognize at once that here was a young genius of whom great things might be expected. I have known no man in whom the poet's heart and imagination were combined with such a brilliant strain of humor and such an unsleeping alertness and adroitness of the critical intelligence." Leslie Stephen, who would publish much of Louis's writing, said that Colvin was "the first outside the home circle to recognise Stevenson's genius, and to give encouragement when encouragement was most needed."[5]

THE "SACRED AND INTIMATE" LETTERS

As soon as Louis was back in Edinburgh he wrote to Frances, "Do you know, I think yesterday and the day before were the two happiest days of my life.... Dear, I would not have missed last month for eternity." He was careful to make clear that he understood his position vis-à-vis Colvin: "I *will* try to be worthy of you and of *him*."

A week later he exclaimed, "It is worth having lived for, to have thrown so much glory and gladness into another's thin existence as you have thrown into mine." He had no intention of letting his parents get wind of this relationship with a woman who was still legally married and also involved with someone else, so her replies were sent to the "Spec," the Speculative Society. "Ha! There is my father gone out. I am off to the Spec."[6]

Occasionally he addressed Frances as "Claire," the name of a character in a story he was struggling to write. Having talked with her about the project, it amused him to call her that.

A month later he was expecting a letter but found nothing at the Spec, and flew into a panic until he discovered that it had simply been mislaid. This prompted a veiled allusion to some earlier romantic connection about which nothing is now known, reproaching himself for having callously ended it.

> Do you know, I have been thinking a little of my wretchedness when your letters did not come, and the whole business has knocked most unpleasantly at my conscience. I too left letters unanswered until they ceased to come, from a person to whom the postage even must have been a matter of parsimony; left them unanswered, on purpose that they might cease. O God! a thing comes back to me that hurts the heart very much. For the first letter, she had bought a piece of paper with a sort of coarse flower-arabesque at the top of it.... I never showed the letters to anyone, and some months ago they became insupportable to me and I burned them. Don't I deserve the gallows?

If this "person" could barely afford postage, it's likely that she was a servant.[7]

By now Louis was regularly addressing Frances as his Madonna. "O blessed life, *O Madonna mia*—no! *nostra*—look down a little gladly on us all."[8]

Soon afterward he hit upon another name for her—Consuelo, the heroine of a novel of that name by George Sand. Consuelo is a Spanish gypsy, abandoned by her lover in Venice, whose superb voice and musical genius make her an opera star throughout Europe. She battles her way to greatness against heavy odds, and although wrongly suspected of immoral behavior, remains pure as a saint until united at last with her true love.

Admittedly, when Louis evoked this comparison he tended to do it, as a critic says, "rather cringingly."

> *O Consuelo de mia alma,* I wish you were here. I am so tired and played out this morning. My head is like lead, and my heart; but I have found the name for you at last—Consuelo. Consolation of my spirit. Consolation. It pleases me to write it and I am as weak as a child this morning; so please excuse this little peal of bells over my triumph.... *Later:* I cannot read or do anything but write to you. And yet I feel I ought not just at present. And I won't.

George Sand's heroine sings a Spanish song that begins *Consuelo de mia alma,* "solace of my soul."⁹

Before long Frances evidently advised Louis to tone it down. He wrote to her the next summer, "Try and forget utterly the R.L.S. you have known in the past; he is no more, he is dead. I shall try now to be strong and helpful, to be a good friend to you and no longer another limp dead-heavy burthen on your weary arms. I think this is permanent: try to believe it yourself, that is the best means to make it so. Try to believe in me, and I shall believe in myself." But he still assured her, "You were the mother of my soul as surely as another was the mother of my body." And on December 25, "Madonna, I give you a son's kiss this Christmas morning, and my heart is in my mouth, dear, as I write the words. Ever your faithful friend and son and priest."¹⁰

A letter three days after that was over the top. "Think of how I cling to you, Madonna, my mother; think of how you must be to me throughout life the mother's breasts to suckle me, and be brave, dear, and be for me a brave mother. If I am to be a son, you must be a mother; and surely I am a son in more than ordinary sense, begotten of the sweet soul and beautiful body of you, and taught all that ever I knew pure or holy or of good report, by the contact of your sweet soul and lovely body." It's hard to believe that the relationship was as platonic as Frances wanted it to seem.¹¹

Once again she must have told Louis to moderate his language, which prompted him to declare his passion instead through suggestive descriptions of works of art. They had seen the Elgin Marbles together, and he wrote afterward to say that he had acquired a framed photograph of the three Fates. "They are wonderfully womanly—they are more womanly than any woman—and those girl draperies are drawn over a wonderful greatness of body instinct with sex.... If all goes to the worst, shall I not be able to lay my head on the great knees of the middle Fate—O these great knees, that awe me and yet make me mad with desire." That is a remarkably erotic response to those cool (and headless) nudes.

Warming to his theme, two days later he enlarged upon it.

> There is something more substantive about a woman than ever there can be about a man. I can conceive a great mythical woman, living alone among inaccessible mountain tops or some lost island in the pagan seas.... I can think of these three deep-breasted women, living out all their days on remote hilltops, seeing the white dawn and the purple even, and the world outspread before them forever and no more to them forever than a sight of the eyes, a hearing of the ears, a faraway interest of the inflexible heart, not pausing, not pitying, but austere with a holy austerity, rigid with a calm and passionless rigidity, and I find them none the less women to the end.
>
> And think, dear, if one could love a woman like that once, see her once grow pale with passion, and once wring your lips out upon hers, would it not be a small thing to die? ... My quiet, deep-kneed, deep-breasted, well-draped ladies of Necessity, I give my heart to you. And they know what is in my heart, and they know whom I love best.[12]

In January 1875 he told Frances that he was writing a novella set in the Italian Renaissance to be entitled "When the Devil Was Well." He explained that he was thinking of a proverb, "When the devil was sick, the devil a monk would be; when the devil was well, the devil a monk was he." "O I like it badly!" he exclaimed. "I wish you could hear it at once."[13]

This story wasn't published until much later (Colvin and Leslie Stephen were both critical of it), but the manuscript has survived, and it's easy to see why Louis wanted Frances to hear it. The poet Sannazarro is painting the portrait of a chaste and beautiful duchess:

> Ippolita came and leant on Sannazarro's chair. He could feel her touch upon his shoulder, and her breath stirred his hair as it came and went. A film stood before his eyes, he could paint no longer; and thus they remained for some troubled seconds in silence. Then Sannazarro laid down his pallette and brushes, stood up and turned around to her, and took

both her hands in his. The sight of her face, white and frightened and expectant, with mild eyes and a tremulous under lip—the sight of her face was to him as if he had seen the thoughts of his own heart in a mirror. Their mouths joined, with a shudder, in one long kiss. This was the time when Sannazarro should have died.

Not long after that Sannazarro is suspected of heresy and tortured on the rack, but "his body was of iron," he recovers from his injuries, and eventually kills the duchess's husband in a duel. After much complicated narration we reach the end. "The figure of a woman came forth into the broken sunlight of the grove. It was Ippolita. His heart stood still for joy." On the manuscript an unidentified person, possibly Bob Stevenson, wrote the comment "*Bravissimo, caro mio!*"[14]

Biographers have generally described Frances as serenely comfortable with this ambiguous relationship, even though Louis was pouring out desperately passionate letters for months on end. Frank McLynn may well be right: "She indulged in emotional brinkmanship, encouraging or at least conniving at a dangerous degree of infatuation by Louis." However, "love" rather than "infatuation" would be the right word.[15]

In fact we have Sidney Colvin's own testimony that Frances was accustomed to attracting younger admirers, though he claimed to believe that it was unconscious. In 1908, five years after the couple finally got married, Colvin's friend Lucas published an anthology of poems and sketches about women entitled *Her Infinite Variety* (Enobarbus's tribute to Cleopatra in *Antony and Cleopatra*). One sketch, "A Thorough-Bred," signed only "X," is known to be by Colvin.

> She cools and soothes your secret smart before ever you can name it; she divines and shares your hidden joy, or shames your fretfulness with loving laughter.... In the fearlessness of her purity she can afford the frankness of her affections, and shows how every fascination of her sex may in the most open freedom be the most honourably secure. Yet in a world of men and women, such an one cannot walk without kindling once and again a dangerous flame before she is aware. As in her nature there is no room for vanity, she never foresees these masculine combustions, but has a wonderful art and gentleness in allaying them, and is accustomed to convert the claims and cravings of passion into the lifelong loyalty of grateful and contented friendship.

That's one way of putting it. Another might be that it was enjoyable to be not just hard to get but impossible to get, while very consciously leading her admirers on.[16]

Louis would dedicate *A Child's Garden of Verses* to Cummy as "my second Mother, my first Wife"; now it was Frances who became "Madonna, my mother." She was the one person to whom he could pour out his feelings in letters as he went on living at Heriot Row. In 1875 he wrote bleakly, "Two birds are building a nest in the holly before my window; you should see them fly up with great straws in their mouths. God prosper them. They are better off than we; they are not obliged to play other people's games, wear other people's clothes, walk with other people's gait, and say other people's silly words after them by leaden rote, under pain of breaking hearts and driving home the gross dagger of disappointment into breasts full of hope."[17]

One year after writing that Louis would meet the woman who would become his wife.

"THE PERFECT FRIEND"

The relationship with the steady, reserved Colvin was just as important to Louis as his adoration of Frances. A decade or so later he addressed Colvin in verse as "the perfect friend":

> I knew thee strong and quiet like the hills;
> I knew thee apt to pity, brave to endure,
> In peace or war a Roman full equipt;
> And just I knew thee, like the fabled kings
> Who by the loud sea shore gave judgment forth
> From dawn to eve, bearded and few of words.[18]

Colvin's unstinting admiration and affection speak well for his character. Introducing his selection of Louis's letters three decades later, he paid tribute to the full range of his friend's temperament:

> He loved, with a child's or actor's gusto, to play a part and make a drama out of life; but the part was always for the moment his very own: he had it not in him to pose for anything but what he truly was. . . . *Divers et ondoyant* [diverse and changeable], the words of Montaigne, beyond other men he seemed to contain within himself a whole troop of singularly assorted characters—the poet and artist, the moralist and preacher, the humourist and jester, the man of great heart and tender conscience, the man of eager appetite and curiosity, the Bohemian, impatient of restraints and shams, the adventurer and lover of travel and of action.

Louis himself remarked in an essay, "We cannot even regard ourselves as a constant; in this flux of things, our identity itself seems in a perpetual variation."[19]

Still later Colvin published some sketches of people he had known, including Louis, and described what Frances had meant to their friend.

> Between him and Mrs. Sitwell there had sprung up an instantaneous understanding. Not only the lights and brilliancies of his nature, but the strengths and glooms that underlay them, were from the first apparent to her, so that in the trying season of his life which followed he was moved to throw himself upon her sympathies with the unlimited confidence and devotion to which his letters of the time bear witness.... Under all this captivating, this contagious gaiety and charm there lay a troubled spirit, in grave risk from the perils of youth, from a constitution naturally frail and already heavily over-strained, from self-distrust and uncertainty as to his own powers and purposes, and above all from the misery of bitter, heart and soul-rending disagreements with a father to whom he was devotedly attached.

Colvin seems always to have treated Louis's adoration of Frances with tolerance and kindness. In 1879 Louis was able to tell him, "I want you to understand that with all my troubles, I am a happy man and happier than often of yore. I have mastered my troubles; they are under my hand; they are now a part of me and under where I sit and rule."[20]

A month later he wrote again to report yet another health setback, but was defiantly optimistic all the same.

> I had a kind of collapse: weakness, languor, loss of appetite, causeless swelled testicle just appearing for the sake of fun you would say. Last but not least, irritation of the spermatic cord caused by sw. t. [i.e., swollen testicle] which was really the devil. I can do no work. It all lies aside. I want—I want—I want a holiday; I want to be happy; I want the moon, or the sun, or something. I want the object of my affections badly, anyway; and a big forest, and fine breathing, sweating, sunny walks; and the trees all crying aloud in a summer's wind; and a camp under the stars.

By now he could speak freely to Colvin about the object of his affections, since that was no longer Frances Sitwell but Fanny Osbourne. He went on defiantly, "Am I a man? By God, I am, although I don't look like it in my literature. A man I am, and they can't crush the sport out of me, were Edinburgh ten times Edinburgh, and a time to spare."[21]

If Frances's moral support was crucial, so was Colvin's professional support. He was extremely well connected in literary and journalistic circles, and played an invaluable role in recommending the young writer to editors. Of those the most important was Leslie Stephen, who would publish no fewer than sixteen of Louis's essays, and a number of stories as well, in the highly regarded *Cornhill Magazine*. Louis was deeply grateful, and wrote later, "If I am what I am and where I am, if I have done anything at all or done anything well, [Colvin's] is the credit. It was he who paved my way in letters; it was he who set before me, kept before me, and still, as I write, keeps before me, a difficult standard of achievement; and it was to him and to Fleeming Jenkin that I owed my safety at the most difficult periods of my life." Jenkin was his Edinburgh professor and impresario of amateur theatricals; by "safety" he must have meant preserving his mental and emotional balance when most under threat.[22]

LOUIS IN LONDON

Colvin's Cambridge professorship was a part-time position, and although he became a fellow of Trinity College and lodged there when in town, his principal residence was in London. Frances too lived in London—at a different address—and often helped him to entertain. She had found employment as secretary to the Working Men's College in Queen's Square, and did some book reviewing as well, so she was able to support herself without help from her estranged husband. When Colvin took up his position at the British Museum in 1884 he would have a residence there.

Colvin arranged Louis's election to the Savile Club, and whenever he was in London he would stay there. It had been founded, Colvin said, "on a principle aimed against the stand-offishness customary in English life, and all members were expected to hold themselves predisposed to talk and liable to accost without introduction." They were notable for their range of interests, "young men drawn from the professions of science or learning, of art, literature, journalism, or the stage." There were some older members too, notably Fleeming Jenkin.

In Edinburgh Louis's Bohemianism made him an outlier; at the Savile he could feel at home among writers and artists, some of them well known, and nearly all of them congenial companions. A visitor years later found a number of old-timers who were happy to share "tales of Louis, in his black shirt and velvet jacket, gesticulating eagerly and shaking his long and unkempt hair, while he made the little circle in the midst of which he talked a momentary center of the universe."[23]

One encounter went badly. As Colvin remembered it, a new member was lunching alone and Louis tried to start a conversation. That was met with a chilly rebuff, at which "Stevenson came away furious, and presently relieved his wrath with the lampoon which is included in his published works."

> I am a kind of farthing dip,
>   Unfriendly to the nose and eyes;
> A blue-behinded ape, I skip
>   Upon the trees of Paradise.
>
> At mankind's feast I take my place
>   In solemn, sanctimonious state,
> And have the air of saying grace
>   While I defile the dinner plate.

Louis didn't name his target, and neither did Colvin, but Edmund Gosse confirmed that it was the then-popular novelist W. H. Mallock. The grudge against Mallock lasted for quite some time. Seven years after this incident Louis sent Gosse a list of "Forthcoming Works by R.L.S." They were to include *Mallock, or, the Creeping Thing: A Romance*. As a happy sequel, between 1970 and 2016 the painter Tom Phillips brilliantly altered pages from *A Human Document,* a terrible novel by Mallock, in successive editions of *A Humument*.[24]

The Savile Club still exists, though in a different location. Its website notes that "Robert Louis Stevenson famously observed to another member the connection between a proficiency at snooker and a misspent youth, and Stevenson was a keen player of the game to the Club's own rules. Savile Snooker was designed to enliven the game and permits out-of-sequence potting of the coloured balls, with a penalty attached for failure, of course. It is said that there is still a strong tradition of playing a very similar game in Samoa, where of course Stevenson settled."

In his sketch of Louis's character, Colvin described an occasion when the horse drawing their cab in London "got the bit between his teeth and bolted for some half a mile along the Thames Embankment; and while I sat with stiffened knees and nerves on the stretch, expecting a smash, I could see that Stevenson actually enjoyed it. Few of us were ever truly happy in a bolting hansom, but Stevenson was so made that any kind of danger was a positive physical exhilaration to him."

Colvin also related a performance that was reminiscent of the "jinks" that Louis and his friends used to perpetrate in Edinburgh. He astonished Colvin's servant by appearing at his house at dawn in disgracefully shabby clothes, "weary and dirty from a night's walking followed by a couple of hours' slumber in a garden outhouse [i.e., shed] he had found open. He had spent the night on the pad through the southern slums and suburbs, trying to arouse the suspicions of one policeman after another till he should succeed in getting taken up as a rogue and vagabond, thereby gaining proof for his fixed belief that justice has one pair of scales for the ragged and another for the respectable. But one and all saw through him, and refused to take him seriously as a member of the criminal classes."[25]

Perhaps Louis's behavior toward Frances can be seen as an example of his attraction to risk-taking and danger. It was certainly dangerous to be openly worshiping the beautiful companion of an older man whom he admired and whose help he would rely on. Fortunately she and Colvin were both wonderfully understanding, and in the years to come Colvin would be an invaluable mentor for Louis's writing career.

CHAPTER 9

"Ordered South"

DEEP DEPRESSION

During the summer of 1873 Louis was emotionally exhausted. He wrote to Elizabeth Crosby, a young woman who had stayed with his family in Edinburgh, "There is no door of escape from this ennui. I try to evade it by constant change; by science, law, literature, perfect sunshine idleness when the weather permits, science again, law again, literature again, and perhaps a little, at the end of the cycle, of what has been mendaciously called 'life.' But leap as I may from one to the other, disgust is always at my back." After she replied (the letter has not survived), he added, "My life is a very distressing one at home, so distressing that I have a great difficulty in keeping up a good heart at all or even in keeping my health together. For nearly a year back I have lived in the most miserable contention with my parents on the subject of religion. . . . To be continually told that you have utterly wrecked the lives of your father and mother, and to see that much of this is true—the wretched truth—is not, you must grant, a very favorable circumstance for cheerful thought. However I must, in Scotch phrase, dree my weird as best I can." The expression means "endure my fate." That was the original meaning of *weird* in Old English, and by the time Shakespeare called the witches "weird sisters" in *Macbeth*, the term was regularly used for the Three Fates.[1]

He didn't mention, of course, another source of anguish: he was in love with a woman he couldn't have.

Louis's parents were still pressing him to get on with his legal career, and even encouraged him to go to London and take a preliminary exam for studying English law, a daunting prospect since it was very different from Scottish. Fortunately Sidney Colvin and Frances Sitwell were aware of the protracted crisis he was enduring and intervened to rescue him. They arranged a consultation for Louis with Dr. Andrew Clark, a distinguished expert on lung diseases (and a Scot from Aberdeen), and evidently told him about their friend's mental state.

Clark found no organic disease, but told Louis firmly not to take the exam, and instead to go directly to the south of France—by himself. "Clark is a trump," Louis told Frances. "He said I must go abroad and that I was better alone." He added, "I had a slight spar with my mother this afternoon about my movements tomorrow. She said 'You shall not have everything your own way, I can tell you.'" Thomas was not the only controlling parent.[2]

As soon as the elder Stevensons heard about the French plan they rushed to London and had an emotional interview with Clark, who insisted on the point. Margaret recorded in her diary, "He tells us that Lou's nervous system has quite broken down, that his lungs are delicate and just in the state when disease might very easily set in. When I asked if I ought to go with him he said, 'No, he wants a complete change of everything, scene, diet and companionship. Strangers will be much more likely to bring him out of himself than if you were with him.'" That was putting it bluntly, but they accepted it.[3]

The very next day, November 5—Guy Fawkes Day—Louis was on his way. A contemporary writer exclaimed, "Railways have all but annihilated space! A traveler may leave the London Bridge Station at 7:40 on a Monday morning, by mail train for Paris, and be at Nice or Menton for supper the following day." Menton was indeed Louis's destination, with happy memories of having stayed there before. As a painting from thirty years later shows, it was still a small seaside village, with the foothills of the Maritime Alps rising behind it; Louis called them "the quiet Alps of the seaboard" (color plate 7).[4]

How long he might stay there had not been determined, but it turned out to be nearly half a year. This was the first time he had ever lived entirely on his own. He wrote to his parents, but poured out his feelings more openly to Frances and to other friends; his letters from this period are among the most revealing that we have.

Right after arriving he received a heartening letter from his cousin Bob, who was studying art in Antwerp. "Talking, I find," Bob wrote, "was talking with you. Talking with other people, I must have always thought, this I will tell Louis, this I won't, so that it was merely collecting material for my real talk with you.

Success means you, life means you, friendship means you, everything means you." Louis was deeply moved, and told Frances, "I am so much astonished, and almost more astonished that he should have expressed it than that he should feel it. He never would have *said* it, I know."[5]

Still, his depression was ongoing and profound. Two days later he wrote to Charles Baxter,

> I am only gradually finding out how nearly done for I have been. I am awfully weary and nervous; I cannot read or write almost at all and I am not able to walk much; all which put together leaves me a good deal of time in which I have no great pleasure or satisfaction. However you must not suppose me discontented. I am away in my own beautiful Riviera and I am free now from the horrible worry and misery that was playing the devil with me at home. A friend in London had a conversation with my father and explained to him a little that I was not the extremely cheerful destroyer of home quiet that he had pictured to himself, and that I really was bothered about this wretched business. . . . It is beastly to have a bad head like this, and to have to pay for half an hour's thinking with a bad night or an hour or two of miserable nervousness.

In this context "nervousness" meant the mental disorder known as neurasthenia, weakness of the nerves, and in the months to come he would refer to it as a breakdown.[6]

The next day he made an attempt to quell his anxiety by merging peacefully into nature, in the manner of the old Romantic poets. As he described it to Frances,

> I sat a long while up among the olive yards today, at a favourite corner where one has fair view down the valley and onto the blue floor of the sea. I had a Horace with me and read a little; but Horace, when you try to read him fairly under the open Heaven, sounds urban, and you find something of the escaped townsman in his descriptions of the country. I tried for long to hit upon some language that might catch ever so faintly the indefinable shifting colour of olive leaves, and above all, the changes and little silverings that pass over them, like blushes over a face, when the wind tosses great branches to and fro; but the Muse was not favourable.

Horace wrote often in praise of his Sabine farm, but Louis's Latin was good enough to detect the artificiality of the escaped townsman.

At this point the episodes of tranquility were always temporary. Two days later,

> I have been to Nice today to see Dr. Bennett [an Edinburgh physician who spent his winters in Nice]. He agrees with Clark that there is no disease; but I finished up my day with a lamentable exhibition of weakness. I could not remember French, or at least I was afraid to go into any place lest I should not be able to remember it, and so could not tell when the train went. I walked about the streets in such a rage with every person who came near me that I felt inclined to break out upon them with all sorts of injurious language; and only didn't, I think, because I knew if I gave way at all that I should give way altogether, and cry, or have a fit, or something. At last I crawled up to the station and sat down on the steps and just steeped myself there in the sunshine, until the evening began to fall and the air to grow chilly.

He added, "I shall not go to Nice again for some time to come."[7]

A few days after this episode he attempted a self-diagnosis. "I hope my letter will neither weary nor frighten you," he wrote to Frances, "and that you will remember, now that I have written to you in all the deformity of my hypochondriasis and with all the sickly vanities—bedside flowers after all that amuse and divert the mind of a person who does not think himself well—remember that I come of a gloomy family, always ready to be frightened about their precious health." At that time "hypochondria" meant what today would be called clinical depression. The point about the family is significant: doctors regularly looked for hereditary causes.[8]

During this time Louis began working on an essay called "Ordered South," which would be published in *Macmillan's Magazine* the next year. The title was conventional; a historian says that in Victorian times "'ordering south' became a standard medical prescription for the well-to-do."[9]

Speaking of himself in the third person, Louis remembers initial exhilaration as he anticipated "an estate out of which he had been kept unjustly, and which he was now to receive in free and full possession." In a sense the South was his true spiritual home. But that mood quickly gave way to lassitude.

> Here, at his feet, under his eyes, are the olive gardens and the blue sea. Nothing can change the eternal magnificence of form of the naked Alps behind Mentone. There is someone by [i.e., nearby] who is out of sympathy with the scene, and is not moved up to the measure of the occa-

sion; and that someone is himself. The world is disenchanted for him. He seems to himself to touch things with muffled hands, and to see them through a veil. His life becomes a palsied fumbling after notes that are silent when he has found and struck them. He cannot recognise that this phlegmatic and unimpressionable body with which he now goes burthened is the same that he knew heretofore so quick and delicate and alive.

He felt ready to welcome death. Quoting this passage, the psychologist Kay Redfield Jamison calls it "one of the most succinct and best descriptions of depression I know."[10]

The only thing that seemed to help was opium, which was legal and easily available. He was familiar with its dangers from De Quincey's *Confessions of an English Opium Eater,* but he needed it now. After encountering the first violet in bloom, he wrote to Frances,

> I do not think so small a thing has ever given me such a princely festival of pleasure. I am quite drunken at heart, and you do not know how the scent of this flower strikes in me the same thought, as I think almost all things will do now, everything beautiful to me brings back the thought of what is most beautiful to me. My little violet, if you could speak I know what you would say! I feel as if my heart were a little bunch of violets in my bosom, and my brain is pleasantly intoxicated with the wonderful odour. I suppose I am writing nonsense but it does not seem nonsense to me.

The next day he told his mother that it had been a drug trip. "I lived all Sunday in the most inexpressible bliss, and when I went to bed at night, there was something almost terrifying in the pleasures that crowded upon me in the darkness." He added, "I shall be more careful how I take such a drug again; I am not quite the figure for much opium I think." Despite chronic ill health, he didn't use it often in the years to come.[11]

A few days later he wrote to Frances, "I dreamed that my mother had written to me that they could join me here about Christmas (I think) and I must own that the dream was not agreeable to me and that I awoke from it with relief." Soon after that he told her, "It is now five months ago since I saw you first; only five months. It seems like my whole life, Consuelo. Ever your faithful friend, Robert Louis Stevenson." He was careful not to use just his first name in signing his letters to Frances.[12]

TWO BRITISH FRIENDS

Sidney Colvin, who had health issues of his own, had already been planning to visit the Riviera, and his arrival in December was just what Louis needed. With this intelligent and sympathetic friend he could enjoy conversation and begin doing some sightseeing. Incidentally, with Colvin Louis seems to have referred to Frances carefully as "Mrs. Sitwell."[13]

Louis had settled at the Hôtel du Pavillon, and the group of guests who dined there grew in size to eleven, most of whom were congenial. Every one of them was either English or Scottish, though there were plenty of opportunities to speak French with other people.

"It is awfully jolly having S.C. here," Louis wrote to Frances; "I shall be miserably dull I fear when he goes again." Soon they spent some time in Monaco, just a few miles away, and he reported,

> I am as happy as can be and wish to notify the fact before it passes. The sea is blue, gray, purple and green, very subdued and peaceful; earlier in the day it was marbled by small keen specks of sun and larger spaces of faint irradiation, but the clouds have closed together now and these appearances are no more.—Voices of children and occasional crying of gulls; the mechanical noise of a gardener somewhere behind us in the scented thicket; and the faint report and rustle of the waves on the precipice far below only break in upon the quietness to render it more complete and perfect.[14]

Louis had visited Monaco previously with his parents, and he wrote now to his mother, "I recollected having been there nearly eleven years ago, and my father throwing stones over the cliff and making me calculate the height." One thing did spoil the view over the Mediterranean. "The pigeon shooting is certainly horrid to behold, and the importunate noise of the guns pervades the garden all afternoon." Those were live pigeons, not clay ones.[15]

In Monaco he and Colvin visited the Monte Carlo Casino, just to see what it was like. In his memoir Colvin recalled an unexpected incident there. "Hearing a sudden 'ping' from near the wall of the room over my right shoulder, I turned and saw that a loser, having left the table, lay writhing on the floor. He had shot himself, fatally as I afterwards learnt, in the stomach. The attendants promptly came forward, lifted him on to an armchair, and carried him out of the room with an air of grave disapproval and shocked decorum."[16]

They soon moved to a different Menton hotel, the Mirabeau, on the other side of the bay, and under Colvin's influence Louis regained his enthusiasm for activity. "He cherished an intense underlying longing for the life of action, danger, and command. 'Action, Colvin, action,' I remember his crying eagerly to me with his hand on my arm as we lay basking for his health's sake in a boat off the scented shores of the Cap St. Martin." At another time they amused themselves by composing a mock advertisement for a Grand Hotel Godam, or in parodic Franglais the Great God-Damn Hotel: "All the agreements of hihg-life [sic] are reunited in this magnificent establishment, newly organized, and entertained upon the footing of the most researched confortable." *Recherché* in French actually means "sought after."[17]

Through Colvin, Louis made a new friend who happened to be in Menton, a fellow Scot named Andrew Lang, six years older than himself (fig. 26). Lang was a poet, critic, and journalist who wrote extensively on anthropology, and would go on to publish popular collections of fairy tales. By chance they had been passengers on the same steamer in the Hebrides years before, but had made no contact at that time. Now they got on well enough, but neither felt the enthusiasm that would later develop.

Louis wrote to his mother, "He is good-looking, delicate, boyish, Oxfordish, etc. He did not impress me unfavourably; nor deeply in any way." Lang's own first impression was recorded many years later. "He looked as, in my eyes, he always did look, more like a lass than a lad, with a rather long, smooth oval face, brown hair worn at greater length than is common, large lucid eyes. I shall not deny that my first impression was not wholly favourable. 'Here,' I thought, 'is one of your æsthetic young men, though a very clever one.'"[18]

An American fan of Stevenson's got a more memorable version of this meeting from Lang himself, expressed in a characteristically "discontinuous and jerky" manner and "amiable growl." The recipient of this account was a theater critic, and may well have been skilled at recalling dialogue (he said he wrote it down in the London Underground immediately after leaving Lang):

> Menton. Promenade. Saw him coming. Didn't like him. Long cape. Long hair. Queer hat. Damned queer. Hands: white, bony, beautiful. Didn't like the cape. Didn't like the hair. Looked like a damned aesthete. Never liked aesthetes, can't stand them. Talked well. Saw that. Still seemed another aesthete Colvin had discovered. Didn't like him at all. Later—oh, yes—but I needn't tell you that. Didn't like him at first. Took time.[19]

Lang was soon captivated, however, by Louis's imaginative talk, and in "Recollections of Robert Louis Stevenson" he would make a striking comment: "Mr.

26. Andrew Lang

Stevenson possessed, more than any man I ever met, the power of making other men fall in love with him. I mean that he excited a passionate admiration and affection, so much that I verily believe some men were jealous of other men's place in his liking."[20]

Over the years Lang and Louis would see each other often at the Savile Club, and Louis addressed him in a poem as "dear Andrew, with the brindled hair," commenting that Lang's writing was equally compelling whether the subject was "reels and rods" or "the old unhappy gods." Lang was indeed an ardent fisherman, and after Louis's death he lamented his friend's lack of interest in sports. "He never played cricket, I deeply regret to say, and his early love of football [i.e., soccer] deserted him. He was no golfer, and a good day's trout-fishing, during which he neglected to kill each trout as it was taken, caused remorse and made him abandon the contemplative boy's recreation." Lang would never have seen a little poem Louis enclosed in a letter to another friend:

> My name is Andrew Lang,
> Andrew Lang,
> That's my name,
> And criticism and cricket is my game.
> With my eyeglass in my eye
> Am not I?
> Am I not
> A lady-dady Oxford kind of Scot?

The "eyeglass" must have been a monocle.[21]

It may seem surprising that Louis and Lang got along so well. Colvin, who was notably reserved himself, described Lang as "fastidiously correct and reserved, purely English in speech with a recurring falsetto note in the voice—that kind of falsetto that bespeaks languor rather than vehemence; full of literature and pleasantry but on his guard, even to affectation, against any show of emotion."[22]

Someone who had known Louis as an undergraduate remembered an encounter in London.

> I happened to be walking with the late Andrew Lang in Bond Street one afternoon. As we walked we came across Stevenson dressed in the height of the eccentricity which, as is well known, he at one time affected—a black shirt, red tie, black brigand cloak, and (I am almost certain) a velvet smoking cap. He came up to us, but Lang said, "No, no; go away, Louis, go away! My character will stand a great deal, but it won't stand being seen talking to a 'thing' like you in Bond Street."[23]

There was also a different kind of friendship. At Louis's hotel were a pair of Russian sisters who were estranged from their husbands. The elder was "tall, very beautiful, dark, and if anything a little appalling looking"; her younger sister immediately began flirting with Louis, which he found unnerving because her intentions remained ambiguous. He was out of his depth with these worldly sophisticates, though mentioning them to Frances evidently provoked jealousy. We don't have her letters, but he wrote reassuringly, "I am only happy in the thought of you, my dear. This other woman is interesting to me as a hill might be, or a book, or a picture—but you have all my heart." Of course she never gave him all of hers.[24]

By now Louis was speaking French with complete ease, and described a conversation with the innkeeper.

> I told him that where one found a kitchen so exquisite one astonished oneself that the wine was not up to the same form. *Eh voilà précisément mon côté faible, monsieur,* he replied with an indescribable amplitude of gesture. *Que voulez-vous? Moi, je suis cuisinier!* ["That is exactly my weak spot, Monsieur. What can I say? Me, I'm a cook!"] It was as though Shakespeare, called to account for some such peccadillo as the Bohemian seaport, should answer magnificently that he was a poet.

Que voulez-vous? literally "What do you want?" is one of those simple but untranslatable French expressions that Louis enjoyed. In *The Winter's Tale* Shakespeare gave landlocked Bohemia a seacoast.[25]

The breakdown was receding into the past, and he reported to Frances that although his dreams were vivid they were no longer scary.

> I dreamed horridly, but not my usual dreams of social miseries and misunderstandings and all sorts of crucifixions of the spirit, but of good, cheery, physical things—of long successions of vaulted, dimly lit cellars full of black water, in which I went swimming among toads and unutterable blind fishes.... Then my dream changed and I was a sort of Siamese pirate, on a very high deck with several others. The ship was almost captured and we were fighting desperately. Then I saw a signal being given and knew they were going to blow up the ship. I leapt right off and heard my captors splash in the water after me as thick as pebbles when a bit of river bank has given way beneath the foot. I never heard the ship blow up, but I spent the rest of the night swimming about among some piles with the whole sea full of Malays searching for me with knives in their mouths. They could swim any distance underwater, and every now and again, just as I was beginning to reckon myself safe, a cold hand would be laid on my ankle—ugh!

Louis was always an imaginative dreamer, but if those were "good, cheery" things, it's hard to imagine what his bad dreams were like.[26]

One day the hotel guests arranged to have their photographs taken, and when it was Louis's turn, one of the Russian ladies told the photographer, *C'est mon fils. Il vient d'avoir dix-neuf ans. Il est tout fier de sa moustache. Tâchez de la faire paraître*—"He's my son. He has just turned nineteen. He is very proud of his moustache; try to make it show up." When Louis sent a copy of the picture home he commented indignantly, "The moustache is clearly visible to the naked eye."[27]

Colvin had gone to Paris for several weeks in order to see Frances, who was staying with a sister there. Bob Stevenson had dinner with him in a café and wrote to Louis,

> He said that he had been much grieved to observe the effect that certain emotions you had gone through lately had had upon you. He said it was a first class thing for you to do and that he knew no other man who was so game for being on the spot as you, and that whatever you had lost, you had gained in him such a friend for life as it is difficult to gain. I thought he was not supposed to be cognizant of what had gone on at all. I am mystified first by you, more by him.

What could the "first class thing" have been? And in what way was Louis "game for being on the spot?" Had there been a showdown concerning Frances, or at least a serious effort to talk things through? At any rate, it was understood that he must drop any hopes he might still be cherishing regarding her. Colvin did remain a faithful friend for life, while the correspondence with Frances seems to have diminished increasingly from then on.[28]

Louis's last day in Menton was March 30, 1874, and after a stay in Paris he was back in Edinburgh in late April. Living abroad had become essential for him, and during the remaining years of his life he would spend four-fifths of his time away from Scotland—in England, in France, in America, and in the South Pacific.

CHAPTER 10

First Steps as a Writer

SOME EARLY TRIALS

Back in his parents' house, Louis resumed his legal studies without enthusiasm. By now he was certain that he wanted to be a writer, but getting started was a daunting prospect. Colvin, who was well connected in publishing, gave good advice: he should begin with essays and move on to short stories, waiting until he was better established to attempt a novel. A new kind of market had developed for short but serious pieces in highbrow periodicals. Starting with the *Saturday Review* in 1856, there were also the *Fortnightly, Contemporary Review, Academy, Portfolio, National Observer, Macmillan's Magazine, Cornhill Magazine,* and *Pall Mall Gazette.* An early effort of Louis's was rejected by the *Saturday Review,* but he would go on to publish in all of the others; "Ordered South" had already appeared in *Macmillan's* while he was in Menton. The editor of the *Cornhill,* Leslie Stephen, was especially encouraging, and over the years would publish no fewer than twenty-four of his essays and stories. Stephen, who enjoyed a high reputation in his time, is best remembered today as the disappointed Mr. Ramsay in *To the Lighthouse* by his daughter Virginia Woolf.

Agreeable as it was to appear in print, payment was modest and there was little prospect of becoming self-supporting in that way. For "Ordered South" Louis received £5, not very different from the monthly allowance he was getting from his parents.

By the end of 1874 he had published four essays on various topics: "On the Enjoyment of Unpleasant Places," "Notes on the Movements of Young Children" (inspired by some girls at the Menton hotel), "Victor Hugo's Romances," and "John Knox and His Relation to Women." The Knox essay is the most interesting, a devastating analysis of the unacknowledged dependence of the Scottish Presbyterian champion on his female admirers.

> Women, [Knox] has said in his "First Blast," are "weak, frail, impatient, feeble, and foolish"; and yet it does not appear that he was himself any less dependent than other men upon the sympathy and affection of these weak, frail, impatient, feeble, and foolish creatures; it seems even as if he had been rather more dependent than most.... He may have rolled out in his big pulpit voice how women were weak, frail, impatient, feeble, foolish, inconstant, variable, cruel, and lacking the spirit of counsel, and how men were above them, even as God is above the angels, in the ears of his own wife, and the two dearest friends on earth [both of those were women]. But he had lost the sense of incongruity, and continued to despise in theory the sex he honoured so much in practice, of whom he chose his most intimate associates, and whose courage he was compelled to wonder at when his own heart was faint. There was a fatal preponderance of self in all his intimacies: many women came to learn from him, but he never condescended to become a learner in his turn.[1]

Louis thought of essays not as formal argument but as personal responses to books and to life. He loved Hazlitt and Lamb, and at one time even projected a biography of Hazlitt, but his hero was Montaigne. "I have never read the whole of Montaigne," he said years later, "but I do not like to be long without reading some of him, and my delight in what I do read never lessens." And although he admired Hazlitt, "he has to me a far away smack of a belittled, sentimental, newspaper Montaigne; and anything that even reminds me of Montaigne is welcome. Heaven knows the distance is immense." What Emerson said of Montaigne's style could apply very well to Louis's: "Cut these words, and they would bleed; they are vascular and alive."[2]

Like those of his predecessors, Louis's essays only seem to be casual and chatty; he put them through endless rewriting. When he collected some of them in *Familiar Studies of Men and Books,* he wrote, "Short studies are, or should be, things woven like a carpet, from which it is impossible to detach a strand."[3]

What Louis would never do was obey a fixed timetable. When the editor of the *Portfolio* proposed to publish a monthly essay of his, he told Colvin, "Do you imagine I could ever write an essay a month, or promise an essay even every three months? I declare I would rather die than enter into any such arrangement. The essays must fall from me, essay by essay, as they ripen." Even after he became a prolific writer, this would never change. Two decades later he told a correspondent, "I am still 'a slow study,' and sit a long while silent on my eggs. Unconscious thought, there is the only method: macerate your subject; let it boil slow, then take the lid off and look in." He added, "The essential part of work is not an act, it is a state."[4]

Thanks to Colvin he did pick up a bit of income with book reviewing. His review of *The Ballads and Songs of Scotland* begins, "Probably there never was published anything with less result, anything that left the reader more entirely where he was. The tempting title is its first merit and its last." The review ends, "We ask ourselves in wonder what possible reason could have induced this unsuccessful enquirer to record, at such great length, the story of his failure?"

Another review shows that he could also respond appreciatively. Quoting an author's comment in *Scottish Rivers* that in one river "we are much mistaken if it be not full of fine fat trouts," he comments, "One can hear the smack of the lips in those words. He had noticed things more closely than most of us, and liked them better, and he could speak of what he thus observed and loved in a way that is full of gusto and most truly human."[5]

During the spring of 1875, staying by himself at Swanston, he tried his hand at a genre that had some prestige at the time, brief prose poems. He told Frances excitedly that one of them about water meadows was "simply a little masterpiece. I desire to repeat that, in case you might think I didn't mean it." When she didn't reply at once he complained, "You might have written to me ere now, Madonna," and a couple of days after that, "I cling to you as a drowning man to a straw."

In his next letter, however, addressed to both Frances and Colvin, he admitted that these efforts might not be much good after all, and then impersonated a schoolboy writing home:

> I am writing *Petits Poèmes en Prose*. Their principal resemblance to Baudelaire's is that they are rather longer and not quite so good. They are ve-ry cle-ver (words of two syllables), O so aw-ful-ly cle-ver (words of three), O so god-dam-nab-ly cle-ver (words of a devil of a number of syllables). I have written fifteen in a fortnight. I have also written some beautiful poetry. I would like a cake, and a cricket bat, and an introduction to the Holy Ghost, if you please, and a passkey to Heaven, and as much money as my friend the Baron Rothschild can spare.

The piece on water meadows is entitled "The Quiet Waters By," from the Scottish metrical version of the twenty-third Psalm. "The water is quiet and clear, and full of lilies and leaping fish; and if I pluck the lilies, the smell of them is as the smell of all the clean waters of the earth. Does the place know me no more?"[6]

The only interesting prose poem is "A Summer Night," which was inspired, as he told Frances, by a night on the town with his cousin Bob.

> The dresses of harlots swayed and swished upon the pavement. Pale faces leapt out of the crowd as they went by the lights, and passed away like a dream in the general dream of the pallid and populous streets. The coarse brass band filled the air with a rough and ready melody; and the fall of alternate feet, and the turn of shoulders and swish of dresses, fell into time with it strangely. Face after face went by; swinging dress after dress brushed on the even stones; out of face after face the eyes stood forth with a sordid animal invitation.

None of these got published.[7]

WILLIAM ERNEST HENLEY

In 1875 an important friendship began. Louis wrote to Frances that Leslie Stephen had come to Edinburgh to give a lecture on Alpine travel—he was an enthusiastic mountaineer—"and took me up to see a poor fellow, a bit of a poet who writes for him, and who has been eighteen months in our Infirmary and may be, for all I know, eighteen months more. Stephen and I sat on a couple of chairs and the poor fellow sat up in his bed, with his hair and beard all tangled, and talked as cheerfully as if he had been in a king's palace, or the Great King's palace of the blue air. He has taught himself two languages since he has been lying there. I shall try to be of use to him."[8]

This was William Ernest Henley, an Englishman one year older than Louis. In his early teens Henley had developed a tubercular condition in his legs, and when he was sixteen his left foot was amputated. By now the right foot was in such bad shape that he was told that it too would have to come off. However, he had read reports of successes in Edinburgh by Dr. Joseph Lister, a pioneer champion of antiseptics to prevent infection. The antiseptic system would become standard—the mouthwash Listerine was named in Lister's honor—but at the time it was a bold gamble to become his patient instead of going ahead with the amputation.

It was a fortunate decision. Lister did save the leg, and with a prosthesis to replace the missing one Henley would regain immense vitality. A drawing of him by "Spy" (color plate 8), published years later, gives a good sense of his muscular alertness. It's a nice touch that in addition to his cane he is holding a cigarette.

Henley was exceptionally well read and an ebullient talker, and Louis immediately fell under his spell. Andrew Lang said, "His 'maimed strength,' his impeded vigour, even his blond upstanding hair and 'beard all tangled,' his uncomplaining fortitude under the most cruel trials, and the candid freshness of his conversation on men and books, won Stevenson's heart." The phrase 'maimed strength' comes from a letter Stevenson wrote to Henley after publishing *Treasure Island:* "I will now make a confession. It was the sight of your maimed strength and masterfulness that begot John Silver."[9]

Louis visited Henley often in the hospital, and would even carry him downstairs for a carriage ride and up again afterward, a startling feat for someone so skinny. Once Henley was released from the hospital he became a valued member of Louis's social circle, calling the amateur actress Anne Jenkin "Queen Anne" and Baxter, who was putting on weight, "Charles the Stout." He also had a name for the little gang of Louis, Bob, Baxter, and Walter Ferrier—"the Four Musketeers."[10]

Henley was more than "a bit of a poet," and that needs to be emphasized, since he became the most valued writer among Louis's friends. His best-known poem, "Invictus" ("Unconquered"), has been jeered at as Victorian bravado, but it was an affirmation of endurance by a man who suffered greatly, experienced a long hospitalization, and would always be physically impaired.

> Out of the night that covers me,
> Black as the pit from pole to pole,
> I thank whatever gods may be
> For my unconquerable soul. . . .
>
> It matters not how strait the gate,
> How charged with punishments the scroll,
> I am the master of my fate,
> I am the captain of my soul.

Many readers have appreciated this poem in the spirit that was intended. Nelson Mandela recited it to his fellow inmates in the Robben Island prison, as reenacted by Morgan Freeman in the film *Invictus.*

While in the infirmary Henley wrote a sequence of twenty-eight poems, *In*

Hospital, whose intensity and directness anticipate the modernism of the next century. They are so impressive, and so little known today, that they deserve to be quoted at some length. "Operation," inspired by Henley's ongoing surgeries, evokes the experience of chloroform, which had only recently been introduced.

> You are carried in a basket,
> Like a carcase from the shambles,
> To the theatre, a cockpit
> Where they stretch you on a table.
>
> Then they bid you close your eyelids,
> And they mask you with a napkin,
> And the anesthetic reaches
> Hot and subtle through your being.
>
> And you gasp and reel and shudder
> In a rushing, swaying rapture,
> While the voices at your elbow
> Fade—receding—fainter—farther. . . .

Even more powerful is "Nocturne":

> At the barren heart of midnight,
> When the shadow shuts and opens
> As the loud flames pulse and flutter,
> I can hear a cistern leaking.
>
> Dripping, dropping, in a rhythm,
> Rough, unequal, half-melodious,
> Like the measures aped from nature
> In the infancy of music;
>
> Like the buzzing of an insect,
> Still, irrational, persistent . . .
> I must listen, listen, listen
> In a passion of attention;
>
> Till it taps upon my heartstrings,
> And my very life goes dripping,
> Dropping, dripping, drip-drip-dropping,
> In the drip-drop of the cistern.

Louis described these poems as "boldly real—not 'realistic,' a word I have learned to hate." By "realistic" he meant the Victorian overload of detail, "art that is like mahogany and horsehair furniture, solid, true, serious, and as dead as Caesar."[11]

The twenty-fifth poem, a sonnet titled "Apparition," is a keenly perceptive portrait of Louis, though he isn't named.

> Thin-legged, thin-chested, slight unspeakably,
> Neat-footed and weak-fingered; in his face—
> Lean, large-boned, curved of beak, and touched with race,
> Bold-lipped, rich-tinted, mutable as the sea,
> The brown eyes radiant with vivacity—
> There shines a brilliant and romantic grace,
> A spirit intense and rare, with trace on trace
> Of passion and impudence and energy.
> Valiant in velvet, light in ragged luck,
> Most vain, most generous, sternly critical,
> Buffoon and poet, lover and sensualist:
> A deal of Ariel, just a streak of Puck,
> Much Antony, of Hamlet most of all,
> And something of the Shorter Catechist.

It's hard to know what was meant by "touched with race"—a Celtic romantic streak, perhaps. The combination of Antony and Hamlet is especially striking. Louis never lost his boldness and courage, nor his introspection.

When Margaret Stevenson saw this sonnet she told Henley, "I must write you a line to thank you for my boy's portrait. I have long wished that you would use your wonderful power of word painting on his behalf, and I was very much pleased when at last the full length picture arrived. But do you really think he is *most* vain? I am not quite prepared to admit that, nor yet the 'sensualist.' I hope you put in that word for the sake of the rhyme—in that case I will forgive you." A few years later Henley put it less diplomatically in "Ballade R.L.S.":

> An Ariel quick through all his veins
> With sex and temperament and style;
> All eloquence and balls and brains;
> Heroic—also infantile.[12]

As the years went by Louis would continue to enjoy Henley's overwhelming personality. In "Talk and Talkers" he is "Burly": "There is something boisterous and piratic in Burly's manner of talk. He will roar you down, he will bury his face in his hands, he will undergo passions and revolt and agony; and meanwhile his attitude of mind is really both conciliatory and receptive." One of Louis's letters to Henley begins "My dear excellent, admired, volcanic angel of a lad, trusty as a dog, eruptive as Vesuvius, in all things great, in all things the soul of loyalty: greeting."[13]

Something else happened to Henley in the Edinburgh Infirmary. He was sharing his room with a young sailor named Boyle, whose sister Anna used to visit him. She and Henley fell in love and later on were married, with Anne Jenkin and Charles Baxter as witnesses (not Louis, who was in Paris at the time). Henley's biographer calls his marriage "the one unmarred experience of his life."[14]

Two years after leaving Edinburgh Henley wrote from London, "We have known each other, Lewis of my heart, but a little while as time goes; and yet how much you have been to me! My life seems to date from that moment when Stephen brought you into the darkened room in the old Infirmary. The love that has filled my life was only a dear and impossible dream then, and but for your help and counsel and companionship would never have been other." This is remarkably similar to what Andrew Lang said about men as well as women falling in love with Louis. (Henley never had any patience with the Frenchified spelling, though, and wrote the name as it was pronounced and originally spelled.)[15]

TEMPORARY LAWYER

Also in 1875, a long-deferred milestone was reached. Louis took the final examination in law, passed it, and was admitted to the Scottish bar. His cousin Henrietta Balfour was riding with his parents in their carriage when they drove up from Swanston to learn the result. After he joined them, "nothing would satisfy Louis but that he would sit on the top of the carriage, that was thrown back open, with his feet on the seat between his father and mother where they were sitting; and he kept waving his hat and calling out to people he passed, whether known or unknown, just like a man gone quite mad. I often wonder what impression it made on the passers-by, as Uncle Tom always used to have good horses and liked them to go very fast."[16]

A formal photograph was taken to commemorate the occasion, in which Louis wears his advocate's gown and wig. At some later date he gave a copy to Charles Guthrie with the inscription "My dear Guthrie, your old comrade Robert Louis Stevenson" (fig. 27). To Frances he sent a brief note: "Madonna, passed.

my dear Guthrie,
your old comrade
Robert Louis Stevenson.

27. Louis as advocate

Ever your R.L.S." The final "S" whirls away in a widening spiral of relief (fig. 28). The stamp at the bottom shows that by the time Guthrie reproduced it in his memoir of his friend, it was the property of the Advocates Library where they both used to study. Margaret put her copy of the photograph into an album that she had kept ever since his infancy, and told him, "There you are, Louis, from

> Madonna,
> Passed.
>
> over
>
> your
> R.
> L.
> S.

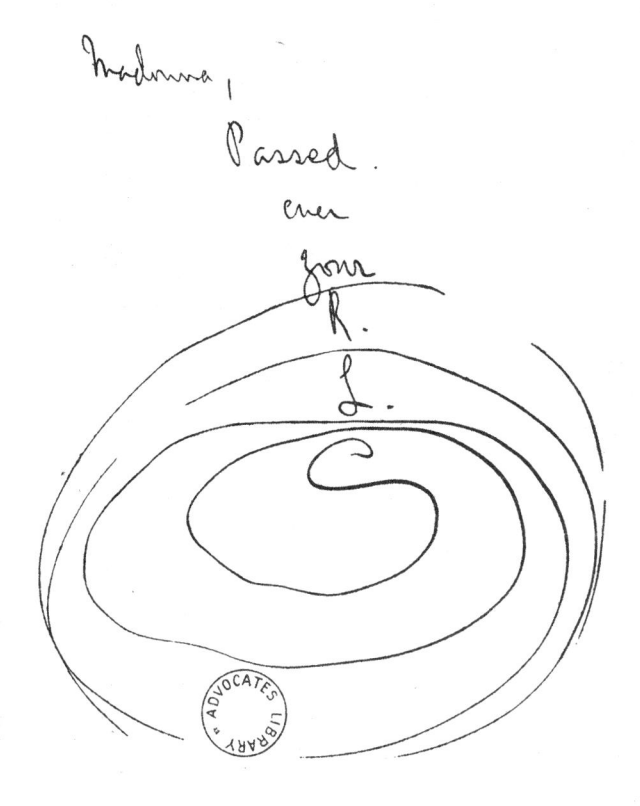

28. Louis to Frances Sitwell

Baby to Bar. My next collection is going to be from Bar to Baronet." He replied, "No, mother, not from Bar to Baronet, but from Bar to Burial."[17]

Delighted, his father rewarded him with the extremely generous sum of £1,000. That was intended to help him set up his practice, but more largely it was a sign of reaching maturity. It's unlikely, however, that the full amount was paid at this time. His parents had kept him on a limited allowance until now, and they probably hoped to control him by continuing to dole it out in installments.

Someone whose brother was also admitted to the bar remembered the "wretchedly cold day" when the ceremony took place. "Stevenson was the picture of misery, blue with cold, untidy, and with his tie all awry. When they met before the ceremony my brother said to him that he looked like a drunken Irishman going to a funeral. Stevenson, hating to face the ordeal, replied, 'I wish I were that Irishman—*coming from* that funeral!'"[18]

After his admission to the bar, Louis spent some time hanging about the courts in hopes of picking up work, but so did a lot of other aspirants, and he didn't try very hard. All he ever secured was a few "courtesy briefs," pro forma and with no work expected. He earned a total of 4 guineas, and stopped going to the courts for good.

Four years later he drafted a short essay entitled "On the Choice of a Profession," a meditation on the accidental way in which most people choose a career, and the process of socialization that makes them accept it. Why, for example, did someone become a banker?

> There is one principal reason, I conceive: that the man was trapped. Education, as practised, is a form of harnessing with the friendliest intentions. The fellow was hardly in trousers before they whipped him into school; hardly done with school before they smuggled him into an office; it is ten to one they have had him married into the bargain; and all this before he has had time so much as to imagine that there may be any other practicable course. It is too late, after the train has started, to debate the needfulness of this particular journey. The door is locked, the express goes tearing overland at sixty miles an hour; he had better betake himself to sleep or the daily paper, and discourage unavailing thought. He sees many pleasant places out of the window: cottages in a garden, anglers by the riverside, balloons voyaging the sky; but as for him, he is booked for all his natural days, and must remain a banker to the end.

"On the Choice of a Profession" is little known because it was discovered long afterward among Louis's papers. Leslie Stephen had rejected it for his *Cornhill Magazine* in 1879, and a decade later it was rejected again by *Scribner's Magazine* in New York. Evidently it represented an unwelcome critique of Victorian values.

In 1872 Louis had exclaimed to Bob, "I want an object, a mission, a belief, a hope to be my wife; and please God, have it I shall." Baxter and Guthrie would go on to distinction in the law; Louis was determined to be a writer and nothing else.[19]

CHAPTER 11

Artists and Boats

PARIS AND BARBIZON

On various occasions in 1874 and 1875, Louis spent some time in France. Brief though the visits were, they convinced him that he must come back and stay much longer. Years later his stepson said that "mentally he was half a Frenchman; in taste, habits, and prepossessions he was almost wholly French. Not only did he speak French admirably and read it like his mother tongue, but he loved both country and people, and was more really at home in France than anywhere else."[1]

Though it would be the French countryside that appealed to Louis most, he did enjoy Paris, especially as he was getting to know it through his cousin Bob. Bob was studying painting in the studio of Charles Durand, who went by the name of Carolus-Duran and had been strongly influenced by the realism of Courbet. Carolus was also an admirer of Velázquez, which was significant for Bob's later career: after giving up on painting he would become an art historian best known for a book on Velázquez. In Paris Bob was living with a model whom he described to Louis as "a burning fiery furnace."[2]

A couple of anecdotes have survived about incidents in cafés. At one of these Louis heard a Frenchman say that the English were cowards. He got up and slapped the man's face. "'*Monsieur, vous m'avez frappé!*' said the Gaul. '*A ce qu'il paraît* [so it seems],' said the Scot, and there it ended."[3]

At another time, when Louis and a group of artist friends were drinking wine in Montmartre, one of them took offense at something and hurled a bottle of wine at the offender. "It was a strong, true shot, and would have hit the mark had not Stevenson sprung to his feet and caught the missile. 'Tut, tut, George,' he said to the thrower. 'If the bottle is passed so quickly, none of us will be able to stand out the evening.'" If that really happened it was unusually athletic of Louis.[4]

Louis also spent some time with Bob in artists' colonies at Barbizon and Fontainebleau north of Paris. He was the one writer in the gang of painters, and found the atmosphere heady although he didn't do much actual writing. As he remembered in "Fontainebleau: Village Communities of Painters," "We were all artists; almost all in the age of illusion, cultivating an imaginary genius and walking to the strains of some deceiving Ariel. Small wonder, indeed, if we were happy!"

He loved their favorite haunt, the Hôtel Siron. "That excellent artists' barrack was managed upon easy principles. At any hour of the night, when you returned from wandering in the forest, you went to the billiard room and helped yourself to liquors, or descended to the cellar and returned laden with beer or wine. The Sirons were all locked in slumber; there was none to check your inroads; only at the week's end a computation was made, the gross sum was divided, and a varying share set down to every lodger's name."

The Barbizon School of Corot and Millet, which specialized in realistic landscape painting, had been active until recently, and Louis remarked that the local scenery had been painted more than enough, whereas Provence and the Rhône Valley were "one succession of masterpieces waiting for the brush." Just a few years later, Cézanne and Van Gogh would be creating masterpieces there .[5]

Through Bob, Louis became friends with an American artist named Will H. Low (he always used the "H," perhaps to avoid the echo of "willow"). The three of them spent a lot of time together, and Low referred to himself, as he recalled in his memoir, as "the third musketeer." He and Louis would often see each other in Paris in later years, and eventually in New York after he had returned home.[6]

Tiring of the social scene at Fontainebleau, Low found lodgings on the river Loing a little to the south in the village of Montigny. Louis enjoyed visiting him there, and wrote, "Montigny has been somewhat strangely neglected. I never knew it inhabited but once, when Will H. Low installed himself there with a barrel of *piquette,* and entertained his friends in a leafy trellis above the weir, in sight of the green country and to the music of the falling water." Low used that trellis in the self-portrait reproduced here (fig. 29), and in his memoir he explained that *piquette* was "a *petit vin,* so light that it would hardly bear transportation to the next village, that was an ideal beverage for the summer months; it was grown on the hills near the village." He added that the big barrel required

29. Will H. Low

several men to transport it and "slaked many a parched throat throughout the summer."[7]

Louis also paid tribute to Montigny in verse.

> A bin of wine, a spice of wit,
> A house with lawns enclosing it,
> A living river by the door,
> A nightingale in the sycamore![8]

At this time he drafted an essay, "Forest Notes: Idle Hours," that re-creates a state of feeling rather than describing a scene. "Ants swarm in the hot sand;

mosquitos drone their nasal drone; wherever the sun finds a hole in the roof of the forest, you see a myriad transparent creatures coming and going in the shaft of light; and even between-whiles, even where there is no incursion of sun-rays into the dark arcade of the wood, you are conscious of a continual drift of insects, an ebb and flow of infinitesimal living things between the trees." Meanwhile the woods are "lit up with such a discharge of violent sunlight, as a man might live fifty years in England and not see." By the time this essay was published in the *Cornhill Magazine* the next year, Louis told Colvin that it was "too sweet to be wholesome."[9]

It's notable that although he was living in a community of landscape painters, he never showed much interest in that genre. Impressionism might have interested him, but that movement was barely underway and he seems not to have been aware of it. Just two years before he arrived in Grez, paintings by Monet, Renoir, Pissarro, Dégas, Morisot, and Cézanne had been exhibited in the Paris show that prompted a satirical critic to coin the term *Impressionism*. What Louis liked was indeed to evoke, in words rather than images, what being in a particular place *felt* like. After *Kidnapped* was published Will Low told him that it gave him a vivid sense of what the Highlands were like. Louis replied that he should take another look at the book, in which there was not a single line "descriptive of landscape."[10]

The one landscape genre that appealed to Louis was Japanese prints, with their crisp bold outlines and vividly distinct colors. When Sidney Colvin gave him several in 1874, he told Bob that they showed "what imaginative truth we sacrifice, to say nothing of decorative effect, by our limping, semi-scientific way of seeing things. Second: the colours are really fun. For themselves, you know; they are their own exceeding great reward; they're not a damned bit like nature and don't pretend to be and they're twice as nice." A decade later, when he could afford it, he acquired thirteen volumes of prints by that artist, calling him "Divine Hokusai!"[11]

What did fascinate Louis were portraits of real people, and his insights were acute. There's a fine example in an essay he wrote a couple of years later about Samuel Pepys. In the course of an affectionate account of the famous *Diary*, he tells us what he sees in the well-known portrait by John Hales (or Hayls), which needs to be reproduced in color (color plate 9).

> Whether we read the picture by the *Diary* or the *Diary* by the picture, we shall at least agree that Hales was among the number of those who can "surprise the manners in the face." Here we have a mouth pouting,

moist with desires; eyes greedy, protuberant, and yet apt for weeping too; a nose great alike in character and dimensions; and altogether a most fleshy, melting countenance. The face is attractive by its promise of reciprocity. I have used the word "greedy," but the reader must not suppose that he can change it for that closely kindred one of "hungry," for there is here no aspiration, no waiting for better things, but an animal joy in all that comes. It could never be the face of an artist; it is the face of a *viveur*—kindly, pleased and pleasing, protected from excess and upheld in contentment by the shifting versatility of his desires.

Louis adds that Pepys "preserved till nearly forty the headlong gusto of a boy."[12]

In the portrait Pepys is holding the manuscript of a song composed by himself, "Beauty Retire," which is mentioned several times in his diary: "Good music we had, and among other things Mrs. Coleman sang my words I set of 'Beauty Retire,' and I think it is a good song and they praise it mightily."[13]

AN INLAND VOYAGE

Of Louis's group of close friends in Edinburgh—Bob, Baxter, Walter Ferrier, and Walter Simpson—the last two remain relatively indistinct in the historical record, though they all enjoyed each other's company. On several occasions, however, Simpson emerges into the light, since he was an ideal traveling companion; he and Louis had previously taken a trip to Germany together, during which Louis had written to his mother, "An opera is far more *real* than real life to me.... I wish that life was an opera. I should like to *live* in one." Seven years older than Louis and a respectable lawyer by then, Simpson was the kind of companion that the elder Stevensons could approve of. He was also a baronet, having inherited the title on the death of his father, who had received it in recognition of his distinguished work in medicine.[14]

Simpson was quiet and reserved, as Louis acknowledged in "Talk and Talkers," where he appears as Athelred (Louis was thinking of the medieval monarch Aethelred the Unready). "Athelred presents you with the spectacle of a sincere and somewhat slow nature thinking aloud. He is the most unready man I ever knew to shine in conversation. You may see him sometimes wrestle with a refractory jest for a minute or two together, and perhaps fail to throw it in the end." In writing, though, Simpson was far from humorless, as reflected in his book on golf that was quoted previously.[15]

A portrait (fig. 30) gives a good sense of Simpson's seriousness. Someone

30. Walter Simpson

who visited the artists' colony described "Sir Salter Wimpson" as "a neutral-tinted blond, with ashen eyes, ashen hair, ashen complexion, ashen mustache; he has funny little fat legs that look about three years old."[16]

He and Louis both enjoyed boating, and they decided to acquire a couple of "canoes" (kayaks) and take an excursion together. Simpson named his boat the *Cigarette,* and Louis's was *Arethusa.* That was a mythological nymph with whom the river god Alpheus fell in love.

The trip took most of September 1876, and covered two hundred miles. They set out from the Belgian port of Antwerp and proceeded southward on the Willebroek Canal. At Brussels, frustrated by endless locks, they took a break and traveled with their boats by train to Maubeuge in France. From there they headed south on the river Oise as far as Pontoise, just north of Paris.

Louis kept a journal along the way. It's now lost, but it formed the basis for his first book, *An Inland Voyage,* two years later, which was published for a modest payment of £20. It's an odd little book, and as Frank McLynn says, "a tribute to Stevenson's literary skill that he was able to make an interesting book out of next to nothing." Claire Harman puts it well: it's a relaxed record of "ordinary life, hardships, rebuffs, oddity, humour, moments of human sympathy."[17]

Traveling always energized Louis, and what mattered was not exciting incidents but the simple experience of movement and change. Two months before this trip he had written to Frances Sitwell, "There are times when people's lives stand still. If you were to ask a squirrel in a mechanical cage for his autobiography, it would not be very gay."[18]

It's also a celebration of freedom. "To know what you prefer," Louis says at the beginning, "instead of humbly saying Amen to what the world tells you you ought to prefer, is to have kept your soul alive." Several people they encountered on the trip confirmed this ideal. The driver of an omnibus (horse-drawn in those days, not motorized) told them, "I drive to the station. Well. And then I drive back again to the hotel. And so on every day and all the week round. My God, is that life?" A canal boatman said, "A man, look you, who sticks in his own village like a bear; very well, he sees nothing. And then death is the end of all. And he has seen nothing."[19]

At one town, due to their scruffy appearance, the travelers were turned away in pouring rain from one hotel after another until a kindly innkeeper and his wife took them in. Louis wrote,

> Madame Bazin came out after a while. She was tired with her day's work, I suppose; and she nestled up to her husband and laid her head upon his breast. He had his arm about her, and kept gently patting her on the shoulder. I think Bazin was right, and he was really married. Of how few people can the same be said! Little did the Bazins know how much they served us. We were charged for candles, for food and drink, and for the beds we slept in. But there was nothing in the bill for the husband's pleasant talk; nor for the pretty spectacle of their married life.[20]

Adventurous though the companions tried to feel, on a river full of hard-working people they were obviously gentlemen on holiday. The point was made by an old man who encountered them resting after they had struggled through a series of locks. "In the fullness of my heart, I laid bare our plans before him. He said it was the silliest enterprise that ever he heard of. Did I not know, he asked me, that it was nothing but locks, locks, locks, the whole way? Not to mention that at this season of the year, we should find the Oise quite dry? 'Get into a train, my little young man,' said he, 'and go you away home to your parents.'"[21]

In his book Louis was circumspect about erotic thoughts, but he remembered this trip in an unpublished poem that describes girls undressing for a swim.

> And stepping free, each breathing lass
> From her discarded ring of clothes
> Into the crystal coolness goes. . . .
> Now bare to the beholder's eye
> Your late denuded bindings lie,
> Subsiding slowly where they fell,
> A disinvested citadel;
> The obdurate corset, Cupid's foe,
> The Dutchman's breeches frilled below.
> Hose that the lover loves to note,
> And white and crackling petticoat.

Louis published a more discreet version in "The Canoe Speaks," which he mentioned to Bob as a poem "on female underclothes which is my own favourite, as that is about the deepest poetry I have." A comment by another friend suggests a Leopold Bloom quality. "Louis has confessed that female underclothing—smocks, hose, garters, drawers—are his fate, and that the noblest sight in the world is a washing."[22]

Given the modest scope of *An Inland Voyage,* the frontispiece by Walter Crane (fig. 31) may seem surprising. The kayakers pass by in the middle distance, not noticing in the foreground a figure from classical mythology, the god Pan. Reclining among rushes, Pan stretches out his goat's legs while resting on an urn that symbolizes the flowing stream. He's holding his panpipes and may have just finished playing a tune.

There was in fact a widespread vogue of Pan at that time. The traditional alternatives to orthodox religious imagery were the gods of Olympus, but they had become tiresomely familiar. Pan represented a different kind of paganism, the amoral and sexual spirit of nature; in Greek *pan* means "all" or "everything," as in "pantheism."

In an early story by E. M. Forster, an English clergyman in Italy claims that Christianity killed the nature spirit, and that sailors at the time of Christ's birth heard a loud voice crying, "The great God Pan is dead." But in Forster's story, an

31. *An Inland Voyage,* frontispiece

English boy falls in love with an Italian youth and escapes into the landscape with the still-living god.[23]

Closer to *An Inland Voyage* is Kenneth Grahame's *The Wind in the Willows,* set on a Thames much like Louis's Oise, in a chapter entitled "The Piper at the Gates of Dawn" that may puzzle readers today. The poetically inclined Water Rat has been helping his friend Otter search for a lost child and suddenly encounters Pan.

> He looked in the very eyes of the Friend and Helper; saw the backward sweep of the curved horns, gleaming in the growing daylight; saw the stern, hooked nose between the kindly eyes that were looking down on them humourously, while the bearded mouth broke into a half-smile at the corners; saw the rippling muscles on the arm that lay across the broad chest, the long supple hand still holding the pan-pipes only just fallen away from the parted lips; saw the splendid curves of the shaggy limbs disposed in majestic ease on the sward; saw, last of all, nestling between his very hooves, sleeping soundly in entire peace and contentment, the little, round, podgy, childish form of the baby otter.[24]

Louis himself, in an essay entitled "Pan's Pipes," emphasized that there was nothing quaint or fey about the goat-footed god.

> For youth and all ductile and congenial minds, Pan is not dead, but of all the classic hierarchy alone survives in triumph; goat-footed, with a gleeful and an angry look, the type of the shaggy world: and in every wood, if you go with a spirit properly prepared, you shall hear the note of his pipe.... Death is given in a kiss; the dearest kindnesses are fatal, and into this life, where one thing preys upon another, the child too often makes its entrance from the mother's corpse. It is no wonder, with so traitorous a scheme of things, if the wise people who created for us the idea of Pan thought that of all fears the fear of him was the most terrible, since it embraces all. And still we preserve the phrase: a panic terror.[25]

The image of Pan was often invoked in Louis's immediate circle. Henley was described by a friend as "the startling image of Pan come to earth and clothed—the great god Pan, with halting foot and flaming shaggy hair, and arms and shoulders huge and threatening, like those of some faun or satyr of the ancient woods." Louis himself, though neither huge nor shaggy, inspired a comparison by Will Low: "It was not a handsome face until he spoke, and then I can hardly imagine that any could deny the appeal of the vivacious eyes, the humor or pathos of the mobile mouth, with its lurking suggestion of the great god Pan at times."[26]

At the end of the narrative *An Inland Voyage* reaches a spiritual high point. The river slows down, and so does interior consciousness.

> Now, when the river no longer ran in a proper sense, only glided seaward with an even, outright, but imperceptible speed, and when the sky smiled upon us day after day without variety, we began to slip into that golden doze of the mind which follows upon much exercise in the open air. I have stupefied myself in this way more than once; indeed, I dearly love the feeling; but I never had it to the same degree as when paddling down the Oise. It was the apotheosis of stupidity.

Rousseau called this state of mind reverie, and Wordsworth called it wise passiveness. Louis was particularly struck by affinities with Eastern thought:

> The central bureau of nerves, what in some moods we call Ourselves, enjoyed its holiday without disturbance, like a Government Office. The great wheels of intelligence turned idly in the head, like fly-wheels, grinding no grist. . . . What philosophers call *me* and *not-me, ego* and *non ego*, preoccupied me whether I would or no. There was less *me* and more *not-me* than I was accustomed to expect. I looked on upon somebody else who managed the paddling; I was aware of somebody else's feet against the stretcher; my own body seemed to have no more intimate relation to me than the canoe, or the river, or the river banks. Nor this alone: something inside my mind, a part of my brain, a province of my proper being, had thrown off allegiance and set up for itself, or perhaps for the somebody else who did the paddling. . . . Thoughts presented themselves unbidden; they were not my thoughts, they were plainly some one else's; and I considered them like a part of the landscape. I take it, in short, that I was about as near Nirvana as would be convenient in practical life; and if this be so, I make the Buddhists my sincere compliments.[27]

Louis may have remembered also Montaigne's praise of *oisiveté,* idleness, in the final chapter of the *Essais:* "'He has passed his life in idleness,' we say; 'I've done nothing today.' What, haven't you been living? That's not just the fundamental, it's the noblest of your occupations."[28]

When *An Inland Voyage* was published, reviewers appreciated the writer's engaging personality and his avoidance of conventional topics: "He is almost a pagan in his fine indifference for dogma and tradition, no less than his freshness of spirit, his vigorous elasticity of temper, his pleasant open-heartedness, his sincerity in the matter of trifles, his genial catholicity as to opinions, his enjoyment of what is near and likable." Still more gratifying was a personal letter from George Meredith, who declared, "It is literature," and closed by saying, "I hope you will feel that we expect much of you." Meredith was the living novelist whom Louis most admired at the time.[29]

All the same, it had been just a trial run, and he wrote to his mother, "I was more surprised at the tone of the critics than I suppose anyone else, and the effect it has produced in me is one of shame. If they liked that so much, I ought to have given them something better, that's all." A couple of months later he added, "I read *Inland Voyage* the other day: what rubbish these reviewers did talk. It is not badly written, thin, mildly cheery, and strained." That may sound like false modesty, but he had much higher aspirations.[30]

The narrative ends at Pontoise, but the journey didn't. The companions continued south to Barbizon, sold off their boats, and proceeded on foot to Châtillon-sur-Loire. That turned out to be the scene of a little adventure. Louis arrived before Simpson did, and in keeping with his bohemian style he was scruffily dressed. Ten years later he described his appearance in an "Epilogue to *An Inland Voyage*": "In person, he is exceptionally lean, and his face is not, like those of happier mortals, a certificate. For years he could not pass a frontier or visit a bank without suspicion. If you will imagine him stooping under his knapsack, walking nearly five miles an hour with the folds of the ready-made trousers fluttering about his spindle shanks, and still looking eagerly around him as if in terror of pursuit—the figure, when realized, is far from reassuring." The point about the trousers was that someone who was well off would have had them personally tailored.

Louis was accordingly detained by a policeman, and when he couldn't produce the necessary papers was imprisoned for vagrancy. However, when Simpson showed up the authorities could see that he was a man of substance and prepared to vouch for his friend. Grudgingly, they were told that they could go free so long as they left town on the next available train, and soon they were relating their story in the dining room at Siron's. Louis enjoyed the affair greatly; it was amusing for the son of a prosperous Edinburgh family to be taken for a tramp.[31]

However, he might have reflected more deeply on how important it was that Simpson was there. Frank McLynn says, "He had still not grasped the fundamental law of French life, that all persons, even beggars, must possess papers." And beyond that, in 1876 he might well have been a German spy, which made Simpson's papers more important than his gentlemanly outfit. The Franco-Prussian War had ended only six years previously, and during their trip they had seen soldiers drilling.[32]

Back when they crossed the Belgian border into France, they had taken refuge from pouring rain in the town of Landrecies—"not the place one would have chosen for a day's rest; for it consists almost entirely of fortifications." Landrecies had sustained a siege by the English in 1543 and another by the Dutch in 1794. "It was just the place to hear the round [i.e., sentries making their rounds] going by at night in the darkness, with the solid tramp of men marching, and the startling reverberations of the drum. It reminded you that even this place was a point in the great warfaring system of Europe, and might on some future day be ringed about with cannon smoke and thunder, and make itself a name among strong towns."[33]

A battle would indeed be fought there in 1914, and that part of Europe would suffer far more in the years to come. If Louis had lived to see that—he would have been sixty-eight in 1918—he might well have been cured of romanticizing war.

CHAPTER 12

Enter Fanny

GREZ-SUR-LOING

When Louis and Walter finished their voyage, they found that the painters had migrated from Barbizon to Grez-sur-Loing, twelve miles away (and fifty miles south of Paris). They stayed at the Hôtel Chevillon, right on the river Loing. Louis had been there the previous year, and described it to his mother at that time: "I have been three days at a place called Grez, a pretty, and very melancholy village on the plain. A low bridge of many arches choked with sedge; great fields of white and yellow water lilies; poplars and willows innumerable; and about it all such an atmosphere of sadness and slackness, one could do nothing but get into the boat and out of it again, and yawn for bedtime."[1]

This time Louis's feelings for the place grew warmer, and in an essay he described what it was like "to awake in Grez, to go down the green inn garden, to find the river streaming through the bridge, and to see the dawn begin across the poplared level. The meals are laid in the cool arbour, under fluttering leaves. The splash of oars and bathers, the bathing costumes out to dry, the trim canoes beside the jetty, tell of a society that has an eye to pleasure."[2]

A group photo (fig. 32) shows a gathering in front of the bridge. In Will Low's memoir some but not all of the people are identified. Louis isn't present. The tallest man is Henley's brother Anthony. Walter Simpson isn't there, but his brother Willie is, at far right. Bob Stevenson stands out in light-colored trousers and striped socks. It's notable that most of them are formally dressed. Perhaps

32. Group at Grez

unusually, a woman is reclining on the boats, but there is no record of who she might have been.

At about this time Bob painted a self-portrait (fig. 33) in which he clenches a pipe beneath his impressive moustache and looks uncharacteristically solemn. Louis may have envied that moustache, since his own was vestigial.

These are the final words of *An Inland Voyage:*

> Now we were to return, like the voyager in the play, and see what re-arrangements fortune had perfected the while in our surroundings; what surprises stood ready made for us at home; and whither and how far the world had voyaged in our absence. You may paddle all day long; but it is when you come back at nightfall, and look in at the familiar room, that you find Love or Death awaiting you beside the stove; and the most beautiful adventures are not those we go to seek.

By the time he wrote that, Louis knew exactly how prophetic it was.

Although the artistic milieu was generally masculine, a few women artists were sometimes in residence at Grez. One of them was an American named Fanny Osbourne with her two children: her teenage daughter Isobel—always known as Belle—and her young son Lloyd.

33. Bob Stevenson

Belle recalled the moment after dinner one evening at the inn when dusk was advancing and she noticed her mother gazing intently at an open window. Someone was arriving from outside and at that moment was framed in the window. "Standing in the opening, the lights from the hanging lamps showing up his figure like a portrait painted against a black background, stood a young man, slender, dark, with a high color and yellow hair worn rather long. He was leaning forward staring, with a sort of surprised admiration, at Fanny Osbourne. Years afterward he told me he had fallen in love then and there. Amid sudden cries of 'There he is!' 'It's Stevenson!' 'Louis!' the stranger vaulted lightly into the room, his friends greeting him noisily."[3]

One month after this encounter Louis wrote an essay entitled "On Falling in Love" which begins: "There is only one event which really astonishes a man and startles him out of his prepared opinions.... It seems as if he had never heard or felt or seen until that moment, and by the report of his memory, he must have lived his past life between sleep and waking." Twelve years later he told Fanny that "the day when I looked through the window" was one of the most memorable of his life.[4]

Louis definitely wanted to remember their first encounter in this way, but of course he could have been romanticizing it in hindsight. At any rate, from then on he would repeatedly evoke love at first sight in his fiction. In a story two years later, "The blood came and went in his arteries and veins with stunning activity; his ears sang; his head turned." And a year after that, "It was only a black dress that caught Dick Naseby's eye, but it took possession of his mind, and all other thoughts departed. He drew near and the girl turned around. Her face startled him; it was a face he wanted; and he took it in at once like breathing air."[5]

A striking photograph of Fanny (fig. 34) was taken at about this time, when she was thirty-six and Louis twenty-six. Richard Holmes describes it well:

> The photograph shows a distinctly romantic heroine, a dark, determined woman with a mass of wild hair brushed impatiently back behind her ears. She wears a velvet-edged jacket over a tight-fitting black dress that carelessly shows off her figure. Knotted round her throat is a large white neckerchief, tied like a man's tie, loose and full, faintly provocative. The eyes are large and frank, the mouth strong and beautifully formed. She combines force of character with a certain indefinable vulnerability.[6]

There was something exotic about Fanny, and although her parents were of northern European descent, a different strain in her ancestry was often suspected. Someone who knew her well called her "a very marked Spanish type," and another mentioned "the almost Indian darkness of her complexion." Years later Louis would write a poem entitled "Dark Women" that celebrates "the clasp of a dusky woman."[7]

An American painter left this impression of Fanny: "A grave and remarkable type of womanhood, with eyes of a depth and a somber beauty which I have never seen equaled—eyes, nevertheless, that upon occasion could sparkle with humor and brim over with laughter. Yet upon the whole Mrs. Osbourne impressed me first of all as a woman of profound character and serious judgment, who could if occasion called have been the leader in some great movement." Walter Simpson's sister Eve met her at this time and recalled, "Mrs. Osbourne smoked with a soothing relish, looking out of her inscrutable eyes straight before her, sphinx-like in her immovableness, but hearkening all the while, and occasionally

34. Fanny Osbourne, later Stevenson

showing a flash of teeth in such a rapid smile that someone said it was like sheet lightning."[8]

Edmund Gosse came to resent what he saw as Fanny's power over Louis, but still he admired her. "She was one of the strangest people who have lived in our time, a sort of savage nature in some ways, but very lovable—extraordinarily passionate, and unlike everyone else in her violent feelings and unrestrained ways of expressing them—full of gaiety, and with a genius for expressing things picturesquely, but not literary. I think R.L.S. must have caught some of his ways of feeling from her." This positive impression is notable, given the difference in personality between Gosse and Fanny; she once described him as "smooth, silken, like a purring cat, very witty, rather maliciously so, but vain beyond belief."[9]

Also, it's not clear what Gosse meant by "not literary." Fanny actually had a keen literary intelligence, discussed Louis's writing in detail with him while it was in progress, and made crucial suggestions for revising such masterpieces as *Kidnapped* and *Dr. Jekyll and Mr. Hyde*.

The New York publisher S. S. McClure got to know the couple ten years later, and said, "When Stevenson met her, her exotic beauty was at its height, and with this beauty she had a wealth of experience and a sense of humor which he had never found in any other woman. When he married her, he married a woman rich in knowledge of life and the world." McClure added an important comment: "She had the kind of pluck that Stevenson particularly admired." Their lives would be full of crises and emergencies, and Fanny would be at her best in managing them.[10]

Her sense of humor was also important, since it's hard to imagine Louis being happy with a humorless companion. Belle's son Austin recalled, "She had an enchanting sense of humor and dearly loved badinage. Seldom laughing aloud, she joined the general hilarity with the running accompaniment of a low and breathless chuckle." That was published in the *Reader's Digest* series "The Most Unforgettable Character I've Met."[11]

Since she was a decade older than Louis, just as Frances Sitwell was, biographers have often suggested that the attraction must have been oedipal. It's impossible to prove or disprove that kind of claim, but in any case the two relationships were drastically different. If Louis did make tentative advances to Frances, they were firmly repelled and left him penitent. His favorite terms for her were "Madonna" and "mother." With Fanny the attraction was mutual.

The psychobiographer Jefferson Singer offers an interesting hypothesis: "Fanny was emotionally volatile, tempestuous, highly opinionated, often black or white about people. Louis had grown up with a father who shared exactly this emotional style. In relationships we often unconsciously seek partners who repeat the emotional dynamic that is familiar to us, even if we have found it problematic and painful. We gravitate toward what we know since we have learned the rules and cues of that particular world."[12]

FANNY'S STORY

By the time Louis met her Fanny Osbourne had already done a lot of living. When a friend said she ought to write her memoirs, "she listened, pondered, and then dismissed the suggestion as impossible, as her life had been like a dazed rush on a railroad express."[13]

She was born in Indianapolis in 1840 to Jacob and Esther Vandegrift, and was christened Frances Matilda by the celebrated Henry Ward Beecher. She never used her full first name and everybody called her Fanny; on the other hand she thought the Dutch name Vandegrift wasn't sufficiently aristocratic and always spelled it Van de Grift. Her father had moved to Indiana from Philadelphia, started a lumber and real estate business, and after saving some money bought a farm while he continued in an office position on a railroad. Fanny was the eldest of six children (five girls and one boy), which as Margaret Mackay suggests may have helped to form "one of her essential traits, an ardent and protective bossiness."[14]

Fanny's sister Nellie, who adored her and eventually wrote her biography, remembered her tireless energy: "She always went leaping up the stairs, even when she was over eighty; fear was absolutely unknown to her." Their father was likewise intense. "One particularly noticed the extraordinarily keen expression of his eyes, which seemed to pin you to the wall when he looked at you. This penetrating glance was inherited by his daughter Fanny, and was often remarked upon by those who met her." That was yet another characteristic that interested Louis. The girls he grew up with had been taught to avoid eye contact.[15]

Nellie quoted Fanny's unpublished account of their early years when "the streets of Indianapolis had no names; it was too lost a place for that." The main street was part of the National Road that ran all the way to the East Coast—"Oh but that that was romantic to me, leading as it did straight out into the wide, wide world!" A special pleasure was the farm. "Our life in the back woods was simple and natural; we had few luxuries, but we had few cares. In our kitchen garden potatoes, cabbages, onions, tomatoes, Indian corn, and numerous other vegetables grew most luxuriantly, and of fruits we had great abundance." A love of gardening remained with Fanny always. In England she would plant many of those crops, and in Samoa she would supervise a plantation.

Something else Nellie remembered was that in spite of her sister's dislike of studying, "she was very precocious, and learned to read at what was considered by her parents' friends as an objectionably early age." Their father was proud of her, and liked to show her off to his friends. One of them asked her, "'What is the shape of the world?' 'Round,' she replied. 'Then why don't we fall off?' he asked, and she answered, 'Because of the attraction of gravitation.' 'This is awful,' he said, in horror at such precocity."

Fanny's grandmother was deeply religious, and Fanny said in the memoir that "her religion was of the most terrible kind—the old-fashioned Presbyterianism which taught that hell was paved with infants' souls, and such horrors. She always said, when she heard of the death of a young child, that the chances were it would become a little angel, which it would not have done if it had lived to be a little older. I was shocked to hear my mother say that she preferred having her children little living devils rather than dead angels."[16]

In her teens Fanny had plenty of admirers. She fell for Sam Osbourne, described by Nellie as "an engaging youth, a Kentuckian by birth, with all the suavity and charm of the Southerner." She was seventeen when they married in 1857, and Sam was twenty; Belle was born a year later.[17]

Sam was always restless; bored with his office job, he decided to seek his fortune in the West. They settled first in a brand-new town called Austin near the Reese River in Nevada. The California gold rush was over by then, and Nevada, where veins of silver had been discovered, was where prospectors headed. Like most of the others Sam wandered in the hills looking for traces of ore and never found any. He certainly never did any actual mining with pick and shovel. He picked up a bit of income with odd jobs, and since he was an inveterate gambler, perhaps he was lucky at that.

Belle had vivid memories of those days, for example when some Indians brought news of a neighbor who went prospecting and had not been heard of since. They had come upon him wandering in the desert, cared for him until he died, and were now bringing his wife "his heart, which they had cut out of his body, dried in the desert air, and preserved for her."[18]

Something Fanny learned to do at this time was to roll her own cigarettes, a practice that Louis would enthusiastically share. She also learned to use a revolver. Her life story wasn't just exotic, it had given her exceptional confidence and independence. Those were qualities that Louis was powerfully drawn to, and they would sustain him during all the challenges and setbacks of their life together.

Giving up on Austin, the family moved in 1864 to Virginia City, where silver had been discovered; the celebrated Comstock Lode lay directly beneath the town. Mark Twain had just left for California after two years writing for the local newspaper, and in *Roughing It* he would call Virginia City "the liveliest town, for its age and population, that America has ever produced," with constant gambling and gunfights. "The thin atmosphere seemed to carry healing to gunshot wounds, and therefore to simply shoot your adversary through both lungs was a thing not likely to afford you any permanent satisfaction, for he would be nearly certain to be around looking for you within the month, and not with an opera glass, either."[19]

Before long there were tensions in Fanny's marriage. As Nellie diplomatically put it, "The wild, free life of the West had carried her young and impressionable husband off his feet, and the painful suspicion now came to her that she did not reign alone in his heart." After they moved to Oakland in California, "her husband's infidelities became so open and flagrant that the situation was no longer bearable."[20]

By then Belle had two younger brothers, Samuel Lloyd—always called Lloyd in later life—and Hervey. Although their father found clerical work and continued to support them, Fanny made up her mind to begin a new life for herself, an extremely daring venture in those days. She and Belle had been studying painting at Virgil Williams's School of Design in San Francisco, and she now took a bold step. With her three children she set out in 1875 for Antwerp, where there was a distinguished art school, intending to continue her studies. The move was not only daring but expensive, and it's not clear how she could afford it. As the biographer Frank McLynn says, Sam was evidently glad "to get rid of his wife and family and enjoy unrestricted dalliance in the Oakland cottage," but his modest salary couldn't have paid for this adventure.[21]

Fanny was fearless, then and always, and traveled with her revolver. She wrote to a friend, "I took my little pistol to the gunsmith to have the rust cleaned off it. The man examined it with the greatest delight, saying that to see it was worth having lived a lifetime."[22]

The school in Antwerp turned out not to accept female students, so they moved to Paris, where Fanny was admitted to the Atelier des Dames and rented a small apartment in Montmartre just below the Sacré Coeur. But at this point disaster struck. Little Hervey came down with scrofula, the old name for tuberculosis of the lymph nodes, and doctors were unable to help. The only account of what this was like was recorded by Lloyd half a century later:

> I was eight; Hervey, a lovely little fellow with long golden curls, was five. We were miserably poor; it seems to me that I was always hungry. I can remember yet how I used to glue myself to the bakers' windows and stare longingly at the bread within. Then my little brother fell ill of a lingering and baffling ailment. Nobody knew what was the matter with him; for weeks he lay dying, while my mother pawned her trinkets to buy him delicacies and toys. Even after all these years the memory of that

ebbing little life recurs to me with an intolerable pathos—the wasted baby hands, the burning toys, the untasted hothouse grapes lying on the counterpane.

On receiving news of Hervey's condition, his father made a hurried trip from San Francisco and arrived a few days before he died. The boy was buried in a pauper's grave in the Père Lachaise cemetery, and they were told that after five years the bones would be "flung into the catacombs."[23]

Fanny's grief must have been shattering. Five years later she wrote to Charles Baxter, whose young daughter had just died, "I have lost a child myself, and I have no word of consolation to offer. I know too well that there is nothing to be said. I thought once that I could not lose my child and live, such sorrow seemed impossible to bear. But I had to bear it, and I lived. I think there is no time day or night when I am awake that the remembrance of it is not with me."[24]

At some point after this loss—just when isn't known—a fellow student said that a change of scene might help, and suggested the artists' colony at Grez. That was why Fanny and her two surviving children happened to be at the Hôtel Chevillon when Louis returned from his inland voyage. Very recently bereaved and still far from sure that she wouldn't return to her husband, she was in no frame of mind for a love affair. However memorable the moment at the window may have been for Louis, it's clear that the relationship took some time to develop.

LIFE AT GREZ

In his memoir Will Low recalled Fanny and Belle at this time. "They were mother and daughter, I was told, though in appearance more like sisters; the elder, slight, with delicately moulded features and vivid eyes gleaming from under a mass of dark hair; the younger of more robust type, in the first precocious bloom of womanhood."[25]

The precocious bloom attracted attention in this masculine milieu, and as for Fanny, she was soon holding court. Two years later a fellow American, Martha Bertha Wright, published a satirical account of life at Grez, "Bohemian Days," that clearly betrays her jealousy of Fanny: "The Queen of Bohemia is generally smoking a cigarette when she is not sleeping, and when dining has her little feet upon the rungs of her neighbor's chair, while she tells strange stories of wild life among the Nevada mines, where she never saw a flower for eight years, and where feverish brandy and champagne were cheaper than cool water and sweet milk." Wright also mentioned Princess Belle, "with eyes so large that the artists always declare them 'out of drawing,' although 'horrid fetching.'"[26]

Right away, as Belle remembered, "Louis brought into our lives a sort of joyousness hard to describe." There were convivial dinners in the dining room or, still better, "in the arbor by the river, the white tablecloth flecked with the shadows of vine leaves, and the air heavy with the scent of roses, mingled occasionally with whiffs of freshly roasted coffee or loaves just out of the oven. Our fare was simple but marvelously well cooked: *pot-au-feu* served in a heavy yellow bowl, yard-long loaves of bread, cheese made in the village, lettuce salad flavored with garlic and tarragon, chickens roasted on a spit before the open fire, all accompanied by bottles of good red wine. We finished off with tall glasses of black coffee and often sat for hours. And such talk—gay, inspiring, electric!" Belle mentions that Simpson and the two Stevensons had a Scottish accent "that grew stronger with excitement."

Conversation was boisterous, and no doubt inebriated, but "Fanny Osbourne's voice was low in tone, and she spoke with very little modulation. Louis described it as sounding like 'water running under ice.'" Belle herself tended to get loud, at which Fanny would make a calming gesture and paraphrase Shakespeare: "A low sweet voice in a woman." Fanny made good use of her speaking style in an impromptu competition. Walter Simpson's sister Eve was visiting and remembered that "Mrs. Osbourne's recitation, in a consistently dead-level voice, of 'George Washington and the Pear Tree' won honours for the most monotonous story." It must have been the cherry tree, of course.[27]

Fanny's sister Nellie preserved a letter she received from Belle at that time:

> There is a young Scotchman here, a Mr. Stevenson, who looks at me as though I were a natural curiosity. He never saw a real American girl before, and he says I act and talk as though I came out of a book—I mean an American book.... He is such a nice-looking ugly man, and I would rather listen to him talk than read the most interesting book I ever saw. We sit in the little green arbor after dinner drinking coffee and talking till late at night. Mama is ever so much better [from losing Hervey] and is getting prettier every day.... Mama swings in the hammock, looking as pretty as possible, and we all form a group around her on the grass, Louis and Bob Stevenson babbling about boats.[28]

Meanwhile Fanny was corresponding with a San Francisco friend, Timothy Rearden, who seems to have had a romantic interest in her, and Rearden picked up hints that she was attracted to Bob. If so, the interest wasn't reciprocated. She

35. Frank O'Meara, by Sargent

told Rearden that on one occasion she and Bob took a long walk during which "he wanted to tell me something, that I would make no mistake in cultivating the acquaintance of his cousin Louis. 'You must have nothing to say to *me,*' he said, 'for I am only a vulgar cad, but Louis is a gentleman, and you can trust him and depend upon him.'"²⁹

True though that was, the subtext was that Bob wanted Belle, not her mother. Meanwhile Belle didn't want Bob but instead Frank O'Meara, third from the right in the group photograph above (fig. 32). A portrait of O'Meara by Sargent confirms his attractiveness (fig. 35). Belle owned the portrait and kept it for the rest of her life. As for Frank, several years later Louis wrote to Low, "I hear he is still the lady-killer."[30]

Fanny also told her San Francisco correspondent, "I was almost driven frantic by Belle's flirtations and their consequences. I had several duels to settle and a suicide or two to look after." That was an exaggeration, of course, but Eve Simpson remembered one duel (she didn't say between whom) that seemed actually about to happen; "Miss Osbourne's eyes had led to this romantic climax." When it turned out that the rivals weren't in earnest, "Louis was sorely annoyed. He hated ridicule when he was engaged on any make-believe, and the chance of a real live duel, about a lady fair too, was not likely to come in his way again in this unromantic century."[31]

One of the artists recalled an occasion when Bob was foretelling everyone's future. "When he came to his cousin he remarked with a satirical little smile, 'There sits Louis, as smug and complacent as any old *type de bourgeois*. I have not the least doubt that he fondly imagines that one of these days they will be publishing all of his dinky, private correspondence—"the letters of R.L.S."—in boards [i.e., hard covers].' And Louis joined as heartily as anyone in the laugh which the sally raised."[32]

Simpson was the only one with any money, and the rest of them knew that the need to make ends meet might force them to give up art. Low remembered Louis saying wryly, "I fall always on my feet, but I am constrained to add that the best part of my legs seems to be my father." In addition to his regular allowance, he could count on emergency supplements whenever he needed them. Low added that this immunity from poverty encouraged a tendency that would persist throughout his friend's life, "the utter incapacity on the part of Louis to deal with questions of money." In fact only once in his life would he ever hold a job, and that was a brief sinecure, serving as Fleeming Jenkin's secretary at the Paris Exposition of 1878.[33]

It seems to have been at this time that Fanny painted a rarely reproduced portrait of Louis reclining by a stream and dozing over a book (color plate 10). Curiously, the bank he's lying on seems to be made of clay, reflected in the yellowish water; but perhaps she was just playing with color combinations. The book is apparently a small atlas, since the open pages reveal colored maps, not text. All his life Louis dreamed of traveling to faraway places, and soon he would do so.

However slowly the relationship between Louis and Fanny may have evolved, by the time she was ready to return to Paris they were in love. Biographers have strangely ignored what was clearly an important element in the relationship:

strong sexual attraction. Whatever Sam Osbourne's faults, Fanny had had that with him. She and Louis had it too, and it would be an essential element in their life together.

Their relationship is a story of deep and lasting love. A wealth of surviving material confirms that Louis was right when he said that marrying Fanny was the best thing he ever did. According to an old friend, "It had on both sides the elements of what we call a grand passion. It was, in a word, an attachment in which the whole nature of each participant was wholly engaged." In a poem long afterward Louis described her diminutive stature—she was nearly a foot shorter than himself—as "high as my heart."[34]

PARISIAN INTERLUDE

When Fanny returned to Paris with Belle and Lloyd, Louis went with them. He felt it necessary to conceal his new relationship from his parents, since she was not only married but might still return to her husband. In Paris they could live together openly, which would have been inconceivable in Britain—Sidney Colvin and Frances Sitwell didn't do it. "What he praised most in the French as a national trait," Lloyd wrote later, "was their universal indulgence towards all sexual problems—their clear-sighted understanding and toleration of everything affecting the relations of men and women. He often said that in this the French were the most civilized people in Europe."[35]

Since Louis's parents had no inkling of Fanny's existence, they couldn't understand why he was staying so long in Paris. From his father he received an ultimatum: "You say you want me to write to you. This is all very fine but you never write to me. . . . I said you should come home. I now say you must come home. If you don't you will be voted a humbug and be regarded as unpopular as the Colorado beetle."

Louis was in a painful position. Twenty-six years old, he was still receiving orders, and since he was dependent on parental support he couldn't afford to assert his independence. In his reply he affected a light tone, and didn't mention the demand that he come home.

> My dear Father, what you say is quite true, I do not seem to be very anxious to write to you, but it is not so easy to write with a bad eye, for my eye continues to be a little bit of a nuisance. I walk about Paris, and can neither read nor write, but the bustle in the streets amuses me vastly; and as I am living along with some fellows, and we partly make our own food,

I have great fun going marketing. . . . Please ask my mother to forward my quarter's allowance to 5 Rue Ravignan, Paris. Ever your affectionate son, Robert Louis Stevenson.

That was Fanny's address.[36]

The eye infection got worse, and a few weeks later Fanny persuaded Louis to consult a specialist in London. She went there with him and took the opportunity to have an operation on her foot, which had been bothering her. While she was convalescing Frances Sitwell and Sidney Colvin met her and were warmly sympathetic. After a visit with them she wrote to her San Francisco friend Rearden,

> I was so out of place in their house that a corner was arranged, or disarranged, for me. They disheveled my curls, tied up my head in a yellow silk handkerchief, wrapped me in yellow shawls, and spread a tiger skin rug over my sofa and another by me. Everything else was a dull pale blue or green, so that I had quite the feeling of being a sort of Pocahontas in my corner. It seemed most incongruous to have the solemn Mr. Colvin, a professor at Cambridge, and the stately, beautiful Mrs. Sitwell sit by me and talk in the most correct English about the progress of literature and the arts. I was rather afraid of them but they didn't seem to mind but occasionally came down to my level and petted me as one would stroke a kitten.

Delighted, Louis sent Frances a one-line letter: "Look here, you and Colvin are God's holy angels."[37]

At this point Fanny went back to Paris and Louis returned home to Edinburgh. He wrote to Henley, "I'll be lonely, dead lonely, for I can't help it; and I'll hate to go to bed, where there is no dear head upon the pillow."[38]

A couple of months later (the dates aren't clear) he returned to Paris and asked his father to accompany him. "Don't be astonished," he wrote to Colvin, "but admire my courage and Fanny's. We wish to be right with the world as far as we can; 'tis a big venture; wish us God speed." Thomas evidently met Fanny, and after he went back to Edinburgh Louis reported joyfully, "That all went off admirably, and is a great thing for Fanny and me."[39]

What could have brought the highly moralistic Thomas Stevenson around? Frank McLynn offers a plausible suggestion. We know that a young woman in Edinburgh had been threatening to reveal her former relationship with Louis, and his parents may have declared that it was his duty to marry her. In that case he might have felt it necessary to inform them that he was already committed to Fanny, and that he fully expected her to secure a divorce from Sam Osbourne.[40]

In the summer of 1878 Louis was in Grez with Fanny again, and his parents were still pressing him to come home. This provoked him to write, "I am now twenty-seven years old, and perhaps a little entitled to follow my own way for a month or so." And then, fearing that this would give offense, he turned up the rhetorical volume: "Do believe that I love you with all my heart—that I think my father the dearest and most honourable of men—and my mother the cleverest and most loving of women—and that I would indeed and most gladly give up almost anything earthly for your sakes." The one thing he would never give up was Fanny.[41]

PARTING

Now, however, came a shock: Fanny abruptly announced that she was returning to America. Sam Osbourne had visited his family twice in France, once at the time of Hervey's death and again a year later. Louis, in Edinburgh at this time, got alarmed. He wrote to Baxter, "The man with the linstock is expected in May; it makes me sick to write it." A linstock held a lighted match used to fire a cannon, and the implication was that his relationship with Fanny might be about to blow up.[42]

Fanny seems to have been thinking about going back for some time. She wrote to Rearden, "I believe that Sam does miss us very much indeed. I had no idea that he would. I thought it would be sort of weight off his mind to have us gone once more. His letter quite touched my heart. . . . I didn't know I should miss him as I do." Of course, she must have expected that Rearden would share this thought with Sam.[43]

There were multiple motives for a reconciliation. One was that Sam had apparently stopped sending money, and Louis was in no position to support her and the children. Another was the affection Belle and Lloyd felt for their father. And even though Sam's infidelities and restlessness were obvious, Fanny felt affection for him too. One writer comments, "He seems to have been enormously attractive to women, Fanny included, for she always took him back after each scrape."[44]

The parting, which took place in London, was anguishing. Half a century later Lloyd recalled, "I had not the slightest perception of the quandary my mother and R.L.S. were in, nor what agonies of mind their approaching separation was bringing." But when Louis saw them off on the boat train, "I had my own tragedy of parting, and the picture lives with me as clearly as though it were yesterday. We were standing in front of our compartment, and the moment to say goodbye had come. It was terribly short and sudden and final, and before I could realize it R.L.S. was walking away down the long length of the platform, a diminishing figure in a brown ulster. My eyes followed him, hoping that he would look back. But he never turned, and finally disappeared in the crowd."[45]

If Lloyd found the parting painful, for Belle it was worse. Sixty years later she claimed that she still didn't understand what had happened. "I don't know why my mother decided to return to California; she never told me, but suddenly we were leaving. This beautiful adventure was over and I thought my heart would break." Any hope that Frank O'Meara would propose marriage was now gone.[46]

Fanny's departure signaled, as Singer says, "a moment of personal defeat in Louis's life. He felt himself a failure in both life and love." Five months later he was staying at Swanston with Henley and wrote an essay entitled "Truth of Intercourse." After talking about friends it moves on to lovers. "Each knows more than can be uttered; each lives by faith and believes by a natural compulsion; and between man and wife the language of the body is largely developed and grown strangely eloquent. The thought that prompted and was conveyed in a caress would only lose to be set down in words." But there is also a darker comment: "How many loves have perished because, from pride, or spite, or diffidence, or that unmanly shame which withholds a man from daring to betray emotion, a lover, at the critical point of the relation, has but hung his head and held his tongue?" Nicholas Rankin comments, "This sounds like regret at having let Fanny go."[47]

Fanny left in August, and one month later Louis set off on an ambitious walking tour. He chose the Cévennes, a mountainous region in the south of France that outsiders seldom visited. He wanted to get far away, and he wanted to be alone.

CHAPTER 13

The Donkey Book

AN INTERIOR PILGRIMAGE

Two years previously Louis had written in the *Cornhill Magazine,* "To be properly enjoyed, a walking tour should be gone upon alone.... When once you have fallen into an equable stride, it requires no conscious thought from you to keep it up, and yet it prevents you from thinking earnestly of anything else."[1]

He was one of those high-strung people—Rousseau was another—who find relief in the steady repetitive movement of walking. Noting that for Walt Whitman "wisdom keeps school outdoors," Louis added a personal note: "Everyone who has been upon a walking or a boating tour, living in the open air, with the body in constant exercise and the mind in fallow, knows true ease and quiet. The irritating action of the brain is set at rest; we think in a plain, unfeverish temper; little things seem big enough, and great things no longer portentous; and the world is smilingly accepted as it is."[2]

There was another motive as well: it ought to be possible to get a book out of the journey. In early September he established himself in the town of Le Monastier-sur-Gazeille and wrote to Baxter, "My dear Charles, I shall soon go off on a voyage, for which I think I shall buy a donkey, and out of which if I do not make a book, may my right hand forget its cunning." That refers to the psalm, "How shall we sing the Lord's song in a strange land? If I forget thee, O Jerusalem, let my right hand forget her cunning."[3]

He did make a book out of it, but above all it was a personal quest. When *Travels with a Donkey in the Cévennes* was published in the next year it carried this dedication: "My dear Sidney Colvin, the journey which this little book is to describe was very agreeable and fortunate for me. After an uncouth beginning, I had the best of luck to the end. But we are all travelers in what John Bunyan calls the wilderness of this world." Bunyan's pilgrim, however, was bound for the Promised Land; Louis was seeking interior peace.

Halfway through the narrative he comments, "Why anyone should desire to visit either Luc or Cheylard is more than my much-inventing spirit can suppose. For my part, I travel not to go anywhere, but to go. I travel for travel's sake. The great affair is to move; to feel the needs and hitches of our life more nearly; to come down off this feather-bed of civilisation, and find the globe granite underfoot and strewn with cutting flints."[4]

"Travel for travel's sake" was in the spirit of the Romantic poets. In "Books Which Have Influenced Me" Louis would say, "Everyone has been influenced by Wordsworth, and it is hard to tell precisely how. A certain innocence, a rugged austerity of joy, a sight of the stars, 'the silence that is in the lonely hills,' something of the cold thrill of dawn, cling to his work and give it a particular address to what is best in us."[5]

The dedication to Colvin continues, "Every book is, in an intimate sense, a circular letter to the friends of him who writes it. They alone take his meaning; they find private messages, assurances of love, and expressions of gratitude, dropped for them in every corner. The public is but a generous patron who defrays the postage."

When Richard Holmes was eighteen he retraced Louis's itinerary with a copy of *Travels with a Donkey* in his pocket, and thirty years afterward re-created the journey in the opening section of *Footsteps: Adventures of a Romantic Biographer*. Still later he evoked the special qualities of Louis's book: "Its themes, though lightly touched on, are central to all his subsequent wanderings: solitude and romance, journeys and homecomings, fathers and sons, loyalties and betrayals, buried treasure and buried evil, and the double life of modern man. It is also, crucially, about marrying his future wife and the companion in all his travels, the remarkable Fanny Vandegrift Osbourne."[6]

On one occasion Louis sleeps on the ground in a forest, and dawn wakens him like the apparition of a goddess. "I have been after an adventure all my life, a pure dispassionate adventure, such as befell early and heroic voyagers; and thus to be found by morning in a random woodside nook in Gévaudan—not knowing north from south, as strange to my surroundings as the first man upon the earth, an inland castaway—was to find a fraction of my daydreams realised."

Holmes comments, "I loved this idea of the 'inland castaway.' It seemed to me such a subtle, almost poetic idea, as if real travel were concerned with disorientation rather than merely distance. It was losing yourself, then finding yourself again: casting yourself, at least for one moment, into the lap of the gods, and seeing what happened."[7]

Like *An Inland Voyage*, *Travels with a Donkey* has a frontispiece by Walter Crane (fig. 36), this time a naturalistic scene with no figures from Greek mythology. Once again there's a reclining figure in the foreground, but it's Louis himself, not the great god Pan. Smoke rises from his inevitable cigarette as he relaxes in his sleeping bag. Further off, much as in *Pilgrim's Progress*, he and his donkey are seen at successive stages of their journey, pausing to greet a white-robed priest at the door of a church, and ending in a sunburst at the summit. Dawn was breaking in the *Inland Voyage* frontispiece too.

MODESTINE

It's not clear why Louis picked Le Monastier as his starting point. Perhaps it's because it's featured in *Le Marquis de Villemer* by George Sand, one of his favorite writers. With characteristic vagueness about numbers, he wrote to Henley that it lay "between nine and ten thousand metres above the sea." Nine thousand meters is 29,500 feet, higher than Mount Everest. Le Monastier is actually at 1,200 meters, a bit less than 4,000 feet.

He stayed there for two weeks, strolling around the village and chatting with the people. He also drafted an extended account of Le Monastier that he thought of using as his first chapter, but realized that it would be better to begin with the journey itself. Fortifying himself before setting out, he put away a breakfast of heroic proportions. "I certainly ate more than ever I ate before in my life: a big slice of melon, some ham and jelly, a filet, a helping of gudgeons, the breast and leg of a partridge, some green peas, eight crayfish, some Mont d'Or cheese, a peach, and a handful of biscuits, macaroons and things."[8]

He would need more equipment than would fit into his backpack, so it was time to acquire a beast of burden. That turned out to be Modestine, a donkey an old man had been using to pull a cart—"a diminutive she-ass, not much bigger than a dog, the colour of a mouse, with a kindly eye and a determined under-jaw." He acquired her for the modest sum of 65 francs and two glasses of beer. In later years he liked to refer to the story of his travels as "the Donkey Book," since she would turn out to be an important character in the story.[9]

36. *Travels with a Donkey,* frontispiece

His travel supplies included a lined school notebook in which he was keeping his journal, an alcohol-burning lamp, a lantern and candles, a revolver in case of danger, tobacco and cigarette papers, a flask for brandy, two changes of warm clothing, a "railway rug," and the sleeping bag. There was also an egg whisk, a present from Henley's wife intended for making brandy eggnogs when staying at inns, but it was more trouble than it was worth and he soon got rid of it. He also packed a leg of cold mutton, a bottle of Beaujolais, and a supply of bread for Modestine and himself. Later on he would sometimes subsist on nothing more than sausage and chocolate.[10]

Since Modestine was small and had been trained to pull a cart, not carry a heavy load, she found the task difficult. In fact she was reluctant to move at all, and he concluded that to get anywhere, "I must instantly maltreat this uncomplaining animal. The sound of my own blows sickened me." He added, "Once, when I looked at her, she had a faint resemblance to a lady of my acquaintance who formerly loaded me with kindness, and this increased my horror of my cruelty." Her sex proved to be a concern when they encountered a male donkey. "He and Modestine met nickering for joy, and I had to separate the pair and beat down their young romance with a renewed and feverish bastinado."[11]

Commentators point out that Modestine must have been in heat, and although Louis describes his cruelty frankly, it's not clear what he expects the reader to make of it. In his journal he mentions an encounter that didn't get into the published version: "As I passed through Costaros, an ugly village on the high road, the people pretended to be hurt and shocked by my brutality. 'Ah,' they cried, 'look how tired she is, the poor beast!'" He doesn't explain why he thought they were only pretending (or, with French *prétendre* in mind, claiming).[12]

Not everyone was sympathetic to Modestine, and an innkeeper gave him practical advice.

> Blessed be the man who invented goads! Blessed the innkeeper of Bouchet St. Nicolas, who introduced me to their use! This plain wand, with an eighth of an inch of pin, was indeed a sceptre when he put it in my hands. Thenceforward Modestine was my slave. A prick, and she passed the most inviting stable door. A prick, and she broke forth into a gallant little trotlet that devoured the miles. . . . And what although now and then a drop of blood should appear on Modestine's mouse-coloured wedge-like rump? I should have preferred it otherwise, indeed; but yesterday's exploits had purged my heart of all humanity. The perverse little devil, since she would not be taken with kindness, must even go with pricking.

A bit later he says that his heart was "as cold as a potato towards my beast of burden." Whereas Louis adored dogs, he regarded Modestine as a convenient machine, "an appurtenance of my mattress, or self-acting bedstead on four castors." In the journal he added, "I could have seen her led to the gelatine manufactory without a pang." That would be the proverbial glue factory. Why is his treatment of the donkey related in this brutal and matter-of-fact way? It casts a pall over the theme of interior pilgrimage.[13]

ON THE ROAD

Louis and Modestine set out from Le Monastier on September 22 and ended at St. Jean-du-Gard on October 3, after covering 140 miles on foot. The route can be followed today on a "Grande Randonnée," a footpath named the Chemin de Stevenson.

Along the way there were numerous hills, the highest of which was the Col or Pic de Finiels at an altitude of just over a mile; he was told that on a clear day the distant Mediterranean could be seen from there. Most people he encountered assumed he must be a peddler, a reasonable guess considering his laden donkey and his backpack. What they were not familiar with was someone hiking with no purpose at all.

Four nights were spent outdoors, and the rest in rustic inns, which had earthen floors and a single bedroom for all travelers.

> The food is sometimes spare; hard fish and omelette have been my portion more than once; the wine is of the smallest, the brandy abominable to man; and the visit of a fat sow, grouting [nosing around] under the table and rubbing against your legs, is no impossible accompaniment to dinner. But the people of the inn, in nine cases out of ten, show themselves friendly and considerate. At Bouchet, for instance, I uncorked my bottle of Beaujolais and asked the host to join me. He would take but little. "I am an amateur of such wine, do you see?" he said, "and I am capable of leaving you not enough."

In describing this episode Louis uses a Scottish expression, "a whang of bread," and speaks of harvesters "cutting aftermath on all sides." We have forgotten that originally an aftermath was a second crop of hay after the first was gathered in.[14]

Shortly after setting out Louis made the sketch reproduced here (fig. 37), labeling it "Château Beaufort from Goudet sur Loire." The thirteenth-century castle was a ruin. "In this pleasant humour," he says, "I came down the hill to

37. Ruined chateau, sketched by Louis

where Goudet stands in the green end of a valley, with Château Beaufort opposite upon a rocky steep, and the stream, as clear as crystal, lying in a deep pool between them. Above and below, you may hear it wimpling over the stones, an amiable stripling of a river, which it seems absurd to call the Loire." He was near the headwaters of that famous river.[15]

Descriptions of weather evoke the experience of traveling in the open. "It was perishing cold, a grey, windy, wintry morning; misty clouds flew fast and low; the wind piped over the naked platform." Or again, "All the way up the long hill from Langogne it rained and hailed alternately; the wind kept freshening steadily, although slowly; plentiful hurrying clouds—some dragging veils of straight rain-shower, others massed and luminous as though promising snow—careered out of the north and followed me along my way."[16]

Occasionally there are mentions of frustrated desire. At one inn a husband and wife got into the bed next to his. "I kept my eyes to myself, and know nothing of the woman except that she had beautiful arms, and seemed no whit abashed by my appearance." In the journal he calls her arms "full white and shapely" and continues, "Whether she slept naked or in her slip, I declare I know not."[17]

Several descriptions, he told his cousin Bob later, were "mere protestations to F., most of which I think you will understand." One of those comes in a chapter entitled "A Night among the Pines."

> And yet even while I was exulting in my solitude I became aware of a strange lack. I wished a companion to lie near me in the starlight, silent and not moving, but ever within touch. For there is a fellowship more quiet even than solitude, and which, rightly understood, is solitude made perfect. And to live out of doors with the woman a man loves is of all lives the most complete and free.

That was the published version. In the journal the implications are even more obvious:

> The woman whom a man has learned to love wholly, in and out, with utter comprehension, is no longer another person in the troublous sense. What there is of exacting in other companionship has disappeared; there is no need to speak, a look or a word stand for such a world of feeling; and where the two watches go so nicely together, beat for beat, thought for thought, there is no call to conform the minute hands and make an eternal trifling compromise of life.

It was, Holmes says, "a proposal of marriage to Fanny Osbourne," but at this point only in his own mind.[18]

Near the end there is another hint.

> The evening began early underneath the trees. But I heard the voice of a woman singing some sad, old, endless ballad not far off. It seemed to be about love and a *bel amoureux,* her handsome sweetheart; and I wished I could have taken up the strain and answered her, as I went on upon

my invisible woodland way, weaving, like Pippa in the poem, my own thoughts with hers. What could I have told her? Little enough; and yet all the heart requires. How the world gives and takes away, and brings sweethearts near only to separate them again into distant and strange lands; but to love is the great amulet which makes the world a garden; and "hope, which comes to all," outwears the accidents of life, and reaches with tremulous hand beyond the grave and death.

Pippa is heard singing in Browning's poem *Pippa Passes;* Milton speaks of "hope which comes to all." By this time Louis's sweetheart was in a strange and distant land.[19]

AMONG THE MONKS

At one point Louis made a detour to visit a monastery called Nôtre Dame des Neiges, Our Lady of the Snows, which had been founded in the year of his birth. Its ninety inhabitants belonged to the Cistercian order known as Trappists. He believed at first that they were forbidden to speak, but found that although they kept silence among themselves they could talk with visitors.

With irony at his own expense, he describes the effect of his early Calvinist indoctrination. "I had not gone very far ere the wind brought to me the clanging of a bell, and somehow, I can scarce tell why, my heart sank within me at the sound. I have rarely approached anything with more unaffected terror than the monastery of Our Lady of the Snows. This it is to have had a Protestant education. And suddenly, on turning a corner, fear took hold on me from head to foot—slavish, superstitious fear."

As it turned out, he had a positive impression of the monks. "Those with whom I spoke were singularly sweet-tempered, with what I can only call a holy cheerfulness in air and conversation." He was also struck by the calm regularity of their lives, rising for prayer in the middle of the night, and busying themselves during the day with useful labor. On the whole they regarded his Protestantism tolerantly, saying only that they hoped he would eventually see the light. This struck him as a refreshing contrast with the dogmatism of Scotland.

Once, however, a visiting priest and a monk who had been a soldier got him talking. "These two men were bitter and upright and narrow, like the worst of Scotsmen, and indeed, upon my heart, I fancy they were worse. The priest snorted aloud like a battle-horse. '*Et vous prétendez mourir dans cette espèce de croyance?*' he demanded"—and you expect to die in a belief like that? Louis tried to defend himself by saying it was the faith of his parents, not mentioning of course that he had shocked them by turning atheist. "'Your father and mother?' cried the priest. 'Very well; you will convert them in their turn when you go home.'" On this Louis comments, "I think I see my father's face! I would rather tackle the Gaetulian lion in his den than embark on such an enterprise against the family theologian." When he wrote that he knew that Thomas Stevenson would be reading it in due course.

Even though he found himself admiring the lifestyle of the monks, self-denial had no appeal.

> The words of a French song came back into my memory, telling of the best of our mixed existence:
>
> > Que t'as de belles filles,
> > Giroflé!
> > Girofla!
> > Que t'as de belles filles,
> > L'Amour les comptera!
> > And I blessed God that I was free to wander,
> > free to hope, and free to love.

The song, from an opera called *Giroflé-Girofla* by Charles Lecocq, means "What a lot of pretty girls you have—love will count them!"[20]

A poem Louis wrote at the monastery echoed the common Protestant view that monastic retreat was a cowardly evasion.

> Aloof, unhelpful, and unkind,
> The prisoners of the iron mind,
> Where nothing speaks except the bell,
> The unfraternal brothers dwell....
>
> Thou, O my love, ye, O my friends—
> The gist of life, the end of ends—
> To laugh, to love, to live, to die,
> Ye call me by the ear and eye![21]

The final section of *Travels with a Donkey* unexpectedly goes into detail about an uprising by Huguenots known as Camisards that was brutally put down in 1702–4. When he was turning his notes into a book that fall, Louis did a lot of reading about them, struck by their similarity to the Scottish Covenanters who had fascinated him since childhood. "Pont de Montvert, or Greenhill

Bridge, as we might say at home, is a place memorable in the story of the Camisards. It was here that the war broke out; here that those southern Covenanters slew their Archbishop Sharpe."

He doesn't romanticize the Camisards' rebellion, but he sympathizes with their sufferings. When the rebels caught up with a priest who had been a torturer, "One by one, Séguier first, the Camisards drew near and stabbed him. 'This,' they said, 'is for my father broken on the wheel. This for my brother in the galleys. That for my mother or my sister imprisoned in your cursed convents.' Each gave his blow and his reason; and then all kneeled and sang psalms around the body till the dawn." As for their victim, he was "a poor, brave, besotted, hateful man, who had done his duty resolutely according to his light."[22]

THE JOURNEY ENDS

The final pages of *Travels with a Donkey* are anticlimactic. Louis sold Modestine for a good deal less than he originally paid for her, and claims that he was unexpectedly stricken with regret.

Up to that moment I had thought I hated her; but now she was gone,

> "And, oh!
> The difference to me!"

For twelve days we had been fast companions; we had travelled upwards of a hundred and twenty miles, crossed several respectable ridges, and jogged along with our six legs by many a rocky and many a boggy by-road. After the first day, although sometimes I was hurt and distant in manner, I still kept my patience; and as for her, poor soul! she had come to regard me as a god. She loved to eat out of my hand. She was patient, elegant in form, the colour of an ideal mouse, and inimitably small. Her faults were those of her race and sex; her virtues were her own.

No one reading this passage by itself would guess that it's describing a donkey, and commentators disagree about the tone. Some think it has to be ironic, quoting as it does a sentimental poem of Wordsworth's about a lost (and probably imaginary) lover. Others think that Louis shares in the sentimentality. The last words in the book are: "I did not hesitate to yield to my emotion." Perhaps he wanted to reassure readers that although he began by abusing Modestine, by the end he felt gratitude and affection.[23]

In any case, reviewers were not reassured. One of them commented, "Donkeys are such proverbially tiresome animals that no one who was not in search of notoriety at any cost to himself would have thought of deliberately choosing one as his sole traveling companion. It is strange how he can dwell with such placid content on the sufferings that he owns to have inflicted on his companion. Raw legs and bleeding skin do not move him in the least." The same writer mentioned hints of "susceptibility towards the softer sex," and suggested that when he recalled the song about *belles filles* while staying with the monks, he was revealing "his true worship." After reading this "delicious article" Louis told Colvin that it represented him "going about the Cévennes roaring for women, and only disquieted at the monastery because it was not a bawdy house."[24]

Another reviewer complained that the author "is, we presume, one of those darlings of fortune who, having no natural hardships of their own, find a piquant gratification in inventing a few artificial ones, that they may know how it feels to be weary, and cold, and footsore, and belated, with the option at any moment of returning to their ordinary life. So Mr. Stevenson turns from life, which is too soft and indulgent, to try how to feels to be a vagabond. It is a caprice like another." There is a good deal of truth to that.[25]

Travels with a Donkey is more impressive than *An Inland Voyage,* but Louis always acknowledged that it's still fairly slight, and also that the persona of the narrator seems artificial. Two decades later he gave a copy to a friend with this inscription:

> It blew, it rained, it thawed, it snowed, it thundered—
> Which was the Donkey? I have often wondered.[26]

As for the family theologian, Thomas Stevenson was unenthusiastic about the book. Even though Louis honored the Camisards and assured the monks that he was true to the faith of his parents, that was not enough. "There are some three or four irreverent uses of the name of God," Thomas told his son, "which offend me and must offend many others." Most readers will find it hard to remember what those could have been. The crisis of five years earlier had subsided and Louis was no longer being called a horrible atheist, but at a deep level his apostasy would always be unforgivable.[27]

FIRST ATTEMPTS AT FICTION

Robert Louis Stevenson is best remembered as a novelist, but until his thirties he found the scope of a novel daunting and was reluctant to attempt one. By the end of 1879 he did have three works of nonfiction in print, the two travel narratives and *Edinburgh: Picturesque Notes.* In addition he had published twelve essays and fourteen short stories, many of them in Leslie Stephen's *Cornhill Magazine.* A historian explains that a demand for such work had been created by a proliferation of new periodicals that needed "to fill columns of white space with agreeable reading matter." They brought in some income, but not nearly enough to live on.[28]

The term "short story" seems to have been used for the first time in 1884 by the American critic Brander Matthews, to describe a distinct kind of condensed and focused narrative, as opposed to a tale that merely happens to be short. Matthews emphasized the excellence of Poe and Hawthorne in this genre; Louis admired and consciously emulated them. Late in life he gave a penetrating description of the new aesthetic: "The dénouement of a long story is nothing; it is just a 'full close,' which you may approach and accompany as you please—it is a coda, not an essential member in the rhythm; but the body and end of a short story is bone of the bone and blood of the blood of the beginning."[29]

The early stories are interesting as first steps in the storyteller's art, but are completely overshadowed by Louis's later achievements. One collection, published later in book form as *New Arabian Nights,* was admired for its experimentalism. In it a prince of Bohemia seeks out adventures in London in imitation of the caliph in the original *Arabian Nights,* which Louis had read and enjoyed as a boy. The critic George Saintsbury praised "the fertility of extravagant incident, grim or amusing or simply bizarre, with the quiet play of the author's humour in the construction of character, the neatness of his phrase, the skill of his description, the thoroughly literary character of his apparently childish burlesque."[30]

Some reviewers thought that the author must have been laughing at the reader, others that he was laughing at himself. A writer in the *Century Magazine* suggested that it might be both:

> The stories are linked together by the adventures of one central character, who is half Monte Cristo and half Haroun al Raschid up to the last page, where in an unexpected fashion he leaves you laughing at him, laughing at yourself, and wondering how long his inventor has been laughing at you both. This is the book on the face of it. But then, in fact, you cannot speak of the book on the face of it, for under the face is a fascinating depth of subtleties, of ingenuities, of satiric deviltries, of weird and elusive forms of humour, in which the analytic mind loses itself.[31]

Scholars have taken these efforts seriously as harbingers of modernism, but Louis didn't. Instead he turned to a now-unfashionable narrative mode that he had always loved—romance, in the old sense of action and adventure, not love affairs. By the time *New Arabian Nights* came out as a single volume in 1882, he had moved far beyond it with his classic Scottish tales "Thrawn Janet" and "The Merry Men," and with *Treasure Island* in its first serialized form.

CHAPTER 14

From Glasgow to San Francisco

A LEAP IN THE DARK

Fanny sailed for America in August 1878, and after that Louis was kept in painful suspense for an entire year by the ambiguous signals she was sending. All of their correspondence is lost, so we can only guess at what went on between them, or even how often they were in communication.

At this time Fanny was separated from Sam, living in Monterey while he stayed in their house in Oakland, but she might still return to him permanently, which would have delighted Belle and Lloyd. On the other hand, she must have realized that coming back from Europe had been a trap. J. C. Furnas puts it well: "Sam Osbourne had her exactly where he wanted her: back home, raising the children, unable to demand a divorce, and unable to control his sexual escapades. All the efforts to escape, all the bids for freedom, had put her right back where she started." More accurately, if she did demand a divorce he wouldn't agree to it.[1]

Louis, meanwhile, was living in Edinburgh, punctuated by visits to London and France. In December there was a moment of hope when he wrote to Baxter, "I HAD GOOD NEWS FROM AMERICA. Glory Halleluiah!" Possibly Fanny suggested that a divorce might now be possible, but if so the hope didn't last.[2]

In February Colvin told Gosse that Louis "had been to pieces" for quite some time, but that "he had got quite a sane letter from an intelligible address in Spanish California, where, after wild storms, intercepted flights and the Lord knows what more, [Fanny] was for the present quiet among old friends of her own, away from the enemy, but with access to the children. What next, who shall tell?" It's not clear what the "intercepted flights" might have been, but as Pope Hennessy says, one thing is clear: if this latest letter from Fanny was remarkable for being sane, the others must have been "desperately odd."[3]

It's also known that Louis was sending Fanny money, because a note of his to Baxter survives asking what would be the best way to send £20 "to Jacob Van de Grift, Riverside, California." That was Fanny's brother, acting as middleman so that Louis would not be in the position of directly supporting another man's wife.[4]

In July Gosse wrote, "How is it thou art feeble? It is a paradox that you, the General Exhilarator, should feel depressed. I take you for my emblem of life, and you talk of feeling lifeless." Louis replied, "My enthusiasm has kind of dropped from me. I envy you your wife, your home, your child—I was going to say your cat. There would be cats in my home, too, if I could but get it! not for me, but for the person who should share it with me. I may seem to you 'the impersonation of life,' Weg, but my life is the impersonation of waiting, and that's a poor creature." Gosse's full name was Edmund William Gosse; Louis made up the nickname by scrambling the initials.[5]

One project he worked on at this time was an essay on Burns that had been commissioned by Leslie Stephen. When "Some Aspects of Robert Burns" came out in the *Cornhill* it outraged the poet's admirers, since it praised his poems only briefly and focused on his behavior with women. The way Louis handled the subject throws some light on his feelings at the time. What he criticized was not Burns's appreciation of sex, but his heartless treatment of the many women he slept with, including the one he reluctantly married.

> It is the punishment of Don Juanism to create continually false positions—relations in life which are wrong in themselves, and which it is equally wrong to break or to perpetuate. . . . He had trifled with life, and must pay the penalty. He had chosen to be Don Juan, he had grasped at temporary pleasures, and substantial happiness and solid industry had passed him by. He died of being Robert Burns, and there is no levity in such a statement of the case; for shall we not, one and all, deserve a similar epitaph?

Louis was determined that when his time came to die of being Robert Louis Stevenson, it would not be after creating false positions and grasping at temporary pleasures.[6]

At the end of July everything changed. A telegram from Fanny arrived and Louis abruptly decided to go to California. Nobody knows what she said. She may have urged him to come, or even warned that if he didn't their relationship would be over. Or it might have been less alarming than that. He was sick of treading water and may simply have made up his mind to act. In the words of an old hymn, "Once to every man and nation comes the moment to decide."

Louis's parents had been expecting him to join them at a spa in the Lake Country, but on July 30 he met them at their train and said he was "called away on business," which they naturally took to mean London. He did go there briefly, but only to tell friends what he was about to do. Gosse remarked later that he would never forget "his feverish unrest, the evidence of the frail condition of his health and his marvelous lack of all preparation for the huge, uncomfortable journey." And writing to Louis himself, Gosse called it "the dismal clammy evening when we bid one another farewell at the corner of Berkeley Square, and I would have betted sixpence with my soul that I should never see your face again."[7]

Louis was unwilling to ask his parents for money for the ambitious journey, and had little cash on hand. During the previous year, with great generosity, he had lent Colvin £400 to help him out in a personal disaster. The Fitzwilliam Museum in Cambridge had asked Colvin to get a collection of prints appraised. When he left the Savile Club in London with the prints a little after midnight, the club porter put his belongings into a cab and the driver immediately galloped off. Although he was soon captured, he had managed to get rid of the loot, and Colvin was personally responsible for the loss of £1,500. With no personal wealth, he accepted responsibility and would gradually pay it back for years to come. It's not clear that Louis ever did recover his £400; right now he was close to broke. The ever loyal Baxter managed to provide a letter of credit for £150 to use in the States, which Louis promised to repay after he could sell some writing, but at present he only had £30 in cash and would have to travel as cheaply as possible.[8]

Today, when a flight from Scotland to San Francisco takes less than eleven hours, it's hard to appreciate how challenging the journey would be. A slow voyage across the often stormy Atlantic would be followed by an exhausting trip by rail across the American continent—three weeks altogether from Scotland to California.

Louis went to Glasgow and booked passage on the steamship *Devonia,* which was scheduled to sail on August 7 from Greenock on the Clyde estuary. On the 6th he wrote to Baxter that he was "in fair spirits," but told Colvin more bleakly,

"I have never been so much detached from life; I feel as if I cared for nobody, and as for myself I cannot believe fully in my own existence. I seem to have died last night.... I have a strange, rather horrible sense of the sea before me, and can see no further into the future." It's true that he had no plan and no idea how to make one.[9]

When he left his friends were appalled, and blamed Fanny. Henley wrote to Baxter, "I hoped she would be brave and generous enough to have given him up—to have shown herself worthy of him by putting herself out of his way for ever. But she's not, and there's an end on't. So far as I can see, the one thing to be feared is that he may be induced to go to Monterey, and there get mixed up once more in the miserable life of alarms and intrigues that he led in Paris."[10]

Still more appalled was Thomas Stevenson, who implored Colvin to intervene. "For God's sake use your influence. Is it fair that we should be half murdered by his conduct? I am unable to write more about this sinful mad business. I see nothing but destruction to himself as well as to all of us. I lay all this at the door of Herbert Spencer. Unsettling a man's faith is indeed a very serious matter." Somehow the theory of evolution was at the root of the trouble.[11]

As Louis relates in his book about the voyage, *The Amateur Emigrant,* he engaged a second-class cabin for £8, £2 more than passengers in steerage paid, which meant that he was furnished with bedding and had a private room with a table to write on. Still, it was only a little enclave in the midst of steerage. Located near the machinery that powered the ship, the steerage was crowded, malodorous, and poorly ventilated.

Alfred Stieglitz's classic photograph (fig. 38), taken on the *Kaiser Wilhelm II* in 1907, makes it clear that steerage passengers got up on deck whenever they could. Still higher up, the wealthy ladies and gentlemen are literally looking down on them.

In Edinburgh Louis had been accustomed to mix with working-class people in a rather touristic way, but now he was one of them, although paying for second class did qualify him as technically a gentleman. "In the steerage there are males and females; in the second cabin ladies and gentlemen. For some time after I came aboard I thought I was only a male, but in the course of a voyage of discovery between decks I came on a brass plate, and learned that I was still a gentleman. Nobody knew it, of course. I was lost in the crowd of males and females, and rigorously confined to the same quarter of the deck."[12]

The description "steamship" may conjure up images of a mighty vessel like the *Queen Mary,* but the *Devonia* was low-slung and modest in size, a vessel of thirty-five hundred tons (the *Queen Mary* was eighty-one thousand). There were

38. *The Steerage,* by Alfred Stieglitz

just 256 passengers. Nicholas Rankin had the inspiration of tracking down the original passenger list in the New York Public Library. Fifty-one people were in the first-class saloon and identified as clerks, divines, and nil—not unemployed, but too rich to need employment. Twenty-two were in the second-class cabin: 15 Scots including Louis, 6 Scandinavians, and an Irishman. The remaining 183 were in steerage. They were Scottish, Irish, German, Scandinavian, and a Russian. Thirty occupations were listed, including brewer, carpenter, lawyer, marble cutter, and silk weaver.

Louis's entry reads:

Name: Robert Stephenson [he always hated that misspelling]
Age: 29
Occupation: Clerk
Country to which they belong: Scotland
Country in which they intend to become inhabitants: USA.[13]

The first-class passengers understood very well the difference between themselves and the rest.

> Through this merry and good-hearted scene [in steerage] there came three cabin passengers, a gentleman and two young ladies, picking their way with little gracious titters of indulgence, and a Lady Bountiful air about nothing, which galled me to the quick. I have little of the radical in social questions, and have always nourished an idea that one person was as good as another. But I began to be troubled by this episode. It was astonishing what insults these people managed to convey by their presence. They seemed to throw their clothes in our faces. Their eyes searched us all over for tatters and incongruities. A laugh was ready at their lips, but they were too well-mannered to indulge it in our hearing. Wait a bit, till they were all back in the saloon, and then hear how wittily they would depict the manners of the steerage.

When this was published after Louis's death Colvin deleted a further comment: "We had been made to feel ourselves a sort of comical lower animal. Such a fine thing it is to have manners!"[14]

This was the time of a "Long Depression" that lasted for six years throughout Europe and the United States. Britain was hardest hit of all. Louis was now confronted with a reality he had been insulated from, and as Furnas says, "There rubbed against him the direct knowledge that to be penniless was more miserable than picturesque; that economic disaster was cruel to individuals as well as abstractly depressing to masses; that alcoholism was incapacitating, not jolly."[15]

In many ways *The Amateur Emigrant* anticipates Orwell's *Down and Out in Paris and London* half a century later.

> Those around me were for the most part quiet, orderly, obedient citizens, family men broken by adversity, elderly youths who had failed to place

themselves in life, and people who had seen better days. . . . Labouring mankind had in the last years, and throughout Great Britain, sustained a prolonged and crushing series of defeats. I had heard vaguely of these reverses; of whole streets of houses standing deserted by the Tyne, the cellar doors broken and removed for firewood; of homeless men loitering at the street-corners of Glasgow with their chests beside them; of closed factories, useless strikes, and starving girls. But I had never taken them home to me, or represented these distresses livingly to my imagination.[16]

In a real sense Louis was escaping from defeats of his own. "We were a company of the rejected. The drunken, the incompetent, the weak, the prodigal, all who had been unable to prevail against circumstances in the one land were now fleeing pitifully to another, and though one or two might still succeed, all had already failed. We were a shipful of failures, the broken men of England." Of Scotland too, of course. "Skilled mechanics, engineers, millwrights, and carpenters were fleeing as from the native country of starvation." What skills was he himself bringing?[17]

Yet a surprising optimism prevailed. "It must not be supposed that these people exhibited depression. The scene, on the contrary, was cheerful. Not a tear was shed on board the vessel. All were full of hope for the future, and showed an inclination to innocent gaiety. Some were heard to sing, and all began to scrape acquaintance with small jests and ready laughter." Louis always enjoyed children, and noted with amusement that they were attracted to each other "like dogs" and went around "all in a band, as thick as thieves at a fair," while the adults were still "ceremoniously maneuvering on the outskirts of acquaintance."

As the title of *The Amateur Emigrant* suggests, he belonged among these people only in a sense. It would be some years before he could support himself by writing, but his parents might resume their subsidies before then, as indeed did happen. His fellow travelers were not just emigrants but immigrants, whereas (despite what the passenger list said) he had no intention of making a home in America. In much the same way, by the time Orwell published his book he had ended his experiment of being down and out.

Still, the voyage was a turning point. "Travel is of two kinds, and this voyage of mine across the ocean combined both. 'Out of my country and myself I go,' sings the old poet: and I was not only travelling out of my country in latitude and longitude, but out of myself in diet, associates, and consideration." The quotation comes from Louis's favorite essayist, William Hazlitt, who doesn't identify the source; perhaps he made it up.[18]

Pope Hennessy stresses Louis's "readiness to muck in with any of his working-class fellows on boat or train, his passionate and almost childlike interest in them, and his acceptance of them as his equals, with nothing but his kind, inquisitive, amiable nature to fall back upon." Louis himself says, "The talk of a workman is apt to be more interesting than that of a wealthy merchant, because the thoughts, hopes, and fears of which the workman's life is built lie nearer to necessity and nature. They are more immediate to human life."[19]

Something else that struck him was the difference between direct experience of life and literary attempts to re-create it. Years later, in an essay entitled "Popular Authors," he recalled a conversation during this voyage:

> The scene is the deck of an Atlantic liner, close by the doors of the ashpit, where it is warm; the time, night; the persons, an emigrant [i.e., Louis] of an inquiring turn of mind and a deck hand. "Now," says the emigrant, "is there not any book that gives a true picture of a sailor's life?" "Well," returns the other, with great deliberation and emphasis, "there is one that is just a sailor's life. You know all about it, if you know that." "What do you call it?" asks the emigrant. "They call it *Tom Holt's Log*," says the sailor. The emigrant entered the fact in his notebook, with a wondering query as to what sort of stuff this Tom Holt would prove to be, and a double-headed prophecy that it would prove to be one of two things: either a solid, dull, admirable piece of truth, or mere ink and banditti. Well, the emigrant was wrong: it was something more curious than either, for it was a work by STEPHENS HAYWARD.

Louis used capital letters to give a little life to the already forgotten Hayward, whose book, when he got hold of it, was neither truthful nor exciting. What was amazing was that this sailor, with his deep experience of the sea, should imagine that Hayward had anything whatever to say.

Louis's melancholy conclusion was that popular writers become popular by encouraging the fantasies of unsophisticated readers—"always acutely untrue to life as it is, often pleasantly coincident with childish hopes of what life ought to be. And this was the work that an actual tarry seaman recommended for a picture of his own existence!" For someone who hoped to become a popular writer himself, that was food for thought.[20]

Always self-critical, Louis had a poor opinion of this essay, as he told the American editor whose deadline forced him to send it in. "How true it is that once start on the wrong foot, all's lost. This paper has been in hand since October [it was now April]; begun and re-begun, and hashed and smashed and doctored; and the damned thing looks as if I hadn't taken any pains to wipe my pen. I am ashamed of it."[21]

There were a few hints of erotic interest on the voyage, but only hints.

The women too often displeased me by something hard and forward, by something alternately sullen and jeering both in speech and conduct. But to begin with, this may have been my own fault, for the game of manners is more easily played with a good partner. . . . May I not construe these taunts and tiffs and sulks as so many challenges into the field of courtship? They are forward and backward to provoke the men, that the first kiss may be taken in a tussle and furiously resented. At least I was not amenable to these advances, if such they were.[22]

When the *Devonia* finally docked it was a relief but not an improvement. In pouring rain Louis and a companion found cheap lodging at a rooming house; neither of them could get any sleep, due to a skin infection they had picked up on the voyage. "My wrists were a mass of sores; so were many other parts of my body. The itching was at times overwhelming; at times, too, it was succeeded by furious stinging pains, like so many cuts with a carriage whip." It was probably scabies, a rash caused by mites that burrow under the skin and provoke an allergic reaction; it lasted for weeks and left him, as he said afterward, "in great part flayed."

The next day he went to a drugstore and was given "a blue pill, a seidlitz powder, and a little bottle of some salt and colourless fluid to take night and morning on the journey. He might as well have given me a cricket bat and a copy of Johnson's dictionary." Back at his lodgings he was so drenched from the rain that he abandoned the clothes he was wearing. "With a heavy heart I said farewell to them as they lay in a pulp in the middle of a pool upon the floor of Mitchell's kitchen. I wonder if they are dry by now."

One point of interest was the landlord's young daughter.

She was a slip of a girl at that attractive period of life when the girl just begins to put on the forms of the woman, and yet retains an accent and character of her own. Her looks were dark, strange and comely. Her eyes had a caressing fixity, which made you inclined to turn aside your own. She was what is called a reading girl, and it was because she saw books in my open knapsack as I sat writing at a table near the bar that she plucked up the courage to address me.

She asked to look at the books, and he gave her one written by himself (he doesn't say which). She was delighted to recognize his picture in it, and read aloud until it was time for him to leave. "I wish her a kind husband who will have, without my wishing it, a most desirable wife, particularly for an author."[23]

The Amateur Emigrant would take a long time to get into print. Colvin and Henley both thought it was inferior work, but they placed it with Charles Kegan Paul, who had previously brought out *An Inland Voyage* and *Travels with a Donkey*. The book was set up in type and Louis corrected the proof sheets, but when his father read it (they were on good terms again by then), he declared, "I think it not only the worst thing you have done, but altogether unworthy of you." He refunded the publisher's advance payment of £100, which Louis had already spent, to prevent publication, and that wouldn't happen until the Edinburgh Edition in 1895.[24]

Even then it was not printed in its entirety. Colvin silently deleted almost one-third of the text, which was not restored until a new edition in 1966. The recovered passages give a vivid sense of the discomforts during the voyage: "An elderly man, but whether passenger or seaman it was impossible in the darkness to determine, lay groveling on his belly in the west scuppers, and kicking feebly with his outspread toes. He had been sick and his head was in his vomit. . . . 'Take care of your knee,' said I to O'Reilly. 'I have got mine in the vomit.'" Also deleted were the itch, the taunting girls, and the landlord's daughter.[25]

Still less acceptable, from Thomas Stevenson's point of view, must have been the revelation that his son ran away from home to join a woman who was not yet divorced and might never be. And it was clear that having broken with his parents, he was subsisting at a near-starvation level, which might suggest callous neglect on their part. They were not callous, exactly, but evidently thought that reducing him to penury might force him to come home. That would contribute to the most dangerous illness of his life.

When the book was finally published it had a dedication to Robert Alan Mowbray Stevenson: "Neither time nor space nor enmity can conquer old affection; and as I dedicate these sketches, it is not to you only, but to all in the old country, that I send the greeting of my heart."

"THE STORY OF A LIE"

One reason Louis needed a writing table was to finish "The Story of a Lie," which he had contracted back in May to deliver to Kegan Paul. He did finish it, and it was a longish story, almost a novella.

Although it's not among his most impressive works, it does resonate strikingly with his life situation at the time. As in an unfinished story called "Edifying Letters of the Rutherford Family," there is tension between a father and son, and this time the son has to surmount obstacles to marry the woman his heart desires. Louis is surely describing himself when he introduces Dick Naseby:

> He was a type-hunter among mankind. He despised small game and insignificant personalities, whether in the shape of dukes or bagmen, letting them go by like seaweed; but show him a refined or powerful face, let him hear a plangent or a penetrating voice, fish for him with a living look in some one's eye, a passionate gesture, a meaning and ambiguous smile, and his mind was instantaneously awakened. "There was a man, there was a woman," he seemed to say, and he stood up to the task of comprehension with the delight of an artist in his art.

One character who briefly interests Dick is an artist in Paris named Peter Van Tromp, who dashes off mediocre sketches in bistros. It doesn't take Dick long to realize that the man is a total humbug, and when he returns to England he assumes that he'll never hear of him again. However, he falls in love at first sight—as happens repeatedly in Louis's fiction—with a beautiful young woman named Esther. Shockingly, she turns out to be none other than the humbug's daughter. She hasn't seen him for years and cherishes a belief that he is a great genius. Dick can't bring himself to disabuse her, but when Van Tromp suddenly shows up Esther sees him for what he is and is furious with Dick for not telling her the truth.

More interesting than the main story is Dick's fraught relationship with his own father, due to misunderstandings but also to profound differences of temperament. Old Naseby is very like Thomas Stevenson: "The universe seemed plain to him. 'The thing's right,' he would say, or 'the thing's wrong'; and there was an end of it. There was a contained, prophetic energy in his utterances, even on the slightest affairs; he *saw* the damned thing; if you did not, it must be from perversity of will; and this sent the blood to his head."

At one point Esther earnestly tells Dick that he is wrong to criticize his father. He exclaims, "My dear, you do not understand; you do not know what it is to be treated with daily want of comprehension and daily small injustices, through childhood and boyhood and manhood, until you despair of a hearing, until the thing rides you like a nightmare, until you almost hate the sight of the man you love, and who's your father after all." Esther responds, "I am sorry for you, it must be very sad and lonely." "'You misunderstand me,' said Dick, chokingly. 'My father is the best man I know in all this world; he is worth a hundred of me, only he doesn't understand me, and he can't be made to.'"

At the age of twenty-nine it was high time for Louis to escape his parents' control—Margaret's may have been passive, but she always supported Thomas. For "The Story of a Lie" Louis concocted a happy ending. Van Tromp and the elder Naseby turn out to be good fellows after all, they both rejoice in Dick's marriage to Esther, and soon there is "a brand-new baby."

That was just wish fulfillment on Louis's part. For all he knew, his parents might never speak to him again, and there was no assurance that he could ever marry Fanny. But he included a striking analysis of the way lovers know each other through mutual idealization (another term might be projection):

> All comprehension is creation. The woman I love is somewhat of my handiwork; and the great lover, like the great painter, is he that can so embellish his subject as to make her more than human, whilst yet by a cunning art he has so based his apotheosis on the nature of the case that the woman can go on being a true woman, and give her character free play, and show littleness, or cherish spite, or be greedy of common pleasures, and he continue to worship without a thought of incongruity. To love a character is only the heroic way of understanding it. When we love, by some noble method of our own or some nobility of mien or nature in the other, we apprehend the loved one by what is noblest in ourselves.

Another moment in the story must reflect Louis's bafflement at the ambiguous signals he had been getting from Fanny. Dick says to Esther, "You know well who I am, and what I am, and that I love you. You say I will not help you; but your heart knows the contrary. It is you who will not help me, for you will not tell me what you want."[26]

This is one of the few stories Louis never chose to reprint after its first publication in a magazine.

ACROSS THE PLAINS

The sequel to *The Amateur Emigrant*—originally they were intended to form a single volume—is *Across the Plains,* relating the railway journey from the New Jersey side of the Hudson to San Francisco.

> I began to exult with myself upon this rise in life like a man who had come into a rich estate. And when I had asked the name of a river from the brakesman, and heard that it was called the Susquehanna, the beauty of the name seemed to be part and parcel of the beauty of the land. As

when Adam with divine fitness named the creatures, so this word Susquehanna was at once accepted by the fancy. That was the name, as no other could be, for that shining river and desirable valley. None can care for literature in itself who do not take a special pleasure in the sound of names; and there is no part of the world where nomenclature is so rich, poetical, humorous, and picturesque as the United States of America.... The names of the states and territories themselves form a chorus of sweet and most romantic vocables: Delaware, Ohio, Indiana, Florida, Dakota, Iowa, Wyoming, Minnesota, and the Carolinas; there are few poems with a nobler music for the ear: a songful, tuneful land.[27]

The long journey was exhausting, and Louis wrote to Colvin a couple of days later, "I am in the cars between Pittsburgh and Chicago, just now bowling through Ohio.... I have already been about forty hours in the cars. It is impossible to lie down in them, which must end by being very wearying." However, he wanted his friends to believe that the venture was working out well. "In America you eat better than anywhere else: fact. The food is heavenly. No man is any use until he has dared everything; I feel just now as if I had, and so might become a man. 'If ye have faith like a grain of mustard seed' [Matthew 17:20]. That is so true! Just now I have faith as big as a cigar case. I will not say die and do not fear man or fortune." To Baxter he wrote from Iowa, "I keep in truly wonderful spirits, all things considered," and to Henley from Nebraska, "Peace of mind I enjoy with extreme serenity; I am doing right; I know no one will think so, and don't care."[28]

Along the way he composed a poem:

> Of where or how, I nothing know;
> And why, I do not care;
> Enough if, even so,
> My traveling eyes, my traveling mind, can go
> By flood and field and hill, by wood and meadow fair,
> Beside the Susquehanna and along the Delaware.[29]

He also wrote another poem that never got published:

> Light as the linnet on my way I start,
> For all my pack I bear a chartered heart.
> Forth on the world without a guide or chart,
> Content to know, through all man's varying fates,
> The eternal woman by the wayside waits.

When Fanny saw this, she must have appreciated "the eternal woman," which echoes *das Ewig-Weibliche* in Goethe's *Faust*.[30]

In Chicago it was necessary to transfer to a different railway line.

> I have never been so dog-tired as that night in Chicago. I sat, or rather lay, on some steps in the station, and was gratefully conscious of every point of contact between my body and the boards. My one ideal of pleasure was to stretch myself flat on my back with arms extended, like a dying hermit in a picture, and to move no more. I bought a newspaper, but could not summon up the energy to read it; I debated with myself if it were worth while to make a cigarette, and unanimously decided that it was not.

The people jammed into the train didn't seem thrilled to be there, and when a musician started to play "Home, Sweet Home" he was told to knock it off.[31]

After eleven days—one more than the Atlantic crossing took—the journey came to a satisfying end.

> The day was breaking as we crossed the ferry; the fog was rising over the citied hills of San Francisco; the bay was perfect—not a ripple, scarce a stain, upon its blue expanse; everything was waiting, breathless, for the sun. A spot of cloudy gold lit first upon the head of Tamalpais, and then widened downward on its shapely shoulder; the air seemed to awaken, and began to sparkle; and suddenly
>
> > "The tall hills Titan discovered,"
>
> and the city of San Francisco, and the bay of gold and corn, were lit from end to end with summer daylight.

"Corn" doesn't mean maize, but in British usage wheat, though more probably it was the golden grass of California. The line of verse is remembered from *The Faerie Queene*, "And the high hills Titan discovered." Louis's mind was full of poetry he had read at one time or another.[32]

Across the Plains would be published in installments in *Longman's Magazine* in 1883, and nine years later as a book. Finally, in the Edinburgh Edition, it would be joined with the suppressed *Amateur Emigrant* as a full account of the journey from Glasgow to San Francisco. But by then Louis was in his grave.

CHAPTER 15

A Year in California

"THE ITCH AND A BROKEN HEART"

On August 30, 1879, Louis arrived at last in Monterey, a hundred miles south of San Francisco. Artist friends had recommended it to Fanny, and she was living there with her children and her sister Nellie, sixteen years younger than herself and only two years older than Belle. "There she found an opportunity," Nellie remembered, "to indulge her skill as a horsewoman, and at any time she might have been seen galloping along the country roads on her little mustang Clavel. She even joined a party of friends who accompanied a band of vaqueros in a great rodeo on the San Francisquito ranch near Monterey."[1]

If Louis had been expecting a joyous reunion, he was bitterly disappointed. Fanny was shocked by his exhaustion and poor health, and still conflicted about Sam, who wanted her back. Also, she was receiving indignant letters from her brother and sisters back east. "Divorces were very rare then," Belle remembered, "and considered disgraceful. Her family were appalled at the idea and wrote frantic protests against it."[2]

Belle told a friend long afterward, "Louis's conduct was not that of a romantic lover who had followed a sweetheart halfway around the world. Although he was gay and full of banter, he was almost coldly casual toward my mother—and her attitude not much different toward him." At point Belle really had no idea what would happen, and Fanny probably didn't either.[3]

Belle's memoir also confirms how deeply she adored her father. "I called him 'Poppa,' and thought him the handsomest, the wisest, the finest man in the whole world. His nose was straight, his blue eyes fine and direct, his complexion fair, but owing to the fashion of that day I never really saw his face, for he wore a beard, golden in color and trimmed to a neat Van Dyke point. When he was laughing, which was often for he was a very cheerful person, he showed remarkably white teeth."

When Fanny first returned from Europe the family lived together in their Oakland house, and when troupes of actors came to San Francisco Sam would take Belle to the theater, where she was dazzled by the "realms of romance." When they went for walks, "tramping over the hills hand in hand, we shouted the words of 'Bowery Girls, Won't You Come out Tonight,' 'Tassels on Her Boots,' and 'Walking Down Broadway.'"

Belle was aware, however, of continual tension between her parents, in "an atmosphere of suppressed feelings that chilled me."

> My mother was sewing; I was curled up on the floor, leaning against my father's knee as he read aloud from *Vanity Fair*. It was a peaceful scene. He had reached the place in the story where Captain Osborne goes to war and his wife Amelia discovers that he has betrayed her with Becky Sharp. I was listening with deep interest, when my mother interrupted in an icy voice, "I wonder that you dare read your own story, Captain Osbourne." My father started, flushed, and cried out, "God Almighty, woman! Can't you ever forget?" And then I was sent out of the room.

Sam Osbourne, who shared the surname of Thackeray's character, had been a captain himself during the Civil War.[4]

Belle recalled an afternoon when a young woman appeared at the front door, and she suspected that this "showy, overdressed creature" was connected in some way with her father.

> As she came up on the porch, nodding and smiling, my mother asked, "Why do you come here?" The woman hesitated, stammered, tossed her head and said, "I came to make a friendly call. There is no reason why I shouldn't." "There is a very good reason why you should not come into my house," my mother said, and then I ran upstairs. From the window of my room I saw the woman walking indignantly down the path, her bustle wagging insolently behind her.[5]

After a discouraging week in Monterey Louis left on horseback and headed up into the rugged coastal mountains. He wrote to Baxter, "My news is nil. I know nothing. I go out camping, that is all I know; today I leave, and shall likely be three weeks in camp; I shall send you a letter from there with more guts than this and now say goodbye to you, having had the itch and a broken heart." The itch was the maddening scabies he had contracted on the *Devonia*.[6]

What happened next was that he came down with a dangerous fever. After a month he was back in Monterey and reported to Gosse what he had been through.

> I was pretty nearly slain; my spirit lay down and kicked for three days. I was up at an angora goat ranch in the Santa Lucia Mountains, nursed by an old frontiersman, a mighty hunter of bears, and I scarcely slept or ate or thought for four days. Two nights I lay out under a tree in a sort of stupor, doing nothing but fetch water for myself and horse, light a fire and make coffee, and all night awake hearing the goat bells ringing and the tree frogs singing when each new noise was enough to set me mad. Then the bear hunter came round, pronounced me "real sick," and ordered me up to the ranch.

The hunter and the rancher took good care of him and undoubtedly saved his life.[7]

There was a welcome sequel. A Monterey doctor supervised Louis's convalescence, and on October 15 he sent a "Private and Confidential" letter to Baxter: "In coming here, I did the right thing. I have not only got Fanny patched up again in health, but the effect of my arrival has straightened out everything. As now arranged there is to be a private divorce in January, after the girls [Nellie and Belle] are married, and yours truly will be himself a married man as soon thereafter as the law and decency permit."[8]

Sam Osbourne did agree to a divorce so long as it was conducted discreetly. His state of mind can only be guessed at, but he was probably tired of being attacked for his infidelities, as well as supporting a family that didn't live with him. It was decided that he would turn over the Oakland house to Fanny and the children, and find lodgings for himself elsewhere until the divorce was finalized. At some point Louis would also leave Monterey and live in San Francisco, where he and Fanny could meet in public places. A writer who has reviewed the evidence concludes convincingly, "Osbourne was a man of responsibility, culture, and refinement, without apparent vindictiveness, who throughout the divorce proceedings behaved with tact and generosity." It's not known if he and Louis ever met face-to-face.[9]

"There were no class distinctions in Monterey," Belle recalled; "we danced with the butcher, the baker, and the—the saloon keeper. Particularly with the saloon keeper, for Adulfo Sanchez was the most popular young man in Monterey. . . . He was young, extraordinarily handsome, and was gifted with a glorious baritone voice. And he fell deeply in love with Nellie." Sanchez's aristocratic Spanish-Mexican family had fallen on hard times. His and Nellie's marriage was a success; they later named their son Louis after their friend, and he wrote a touching poem, "To My Name-Child."[10]

A regular visitor to Monterey was a San Francisco artist named Joe Strong, who "looked like a young German with his twisted yellow mustache and close-cropped hair." Before long he and Belle would get married, but in high secrecy since Fanny was opposed to the match. She had had ideas about somebody else for her daughter and disapproved of Joe, who was all too like Sam: charming, unreliable, a heavy drinker, and compulsively unfaithful. Unfortunately, that seems to be why Belle was attracted to him.[11]

After Fanny attempted to put her foot down, Joe hastened to get Sam's blessing and then came down to Monterey with a marriage license. On August 9 — three weeks before Louis's arrival — he and Belle had gone secretly to a cottage where a minister married them.

Once the truth came out, the couple moved into a San Francisco apartment that Sam found for them, and in her memoir Belle described her joy: "My dear father! When I remember him, it is always with his arms open wide to love and comfort me. He helped us to arrange the rooms, invited us to dinner, and when we parted, filled my handbag with twenty dollar gold pieces. Bless him!"[12]

Joe got commissions to paint portraits, and Belle brought in income with fashion ads, newspaper illustrations, and birthday cards. Bob Stevenson still had fond memories of Belle, to whom he had been strongly attracted at Grez, and he wrote to Louis, "Never mind my letters to Belle, it is of no consequence now. No, Belle is married. I hope she will be happy. I think she is a person to get to like a man she is with. I cannot think or look forward to being any cause of future disagreement; besides, I have accustomed myself to regard the world as a place not to be happy in."[13]

As for Lloyd, who was now ten, he shared Belle's affection for their father. "He was a tall, very fine-looking man, with a pointed golden beard and a most winning and lovable nature; I loved him dearly and was proud of his universal popularity." When Sam came down to Monterey for a visit Lloyd was bewildered when he overheard Fanny saying "with an intensity that went through me like a knife, 'Oh, Sam, forgive me!'"

Soon after that Louis took Lloyd for a walk and told him solemnly, "I want to tell you something. You may not like it, but I hope you will. I am going to

39. Monterey rooming house

marry your mother." There was a stunned silence, and then Lloyd put his hand into Louis's. As he recalled long afterward, "A rapturous sense of tenderness and contentment came flooding over me." It would be years before anything like that would come flooding over Belle.[14]

Louis felt increasingly at home in Monterey. To preserve propriety he didn't live with Fanny, but stayed in a rooming house on the unpaved main street (fig. 39). At the far right in the picture, a white "X" marks his room, and the sign beneath the second-floor windows says STEVENSON HOUSE; by the time this picture was published in 1911 the house had become a shrine to his memory.

His closest friendship was formed with one of the most remarkable characters in Monterey, a restaurant owner named Jules Simoneau (fig. 40). In a letter to Colvin he described Simoneau as "a jolly old Frenchman, the stranded fifty-eight year old wreck of a good-hearted dissipated and once wealthy Nantais [from Nantes] tradesman," and to Henley he called him "a most pleasant old boy with whom I discuss the universe and play chess daily." They corresponded from time to time in later years, and when a monument to Louis was dedicated in San Francisco in 1897, Simoneau was a guest of honor. Simoneau's Mexican wife Martina used to call their friend "Don Roberto Luís."[15]

Many years later Simoneau told a visitor that he remembered Louis well. "I 'ave been good fren' to good many men. Only one nevaire forget. Louis Stevenson, 'e nevaire forget." Simoneau added "in his Gallic way and with many a Gallic gesture, 'Louis 'e was brave. 'E was ver' poor. 'E was ver' seeck. Oui! Sometam 'e was ver' *ongry*. But always 'e laugh. Always 'e keep ze smile! Always 'e try to work, even w'en it seem 'is heart break. Zat was Louis. 'E was *brave!*'"[16]

40. Jules Simoneau

Soon Louis was a regular member of a group that met at Simoneau's. When he wrote about his time there in "The Old Pacific Capital: Monterey," he recalled, "We have sat down to table, day after day, a Frenchman, two Portuguese, an Italian, a Mexican, and a Scotchman. We had for common visitors an American from Illinois, a nearly pure blood Indian woman, and a naturalised Chinese; and from time to time a Switzer and a German came down from country ranches for the night. No wonder that the Pacific coast is a foreign land to visitors from the Eastern States, for each race contributes something of its own." The title of the essay recalls that until 1846 Monterey had been the capital of Alta California under Mexico, and before that under Spain.[17]

With his health improving and in serious need of income, Louis did a lot of writing. He completed *The Amateur Emigrant,* the story "The Pavilion on the Links," and an essay on Thoreau that's notable for this judgment: "Not one word about pleasure, or laughter, or kisses, or any quality of flesh and blood. It was not inappropriate, surely, that he had such close relations with the fish."[18]

In addition he drafted several chapters of a novel to be called "A Chapter in the Experience of Arizona Breckenridge," or else perhaps "A Vendetta in the West." Like many of his projects, nothing ever came of that one.[19]

The scenery was altogether new to Louis, and the ocean haunted his imagination.

> Even in quiet weather, the low, distant, thrilling roar of the Pacific hangs over the coast and the adjacent country like smoke above a battle.... Sandpipers trot in and out by troops after the retiring waves, trilling together in a chorus of infinitesimal song.... The one common note of all this country is the haunting presence of the ocean. A great faint sound of breakers follows you high up into the inland canyons; the roar of water dwells in the clean, empty rooms of Monterey as in a shell upon the chimney; go where you will, you have but to pause and listen to hear the voice of the Pacific.

As always in Louis's writing, this is not scenic description, it's an evocation of what one would hear and feel. And what other writer would think of "infinitesimal song?"[20]

The title "The Old Pacific Capital" makes Monterey sound romantic, but most of the time it didn't really seem that way, especially after Fanny and the children departed. When he himself had left, Louis told Henley, "It was time I was out of Monterey. The place breathed on me. To live alone in such a hole, the one object of scandal, gossip, imaginative history—well, it was not good."[21]

The improvement in health turned out to be temporary. In December he wrote to Gosse, "I have been sweated not only out of my pleuritic fever, but out of all my eating cares and the better part of my brains (strange coincidence) by aconite. I have that peculiar and delicious sense of being born again in an expurgated edition, which belongs to convalescence." Pleuritic fever meant pleurisy, yet another lung disorder that he was subject to. Aconite was a traditional remedy for all sorts of complaints, but of doubtful efficacy and potentially dangerous since it contains alkaloids that can be highly toxic. Shepherds called the plant wolfbane and used it to poison wolves.[22]

Fanny's divorce was officially certified on December 12 at the Nineteenth Judicial District Court in San Francisco, and Louis reported to Colvin, "Fanny has divorced her Master; he behaved well and was to support her till we married, and of course we were to hurry nothing so as to avoid scandal for him. And now he has lost his government appointment [as a court stenographer], and as he never saved anything, he is on his back." This was indeed the end of any contributions from Sam, who would remarry after a while and then vanish, leaving his second wife bewildered. Louis, already struggling to make ends meet with miscellaneous writing, was now faced with supporting Fanny and Lloyd.[23]

Henley, who had been arguing against the marriage, now sent a generous letter. "Hurray, my Louis! Compliments, congratulations, love, best wishes, etcettery! I am very glad, thou art very glad, he is very glad, we are very glad, and so on! Make haste and get married and come home and live happily ever afterwards. That is all we ask." It was a conciliatory gesture to spell the name "Louis" instead of "Lewis" as Henley usually did.[24]

"YON DISTRESSFUL CITY BESIDE THE GATES OF GOLD"

Three days before Christmas Louis moved to San Francisco, but it was understood that he should wait to live with Fanny until they could be legally married. This wasn't Calvinist Edinburgh, but it wasn't Paris either.

At 608 Bush Street, close to Chinatown (fig. 41), he saw a notice advertising furnished rooms, and made an agreement with the landlady, Mrs. Mary Carson. "When I came to know him," she said later, "I loved him like my own child." Mary was a native of Waterford in Ireland; her husband William was a machinist who went by the name of "Speedy." His name appears in the city directory for 1880, and so does "Stevenson, Robert L., author, 608 Bush." The Carsons must have reported his occupation in that way.[25]

San Francisco was still a young city, and Louis was struck by its provisional nature, as he wrote in "A Modern Cosmopolis."

> I wonder what enchantment of the Arabian Nights can have equaled this evocation of a roaring city, in a few years of a man's life, from the marshes and the blowing sand. Such swiftness of increase, as with an overgrown youth, suggests a corresponding swiftness of destruction. The

41. 608 Bush Street, San Francisco

sandy peninsula of San Francisco, mirroring itself on one side in the bay, beaten on the other by the surge of the Pacific, and shaken to the heart by frequent earthquakes, seems in itself no very durable foundation.

The great earthquake would indeed come in 1906. Louis had noted presciently, "No one feels safe in any but a wooden house. Hence it comes that in that rainless clime, the whole city is built of timber—a woodyard of unusual extent and complication; that fires spring up readily, and served by the unwearying trade wind, swiftly spread." Fire would cause far more damage than the earthquake itself, and one of its victims was the Carson house on Bush Street.

Living in poverty, he didn't admire the commercial culture. The Stock Exchange, he wrote, was "the heart of San Francisco: a great pump we might call it, continually pumping up the savings of the lower quarters into the pockets of the millionaires upon the hill." These memories would be recalled in his novella *The Wrecker*. His politics may have been conservative, but never in a simple or programmatic way.[26]

Naturally he was homesick, as he recalled in verse:

> It's forth across the roaring foam and on towards the west,
> It's many a lonely league from home, o'er many a mountain crest,
> From where the dogs of Scotland call the sheep around the fold,
> To where the flags are flying beside the Gates of Gold.
>
> Where all the deep-sea galleons ride that come to bring the corn,
> Where falls the fog at eventide and blows the breeze at morn;
> It's there that I was sick and sad, alone and poor and cold,
> In yon distressful city beside the Gates of Gold.[27]

Louis made a friend in San Francisco who turned out to be an important influence for the future. That was a poet and fiction writer named Charles Warren Stoddard, who published regularly in San Francisco newspapers, and was a friend of Joe Strong and Jules Simoneau. Stoddard introduced Louis to Melville's *Typee* and *Omoo*—"the books," Belle said, "that first turned his thoughts towards the islands."[28]

After he returned to Britain Louis sent Stoddard some verses in Scots:

> Far had I rode an' muckle seen,
> An' witnessed mony a ferlie,
> Afore that I had clappit e'en
> Upo' my billy, Charlie.
>
> Far had I rode an' muckle seen,
> In lands accountit foreign,
> An' had foregather'd wi' a wheen
> Or I fell in wi' Warren.
>
> Far had I rode an' muckle seen,
> But ne'er was fairly doddered
> Till I was trystit as a frien'
> Wi' Charlie Warren Stoddard!

Muckle is "much," a *ferlie* is a marvel, and *wheen* is "a good few."[29]

There is no record of what Louis thought of Stoddard's *Summer Cruising in the South Seas,* which has been described as "a collection of swooning prose sketches" featuring romantic relationships between older men and young male companions. In Stoddard's reminiscences of Louis one may suspect a note of disappointment. "His familiars grew to think of him and to look upon him as being but a disembodied intellect; his was the rare kind of personality that inspires in the susceptible heart a deep though passionless love. I take him to have been the last man in the world to awaken or invite passion." Not Stoddard's kind of passion, at any rate.[30]

Louis wasn't disembodied, but he was shockingly emaciated. Someone who knew him at the time recalled, "He was a touching sight in those piteous days. His face was ghastly in its pallor, his clothes seemed to have been flung upon him, and his trousers and shoe tops disagreed by at least two inches. Men were seen to jump at the sound of his cough and to rub their eyes at the first sight of him."[31]

His friends back home were starting to realize that his condition was terrible, and began trying to lure him back with affection rather than hectoring. Shortly after Christmas this came from Gosse:

> Why do you write such letters to wring my heart? Here am I crying over your letter just received. It is too bad of you. Come straight back to us from that Monterey. You will be all right again on British ground. I cannot bear to think of you all alone in the midst of strangers, fretting and tiring yourself to pieces. Do come home. You don't know how glad we shall all be to see you, how delightfully dull and humdrum everything is here. We haven't the originality to think of dying. It's never done here, in our set. I hate you for making me so miserable.

A bit earlier Louis had written, "Your kind letter, coming when it did, was an act of friendship of far greater importance than you could have dreamed when you wrote. It is the history of our kindnesses that alone makes this world tolerable."[32]

In happier moods Louis enjoyed what he called in one of his stories "the draughty, rowdy city of San Francisco," whose sights included a street lined with brothels—"little houses, rather impudently painted, and offering to the eye of the observer this diagnostic peculiarity, that the huge brass plates upon the small and highly-coloured doors bore only the first names of ladies—Norah or Lily or Florence."[33]

He was happily picking up Americanisms, and when they got into his correspondence some British friends were shocked. Walter Ferrier told a sister who was about to visit America, "One thing you must steadily avoid—*don't become a Yankee!* Louis Stevenson is a vile Yankee now, I suppose—he doesn't talk about being 'ill,' but says he, 'I have been very *sick*'—can you vomit?" In British usage "being sick" does mean vomiting.[34]

Cut off from any subsidy from his parents, Louis was desperate to sell his writing for whatever he could get. He thought newspaper journalism might be promising, since San Francisco had six dailies and three weeklies, but so far as is known he only sold a couple of short pieces. At this point he told Baxter to sell off most of his books that were still at Heriot Row, and when Colvin offered a loan to tide him over, he replied, "You don't understand; this is a test. I must support myself, at what rate I have still to see." He was excited when "The Pavilion on the Links" was accepted by Leslie Stephen, and wrote to Henley, "That was good news. The Dooke de Korneel, K.C.B., taken a blood and thunder!" That expression apparently meant that this story was more melodramatic, if not exactly blood and thunder, than his previous work. "Korneel" was the *Cornhill;* K.C.B. stands for Knight Commander of the Bath, an honor Stephen didn't hold, though in 1902 it would in fact be conferred.[35]

In those days Oakland, where Fanny was living, was thinly settled. There were as yet no improved roads or sidewalks, and quite ordinary houses might have extensive gardens and grounds. The photograph (fig. 42) shows Fanny on the vine-covered porch, with a glimpse of the garden she loved to cultivate; Belle later wrote, "Of all the lovely gardens she left in her trail through life, I think the one at East Oakland was the most gorgeous." Fanny also set up a rifle range.[36]

A dairyman who had been a neighbor recalled,

> The Osbournes were nice people. We all liked Sam—he was a smart, refined, pleasant gentleman, always ready to stop and talk. His wife we didn't know so well. She spent lots of time in her studio—a little dark rather foreign-looking lady. Stevenson came there as any other visitor would come to any other home. He was very sick at first, and Mrs. Osbourne took care of him. When he began to improve we often saw him about the place. He walked in the garden, keeping to himself. We knew that Sam and his wife weren't happy; that he was mixed up with a woman in San Francisco. Well, seems like his wife fell in love with Stevenson. They got married and moved away. That's how things work out sometimes.[37]

In the spring of 1880 Louis experienced an attack of illness so frightening that Fanny abandoned discretion and took him in, shocking though that must

42. Fanny at her Oakland cottage

have been to conventional proprieties. For the first time he coughed up blood, which would happen repeatedly in the years to come. When he was recovering he wrote to Gosse, "I have been very, very sick; on the verge of a galloping consumption, cold sweats, fever, and all the ugliest circumstances of the disease; and I have cause to bless God, and my wife that is to be, and one Dr. Bamford (a name the Muse repels) that I have come out of all this, and got my feet once more upon a little hilltop, with a fair prospect of life and some new desire of living."[38]

He began writing in earnest again, and in the afternoons would read aloud what he had done that morning. As Nellie recalled, "While we sat in a circle, listening in appreciative silence, he nervously paced the room, reading aloud in his full sonorous voice—a voice that always seemed remarkable in so frail a man—his face flushed and his manner embarrassed, for far from being overconfident about his work, he always seemed to feel a sort of shy anxiety lest it should not be up to the mark."

When especially fatigued he preferred to dictate to Nellie. "He had a habit of walking up and down the room, his pace growing faster and faster as his enthusiasm rose. We feared that this was not very good for him, so we quietly devised a scheme to prevent it, without his knowledge, by hemming him in with tables and chairs, so that each time he sprang up to walk he sank back discouraged at the sight of the obstructions."[39]

Louis also got to know Fanny's closest friends, Dora and Virgil Williams. Virgil was director of the California School of Design (today the San Francisco Art Institute), where both Fanny and Belle had studied, and Dora was an artist. Her sketch of Fanny at this time (fig. 43) is more affecting than any of the photographs we have.

Dora left a description of Louis when Fanny brought him to meet them. "While we were earnestly talking, and Stevenson had for the moment paused in his walk and was leaning his slight figure on the mantelpiece, my husband came in and glanced at him very curiously. I hastened to introduce them to each other. He afterwards told me that he thought some tramp had got into the room and I could not get him out, so peculiar and foreign was the appearance of my visitor. From that hour, however, they became fast friends."[40]

A year later, when Louis and Fanny were married and living in Scotland, he wrote to Virgil: "If there was ever a place where I most needed friends it was San Francisco, for there I was sick, sad and poor; and if ever I found friends equal to my need it was in you and your wife, whose house was made a home to me in the worst hours of my life. No one but myself can ever know how much I suffered; and so none can tell how opportune were the confidence, the welcome, and the unwearying, invariable friendship that I had from you and Mrs. Williams."[41]

Louis's parents had stayed in touch with Baxter and Colvin, who finally made them understand their son's precarious condition. Equally important, they made it clear that he would soon marry Fanny and not just live with her. Thomas now wrote to Louis, "I had entirely misunderstood the present state of matters, which if Colvin was correct gives of course a very different aspect to it.

43. Fanny, sketched by Dora Williams

The actors have apparently changed their positions from what I had supposed, and certainly materially for the better."[42]

Soon after this Louis was able to report to Colvin, "My dear people telegraphed me in these words: 'Count on 250 pounds annually.' You may imagine what a blessed business this was." He added that he had doggedly written *The Amateur Emigrant* "in a circle of hell unknown to Dante, that of the penniless and dying author. For dying I was, although now saved. Another week, the doctor said, and I should have been past salvation." The sum of £250 a year would be enough to live on without other income, and as Jenni Calder says, "It meant more than just money, it meant his father's blessing."[43]

With money to spend, he could finally do something about his teeth, which were giving so much trouble that he decided to have them all extracted—not uncommon at a time when dental hygiene was often ignored. He mentioned almost casually to Baxter that he would postpone marriage briefly for that reason: "I am waiting till I get in my new teeth—the old ones having been gently removed with a pair of pliers." The new ones wouldn't work out well, and three years later he would report to his mother from France, "I had to get a new plate of teeth; my mouth was in a dreadful state. It was horrid costly but could not be helped."[44]

For the wedding Louis and Fanny were careful to choose a Presbyterian minister, William Anderson Scott, who performed the ceremony at his San Francisco home. His marriage registry records:

> Married by me at my residence 19th May 1880, Robert Louis Stevenson, born in Edinburgh, Scotland, white, single, 30 years old, resides in Oakland, California.
> Fannie Osbourne, born in Indianapolis, Indiana, 40 years, widowed, white, resides in Oakland.

Margaret Mackay comments, "It is touching that Fanny, though bravely admitting to forty years, lost courage and described herself as 'widow.'" But perhaps the Reverend Scott would have refused to marry a divorcée.[45]

A formal portrait of Fanny was made at this time (fig. 44), with her unruly hair carefully dressed under a ladylike hat and (as in the Williams sketch) wearing a cross. In photographs she always did look solemn.

The newlyweds entered this union with their eyes open. A fragmentary essay that Louis drafted in San Francisco shows deep understanding of the relationship they were now confirming.

> In all our daring, magnanimous human way of life, I find nothing more bold than this. To go into battle is but a small thing by comparison. It is the last act of committal. After that, there is no way left, not even suicide, but to be a good man. She will help you, let us pray. And yet she is in the same case; she, too, has daily made shipwreck of her own happiness and worth; it is with a courage no less irrational than yours that she also ventures on this new experiment of life. Two who have failed severally now join their fortunes with a wavering hope.[46]

Biographers have suggested that Fanny was lucky to get Louis, but the reverse was equally true. He commented a year later that she had married him

44. Fanny at the time of her marriage

"when I was a mere complication of cough and bones, much fitter for an emblem of mortality than a bridegroom." Nellie said that "she married him when his fortunes, both in health and finances, were at their lowest ebb, and she took this step in the almost certain conviction that in a few months at least she would be a widow. The best that she hoped for was to make his last days as comfortable and happy as possible."[47]

Fanny certainly didn't imagine that she was uniting herself with a future celebrity. "She married Louis," Belle said, "not expecting that he would live, but hoping by her devotion to prolong this life now so dear to her. Though she admired his work, she had no idea he would ever become famous." In fact his later achievements had much to do not just with Fanny's belief in him, but with her intelligent criticism and advice. Nellie also said, "Her profound faith in his genius before the rest of the world had come to recognize it had a great deal to do with keeping up his faith in himself."[48]

Belle added a moving reminiscence: "I remember coming through the hall, and stopping suddenly at a light joyous sound. With a catch at my heart, I realized it was the first time I had ever heard my mother laugh." As Nellie commented in quoting this, Belle never grasped until then "what a sad and bitter life Fanny Osbourne's had been."[49]

More than any of Louis's biographers, Richard Holmes does justice to this remarkable union. "When one considers other Victorian literary marriages—Hardy's, say, or Dickens's—Stevenson's is something phenomenal, dynamic, explosive. It contained energies, tempests, fireworks, and sheer anarchic excitement that would have obliterated any conventional household. To find anything like his relationship with Fanny—and the comparison is significant in the largest way—one would have to look forward to Lawrence and Frieda."[50]

HONEYMOON IN A MINING CAMP

Shortly before the marriage Louis had written to Colvin, "My health: I am now out of danger; in but a short while (i.e. as soon as the weather is settled) F. and I marry and go up to the hills to look for a place; 'I to the hills will lift mine eyes, from whence doth come mine aid.'" That was from the Scots metrical version of Psalm 121.[51]

The hills meant the Sierras, where the mountain air would be healthier for Louis than the fogs of San Francisco. Virgil and Dora Williams had a country place—they called it a ranch—on the flank of Mt. Saint Helena, seventy miles north of the city, and they encouraged the newlyweds to go there. Accompanied by Lloyd, they traveled by train to Calistoga, whose name was a combination of "California" and "Saratoga"; its hot springs reminded people of Saratoga Springs in New York.

Louis took a great interest in Napa wines, which were just getting established, and also had his first experience of the recently invented telephone. When he asked to meet a celebrated stagecoach driver named Clark Foss he was told that Foss was out of town but that they could still talk.

> Next moment, I had one instrument at my ear, another at my mouth, and found myself, with nothing in the world to say, conversing with a

man several miles off among desolate hills. Foss rapidly and somewhat plaintively brought the conversation to an end, and returned to his night's grog at Fossville while I strolled forth again on Calistoga high street. But it was an odd thing that here, on what we are accustomed to consider the very skirts of civilization, I should have used the telephone for the first time in my civilized career. So it goes in these young countries; telephones, and telegraphs, and newspapers, and advertisements running far ahead among the Indians and the grizzly bears.

That comes from the book that resulted from the stay, *The Silverado Squatters*.[52]

In Calistoga they became friendly with the storekeeper, a Russian Jew named Morris Friedberg to whom Stevenson gave the alias Kelmar in his book. Everyone was in debt to Kelmar, and he exploited that fact to keep selling them goods that would get them even deeper in debt. Here as elsewhere Stevenson showed no sign of antisemitism. "The village usurer," he wrote, "is not so sad a feature of humanity and human progress as the millionaire manufacturer, fattening on the toil and loss of thousands, and yet declaiming from the platform against the greed and dishonesty of landlords." He commented that Kelmar "had something of the expression of a Scotch country elder, who by some peculiarity should chance to be a Hebrew." Years later, responding to some comment by a friend, he said, "What a strange idea, to think me a Jew-hater! Isaiah and David and Heine are good enough for me; and I leave more unsaid. Were I of Jew blood, I do not think I could ever forgive the Christians; the ghettos would get in my nostrils like mustard or lit gunpowder."[53]

With Kelmar's help they identified a place on the mountainside where they could live rent-free in an abandoned miners' bunkhouse. Until recently mercury and silver had been extracted there, and a briefly thriving town was given the optimistic name of Silverado, but the vein of ore was played out and the miners were gone.

Louis peered through chinks in the wall of an abandoned mill in the town.

It stands deserted, like the temple of a forgotten religion, the busy millers toiling somewhere else. All the time we were there, mill and mill town showed no sign of life. That part of the mountainside, which is very open and green, was tenanted by no living creature but ourselves and the insects, and nothing stirred but the cloud manufactory upon the mountain summit. It was odd to compare this with the former days, when the engine was in full blast, the mill palpitating to its strokes, and the carts came rattling down from Silverado, charged with ore.[54]

They moved into a vacant shack with one room on top of another on the side of a cliff. Behind it was a tunnel that would serve them as refrigerator and wine cellar. "There were four of us squatters—myself and my wife, the King and Queen of Silverado; Sam, the Crown Prince; and Chuchu, the Grand Duke." Fanny's son, twelve years old by now, was still going by the name he shared with his father, but he would soon prefer his middle name and be known thenceforth as Lloyd. As for the Grand Duke, a setter crossed with spaniel, "he was the most unsuited for a rough life. He had been nurtured tenderly in the society of ladies; his heart was large and soft; he regarded the sofa cushion as a bedrock necessary of existence. Though about the size of a sheep, he loved to sit in ladies' laps; he never said a bad word in all his blameless days; and if he had seen a flute, I am sure he could have played upon it by nature. It may seem hard to say it of a dog, but Chuchu was a tame cat."[55]

There were two rows of miners' bunks in the abandoned shack, and they piled hay for cushioning into the ones they would use. A visit from Belle and her husband produced a drawing by Joe that was subsequently engraved as frontispiece for *The Silverado Squatters* (fig. 45). Louis is shown reclining and writing while Fanny is sewing. The table was the only conventional item of furniture; they sat on trunks and packing cases. It's evident that the bunk Louis is on has been widened to accommodate Fanny as well. Since she was the one who did the carpentry (he tended to hit the nail on the thumb), that was presumably her handiwork. There's an open suitcase on the floor full of books, one of which has been carelessly dropped. Beneath the table is a pair of shoes; they went barefoot whenever possible. At the bottom, in deliberate imitation of the *Inland Voyage* frontispiece, a cherubic wine god nestles among Napa grapes and gazes apprehensively at a tangle of rattlesnakes.

Louis had a dim view of Belle's husband, and mentioned him in the book without actually naming him. "We brought with us a painter guest, who proved to be a most good-natured comrade and a capital hand at an omelet." Joe's good nature would never be in question, but his fecklessness and infidelities would eventually end the marriage.[56]

This casual reference comes immediately before a romantic re-creation of sense experience in a chapter entitled "A Starry Drive."

> I have never seen such a night. It seemed to throw calumny in the teeth of all the painters that ever dabbled in starlight. The sky itself was of a ruddy, powerful, nameless, changing colour, dark and glossy like a serpent's back. The stars, by innumerable millions, stuck boldly forth like

45. *The Silverado Squatters,* frontispiece

> lamps. The Milky Way was bright, like a moonlit cloud; half heaven seemed milky way. The greater luminaries shone each more clearly than a winter's moon. Their light was dyed in every sort of colour—red, like fire; blue, like steel; green, like the tracks of sunset; and so sharply did each stand forth in its own lustre that there was no appearance of that flat, star-spangled arch we know so well in pictures, but all the hollow of heaven was one chaos of contesting luminaries—a hurly-burly of stars.

That is not painterly depiction, but re-creation of emotion. Or not painterly in a conventional sense; Louis never saw a Van Gogh.

Relishing adventure, he was impressed by ubiquitous rattlesnakes and claimed to be not frightened.

> The place abounded with rattlesnakes—the rattlesnake's nest, it might have been named. Wherever we brushed among the bushes, our passage woke their angry buzz. One dwelt habitually in the wood pile, and sometimes, when we came for firewood, thrust up his small head between two logs and hissed at the intrusion. The rattle has a legendary credit; it is said to be awe-inspiring, and, once heard, to stamp itself for ever in the memory. But the sound is not at all alarming; the hum of many insects and the buzz of the wasp convince the ear of danger quite as readily. As a matter of fact, we lived for weeks in Silverado, coming and going, with rattles sprung on every side, and it never occurred to us to be afraid. I used to take sun baths and do calisthenics in a certain pleasant nook among azalea and calcanthus, the rattles whizzing on every side like spinning-wheels.[57]

If that sounds implausible, it should. Nellie, who knew California much better than Louis did, suggested that "he often mistook the buzzing noise made by locusts, or some other insect, for the rattle of the snakes." She also commented, "The old bunkhouse seemed to me an incredibly uncomfortable place of residence."

It amused Nellie to hear him practicing his Americanisms.

> One day Louis came in with his pockets full of twenty dollar gold pieces, with which he had supplied himself for the journey. He thought this piece of money the handsomest coin in the world, and said it made a man feel rich merely to handle it. In a jesting mood, he drew the coins from his pockets, threw them on the table, whence they rolled right and left on the floor, and said: "Just look! I'm simply lousy wid money!"[58]

The only neighbors were a hunter named Rufe Hanson, his wife, and her brother. Louis was greatly impressed by Rufe. "He was fit for any society but that of fools. Quiet as he was, there burned a deep, permanent excitement in his dark blue eyes, and when this grave man smiled, it was like sunshine in a shady place." That could never have been said of Rufe's brother-in-law, who did odd jobs and always did them badly. Pondering this complacent dolt roused Louis to extended analysis:

> His clumsy utterance, his rude embarrassed manner, set a fresh value on the stupidity of his remarks. I do not think I ever appreciated the meaning of two words until I knew Irvine—the verb *loaf,* and the noun *oaf;* between them they complete his portrait. He could lounge, and wriggle, and rub himself against the wall, and grin, and be more in everybody's way than any other two people that I ever set my eyes on. . . . Above all things, he was delighted with himself. You would not have thought it, from his uneasy manners and troubled, struggling utterance, but he loved himself to the marrow, and was happy and proud like a peacock on a rail. He had the soul of a fat sheep, but regarded as an artist's model, the exterior of a Greek god.[59]

A chance meeting with a fellow Scot inspired home thoughts.

> Of all mysteries of the human heart, this is perhaps the most inscrutable. There is no special loveliness in that gray country, with its rainy, sea-beat archipelago; its fields of dark mountains; its unsightly places, black with coal; its treeless, sour, unfriendly looking corn lands; its quaint, gray, castled city, where the bells clash of a Sunday, and the wind squalls, and the salt showers fly and beat. I do not even know if I desire to live there; but let me hear, in some far land, a kindred voice sing out, "Oh, why left I my hame?" and it seems at once as if no beauty under the kind heavens, and no society of the wise and good, can repay me for my absence from my country.[60]

From Calistoga Fanny sent a carefully calculated letter to the mother-in-law she had yet to meet. Apologizing for not having written sooner, she explains that she has been suffering from a series of illnesses, including blood poisoning caused by a bout of diphteria; she probably understood that appealing to health problems was a way to ingratiate herself with the elder Stevensons. She then comments on coping with her husband's illnesses: "Taking care of Louis is, as you must know, very like angling for sly trout; one must understand when to pay out the line, and exercise the greatest caution in drawing him in." To this she adds a compliment: "I am sure, now, that he is on the high road to recovery and health, and I believe that his best medicine will be the meeting with you and his father, for whom he pines like a child." And finally, she comments that the photograph of her that had been sent to Margaret was unflattering—"unfortunately all photographs of me are"—but "Louis thinks me, and to him I believe I am, the most beautiful creature in the world. It is because he loves me that he thinks that, so I am very glad."[61]

Though the stay at Silverado provided enough material for a book, it was over in less than two months. The family arrived in early June and were back in San Francisco before the end of July. Many years later a writer interviewed old-timers who remembered Louis, but she didn't learn much. One man had driven Louis up from Calistoga in a wagon, "and I says to him, 'What the hell's your hurry?' Didn't seem to me he had so much to do that we had to race up the mountain. Fact is, I thought him kind of a fool, livin' in that old shack awritin' books. I didn't think he was hardly as smart as I."

Equally unhelpful was a rancher's daughter:

> I was just a youngster, but I can see Mr. Stevenson now, sitting on our front porch talking with my father and mother. How he squinted his black eyes and looked me up and down! I was one of those long-legged skinny little girls that would get self-conscious at the least little thing. His looking at me so hard gave me the creeps; I remember to this day how I felt. I refused to talk to him or eat dinner with him. Can you beat that?[62]

Today the area is the site of Robert Louis Stevenson State Park, and a trail to the summit passes by the site of the shack, which was demolished long ago.

Now that Louis and his parents were reconciled, it was time to return to Scotland, and he left San Francisco by train with Fanny and Lloyd on July 29. On August 7 in New York they embarked on the Royal Mail liner *City of Chester* for Liverpool, traveling first class thanks to the elder Stevensons' generosity. It was exactly one year since he had left Glasgow for New York.

CHAPTER 16

Edinburgh and Davos

MEETING THE PARENTS

On August 17, 1880, the *City of Chester* docked in Liverpool. Thomas and Margaret Stevenson were there to welcome the newlyweds, and also Sidney Colvin, who had decided on impulse to join them. This first meeting between Fanny and Louis's parents could not have gone better. "She made an immediate conquest of them," Colvin wrote later, "especially of that character so richly compounded between the stubborn and the tender, the humorous and the grim, his father." It was fortunate that although Thomas Stevenson was a staunch Tory, he held the unusual belief, as Louis described it, that there ought to be a law "under which any woman might have a divorce for the asking, and no man on any ground whatever." As for Louis's health, Colvin added, it had clearly improved, and "he didn't seem to me a bit like a dying man in spite of everything."[1]

At Heriot Row, Margaret—who was only ten years older than her new daughter-in-law—wrote in her diary, "Fanny fitted into our household from the first. It was quite amusing how entirely she agreed with my husband on all subjects, even to the looking on the dark side of most things, while Louis and I were more inclined to take the cheery view." Thomas was definitely taken with Fanny, and not just because she was making an effort to be ingratiating. Her perspective was more sober, even at times more gloomy, than Louis's determined optimism, and Thomas started calling her by the pet name Cassandra.[2]

Fanny herself wrote to Dora Williams,

> I am glad to say that Louis's father and mother and all relations like me, and I like them. His mother, I am sure, plays dolls with me. She buys everything she can in shops for me, and is continually searching in drawers and boxes for things of her own to give me. When everything else is exhausted she puts on her dressing gown and has a good time trying her own things upon me from jewelry to caps, just as a child plays with a doll. Speaking of clothes I amused myself while the rest were at church by looking through Louis's wardrobe. I found a room filled with every manner of garment that a man could possibly wear under any circumstances, and some too gorgeous to wear at all.

She understood, of course, that Louis wore disreputable clothes as a rebellion against his upbringing and class. It's interesting also that although she had been raised a Presbyterian, she didn't feel obligated to accompany the family to church.[3]

Fanny's affection for Thomas was unfeigned, and forty years later she would write, "I shall always believe that something unusual and great was lost to the world in Thomas Stevenson. One could almost see the struggle between the creature of cramped hereditary conventions and environment, and the man nature had intended him to be. Fortunately for my husband, he inherited from his tragic father his genius and wide humanity alone. The natural gaiety of Margaret Stevenson, who lived as a bird lives, for the very joy of it, she passed down to her son." That's generous but perhaps not entirely accurate. Louis inherited both temperaments, the tragic depth as well as the joy in living.[4]

Fanny understood right away that frankness on her part would be appreciated. Her grandson Austin remembered her account of the very first dinner at Heriot Row: "Finding the roast overdone, [Thomas] lost his temper and shouted at the maids, crinkling in their starched aprons. His daughter in law rose from her chair, her face white and her eyes big with wrath, for nothing roused her fury more than injustice. 'You are a spoiled old man,' she said in a voice like water running under ice. 'You are taking a cruel advantage of these helpless people who cannot answer back. If you ever again raise your voice against these faithful women I shall instantly leave this house and never set foot in it as long as I live!'" Although Fanny was capable of overdramatizing her stories, this probably reflects what did happen (Austin borrowed the water under ice from something Louis once said). "Nonplused, the old man stared at her in admiration. 'Sit ye doon, lassie,' he said, laughing. 'I see ye're a stormy petrel!' From then on peace reigned."[5]

Fourteen years later, in Samoa, Fanny found a poem "to my wife, on her birthday" pinned to her mosquito netting in the morning. It was entitled "To the Stormy Petrel." A seabird that was believed to make an appearance during storms, the term was applied to a person who enjoys conflict.[6]

Louis may well have approved of her outburst at dinner. Years earlier he told Frances Sitwell that he was ashamed of having been rude to a servant at the table: "Nothing can be more disgusting than for a man to speak harshly to a young woman who will lose her place if she speak back to him." He added that it took him four days to apologize "because I was doing a thing that would be called ridiculous in thus apologizing. I did not know I had so much respect of middle-class notions before; this is my right hand which I must cut off. Hold the arm please."[7]

Rosaline Masson remembered that Thomas was fond of telling Fanny, "I doot ye're a besom"—a broom made of rough twigs. Masson explained, "The word applied to a woman indicates that she is somewhat tart in temper, and what might be described as 'a handful.'" After one of Louis's uncles met Fanny he said, "Yes, Louis, you have done well. I married a besom myself and have never regretted it."[8]

An important development was relief from financial anxiety. It was made clear that the promised £250 per year would often be supplemented; it was a minimum, not a maximum. Eventually, when Louis's books became popular, he would have an impressive income of his own, but during the 1880s it was critical to count on continued support.

At this time Walter Simpson gave them a black Skye terrier, called at first Wattie in Walter's honor, later Woggs, and eventually and mysteriously Bogue. He was much loved and would make frequent appearances in Louis's correspondence from then on, though his friends didn't share his fondness. Graham Balfour said that Woggs was "entirely devoted to his master and mistress, and at odds with the world at large"; Colvin described him as "the most engaging, petted, ill-conducted and cajoling little thorough-bred rascal of his race."[9]

With a harsh winter in prospect, it was time to think of a better climate for Louis's health. He had already experienced the pure, dry air of Silverado, and the destination now was to be Davos in the Swiss Alps, a favored retreat for people known to be "lungy." It had been urgently recommended by his uncle George Balfour, the family physician, who suspected tuberculosis. In fact doctors would always have trouble deciding what was wrong with his health, and Henley told him later, "All you seem to get from your doctors is long words and permission to travel."[10]

On the way to the Continent they stopped off in London, where they inevitably exhausted their funds. The ever-tolerant Colvin wrote to Baxter to join him in helping out, and commented, "I find those absurd Louis's have in the innocence of their hearts been spending more money than they knew (imagine taking the best of quarters at the Grosvenor Hotel) and haven't got anything like money to take them to Davos." Baxter immediately sent £40, but in France a week later Louis wrote to his father that the Grosvenor had charged £46 and they were broke once again. His tone implied that the shortfall was inexplicable, but Fanny added in a postscript, "It was foolish to go to so dear a hotel, but I knew nothing about English hotels and did not begin to suspect it for a day or two; by that time Louis was so hunted to death by fiends slightly disguised as friends that he hadn't the strength of mind to move."[11]

"MY ALPINE EXILE"

Davos is well known today for its ski resort and the World Economic Forum, and for Thomas Mann's 1924 novel *The Magic Mountain,* but in those days it was just beginning to be developed, and has been described as nothing more than "a dismal health resort." Known properly as Davos-Platz—"Davos Place," as opposed to Davos Burg down below—it is located in the Grisons in eastern Switzerland, at an altitude of one mile.[12]

Louis had romantic feelings about Edinburgh and the Scottish Highlands, and loved the climate and scenery of the Riviera and California. He never felt that way about Switzerland, which at an earlier time he had called "the place of my pet abhorrence." In a poem sent to a friend in Venice he imagined "sea-grey lagoons, sea-paven highways, / Dear to me here in my Alpine exile."[13]

A photograph taken a couple of decades later (fig. 46) conveys the bleakness of the scene. The mountains, barren in summer and icy in winter, struck Louis as picturesque in the most boringly conventional way: "The Alps are very carefully made, with a view to strong effect; they are quite a success." The Landwasser that flows through the town was likewise boring—"Still hurry, hurry, to the end, / Good God, is that the way to run?"[14]

Germ theory was a very recent development, just beginning to gain acceptance. If disease was indeed transmitted through the air by microscopic organisms, then it might follow that cold dry air was the safest environment to avoid contagion or, if already infected, to manage the disease. In *Illness as Metaphor* Susan Sontag explains, "There was a notion that tuberculosis was a wet disease, a disease of humid and dank cities. The inside of the body became damp ('mois-

46. Davos

ture in the lungs' was a favored locution) and had to be dried out. Doctors advised travel to high, dry places—the mountains, the desert."[15]

The pulmonary specialist at Davos was Dr. Karl Ruedi. Louis liked him immensely, and Lloyd mentioned one reason why: "The doctor, who had learnt his fluent English in Colorado, could change in a moment from cultured French to this strange, nasal jargon and all its racy frontier idiom."[16]

After a week Louis wrote to his parents that he had received a preliminary diagnosis. "Ruedi says I have chronic pneumonia, infiltration and a bronchitic tendency; also spleen enlarged; says I am just the party [i.e., type] for Davos." Specialists often doubted that he actually had tuberculosis. As previously mentioned, it's possible that he suffered from a different lung condition that was hereditary rather than infectious, but a physician who has studied the evidence says, "The exact diagnosis is less important than the way the illness was perceived by Stevenson, by his family, and by the many doctors who treated him."[17]

The routine prescribed by Ruedi was unexciting in the extreme. "I have a glass of milk in bed half past six, but never, in fact, much before seven; breakfast with meat between seven and eight; one smoke; work nine to eleven; eleven, glass of milk; eleven to one, out; lunch; (one smoke) to three, out; four to five, work (if I like, I never have liked); six, dinner (one smoke); half past nine, bed, after another glass of milk. It's like a Trappist monastery, only too much food instead of too little."

Before long Louis quietly made up the deficiency of tobacco and alcohol. Fanny, meanwhile, was obeying a different regimen. "She eats meat, meat, meat; and drinks wine, wine, wine. No bread, no butter, no soup, no potatoes, nothing that she likes at all. He said she was threatened with OBESITY. This word is like a dart through her liver."[18]

By now Louis was frequently coughing up blood, and he sometimes referred to his affliction as "my old friend Bluidy Jack." In December he wrote to Henley to complain about garbled proofs of an article: "Your printer is a bloody insolent dog, whom I could smite on the mouth. Who is he to alter my punctuation? I made two tablespoonfuls of bad blood over the bitch." The fussiness about punctuation is characteristic, and so is the grim precision of "two tablespoonfuls."[19]

A few months later Louis told Henley glumly that he had become "a professional sickist." That makes it all the more impressive that he never lost his eagerness for experience. Chesterton commented, "Of all human things the search for health is the most unhealthy. And it is truly a great glory to Stevenson that he, almost alone among men, could go on pursuing his bodily health without once losing his mental health."[20]

In his unquenchable enthusiasm for life, Louis was defying the stereotype of the "consumptive," who as Sontag describes it would alternate between hectic energy and lassitude, and would be gradually self-consumed until an early death. Often this was idealized as a spiritual transfiguration, but that was no consolation for people who had simply contracted an incurable bacterial infection. After antibiotics did cure tuberculosis, the metaphorical typecasting moved on to cancer. In Sontag's view, "The healthiest way of being ill is the one most purified of, most resistant to, metaphoric thinking." Louis defied typecasting, and succeeded magnificently.[21]

He did have a different kind of anxiety, as Fanny explained in a postscript to one of his letters home, and that was a threat of psychic breakdown. "Louis is learning to be very sedate and quiet, and does not give way to excitability about small things so much. I know it distressed his father, who thought it like his Uncle Alan. He thought so himself, and has been trying with a great deal of success to master it."[22]

Understandably, Fanny herself was experiencing stress, and in March she went to Paris to consult doctors about puzzling symptoms of her own. Louis wrote to his mother, "I have a notion there is a good deal of nervousness in her

47. Veranda of a Davos hotel

ill health." That meant neurosis, which was then thought to be a disease of the nerves.[23]

Claire Harman says that the pair of them were always "hysterically alert to each other's mortality," but considering how serious their illnesses sometimes were, and how little understood by doctors at the time, that seems excessive. Fanny experienced alarming heart palpitations whenever she lived at high altitude, as well as rheumatism, gall bladder attacks, and liver trouble. The medicines that were prescribed generally did more harm than good.[24]

Life in the Davos hotels was dull; a photograph (fig. 47) shows patients heavily bundled up on a porch open to the frigid air. Some people did try to have fun, as Lloyd remembered: "The uncertain tenure of life engendered recklessness even in the staidest. There were wild love affairs, tempestuous jealousies, cliques and coteries of the most belligerent description, and an endless amount of gossip and backbiting. The dead were whisked away very unobtrusively. People you had not seen for some time could usually be found in the cemetery."[25]

By now Louis felt free to discuss religion with his parents, more comfortably no doubt in writing than in person. He wrote to his mother the day after Christmas, "I wonder if you or my father ever thought of the obscurities that lie upon human duty from the negative form in which the ten commandments are stated; or how Christ was so continually substituting affirmatives. It is much more important to do right than not to do wrong. Faith is, not to believe the Bible, but to believe in God."

The ending of the letter is a touching expression of gratitude for their acceptance of Fanny. "I believe I have been only twice away before on Xmas. I am glad it comforts you to know me to be with my wife. I cannot tell you what a change it is to me; may God bless her, and spare us long in love to each other. I send you both my most affectionate love, except what I keep for my wife, and remain, your affectionate son, Robert Louis Stevenson." The signature may seem strangely formal, but he often signed letters to his parents "R.L.S."[26]

There was a prominent writer at Davos, the poet and critic John Addington Symonds, and Louis found him entertaining. In "Talk and Talkers" he described Symonds ("Opalstein") as "the best of talkers, singing the praises of the earth and the arts, flowers and jewels, wine and music, in a moonlight, serenading manner, as to the light guitar." They spent a good deal of time together, but Symonds was not an easy companion. Louis told Gosse that conversing with him was an "adventure in a thorn wood."[27]

Symonds was not impressed by Louis, who wasn't yet established as much of a writer. Symonds himself had published studies of Dante and the ancient Greek poets, and was now at work on his monumental seven-volume *Renaissance in Italy*. He wrote to a friend that the more he saw of Louis, "the less I find of solid mental stuff. He wants years of study in tough subjects. After all a university education has some merits. One feels a want of it in men like him." Symonds was a graduate of Balliol College, Oxford; apparently the University of Edinburgh didn't count as a real university.[28]

To be sure, Louis always admitted that there was some truth to that criticism. He once said, "I denied myself many opportunities; acting upon an extensive and highly rational system of truantry, which caused me a great deal of trouble to put in exercise—perhaps as much as would have taught me Greek—and sent me forth into the world and the profession of letters with the merest shadow of an education."²⁹

Lloyd confirmed that Symonds's attitude was wounding to Louis's self-confidence.

> The influence of such men—academic, and steeped in the classics—was always subtly harmful to Stevenson, who had what we would call now an inferiority complex when in contact with them. Their familiarity with the ancient Greeks and Romans seemed to emphasize his own sense of shortcoming; made him feel uneducated, and engaged in unimportant tasks; put him out of conceit with himself and his work. Even as a boy I could feel the veiled condescension Symonds had for him.

Lloyd added that if Symonds ever read *Treasure Island,* which he probably didn't, "I doubt if he would have found anything to admire in it, but rather a renewed concern that so brilliant and unschooled a mind should waste itself."³⁰

Symonds may also have felt the same kind of disappointment that Charles Warren Stoddard did in San Francisco. His wife was living with him at Davos, but he was well known to be homosexual; in the twentieth century his poems on that theme were published, with male pronouns restored in his translation of Michelangelo's love sonnets. He had also published *A Problem in Greek Ethics,* a pioneer study in gay history.

Louis didn't manage to do much writing at Davos, but as usual kept dreaming up projects, one of which was to be a major contribution to history. He wrote to his father, "There is a noble book to be written on the Highlands from then to now, social, religious and military. This book can be ready in a year and will pay as I go on, I hope. It will be solid and popular both, a vast stirring book to think of." He asked Thomas to send a large collection of historical sources, and even vowed to learn Gaelic (he never did). It was characteristic to imagine that a "vast stirring book" could be turned out in a single year, and characteristic also that it never got written. The reading was far from wasted, however. It would become the foundation of *Kidnapped* six years later, and still later of *Catriona, The Master of Ballantrae,* and *Weir of Hermiston.*³¹

Whenever he felt up to it, Louis attempted to enjoy outdoor recreations. In March 1881 he published an anonymous piece entitled "The Misgivings of Convalescence," which anyone who knew him would have recognized as deeply personal, but which was presented as the condition of "any phthisical young man." "Phthisis" was an old name for tuberculosis. The Riviera, he claimed to believe, was a "languorous land" that encouraged passivity, whereas "a man who puts his pleasure in activity, who desires a stirring life or none at all, will be certain to do better in the Alps. The continual, almost painful bracing [i.e., strengthening climate], the boisterous inclemencies, the rough pleasure of tobogganing, the doctor exciting him to be up and walking and to walk daily further, the glittering, unhomely landscape, the glare of day, the solemn splendours of the night, spur him to the gallop in his quest of health."[32]

He even took up tobogganing, writing to Baxter in the style of Alfred Jingle in Dickens's *Pickwick Papers*:

> Not been well; then been better; then double summersault, landing twice on crown of head, speed calculated forty-five miles an hour; consequent stiff neck and blasted depressing hemorrhage this morning. Otherwise cheery; wish I were a bird; seductive Rutherfords [their Edinburgh pub]; fifteen minutes talk, return, wish I were bird. Breathless style; unwillingness to write; wish were bird; sincerely yours R.L.S.
>
> It had better be explained that I am neither drunk nor mad; but only hideously lazy.[33]

There was a surprising visit at this time from Frances Sitwell, occasioned by a tragic development. At Cockfield Rectory, Louis and her young son Bertie had very much hit it off, and in a letter from California he asked, "How is Bert and what is he doing? Give him my love." Now, just half a year later, as he reported to his parents, "A telegram came from Mrs. Sitwell asking us to take rooms for herself and her son, as the latter had been ordered to Davos at once. He had been ill two weeks, she said, so imagine the shock when the carriage drove up and two men lifted out a ghastly dying boy."

The condition was diagnosed as "quick consumption," and it was especially distressing that "the poor boy has no idea that anything serious is wrong, and yet we know that any breath may be his last. His poor mother must sit by him and smile and talk of what they will do tomorrow, of ordering a toboggan for him, of the music he has brought with him, of the future that for him means perhaps a few hours, at the most a few days. The doctor has told her plainly what to expect."[34]

In a letter to Colvin, Louis admitted that he was so shocked by this crisis that he alternated between "a stiff disregard, and a kind of horror; sometimes I am brutally cynical and indifferent, sometimes (as last night) I get waked up by whiffs of intolerable dismay and agony.... It has helped to make me more conscious of the wolverine on my own shoulders, and that also makes me a poor judge and poor adviser." Less than three months after arriving Bertie died. Louis told his parents, "It seems strange that I should have suffered so much and be in a fair way to recovery and he, who suffered as good as nothing, should now be dead. His mother is wonderfully well, although absolutely dead-broke with fatigue. What a strange disease this phthisis is, it takes so many various forms and goes at such a varying speed."[35]

By now he was thoroughly fed up with Davos, and told Colvin, "I have not, I believe, remained so long in any one place as here in Davos. That tells on my old gipsy nature." In May he headed home, and on the way even Paris was depressing. To his parents he complained of "the exhalations of the most putrid city in the universe"; Fanny added in a postscript, "They did something to drains in the next house to us, and the typhoid germs leaped at my throat at once." In a letter to Fleeming Jenkin Louis called Paris "the temple of stenches; at night they make smells by steam; *awful* smells."[36]

After two weeks they left for London and then Scotland. It would turn out to be an exceptionally productive summer: *Treasure Island* would be conceived and partly written in what for Louis was record speed.

CHAPTER 17

A Breakthrough in the Highlands

"BABES IN THE WOOD"

The family, joined by Margaret Stevenson, would spend the next five months in Scotland, first at Pitlochry in Perthshire and then at Braemar in Aberdeenshire. When Louis and Fanny passed through London on their way, they struck friends who were there as naïve about money. Charles Baxter, who together with William Ernest Henley was becoming Louis's de facto business agent, wrote from Edinburgh to ask how they were managing, and Henley replied,

> [Fanny] is not extravagant—only careless and thriftless; she doesn't spend on herself at all. Louis is the same precisely, and as neither of them appears to think economy a practicable duty, or even the semblance of it a possible assumption, the money goes. What I want to say, my dear Charles, is this: *Don't allow yourself to dislike Mrs. S. more than you can help;* and if you are hard on either of them—as, professionally, you may chance to have to be—bear rather on Louis than on her.

What worried Henley most was not so much financial carelessness as mood swings.

> Louis, I am afraid, is not morally so strong as he used to be. His illness and his adventures together—and perhaps his marriage, I know not— seem, from what I can gather, to have a little sapped and weakened, and set up a process of degeneration in his moral fibre. Thus, he has terrible

fits of remorse and repentance, but he is lavish and thriftless all the same. You will have, therefore, to deal with a sick child, who is the husband of a schoolgirl of forty. You know at the best the said child was never easy to manage.[1]

A week later Henley reported to Baxter that although a doctor found Louis's lungs in good shape, his mental state seemed precarious.

> For the moment, though, his nerves are all to pieces. He is more the Spoiled Child then it is possible to say. And, for the time being, it will be well for you, *and for his father and mother,* to receive him with open arms. Make no references to coins [their usual term for money], and take all the care you can of him. He and I exchanged a few words on the subject of coins. I told him you were a little annoyed, and he was very remorseful. Nothing is more evident than that he is tolerably irresponsible.... He is curiously excitable and unstrung; emotion is always excessive with him, and any provocation to sentiment ought steadily to be avoided.
>
> What I hope, therefore, is this: that you'll make no change of any sort in your manner to him, but you'll content yourself for the moment with being better and more charming than ever; and that you'll see your way to advising *père et mère* to be the same, to avoid reproaches and regrets like poison, to ask no account of past days, and to make life at Braemar as quiet, as healthy, as uneventful, as studious for him as they possibly can.... And, another thing—be as kind and nice to Mrs. Louis as ever you can. I have seen much of her, and I have modified a good deal. I like her some, and I can't help pitying her much. My wife's feeling is the same....
>
> They are a couple of Babes in the Wood. *Voilà. C'est pas plus malin que ça* [it's no worse than that]. And, for the life of us, we can't venture for the moment on whipping their bottoms and sending them to bed.

Perhaps this was ungenerous, but Henley cared deeply about Louis and was learning to appreciate Fanny. He himself had to work extremely hard to make ends meet, and found it difficult to sympathize with somebody who could expect a parental bailout whenever he spent beyond his means.[2]

As for Fanny, she was no babe in the woods, but she was going along with what seemed to be the norm in this new environment. In Paris before she met Louis she had understood very well how to economize, even when her beloved son Hervey was dying, but for now she was in no position to take charge.

RAIN, MORE RAIN, AND THREE STORIES

They reached Pitlochry on June 2 and rented a farmhouse called Kinnaird Cottage. Margaret stayed with them, as did Lloyd, and Thomas visited whenever he could get away from his work in Edinburgh. Unfortunately the weather was terrible, and threatened to undo the improvement in health that Louis had made at Davos. "Scots accustomed to dreary weather," Gavin Bell remarks, "are fond of joking that they consider themselves lucky if summer falls on a weekend."[3]

Louis tried to be optimistic, but he had a persistent cold that was accompanied by hemorrhages. He wrote to Colvin, "If I could but heal me of my bellowses, I could have a jolly life—have it, even now, when I can work and stroll a little, as I have been doing till this cold. I have so many things to make life sweet to me, it seems a pity I cannot have that one other thing—health."[4]

Unexpectedly, the impulse to write fiction revived. Louis and Fanny began amusing themselves by writing Gothic tales and reading them aloud. During the two months at Pitlochry he completed no fewer than three stories, two of which are among his very best.

"The Pavilion on the Links," already mentioned, was set in Scotland but could have been in almost any seaside location. Now he turned seriously to his own country and its past, which had fascinated him from his earliest days.

"The Body Snatcher" was the first of the three stories, and in his own opinion the least successful. It was based on real events, a series of crimes that occurred back in 1828. At a time when it was difficult for medical teachers to acquire cadavers for dissection, a lecturer named Robert Knox became the favorite customer of a pair of "resurrectionists," William Burke and William Hare, who furnished bodies for his demonstrations in a lecture hall. After he bought sixteen cadavers it emerged that far from dying of natural causes, they had been murdered by suffocation.

At the trial Hare turned king's evidence—in effect a plea bargain—and Burke was hanged. Appropriately, his own corpse was publicly dissected, and his skeleton is still on view in the Anatomical Museum of the Edinburgh Medical School. As for Knox, it was never proved that he knew how the cadavers had been obtained, but his career was ruined and he left Edinburgh soon afterward.

What fascinated Louis in this story was the symbiosis between respectable professionalism and the criminal underworld. In "The Body Snatcher," the medical lecturer employs a pair of assistants to obtain cadavers. One of them, Macfarlane, is coolly indifferent to the likelihood that these were victims of murder.

The other, Fettes, exclaims, "Hell, God, Devil, right, wrong, sin, crime, and all the old gallery of curiosities—they may frighten boys, but men of the world, like you and me, despise them." All the same, Fettes has a conscience, which he drowns in alcohol. "For his day of work he indemnified himself by nights of roaring, blackguardly enjoyment; and when that balance had been struck, the organ that he called his conscience declared itself content."

One night they pull back the covering from a newly delivered corpse, believing it to be that of a recently deceased prostitute, and recognize instead a man named Gray, who long before had threatened to blackmail them and was murdered by Macfarlane himself. Now he reappears as a revenant to accuse them. "A wild yell rang up into the night; each leaped from his own side into the roadway: the lamp fell, broke, and was extinguished; and the horse, terrified by this unusual commotion, bounded and went off toward Edinburgh at a gallop, bearing along with it, sole occupant of the gig, the body of the dead and long-dissected Gray."

That's how the story ends, but we have been prepared for it by a previous encounter that we couldn't understand until now. Long after this terrifying reappearance of Gray, Macfarlane and Fettes meet by chance in an English pub. Fearing exposure, Macfarlane offers to buy his silence, but Fettes spurns him with contempt. At this point, seeing other customers staring at him,

> Macfarlane made a dart like a serpent, striking for the door. But his tribulation was not yet entirely at an end, for even as he was passing Fettes clutched him by the arm and these words came in a whisper, and yet painfully distinct, "Have you seen it again?" The great rich London doctor cried out aloud with a sharp, throttling cry; he dashed his questioner across the open space, and, with his hands over his head, fled out of the door like a detected thief.

The next day his spectacles are found shattered on the threshold.[5]

Louis began this story in 1881 but dropped it, as he told Colvin, "in a justifiable disgust, the tale being horrid." Three years after that the editor of the *Pall Mall Gazette* asked him for a horror story that would make readers' flesh creep, and he offered "The Body Snatcher," commenting that it was "bloodcurdling enough; perhaps too much so." It appeared in the magazine's "Christmas Extra," and Chesterton remembered with amusement that it was advertised in the streets "in a way as horrible as the story itself. Six plaster skulls were made by a theatrical property man. Six pairs of coffin lids, painted dead black with white skulls and crossbones in the centre for relief, were supplied by a carpenter. Six long white surplices were purchased from a funeral establishment. Six sandwich-men were hired at double rates. The rest can be guessed. But the police suppressed the nuisance." Sandwich men were so called because they were sandwiched, front and back, by a pair of advertising placards.[6]

"The Body Snatcher" was never reprinted in Louis's lifetime. More memorable was "Thrawn Janet," whose origins lay in the chilling tales of the Devil and his works that Cummy used to relate. Since then Louis had read widely in seventeenth-century treatises on witchcraft, for example, *Satan's Invisible World Discovered* by a Glasgow professor of philosophy.[7]

This story too began as a social entertainment when the family was confined to Kinnaird Cottage by foul weather. In Fanny's account,

> Although it was the seventh of June when we moved into the cottage, as yet we had had nothing but cold rains and penetrating winds; and in all innocence I asked when the spring would begin, "The spring!" said my mother in law, "why, *this* is the spring." "And the summer," I inquired anxiously, "when will the summer be here?" "Well," returned my mother in law doubtfully, "we must wait for St. Swithin's day; it all depends on what kind of weather we have then." St. Swithin's day came and went in a storm of wind and rain. "I am afraid," confessed my mother in law, "that the summer is past, and we shall have no more good weather."

That date is July 15, and Margaret was remembering an old tradition: "St. Swithin's day if thou dost rain / For forty days it will remain, / St. Swithin's day if thou be fair / For forty days 'twill rain nae mare."

Fanny went on to relate the inception of "Thrawn Janet."

> That evening is as clear in my memory as though it were yesterday—the dim light of our one candle, with the acrid smell of the wick that we had forgotten to snuff, the shadows in the corners of the "lang, laigh, mirk chamber, perishing cauld," the driving rain on the roof close above our heads, and the gusts of wind that shook our windows. By the time the tale was finished my husband had fairly frightened himself, and we crept down the stairs clinging hand in hand like two scared children.

Her quotation was taken from "Thrawn Janet" itself—"the long, low, dark chamber."[8]

Unlike Louis's earlier stories, this one is brief and intense; Henry James called it "a masterpiece in thirteen pages." It's told not by a sophisticated narrator but by a villager recalling the events fifty years later. He speaks in the Scots dialect, which is managed so deftly that the flavor and energy come through even if some words are unfamiliar.[9]

Young Mr. Soulis arrives in the village of Balweary to be its new minister. Full of book learning, he has no patience with the superstitions of the country folk, while they think he has "nae leevin' experience in religion." Living experience, with a vengeance, is what he gets.[10]

Soulis takes as housekeeper an old woman named Janet McClour who is widely suspected of being a witch, especially after she suffers a stroke, speaks indistinctly, and carries her head twisted against her shoulder. That's when the villagers start calling her Thrawn Janet, meaning "crooked." To establish whether she's really a witch they put her to the traditional test of dunking in a river to see whether she will float or drown. She survives, but they're not convinced.

One day Soulis encounters an uncanny black man who gazes at him coolly, says not a word, and dashes away. It was a common belief in the countryside that Satan often appeared as a black man. Scott had invoked the tradition in *The Heart of Midlothian,* in which "the apparition of a tall black man" falls into a river and participants in a religious meeting rush to try to save him. Instead they risk being dragged in and drowned themselves, until one of them cries out, "Quit the rope, it is the Great Enemy! He will burn, but not drown!" After that, "he went down the water screeching and bullering like a Bull of Bashan, as he's ca'd in Scripture."[11]

That night Soulis hears loud banging in Janet's room, followed by a violent wind outside and then silence. When he opens her door, this is what he sees:

> The minister's heart played dunt an' stood stock-still; an' a cauld wund blew amang the hairs o' his heid. Whaten a weary sicht was that for the puir man's een! For there was Janet hangin' frae a nail beside the auld aik cabinet: her heid aye lay on her shoother, her een were steeked, the tongue projekit frae her mouth, and her heels were twa feet clear abune the floor.
>
> "God forgive us all!" thocht Mr. Soulis; "poor Janet's dead."
>
> He cam' a step nearer to the corp; an' then his heart fair whammled in his inside. For by what cantrip [spell] it wad ill-beseem a man to judge, she was hingin' frae a single nail an' by a single wursted thread for darnin' hose.

Soulis locks the door, goes downstairs, and tries to pray. But then he hears something coming slowly down the stairs, and it's Janet.

"Witch, beldame, devil!" he cried, "I charge you, by the power of God, begone—if you be dead, to the grave—if you be damned, to hell."

An' at that moment the Lord's ain hand out o' the Heevens struck the Horror whaur it stood; the auld, deid, desecrated corp o' the witch-wife, sae lang keepit frae the grave and hirsled round by deils, lowed up like a brunstane spunk and fell in ashes to the grund; the thunder followed, peal on dirling peal, the rairing rain upon the back o' that; and Mr. Soulis lowped through the garden hedge, and ran, wi' skelloch upon skelloch, for the clachan.

Skellochs are screams; the clachan is the village.

In the morning the villagers see the black man departing over the hills. "There's little doubt," the narrator concludes, "but it was him that dwalled sae lang in Janet's body; but he was awa' at last; and sinsyne the deil has never fashed us in Ba'weary. But it was a sair dispensation for the minister; lang, lang he lay ravin' in his bed; and frae that hour to this, he was the man ye ken the day."

We now understand the description of Soulis at the very beginning of the story: "A severe, bleak-faced old man, dreadful to his hearers, he dwelt in the last years of his life, without relative or servant or any human company, in the small and lonely manse under the Hanging Shaw. In spite of the iron composure of his features, his eye was wild, scared, and uncertain; and when he dwelt, in private admonitions, on the future of the impenitent, it seemed as if his eye pierced through the storms of time to the terrors of eternity."

In an essay on Louis's writing, James made this comment:

> It would never have occurred to us that the style of *Travels with a Donkey* or *Virginibus Puerisque* [an essay collection] and the idiom of the parish of Balweary could be a conception of the same mind. If it be a good fortune for a genius to have had such a country as Scotland for its primary stuff, this is doubly the case when there has been a certain process of detachment, of extreme secularisation. Mr. Stevenson has been emancipated: he is, as we may say, a Scotchman of the world.

It's true that Louis was a freethinker and didn't share his narrator's belief in the Devil, but he shared a recognition of a dark element in human nature, a theme he would return to again and again. "No Southerner," his fellow Scotsman Andrew Lang said of this story, "can appreciate all its merits, the thing is so absolutely and essentially Scots."[12]

In early July Louis wrote to Colvin that Leslie Stephen had accepted "Thrawn

Janet" for publication, while "The Body Snatcher" had been abandoned, and "my third, 'The Merry Men,' I am more than half through and think real well of. It is a fantastic sonata about the sea and wrecks, and I like it much above all my other attempts at story telling." He may have been teasing Colvin with the Americanism "think real well of." At the end of the letter he listed titles for the story's five sections and labeled them, with another Americanism, "Tip Top Tale."[13]

Louis has been called "one of the great open-air writers," but only now was he discovering that gift. "The Merry Men" was inspired by vivid memories of the little island of Earraid where he had spent time in his teens while the Dhu Heartach lighthouse was being constructed. Years later he told Graham Balfour that instead of beginning with a plot or characters, "you may take a certain atmosphere and get actions and persons to express and realise it. I'll give you an example: 'The Merry Men.' There I began with the feeling of one of those islands on the west coast of Scotland, and I gradually developed the story to express the sentiment with which that coast affected me."[14]

Like "Thrawn Janet," this story has a narrator who is a witness to the action. Charles Darnaway, a recent graduate of the University of Edinburgh, has been visiting his uncle Gordon Darnaway on the remote island of Aros (the fictionalized name for Earraid). He knows that a ship from the Spanish Armada was wrecked upon the reefs there long ago, and he dreams of locating its treasure. Also, he is in love with his cousin Mary Ellen, Gordon's daughter. The historical moment isn't clear, but William Robertson is mentioned as head of the University of Edinburgh. Robertson died in 1793, so that indicates the eighteenth century.

Charles's hopes of discovering the sunken treasure seem to bear fruit when he's groping in shallow water and comes upon a rusty shoe buckle that might have been Spanish.

> The sight of this poor human relic thrilled me to the heart, but not with hope nor fear, only with a desolate melancholy. I held it in my hand, and the thought of its owner appeared before me like the presence of an actual man. His weather-beaten face, his sailor's hands, his sea-voice hoarse with singing at the capstan, the very foot that had once worn that buckle and trod so much along the swerving decks—the whole human fact of him, as a creature like myself, with hair and blood and seeing eyes, haunted me in that sunny, solitary place, not like a spectre, but like some friend whom I had basely injured. . . . My uncle's words, "the dead are down there," echoed in my ears; and though I determined to dive once

more, it was with a strong repugnance that I stepped forward to the margin of the rocks.

When Charles reenters the water, a wave bowls him over.

> I was flung sprawling on my side, and instinctively grasping for a fresh support, my fingers closed on something hard and cold. I think I knew at that moment what it was. At least I instantly left hold of the tangle, leaped for the surface, and clambered out next moment on the friendly rocks with the bone of a man's leg in my grasp. . . . It was not until I touched that actual piece of mankind that the full horror of the charnel ocean burst upon my spirit. I laid the bone beside the buckle, picked up my clothes, and ran as I was along the rocks towards the human shore. I could not be far enough from the spot; no fortune was vast enough to tempt me back again.

His uncle Gordon, however, is profoundly tempted by what horrifies Charles. Every time there's a storm he watches from a cliff in hopes of seeing a vessel dashed to destruction, so that he can scavenge for things that wash ashore. His house is furnished incongruously with elegant items acquired in that way.

Still more shocking is something else that Charles discovers. Walking among the dunes, he comes upon what is clearly a recent grave, and guesses that his uncle must have murdered a survivor from a shipwreck. It turns out to be true. Gordon has been tortured ever since by a consciousness of sin that heavy drinking fails to suppress, and he declares that he belongs to the Devil.

> If it wasnae sin, I dinnae ken that I would care for't. Ye see, man, it's defiance. There's a sair spang o' the auld sin o' the warld in yon sea; it's an unchristian business at the best o't; an' whiles when it gets up, an' the wind skreights—the wind an' her are a kind of sib, I'm thinkin'—an' thae Merry Men, the daft callants, blawin' and lauchin,' and puir souls in the deid thraws warstlin' the leelang nicht wi' their bit ships—weel, it comes ower me like a glamour. I'm a deil, I ken't. But I think naething o' the puir sailor lads; I'm wi' the sea, I'm just like ane o' her ain Merry Men.

We've forgotten that *glamour* originally meant "magic, enchantment, spell." It was by extension that it later came to mean being enchanting to other people.

The "Merry Men" was the ironic local name for reefs that boom loudly in stormy weather. Charles says, "Whether they got the name from their movements, which are swift and antic, or from the shouting they make about the turn of the tide, so that all Aros shakes with it, is more than I can tell.... It seemed even human."

As a tormented sinner, Gordon fears the ocean as the agent of divine retribution, and tells Charles that however dreadful "bogles"—bogies, ghosts or specters—may be on land, those in the sea are worse. "'O, sirs,' he cried, 'the horror—the horror o' the sea!'" The story ends when he goes mad.

Though Charles is an enlightened university student, he can't help feeling that "Heaven's will was declared against Gordon Darnaway." And only now do we understand something he said at the beginning of the story. "Since I became the witness of a strange judgment of God's, the thought of dead men's treasures has been intolerable to my conscience."[15]

When Henley read "The Merry Men" he told Colvin, "It contains some stunning dialogue, heaps of good descriptive writing, no end of real imagination, and a character who is a veritable creation. You will enjoy it greatly, and be prouder of our young man than ever." Louis was one year younger than Henley. To Louis himself Henley wrote, "I have read 'The Merry Men.' You are right about it. 'Tis your finest story." After suggesting possible revisions he added, "I think you have been lavish of your imagination, and might have made, and early, a two-volume romance out of what you have disposed of in five chapters. And this is a great grief. For I expected a book." Henley didn't realize that the sea, its terrors, and the quest for treasure were about to return in *Treasure Island*.[16]

As with "Thrawn Janet," the imaginative re-creation of Scottish superstition was disturbing even to Louis himself. Six years later he told a friend, "I do not think it is a wholesome part of me that broods on the evil in the world and man, but I do not think that I get harm from it; possibly my readers may, which is more serious; but at any account, I do not purpose to write more in this vein." That was in response to his correspondent wondering "whether in the course of your very thorough researches some evil may not stick to your soul."[17]

Still later, Louis noticed Belle reading a book and asked her to read aloud from it. She recorded in her journal,

> As it happened, I was reading "The Merry Men"; he laughed a little when he recognized his own words. I went on and finished the story. "Well," he said, "it is not cheerful; it is distinctly not cheerful!"
>
> "In these stories," I asked, "do you preach a moral?"
>
> "Oh, not mine," he said. "What I want to give, what I try for, is God's moral!"
>
> "Could you not give God's moral in a pretty story?" I asked.

"It is a very difficult thing to know," he said; "it is a thing I have often thought over—the problem of what to do with one's talents." He said he thought his own gift lay in the grim and terrible—that some writers touch the heart, he clutched at the throat.

The grim and terrible was by no means his only gift, but it did liberate him from the restrained and conventional narratives he had written thus far.[18]

In a very different vein, during this summer he got the idea for what would become *A Child's Garden of Verses*. Margaret wrote in her diary, "I had Kate Greenaway's children's birthday book. Lou took it up one day and said, 'These are rather nice rhymes, and I don't think they would be difficult to do,' and he proceeded to try."[19]

At this time he put his name forward for a professorship of history at the University of Edinburgh, which would have been a part-time job like Colvin's at Cambridge, and solicited recommendations from friends. Biographers have regarded the application as absurd, given his lack of academic qualifications, but Roslyn Jolly has demonstrated that that judgment is anachronistic. Traditionally historians were appreciated for compelling narratives, which Louis certainly could have produced, and the modern scholarly demand for objectivity grounded in data was only just emerging. Barry Menikoff notes that the winner of the position and the runner-up were completely undistinguished; as an avid student of history, Louis was probably better qualified than they were.[20]

In a way he was looking forward, not back; in our own day many of the best historians are telling stories once again. And they make clear, as older historians often didn't, that historical evidence is always ambiguous and cries out for interpretation. Three years after this attempt Louis wrote, "The art of narrative, in fact, is the same, whether it is applied to the selection and illustration of a real series of events or of an imaginary series. On a more careful examination 'truth' will seem a word of very debatable propriety, not only for the labours of the novelist, but for those of the historian."[21]

After the application was turned down, Edmund Gosse, who had loyally produced a letter of recommendation, thought that "the round Louis was well out of such a square hole as a chair in a university."[22]

BRAEMAR

After two months at Pitlochry the family moved to a stone cottage near Braemar (fig. 48), seventy-five miles north of Edinburgh, where they hoped the

48. The Braemar cottage

climate would be better for Louis's health. Fanny recalled, however, "It was a season of rain and chill weather that we spent in the cottage of the late Miss M'Gregor, though the townspeople called the cold, steady, penetrating drizzle 'just misting.' In Scotland a fair day appears to mean fairly wet. 'It is quite fair now,' they will say, when you can hardly distinguish the houses across the street." Louis wrote to Gosse, who was about to visit, "If you had an uncle who was a sea captain and went to the North Pole, you had better bring his outfit."[23]

One point of interest was that Queen Victoria's beloved Balmoral Castle was not far away, and she could sometimes be seen riding by in her carriage, bundled up against the chill. Fighting off his latest cold, Louis wrote to Frances Sitwell, "It is really extraordinary that I should have recovered as well as I have, in this blighting weather; the wind pipes, the rain comes in squalls, great black clouds are continually overhead, and it is as cold as March. The queen knows a thing or two, I perceive; she has picked out the finest habitable spot in Britain."[24]

In a letter to Dora Williams, Fanny described the queen, who was sixty-two at the time. "She is a purple old lady, with much more of the queen than I had imagined in her appearance; but the man for my money is John Brown. He is a large, fine, handsome, gray haired man, with a kilt and the appearance generally of a duke; I doubt if any of the dukes look so dukey." Brown was Victoria's faithful attendant or gillie, and there were already rumors about the nature of their relationship; Prince Albert had died twenty years previously.[25]

When Gosse arrived in August the whole family was there, as well as Cummy. He wrote to his wife, "This is a most entertaining household. All the persons in it are full of character and force; they use fearful language towards one another and no quarrel ensues." Even Cummy was delighted, for Gosse, remembering his pious upbringing, read eloquently from the Bible when the family assembled for prayers. "She turned fiercely on R.L.S. and said, 'He's the only one of your fine friends who can do justice to the Word of God.'" Gosse admitted that he had adopted "a rather stagey manner of reading aloud."[26]

Another visitor was Alexander Japp, a Scot who had become a publisher in London; he got on especially well with Louis's father, and they often took long walks together. On one such occasion "Thomas Stevenson, with a strange, sad smile, told me how much of a disappointment, in the first stage at all events, Louis (he always called his son Louis at home) had caused him by failing to follow up his profession at the Scottish Bar." Thomas believed deeply in the importance of professions, and thought of writing as a mere hobby. Walter Scott had been a lawyer and judge as well as novelist. Recounting this conversation, Japp commented, "One cannot help feeling how much Stevenson's very air and figure would have been out of keeping among the bewigged, pushing, sharp-set, hard-featured, and even red-faced and red-nosed company who daily walked the Parliament House, and talked and gossiped there, often of other things than law and equity."[27]

A CLASSIC IS BORN

To amuse themselves during the endless rain, Louis and Lloyd drew a map of an imaginary island and made up stories about it. As Louis remembered, "It was elaborately and (I thought) beautifully coloured; the shape of it took my fancy beyond expression; it contained harbours that pleased me like sonnets; and with the unconsciousness of the predestined, I ticketed my performance *Treasure Island*." The tale may have been predestined, but its title wasn't. Originally he called his story *The Sea Cook* after Long John Silver, the former pirate who joins the treasure-seeking voyage disguised as a cook. *The Sea Cook* is almost as unpromising a title as *Trimalchio at West Egg*, which Fitzgerald originally wanted for his masterpiece *The Great Gatsby*. It was a publisher who told Louis that *Treasure Island* would be more effective.

Louis added that the story "seemed to me as original as sin." There were plenty of melodramatic sea stories in existence, as well as histories of eighteenth-century piracy that he had devoured, but those are forgotten today while *Treasure Island* is a world classic, translated into scores of languages and reissued in countless editions.

It was especially gratifying that the project brought out the adventure-loving romantic in Thomas Stevenson.

> I had counted on one boy, I found I had two in my audience. My father caught fire at once with all the romance and childishness of his original nature. His own stories, that every night of his life he put himself to sleep with, dealt perpetually with ships, roadside inns, robbers, old sailors, and commercial travelers before the era of steam. He never finished one of these romances; the lucky man did not require to! But in *Treasure Island* he recognised something kindred to his own imagination; it was *his* kind of picturesque; and he not only heard with delight the daily chapter, but set himself actively to collaborate.[28]

Treasure Island is constructed with consummate art, but the best art conceals art. The story is told by Jim Hawkins, recalling his boyhood in a seaside inn kept by his parents in the west of England. One day a gruff old sailor arrives.

> I remember him as if it were yesterday, as he came plodding to the inn door, his sea-chest following behind him in a hand-barrow—a tall, strong, heavy, nut-brown man, his tarry pigtail falling over the shoulder of his soiled blue coat, his hands ragged and scarred, with black, broken nails, and the sabre cut across one cheek a dirty, livid white. I remember him looking round the cove and whistling to himself as he did so, and then breaking out in that old sea-song that he sang so often afterwards:
>
> > "Fifteen men on the dead man's chest—
> > Yo-ho-ho, and a bottle of rum!"
>
> in the high, old tottering voice that seemed to have been tuned and broken at the capstan bars.[29]

Calling himself Billy Bones, the sailor takes over the inn, swilling rum and tyrannizing over patrons who can't help enjoying his tales of the high seas. However, a visitor brings a message that puts him on guard, and shortly after, Jim is accosted by a blind man tapping with a stick along the road to the door of the inn.

What follows is a powerfully managed sequence of danger and suspense. Jim describes the encounter: "'I hear a voice,' said he, 'a young voice. Will you give me your hand, my kind young friend, and lead me in?' I held out my hand, and the horrible, soft-spoken, eyeless creature gripped it in a moment like a vise. I was so much startled that I struggled to withdraw, but the blind man pulled me close up to him with a single action of his arm." A critic comments, "He is the nightmare of every child, and perhaps of every adult."[30]

The uncanny visitor demands to be taken to Billy Bones, and gives him a piece of paper. Billy sinks back in shock. He has recognized Blind Pew, an old shipmate who is delivering the "Black Spot" that tells a pirate he is about to die. "'And now that's done,' said the blind man; and at the words he suddenly left hold of me, and with incredible accuracy and nimbleness skipped out of the parlour and into the road, where, as I still stood motionless, I could hear his stick go tap-tap-tapping into the distance."

No sooner does Billy try to stand up than he collapses and dies of a stroke. Since he has never paid for his lodging, Jim and his mother (his father is dead by now) start to go through his belongings until they hear noises outside; it's Pew returning with his gang. They flee from the inn just before the pirates burst in. Suddenly galloping horses are heard. The gang had been detected as likely smugglers, and revenue officers are rushing to arrest them. As the rest of the pirates dash away, Pew is left staggering and alone in the road, listening in terror to the horses bearing down. From a hiding place Jim sees what happens:

> There he remained behind, tapping up and down the road in a frenzy, and groping and calling for his comrades. . . . He turned with a scream and ran straight for the ditch, into which he rolled. But he was on his feet again in a second and made another dash, now utterly bewildered, right under the nearest of the coming horses. The rider tried to save him, but in vain. Down went Pew with a cry that rang high into the night; and the four hoofs trampled and spurned him and passed by. He fell on his side, then gently collapsed upon his face and moved no more.

The intensification of threats has been superbly managed. First came the strange but apparently harmless Billy Bones, then the disturbing Blind Pew, then Billy's death, then the pirates' invasion, and finally the eruption of violence as the horses crush Pew in the road.[31]

When he composed these opening chapters, Louis had achieved a new level of narrative power. Using a first-person narrator was not common at the time. It wasn't just a choice of "point of view"; in this tale of adventure it puts the reader into the midst of the action, startled into terror when Jim is startled. The artist

N. C. Wyeth had a gift for dramatizing critical moments, and his 1919 illustration (color plate 11) shows Pew with the inn behind him as the horses thunder toward him. The image is faithful to Jim's first impression: "He was hunched, as if with age or weakness, and wore a huge old tattered sea cloak with a hood that made him appear positively deformed."

Before fleeing the inn Jim and his mother grabbed what they could from Billy's sea chest, and a parcel he happened to take turns out to be exactly what the pirates had come to find: the map of an island showing where a pirate named Captain Flint had buried a treasure. When Trelawney, the local squire, sees this map he resolves to charter a ship and find the treasure, taking with him his friend Dr. Livesey. Jim will go as cabin boy.

At Bristol they charter a ship called the *Hispaniola* and engage an experienced captain for it. They also meet a jolly tavern keeper who offers to recruit a crew. This is Long John Silver, with whom Jim and his companions are immediately charmed.

> His left leg was cut off close by the hip, and under the left shoulder he carried a crutch, which he managed with wonderful dexterity, hopping about upon it like a bird. He was very tall and strong, with a face as big as a ham—plain and pale, but intelligent and smiling. Indeed, he seemed in the most cheerful spirits, whistling as he moved about among the tables, with a merry word or a slap on the shoulder for the more favoured of his guests.

As usual in Louis's writing, there are visual details but also vivid evocation of motion and sound—the hopping, the whistling, the friendly shoulder slaps. He always deplored heaping up descriptive details as "realist" novelists did. "I have a better method—the kinetic, whereas Balzac continually allowed himself to be led into the static." And what other writer would have thought of "a face as big as a ham?" The image is strange and disturbing, suggesting size certainly, and perhaps something blank and inhuman as well.[32]

Billy Bones had warned Jim to be on the lookout for a man with one leg. Also ominous is the fact that the one-legged Silver has a parrot named Captain Flint that keeps squawking "Pieces of eight." But even with these clues, the squire and doctor never dream that Silver was once a pirate with Flint, much less that the crew he has assembled were pirates too. It is only by chance that Jim exposes their treachery, in an incident inspired by Louis's father.

As a young man Thomas Stevenson had traveled by ship on a lighthouse-building expedition. Soutar, the captain, was a trusted right-hand man, but "my father crept one rainy night into an apple barrel on deck, and from this place of ambush overheard Soutar and a comrade conversing in their oilskins. The smooth sycophant of the cabin had wholly disappeared, and the boy listened with wonder to a vulgar and truculent ruffian." We're not told exactly what Thomas heard, but clearly it exposed Soutar's duplicity.[33]

After the *Hispaniola* is far out to sea, Jim climbs into an apple barrel and makes a fearful discovery.

> Sitting down there in the dark, what with the sound of the waters and the rocking movement of the ship, I had either fallen asleep or was on the point of doing so when a heavy man sat down with rather a clash close by. The barrel shook as he leaned his shoulders against it, and I was just about to jump up when the man began to speak. It was Silver's voice, and before I had heard a dozen words I would not have shown myself for all the world, but lay there, trembling and listening, in the extreme of fear and curiosity, for from these dozen words I understood that the lives of all the honest men aboard depended upon me alone.

The pirates' plan is to wait until the *Hispaniola* reaches the island, kill Jim's companions and the few non-conspirators in the crew, and recover the treasure for themselves.[34]

In *Treasure Island* we live through each suspenseful moment just as Jim does. The ability to create that kind of narrative tension is rare, and readers of all ages responded to it; the prime minister, William Ewart Gladstone, said that the book kept him up all night. Leslie Stephen commented, "Stevenson had a schoolboy for audience; his father became a schoolboy to collaborate; and when published it made schoolboys of Gladstone and of the editor of the cynical *Saturday Review*."[35]

As already mentioned, the conception of Silver had an immediate inspiration: Louis based him on his friend Henley. "I had an idea for John Silver from which I promised myself funds of entertainment: to take an admired friend of mine (whom the reader very likely knows and admires as much as I do), to deprive him of all his finer qualities and higher graces of temperament, to leave him with nothing but his strength, his courage, his quickness, and his magnificent geniality, and to try to express these in terms of the culture of a raw tarpaulin." Louis freely acknowledged to Henley himself what he'd done. "I will now make a confession. It was the sight of your maimed strength and masterfulness that begot John Silver." He added tactfully, "Of course, he is not in any other quality or feature the least like you; but the idea of the maimed man, ruling and dreaded by the sound, was entirely taken from you."[36]

For the imaginary island, whose location is presumably in the Caribbean, Louis drew on his own recent memories. Much of the scenery was inspired by California, with live oaks and redwoods and the booming surf of Monterey. "I have never seen the sea quiet round Treasure Island," Jim says. "The sun might blaze overhead, the air be without a breath, the surface smooth and blue, but still these great rollers would be running along all the external coast, thundering and thundering by day and night; and I scarce believe there is one spot in the island where a man would be out of earshot of their noise." There is a reminiscence of Silverado too. "Here and there I saw snakes, and one raised his head from a ledge of rock and hissed at me with a noise not unlike the spinning of a top. Little did I suppose that he was a deadly enemy and that the noise was the famous rattle."[37]

It was Louis's habit to read aloud from his work to family and friends. Gosse reported to his wife, "Louis has been writing, all the time I have been here, a novel of pirates and hidden treasure, in the highest degree exciting. He reads it to us every night, chapter by chapter." At a later time Gosse recalled, "I look back to no keener intellectual pleasure than those cold nights at Braemar, with the sleet howling outside, and Louis reading his budding romance by the lamplight, emphasizing the purpler passages with lifted voice and gesticulating finger."[38]

The visitor Alexander Japp likewise admired Louis's performance. "His fine voice, clear and keen in some of its tones, had a wonderful power of inflection and variation, and when he came to stand in the place of Silver you could almost have imagined you saw the great one-legged John Silver, joyous-eyed, on the rolling sea."[39]

In creating this tale Louis was rebelling against two tendencies in fiction that were then admired: subtle psychological analysis, and observation of society and manners. He also deplored "the novel with a purpose"—what today might be called a "message"—in which "we see the moral clumsily forced into every hole and corner of the story, or thrown externally over it like a carpet over a railing."[40]

Critics have complained that the characters in *Treasure Island* lack psychological depth, but that's not the only appeal that narrative can have. The characters in the *Iliad* and the tales of King Arthur are vivid and unforgettable, but they too could be said to lack psychological depth. *The Lord of the Rings,* long condescended to by critics, has outlived most of the Pulitzer and Booker Prize winners of its time.

Treasure Island was conceived as a romance in the traditional sense—not a love story, but a tale of heroism and adventure. In "A Gossip on Romance" Louis declared, "The great creative writer shows us the realization and the apotheosis of the daydreams of common men. His stories may be nourished with the realities of life, but their true mark is to satisfy the nameless longings of the reader, and to obey the ideal laws of the daydream." Unlike daydreaming, however, literary romance should have satisfying coherence and structure. "The right kind of things should fall out in the right kind of place; the right kind of thing should follow; and not only the characters talk aptly and think naturally, but all the circumstances in a tale answer one to another like notes in music."

A story, Louis continued, shouldn't seem improbable or bizarre as dreams often do, but totally believable even while emphasizing action. "The interest turns not upon what a man shall choose to do, but on how he manages to do it; not on the passionate slips and hesitations of the conscience, but on the problems of the body and of the practical intelligence, in clean, open air adventure, the shock of arms or the diplomacy of life." He gave an illustration of what he disliked: "English people of the present day are apt, I know not why, to look somewhat down on incident, and reserve their admiration for the clink of teaspoons and the accents of the curate. It is thought clever to write a novel with no story at all, or at least with a very dull one."[41]

C. S. Lewis once made a spirited defense of adventure stories, suggesting that in a family of self-consciously literary people the only imaginative experience "may be occurring in a back bedroom where a small boy is reading *Treasure Island* under the bedclothes by the light of an electric torch." In that kind of reading, Lewis said, the story should turn on imminent dangers and hairbreadth escapes; it should excite curiosity and finally satisfy it; and the reader should participate vicariously. "To have lost the taste for marvels and adventures is no more a matter of congratulation than losing our teeth, our hair, our palate, and finally our hopes."[42]

Although C. S. Lewis spoke of "a small boy," it would be wrong to dismiss *Treasure Island* as nothing more than a boys' book. Italo Calvino made a shrewd comment: in an era of literary sophistication that despised heroism and romance, this was the only way to create an adventure "without turning it into parody and destroying it: to see it through the eyes of a boy." Calvino added that what makes it succeed is the engrossing style, *miracolosamente semplice e pulito*—"miraculously simple and clean." The narrator is a boy, but the narrative is the work of a master.[43]

BACK TO DAVOS

The writing continued rapidly at Braemar until the midpoint of the story, and then Louis hit a wall. In part it was a matter of solving a technical problem of narration, but beyond that he needed time to get perspective. He knew that *Treasure Island* was good, and he wanted it to be great. The second half wouldn't be written until they were back in Davos for the winter.

The reason for going there was that Dr. George Balfour arrived for a visit and was concerned to discover how ill his nephew was. Dr. Balfour sent for a "respirator," an odd-looking mask in which the patient was to inhale medicinal vapors, and ordered Louis to leave at once for the Alps. Louis reported the situation to Henley in verse:

> Dear Henley, with a pig's snout on
> I am starting for Londón,
> Where I likely shall arrive
> On Saturday, if still alive....
> I shall remain but little time
> In London, as a wretched clime,
> But none so wretched (for none are)
> As that of bloody old Braemar.

When Colvin published the letter that contains this poem two decades later, he altered "bloody" to "beastly," as less offensive to Victorian sensibilities. Fanny wrote to Frances Sitwell, "Tomorrow we shake the mud (not the dirt, it has been too wet for that) of Braemar from our feet, and leave it, I hope forever."[44]

The publisher Japp's visit had a remarkable outcome. He had come to Braemar to talk with Louis about Thoreau, but when he left he took with him the first half of *Treasure Island,* and undertook to arrange for its serial publication while awaiting the conclusion. Louis had never written a novel, and when they went to Braemar had no particular plans to do so. Years later he said, "Had not Japp come on his visit, had not the tale flowed from me with singular ease, it must have been laid aside like its predecessors, and found a circuitous and unlamented way to the fire."[45]

CHAPTER 18

Alpine Cold, and Treasure Island

WAR GAMES AND BITTER WEATHER

Arriving at Davos in October 1881, Louis and Fanny wanted to avoid the forced sociability of a hotel, so they rented a house of their own called the Chalet am Stein, named for a boulder on the hill above it. They would be there for six months. On the whole it was a depressing time, but it also marked a major step forward in Louis's career as a writer.

After the emotional drama of family life in Scotland, it was a relief to be on their own with only the affectionate Lloyd as company. An essay Louis wrote at this time includes these reflections:

> Marriage is one long conversation, chequered by disputes. The disputes are valueless; they but ingrain the difference, the heroic heart of woman prompting her at once to nail her colours to the mast. But in the intervals, almost unconsciously and with no desire to shine, the whole material of life is turned over and over, ideas are struck out and shared, the two persons more and more adapt their notions one to suit the other, and in process of time, without sound of trumpet, they conduct each other into new worlds of thought.

It's unlikely that Louis would have written "the heroic heart of woman" before he knew Fanny.[1]

In a letter to Henley he quoted from a Renaissance poem in Latin entitled *Loquitur Puella Fuscula,* "the dusky girl speaks":

> *Quod sim fuscula, quod nigella, et ipsae*
> *Fusco in pectore nigricent papillae,*
> *Quid tum? Nox nigra* etc. etc.

That means "Because I am dusky, because I am black, and the very nipples on my dusky breast are black—what of that? Night is black." Louis's discreet "etc." refrains from quoting what follows: "Settled in bed, together, quiet, we'll have our sex, and bound in bed we'll lay the shadows to rest until Venus at sunrise shakes us out of sleep." Louis often referred to Fanny as dusky.[2]

Whether or not the dry air was beneficial for Louis's health, he always detested being cold, and never more than now. The day after Christmas he wrote to his mother, "The cold was beyond belief. I have often suffered less at a dentist's." Those were the days before dental anesthesia. There was also roaring wind, which he had hated since he was a small child listening to it fearfully in the night. Fanny wrote in February, "There is a horrible Föhn [the Alpine equivalent of the Mistral] blowing. We have had almost none this year; I had forgotten how bad they were. It is very depressing, moaning and howling and poisonous."[3]

Two months later, thoroughly discouraged by Davos, Louis wrote nostalgically to Henley about "the old and, on the whole, the good days in Bristo Street," where Henley used to live in Edinburgh in 1876. In his reply Henley took exception to "on the whole."

> Of course the days in Bristo Place were good and happy days. Who ever said they weren't? Who is there that would have the heart, or the face, to regret such a past as ours? Did we not live? did we not love? did we not drink? and talk, and write? were we not friends? did we not suffer and enjoy and fool? Answer me that! How should the days have been other than good? I protest that if you've qualified your opinion of those times by so much as a single "if" I shall be an angry man. A little more, and you'll out-Colvin Colvin.

Colvin's cool judiciousness was well known to both of them.[4]

Life at Davos was dominated by medical concerns, and Fanny as well as Louis suffered new ailments in addition to his condition that had brought them there. These were reported so regularly that Henley wrote teasingly,

> Your kneecap? Did I dream that you had slipped it? How? I can't help thinking that somebody told me you had disarranged some part of your anatomy. Was it your diaphragm? or was it Mrs. Louis's diaphragm? or

was it your finger that fractured? Did you have an abscess in your ear? or was it Sam [i.e., Lloyd]? Or was it Woggs that slipped his kneecap in jumping off a tombstone, that time when you burst your diaphragm in calling for doctors because Mrs. Louis had broken her finger, and Sam was busily getting rid of his gallstones?[5]

Woggs did figure as an important member of the household, and is often mentioned in correspondence. He was notorious for fouling carpets and even chewing them up. Louis wrote to Colvin, "A worse-hearted, worse-smelling, chuckle-headed Beelzebub in carpet ravelings was never thought of. He is only fit to be thrown into some black pot of the ocean, to glut the appetite of the 'griesly Wasserman!' But we adore him; can't help it, it appears." The quotation is an example of Louis's phenomenal memory; it comes from the description of a sea monster in Spenser's *Fairie Queene:*

> The dreadful fish, that hath deserved the name
> Of Death, and like him looks in dreadful hue,
> The griesly Wasserman, that makes his game
> The flying ships with swiftness to pursue.[6]

Louis and Fanny composed a joint letter supposedly dictated by Woggs, responding to a correspondent's assumption that their dog was female:

> I am *not* a lady dog. I am more proud of not being a lady dog than anything else in the world, except, perhaps, not being a human boy. . . . Missis has a son, only of the common breed, but most shamefully pampered. Meat twice a day, I assure you, and unlimited porridge and milk in the evening; he is never shut out of doors during meals, nor have I ever seen him kicked out of the way. People actually apologize when they fall over him. Did Missis tell you that I have a nose like a blackberry, and eyes like Highland pools, and that I can sing like a nightingale?[7]

An enjoyable recreation was war games that Louis and Lloyd played by the hour. Leslie Fiedler comments, "An only child and one isolated by illness, Stevenson had never been able to feel himself anything but a small adult (his parents observed him, noted down his most chance remarks with awful seriousness); against the boy Lloyd he was able to define himself as a boy."[8]

There had been toy soldiers on the counterpane when Louis was a child, and real warfare had fascinated him from earliest days. When he was four Margaret noted in her Baby Book that he was eager to hear news from Crimea. "Lou is quite mad on the subject of soldiers and the War. He prays night and morning for our poor soldiers that are fighting at Sebastopol and that they may get the victory. This is quite of his own accord."[9]

The Davos version of the counterpane was a scale-model *Kriegspiel* such as military academies used for teaching the subtleties of strategy. Six hundred lead soldiers were deployed on the attic floor, which was laid out as a map with hills, towns, rivers, bridges, and so on. Troops could march one foot per day, or four inches if pulling artillery; once within range they would fire at each other with miniature pellets from miniature cannons.

> Proudly they perished one by one:
> The dread Pea-cannon's work was done![10]

"We played the game," Lloyd remembered, "with a breathlessness and intensity that stirs me even now to recall." Louis told him that if only he had enjoyed good health he would certainly have gone into the army, and when Lloyd said he admired Lord Wolseley more than any man living, Louis smiled and agreed. Viscount Wolseley was a field marshal who had fought in various colonial campaigns as well as Crimea. Louis once told his cousin Bob that when he tried to read Tennyson's "Ode on the Death of the Duke of Wellington" aloud, "I had a hand at my throat tightening steadily as I read, until I could articulate no more and had to throw the book away. That is one of the experiences in life worth having."[11]

Lloyd remembered that Louis loved to talk with retired army officers, who were impressed by his fund of knowledge. "I would overhear something like this: 'Extraordinary man, sir—that writing fellow—that Stevenson. Absolutely knows everything that ever happened anywhere. Knows India like a book, sir; knows South Africa; might have been himself in the Punjab with Lawrence; knows even the modest part I took myself in the siege of Cheetahpore; and I was greatly gratified to amplify his knowledge in a few particulars and explain in detail the whole campaign in Eastern Oudh!'"[12]

Having Lloyd for company furnished another form of entertainment. Lloyd had acquired a miniature printing press and was producing compositions of his own, with titles such as *The Black Canyon; or, Wild Adventures in the Far West: A Tale of Instruction and Amusement for the Young* "by Samuel L. Osbourne, printed by the author, Davos Platz."[13]

Soon they were collaborating on poems, most memorably "Robin and Ben: or, The Pirate and the Apothecary." When Robin returns home after a lawless career on the high seas, he is shocked to find himself shunned by his fellow townsmen, and broods in a tavern.

> His soul was wounded; proud and glum,
> Alone he sat and swigged his rum,
> And took a great distaste to men
> Till he encountered Chemist Ben.
> Bright was the hour and bright the day
> That threw them in each other's way.

However, Ben explains how he has done so well in the world:

> "Here is the key to right and wrong:
> Steal little, but steal all day long;
> And this invaluable plan
> Marks what is called the Honest Man."
> Out flashed the cutlass, down went Ben
> Dead and rotten, there and then.[14]

Louis created simple woodcuts to illustrate the poems, using a penknife on ordinary boards and teaching himself as he went along. In the picture reproduced here (fig. 49), Ben lies dead beneath a lurid sun while Robin stands over him with the fatal cutlass. The crude graphic style is well suited to the doggerel.

Long afterward Lloyd published the Davos poems as a collectors' item. In his preface he recalled gloomier moods from those days too—moods that were generally provoked by anxiety about money.

> The little boy thought it was a very jolly place. He loved the tobogganing, the skating, the snow-balling; loved the crisp, tingling air, and the woods full of Christmas trees, glittering with icicles. Nor with his toy theatre and printing-press was the indoor confinement ever irksome. He but dimly appreciated that his stepfather and mother were less happy in so favoured a spot. His mother's face was often anxious; sometimes he would find her crying. His stepfather, whom he idolised, was terribly thin, and even to childish eyes looked frail and spectral. The stepfather was an unsuccessful author named Robert Louis Stevenson, who would never have got along at all had it not been for his rich parents in Edinburgh. The little boy at his lessons in the room which they all shared grew used to hearing a sentence that struck at his heart. Perhaps it was

49. "Robin and Ben"

the tone it was uttered in; perhaps the looks of discouragement and depression that went with it: "Fanny, I shall have to write to my father."[15]

THE PROLIFIC WRITER

Louis's immediate task was to complete *Treasure Island,* since Alexander Japp had placed it with a magazine called *Young Folks* and serialization was already underway. The author was identified as Captain George North; Louis's literary friends had urged him not to compromise his reputation as a serious writer. He went along for the time being, but wrote indignantly to Henley,

> To those who ask me (as you say they do) to do nothing but refined, high toned, bejay, bedam masterpieces, I will offer the following bargain: I agree to their proposal, if they give me £1,000 a year, at which I value *mon possible,* and at the same time effect such a change in my nature that I shall be content to take it from them instead of earning it. If they cannot manage these two trifling matters, by God, I'll trouble them to hold their tongues and shut their jaw, by God. That kind of business com-

mences to tickle me the wrong way. I will swallow no more of that gruel. Let them write their dam masterpieces for themselves, and let me alone. I don't want to hear more of such effeminate, unjust, cultchaw [i.e., "culture"], filthy, pragmatical, affected snot—and so you may inform the crew.[16]

Louis detested deadlines and avoided them when he could, but this time a deadline produced superb results, and he was surprised by how easily the final chapters came. "Down I sat one morning to the unfinished tale; and behold! it flowed from me like small talk; and in a second tide of delighted industry, and again at a rate of a chapter a day, I finished *Treasure Island*."[17]

The technical problem that had stalled the novel at Braemar was that Jim Hawkins gets separated from his companions Squire Trelawney and Dr. Livesey, and since this was a first-person narrative, he was in no position to report events that happened when he wasn't there. The solution Louis came up with, and would use repeatedly in later writing, was to have a second narrator pick up the tale. Dr. Livesey takes over for three chapters, after which Jim resumes.

Making Jim the narrator was more than just a device to create immediacy; *Treasure Island* was becoming what the Germans call a Bildungsroman, a novel tracing the education and psychological growth of its central character. We share in Jim's growing understanding of whom to trust and whom to distrust, above all the engaging but ruthless Long John Silver. At one point after Jim has rashly run away from his companions, he hears Silver's voice and ventures closer to spy from a hiding place in the bushes. A few of the sailors are not members of Silver's gang, and at this moment one of them is refusing to take part in the pirates' plot. "Kill me if you can," he says, "but I defies you," and begins to walk away. Instantly Silver hurls his crutch at the man, knocking him down, and then pounces.

> Silver, agile as a monkey even without leg or crutch, was on the top of him next moment and had twice buried his knife up to the hilt in that defenseless body. From my place of ambush, I could hear him pant aloud as he struck the blows.... The monster pulled himself together, his crutch under his arm, his hat upon his head. Just before him Tom lay motionless upon the sward; but the murderer minded him not a whit, cleansing his blood-stained knife the while upon a wisp of grass. Everything else was unchanged, the sun still shining mercilessly on the steaming marsh and the tall pinnacle of the mountain, and I could scarce persuade myself that murder had been actually done and a human life cruelly cut short a moment since before my eyes.[18]

Louis was developing a gift for creating characters who are attractive but also dangerous. "The admirable John Silver," Henry James said, "is one of the most picturesque and indeed in every way most genially presented villains in the whole literature of romance. He has a singularly distinct and expressive countenance, which of course turns out to be a grimacing mask. Never was a mask more knowingly, vividly painted."[19]

Later on Louis wrote a whimsical dialogue entitled "The Persons of the Tale," in which Silver and the ship's captain step outside of the novel for a conversation. Silver gets to make an important point to the captain: "What I know is this: if there is sich a thing as a Author, I'm his favourite chara'ter. He does me fathoms better'n he does you—fathoms, he does. And he likes doing me. He keeps me on deck mostly all the time, crutch and all; and he leaves you measling in the hold, where nobody can't see you, nor wants to, and you may lay to that! If there is a Author, by thunder, he's on my side, and you may lay to it!"[20]

Even though Silver is an attractive villain, he *is* a villain, and since the whole story is told by Jim in retrospect, we know that his treachery will fail in the end. In a clever feat of plot design, Jim's actions play a crucial role in making that happen, starting with the episode of the apple barrel when he overheard the pirates plotting. Often in the right place at the right time, he finds inner resources he didn't know he had. "There's a kind of fate in this," Dr. Livesey says when it's nearly over. "Every step, it's you that saves our lives."[21]

One such incident confirms Louis's genius for creating narrative tension. Two sailors have been left on the ship while the rest of the pirates have gone ashore in search of the treasure, but the two men quarrel and one is killed while the other, Israel Hands, lies on deck gravely wounded. From the beach Jim sees the ship adrift and resolves to get to it in a little makeshift boat he has found, hoping to recover it if possible. When he clambers aboard, Israel Hands attacks him with a knife, but the ship gives a lurch, he misses his aim, and Jim scrambles for safety up the mast. Unable to reach him, Hands offers to make peace, comparing himself to a vessel striking sail in sign of surrender.

> "Jim," says he, "I reckon we're fouled, you and me, and we'll have to sign articles. I'd have had you but for that there lurch, but I don't have no luck, not I; and I reckon I'll have to strike, which comes hard, you see, for a master mariner to a ship's younker like you, Jim."
>
> I was drinking in his words and smiling away, as conceited as a cock upon a wall, when, all in a breath, back went his right hand over his shoulder. Something sang like an arrow through the air; I felt a blow and then

a sharp pang, and there I was pinned by the shoulder to the mast. In the horrid pain and surprise of the moment—I scarce can say it was by my own volition, and I am sure it was without a conscious aim—both my pistols went off, and both escaped out of my hands. They did not fall alone; with a choked cry, [Hands] loosed his grasp upon the shrouds and plunged head first into the water.

Owing to the cant of the vessel, the masts hung far out over the water, and from my perch on the cross-trees I had nothing below me but the surface of the bay. Hands, who was not so far up, was in consequence nearer to the ship and fell between me and the bulwarks. He rose once to the surface in a lather of foam and blood and then sank again for good. As the water settled, I could see him lying huddled together on the clean, bright sand in the shadow of the vessel's sides. A fish or two whipped past his body. Sometimes, by the quivering of the water, he appeared to move a little, as if he were trying to rise. But he was dead enough, for all that, being both shot and drowned, and was food for fish in the very place where he had designed my slaughter.

Every sentence drives the movement forward, in what George Saunders (referring to Russian writers) has called "a series of incremental pulses, each of which does something to us. Each puts us in a new place relative to where we just were."[22]

At first, with Jim high up on the mast, it seems that the danger is past and he complacently relaxes. Then comes instantaneous violence, which happens in a blur. He sees the sailor's hand go behind his shoulder, "something" whizzes through the air too fast to see what it is, and he's pinned to the mast in pain. When his pistols go off it's not even self-defense, and it's by mere luck that Hands is hit.

Hands cries out—a "choked" cry—and then loses his grip on the ropes and plunges into the sea. After the intense action, stillness. But as in a nightmare, the menace won't stop; he is rising to the surface again. Then the "lather of foam and blood" is reassuring, and he sinks a second time, for good. We know that the water is clear because "the clean, bright sand" on the bottom is fully visible. Nothing is moving now except a couple of fish, which don't just "swim" past but "whip" past the body.

Or is it over even now? Hands seems to be moving yet again! No, that's an illusion, it's only that the water is quivering. He is doubly dead, "both shot and drowned," and the fish will soon devour him.

Eventually treasure does get recovered, a mass of exotic coins worth no less than £700,000, an enormous fortune in those days—"doubloons and double guineas and moidores and sequins, the pictures of all the kings of Europe for the last hundred years, strange Oriental pieces stamped with what looked like wisps of string or bits of spider's web, round pieces and square pieces, and pieces bored through the middle, as if to wear them round your neck." With much labor they get the coins into the ship, not bothering to take all of the heavy bars of silver and miscellaneous weapons that had also been buried.

The treasure-seekers might be triumphant, but Jim is not. He reflects, "That was Flint's treasure that we had come so far to seek and that had cost already the lives of seventeen men from the *Hispaniola*. How many it had cost in the amassing, what blood and sorrow, what good ships scuttled on the deep, what brave men walking the plank blindfold, what shot of cannon, what shame and lies and cruelty, perhaps no man alive could tell."

When they sail away, marooning the surviving pirates on the island, they take Silver with them, but it's understood that in England he will have to stand trial. During a stop for supplies on the South American mainland, however, he makes his escape, and no reader is likely to be sorry about that.

Strikingly, the mood at the end is somber rather than triumphant. Jim has grown up, but with plenty of psychic scars. He has witnessed treachery and death at close hand, has killed a man at point-blank range, and has escaped his own death by good luck more than anything. The last words in the book are the voice of Silver's parrot.

> The bar silver and the arms still lie, for all that I know, where Flint buried them; and certainly they shall lie there for me. Oxen and wain-ropes would not bring me back again to that accursed island; and the worst dreams that ever I have are when I hear the surf booming about its coasts or start upright in bed with the sharp voice of Captain Flint still ringing in my ears: "Pieces of eight! Pieces of eight!"[23]

It's important to note that due to Victorian conventions, much of real life had to be left out of *Treasure Island*. A few years later Louis composed a sailors' song purportedly heard in a London pub:

> It's there we trap the lasses
> All waiting for the crew;
> It's there we buy the trader's rum
> What bores a seaman through.

The rum got into *Treasure Island,* the lasses didn't. Although one wouldn't expect female characters to play an important role in a quest for treasure, it's still striking that Jim's mother is the only woman in the entire book. In later novels, *Catriona* above all, Louis would try hard to give women a major role, but like other writers at the time he felt seriously inhibited by obligatory prudery. Publishers made their biggest profits by selling to lending libraries, which rejected outright any novel that hinted at sex. Louis told Colvin, "This is a poison bad world for the romancer, this Anglo-Saxon world; I usually get out of it by not having any women in at all." Even when he did create female characters later on, he took great care to avoid sexually suggestive implications.[24]

Victorian taboos were so strict that Louis's pirates couldn't even swear, though he himself, as Lloyd recalled, "could swear vociferously." While he was writing *Treasure Island* he complained to Henley, "Buccaneers without oaths—bricks without straw." He solved the problem by never actually quoting what they said: "With a dreadful oath he stumbled off." No doubt he appreciated Dickens's solution in *Great Expectations,* which was to write "bless" whenever Bill Barley, an old sea dog, would have said "damn"—"Here's old Bill Barley, bless your eyes. Here's old Bill Barley on the flat of his back, by the Lord. Lying on the flat of his back, like a drifting old dead flounder, here's your old Bill Barley, bless your eyes. Ahoy! Bless you."[25]

The last of the seventeen installments of *Treasure Island* was published in *Young Folks* in January 1882, for a total payment of £30. For book publication Henley, as de facto agent, negotiated a contract with Cassell for £100; that may not sound like much, but it was a lot at the time, equivalent to £6,500 today. At that time Henley had an editorial position at Cassell's, and had thrown the *Young Folks* installments on the chief editor's desk with the exclamation, "There is a book for you!" Louis wrote to thank him: "Bravo, Bully Boy! Bravo! You are the Prince of Extortioners. Continue to extortion." To his parents he described it as "a hundred pounds, all alive, oh! A hundred jingling, tingling, golden, minted quid." Not only did he get £100 from Cassell, but they agreed to a royalty of £20 for every thousand copies after the first four thousand.[26]

The author was now identified as Robert Louis Stevenson, not Captain George North, and the book bore a dedication to Lloyd: "To S.L.O., an American gentleman in accordance with whose classic taste the following narrative has been designed, it is now, in return for numerous delightful hours, and with the kindest wishes, dedicated by his affectionate friend, the author." The American gentleman was fifteen at the time.

The map of the island, which had begun as a casual amusement at Braemar by Louis and Lloyd, was much more than a decorative feature. If it's properly reproduced one can follow every twist and turn of the story on it, and for the book version draftsmen in Thomas Stevenson's engineering office produced the map shown here (color plate 12).

Within three years of the 1883 first edition, four more were released, for a total sale of sixteen thousand copies, and by 1891 nearly forty thousand were in print. Louis therefore earned at least £600 from *Treasure Island,* and his heirs would continue to receive royalties until the book went out of copyright in 1944.[27]

As a relatively short novel, it was responsive to a recent development in publishing. The three-volume format that had been the norm suddenly ceased to exist. Novels now came out as single volumes at modest prices—5 shillings in this instance. Oscar Wilde was looking back at the older practice when he made Miss Prism say in *The Importance of Being Earnest,* "Do not speak slightingly of the three-volume novel, Cecily. I wrote one myself in earlier days."[28]

FAREWELL TO DAVOS

By now Louis had produced an impressive body of work. In addition to *Treasure Island,* there were *The Silverado Squatters* and "Thrawn Janet," as well as the important essays "Talk and Talkers" and "A Gossip on Romance." In addition he published collected editions of his earlier essays under the titles *Virginibus Puerisque* ("For Girls and Boys") and *Familiar Studies of Men and Books,* and there were new stories entitled *New Arabian Nights.* In spite of working by fits and starts, he had accomplished a great deal and would continue to do so. During the twenty years from 1874 to 1894 he turned out an average of four hundred pages a year.

Henley told him, "I like the style of the new essays better than that of the others—the earlier ones. It is clear, more sufficient, less foppish or rather less tricksy (not tricky, mind) and more like Style; has more distinction, in fact, and less personality."[29]

It amused Louis to make fun of Henley in "Talk and Talkers," which featured a number of his friends under aliases (as already mentioned, Henley was "Burly"). He wrote just before the essay came out in the *Cornhill,* "I have gibbeted you and Bob and a crowd of others in an article, my dear sir. By God, we'll see who's uppermost. I have made the flesh smoke; the sound of my lashes is audible in the ends of the earth. I perceive you wince, sir—why? Does it hurt? Ah, sir, more is coming. I shall tear the bandage from the world's eyes and show you as you are."³⁰

Despite these achievements, however, periods of intensive work were often followed by slumps. In March Louis told Baxter, "I am getting a steady, slow, sluggish stream of ink over paper," and to Henley he described himself as "dead in the head," concluding, "Pity the sorrows of an idiot thirty-one years old. Rbrt Ls Stvnsn of Sctlnd. Gd hlp hm, qut dmbfndrd. Nthng bt cnsnnts."³¹

At this time he composed a poem entitled "The Celestial Surgeon."

> If I have faltered more or less
> In my great task of happiness;
> If I have moved among my race
> And shown no glorious morning face;
> If beams from happy human eyes
> Have moved me not; if morning skies,
> Books, and my food, and summer rain
> Knocked on my sullen heart in vain:
> Lord, thy most pointed pleasure take
> And stab my spirit broad awake;
> Or, Lord, if too obdurate I,
> Choose thou, before that spirit die,
> A piercing pain, a killing sin,
> And to my dead heart run them in!

After this poem was published the bishop of Oxford praised its "graceful, noble lines" and declared, "Surely no poet of the present day, and none perhaps since Dante, has so truly told of the inner character of accidie, or touched more skillfully the secret of its sinfulness." Evidently the bishop was not a careful reader of poetry. While the poem does evoke sloth (*accidie* or *acedia*), one of the Seven Deadly Sins, Louis was begging the Almighty to *make* him sinful as a relief from torpor.³²

Happily, however, the health cure eventually succeeded, and in April he told Henley, "My lungs are said to be in a splendid state. A cruel examination, and exanimation I may call it, had this brave result. Tayaut [French for "tally ho"]. Hillo. Hey. Stand by. Avast! Hurrah!" Dr. Ruedi declared that it was permissible to leave Davos, which Louis gladly did, never to return.³³

CHAPTER 19

Two Years on the Riviera

ORDERED SOUTH ONCE MORE

Reunited with the elder Stevensons, the family spent a pleasant summer at Kingussie in the Scottish Highlands, though Louis was lonely at first because Fanny stayed on at Heriot Row to await the arrival of Lloyd. He sent her a whimsical poem that began "Where is my wife? where is my Woggs?" and continued with verses playing anagrammatically on Fanny's name:

> I am as good as death
> When separate from F.
> I am far from gay
> When separate from A.
> I loathe the ways of men
> When separate from N.
> Life is a murky den
> When separate from N.
> My sorrow rages high
> When separate from Y.
> And all seems uncanny
> When separate from Fanny.

He signed the letter "Uxorious Billy far from you." A couple of months previously he had written to a young admirer seeking advice, "By your 'fate,' I believe I meant your marriage, or that love at least which may befall anyone of us at the shortest notice and overthrow the most settled habits and opinions. I call that your fate because then, if not before, you can no longer hang back, but must stride out into life and act."[1]

When autumn arrived, unfortunately, Louis began to hemorrhage. They hastened to London to consult Dr. Clark. Louis told Henley, "I carried the art of spitting blood to a pitch not previously dreamed of in my philosophy" (he was remembering Hamlet telling Horatio, "There are more things in heaven and earth than are dreamt of in your philosophy"). As before, Clark's advice was to spend the winter on the Riviera.[2]

At this time news arrived that Louis's books were beginning to be popular in the United States. He wrote delightedly to his parents,

> In eighteen hundred and eighty-three
> America discovered me!

and added, "I am Columbus outside in," which is to say in reverse. One wonders, however, if Thomas and Margaret had ever heard of the American jingle "In fourteen hundred and ninety-two / Columbus sailed the ocean blue."[3]

They stayed at first near Marseille and then at Hyères, ninety miles west of Nice. When Edith Wharton had a house there forty years later it was still "an old Provençal town set well away from the seaside, which had kept its customs, its rural and provincial atmosphere, and its regional dialect."[4]

After they arrived at the Hôtel des Îles d'Or, Louis wrote to his parents, "My dear people, this is a beautiful and charming spot. We are going to try to find a cheaper hotel and stay for a while. It agrees well with me, I think; and I believe Fanny is going to get over her last bad turn, thanks to the warm weather. The weather is sublime; it is really. It could not be beaten. My mind seems hopelessly addled.... My mind is quite extinct."[5]

It didn't take long to realize that they didn't really care for hotel life, and in March they rented a house known as the Chalet La Solitude. The house (fig. 50) had an unusual history. It had been constructed for the Paris Exposition of 1878, when Louis had acted as his mentor Fleeming Jenkin's secretary, and was a model intended to be reproduced on a larger scale. After the exposition closed it had been moved to Hyères. Louis would not have been pleased that when the Stevenson Club of London later attached a memorial plaque to the house, they identified him as "English author."[6]

"I now draw near to the middle ages," Louis wrote to Will Low. "Nearly three years ago that fatal Thirty struck, and yet the great work is not done—not yet even conceived. But so, as one goes on, the wood seems to thicken, the footpath

50. La Solitude, Hyères

to narrow, and the House Beautiful on the hill's summit to draw further and further away." He was remembering *Pilgrim's Progress,* in which Christian is given hospitality in the House Beautiful by Prudence, Piety, and Charity—not necessarily favorite guides in Louis's own case.[7]

Still, the pleasant climate and surroundings were seductive, and by November he could write to his Monterey friend Jules Simoneau that apart from health worries, "I have no wish that is not fulfilled; a beautiful small house in a large garden; a fine view of plain, sea and mountain; a wife that suits me down to the ground; and a barrel of good Beaujolais."

He also offered a balance sheet contrasting the English and French.

The English:	*The French:*
hypocrites	free from hypocrisy
good, stout reliable friends	incapable of friendship
dishonest to the root	fairly honest
fairly decent to women	rather indecent to women

He especially deplored the French treatment of women, though he added, "The race of man was born tyrannical; doubtless Adam beat Eve."[8]

It's remarkable that doctors who treated lung conditions regarded "good air" as the one essential thing. The mechanism of infection wasn't well understood, and researchers were just beginning to suspect that malaria ("bad air") had anything to do with mosquitoes. When the pirates in *Treasure Island* fall ill after carousing in a swamp, Dr. Livesey tells them severely, "That comed—as you call it—of being arrant asses, and not having sense enough to know honest air from poison, and the dry land from a vile, pestiferous slough."[9]

Whatever the quality of the air, the Riviera suffered recurring epidemics of cholera as well as typhus, and Hyères was especially unsanitary. Blowing dust got into Louis's eyes and provoked a case of ophthalmia that forced him to wear dark glasses and give up reading. And there were more hemorrhages. It was believed that the slightest activity might provoke them, and he was ordered to stay in bed with one arm bound to his side.

Difficult though this regimen was, in later years he remembered Hyères fondly. In Samoa in 1891, by which time his health was immensely improved, he wrote to Colvin that he had just had an imaginary conversation with him. "I was toiling, the sweat dripping from my nose in the hot fit after a squall of rain; methought you asked me—frankly, was I happy. 'Happy (said I), I was only happy once: that was at Hyères; it came to an end from a variety of reasons, decline of health, change of place, increase of money, age with his stealing steps. Since then, as before then, I know not what it means. But I know pleasure still.'" Perhaps he also had in mind that at Hyères he and Fanny were living alone together (Lloyd was at school in England much of the time), which they never did afterward. Yet the awareness that death might strike at any moment was keen. "Age with his stealing steps" comes from the Gravedigger's song in *Hamlet* as he tosses up a skull from Ophelia's open grave.[10]

Actually they were not completely alone, since they acquired a valuable servant, Valentine Roch. She would remain with them for six years, eventually marrying and settling in California, but like servants in most writings of the time she remains indistinct. Lloyd, however, was greatly taken with Valentine, and described her as "our vivacious cook and maid of all work. She was a charming girl, far above her class, with a sparkling sense of humor, who reviewed the whole neighborhood and nightly brought its annals up to date."[11]

Fanny, like Louis, was often ill. In a series of letters he told his parents, "Fanny very bad. I have never seen so bad a turn"—"Fanny has been pretty bad again"—"Fanny has been ill again; we got the doctor who did very well, and is experimenting away upon her with red-hot needles: 'tis his mania, and I don't imagine it can do harm." She herself wrote, "I have had some bad times, but the doctor here is certain he can cure me entirely with what he calls 'thermal cautery.' He heats a sort of little hammer red hot and burns spots upon me with it." Cauterization is still used for a wide variety of conditions, but it's impossible to know what Fanny's may have been.[12]

Some biographers have reproached Fanny for what they describe, without evidence, as hypochondria, but many of her afflictions were very real, as was distressingly common in those days. Also, there was the psychological pressure of looking after Louis. Thirty years after his death Lloyd told an inquirer, "As to my mother, whatever you may find to criticize in her, remember always that it was she who kept Stevenson alive; and in keeping him alive—guarding him, watching over him, subordinating her whole life to him—she necessarily offended many people. Her life in many ways was a very sad one—a life of unending apprehension. Death was always snatching at Stevenson, and there she was always interposing herself."[13]

"TUSHERY"

Writing was the best relief. It was while lying in bed at Hyères that Louis composed most of *A Child's Garden of Verses*. Inert and in near darkness because of the eye affliction, he had a board laid across his bed with sheets of paper pinned to it. "On these," Fanny remembered, "or on a slate fastened to the board, he laboriously wrote out in the darkness, with his left hand, many more of the songs of his childhood." He had crippling writer's cramp in his right hand. In the notebook that contains drafts of the poems there are also such notes as this: "I wonder if we might not have the chloral mixture in smaller doses to be taken more frequently in case of persistence? so that one could, in case of necessity, take a dose every thirty minutes."[14]

Louis never had great ambitions as a poet, which is just as well, since when he strove to be "poetical" he was never at his best. "He scribbled verses," Belle said, "to pass the time. He thought so little of these that the *Child's Garden of Verses* and *Underwoods* would not have been printed had not many a poem been rescued from the margins of magazines, the fly-leaves of a book he was reading, and even the wastepaper basket."[15]

A year after the serialization of *Treasure Island,* the editor of *Young Folks* asked for another novel, and Louis jumped at the chance for easy money. This would be *The Black Arrow: A Tale of the Two Roses,* set during the medieval Wars of the Roses and, like *Treasure Island,* purportedly written by "Captain George North." He noted in his diary that he began writing on May 26, 1883; the serialization started just one month later and ran through late October.

The Black Arrow is not very good, and he knew it wasn't. When he sent the manuscript to Colvin Louis called it "dullish and put-up, and as unlike the reality of *Treasure Island* as possible." Still, it's worth glancing at as an example of the kind of potboiler that was popular at the time, and a dependable source of income for a writer who could play that game. Readers of *Young Folks* actually thought it was better than *Treasure Island,* which reveals a lot about the readers of *Young Folks*.[16]

When he began writing Louis reported cheerfully to Henley that it was going to be "a whole tale of tushery. And every tushery touches me so free, that may I be tushed if the whole thing is worth a tush. *The Black Arrow: A Tale of Tunstall Forest* is his name: tush! a poor thing!" "Tush" was a dismissive expression for something trivial, and Louis seems to have made up the word *tushery*. This novel has been described as "clogged with archaic language," and that's putting it mildly—"Ye were a good friend to me-ward"; "Toss-pot and Shuttle-wit run in, but my Lord Good-Counsel sits o' one side, waiting"; "Give ye good day, good ferryman. Launch me your boat, I prithee; we are sore in haste." The narration is formulaic too. "The old rogue made a humorous grimace, and although Dick was displeased to lie under so great favours to so equivocal a personage, he was yet unable to restrain his mirth."[17]

For book publication five years later Louis added a dedication to Fanny.

> No one but myself knows what I have suffered, nor what my books have gained, by your unsleeping watchfulness and admirable pertinacity. And now here is a volume that goes into the world and lacks your imprimatur: a strange thing in our joint lives; and the reason of it stranger still! I have watched with interest, with pain, and at length with amusement, your unavailing attempts to peruse *The Black Arrow;* and I think I should lack humour indeed if I let the occasion slip and did not place your name in the fly-leaf of the only book of mine that you have never read—and never will read.

That's surely a strange way of presenting a book to the public! Still later Louis wrote to an acquaintance, "I find few greater pleasures than reading my own works, but I never, O I never read *The Black Arrow.*"[18]

At Hyères he also worked on a novel called *Prince Otto,* which was serialized in *Longman's Magazine* and then published in book form by Chatto and Windus. He was hoping, he said in the dedication to Nellie Sanchez, "by hook or crook, this book or the next, to launch a masterpiece."

The struggle to get *Prince Otto* into shape was exasperating. At one point he told Henley, "It is queer and a little, little bit free; and some of the parties are immoral; and the whole thing is not a romance, nor yet a comedy, nor yet a romantic comedy; but a kind of preparation of some of the elements of all three in a glass jar." So far as comedy goes, "None of it is exactly funny, but some of it is smiling."[19]

Louis wanted very badly to believe in *Prince Otto,* and he wrote to Will Low, "There is a good deal of stuff in it, both dramatic and, I think, poetic; and the story is not like these purposeless fables of today, but is, at least, intended to stand firm upon a base of philosophy—or morals—as you please. It has been long gestated, and is wrought with care." The gestation and the careful writing were real enough. Years later he told another correspondent, "*Otto* was my hardest effort, for I wished to do something very swell, which did not quite come off. Whole chapters of *Otto* were written as often as five and six times, and one by my wife—my wife's version was the second last." He was addressing an American, which is presumably why he used the word "swell."[20]

When the novel was finally published the response was lukewarm. One reviewer said, "We all expected that *Prince Otto* was to prove the magnum opus. Well, we were wrong." The few positive reviews were by friends (concealed by anonymity) and even they were carefully vague. Andrew Lang wrote in the *Pall Mall Gazette,* "It is a book to be drunk in one long breath, like a draught of sunny Moselle from a tapering, iridescent Venetian goblet. . . . We should call it a philosophical-humouristical-psychological fantasy."[21]

Disappointing though this novel is, it's interesting to think about what Louis was trying to do. The story is set at the time of the revolutions of 1848, and an imperious prime minister named Gondremark is obviously intended to suggest Bismarck. The feckless Prince Otto has no interest in exerting authority, and his fictional principality of Grünewald succumbs to a revolution. The very first words erase his domain before the story even begins: "You shall seek in vain upon the map of Europe for the bygone state of Grünewald. . . . Less fortunate than Poland, she left not a regret behind her, and the very memory of her boundaries has faded."

When *Prince Otto* was published Henry James—a personal friend by that time—tried to put the best face on Louis's work: "As in his extreme artistic vivacity he seems really disposed to try everything, he has tried once, by way of a change, to be inhuman, and there is a hard glitter about *Prince Otto* which seems to indicate that in this case, too, he has succeeded."[22]

The one interesting character is the Countess Von Rosen, who was based on the alarmingly flirtatious Russian sisters in Menton. She has a lot in common too with Fanny Stevenson, who took pains advising Louis on the characterization and did some rewriting herself. He reported to Henley, "Triumph of triumphs, my wife—my wife who hates and loathes and slates [criticizes] my women—admits a great part of my Countess to be on the spot."[23]

The countess is notable for her sexual magnetism, which she deploys on all occasions. She is also amoral, declaring, "I have broken all the ten commandments; and if there were more tomorrow, I should not sleep till I had broken these." Something Louis said to Henley indicates what he wished he had been free to do. "To be quite frank, there is a *risqué* character: the Countess von Rosen, a jolly, elderly—how shall I say?—fuckstress; whom I tried to handle so as to please this rotten public, and damn myself the while for ruining good material. I could, an if I dared, make her jump."[24]

In a letter to Bob years later, Louis recalled their early days in Edinburgh and commented, "The damned thing of our education is that Christianity does not recognize and hallow Sex. It looks askance at it, over its shoulder, oppressed as it is by reminiscences of hermits and Asiatic self-torturers. When I came to myself fairly about twenty-five, I recognized once for all the Lingam and the Yoni as the true religious symbols." In Hindu usage those are the male and female sexual organs. If Louis had lived into the time of D. H. Lawrence, he might well have written more openly about sexuality. As it stands, *Prince Otto* only confirms that James was right and that he had to try everything once; this was a kind of fiction he would never attempt again.[25]

Prince Otto has had few readers in recent times, but one was Nabokov, who embedded numerous allusions to it in *Pale Fire*. His Zembla is an imaginary state much like Grünewald, and his Kinbote has much in common with Otto.[26]

A FRIEND'S DEATH, AND RENEWED ILLNESS

In September news arrived that Walter Ferrier, one of the founding members of the Liberty, Justice, and Reverence society at the university, had died at the age of thirty-three. The news hit Louis hard, though it was all too foreseeable; Ferrier's early promise had been ruined by alcoholism. "My poor, besotted gentleman," he wrote to Henley. "O what regrets, what regrets! I cannot write about James Walter yet awhile; I wish to God I could have gone to his funeral even. Christ pity us: the hearse to take him away, that old fount of laughter."

A few days later Louis wrote again, "The last time that I saw him before leaving for America—it was a sad blow to both of us—I waited hours for him, and at last he came. 'My God,' I said, 'you have had too much again.' He did not deny it, as he did in the old days. He said 'Yes,' with a terrible simplicity. This fresh humiliation, after all the brave words and projects, accepted so plainly and so humbly, it went to my heart like a knife."[27]

To Ferrier's sister Elisabeth Anne ("Coggie") Louis wrote, "I did not know how much he had suffered; it is so that we are cured of life." Two months after this his grief had not abated, and he wrote again to Coggie, "I feel as if the earth were undermined, and all my friends have lost one thickness of reality since that one passed. Those are happy that can take it otherwise: with that I find things all beginning to dislimn"—that is, grow indistinct.[28]

Meanwhile, even when housebound by ill health, Louis kept up his usual stream of playful correspondence. After asking Bob to remember him to an artist friend named William Bazett Murray, it occurred to him that "Bazett" would make a fine expletive, and he proceeded to illustrate some of its uses.

> "O Bazett!" It would be a good oath. "Bazett" howled the infuriated ruffian. "Bazett!" said the licentious poet. "Bazett!" ejaculated the milkmaid as she pulled up her petticoat before the ardent miller. "You can have me, if you want, like a man," observed the modest prostitute, "but don't you try to come Bazett over me." "He was a very nice gentleman," said the ingenuous maid, "and gave me a shilling and a pair of gloves and half a pound of candy and took me to a circus and a coffee shop; but when it came to Bazett"—and she concluded the phrase with an animated pantomime.[29]

By the time spring arrived in Hyères, Louis's health seemed much improved. He and Fanny were contented with their life, and he wrote to his mother, "The great Cassandra is in pretty good feather; I love her better than ever and admire her more; and I cannot think what I have done to deserve so good a gift. This sudden remark came out of my pen; it is not like me; but in case you did not know, I may as well tell you that my marriage has been the most successful in the world. I say so, and being the child of my parents, I speak with knowledge. She is everything to me: wife, brother, sister, daughter and dear companion; and I would not change to get a goddess or a saint. So far, I think, after four years of matrimony."[30]

Just one month later, however, disaster struck: Louis suffered the most dangerous bronchial attack of his life. Fanny wrote to Henley, "I suppose that Louis has ruptured a blood vessel. The blood spurted all over everything in a moment. He was almost strangled with it. I caught nearly a pint of blood in a basin besides what went on towels and things and everywhere." And the next morning, "after sleeping about three hours he awoke and literally poured forth another volume of blood equal in quantity to the first. If it is not the end, Henley, it is the beginning of the end."

Henley immediately met with Baxter and Bob Stevenson in London, and they dispatched a distinguished Dr. Mennell to hurry to Hyères; the local doctor didn't inspire much confidence. Mennell's diagnosis was that Louis had broken several small arteries rather than a major one and would recover if kept absolutely quiet. As usual Fanny took on the job of nursing him, as she reported to Henley: "He will allow no one to touch him but me, and as he is forced to lie perfectly inert it is difficult to lift even his light weight in and out of bed. I have hurt my back a little doing it." At this time she was addressing Henley affectionately as "my dear Wild Man of the Woods" and "you great noisy swearing creature."[31]

By the end of the month Louis was well enough to write to Baxter, "I'm a wheen [a little bit] be'er. The devil an' me's no dune yet." Even so, he signed another letter by alluding to a hymn, "Yours ever, There-is-a-fountain-filled-with-blood Stevenson." To Bob Stevenson he wrote, "I am myself no more. Of that lean, feverish, voluble and whiskyfied young Scot, who once sparked through France and Britain bent on art and the pleasures of the flesh, there now remains no quality but the strong language."[32]

The last straw was a new cholera epidemic on the Riviera. It was time to go. After a brief stay at a health resort in Auvergne they were back in Britain, and would remain there for the next three years.

1. Louis in Sydney, Australia

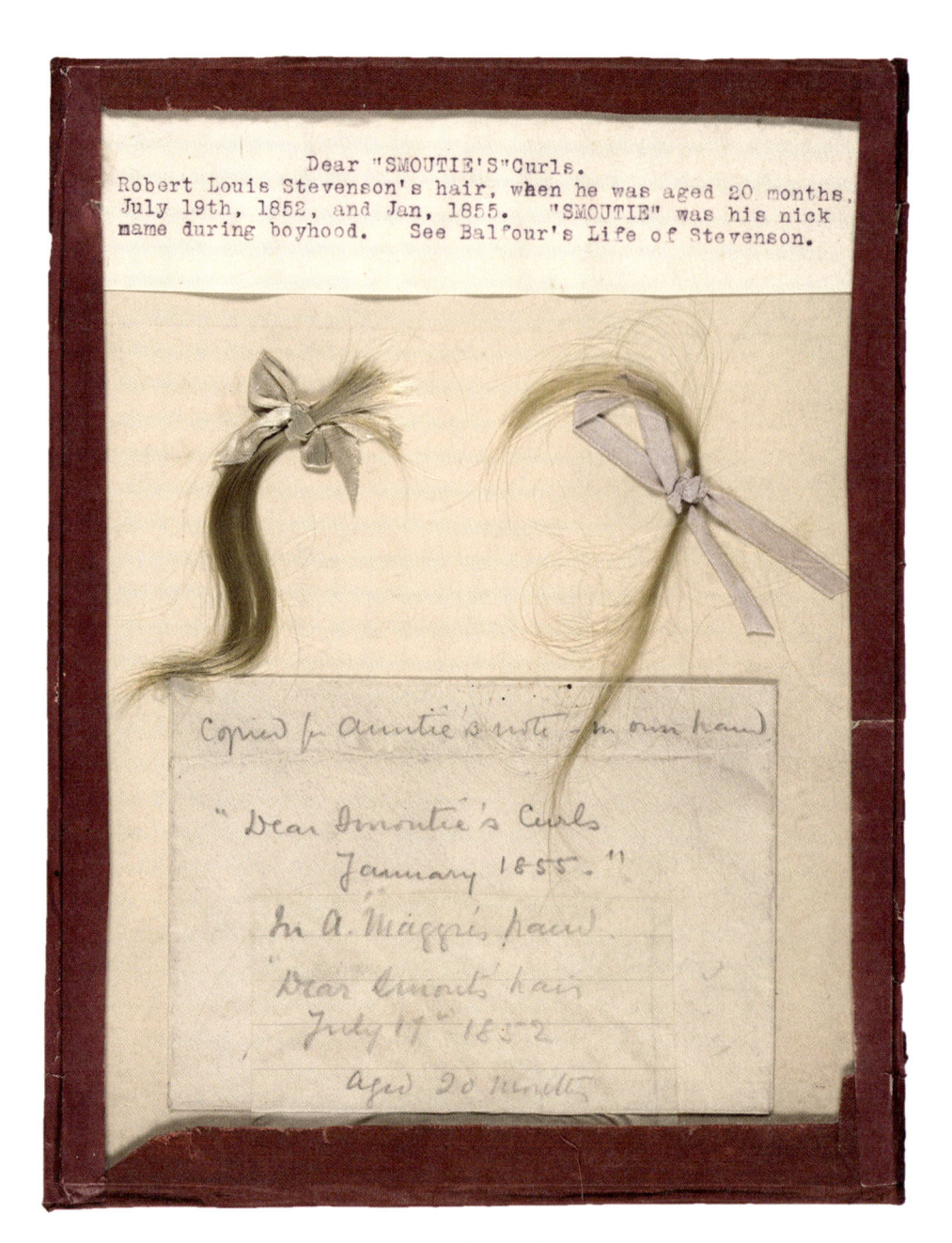

Dear "SMOUTIE'S" Curls.
Robert Louis Stevenson's hair, when he was aged 20 months,
July 19th, 1852, and Jan, 1855. "SMOUTIE" was his nick
name during boyhood. See Balfour's Life of Stevenson.

Copied fr Auntie's note in own hand

"Dear Smoutie's Curls
       January 1855."

In A. Maggie's hand

"Dear Smout's hair
     July 19th 1852

   Aged 20 months

2. Locks of Louis's hair

3. "The Lamplighter"

4. A Skelt illustration

5. Skerryvore Lighthouse

6. *Snowballing outside Edinburgh University,* by Samuel Bough

7. Menton harbor, by Albert Marquet

8. William Ernest Henley, by "Spy"

9. Samuel Pepys, by John Hayls

10. Louis at Grez, by Fanny

11. Blind Pew, by N. C. Wyeth

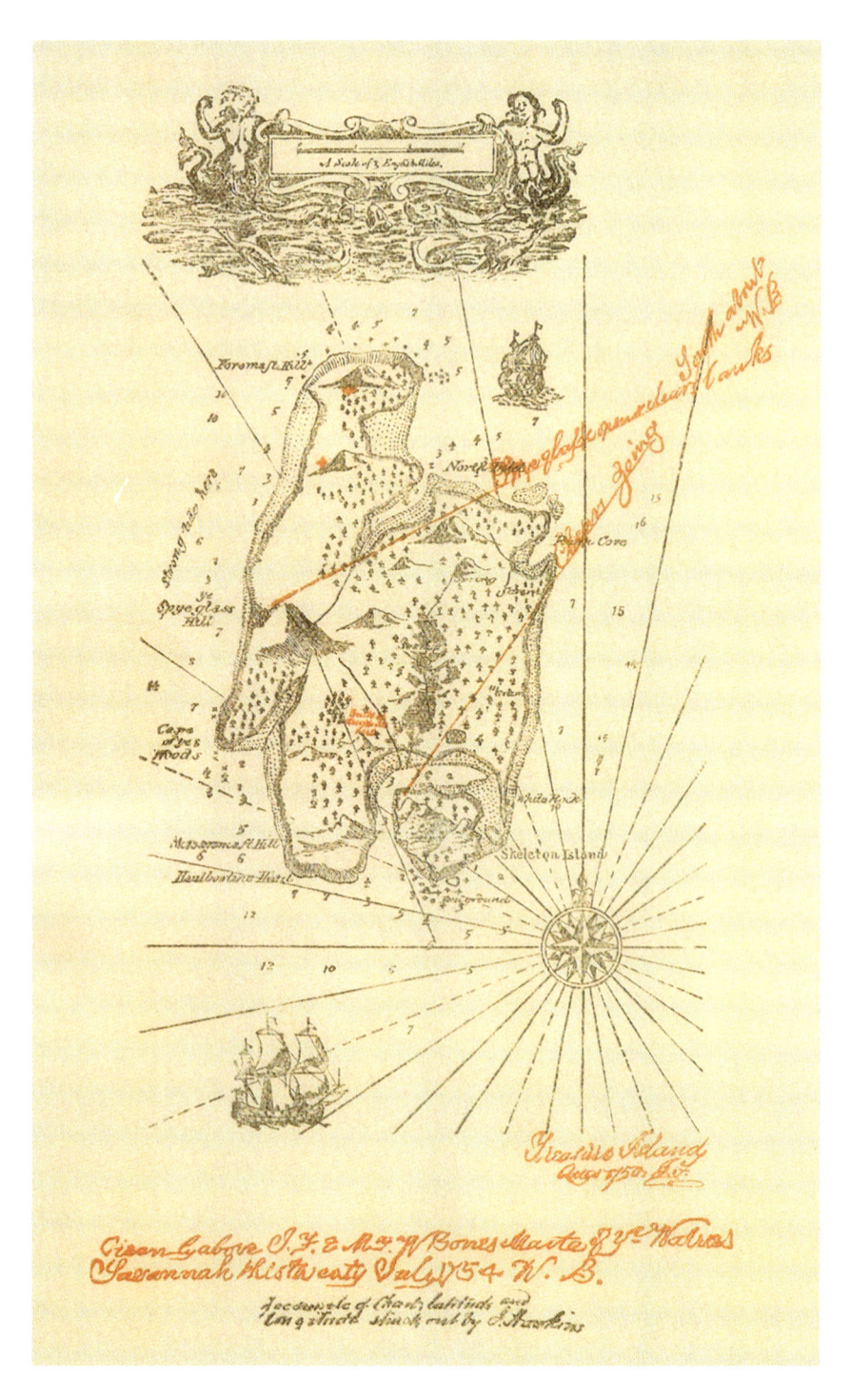

12. Map of Treasure Island

13. Louis and Fanny, by Sargent

14. David and Alan, by Wyeth

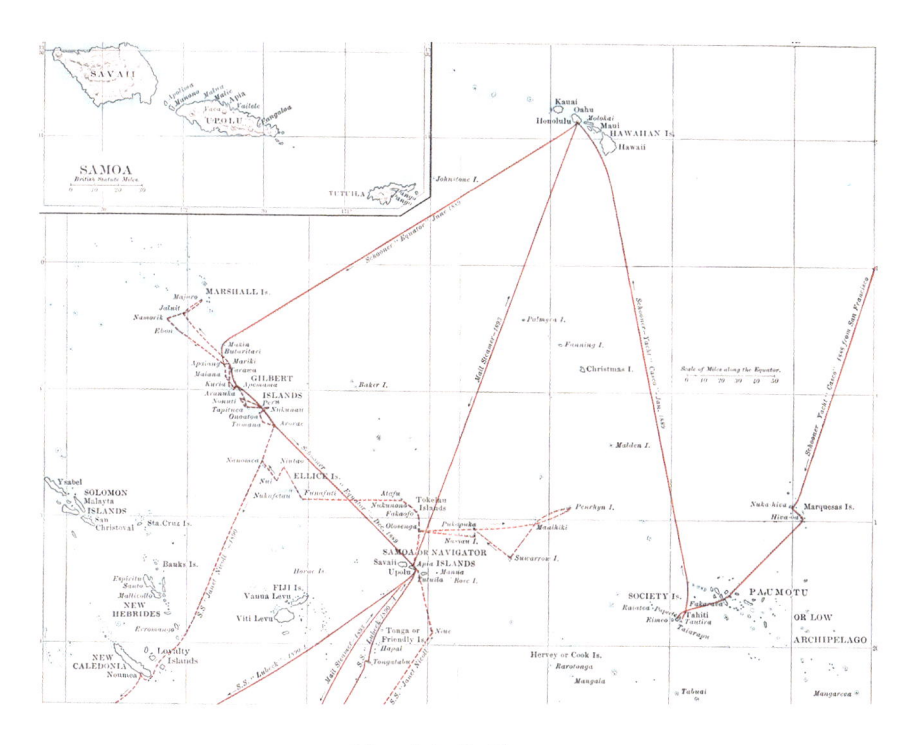

15. Map of the Pacific voyages

16. Upolu

17. Louis, by Girolamo Ballatti Nerli

CHAPTER 20

A Home in England

SKERRYVORE

Louis and Fanny chose to settle in Bournemouth on the English south coast. Easily reached by train from London, it was a popular health resort. "As all the world knows," a contemporary writer said, "invalids are the staple industry of Bournemouth. The place is sheltered and warm, and the air of its pine woods delightful and beneficial, so there is a large floating population of sick folk catered to by the remainder of the inhabitants."[1]

Louis and Fanny would live there for three years, from July 1884 to August 1887, after what had been a peripatetic existence. He compiled a list of towns in which he had spent at least one night: seventy-four in France, fifty in Scotland, forty-six in England, and another forty in other parts of Europe.[2]

After a few months in a rented house they moved into one that was bought for them by Louis's parents. They gave it the name Skerryvore, which was rich with associations. To this day the Skerryvore Lighthouse (color plate 5) is the tallest in Scotland, eleven miles out to sea beyond the Inner Hebrides; it had been built in the 1840s by Thomas Stevenson and his brother Alan. Louis told a correspondent, "We are all very proud of the family achievements, and the name of my house here in Bournemouth is stolen from one of the sea-towers of the Hebrides which are our pyramids and monuments." In the garden they set up a model of the lighthouse, in which an actual light was lit at night.[3]

A visitor described Skerryvore as "a two-story villa of yellow brick, overgrown with ivy, and capped with many high-pitched gables of blue slate. It turns its back on the road, and overlooks a garden which scrambles over the edge of the ravine." An etching (fig. 51) shows three figures in the foreground who are presumably Fanny (taller than she actually was), Louis, and Woggs. The seagulls indicate the nearness of the sea.[4]

Fanny adored it there; she had been on the move her entire life and was sick of it. She wrote to her friend Dora Williams, "It is very comfortable to know that we have a home really and truly and will no more be like Noah's dove, flying about with an olive branch." She threw herself enthusiastically into decorating, and wrote to Margaret, "Skerryvore will not look much like other people's houses, but it will please me so much more than if it did. I have never had such a chance to revel in color before."[5]

Louis's feelings were more mixed; he told Gosse, "I am now a beastly householder." Lloyd, who lived with them there when not at school, remembered that in later years Louis never once mentioned Skerryvore with regret. "The Victorianism it exemplified was jarring to every feeling he possessed. Of all men he was least fitted for ordinary English suburban life. Not that he saw much of it; he was virtually a prisoner in that house the whole time he lived in it. His health throughout was at its lowest ebb; never was he so spectral, so emaciated, so unkempt and so tragic a figure."[6]

It was at this time that Lloyd stopped using his original first name, Sam, which he shared with his father. He may have made the change because of a scandal concerning the elder Sam, who had suddenly deserted his second wife and disappeared forever, taking his latest girlfriend with him. Fanny told Colvin, "I believe that Louis feels a sort of joy in knowing that the boy now belongs to him entirely." As for Belle, she and her husband Joe were now living in Hawaii, and it would be another four years before they would be reunited with the Stevensons.[7]

Although Louis named the house to please his father, he felt disappointment and even guilt at having rejected the family profession.

> Say not of me that weakly I declined
> The labours of my sires, and fled the sea,
> The towers we founded and the lamps we lit,
> To play at home with paper like a child.

The regret may have been exaggerated, but even later on, when he was a literary celebrity, the conflicted feelings remained. In the last year of his life, with several popular novels to his credit by then, he told Will Low, "Small is the word; it is a

51. Skerryvore

small age, and I am of it. I could have wished to be otherwise busy in this world. I ought to have been able to build lighthouses and write *David Balfours* too."[8]

For the first time since she lived in Oakland, Fanny was able to indulge her passion for gardening. Louis asked Will, who had returned home to America, to send seeds that were not available in England—sugar peas, sweet corn, and cantaloupe. For himself the piano was a new enthusiasm. "He is enjoying the piano immensely," Fanny told his parents, "and is learning to play in a way." He never considered taking lessons, but picked out the notes with one finger and eventually with two. He wrote to Henley, "To be seated at a piano, to experiment on a lot of black dots, to have an inspiration and find out some shadow of what is meant, is HEAVEN." To Colvin he said, "You should hear me labouring away at Martini's celebrated, beroomed gavotte or Boccherini's beroomed, famous minuet. I have 'beroomed' on the brain, and sign myself, Sir, The Beroomed Stevenson." In German *berühmt* means "famous." Two weeks later he admitted that he was still limited to "the manly and melodious forefinger."[9]

He did have genuine musical taste. Working on a Bach gavotte, he wrote to Bob, "'Tis strange why Bach is thought dry—he is much less dry than anybody else, offering such rewards to the human mind at every step." He often talked enthusiastically about concerts he had attended years before, and Lloyd thought it was a great pity that gramophones didn't come into widespread use until after his death.[10]

An important member of the household was Valentine, who had remained with the family after they left Hyères. She contributed a reminiscence to *I Can Remember Robert Louis Stevenson:* "Whenever my thoughts take me back to those happy days at Skerryvore, I feel grateful to the Fates which granted me those few years of close companionship with one who is beloved of all who knew him. From him I learned that life is not for self if we want happiness—and that it is only in service that we fulfill our destiny." Valentine admitted that at times there were tensions, though she didn't explain what they were. When she was "good" Louis called her Joe, and when bad she was Thomassine. He once handed her a piece of paper on which he had written:

> A dearer I do not know than Joe,
> A sadder girl has rarely been than Thomassine.
> Joe is my friend—so may she always be,
> And for Joe's sake that darker Thomassine wants a true friend in me.

Valentine added that she and other servants experienced from him "love that radiated to all around him." She made no mention of Fanny.[11]

52. Fanny in Bournemouth

PORTRAITS

Several portraits were made at this time. Fanny (fig. 52) is shown relaxed, with her hair done up more carefully than usual, and with her characteristic direct gaze; her wedding ring is conspicuously evident. The photograph of Louis (fig. 53) is more stylized. It was taken by Sir Percy Shelley, son of the poet, and no doubt carefully posed by him.

People at the time often complained that photographs misrepresented them. The formal conditions of Victorian studios, together with the extended exposures that were necessary, meant that sitters had to assume fixed and often uncharacteristic expressions. Charles Darwin said, "All my photographs and por-

53. Louis in Bournemouth

traits make me look either silly or stupid or affected," and on another occasion, "If I really have as bad an expression as my photograph gives me, how I can have one friend is surprising." For someone as volatile as Louis, no portrait could really convey his personality. He wrote to an admirer who asked for a photograph, "The truth is I have no appearance; a certain air of disreputability is the one constant character that my face presents; the rest change like water. But still I am lean, and still disreputable."[12]

During this period Fanny commented, "A friend of mine said, 'Louis is never what one would call a handsome man, and is sometimes positively plain; but then he is sometimes absolutely beautiful.' I think this is a very good description that applies to more than his personal appearance."[13]

The best portrait is not by a photographer at all, but by a painter. John Singer

Sargent, who had once shared a Paris studio with Bob Stevenson, came down from London to Bournemouth to paint it. He struck Louis as "a charming, simple, clever, honest young man," but his first attempt, with Louis seated in an armchair, didn't turn out well. "He represents me as a weird, very pretty, large-eyed, chicken-boned, slightly contorted poet. He is not pleased; wants to do me again in several positions; walking about and talking is his main notion. We both lost our hearts to him."[14]

The second attempt (color plate 13) was more interesting. Louis wrote to Will Low,

> Sargent was down again and painted a portrait of me walking about in my own dining room, in my own velveteen jacket, and twisting as I go my own moustache; at one corner a glimpse of my wife in an Indian dress and seated in a chair that was once my grandfather's, but since some months goes by the name of Henry James's, for it was there the novelist loved to sit—adds a touch of poesy and comicality. It is, I think, excellent, but is too eccentric to be exhibited. I am at one extreme corner; my wife, in this wild dress and looking like a ghost, is at the extreme other end; between us an open door exhibits my palatial entrance hall and a part of my respected staircase. All this is touched in lovely, with that witty touch of Sargent's; but of course it looks damn queer as a whole.

They kept the painting, which wasn't sold until Fanny's death three decades later; it is now in the Metropolitan Museum in New York.[15]

Sargent was able to capture, as no one else ever did, Louis's restless moving about and his posture as he did it. Someone who knew him said,

> He walked with a long and curiously marked step, light but almost metrical, in accord, it seems, with some movement of his mind. It was his constant habit to pace to and fro as he conversed, and his step and speech seemed in harmony. He did not stoop, but in walking his body was somewhat inclined forward, and in his attitude generally there was something unusual, distinguished, almost fantastic. His bearing remains in my memory as unlike that of any other human being I ever saw.

Rosaline Masson agreed that "Mr. Sargent has caught the charm, the genius, the long fingers, the thinness, the restlessness, the damn queerness, the very spirit of the man himself."[16]

Sargent himself called his painting "the picture of the caged animal lecturing about the foreign specimen in the corner." That would be Fanny, who like

Sargent was American. He had suggested that she wear the sari for its colorful effect, and although she does look ghostlike, one feature is fully visible—her naked foot poking out beneath the gown. She went barefoot whenever she could, and in Samoa would rejoice in never having to wear shoes at all.[17]

"MY HEALTH HAS BEEN HELLISH"

No sooner had they arrived in Bournemouth than Louis had an attack of hemorrhaging so scary that they hurried to London to see a specialist. When the episode was over he reported to Low, "My health has been hellish. I had a real blood vessel business, or if not that something equally bloody, two basins being filled; thereafter three weeks without moving a hand and an unparalleled effect of real tedium."[18]

Less alarming, but certainly disturbing, was the discovery of a parasite. "I have been detected in the felonious possession of many yards of tapeworm. I was instantly arrested and the goods have been restored to their maker, much good may they do him. The worm was very like me in figure; in the face there was only a family resemblance. I may now say, and that gladly, that I have had every infamous complaint. 'Tis a strange world." Fanny, who had become a devoted reader of the medical journal the *Lancet,* suspected back at Hyères that their salad greens might be infested with tapeworm eggs.[19]

In November it was flu for a change. Louis wrote to Henley, "Do you know anyone that wants a cough: a hacking, hewing, tickling, leacherous, choking, nauseating, vomitable cough; a cough that springs like a rattle, rakes like a barrow [perhaps a misreading for "harrow"], and deracinates the body like a shot of dynamite?" Fanny added a postscript: "Louis is far too ill to do any work at all. His cough never ceases."[20]

Ill health naturally provoked depression, as when Louis wrote on another occasion, "I awoke this morning with collywobbles and had to take a small dose of laudanum with the usual consequences of dry throat, intoxicated legs, partial madness, and total imbecility." Collywobbles meant an upset stomach, but more generally nervous anxiety. At one point Fanny told Colvin, "I had to lift Louis in and out of bed ten times in one night. He was quite off his head and would not be contradicted because he was bleeding at the lungs at the same time and got into furies when I wasn't quick enough."[21]

A visitor to Skerryvore later recalled Louis "rolling a limp cigarette in his long, limp fingers, and talking eagerly all the while." Then came a striking impression of Fanny:

Opposite him sits Mrs. Stevenson, the tutelary genius of Skerryvore, a woman of small physical stature, but surely of heroic mould. Her features are clear-cut and delicate, but marked by unmistakable strength of character; her hair of an unglossy black, and her complexion darker than one would expect in a woman of Dutch-American race. I have heard her speak of a Moorish strain in her ancestry, whether seriously or in jest I know not. Beneath a placid though always alert and vivacious exterior, Mrs. Stevenson conceals much personal suffering and continual anxieties under which many a stronger woman might well break down.[22]

A constant concern was too much socializing, which exhausted Louis and provoked dangerous attacks. During a visit to London Fanny wrote to Margaret, "Louis knows far too many people to get a moment's rest. Company comes in at all hours from early morning till late at night, so that I almost never have a moment alone, and if we do not soon get away from London I shall become an embittered woman. It is not good for my mind, nor my body either, to sit smiling at Louis's friends until I feel like a hypocritical Cheshire cat, talking stiff nothings with one and another in order to let Louis have a chance with the one he cares the most for, and all the time furtively watching the clock and thirsting for their blood because they stay so late."[23]

In protecting him Fanny was just following the orders of his doctors. "He must be perfectly tranquil, trouble about nothing, have no shocks or surprises, not even pleasant ones; must not eat too much, drink too much, laugh too much; may write a little, but not too much; talk *very* little, and walk no more than can be helped." Fanny's medical reading made her understand, as most doctors at the time still didn't, that colds and flu are contagious. The doctors assured her that "it was absolutely impossible to catch a cold from anything but an open window, or wet feet, or a draft." Louis was indeed highly susceptible to viruses of all kinds; immune deficiency syndrome has been suggested.[24]

Colvin appreciated, as some of Louis's other friends did not, how essential Fanny's love and care were. "Strength and staunchness were, as I saw her, her ruling qualities.... Against those of his friends who might forget or ignore the precautions which his health demanded she could be a dragon indeed, but the more considerate among them she made warmly her own and was ever ready to welcome." Colvin added memorably that Fanny's eyes "were full of sex and mystery."

He also recorded an encounter at Skerryvore during which Louis revealed feelings that he usually hid. "I had followed him from the house into the garden.

He was leaning with his back to me looking out from the garden gate; as he heard me approach he turned round upon me a face such as I never saw on him save that once—a face of utter despondency, nay tragedy, upon which seemed stamped for one concentrated moment the expression of all he had ever had, or might yet have, in life to suffer or to renounce. Such a countenance was not to be accosted, and I left him."[25]

Six years later, describing a vigorous ride on horseback through a Samoan mangrove swamp, Louis commented on how much he had changed from "the pallid brute that lived in Skerryvore like a weevil in a biscuit."[26]

FRIENDS

At one point Fanny wrote to Colvin, "We have had a good deal of wearing company for some time. Our own house was full, and we had also a couple of dependencies in the neighborhood. Louis's mother and father were here. Aunt Alan [Stevenson], and Miss Ferrier and Henley; we have also had Teddy Henley [his brother] for a couple of nights. Bob and his family, and [his sister] Katharine and hers, are also in the neighborhood—and Sam's here. It has been such a difficult party that I quite broke down under the strain."

It struck Colvin that Louis's parents wore him out even more than his friends did. He told Henley, "I have very disquieting accounts from Bournemouth. If ever I am hung it will be for throttling Mrs. T.S. [Thomas Stevenson], and I shall go smiling and with a good conscience to the gallows. It appears that after having crushed and exhausted him with three weeks of their society, she has left him the legacy of an influenza cold, which has congested all his organs as in the old Hyères time." Having paid for the house, Louis's parents felt free to monopolize his time as often as they liked.[27]

It was a particular pleasure to spend time with Bob, however. A Skerryvore friend remembered that whenever the cousins were together, "R.L.S. became younger, gayer, and more extravagantly amusing than at other times." Fanny commented, "I wish we could roll them into one. If Louis knew half as much as Bob, or Bob could write half as well as Louis, what an art critic they would make!" By now Bob had given up as a painter and was launching his career as an art historian.[28]

The cousins even found opportunities to play at war games, incorporating the actual landscape and not lead soldiers. After one visit Louis described to Bob the campaign he was developing: "My headquarters were to move on Hernebridge Station, and the station was my first real objective. There, in case you were to hold St. Catherine's Hill, which I didn't think you would, I got a certain cover from the railway, and got command of the necessary bridge."[29]

Edmund Gosse occasionally visited Bournemouth, and in his memoirs he remembered Louis with warm appreciation: "I pause to think how I can render in words a faint impression of the most inspiriting, the most fascinating human being that I have known." The conclusion is equally generous: "He was the most unselfish and the most lovable of human beings."[30]

Gosse had painfully suppressed homoerotic feelings that he eventually acknowledged. Henley was in the habit of referring to him as "Becky" with the pronoun "she," as he did with men whom he regarded as effeminate. Gosse was married, but he did cherish an intense passion for a sculptor named Hamo Thorneycroft, which his wife seems to have understood and approved. When Lytton Strachey was asked whether Gosse was homosexual, he replied, "No, but he's Hamo-sexual."[31]

Long afterward, when John Addington Symonds published a revealing set of sonnets, Gosse told him that they were "absolutely in accordance with my own experience. The position of a young person so tormented is really that of a man buried alive and conscious, but deprived of speech. He is doomed, by his own timidity and ignorance, to a repression which amounts to death, because so far as he can see it is final, as final as blindness or mutilation could make it. This corpse however is obliged to bustle around and make an appearance every time the feast of life is spread."[32]

There were also new friends. Among them were Sir Percy Shelley, already mentioned for his photograph of Louis, and his wife Jane, who liked to think of Louis as a reincarnation of her husband's father Percy Bysshe Shelley. He acknowledged that there was a resemblance: "I have before me four photographs of myself done by Shelley's son: my nose is hooked, not like the eagle indeed, but like the accipitrine [hawk] family in man. . . . I have a look of him, all his sisters had noses like mine; Sir Percy has a marked hook; all the family had high cheekbones like mine."[33]

Fanny told Colvin, "Lady Shelley is delicious; naturally no longer young, suffering from the effects of a terrible accident that has left her a hopeless invalid, but with all the fire of youth, and as mad as some other people you know, and ready to plunge into any wild extravagance at a moment's notice." "Some other people" no doubt included Louis.[34]

Another new friend was a neighbor in her twenties named Adelaide Boodle, who worshiped Fanny. In a memoir entitled *R.L.S. and His Sine Qua Non* she recalled, "The chief thing about his wife that struck me in that first interview was the depth and tenderness that glowed in her unfathomable eyes." Before long Adelaide learned something else: "But how those glorious eyes could flash with righteous anger! The mere mention of cruelty in any shape would bring all the smouldering fires to a blaze."

Adelaide revealed that she aspired to be a writer, and it was agreed that she should receive instruction first from Fanny and afterward from Louis. Fanny was tactful and kind. Louis, though kind, was vehement in denouncing anything weak or conventional. When Adelaide brought him a piece of writing,

> The *Sine qua non,* to all appearances sound asleep, was lying on the divan. With a red silk pillow as her background, she looked so superbly beautiful that, for a moment, my attention wandered. Suddenly there was a low (but crescendo) rumble of thunder: "Oh, but this work is disgracefully bad! It could hardly be worse. What induced you to bring me stuff like this?" The *Sine qua non,* like a couching lioness bereaved of her whelps, sprang to the rescue. All in a moment she reared her glorious head, and from the divan at the far end of the room rang out this scorching denunciation: "Louis! You are a brute! I told you it would kill the child—and it *will.*"

He then knelt down, took Adelaide's hand, and exclaimed, "Fanny is right. I really am a brute. But I did not mean to be so cruel. Oh, but the work *is* bad you know—very bad, and you must never, never write like that again."

As an exercise he told Adelaide to compose a description of her garden. After reading it he delivered his judgment:

> You should have used fewer adjectives and many more descriptive verbs. If you want me to see your garden, don't, for pity's sake, talk about "climbing roses" or "green, mossy lawns." Tell me, if you like, that roses twined themselves round the apple trees and fell in showers from the branches. Never dare to tell me again anything about "green grass." Tell me how the lawn was flecked with shadows. I know perfectly well that grass is green. So does everybody else in England. What you have to learn is something different from that. Make me see what it was that made your garden distinct from a thousand others. And by the way, while we are about it, remember once for all that "green" is a word I flatly forbid you to utter in a description more than, perhaps, once in a lifetime.

When Adelaide returned with her revision he said approvingly, "In the description I found only one word to change, and one comma that ought to have been a semicolon."

She recalled some valuable rules for composition that he gave her: "Don't bother your head about English grammar; it's a poor study at best"; "Read every sentence aloud to yourself"; and "Never let a long sentence get out of hand. If it begins to run loose, tie it in a knot with a good strong inversion: swing it round on a pivot."[35]

Sargent's painting of Louis and Fanny provoked this opinion from Adelaide: "Most people, naturally enough, and doing only as [Fanny] would have had them do, would have placed R.L.S. in the foreground, sketching her in, as Mr. Sargent did, like a kind of lurking shadow. This, in her own eyes, would have been her true position. But how different the picture would have been could [Louis] himself have painted it! How proud he was of his 'critic on the hearth,' how dependent (almost like a child in this) upon her good opinion!" The joke about the critic was an allusion to Dickens's novella *The Cricket on the Hearth.*

Adelaide recalled an incident when Fanny had gone to London and Louis undertook to look after the garden, hacking enthusiastically at her raspberries and destroying every shoot that would have produced fruit. When Fanny returned she was deeply distressed, but as Louis approached she said to Adelaide, "Hush, Louis must never know what he has done. He did it to surprise me, and thinks it has been a splendid day's work." He never figured it out, and talked eagerly about the raspberries they were going to harvest.[36]

A painful loss at this time was the ever quarrelsome Woggs, whom Louis and Fanny doted on. In Graham Balfour's account, "Having been sent to hospital to recover from wounds received in battle, he broke loose, in his maimed state attacked another dog more powerful than himself, and so perished. His master and mistress were inconsolable, and never, even in Samoa, could bring themselves to allow any successor." Actually, there would be at least one more dog, but none that took Woggs's place in their hearts.[37]

"THE PRINCE OF MEN," HENRY JAMES

The most important friend Louis made at Bournemouth was also the most surprising. It would be hard to imagine two novelists more unlike each other in style and themes than Louis and Henry James, but they became warm admirers of each other's writing and fast friends as well. Perhaps it was because they were such an odd couple that they hit it off. They didn't think of each other as rivals, but as fellow workers in different regions of literature. During Louis's final years only three of his significant friendships would continue undiminished. Two were with Baxter and Colvin, whom he had known for the whole of his adult life, and the other was with James.

James came down frequently from London to Bournemouth because his sister Alice was there. Bedridden much of her life with "nervous attacks" in what has been described as "her career as a patient," Alice had gone to Bournemouth in hope of improved health. A year after Louis and Fanny arrived there Fanny reported to his parents, "We have had a very pleasant visitor. One evening a card was handed in with 'Henry James' upon it. I had always been told that he was the type of an Englishman, but except that he looks like the Prince of Wales I call him the type of an American. He is a gentle, amiable, soothing, sleepy sort, fat and dimpled. We find ourselves excessively fond of him." The gentle amiability made a nice complement to Louis's effervescence.[38]

The best known portraits of James show him years later as a grand old man. Sargent made the drawing reproduced here (fig. 54) when James was forty-three, at just the time when he and the Stevensons were becoming friends. He was seven years older than Louis and three years younger than Fanny.

The two men had in fact met before, at a luncheon in London with Gosse and Lang in 1879. Afterward James described Louis to a friend as "a shirt-collarless Bohemian and a great deal (in an inoffensive way) of a *poseur.*" Louis was equally unenthusiastic, telling Henley that James was "a mere club fizzle (*fizzle* perhaps too strong, on representations from the weaker vessel) and no out-of-doors, stand-up man whatever—as the Highlander would say." Fanny (the biblical "weaker vessel") had defended James's writing.[39]

More significantly, the two writers had already had an exchange in print about writing. In his essay "The Art of Fiction" James had contrasted two novels that struck him as equally admirable. One was Edmond de Goncourt's *Chérie.* As for the other, "I have just been reading, at the same time, the delightful story of *Treasure Island,* by Mr. Robert Louis Stevenson. One of these works treats of murders, mysteries, islands of dreadful renown, hairbreadth escapes, miraculous coincidences, and buried doubloons. The other treats of a little French girl who lived in a fine house in Paris, and died of wounded sensibility because no one would marry her. I call *Treasure Island* delightful, because it appears to me to have succeeded wonderfully in what it attempts." James went on to declare that the function of art is to compete with life.[40]

This claim moved Louis to publish a response, "A Humble Remonstrance," in which he argued that the passions and afflictions of real life "waste and slay

54. Henry James, by Sargent

us." Not so with literature. "Life is monstrous, infinite, illogical, abrupt and poignant; a work of art, in comparison, is neat, finite, self-contained, rational, flowing and emasculate. Life imposes by brute energy, like inarticulate thunder; art catches the ear, among the far louder noises of experience, like an air artificially made by a discreet musician." He added, "The novel, which is a work of art, exists not by its resemblances to life, which are forced and material, as a shoe must still consist of leather, but by its immeasurable difference from life, which is designed and significant." The word *flowing* is important. We expect a work of fiction to move forward steadily and intelligibly, whereas life does not.[41]

After reading "A Humble Remonstrance" James sent Louis a personal letter, saying that they agreed far more than they disagreed, and assuring him of "hearty sympathy, charged with the assurance of my enjoyment of everything you write." It was a luxury, he added, "to encounter someone who *does* write—who is really acquainted with that lovely art."[42]

Louis hastened to reply: "I am rejoiced indeed to hear you speak so kindly of my work: rejoiced and surprised. I seem to myself a very rude, left-handed countryman; not fit to be read, far less complimented, by a man so accomplished, so adroit, so craftsmanlike as you." He saw that they were in agreement about the crucial importance of language and style, the foundation of everything that matters in literature. "People suppose it is the 'stuff' that interests them: they think for instance that the prodigious fine thoughts and sentiments in Shakespeare impress by their own weight, not understanding that the unpolished diamond is but a stone. They think that striking situations or good dialogue are got by studying life; they will not rise to understand that they are prepared by deliberate artifice and set off by painful suppressions."[43]

In "A Gossip on Romance," as mentioned earlier, Louis had described the kind of narrative he wanted to write, in which "the interest turns not upon what a man shall choose to do, but on how he manages to do it; not on the passionate slips and hesitations of the conscience, but on the problems of the body and of the practical intelligence." The first in each of these alternatives could apply very well to James's novels, of which Henry Adams said, "He taught the world to read a volume for the pleasure of seeing the lights of his burning-glass turned on alternate sides of the same figure."[44]

Now James became a daily visitor at Skerryvore, occupying the armchair inherited from Louis's grandfather that appears in the Sargent portrait. When he returned to London Fanny said, "After ten weeks of Henry James the evenings seem very empty, though the room is always full of people. As time passed we came to have a real affection for him, and parted from him with sincere regret." From London James wrote that he hoped to return to Bournemouth soon, and "as nearly as possible at that moment, my sedentary part shall press the dear old fireside chair. There is a fundamental affinity between them which yearns to be gratified." It may not be obvious that James was exploiting a double meaning in British usage; in his 1755 *Dictionary* Samuel Johnson defined "fundament" as "the back part of the body."[45]

When later on James presented them with a handsome mirror, Louis thanked him with a poem, "The Mirror Speaks":

> Now with an outlandish grace,
> To the sparkling fire I face

> In the blue room at Skerryvore.
> Where I wait until the door
> Open, and the Prince of Men,
> Henry James, shall come again.

James wrote to a friend at this time, "I have a great resource for the evening in the presence here of Robert Louis Stevenson, who is an old acquaintance of mine ripening now into friends. I suppose you know his charming writings—and the adorable tale of *Treasure Island*. He is deadly consumptive, and has not for two years been out of the house; is also married to a Californian divorcee older than himself, and wears on his emaciated person ancient seal skin garments of hers. But his face, his talk, his nature, his behaviour, are delightful, and I go to see him every night." James was fascinated by Fanny as an exotic type of American altogether different from his New England acquaintances. He told Owen Wister, famous later for the Western novel *The Virginian*, "If you like the gulch and canyon you will like her."[46]

The friends' openness and affection are apparent in a letter Louis sent to James at the end of 1886:

> My wife is peepy and dowie [sad and dismal]: two Scotch expressions with which I will leave you to wrestle unaided, as a preparation for my poetical works. She is a woman (as you know) not without art: the art of extracting the gloom of the eclipse from sunshine; and she has recently laboured in this field not without success or (as we used to say) not without a blessing. It is strange: we fell out my wife and I the other night; she tackled me savagely for being a canary bird; I replied (bleatingly) protesting that there was no use in turning life into *King Lear;* presently it was discovered that there were two dead combatants upon the field, each slain by an arrow of the truth, and we tenderly carried off each other's corpses. Here is a little comedy for Henry James to write! The beauty was each thought the other quite unscathed at first. But we had dealt shrewd stabs. . . . Well, here are the kindest recollections from the canary bird and from King Lear, from the Tragic Woman and the Flimsy Man.

This was by no means a private communication; Fanny added a postscript, "It is odd, but the doleful woman became such through too much cheerful society, too long continued; nothing more serious than that." She signed her note "Ever the D.W." (Doleful Woman).[47]

James replied, "I was charmed by your account of the concussion between your high spirits and your wife's moderate ones, and would have given much to assist at the debate, which I should have endeavoured to keep within parliamentary limits . . . I salute you both, and am ever, my dear Louis, very faithfully yours, and your sterner consort's, Henry James." When Colvin was assembling Louis's letters for publication after his death, he asked James whether this one should be omitted as likely to offend Fanny. James replied, "Fanny S. will be a bigger fool than I ever took her for if she resents the lively description of their domestic broil. It helps to commemorate her and makes her interesting—and just so, I feel sure, she will rejoice."[48]

Henry James's sister Alice never met the Stevensons at Bournemouth, but her famous diary has a glance at Fanny in London as an example of vulgar Americans who "swarm in the West and Southwest" and were looked down on by cultivated Bostonians like herself. Homegrown vulgarity had at least the advantage of familiarity:

> What a blessed arrangement 'tis that our own vulgar ones are mitigated for us by the power to divine more or less the circumstances responsible for 'em and are consequently simply relative in their offensiveness—but how can they be anything but *absolute* to the foreigner? I had such a curious impression of a type in seeing Mrs. R. L. Stevenson in London. From her appearance Providence or Nature, whichever is responsible for her, designed her as an appendage to a hand organ, but I believe she is possessed of great wifely virtues and I have heard some excellent letters written by her to Henry—but such egotism and so naked!! giving one the strangest feeling of being in the presence of an unclothed being.

The implication seems to be that Fanny's dark complexion made one think of a gypsy, possibly even an organ grinder's monkey. Alice James's condescension makes her brother's openness and sympathy all the more admirable.[49]

The Bournemouth friendships were gratifying, but all the same, Louis actively disliked living there. Like Davos, the town was a stodgy haven for invalids. But just as in Davos, confinement and inactivity stimulated an extraordinarily productive period of writing, and by the time he left Bournemouth he would be recognized as a major author.

CHAPTER 21

A Torrent of Writing

LOUIS AS MODERNIST

From 1884 to 1887 Louis produced an astonishing number and range of publications. Most notable were *Kidnapped* and *Dr. Jekyll and Mr. Hyde*. In addition there were *The Silverado Squatters, Prince Otto, A Child's Garden of Verses,* other poems collected as *Underwoods,* stories collected as *More New Arabian Nights* and as *The Merry Men and Other Tales and Fables,* the essay collection *Memories and Portraits,* and a *Memoir of Fleeming Jenkin* (his Edinburgh mentor had died at this time, at the early age of fifty-two). Prolific as this output was, he enjoyed telling friends that he was completing other works as well, such as *Herbert and Henrietta: or The Nemesis of Sentiment, Happy Homes and Hairy Faces,* and *A Pound of Feathers and a Pound of Lead*.[1]

This torrent of writing may seem surprising, since as Rosaline Masson noted in her biography of Louis, he had been almost constantly incapacitated by illness since sailing to America in 1879.

> He had been a chronic invalid, submitting to an invalid's life, at Monterey and San Francisco; in the Highlands—Pitlochry and Braemar; at Davos; at Stobo Manse; at Kingussie; again at Davos; in France—St. Marcel and Hyères—ever seeking for health, never finding it. And now at Bournemouth there awaited him a life of accepted invalidism spent chiefly in the sickroom, suffering constant pain and weakness, often forbidden for days or even weeks to speak aloud, and having to whisper or

write on paper all he wanted to say to his wife or his friends. And yet these three years proved a very industrious and successful time in Stevenson's life.

But it's equally possible that if he had been more active, he would have written less.[2]

George Eliot once wrote, "To know intense joy without a strong bodily frame, one must have an enthusiastic soul." Louis didn't care for Eliot's novels—he thought they were too preachy—but he did have an enthusiastic soul, and experienced joy even at the darkest times. Although he often declared that action was more important than writing, for him writing *was* action.[3]

Louis remarked that he was living in an age of transition, and that was a widely used term when traditional assumptions about art were giving way to modernism. Reacting against the dense and earnestly moralizing Victorian novels, writers were now emphasizing individuality of vision and skillfully crafted style. The author of *Treasure Island* and *Kidnapped* would never have espoused the slogan "Art for art's sake," but the contemporary critic William Archer was right to call him "a modern of the moderns, both in his alert self-consciousness and in the particular artistic ideal which he proposes to himself. He professes himself an artist in words." Alan Sandison takes this statement as the keynote for his *Robert Louis Stevenson and the Appearance of Modernism,* showing convincingly that "his experiments, his ceaseless questing among forms, ensured that of all his contemporaries his works show the greatest and most radical diversity."[4]

Louis did take offense at Archer's suggestion that he indulged too freely in "aggressive optimism." Louis wrote to Archer to say that far from devoting his life to manly exercise, as Archer had assumed, he had been a perpetual invalid, and his art was compensation for that. "To have suffered, nay, to suffer, sets a keen edge on what remains of the agreeable. This is a great truth, and has to be learned in the fire. Yours very truly, Robert Louis Stevenson." Archer quickly made amends, and they became friends.[5]

At this time Louis fell under the spell of Dostoevsky, reading *Crime and Punishment* in French translation since there was no English version as yet. In a letter to Henley he exclaimed, "Dostoieffsky is of course simply immense—it is not reading a book, it is having a brain fever to read it." When his Davos friend Symonds asked if he had read it, he described its profound impact on him:

> *Raskolnikoff* is the greatest book I have read easily in ten years; I am glad you took to it. Many find it dull; Henry James could not finish it. All

I can say is, it nearly finished me. James did not care for it because the character of Raskolnikoff was not objective; and at that I divined a great gulf between us, and on further reflection, the existence of a certain impotence in many minds of today, which prevents them from living *in* a book or a character and keeps them standing afar off, spectators of a puppet show. To such I suppose the book may seem empty in the centre; to the others it is a room, a house of life, into which they themselves enter and are tortured and purified.

(Dante Gabriel Rossetti entitled a cycle of love sonnets *The House of Life*.) It was a telling criticism to diagnose a certain impotence of imagination in James. It had amused Louis to describe his own characters in *Treasure Island* as puppets, but the goal of the artist must be to convince readers that the characters are alive and real.[6]

During Louis's illnesses in Hyères, Fanny had entertained him with stories she used to make up during her daily walk. As she described them later, they were "a sort of Arabian Nights Entertainment where I was to take the part of Scheherazade and he the Sultan." Now they decided to re-create as many as they could recall, and they set to work as a team. Louis wrote "Zero's Tale of the Explosive Bomb," while Fanny wrote "The Destroying Angel" and "The Fair Cuban"; the remaining eleven stories were written in collaboration. They were published in 1886 as *More New Arabian Nights: The Dynamiter,* with a title page listing the authors as Robert Louis Stevenson and Fanny Van de Grift Stevenson.[7]

Fanny was proud of her contribution, and it made her angry when people assumed it must really have been by Louis alone. One reviewer who did notice her name made her angry for a different reason, as she told Margaret Stevenson: "It is rather hard to be treated like a comma, and a superfluous one at that—and in one paper, which I will send you, the only one in which I am mentioned, the critic refers to me as 'undoubtedly Mr. Stevenson's sister.' *Why* pray? Surely there can be nothing in the book that points to sister in particular." Audrey Murfin has shown that critics and biographers, right up to our own time, have consistently assumed that Fanny's contribution was either trivial or made the book worse. They also ignore the fact that she and Louis worked steadily together throughout the process of revision.[8]

The collection relates the experiences of three young would-be detectives who blunder through life, beguiled by a mysterious woman who plays the role of Scheherazade. Presiding over it all is Theophilus Goodall, whom we know from *New Arabian Nights* to be Prince Florizel of Bohemia. A friendly reviewer of the new book said that "Mr. Stevenson [no mention of Fanny] flushes a regular three-volume covey of incident, pursues it for a while—for a chapter, a page, a few lines—and then gaily tosses it aside. *The Dynamiter* contains a whole library of possible novels. Its charm lies in this wanton profusion of a spendthrift whose resources seem inexhaustible."[9]

As for dynamite, there's not much of that until the eighth chapter, "Zero's Tale of the Explosive Bomb," but for some reason the collection has always been known by its subtitle. That was inspired by a recent incident when a piece of luggage exploded in the cloakroom at Victoria Station, and bombs that had failed to go off were discovered in other stations. The perpetrators were Fenians protesting English opposition to Irish home rule, an opposition that Louis wholeheartedly shared. That scheme and later ones all fail, due to the incompetence of the bomb makers, and in the end the terrorist blows himself up.

Chesterton's criticism is unanswerable: "It is really impossible to use a story in which everything is ridiculous to prove that certain particular Fenians or anarchist agitators are ridiculous. Nor indeed is it tenable that men who risk their lives to commit such crimes are quite so ridiculous as that."[10]

More New Arabian Nights did remarkably well commercially. When it was published in 1886 nearly eighteen thousand copies were sold in the first month, followed by another printing of five thousand. Some recent critics have admired its modernist playfulness, but be that as it may, this would be the last time that Louis chose to tease his readers. The major works still to come—*Kidnapped, Dr. Jekyll and Mr. Hyde, The Master of Ballantrae, Catriona, Weir of Hermiston*—all narrate events as if they are absolutely real.[11]

"VERSES BY A PROSE WRITER"

A Child's Garden of Verses was published in 1885, and would turn out to be Louis's high point as a poet. In 1887 he brought out *Underwoods,* a collection of poems he had been writing over the years, and its reception was lukewarm. One reviewer concluded, "The author of *Underwoods* is a man of fine poetic culture, but not a poet," even though "as verses by a prose writer they deserve high praise." Louis took this in good part, and wrote to say, "Your article is very true and very kindly put: I have never called my verses poetry. They are verse, the verse of a speaker not a singer; but that is a fair business like another." The title *Underwoods,* he explained in his preface, was borrowed from Ben Jonson to suggest minor growths beneath the principal works.[12]

Diction would always be a problem in Louis's poems. As was fashionable at the time, he often affected archaic language that was thought to be "poetical," and in *Underwoods* we find "I prithee," "thou sawest," "little boots it," "the unfoughten field," "sing earlier, Muse," "fire-ypainted walls," "I pause at whiles," "man appears and evanishes," and "I trow."[13]

His limitations as a lyric poet are evident if we compare his translation of Martial's elegy for a slave girl with an earlier version by Leigh Hunt. This is Louis:

> Here lies Erotion, whom at six years old
> Fate pilfered. Stranger (when I too am cold
> Who shall succeed me in my rural field),
> To this small spirit annual honours yield.

And this is Hunt:

> Underneath this greedy stone
> Lies little sweet Erotion,
> Whom the Fates, with hearts as cold,
> Nipped away at six years old.
> Thou, whoever thou may'st be,
> That hast this small field after me,
> Let the yearly rites be paid
> To her little slender shade.

The tenderness makes Louis's version seem like a mechanical exercise.[14]

It's important to note that most of these poems were occasional, dashed off casually or included in letters to friends. When *Underwoods* was published Henry James wrote to his brother William that two poems addressed to himself (one was "The Mirror Speaks," mentioned earlier) were "the poorest things in the book. Both were scribbled off at the moment—the first put on my plate one day I went to dine with him at Bournemouth—and I never dreamed that he had kept copies of them and would publish them."[15]

Still, few novelists have written poetry at all—Scott, Hardy, and Lawrence stand out as exceptions. Minor or not, Louis's poems fill 450 pages in a modern edition, and they are especially valuable for biography. His warm feeling for friends and loved ones appears throughout, and there are some memorable poems in the Lallan Scottish dialect. He told Colvin that these were "better than my English verse; more marrow and fatness."[16]

Most of those are in the Standard Habbie stanza that Burns used so well (named after a famous piper, Habbie Simpson). In "The Maker to Posterity" Louis imagines readers puzzling over the dialect:

> "What tongue does your auld bookie speak?"
> He'll spier; an' I, his mou to steik:
> "No bein' fit to write in Greek,
>   I wrote in Lallan,
> Dear to my heart as the peat reek,
>   Auld as Tantallon."

"His mou to steik" means "his mouth to shut"; Tantallon Castle is a ruin on the coast of East Lothian, not far from Edinburgh.

In a note Louis commented that Burns's western Ayrshire dialect "has always sounded in my ear like something partly foreign; and indeed I am from the Lothians myself. It is there I heard the language spoken about [i.e., during] my childhood, and it is in the drawling Lothian voice that I repeat it to myself."[17]

He often found opportunities to deplore the Edinburgh winter, as in "To Charles Baxter," written when returning from France:

> I've seen 's hae days to fricht us a',
> The Pentlands poothered weel w' snaw,
> The ways half smoored wi' liquid thaw
>   An' half congealin',
> The snell an' scowtherin' northern blaw
>   Frae blae Brunteelan'.

"Snell" is "bitter," and "scowthering" is "singeing" or "burning." Burntisland is a town on the northern shore of the Firth of Forth, directly across the water from Edinburgh.[18]

Some of the most impressive poems appeal to folk tradition, much as Yeats would soon be doing in Ireland. One of them is "The Spaewife," which means a fortune-teller:

> O, I wad like to ken—to the beggar wife says I—
> The reason o' the cause an' the wherefore o' the why,
> Wi' mony anither riddle brings the tears into my e'e.
> —*It's gey an' easy speirin', says the beggar-wife to me.*

That means "It's very easy asking"—but not, of course, answering.[19]

NOT A PLAYWRIGHT

The dream of a bonanza in the theater seduced many writers who had no relevant experience. Henry James was one of them. He wrote five plays but only saw one produced, and when he took his bow on opening night he was hissed.

Despite Louis's participation in the Jenkin theatricals, in later life he seldom went to plays or showed much interest in them; he read Shakespeare as literature, not drama. The last time he ever went to a theater seems to have been in San Francisco in 1880, and that was to see the Gilbert and Sullivan operetta *The Pirates of Penzance,* perhaps because the title appealed to him.

His venture in playwriting came about because Henley goaded him into it, convinced that between them they could produce a hit. Henley made repeated visits to Bournemouth for this purpose, and impressed young Lloyd as "a great, glowing, massive-shouldered fellow with a big red beard and a crutch; jovial, astoundingly clever, and with a laugh that rolled out like music. Never was there such another as William Ernest Henley; he had an unimaginable fire and vitality; he swept one off one's feet."[20]

The subject Louis and Henley settled on was the career of William Brodie, an eighteenth-century criminal known as "Deacon Brodie," not for a religious appointment but as elected head of his workingmen's guild. A master craftsman by day, Brodie became a skilled burglar at night. In due course one of his confederates betrayed him, and since burglary was a capital offense, he was hanged in 1788.

In Louis's childhood bedroom was an actual cabinet made by Brodie, and Cummy had told him bloodcurdling stories concerning it. "Weighed upon by the opaque and almost sensible darkness, I listened eagerly for anything to break the sepulchral quiet. But nothing came, save, perhaps, an emphatic crack from the old cabinet that was made by Deacon Brodie, or the dry rustle of the coals on the extinguished fire."[21]

When Henley heard about Brodie he seized upon the story as their road to riches, and they had started working on a play in 1878. Now it was time to address the project in earnest. "We were enveloped in a gorgeous dream," Lloyd recalled. "R.L.S. was no longer to plod along as he had been doing; Henley was to abandon his grinding and ill-paid editorship; together they would combine to write plays—marvelous plays that would run for hundreds of nights and bring in thousands of pounds."[22]

Henley's letters are filled with pipe dreams about this play. In one of them he wrote, "Put £5 per night as the minimum, and take a run of a hundred nights as a fair average, and we divide £525 between us. Exclusive all this, mind, of the provinces and what we may make in the States." A couple of weeks later he was even more sanguine: "I expect to clear between six and seven hundred as my share of the *Deacon*—our first play."[23]

Deacon Brodie, or, The Double Life: A Melodrama in Five Acts had only modest success. Prominent actors and theater managers turned it down, but in 1882 it did have a brief run in the Yorkshire city of Bradford, followed by Aberdeen and Glasgow in 1883 and London in 1884. Then it fizzled out. Reading the play today, it's easy to see why. It's not so much melodramatic as sentimental, set in the final days when Brodie's crimes are exposed and his repentance comes too late. Everything centers on his failure to repay money he had borrowed from his sister Mary; he had lost it all by gambling, and burglary wasn't sufficient to make up the difference. "My sister—my kind, innocent sister! She will come smiling to me with her poor little love-story, and I must break her heart. Broken hearts, broken lives! . . . I should have died before."

In another scene Brodie beseeches Mary's fiancé to forgive him, and likewise his mistress Jean who has borne his child. "O, as God sees me, I will strive to make a new and a better life, and to be worthy of your friendship, and of your tears . . . your tears. And to be worthy of you too, Jean; for I see now that the bandage has fallen from my eyes; I see myself, O how unworthy even of you." Surely it was Henley, and not Louis, who made Brodie say "*even* of you."[24]

Henley wrote bitterly to Baxter, "I don't expect we shall ever get to work on the thing again, nor for that matter on anything else. The match is no longer equal. Louis has grown faster than I have." He was becoming jealous of his friend's success, and they would drift increasingly apart. When Colvin told Louis that *Deacon Brodie* wasn't any good, Louis agreed but said, "It is about Henley, not *Brodie* that I care." He added flatly, "The *Deacon* is damn bad."[25]

There were two further plays, *Admiral Guinea* and *Beau Austin*, which were even worse. After rereading them Louis told Henley, "The reperusal of the *Admiral* was a sore blow; eh, God man, it is a low, black, dirty, blackguard, ragged piece: vomitable in many parts—simply vomitable. Pew is in places a reproach to both art and man." That was an attempt to resurrect Blind Pew from *Treasure Island*. *Beau Austin* did get produced in London in 1890, with the distinguished Beerbohm Tree in the title role, but it too fell flat. Henley began referring to Tree as "the Barebum."[26]

There was one final collaboration, *Macaire: A Melodramatic Farce*, set in a French inn. It ends when the title character is shot by a policeman and dies exclaiming, "Death——what is death?"

CHAPTER 22

Creating a Myth

JEKYLL AND HYDE

In several stories Louis had explored the theme of an ominously double self, versions of which had been current in Western culture for a long time. The German writer Jean Paul Richter coined the term *doppelgänger* as far back as 1796, and E.T.A. Hoffmann made it the title of a story in 1821. Most immediately relevant for Louis was James Hogg's *Confessions of a Justified Sinner,* published in Edinburgh in 1824, in which a murderer blames his crimes on a mysterious element in himself that has taken over: "I was a being incomprehensible to myself. Either I had a second self, or else my body was at times possessed by a spirit over which it had no control." The expression "justified sinner" reflects the Calvinist doctrine that people who are "elect" can commit crimes with impunity because they receive justification through divine grace. Louis didn't believe in that doctrine any more than Hogg did, but both of them grew up in a culture that was permeated by it.

In the fall of 1885 a startling expression of the doppelgänger theme surfaced from Louis's unconscious. As Fanny told Graham Balfour, "In the small hours of one morning I was awakened by cries of horror from Louis. Thinking he had a nightmare, I awakened him. He said angrily, 'Why did you wake me? I was dreaming a fine bogey tale.'" Bogies—the Scottish word for ghosts or specters—had been part of his consciousness since his earliest days, featured in the stories that Cummy used to tell and that he recalled in *A Child's Garden of Verses:* "Now my little heart goes a-beating like a drum, / With the breath of the Bogie in my hair."[1]

In his autobiographical essay "A Chapter on Dreams," Louis described the origin of *Jekyll and Hyde*.

> I had long been trying to write a story on this subject, to find a body, a vehicle, for that strong sense of man's double being which must at times come in upon and overwhelm the mind of every thinking creature.... For two days I went about racking my brains for a plot of any sort; and on the second night I dreamed the scene at the window, and a scene afterward split in two, in which Hyde, pursued for some crime, took the powder and underwent the change in the presence of his pursuers.... All that was given me was the matter of three scenes, and the central idea of a voluntary change becoming involuntary.

The "powder" is a chemical with which Dr. Jekyll concocts a drink that transforms him into the horrifying Mr. Hyde.[2]

A first draft emerged with astonishing speed. According to Lloyd, although Louis usually worked slowly, he now produced thousands of words a day for a week. "It was a stupendous achievement; and the strange thing was that instead of showing lassitude afterward, he seemed positively refreshed and revitalized." He then read the draft aloud to Fanny and Lloyd. "Stevenson, who had a voice the greatest actor might have envied, read it with an intensity that made shivers run up and down my spine."

Lloyd was spellbound, but he was surprised to see that Fanny was reluctant to respond.

> Her praise was constrained; the words seemed to come with difficulty; and then all at once she broke out with criticism. He had missed the point, she said; had missed the allegory; had made it merely a story—a magnificent bit of sensationalism—when it should have been a masterpiece. Stevenson was beside himself with anger.... The scene became so painful that I went away, unable to bear it any longer. It was with a sense of tragedy that I listened to their voices from the adjoining room, the words lost but fraught with an emotion that struck at my heart. When I came back my mother was alone. She was sitting, pale and desolate before the fire, and staring into it.

Fanny's point was that Louis had ruined the story by turning it into a mere tale about a secret life, much like Deacon Brodie's during his burglary escapades. What was needed was not just a character wearing a disguise, but something far more profound: a character struggling with a deeper hidden self that breaks loose and fights for supremacy.

After a while Louis returned and exclaimed, "You are right! I have absolutely missed the allegory, the very essence of it!" and threw the manuscript into the fire. Fanny and Lloyd were aghast, but he explained that there was no point tinkering with the unsatisfactory version; he needed to start afresh. After another three days of "feverish industry" he returned triumphantly with a preliminary draft of "the *Jekyll and Hyde* that everyone knows; that, translated into every European tongue and many Oriental, has given a new phrase to the world."[3]

What Louis created was not so much allegory as myth, open-ended and disturbing. When a clergyman complained that the story needed an explanatory key, Louis replied, "I have said my say as I was best able; others must look for what was meant."[4]

At the beginning the narrative focuses on Dr. Jekyll's lawyer, Mr. Utterson. Jekyll has just revised his will, and Utterson is mystified by his client's stipulation that in case of his disappearance, his heir should be an unknown person called Edward Hyde. Utterson is an unimaginative, pragmatic witness to what will be a shocking story.

Most interpretations of *Jekyll and Hyde* have been thematic, but the story lives because it's so brilliantly told. When Nabokov included it in a course he taught at Cornell, he said in his catalogue description, "Special attention will be paid to individual genius and questions of structure." Nabokov added that he would concentrate on "such combinations of details as yield the sensual spark without which a book is dead. In that respect, general ideas are of no importance."[5]

It's true that what makes *Jekyll and Hyde* great is Louis's artistic skill. "Each apparently incredible or insignificant detail," a reviewer in the *Times* said when it was published in 1886, "has been thoughtfully subordinated to his purpose. We may compare it with the sombre masterpieces of Poe, and we may say at once that Mr. Stevenson has gone far deeper. He has weighed his words and turned his sentences so as to sustain and excite throughout the sense of mystery and horror."[6]

It is not generally realized that the title Louis gave his story was *Strange Case of Dr. Jekyll and Mr. Hyde*. Publishers have generally added "The" to the title, but Louis didn't. Perhaps he wanted to avoid suggesting that this was just one "case" among many, and was also highlighting the word "strange." One might imagine that he was thinking of Sherlock Holmes's "cases," but Conan Doyle didn't publish his first Holmes story until the following year.

Borges put his finger on the crucial point: "The allegorical tale pretends to be a detective story; no reader guesses that Hyde and Jekyll are the same person." Instead we struggle to solve the mystery along with Jekyll's friends, and share in their horrified amazement when they finally witness Jekyll turning into Hyde. For this reason even the best movie versions are deeply compromised. There's no avoiding showing the transformation right from the start.[7]

The story is told through a series of narrators. At the beginning a conventional anonymous narrator introduces us to Utterson and Jekyll. Partway into the tale there is a second narrator, a friend of Jekyll's and Utterson's named Dr. Lanyon. Only at the end does everything become clear, in a letter by Jekyll himself entitled "Henry Jekyll's Full Statement of the Case." The succession of narrators, with progressively deepening perspectives, intensifies the power of the story as it gradually comes into focus. Louis would return to this technique in *The Master of Ballantrae*.

Hyde is represented in the novel as somehow disquieting to look at, but nothing like the grotesque monster of film versions. When Nabokov lectured on *Jekyll and Hyde* he began, "You will ignore the fact that ham actors under the direction of pork packers have acted in a parody of the book."[8]

One day Utterson is surprised to encounter a peculiar character using a key to enter Jekyll's house from a back alley. As yet he has no idea that this is the mysterious Hyde named in Jekyll's will. Later on, when he does know it was Hyde, he recalls this moment:

> Mr. Hyde was pale and dwarfish, he gave an impression of deformity without any nameable malformation, he had a displeasing smile, he had borne himself to the lawyer with a sort of murderous mixture of timidity and boldness, and he spoke with a husky, whispering and somewhat broken voice; all these were points against him, but not all of these together could explain the hitherto unknown disgust, loathing, and fear with which Mr. Utterson regarded him. "There must be something else," said the perplexed gentleman. "There is something more, if I could find a name for it. God bless me, the man seems hardly human! Something troglodytic, shall we say?"

With his interest in theories of evolution, Louis was echoing contemporary speculations about evolution in reverse, a theory that criminals were degenerate throwbacks to the savage past of the human race. He had recently invoked this idea in a short story called "Olalla," in which the criminal past of a Spanish family is reborn atavistically in their descendants.[9]

Just as relevant is the Calvinist perspective that underlay the stories "Thrawn Janet" and "The Merry Men." "O my poor old Harry Jekyll," Utterson exclaims when he grasps that Hyde has some kind of hold on Jekyll, "if ever I read Satan's signature upon a face, it is on that of your new friend." Hyde is smaller than Jekyll and seems younger, which leads Utterson to wonder if he is an illegitimate son who is perhaps blackmailing him. He and Lanyon dedicate themselves to figuring out who Hyde is—still not dreaming that he and their friend Jekyll are one and the same.

When we finally read the third narrator's account, "Henry Jekyll's Full Statement of the Case," we get a complete understanding at last, just as Lanyon and Utterson do. Aware of increasing temptations to indulge in illicit behavior, Jekyll came up with what he hoped would be a solution: to concoct a drug that would split his good and bad selves apart. Then the bad one could indulge in occasional misdeeds while the good one would be liberated.

> If each, I told myself, could but be housed in separate identities, life would be relieved of all that was unbearable; the unjust might go his way, delivered from the aspirations and remorse of his more upright twin; and the just could walk steadfastly and securely on his upward path, doing the good things in which he found his pleasure, and no longer exposed to disgrace and penitence by the hands of this extraneous evil. It was the curse of mankind that these incongruous faggots were thus bound together—that in the agonised womb of consciousness, these polar twins should be continuously struggling.

But after he creates the potion and drinks it, Jekyll finds that he is no longer in control.

> There was something strange in my sensations, something indescribably new and, from its very novelty, incredibly sweet. I felt younger, lighter, happier in body; within I was conscious of a heady recklessness, a current of disordered sensual images running like a mill-race in my fancy, a solution [i.e., dissolving] of the bonds of obligation, an unknown but not an innocent freedom of the soul. I knew myself, at the first breath of this new life, to be more wicked, tenfold more wicked, sold a slave to my original evil; and the thought, in that moment, braced and delighted me like wine.[10]

Early in the story Hyde casually tramples a girl in the street and walks calmly on while she lies screaming in pain. At this stage he is more callous than vicious, but that will change. A year later a maidservant gazes dreamily out of her window—this is "the scene at the window" that Louis saw in his dream—and is horrified to see Hyde encounter "an aged and beautiful gentleman with white hair" who pauses to ask directions.

> All of a sudden [Hyde] broke out in a great flame of anger, stamping with his foot, brandishing the cane, and carrying on (as the maid described it) like a madman. The old gentleman took a step back, with the air of one very much surprised and a trifle hurt; and at that Mr. Hyde broke out of all bounds and clubbed him to the earth. And next moment, with ape-like fury, he was trampling his victim under foot and hailing down a storm of blows, under which the bones were audibly shattered and the body jumped upon the roadway. At the horror of these sights and sounds, the maid fainted.

When Utterson is shown the cane later on, he's shocked to recognize it as one he himself had given to Jekyll—but he still supposes that Hyde and Jekyll are different individuals.[11]

These eruptions of violence apparently struck Hollywood screenwriters as not sensational enough, and they inaugurated a tradition of reading *Jekyll and Hyde* as a story of sexual predation in the London underworld. The movie versions have been described as "smoky with sex in the interpolated orgy scenes." Recent criticism has seized upon hints in surviving drafts of the story—the original draft underwent a lot of revision—to elaborate on this interpretation. In one version Jekyll says, "From a very early age I became in secret the slave of disgraceful pleasures," and in another, "I became in secret the slave of certain appetites." Some readers suspected that this meant sexual misbehavior; Gerard Manley Hopkins suggested to a friend that "the trampling scene is perhaps a convention: he was thinking of something unsuitable for fiction."[12]

Hopkins no doubt meant that the appetites were homosexual. Louis's Davos friend Symonds, a painfully closeted homosexual, did apply *Jekyll and Hyde* to himself in that way:

> It makes me wonder whether a man has a right so to scrutinize "the abysmal deeps of personality." It is indeed a dreadful book, most dreadful because of a certain moral callousness, a want of sympathy, a shutting out of hope. The art is burning and intense. As a piece of literary work, this seems to me the finest you have done—in all that regards style, invention, psychological analysis, exquisite fitting of parts, and admirable employ-

ment of motives to realize the abnormal. But it has left such a deeply painful impression on my heart that I do not know how I am ever to turn to it again. The fact is that viewed as an allegory it touches one too closely. Most of us at some part of our lives have been upon the verge of developing a Mr. Hyde.[13]

Louis's own view was that although such interpretations weren't necessarily mistaken—his story is an open-ended myth—they were reductive. He told one correspondent, "People are so filled full of folly and inverted lust that they can think of nothing but sexuality. The hypocrite let out the beast Hyde—who is no more sexual than another, but who is the essence of cruelty and malice, and selfishness and cowardice: and these are the diabolic in man—not this poor wish to have a woman that they make such a cry about."[14]

When Louis replied to Symonds he made clear what he thought was important: "*Jekyll* is a dreadful thing, I own; but the only thing I feel dreadful about is that damned old business of the war in the members. This time it came out; I hope it will stay in, in future." The reference is to the dualism preached by St. Paul—"I see another law in my members, warring against the law of my mind, and bringing me into captivity to the law of sin which is in my members." That was no occasional or exceptional state, but the constant condition of the human race. In the King James translation "members" means the entire body, not just the sexual parts.[15]

Jekyll's original intention was to allow his Hyde avatar nothing more than occasional episodes, but he is alarmed to realize that Hyde is increasingly taking over. "You must suffer me to go my own dark way," he tells a friend, using explicitly religious language. "I have brought on myself a punishment and a danger that I cannot name. If I am the chief of sinners, I am the chief of sufferers also." St. Paul called himself the chief of sinners, and Bunyan entitled his autobiography *Grace Abounding to the Chief of Sinners*.[16]

Jekyll makes one last desperate attempt to banish Hyde, vowing to devote himself entirely to good works, but as he relates in his "Full Statement," after two months the temptation is too great. He swallows his potion again, and that's when he beats the white-haired gentleman to death. We first saw that event from the outside; now Jekyll recalls what it felt like. "Instantly the spirit of hell awoke in me and raged. With a transport of glee, I mauled the unresisting body, tasting delight from every blow; and it was not till weariness had begun to succeed, that I was suddenly, in the top fit of my delirium, struck through the heart by a cold thrill of terror." By now any distinction between Jekyll and Hyde has collapsed.

Jekyll ends the story by choosing suicide as the only way out before he turns permanently into Hyde. "Here then, as I lay down the pen and proceed to seal up my confession, I bring the life of that unhappy Henry Jekyll to an end."

Those are the last words of the story, but by the time we read them we already know that Jekyll is dead. In the preceding chapter, "The Last Night," Utterson and Jekyll's butler hear weeping from inside a locked room and resolve to break down the door with an ax.

> There lay the body of a man sorely contorted and still twitching. They drew near on tiptoe, turned it on its back and beheld the face of Edward Hyde. He was dressed in clothes far too large for him, clothes of the doctor's bigness; the cords of his face still moved with a semblance of life, but life was quite gone; and by the crushed phial in the hand and the strong smell of kernels [cyanide] that hung upon the air, Utterson knew that he was looking on the body of a self-destroyer. "We have come too late," he said sternly, "whether to save or punish. Hyde is gone to his account; and it only remains for us to find the body of your master."

At this point they still fail to grasp that the dead man *is* the master. In death Jekyll has become entirely Hyde.[17]

When Charles Longman read the manuscript he was eager to publish it, but thought that it would lose effectiveness by being broken into installments for his magazine—"It was a tale which should be read straight through, not at an interval of a month." Accordingly he proposed to publish it as a book, which Louis approved of so long as he wouldn't lose money. That was taken care of by a generous advance payment against future royalties. Given its brevity, the book was made to look more substantial by the use of large type and wide margins.[18]

The reception was extraordinary. Longman's sold forty thousand copies in England within the first six months, as a cheap shilling paperback and a slightly more expensive hardback. In America *Scribner's* sold seventy-five thousand at an even cheaper price of 25 cents. Unfortunately there was no international copyright until 1891, so Louis got no income from that.

Graham Balfour commented later, "Its success was probably due rather to the moral instincts of the public than to any conscious perception of the merits of its art. It was read by those who never read fiction, it was quoted in pulpits, and made the subject of leading articles in religious newspapers." One writer declared, "It is an allegory based on the twofold nature of man, a truth taught us by the apostle PAUL in Romans 7, 'I find then a law that, when I would do good, evil is present with me.' . . . May GOD grant that this book may be a warning to

55. Richard Mansfield as Jekyll and Hyde

many who are trifling with sin, unconscious of its awful power to drag them down to the lowest depths of hell."[19]

Louis was pleased with the popularity of *Jekyll and Hyde,* but he was far from regarding it as his masterpiece. A few years later he even called it "the worst thing I ever wrote." Still, it was a satisfaction to have found a literary vehicle for the theme of doubleness that had always haunted him.[20]

The story was soon adapted as a stage play, with Richard Mansfield starring as both Jekyll and Hyde. A photograph taken at the time (fig. 55) captures the duality of the character; as a commentator says, "The scandal is that the monster operates as a double exposure, not severed from Jekyll at all."[21]

In the summer of 1888 Mansfield's stage production moved from America to London, and less than a week after that Jack the Ripper began his career of serial killing. A writer in the *Pall Mall Gazette* commented, "There certainly seems to be a tolerably realistic personification of Mr. Hyde at large."[22]

Remarkably enough, *Strange Case of Dr. Jekyll and Mr. Hyde* was not the only novel that Louis published in 1886. The other was *Kidnapped,* a brilliant historical fiction set in eighteenth-century Scotland, which dramatizes a very different kind of dividedness—not within the self, but within a national culture. That the two novels should appear in a single year is a testimony to the breadth of his genius.

CHAPTER 23

Kidnapped

THE HIGHLANDS

Louis's best writing came from sudden inspiration. That had happened with *Treasure Island* and with *Dr. Jekyll and Mr. Hyde.* In early 1885 he made a start on *Kidnapped.* "I began it," he said later, "partly as a lark, partly as a potboiler," and he set it aside while he turned to other projects. When he returned to it a year later the inspiration arrived. "Suddenly it moved. David and Alan stepped out from the canvas, and I found I was in another world." David Balfour—to whom Louis gave one of his own names—and Alan Breck Stewart are the odd couple at the heart of a tale every bit as surprising and thrilling as *Treasure Island.* "In one of my books, and in one only," Louis said later, "the characters took the bit in their teeth; all at once they became detached from the flat paper, they turned their backs on me and walked off bodily; and from that time my task was stenographic—it was they who spoke, it was they who wrote the remainder of the story." Graham Balfour confirmed that he was referring to *Kidnapped.*[1]

However Louis's best fiction may have originated, it sprang from long-meditated themes. His love of tales of piracy was waiting for *Treasure Island;* his dread of interior conflict was waiting for *Jekyll and Hyde.* The roots of *Kidnapped* reached back to his earliest days, when his family spent extended vacations at Bridge of Allan, a popular health resort northwest of Edinburgh. Nearby were Stirling Castle, which had endured eight sieges over the years, and the battlefield of Bannockburn, where a Scottish army defeated the English in the fourteenth century. Bridge of Allan was also close to the imaginary line that divided the Lowlands from the Highlands, as shown on the map (fig. 56). It wasn't an actual physical boundary, or an administrative one either, but reflected an awareness that the cultures on either side were profoundly different from each other. In *Kidnapped* a character mentions "the Highland line."[2]

Louis was there at least ten times between the ages of three and twenty-five, and eagerly devoured tales of the romantic past. At Davos he planned to write a formal history of the Highlands, and although that never happened, the reading he did for it was still fresh in his mind when he began *Kidnapped*.

As their name implies, the Highlands of Scotland are very different, geographically and geologically, from the fertile Lowlands. They are dominated by mountain ranges, and Ben Nevis, at 4,400 feet, is the highest mountain in the British Isles. Population was sparse, supported mainly by cattle raising and subsistence farming. In a book about "Britishness" Linda Colley says that Lowland Scots "traditionally regarded their Highland countrymen as members of a different and inferior race, violent, treacherous, poverty-stricken and backward." Conversely, Highlanders regarded the urban and commercial Lowlanders as a threat to their way of life.[3]

As everyday garments men in the Highlands wore kilts, which were originally full-length cloaks but in the eighteenth century had been modified to knee-length skirts (women wore dresses, not kilts). The common language of the Highlands was Gaelic, completely different from the Lallans ("Lowland") Scots that Louis enjoyed using; he never learned Gaelic.

In the Lowlands most of the landlords, merchants, lawyers, clergy, and professors had welcomed the 1707 union of Scotland with England. They spoke English, and many of them pursued careers in London. That was the class to which both sides of Louis's family belonged. He never felt that he belonged, however, and he identified in imagination with the culture of the Highlands, which appealed to him as romantic, passionate, and risk-taking—everything Edinburgh was not. "In spite of the difference of blood and language," he once wrote, "the Lowlander feels himself the sentimental countryman of the Highlander."[4]

Clann is the Gaelic word for "family," and clan membership was fundamental to Highland life. "The Highlands were tribal," the historian T. C. Smout says, "in the exact sense that nineteenth-century Africa was tribal." A clan might coincide geographically with a particular region, but some chieftains had no land at all; the basis of allegiance was blood relationship. Clan members owed military service to their chief if summoned, a feudal obligation that had not existed in England since the Middle Ages. The obligation of service operated in both directions. Smout explains, "Since all the clansmen from the chief downwards

56. The Lowlands and Highlands

were blood relations of each other, it followed that the chiefs were expected to feel fatherly obligations even towards the poorest and weakest, and all the clansmen were expected to give unstinted help to each other in time of crisis."[5]

There were at least 120 clans in Scotland (including some in the Lowlands), depending how they're counted—possibly more than 200. Among the most famous Highland clans were the Campbells and Stewarts in the south, the Mackenzies and Macdonalds further north, and in the western Hebrides the Macleans and Macleods. The map indicates the principal locations of a number of clans.

As Fernand Braudel showed in his classic study of the Mediterranean, mountain people everywhere have resisted control from outside, fragmenting into tribes or clans and engaging in endless feuds. Clan solidarity was intense in the Highlands; a character in *Kidnapped* comments that "they all hing together like bats in a steeple."[6]

Louis empathized with their defense of a traditional culture. Walter Scott's novels celebrated the heroic past—that was why Louis's father loved them—but he acknowledged the historical fatality of its passing, and understood that the defeat of the clans made the development of modern Scotland possible. Louis felt deeply disaffected from modern Scotland, and lost causes always fired his imagination.

Kidnapped is set in 1751, at a time in history that may need some context today. After King James of Scotland succeeded Queen Elizabeth in 1603 as James I, his line—the Stuarts—had occupied the British throne, ruling over England and Wales as well as Scotland. In 1714, however, the next Stuart in the succession was a Catholic. He would have become King James III, but Parliament had declared Catholicism to be disqualifying, and a Protestant imported from Germany was crowned instead as George I. From then on, many Scots claimed allegiance to the displaced Stuart heir, who was known as the Pretender. His supporters were called Jacobites, from Jacobus, the Latin form of James.

In 1715 James led an armed rebellion to recover the throne, but was defeated in battle in the north of England and spent the rest of his days in France. There was a second rebellion in 1745, led by his son Charles Edward Stuart—"Bonnie Prince Charlie"—and it too was put down. Many Scots continued privately to toast the Pretender as "the king over the water," but England cracked down, constructing forts throughout Scotland to maintain control. English soldiers—the notorious redcoats—patrolled everywhere, and in effect the Highlands became occupied territory.

To symbolize the suppression of the Highland clans, many of whose chieftains were dispossessed and driven into exile, the tartan patterns that indicated membership in a particular clan were made illegal. When Samuel Johnson toured the Highlands with James Boswell in 1773 he confirmed that "the plaid is rarely worn." They encountered just one man "completely clothed in the ancient habit, and by him it was worn only occasionally and wantonly."[7]

Louis identified so deeply with the defeated Highlanders that he searched repeatedly for evidence that the name Stevenson was adopted by some members of the Macgregor clan, who sought to hold on to their possessions by changing their name. Graham Balfour wrote, "To have proved himself a disguised clansman of Rob Roy, and to have had James More for the black sheep of the family, was a dream which it was worth a world of pains to verify. For these shadowy speculations there seems to be no ground in history." Rob Roy Macgregor was a celebrated outlaw at the beginning of the eighteenth century, and hero of Scott's *Rob Roy*; his son Robin Oig makes an appearance in *Kidnapped*. As for James More, Louis would introduce him in *Catriona*, the sequel to *Kidnapped*, and have David Balfour fall in love with More's daughter.[8]

All of this history had been fermenting for years in Louis's mind, and now he suddenly saw how he could transmute it into fiction. In *Treasure Island* Jim Hawkins was plunged into a gripping imaginary situation; in *Kidnapped* David Balfour would be plunged into a fraught situation that really existed in Scotland's past.

FROM HISTORY TO STORY

The difficulty in any historical novel is to make the narrative alive and compelling, introducing enough context to keep the reader oriented without bogging down in details. *Kidnapped* sweeps the reader along from beginning to end, and as in *Treasure Island*, the narrative rises repeatedly to tension and danger. As is true of nearly all of Louis's best fiction, the story is told by a first-person narrator. We live through David's experiences as he himself does, sharing in his bewilderment or fear. And more profoundly than Jim Hawkins in *Treasure Island*, David has to learn not only whom to trust, but also who he is.

As the story begins, David has just turned seventeen in the western Lowlands when his father dies, leaving him an orphan. The local minister then gives him a letter from his father that advises him to go and meet Ebenezer Balfour, an uncle he never knew he had, who lives on the family estate near Edinburgh. Ebenezer turns out to be a miser and misanthrope, living alone in a half-ruined mansion, but he tells his nephew that "there's a wee bit siller that I half promised ye before ye were born," amounting to the handsome sum of 40 guineas.

> My uncle counted out into my hand seven and thirty golden guinea pieces; the rest was in his hand, in small gold and silver; but his heart failed him there, and he crammed the change into his pocket.
> "There," said he, "that'll show you! I'm a queer man, and strange wi' strangers; but my word is my bond, and there's the proof of it."
> Now, my uncle seemed so miserly that I was struck dumb by this sudden generosity, and could find no words in which to thank him.

What follows is a fine example of Louis's narrative art, in which a placid scene is interrupted by sheer terror. Ebenezer instructs David to go up a stone staircase and bring down a chest filled with papers, which will presumably confirm their family relationship. While he is groping his way up in the dark, however, a flash of lightning reveals that he is in mortal danger. Immediately in front of him the stairs end in mid-air, high above a stone courtyard; one step further would mean a fatal plunge. "The mere thought of the peril in which I might have stood, and the dreadful height I might have fallen from, brought out the sweat upon my body and relaxed my joints."

David climbs back down and silently approaches his uncle. "I stepped forward, came close behind him where he sat, and suddenly clapping my two hands down upon his shoulders—'Ah!' cried I. My uncle gave a kind of broken cry like a sheep's bleat, flung up his arms, and tumbled to the floor like a dead man." Chesterton commented that this novel is full of "snapping phrases that seem to pick things off like pistol shots."[9]

Only now do we appreciate the irony of Ebenezer's refusing to hand over the loose change, even when he expected David to be dead just minutes later. It's a deft characterization of a miser who even in that moment can't help keeping something back.

By chance David makes a shocking discovery: his late father, not Ebenezer, was the elder brother and ought to have been the heir—which means that the estate should now belong to David. He resolves to be on his guard from now on, but is no match for Ebenezer, who tricks him into visiting a ship where he is suddenly knocked unconscious. That is the kidnapping of the title. When he revives he's at sea, on his way to be sold into servitude in the Carolinas.

Good luck rescues David. The ship runs down a small boat, and a man saves himself by climbing aboard; this is Alan Breck Stewart, a Highlander carrying money from the clans to his exiled chieftain in France. Soon David overhears the sailors plotting to murder Alan for the money, and the two of them prepare for the attack with weapons that are stored nearby.

> It came all of a sudden when it did, with a rush of feet and a roar, and then a shout from Alan, and a sound of blows and someone crying out as if hurt. I looked back over my shoulder and saw Mr. Shuan in the doorway, crossing blades with Alan.
> "That's him that killed the boy!" I cried.
> "Look to your window!" said Alan; and as I turned back to my place, I saw him pass his sword through the mate's body.

Graham Greene, who was proud of being related to the Stevensons, noted how different this passage is from conventional writing: "No similes or metaphors there, not even an adjective."[10]

The victory forges a powerful bond. "'David, I love you like a brother. And O, man,' he cried in a kind of ecstasy, 'am I no a bonny fighter?'"

Soon a storm wrecks the ship on a reef, and after struggling ashore David is caught up in an actual historical event. At Bridge of Allan Louis had been fascinated by the 1751 Appin murder, named for a town in the western Highlands. The Campbell clan was loyal to Britain, and Colin Campbell was in the Appin region to evict tenants for nonpayment of taxes to the British crown. He was shot dead on the highway, and the identity of the assassin is unknown to this day.

David happens to encounter Campbell's party on the road, and with no idea who they are, he stops them to ask for directions. Just then the shot rings out and Campbell falls dead. David is terrified, aware that since it was he who had stopped Campbell, he is sure to be suspected as an accessory to the murder. He begins to run, not knowing where he's going, and it's a complete surprise when he encounters Alan Breck.

Alan swears that it wasn't he who fired the shot, but as a Stewart he is an enemy to the Campbells and will be hunted down. Fortunately, he knows this mountainous region by heart. If they can reach Edinburgh far to the east, Alan will find a ship to carry him to France, and David can recover his stolen inheritance. Incidentally, "Stuart" and "Stewart" are variant spellings of the same name, which is why Alan Breck Stewart can say proudly, "I bear a king's name."[11]

The complex relationship between David and Alan is one of the finest things in all of Stevenson. Not only do they have little in common, they really ought to be enemies. David is loyal to the Whig government of Britain that was supported by the modernizing, commercial Lowlands; Alan is a Jacobite on his way to deliver Appin rents to his exiled kinsman and clan chief. David is heir to a

Lowlands estate that he hopes to recover from his treacherous uncle; Alan has no land or title and has lived for years as a swashbuckling soldier of fortune.

The better they get to know each other, the more obvious their differences will be. Nevertheless, Alan's fidelity to the cause he believes in is powerfully attractive to the idealistic David. Conversely, David is inexperienced and cautious, yet he joins forces with Alan in a moment of crisis. From now on they will be companions in a flight through the mountains to save their lives, with an ever-deepening emotional bond.

The relationship is somewhat like Jim Hawkins's with Long John Silver, but with far greater depth and psychological truth. Leslie Fiedler puts it well: "The relationship of the Boy and the Scoundrel, treated as a flirtation in the earlier book, becomes almost a full-fledged love affair, a pre-sexual romance. The antagonists fall into lovers' quarrels and make up, swear to part forever, and remain together. David must measure the Scoundrel against himself, and the more unwillingly comes to love that of which he must disapprove."[12]

Jefferson Singer extends the thought further. In this friendship Louis brings together the Lowland culture that formed him and the Highland one he wished he belonged to. More immediately, David and Alan represent essential elements within himself.

> The purity of Alan's feelings rebuffs the deadening of emotion that Stevenson associated with his own late nineteenth-century world of technology and bureaucratic monotony. Alan's authenticity in the expression of his feelings was central to Stevenson's understanding of his own volatile nature, and perhaps to his father's as well. Quick to love, quick to anger, ready to sacrifice for a friend or a principle, this way of being spoke deeply to Stevenson.

Louis's stepson Lloyd said that he was "as chivalrous and impulsive as Alan Breck, with whom he had not a little in common."[13]

Alan Breck Stewart, like many of the characters in *Kidnapped,* actually existed. Breck was a nickname meaning "spotted," in reference to scars on his face. He is deftly characterized when he first leaps aboard the ship:

> He was smallish in stature, but well set and as nimble as a goat; his face was of a good open expression, but sunburnt very dark, and heavily freckled and pitted with the smallpox; his eyes were unusually light and had a kind of dancing madness in them, that was both engaging and alarming; and when he took off his great-coat, he laid a pair of fine silver-mounted

pistols on the table, and I saw that he was belted with a great sword. His manners, besides, were elegant, and he pledged [toasted] the captain handsomely. Altogether I thought of him, at the first sight, that here was a man I would rather call my friend than my enemy.[14]

The narrative of "the flight in the heather" is a tour de force, evoking the experience of struggling through a forbidding landscape where danger of capture is ever-present. Realist novels were full of descriptive details; Louis knew how to evoke reality without the details, making it all the more vivid. At a dinner in London the painter John Everett Millais called across the table to Sidney Colvin, "You know Stevenson, don't you? Well, I wish you would tell him from me, if he cares to know, that to my mind he is the very first of living artists. I don't mean writers merely, but painters and all of us: nobody living can see with such an eye as that fellow, and nobody is such a master of his tools."[15]

An example of this skill comes when David and Alan have to cross a valley infested by redcoats. "Quickness was not all, but a swift judgment not only of the lie of the whole country, but of the solidity of every stone on which we must set foot; for the afternoon was now fallen so breathless that the rolling of a pebble sounded abroad like a pistol shot, and would start the echo calling among the hills and cliffs." A critic brings out how skillfully this is done: "Here we learn that the scene is a stony valley walled by hills and cliffs on a very still afternoon; yet the scene is presented purely in terms of the personal danger of the fugitives, the qualities they will need to survive, and their calculation of the risk of making a noise." There are no visual details at all, yet we see and feel it just as David does. "The terrain traversed by David," Jenni Calder says, "is a felt landscape, literally felt by his feet and his hands and knees as he struggles through it."[16]

The journey through the mountains is punctuated by crises. One of these comes when the fugitives have to cross a dangerous torrent before soldiers overtake them. They manage to reach a rock in midstream, where David is paralyzed by fear; Alan leaps to the opposite bank and commands him to follow.

> I had this good example fresh before me, and just wit enough to see that if I did not leap at once, I should never leap at all. I bent low on my knees and flung myself forth, with that kind of anger of despair that has sometimes stood me in stead of courage. Sure enough, it was but my hands that reached the full length; these slipped, caught again, slipped again; and I was sliddering back into the lynn, when Alan seized me, first by the hair, then by the collar, and with a great strain dragged me into safety.[17]

As with *Treasure Island,* the illustrator N. C. Wyeth excelled at capturing such moments. In deciding which episodes in a novel to illustrate, his son Andrew recalled, "Pa would reread it carefully and underline the passages that he felt were the essence of the story." On the picture reproduced here (color plate 14) a commentator says, "The illustrator shows the boy stranded on a rock in the middle of a dangerous current, unable to move forward or backward until Alan Breck forces him to take a blind leap to safety. Wyeth focuses attention on a moment of choice, involving that combination of trust and daring which will be vital to David's ultimate salvation."[18]

Splendid though the illustration is, Louis's account is still better. In his own terms it's kinetic, whereas the picture is static. The right words can be worth more than a thousand pictures. "Sliddering," meaning to slip or slide, came from an Old English word that survived in Scots.

One of the most memorable moments comes near the end of their flight, when the fugitives are dragging themselves along with exhaustion. Frayed nerves provoke a quarrel in which each feels insulted, and David absurdly demands a duel.

> But before I could touch his blade with mine, he had thrown it from him and fallen to the ground. "Na, na," he kept saying, "na, na—I cannae, I cannae."
>
> At this the last of my anger oozed all out of me; and I found myself only sick, and sorry, and blank, and wondering at myself. I would have given the world to take back what I had said; but a word once spoken, who can recapture it? I minded me of all Alan's kindness and courage in the past, how he had helped and cheered and borne with me in our evil days; and then recalled my own insults, and saw that I had lost for ever that doughty friend. At the same time, the sickness that hung upon me seemed to redouble, and the pang in my side was like a sword for sharpness. I thought I must have swooned where I stood.[19]

Henry James greatly admired this episode. "The quarrel of the two men on the mountainside is a real stroke of genius, and has the very logic and rhythm of life—a quarrel which we feel to be inevitable, though it is about nothing, or almost nothing, and which springs from exasperated nerves and the simple shock of temperaments." But it was an exaggeration to say that the episode is about "almost nothing." Their brief but intense relationship is about to end, foreshadowed here in a kind of anticipated grief.[20]

What Alan says next is truly moving. "He came near sobbing. 'Davie,' said he,

'I'm no a right man at all; I have neither sense nor kindness; I could nae remember ye were just a bairn, I couldnae see ye were dying on your feet; Davie, ye'll have to try and forgive me.'"

When they reach Edinburgh Alan prepares to make his escape. David, with the help of a Balfour family lawyer, exposes his uncle's treachery and secures a large stipend to be paid until Ebenezer dies and leaves the entire estate to him. Yet it is a strangely anticlimactic conclusion; James said that the story "stops without ending."[21]

It is also a melancholy conclusion. When Alan is about to depart,

> We stood a space, and looked over at Edinburgh in silence.
> "Well, goodbye," said Alan, and held out his left hand.
> "Goodbye," said I, and gave the hand a little grasp, and went off down hill.
> Neither one of us looked the other in the face, nor so long as he was in my view did I take one back glance at the friend I was leaving. But as I went on my way to the city, I felt so lost and lonesome, that I could have found it in my heart to sit down by the dyke, and cry and weep like any baby.... There was a cold gnawing in my inside like a remorse for something wrong.[22]

David has his inheritance now and is making plans to become a lawyer, but the gain feels like a loss, as he leaves behind the romantic world of wildness, adventure, and risk. The relationship with the most compelling person he ever met has ended. No wonder the mood is of heartache rather than triumph.

The working manuscript of *Kidnapped* has survived, and comments by Fanny give evidence of her literary intelligence. She wrote in the margin, "Overdone!" and again, "Overdone, and a little too good! No weeping, please." She also urged Louis to delete the word "very" which kept showing up. Accordingly he made the changes:

> To be sure, I laughed ~~very hard~~ over this....
> "What?" cried the voice ~~very~~ sharply.

Those were shrewd corrections, and so was Fanny's reaction to this sentence: "The ship was bound for the Carolinas; and my children, you must not suppose that I was going to that place merely as an exile." As she reminded Louis, it was crucial for David to tell the story as he experienced it at the time. "*No children,*" she exclaimed in the margin—"this is not Aunt Jenny's tales to her children and nieces. You destroy the illusion the moment you jump to the present. I am seeing a boy all the time just as he goes along. Don't cut his throat, or you give me two narrators to follow, both man and boy. You were just boasting that he talked like a boy telling his story and now he's an old man!"[23]

Like *Treasure Island, Kidnapped* was serialized in *Young Folks,* starting in May 1886, and soon afterward was published in book form by Cassell. Louis received £150 from Cassell, plus 15 percent royalties on future sales. Critical reception was enthusiastic. The *Athenaeum* called *Kidnapped* "such really vital, really organic work as Mr. Stevenson has never given us in his stories for adults, such as *Prince Otto* and *The New Arabian Nights,*" and the *St. James's Gazette* said, "The simplicity which is the highest art, a mastery of language, and a subtle and sympathetic power of compelling attention, are all at the command of Mr. Stevenson."[24]

Henry James commented, in a note in his personal copy, on "this coquetry of pretending he writes 'for boys.'" *Kidnapped* is very much an adult novel, with sophisticated narration and complicated historical and political tensions. If anything, it's remarkable that it can be read and appreciated by the young.[25]

CHAPTER 24

Farewell to Europe

The year 1887 was a turning point in Louis's life in two major ways. His father died in May, and three months later he departed for America, accompanied by Fanny, Lloyd, his newly widowed mother, and their maid Valentine. He had no idea how long he would be away, but it would turn out to be forever.

During the previous two years Thomas had been showing increasing signs of dementia; he often struggled to find a word, or would give up and leave a thought unfinished. In March 1886 Louis told Colvin, "He has many marks of age, some of childhood. The change (to my eyes) is thoroughly begun; and a very beautiful, simple, honourable, high-spirited and childlike (and childish) man is now in process of deserting us piecemeal." A year later he wrote to Anne Jenkin, "My father is still very yellow [he had jaundice], and very old, and very weak, but yesterday he seemed happier, and smiled, and followed what was said; even laughed, I think. When he came away he said to me, 'Take care of yourself, my dearie,' which had a strange sound of childish days, and will not leave my mind."[1]

Thomas and Margaret had been staying in lodgings of their own in Bournemouth, but in April his condition had deteriorated so badly that he was sent home to Edinburgh, in a private railway carriage that could stop along the way if necessary. On May 4 Louis and Fanny also set off for Edinburgh, but when they got there Thomas gave no sign of recognition. Margaret wrote in her diary,

"Lou arrived this afternoon and his father does not know him." Louis himself described the final encounter in "The Last Sight":

> Once more I saw him. In the lofty room
> Where oft with lights and company his tongue
> Was trump to honest laughter, sat attired
> A something in his likeness. "Look!" said one,
> Unkindly kind, "look up, it is your boy!"
> And the dread changeling gazed at me in vain.

Thomas Stevenson died on May 8 at the age of sixty-nine.[2]

Louis was not able to attend his father's funeral, having succumbed to illness brought on by stress and grief. Fanny told Colvin that he stayed away at the insistence of his physician uncle George: "A poisonous sun is shining; I believe they call it fair weather. . . . I must say that Dr. Balfour has acted most kindly to Louis. He kept him out of Heriot Row even the night his father died, which is more than I could have done myself. He did all he could to keep Louis in check, and is watching him most carefully now." She appreciated the doctor's straightforward opinion of future prospects: "He says frankly that though Louis may have ups and downs he can never really be better, and will always have hemorrhages more or less bad according to the care he takes of himself. He says just what Ruedi [at Davos] always said, that it is fibroidal disease of the lungs, for which there is no cure, only palliation."[3]

As Louis and Fanny were leaving Edinburgh for Bournemouth, there was an encounter that Rosaline Masson described:

> Late in May, two friends walking along Princes Street saw an open cab coming slowly towards them westward along the broad roadway, a man and a woman in it. As it passed, a slender, loose-garbed figure stood up in the cab, waved a wide-brimmed hat, and called out "Goodbye!" It was Louis Stevenson. The cab passed as they waved back to him, and as he stood, looking back at them over the back of the cab, still waving his hat, the long line of Princes Street, with the grey and green of the Castle Rock and the gardens on one side, and Princes Street itself glittering in the sunshine on the other, was at its very best. It was Edinburgh's last sight of Louis Stevenson, and Louis Stevenson's last look back at the city of his birth.[4]

He was eager to leave not just Edinburgh but Bournemouth, and seized on a doctor's recommendation that he should seek a more healthful climate in America. Fanny was stricken at the prospect of leaving her "little nest," the only house she had ever owned, and wrote to Lloyd, who was at school at the time, about how wrenching it would be to go. "Life had been too happy in Skerryvore—the envying gods had struck it down."

Lloyd wondered if Louis would be equally distressed, but far from it: "The prospect of Colorado or New Mexico seemed to fill him with joy. Were we not to live in the wilds with rifles on our walls and bear skins on our mud floors! Sombreros, ha, ha! Mustangs, silver spurs, spaciousness, picturesque freedom! There was not a word about cozy nests, nor envying gods, nor eternal farewells to happiness. None whatever. *Vive la vie sauvage!* He was plainly glad to be off, and the sooner the better."[5]

The chief obstacle was anxiety about Margaret's situation. She was still at home in Edinburgh, and in July Louis wrote to her, "Not only would we not go to America without you, we should not persist in trying it if we did not believe it would be, on the whole, the best for you. I have been a bad enough son all round; I would now be a decently good one if possible. Your loving son, R.L.S." She was very willing to go. She had no wish to live alone at Heriot Row, and was more adventurous than might have been expected.[6]

By August plans to leave were definite, and Louis wrote to Colvin, "Here I am in this dismantled house hoping to leave tomorrow, yet still in doubt; this time of my life is at an end. The last day—the last evening—in the old house, with a sad, but God knows, nowise a bitter heart; I wish I could say with hope." He told Henley, "My spirits are rising again after three months of black depression: I almost begin to feel as if I should care to live; I would by God! And so I believe I shall." Henley replied, "Your news is inexpressibly refreshing. With heart that way I have no fear of the issue." He added, "Trust me, we shall live to reform the drammy yet." Collaborating to reform the drama was a burden Louis had no wish ever to shoulder again.[7]

After they left for London, Fanny sent a note to their protégée Adelaide Boodle in which she described a surprising burst of emotion from Louis. "It had suddenly come upon him that he loved Skerryvore, Westbourne, Bournemouth, even the Poole Road, with an almost morbid sentimentality. When he said farewell to Mary Anne, for whom he has much respect and liking, it all came over him like a flood, and he burst into tears. Agnes, who had been wreathed in smiles, looked at Louis, then at her mother, who was crying, and broke into a perfect roar like a child, so that Louis had to be hurried away, Agnes's loud weeping and wailing remaining with him as a lasting memory."[8]

Agnes and Mary Anne were servants in the Bournemouth household. People known as "the help" were rarely noticed in correspondence and novels of that time, and yet they must have been present for most of every day. Agnes was also mentioned in a letter Louis sent Fanny when she had gone to London to buy some things they needed: "Valentine and Agnes are out on messages. . . . Valentine very pretty in her cap, and the pair quite a neat turn-out." There was no other mention of Mary Anne.[9]

On August 22, 1887, the family sailed from London on the SS *Ludgate Hill*. A large number of friends had come to say goodbye, one of whom was Gosse, who found Louis "less emaciated than I feared."

> He is in mourning for his father, and was quite stylishly dressed in a black velvet coat and waistcoat and black silk necktie and dark trousers, so that instead of looking like a Lascar [Southeast Asian sailor] out of employment, as he generally does, he looked extremely elegant and refined, his hair over his shoulders but very tidy and burnished like brass with brushing. He prowled about the room in his usual noiseless panther fashion, talking all the time, full of wit and feeling and sweetness, as charming as ever he was, but with a little more sadness and sense of crisis than usual.

Others who were there included Henry James, William Archer, Colvin, Henley, "Aunt Alan" Stevenson, Cummy, Coggie Ferrier, and Bob Stevenson's sister Katharine de Mattos. Colvin said later, "Leaving the ship's side as she weighed anchor, and waving farewell to the party from the boat which landed me, I little knew what was the truth, that I was looking on the face of my friend for the last time."[10]

Five years after this departure Louis wrote from Samoa to their Bournemouth friend Ida Taylor, "You remember how you always said we were but an encampment of Bedouins, and that you would awake some morning to find us fled forever." That was a long-standing way of life for Louis. Five years previously he had written to his mother, "You must understand that I shall be a nomad, more or less, until my days be done."[11]

Skerryvore was rented out for the time being, since they might return someday, but that would never happen. Today the house no longer exists. During the Second World War it was destroyed by a random German bomb. The site is now occupied by a commemorative garden at the end of R. L. Stevenson Avenue, with the model lighthouse still there.

CHAPTER 25

An Adirondack Winter

LIONIZED IN NEW YORK

The SS *Ludgate Hill* had been chosen for spaciousness and fresh air rather than ocean-liner luxury, but only when it paused at Le Havre did the Stevenson party realize why their tickets were so inexpensive: the cargo was mostly livestock. Some people might have found that disagreeable, but not Louis. After the voyage he wrote to Colvin, "O it was lovely on our stable-ship, chock-full of stallions. It was a thousandfold pleasanter than a great big Birmingham liner like a new hotel; and we liked the officers, and made friends with the quartermasters, and I (at least) made a friend of a baboon (for we carried a cargo of apes) whose embraces have pretty near cost me a coat." To Bob he wrote, "I was so happy on board that ship, I could not have believed it possible. I had literally forgotten what happiness was, and the full mind—full of external and physical things, not full of cares and labours and rot about a fellow's behavior. My heart literally sang."[1]

During the voyage he had a chance to assemble some previously published essays for the collection *Memories and Portraits,* and he composed a dedication for the title page:

> To my mother
> In the Name of Past Joy and Present Sorrow
> I Dedicate These Memories and Portraits
> S. S. Ludgate Hill, within sight of Cape Race

Cape Race is a point on the southern tip of Newfoundland.

By the time he left Britain Louis was a well-known writer; in New York he was astonished to find himself a celebrity. Besieged by interviewers, he wrote to Colvin, "My reception here was idiotic to the last degree; if Jesus Christ came, they would make less fuss." Americans at that time were given to lionizing British celebrities, as had happened recently with Oscar Wilde and years earlier with Dickens. The contrast was staggering between this welcome and Louis's previous arrival in New York, when he shivered through his first night in wet clothes in a cheap boardinghouse.

A Stevenson myth was developing, and journalists competed to interview the great man and describe him. Thus the *Sunday World:*

> Unconsciously the attention of the visitor has already been fixed on his host's hands and eyes. The latter are very wide apart and look as if they could see to one side as well as ahead. Their deep brown has nothing mournful in it, they are too active-looking for that; and yet they do not flash, but move slowly and seem all the while to be reading something— not necessarily a book, but a shadow, perhaps, or a storm on the Scottish coast, or a shipwreck, or a temptation in a human soul.[2]

Not only was Louis famous, his books were bringing in impressive income for the first time. He had been earning a few hundred pounds a year from his writing, but now the *New York World* offered $10,000 for fifty-two weekly articles, which he had sense enough to turn down as an impossible task. Instead he accepted $3,500 from *Scribner's Magazine* for twelve monthly essays. He produced all of them on time, and many are among his best.

And even without these lucrative payments, Louis's financial circumstances were already secure for the first time, thanks to his father's will. By Scottish law a third of a man's estate went to his widow, a third to his children, and the final third to bequests of his choice. Louis could have insisted on receiving his share at this time, but he didn't, preferring to leave it in his mother's hands and to wait for his full inheritance after her death. Since he predeceased her he never did receive it, and it went in the end to his own heirs. What he did get at this time, however, was the handsome sum of £3,000, which had been separately provided for in the will.[3]

When Louis was reunited in New York with his artist friend Will Low and his French wife Berthe he said, "I'm just an obscure 'literary gent' at home, and this wave of notoriety frightens me. It cannot mean much from some of its indications; and what if I should grow to like it?" Someone who was present at their

57. Stevenson medallion, by Saint-Gaudens

reunion recalled, "The Lows and the Stevensons were old and dear friends, and they had not seen each other in a long time. Such handshaking and such embracing you would not expect to see outside of France. The men threw their arms around each other's necks with all the effusion of schoolgirls, but with infinitely more depth to their emotions."[4]

The sculptor Augustus Saint-Gaudens was a friend of Low's, having shared a studio with him in Paris, and said that if Louis ever came to New York he would gladly make his portrait. This now happened at Louis's hotel while he reclined in bed with the inevitable cigarette. Saint-Gaudens modeled his likeness in clay in five sessions of three hours each, and numerous bronze medallions (fig. 57) were afterward cast from the mold.

The sculptor chose to emphasize physical weakness, with bony fingers and sunken chest contrasted against plump pillows and a firm bedhead. Victorian novels and paintings are filled with sickroom scenes that affirm the nobility of illness, but it was Louis's energy that most impressed people who met him, and his letters show that he was actually feeling exceptionally vigorous at this time. Reading and writing in bed was his regular custom, and he merely continued to do so while posing.

Saint-Gaudens's motives for representing Louis as ailing can only be guessed, but he sent a remarkable letter immediately afterward to Low: "My episode with Stevenson has been one of the events of my life and I now understand the state of mind [name unclear] gets in about people. I'm in that beatific state." That declaration was accompanied by a sketch of himself kneeling in adoration before a haloed Stevenson.[5]

After Louis's death a bas-relief based on this image was mounted in St. Giles's Church in Edinburgh, with a pen tactfully replacing the cigarette. When Cummy saw it "she stamped her foot, and swept the thing away with an impatient gesture. 'Why will they be showing Master Lou in bed?' she said. 'I didn't love him because he was a sickly child.'"[6]

On a subsequent visit to New York Louis met Mark Twain, whom he had always admired. When they were about to meet he wrote to Twain that he had read *Huckleberry Finn* no fewer than four times "and am quite ready to begin again tomorrow." He added that during a sleepless night his father once picked up a copy of *Roughing It,* and "next morning he told me he had to put it aside. 'I was frightened,' he said, 'I was positively frightened; it cannot be safe for a man of my time of life to laugh so much.'"[7]

The two writers now spent an afternoon chatting on a bench in Washington Square. Unfortunately Louis left no account of what they said, and Twain, who seems to have done most of the talking, recorded only comments that they exchanged on a couple of minor American authors. It's easy to imagine that they also talked about their mutual success with "boys' stories" that were altogether adult in implication. Writing to Twain five years later, Louis recalled "that very pleasant afternoon we spent together in Washington Square among the nursemaids like a couple of characters out of a story by Henry James." James's fifth novel, published in 1880, was *Washington Square*.[8]

Twain did describe the impression Louis made on him, however.

> His business in the Square was to absorb the sunshine. He was most scantily furnished with flesh, his clothes seemed to fall into hollows as if there might be nothing inside but the frame for a sculptor's statue. His long face and lank hair and dark complexion and musing and melancholy expression seemed to fit these details justly and harmoniously, and the altogether of it seemed especially planned to gather the rays of your

observation and focalize them upon Stevenson's special distinction and commanding feature, his splendid eyes. They burned with a smouldering rich fire under the penthouse of his brows, and they made him beautiful.[9]

Louis also met William Tecumseh Sherman, notorious for the Civil War march through Georgia. Always an admirer of military fame, he had enjoyed Sherman's memoirs and asked Saint-Gaudens for an introduction. The great man had never heard of him and wondered if he might be one of his own former soldiers, but Louis wasn't disappointed in the least. "It was magnificent," he told Low, "to simply stand in the presence of one who has done what he has, and then to find him so genial and human."[10]

In New York Louis also made a valuable professional connection. When he was in Bournemouth an American publisher named S. S. McClure was visiting London and proposed getting together, but it never happened because Louis characteristically mislaid McClure's London address. Remembering that, he now invited McClure to drop in at his hotel. In his autobiography McClure recalled, "He received us in bed, very much in the attitude of the St. Gaudens medallion, for which he was then posing. Though he was in bed he did not seem ill; he looked frail but not sick. The thing about his appearance that most struck me was the unusual width of his brow, and the fact that his eyes were very far apart."[11]

McClure had a classic rags to riches story. After a boyhood on an Irish farm, his family came to America, where he put himself through Knox College in Illinois and went on to become a leading New York publisher. He would narrate his story in 1914 in *The Autobiography of S. S. McClure;* if the book seems unusually well written, it ought to, since it was ghostwritten by Willa Cather. He had published her early work and made her his managing editor, and she always held him in high esteem. She used to say that learning to speak in his voice prepared her to create the male narrator of *My Ántonia*.[12]

On McClure's desk in the photograph (fig. 58) are copies of *McClure's Magazine,* a pioneering venture in investigative journalism which he would found in 1894; he also established the first U.S. newspaper syndicate. For Louis this was a very different kind of relationship from the gentlemanly tradition of publishing in Britain, where authors accepted whatever payment their publishers chose to offer. American editors were aggressively entrepreneurial, lining up authors competitively, suggesting ideas for articles, and offering lucrative contracts. Over the years McClure published such writers as Jack London, Upton Sinclair, Rudyard Kipling, and Conan Doyle, in addition to Cather and Stevenson. Nothing came of his connection with Louis at this time, but in later years he would serialize

58. S. S. McClure

two relatively minor novels, *St. Ives* and *The Ebb-Tide*, in his magazine, and would publish Louis's account of beginning *Treasure Island* at Braemar.[13]

During one of McClure's visits they signed a contract to publish *The Black Arrow* in book form (in England it had appeared only as a magazine serial). It then emerged that *The Black Arrow* was already under contract to Charles Scribner. So far as can be ascertained, Louis genuinely *forgot* that he had done that. McClure commented in his autobiography, "Stevenson was the last man to inform one about his business affairs, even when he was informed as to them himself, which was not often." Charles Baxter was generously handling Louis's finances, but always from afar, and seldom with adequate information.[14]

59. The Saranac Lake sanatorium

SARANAC LAKE

The experience of Davos seemed to confirm that cold dry air was good for Louis's health, and the first thought was to settle in Colorado, which had been recommended by Dr. Ruedi since he had once lived there himself. However, Fanny often experienced heart trouble at high altitude, and they settled instead on the town of Saranac Lake in upstate New York, a hundred miles south of Montreal. A small hamlet at the time, it had an excellent sanatorium run by a specialist named Edward Livingston Trudeau. A photograph taken while the Stevensons were there (fig. 59) shows how simple and isolated it was. The sanatorium and town had few charms and virtually no social life—a far cry from Davos.

They rented a house known as the Baker cottage, owned by a woodsman named Andrew Baker who continued to live with his family in the back. The lake was not in view, but Louis was delighted to find a stream close by. He wrote to Henry James, "I like water (fresh water I mean) either running swiftly among stones or else largely qualified with whisky." There was a sitting room with a fireplace, bedrooms for Margaret and for Louis and Fanny, and "servants' rooms" on the small second floor that were occupied by Lloyd and Valentine.[15]

A picture of the house taken ten years later (fig. 60) shows a pleasant summertime scene, but they arrived in the fall and departed in the spring, so what

60. The Baker cottage

they experienced was mostly winter, when the temperature dropped as low as 48 degrees below zero and snow sometimes covered the first-floor windows. They were there during the Great Blizzard of '88, one of the most severe in American history, when the railways shut down and people were trapped in their homes for a week. If the kitchen floor was washed with hot water it immediately became a sheet of ice, and it was impossible to stay comfortable except in a bed warmed with heated soapstones; they also carried the stones in their pockets when they went outside. Fanny's sister Nellie heard that even in bed, when Valentine reached for a handkerchief she had put under her pillow she found it frozen solid. The cold was far worse than during the two winters at Davos.[16]

Fanny quickly decided to travel to Montreal and buy snowshoes, fur hats, and heavy buffalo coats. A photograph (fig. 61) shows her, Lloyd, and Louis bundled up. Lloyd, with spectacles flashing, has grown a mustache in emulation of Louis (and for some reason is wearing a necktie); Fanny is looking down at their new dog Sport.

Lloyd remembered Saranac Lake with distaste. "Sleighs, snowshoes, and frozen lakes; *voyageurs* in quaint costumes and with French to match; red-hot stoves and streaming windows; guides who spat, and looked like [Fenimore Cooper's] Leatherstocking; consumptives in bright caps and many-hued woolens gaily to-

61. Lloyd, Fanny, and Louis at Saranac Lake

bogganing at forty below zero; buffalo coats an inch thick; snowstorms, snow drifts, Arctic cold; the sensation of rubbing snow on your congealed ears and unfortunate nose—such was our new home in which R.L.S. was hoping to regain his health."[17]

Fanny didn't care for the place any more than Lloyd did. Her own health was often bad, and she went away for extended periods, visiting her family in Indiana and friends in San Francisco. There she saw Nellie and also Belle and her husband Joe, who came over from Hawaii and brought their seven-year-old son Austin with them.

There was also a poignant meeting with Sam Osbourne's current wife, known as Paulie (her maiden name was Rebecca Paul). Sam had vanished without a trace—some people suspected suicide—and Paulie had given up hope that he would ever reappear. As Nellie described it, "When she met Mrs. Stevenson in San Francisco she fell on her knees before her and burst into bitter weeping, saying: 'You were right about that man and I was wrong.'" Afterward Fanny wrote to Louis, "Imagine how humble I felt in my good fortune when I sat side by side with that poor woman whose case might have been mine—but for you."[18]

Dr. Trudeau, the founder and head of the Saranac Lake sanatorium, was an impressive person. Two years older than Louis, he was in his teens when a brother died of rapidly advancing tuberculosis, which inspired him to go to medical school; later he discovered that he too suffered from the disease in a milder form. Since mountain air was recommended for therapy, he began spending time in the Adirondacks boating and hunting. A photograph taken in 1873 (fig. 62) shows him at that time.

In 1884 Trudeau returned to Saranac Lake and founded the Adirondack Cottage Sanitarium. Just two years previously it had been discovered that tuberculosis is contagious, caused by a bacterial infection. This was an era when even a single researcher, working alone, could achieve major results. Trudeau made it his mission to isolate the bacillus, grow it experimentally, and find some agent that could counteract it in living animals. When he died from the disease in 1915 that had not yet been achieved, but in 1944 the discovery of streptomycin would finally conquer it. In his own day, as he said in his autobiography, it used to kill "one in seven of the human race."

Trudeau did succeed, however, in isolating the bacillus under a microscope, which allowed him to diagnose tuberculosis with certainty even in people who might be troubled only by a persistent cough. Conversely, in Louis he found no evidence that it was the cause of his bronchial attacks, and saw no need for treatment. The two men passed social evenings together. "Mr. Stevenson was so attractive in conversation that I found myself, as it was growing dark, very often seated by the big fireplace in the Baker cottage having a good talk. His striking personality, his keen insight into life, his wondrous idealism, his nimble intellect and his inimitable vocabulary in conversation, have grown on me more and more as the years roll by."[19]

Long after Louis's death, however, Trudeau apparently had second thoughts about the nature of his illness. He wrote, "It is a mistake to say that he never had tuberculosis. Although, while I took care of him, he had none of the active symptoms, such as hemorrhage, or fever, or tubercle bacilli, yet he undoubtedly had

62. Dr. Trudeau

tuberculosis. It may have become active again after he left Saranac, so there is no telling just how much that disease may have contributed to his mortal illness at Samoa." It's not clear why Trudeau came to this conclusion. It would be a sudden stroke, not a "mortal illness," that killed Louis, and until that moment he seemed healthier and stronger than he had ever been in his life.[20]

There must have been regular contact with other local people at Saranac Lake, but little trace of it survives. A visitor in 1911 found Mrs. Baker still living in her cottage and asked her eagerly for reminiscences. There was just one. "Every time I paused for a reply, she merely told me once again that Louis *would* burn holes in the sheets and that nothing could be done about it. He liked to stay in bed; he never stayed in bed without smoking cigarettes; he dropped the ashes on the sheets; the sheets were full of holes. That was all that she remembered of Robert Louis Stevenson."[21]

There is also a note that Louis sent to a butcher named Harry Oldfield:

> Mr. Robert Louis Stevenson presents his compliments to Mr. Oldfield and begs to return him the remainder of a joint of mutton which he refuses either to eat or pay for. Fillet of beef had been ordered as far back as Monday; Mr. Stevenson can readily understand there might arise some difficulty in supplying that, but at least Mr. Oldfield knew that Mr. S. would want something on Thursday; and Mr. S. prefers to hope it was in error that Mr. O. sent him anything so perfectly uneatable as the joint which he now has the pleasure to return.

Harry Oldfield evidently kept this note.[22]

TWO PROBLEMATIC NOVELS

Louis began two full-length novels during the bitter winter at Saranac Lake, but when they were published readers found them disappointing, and still do.

One was a collaborative effort with Lloyd called *The Wrong Box,* a farcical tale in which a dead body keeps getting delivered to inappropriate addresses. Lloyd had begun developing the tale on his own, and when he produced a first draft Louis proposed a collaboration:

> "Some of it is devilishly funny, and I have burst out laughing again and again." After a pause [Louis] added, through the faint cloud of his cigarette smoke, "But of course it is unequal; some of it is pretty poor. Why, I could take up that book, and in one quick, easy rewriting could make it *sing!*" Our eyes met; it was all decided in that one glance.

The collaboration had the advantage of shared enjoyment, an adult version of the Davos war games. "It was exhilarating to work with Stevenson," Lloyd said, "he was so appreciative, so humorous, brought such gaiety, camaraderie, and good will to our joint task." Lloyd remembered a characteristic comment: "It's glorious to have the ground ploughed, and to sit back in luxury for the real fun of writing—which is rewriting." Everything Louis wrote went through numerous drafts, and was sometimes published to meet a deadline before he felt satisfied with it.[23]

In March 1889, a year after the Stevensons had left Saranac Lake, the manuscript was sold to *Scribner's* for the impressive sum of $5,000, and there was a separate British edition from Longman's. Reviews were chilly. The *Athenaeum* captured the general reaction: "If there are readers who can get through more than a quarter of the small volume and find it amusing, they must be wondered at and not envied." There was a facetious note in the book's preface: "The authors can but add that one of them is old enough to be ashamed of himself, and the other young enough to learn better." That prompted another reviewer to comment, "We do not know who Mr. Osbourne is, but as he is young enough to learn better there is hope that he may improve. As for Mr. Stevenson, who is old enough to be ashamed of himself, we are very glad to hear it. He ought to be ashamed of himself."[24]

The other novel, *The Master of Ballantrae,* was more ambitious, and the first of twelve monthly installments appeared in *Scribner's Magazine* in December 1887. It tells the story of the conflict between two brothers, sons of Lord Durrisdeer at Ballantrae, a town in the west of Scotland that Louis had once visited. James, the elder, known as "the Master," is charismatic and high-handed; Henry is dependable but boring. During the Jacobite rebellion of 1745, which previously supplied the background of *Kidnapped,* James joins the rebels while Henry remains at home. After news arrives that James has been killed, Henry marries his brother's fiancée, in a union more dutiful than romantic. But the report of James's death turns out to have been mistaken, and he unexpectedly returns.

As narrator Louis chose Ephraim Mackellar, the loyal but unimaginative steward of the estate, whose straightforward account makes eruptions of melodrama all the more powerful. A crisis is triggered one evening when James insults Henry:

> "With all those solid qualities which I delight to recognise in you, I never knew a woman who did not prefer me—nor, I think," he continued, with the most silken deliberation, "I think—who did not continue to prefer me."
>
> Mr. Henry laid down his cards. He rose to his feet very softly, and seemed all the while like a person in deep thought. "You coward!" he said gently, as if to himself. And then, with neither hurry nor any particular violence, he struck the Master in the mouth.
>
> The Master sprang to his feet like one transfigured; I had never seen

the man so beautiful. "A blow!" he cried. "I would not take a blow from God Almighty."

They leave the house to fight a duel. Unexpectedly, Henry is the better swordsman and stabs James in the chest. He and Mackellar hasten indoors to tell Lord Durrisdeer that James is dead, but when they return to bury the body it has vanished.

> "Ah!" says Mr. Henry; and suddenly rising from his seat with more alacrity than he had yet discovered, set one finger on my breast, and cried at me in a kind of screaming whisper, "Mackellar"—these were his words—"nothing can kill that man. He is not mortal. He is bound upon my back to all eternity—to all eternity!"

We learn that James had an appointment with smugglers to leave for France that very night, and they have carried him away.[25]

This is the high point of *The Master of Ballantrae,* and we are still not quite halfway through it. Virtually everything that follows is unconvincing, including a preposterous episode on a pirate ship, a buried treasure in the Adirondack forest, and a fakir from India who buries James when—yet again—he seems dead but is only in a trance. At the end both brothers die.

Some critics have called this novel a masterpiece, and it certainly might have been one, but most readers have felt that it fails to deliver on its promise. J. M. Barrie's verdict seems right. He wrote to Louis, "I think *The Master of Ballantrae* the best thing you have done—I mean the Scotch part of it only. I felt when reading it that the rest of us had better go and turn ploughmen. The second half, however, seems to me not worth your while."[26]

This novel suffered from having to meet deadlines, since before it was finished it was already being serialized. When he did complete it, months after leaving Saranac Lake, Louis wrote to his editor, "I am quite worked out, and this cursed end of *The Master* hangs over me like the arm of the gallows."[27]

THE BREACH WITH HENLEY

The most memorable thing that happened at Saranac Lake was the shocking rupture of one of Louis's closest friendships, with William Ernest Henley. It seems to have taken both of them by surprise, beginning with a misunderstanding that turned poisonous, and since mail took a week or more to travel in each direction, there was no way to talk things through directly. In any case, the immediate provocation seems inadequate to the violence of the rupture. Third parties, in particular Baxter, found it hard to understand what was happening, let alone why. One thing is clear: submerged resentments had been brewing for a long time, and a single spark caused an explosion. In retrospect nobody emerged from it well, and definitely not Louis.

The provocation came soon after Louis broke the news to Henley that the production of their play *Deacon Brodie* had failed in Philadelphia, which was made worse when Henley's brother Teddy, who played Brodie, got drunk and disgraced himself in fistfights. Louis told Baxter that "the drunken whoreson bugger and bully" had been living in expensive hotels "and smashing inoffensive strangers in the bar."[28]

Henley was well aware that Teddy was a difficult character, but the playwriting project had been a preoccupation of his for years. Louis never wanted to do it, and felt increasingly that they were never going to get anywhere; from his perspective it was only out of loyalty to his friend that he kept on collaborating at all. From Henley's perspective, they could have achieved great success, and the reason they didn't was Louis's failure to commit himself wholeheartedly.

Probably a more important source of resentment was that Louis had exploited Henley for years as an informal literary agent. In 1883 Louis wrote to Gosse from the Riviera that Henley "acts for me in all matters. He is my unpaid agent: an admirable arrangement for me, and one that has rather more than doubled my income on the spot." Even before leaving for America, Louis had been away from Britain a lot, and trusted Henley to use his literary connections to find publishers for his writing.[29]

It's also true that Louis lent Henley money from time to time, but in a spirit of *noblesse oblige,* and it was money from his parents, not earned by himself. Meanwhile Henley was forced to support himself by editorial work instead of developing his own career. He was a poet, but only occasionally, and had not yet collected any of his poems in book form. His only publications were book reviews that he ground out constantly for a very modest income. And now that Louis was rich and famous, Henley may well have foreseen that with his usefulness declining, the friendship might be cooling as well. From that perspective, when a quarrel unexpectedly erupted between Katharine, Bob Stevenson's sister and Louis's cousin, and Fanny, he may have seized upon it as an excuse for demanding a new commitment of loyalty from Louis. Conversely, Louis might have become genuinely weary of the relationship, and seized an occasion to take a stand. It may be that both he and Henley were using the Katharine-Fanny quarrel as a front for their own unacknowledged resentments.

Something else was involved: Henley had been in the habit of saying unkind things about Louis behind his back, and Louis knew it. He wrote to Baxter,

> I have forgiven, and forgiven, and forgotten and forgotten; and still they get their heads together, and there springs up a fresh enmity or a fresh accusation. An accusation brought against my wife of a description to cut us both to the soul. . . . I cannot say it is anger that I feel, but it is despair. My last reconciliation with Henley [presumably about playwriting] is not yet a year old; and here is the devil again. I am weary of it all—weary, weary, weary. . . . The tale of the plays which I have gone on writing without hope, because I thought they kept him up, is of itself something; and I can say he never knew—and never shall know—that I thought these days and months a sacrifice. . . . Well, I send it [i.e., this letter]. Take it for what it is: a very desolate cry."[30]

The fatal spark was struck by Henley in a letter sent to Louis at Saranac Lake. The letter concerned Henley's friendship with Katharine de Mattos, estranged from the husband whose name she bore, whose idea for a story may or may not have been stolen by Fanny. In fact Louis had known her far longer than Henley had; she was one year younger than Louis, and they had always been close. After they read a romantic novel together in an old castle in their teens, Louis remembered the occasion as "a boy and girl romance."[31]

In a poem "To K. de M." in *Underwoods,* published just one year before the quarrel erupted, he identified Katharine with their native landscape:

> A lover of the moorland bare
> And honest country winds, you were;
> The silver-skimming rain you took,
> And loved the floodings of the brook. . . .
> And on the heath, afar from man,
> A strong and bitter virgin ran.

That last line is oddly mysterious.[32]

Louis dedicated *Dr. Jekyll and Mr. Hyde* to Katharine, with still another evocation of their youth:

> It's ill to loose the bands that God decreed to bind;
> Still will we be the children of the heather and the wind;
> Far away from home, O it's still for you and me
> That the broom is blowing bonnie in the north countrie.

Louis told Katharine in a letter, "You know very well that I love you dearly, and that I always will. I only wish the verses were better, but at least you like the story; and it is sent to you by the one that loves you—Jekyll and not Hyde."[33]

Over the years Katharine occasionally tried her hand at writing and asked Louis for criticism. He delivered it severely: "Now, for the introduction, I am going to be rude. It's all bad. It is woolly, hard to follow, and disorderly. You have to learn to write first a good deal better. Do you understand me when I say you are writing with gloves on just now? You must learn to write with the quick of your fingers."[34]

In Bournemouth Katharine and Fanny had become good friends, which mattered a lot to Fanny since she knew that some of Louis's friends had mixed feelings about her. When the crisis erupted four people were involved, all of whom had been close until that time—Katharine; Henley as her self-appointed champion; Fanny, whose good faith was under attack; and Louis, in furious defense of his wife.

In March 1888, while they were living at Saranac Lake, Fanny published a short story called "The Nixie" in *Scribner's Magazine*. When Henley read it he sent Louis a letter that began with ordinary chat but went on, "I read 'The Nixie' with considerable amazement. It's Katharine's; surely it's Katharine's? The situation, the environment, the principal figure—*voyons!* There are even reminiscences of phrase and imagery, parallel incident—*que sais-je?* It is all better focused, no doubt, but I think it has lost as much (at least) as it has gained; and why there wasn't a double signature is what I've not been able to understand."[35]

This is what had happened. At Bournemouth Katharine and Fanny discussed an idea for a story, which Katharine may have already begun to write, about a man who meets a young woman on a train without realizing she has escaped from a lunatic asylum. Fanny said it would be more interesting if she were a nixie, a supernatural water sprite in German mythology, and after their discussion Fanny believed that Katharine had yielded the project to her. But when "The Nixie" was published under Fanny's name only, Henley—almost certainly encouraged by Katharine, with whom he was close—sent the accusatory letter. He himself affected to believe that what he said was just a remark made in passing, and concluded, "Louis, dear lad, I am damn tired. . . . You have loved me much. Let us go on so till the end. . . . Forgive this babble, and take care of yourself, and *burn this letter*. Your friend, W.E.H."

However, he had written "Private and Confidential" at the beginning of the letter, and that, together with the directive to burn it, seemed to indicate to Louis that Henley's intent was far from casual and that he was being forbidden to show the letter to anyone, even Fanny. He took this to mean that his wife was being defamed and that he was supposed to ignore it.

A further complication was that Louis suspected Henley of romantic involvement with Katharine, which might have distorted his judgment in taking her side. That probably wasn't true, but Baxter, who did his best to mediate, saw the suspicion as a fatal complication. He told their mutual friend Charles Guthrie, "Coupled with Henley's enmity to Mrs. Louis, you can here see the origin of the heat and fury with which he rushed to the attack. He would have resented what he thought a theft in any case, but not with so much of what you term 'chivalry.'" Baxter agreed with Louis that Henley had been egocentric and insulting, but argued that the offense was inadvertent and that he was genuinely eager to be reconciled after he understood how his letter had enraged Louis. Henley's biographer says, "From the whole pitiful imbroglio Charles Baxter is the one who emerges with the most credit."[36]

As for Katharine, she attempted to smooth things over and wrote to Louis, "As Mr. Henley's very natural but unfortunate letter was written without my wish or knowledge, I have refused to let him go further in the matter. He had a perfect right to be astonished, but his having said so has nothing to do with me. If Fanny thinks she had a right to the idea of the story I am far from wishing to reclaim or to criticize her in any way." Henley himself wrote, "I will only say again, forgive me, and have faith in me yet. I am not ungrateful nor disloyal. Surely you should know that much of me by now? And the old affection, the old kinship, the old affinity (*enfin!*) is as living and dear as ever." It was too late.[37]

Fanny, of course, took it still more personally, and if she feared that her conduct was in any way at fault, that might have increased her defensiveness. Her letter to Baxter was over the top: "I do not see how it is possible for me to return to England after the disgrace that has been put upon me by Louis's friends.... If it so happens that I must go back to perfidious Albion, I shall learn to be false. For Louis's sake I shall pretend to be their friend still—while he lives; but that in my heart I can ever forgive those who have borne false witness against me! while they eat their bread from my hand—and oh, they will do that—I shall smile and wish it were poison that might wither their bodies as they have my heart."[38]

Katharine then sent Louis a letter that was more or less an apology. "How deeply sorry I am it is useless to try to say, and impossible not to remember all your past kindness which is now turned into a lifelong distrust of me. If I have failed to understand anything said to me at Bournemouth or put a wrong construction on things I am more grieved than ever, but I cannot say it has been intentional." Baxter's conclusion, however, was that even if Henley had acted thoughtlessly, Katharine had goaded him to do it. He told Louis, "If there *has* been bad behaviour, hers has certainly been not the least, and I regard her as the wicked mainspring of all this distress."[39]

In the future there would be occasional routine communications between Louis and Henley, but the friendship was dead. Henley never knew that Louis authorized Baxter to go on helping him financially while keeping the source of the money secret. But Louis's motives in doing that are far from clear. He may have believed he was acting nobly even though he had been cruelly injured. Or he may even have understood—finally—how much he had taken Henley's help for granted over the years, without ever properly acknowledging it. If he was really prepared to break with his old friend now that he was wealthy and famous, Henley's sense of injury was well justified.

Yet another of Louis's deepest relationships was fatally wounded by the scandal. Since Katharine was Bob Stevenson's sister, it's not surprising that he took her side. It's now known that Bob actually helped her and Henley with their letters to Louis. Bob and Louis, the inseparable companions of their Edinburgh youth, the "Stennis *frères*" as they were playfully known at Grez, corresponded only rarely and casually from this time on.

Since Louis never returned to Britain, there was no chance for a face-to-face reconciliation with any of the parties concerned. In 1890 he wrote to Baxter from New Caledonia, "Even Bob writes to me with an embarrassment which communicates itself to my answers. Our relation is too old and close to be destroyed; I have forgiven him too much—and he me—to leave a rupture possible; but there it is—the shadow. I bore you with these regrets. But I did not ever care for much else than my friends; and some they are dead etc., and I am at the end of the world from what remains: gone, all are gone." Louis was recalling a poem by Charles Lamb: "How some they have died, and some they have left me.... All, all are gone, the old familiar faces."[40]

"THE DREAM OF A LIFE REALISED"

When spring finally arrived at Saranac Lake the family was eager for a change. The plan they decided on, now that they had plenty of money, was to charter a yacht and sail the high seas. Lloyd remembered poring over nautical guides to the Pacific. "As the snow drove against our frozen windows, as the Arctic day closed in gloomy and wild, and snowshoes and buffalo coats were put by to steam in corners, we gathered round the lamp." They, or at least he, fantasized especially about "undraped womanhood, bedecked with flowers, frisking in vales of Eden, while we were wooled to the neck like Polar explorers."[41]

McClure encouraged the idea of a sailing adventure. He recalled much later that when Louis mentioned it, "I thought at once of *An Inland Voyage* and *Travels with a Donkey,* and told him that if he would write a series of articles describing his travels, I would syndicate them for enough money to pay the expenses of his trip. The next time I went to Saranac, we actually planned out the South Pacific cruise, talking about it until late into the night." McClure wasn't prepared to fund the voyage in advance, but he expected to pay generously for the account of it that Louis would write, first in installments and afterward in book form. As it turned out, Louis never did produce that kind of book, and the expectation of writing about his travels for McClure came to nothing.[42]

Meanwhile there was enough money on hand to fund an ambitious voyage; Margaret, who was eager to go along, may have contributed. If the plan with McClure worked out, more income would be generated in due course, but that wasn't essential for making the trip. Fanny, who was in California at the time, undertook to locate a suitable vessel, but at first without success. It seemed that they would have to settle for a less thrilling Atlantic voyage. Then she sent a telegram: "Can secure splendid sea-going schooner yacht *Casco* for [an] even hundred and fifty a month with most comfortable accommodation for six aft and six forward. Can be ready for sea in ten days. Reply immediately." Louis fired off his reply: "Blessed girl, take the yacht and expect us in ten days." As they prepared to leave for the West Coast in May, he wrote to Baxter that he was looking forward to "the dream of a life realised." It's as if he rejected the engineering his family was famous for, but kept the sea that had been the scene of their life's work.[43]

CHAPTER 26

Sailing the High Seas

SETTING FORTH

After leaving Saranac Lake, Louis went with Margaret and Lloyd to New York before joining Fanny in San Francisco. Parting from Will Low, Louis told him, "I loved the Pacific in the days when I was at Monterey, and perhaps now it will love me a little. I am going to meet it; ever since I was a boy, the South Seas have laid a spell upon me." Writing to William Archer, he signed himself

> Robert Louis Stevenson
> Pirate Captain
> (for seven months)
> of Another Man's Yacht.

The only sailing he had previously done was brief outings near the Scottish and Riviera coasts.[1]

A few months before heading to San Francisco he had recalled his journey in the amateur emigrant days: "I dread worse than almost any other imaginable peril that miraculous and really insane invention, the American Railroad Car. I fear the railroad car as abjectly as I do an earwig, and, on the whole, on better grounds." This time, however, thanks to his inheritance and to income from publishers, there was plenty of money and the five-day trip was pleasant, with a private stateroom and dressing room. Margaret and Lloyd accompanied him, Fanny joined them at Sacramento, and they arrived in San Francisco on June 7.[2]

The vessel Fanny had secured was the impressively grand *Casco*, ninety-four

63. The *Casco*

feet long with a beam or width of twenty-two feet. Although built originally for racing rather than cruising, it had already been as far as Tahiti, forty-two hundred miles away. As a photograph shows (fig. 63), the boat was gaff rigged, an arrangement common at the time in which the top of each sail is supported by a small projecting boom rather than directly joining the mast. The owner, Dr. Samuel Merritt, had named his yacht after Casco Bay in his native state of Maine.

Dr. Merritt was an impressive individual who became rich in real estate and had recently served as mayor of Oakland; Lake Merritt was named in his honor after he led a campaign to dam a tidal estuary that had been full of sewage. He was reluctant at first to trust his boat to these strangers, but after Fanny arranged a meeting all difficulties vanished. "'I'll go ahead now with the yacht,' said the doctor; 'I'd read things in the papers about Stevenson and thought he was a kind of crank; but he's a plain, sensible man that knows what he's talking about just as well as I do.'" Virgil and Dora Williams helped out by assuring Merritt that they had just cashed a check of Louis's for $10,000.[3]

The captain would be a highly experienced sailor named Albert Otis, who agreed to the assignment after Merritt promised him complete control of the voyage and the right of approval for any destinations they would visit. Otis had read *Treasure Island* "with much pleasure," but the first sight of its author gave him pause.

> Imagine a man of medium height, so painfully thin that his clothes seemed a burden to him, his brown hair falling to his shoulders around a face of deathlike whiteness, but alight with the most fascinating brown eyes I had ever seen. As soon as I was alone the thought returned to me with some force that before sailing I had better make the necessary arrangements for his death at sea; in fact, as I looked him over in my mind, without the tonic of his sustaining eyes, I did not believe it would be possible for him to make the trip and return alive.[4]

Belle came over from Honolulu to see them off, and accompanied Fanny to make final arrangements. "I remember my surprise at [Fanny's] levity when Dr. Merritt said finally, 'Now that's settled and I'm glad, Little One!' and she answered, 'So am I, Big One!'" Fanny took charge of provisioning the vessel for the long voyage, ordering barrels of flour and sugar, hams and bacon and dried beef, coal for cooking, kerosene for light, and cigarette materials.[5]

Belle's reunion with her brother, who was now a foot taller than she (fig. 64), came as something of a shock. "My brother Lloyd was nineteen then, and very English in speech and manner. I tried to see in this six-foot stranger with the lean intellectual face and eyeglasses, the little towheaded brother I had parted with nine years before. His witty talk, his fine manners and his unusually musical voice made a deep impression on me. Though I had looked forward eagerly to seeing him again, all I recall of my brother that morning on the *Casco* is that he wore gold rings in his ears like a sailor."[6]

The party that set sail consisted of Louis, Fanny, Margaret, Lloyd, and their maid Valentine Roch. The *Casco* was luxuriously appointed, and Margaret was impressed. "From the deck you step down into the cockpit, which is our open-air drawing room. It has seats all round, nicely cushioned, and we sit or lie there

64. Lloyd Osbourne

most of the day. The compass is there, and the wheel, so the man at the wheel always kept us company." Down below there were berths on which "we three women are laid away as on shelves each night to sleep," while Louis had a cabin of his own, "very roomy, with both a bed and a sofa in it, so that he will be very comfortable." In a central space sofas and a table were covered with "crimson Utrecht velvet," and beneath them was a carpet of "crimson Brussels."

The sailors were multinational. "The captain is Albert Otis, American. The crew are: Charles Olsen, Russian; John Lassen, Swede; Fred Schröder, Swede; Charles Wallin, Finn; Antone Cousina (steward and cook), Japanese; and Valentine Borch (cabin boy), Swiss." Valentine (Margaret misheard her surname) wasn't a boy, of course. The cook, who had changed his name because of anti-Japanese prejudice, got drunk and belligerent and would later be replaced.[7]

Since the prevailing wind was unfavorable on the day of their departure, on June 28, 1888, the *Casco* was towed out to sea by a tug. Louis was living a dream from *A Child's Garden of Verses*. In "My Ship and I" he had sailed a toy ship on a pond, "But when I'm a little older, I shall find the secret out / How to send my vessel sailing on beyond." Another poem was "Foreign Lands":

> I should like to rise and go
> Where the golden apples grow;
> Where below another sky
> Parrot islands anchored lie.[8]

Back in Britain, Louis's friends were appalled to learn that he was heading into the Pacific instead of returning to their literary milieu, which they considered the only possible place for a writer. Almost unanimously they predicted he would never write anything again. Even Charles Warren Stoddard in San Francisco, though he had written fondly about the Pacific himself, declared melodramatically, "After a phenomenal success in letters which made him an idol of the reading world, a world from which he had vainly striven to banish himself, he suddenly weighed anchor and descended into the abysmal waters of the sea." Back in Britain, of course, Louis had never been idolized; that arrived recently with his reception in America, and his feelings about it were very mixed.[9]

Only Henry James was fully sympathetic, even though he felt genuinely bereft. "My dear Louis," he wrote, "you are too far away—you are too absent—too invisible, inaudible, inconceivable. Life is too short a business and friendship too delicate a matter for such tricks. This is a selfish personal cry: I wish you back; for literature is lonely and Bournemouth is barren without you. Your place in my affection has not been usurped by another—there is not the least little scrap of another to usurp it." James added that the accomplishments of their literary circle were not so wonderful after all. "Lang, in the *Daily News* every morning, and I believe in a hundred other places, uses his beautiful thin facility to write everything down to the lowest level of Philistine twaddle."[10]

On conventional maps the islands of the Pacific are disproportionately large, which makes it difficult to grasp how enormous the distances between them are. If shown at proper scale, as on the globe illustrated here (fig. 65), they would be mere flyspecks. By the time Captain Cook arrived at the Hawaiian archipelago in 1778, Spanish galleons traveling between Manila and South America, taking advantage of prevailing winds north and south of the islands, had gone right past it unknowingly for nearly two hundred years.[11]

The vast distances pointed to a serious danger: Captain Otis was the only qualified navigator, and if a storm should sweep him overboard there was small chance that the *Casco* could find its way to any port. Ten days out of San Francisco the weather turned ominous, and he realized it must be "one of those great re-

65. Map of the Pacific

volving storms frequently encountered in the Pacific"—a typhoon, known elsewhere as a hurricane. Everything depended on establishing which side of the storm they were on, so he made a guess and headed westward under full sail. The captain of another ship from San Francisco guessed wrong, had all his sails torn to pieces, and was lucky to survive.

Even so, the *Casco* encountered a ferocious squall, and the passengers paid a price for ignoring orders to keep the portholes covered with thick panes of glass known as deadlights. Otis himself related years later, "Before the *Casco* could be brought into the wind, she was struck and knocked down until the wind spilled out of her sails, with the sea pouring over the cockpit in a torrent. The deadlights were at least eighteen inches below the surface of the deep salt sea. The vigour with which two streams of water, under great pressure, poured into the cabins proved a new and startling experience to the inmates." Once they made landfall he took care to hire a first mate who also understood navigation.

On another occasion the sails were double-reefed—tied down to make them smaller—while the vessel was "swept like a toy across the sea." The passengers had to stay below, and on deck the crew survived only by being lashed in their places. "Was there danger?" an interviewer asked Otis. "Yes, a little." "How did Stevenson take it?" "Why, man, he never turned a hair; in fact I am convinced that he enjoyed it." Otis was right; wild weather exhilarated Louis, and he said that he laughed at the name of "the Pacific (aw-haw-haw) Ocean."[12]

After the voyage ended Louis wrote to Colvin, "I cannot say why I like the sea; no man is more cynically and constantly alive to its perils; I regard it as the highest form of gambling; and yet I love the sea as much as I hate gambling. Fine, clean emotions; a world all and always beautiful; air better than wine; interest unflagging: there is upon the whole no better life." At another time he declared, "Danger, enterprise, hope, the novel, the aleatory are dearer to man than regular meals." An aleatory outcome is unpredictable because governed by chance—*alea* is Latin for dice.[13]

Louis expected that at some point he would write about the voyage, as he told Baxter later on: "I shall have a fine book of travels, I feel sure; and will tell you more of the South Seas after a very few months than any other writer has done—except Herman Melville perhaps, who is a howling cheese." That expression meant "the best thing"; Lang remembered him calling Julius Caesar "the howlingest cheese who ever lived."[14]

Sometimes there were flashbacks to the world Louis had left behind. In a letter to Baxter to be mailed from the next port, he recalled their youthful evenings together in Rutherford's pub:

> The night was warm as milk; and all of a sudden I had a vision of—Drummond Street. It came on me like a flash of lightning; I simply returned thither, and into the past. And when I remembered all that I hoped and feared as I pickled about Rutherford's in the rain and east wind; how I feared I should make a mere shipwreck, and yet timidly hoped not; how I hoped (if I did not take to drink) I should possibly write one little book etc. etc. And then, now—what a change! I feel somehow as if I should like the incident set upon a brass plate at the corner of that dreary thoroughfare, for all students to read, poor devils, when their hearts are down. And I felt I must write one word to you.[15]

There were also moments of self-analysis. One day when Louis was on deck reading *Don Quixote,* he looked up and said to Lloyd, "That's me." Lloyd expanded the thought in his memoir: Louis was "intolerant of evil; almost absurdly chivalrous; passionately resentful of injustice; impulsive, headstrong, utterly scornful of conventions when they were at variance with what he considered right—his was a nature that was surely to be misjudged and as surely ridiculed by many." Nicholas Rankin adds that Louis was Sancho as well as Quixote, "with a streak of matter-of-fact realism that allowed him to see his own gallantry as both tragic and comic." He told Lloyd that *Don Quixote* was "the saddest book I have ever read."[16]

Louis wasn't the only one who had dreamed of tropical islands. Just before leaving San Francisco Margaret wrote to her sister Jane,

> Isn't it wonderful that I am going to see all these strange, out-of-the-way places? I cannot yet realise it. I remember so well repeating as a little girl at school,
>
>> Full many are the beauteous isles
>> Unseen by human eye,
>> That sleeping 'mid the ocean's smiles,
>> In sunny silence lie.
>
> I always longed so much to see them, and I can hardly believe that all those childish longings are to come true.

The lines come from "The Isle of Palms," in which young Mary and her lover live blissfully on an idyllic island where they have been shipwrecked. No doubt it was assigned in school because of its pious moral:

> Our Saviour!—What angelic grace
> Stole with dim smiles o'er Mary's face,
> While through the solitude profound
> With love and awe she breathed that holy sound![17]

NUKUHIVA

Continuing in a southwesterly direction, the *Casco* made its first landfall after three weeks at the island of Nukuhiva in the Marquesas, thirty-five hundred miles from Hawaii. Melville had lived there in 1842, and made it the setting for the semi-fictionalized memoir *Typee,* to which Louis had been introduced by

Stoddard. Melville's other South Seas book was *Omoo*, a Marquesan word meaning someone who wanders from one island to another. Louis was an Omoo now.

In the travel book he did eventually write, *In the South Seas,* he described this moment: "The first experience can never be repeated. The first love, the first sunrise, the first South Sea island, are memories apart and touched a virginity of sense." When the *Casco* dropped anchor "it was a small sound, a great event; my soul went down with these moorings whence no windlass may extract nor any diver fish it up."[18]

This was Louis's first encounter with Polynesian culture, and the beginning of his sympathy with the islanders at a time when that culture was being destroyed; the Marquesas were nominally independent but by now controlled by France. He recorded a conversation with a teenage mother nursing her little baby. When she questioned him about England he described, "as best I was able, and by word and gesture, the overpopulation, the hunger, and the perpetual toil." She sat for a time silent, "gravely reflecting on that picture of unwonted sorrows." And then,

> It struck in her another thought always uppermost in the Marquesan bosom, and she began with a smiling sadness, and looking on me out of melancholy eyes, to lament the decease of her own people. "*Ici pas de kanaques* [there are no kanakas here]," said she; and taking the baby from her breast, she held it out to me with both her hands. "*Tenez*—a little baby like this; then dead. All the Kanaques die. Then no more." The smile, and this instancing by the girl-mother of her own tiny flesh and blood, affected me strangely; they spoke of so tranquil a despair.

Foreigners sometimes used the term *kanaka* as a racist put-down, but it wasn't originally negative. In the Polynesian languages it simply meant "people," and Richard Henry Dana had observed in *Two Years before the Mast* that islanders everywhere called themselves by that name—"they were the most interesting, intelligent, and kind-hearted people that I ever fell in with."[19]

Louis was struck by the matter-of-fact way in which the islanders referred to cannibalism, which had been practiced until very recently. He was introduced to a chief who was notable as "the last eater of long pig in Nukuhiva."

> Not many years have elapsed since he was seen striding on the beach of Anaho, a dead man's arm across his shoulder. "So does Kooamua to his enemies!" he roared to the passers-by, and took a bite from the raw flesh. And now behold this gentleman, very wisely replaced in office by the

French, paying us a morning visit in European clothes. He was the man of the most character we had yet seen: his manners genial and decisive, his person tall, his face rugged, astute, formidable, and with a certain similarity to Mr. Gladstone's—only for the brownness of the skin, and the high-chief's tattooing, all one side and much of the other being of an even blue.

Kooamua enjoyed a tour of the *Casco,* and commented that as a chief he had to observe exact sobriety, but a few days later they encountered him hopelessly drunk "in a state of smiling and lopsided imbecility."[20]

Margaret was open-minded about everything she was seeing, including the exposed skin and tattoos that missionaries denounced. "Two most respectable-looking old gentlemen wore nothing but small red and yellow loincloths and *very* cutty sarks [short skirts] on top. There were even some who wore less! The display of legs was something we were not accustomed to; but as they were all tattooed in most wonderful patterns, it really looked quite as if they were wearing openwork silk tights. . . . Fanny and I feel very naked with our own plain white legs when we are bathing." Margaret had no prejudice concerning skin color, either. She mentioned one man who wore a garment "leaving an ample stretch of brown satin skin exposed to view. What wonderful skins they all have, by the way!"[21]

It amused her that the Marquesans invented new names for the visitors.

Louis was at first "the old man," much to his distress; but now they call him "Ona," meaning *owner* of the yacht, a name he greatly prefers to the first. Fanny is *Vahine,* or wife; I am *the old woman,* and Lloyd rejoices in the name of *Maté Karahi,* the young man with glass eyes (spectacles). Perhaps it is a compliment here to call one old, as it is in China. At any rate, one native told Louis that he himself was old, but his mother was not!

The name "Ona" was important. That implied that Louis was a rich man traveling solely for pleasure, as contrasted with the unscrupulous traders who were constantly trying to cheat the Polynesians.[22]

TAHITI

Leaving Nukuhiva, the *Casco* proceeded—at Louis's insistence—to the Tuamotus, known at the time as the Dangerous Islands, and then onward to Tahiti. He always used the French pronunciation "Ta'iti," and on these islands his fluent

French was invaluable. They now acquired a Chinese cook, Ah Fu, who was intelligent and resourceful; he would stay with the family for several years. They enjoyed hearing expressions he had picked up from sailors. When a pirate named Bully Hayes was mentioned, Ah Fu exclaimed, "I know that fella plenty." Louis agreed that he was a very bad man, and Ah Fu said, "Him son of a bitch."[23]

Papeete, the capital, was discouragingly commercialized, and they headed overland to the village of Tautira. There Louis developed a high fever, and the local chief's sister Moë invited the family to live with her for as long as necessary. Fanny believed that her attention and care saved his life. This led to a warm friendship between Louis and Moë's brother Ori a Ori (fig. 66). Fanny wrote to Colvin, "Ori is the very finest specimen of a native we have seen yet: he is several inches over six feet, has perfect though almost gigantic proportions, and looks more like a Roman emperor in bronze than words can express." Soon he and Louis exchanged names, which made them brothers.[24]

Not long afterward he wrote a poem based on a Tahitian ballad and dedicated it to Ori.

> Ori, my brother in the island mode,
> In every tongue and meaning much my friend,
> This story of your country and your clan,
> In your loved house, your too much honoured guest,
> I made in English. Take it, being done;
> And let me sign it with the name you gave—
>
> TERITERA

Teritera was Ori's clan name, while Ori took the name Rui—"the nearest they can come to Louis," he explained in a letter to a friend, "for they have no L and no S in their language."[25]

The *Casco* came up the coast from Papeete, and everyone was preparing to leave when a startling problem stopped them. At each island they had visited Margaret kept urging Captain Otis to go to church, and he always refused. Now some Tautira women were guests on board and one of them offered a prayer to deliver the ship from the perils of the sea. As Fanny's sister Nellie heard the story,

> [Otis] stood leaning disgustedly against the mast while the prayer was said. After the visitors left he made some impatient exclamation against "psalm-singing natives," and struck the mast a hard blow with his fist. It went through into decayed wood, and the captain was aghast. Mrs. Stevenson, on her part, was triumphant, and she always loved to tell that

66. Ori a Ori

story and dwell on the expression of the captain's scoffing face as he saw a prayer answered. Both masts were found to be almost entirely eaten out with dry rot, and if either had gone by the board off the reefs of one of the islands nothing could have saved the *Casco* from going to the bottom.

Preparations to leave San Francisco had been hasty, and Otis had relied on a previous captain's assurance that everything was sound. In fact they had been in grave danger the whole time, and only luck got them through stormy weather without disaster.[26]

The success of the prayer should be qualified by something Louis came to understand, that islanders who converted to Christianity went right on holding their previous beliefs as well. Ori and Moë, he wrote, "were persons perfectly intelligent: gentlefolk, apt of speech. The sister was very religious, a great churchgoer, one that used to reprove me if I stayed away; I found afterwards that she privately worshipped a shark."[27]

It was necessary for the *Casco* to return cautiously to Papeete, where there was a long delay waiting for repairs. Ori refused to hear of the Stevenson party going along. "You are my brother," he declared; "all that I have is yours. I know that your food is done, but I can give you plenty of fish and taro. We like you, and wish to have you here. Stay where you are until the *Casco* comes, be happy, *et ne pleurez pas*—don't cry." At this, Fanny said, "Louis dropped his head into his hands and wept."[28]

The extended stay at Tautira gave Louis a chance to recover his health, and also to get some work done. He pushed ahead with *The Master of Ballantrae* and nearly finished it, re-creating eighteenth-century Scotland and a frigid North American winter while living on a tropical island.

At Papeete a mast in good condition was eventually obtained from a wrecked French ship, and it was time to set sail again. Just before they departed Otis took on as mate a German who called himself the Baron von der Goltz. Louis recorded a conversation:

> *Captain:* "Hullo, Mr. Goltz, you are drunk." *The Baron:* "Do you mean to insinuate that I have been drinking?" *Captain:* "I know nothing about that, but you're drunk." *The Baron* (with passion): "Speak to me kindly, Captain, or I shall weep!"[29]

Some months later they received a letter from Ori, which Fanny translated from French and sent to Frances Sitwell:

> To Teritera (Louis) and Tapina Tutu (myself) and Aromaiterai (Lloyd) and Teiriha (Mrs. Stevenson), Salutation in the true Jesus. I make you to know my great affection. At the hour when you left us, I was filled with tears, my wife Rui Tehini also, and all of my household. When you embarked I felt a great sorrow. It is for this that I went upon the road, and

you looked from that ship, and I looked at you on the ship with great grief until you had raised the anchor and hoisted the sails. When the ship started, I ran along the beach to see you still; and when you were on the open sea I cried out to you, "Farewell Louis"; and when I was coming back to my house I seemed to hear your voice crying, "Rui farewell." It is your eyes that I desire to see again. It must be that your body and my body shall eat together at our table: there is what would make my heart content.

After reading this, Fanny said, "Louis has left in tears, saying that he is not worthy that such a letter should be written to him."[30]

CHAPTER 27

Hawaii

HONOLULU

From Tahiti it was another twenty-six hundred miles, northward this time, to Honolulu, as shown on a map in Graham Balfour's biography (color plate 15). By now it was January 1889, nine months out from San Francisco. "One stirring day," Louis wrote to his cousin Bob, "was that in which we sighted Hawaii. It blew fair but very strong, we carried jib, foresail and mainsail, all single-reefed, and she carried her lee rail under water and flew. The swell, the heaviest I have ever been out in—I tried in vain to estimate the height, I am sure *at least* fifteen feet—came tearing after us about a point and a half off the wind. I never remember anything more delightful and exciting. Pretty soon after, we were lying absolutely becalmed under the lee of Hawaii." It obviously pleased Louis to have picked up authentic nautical lingo—single-reefed, lee rail under water, a point and a half off the wind.[1]

To Baxter, Louis reported that they had paid off the *Casco,* which would return to its owner in San Francisco, and had had a wonderful voyage, though not everyone enjoyed it equally. Fanny never got over seasickness, whereas Margaret loved every minute and was seldom sick. "My wife is no great shakes; she is the one who has suffered most. My mother has had a Huge Old Time."[2]

On hand to welcome them were Belle and Joe Strong, who had been in Honolulu with their son Austin since 1882 when a plantation owner commissioned Joe to make paintings of island life. Joe's parents had been missionaries in Hawaii and he knew the islands well. The couple seemed to be managing successfully, but that wouldn't last; Joe has been described as "an artist who found art useful as a means of avoiding work." They had had a second son, named Hervey in memory of Belle's brother who died in Paris, but he died before his first birthday.[3]

There was a rather mysterious parting in Honolulu: after six years with the family, Valentine Roch left. Louis wrote to Baxter, "Valentine leaves us here, to mutual glee. Stop her private wages, and be ready (when she applies) to give her her little stock [probably wages he had invested for her]. It has been the usual tale of the maid on board the yacht." That may mean involvement with a member of the crew, though it's not obvious why it would be a firing offense.[4]

In the reminiscence that Valentine contributed to *I Can Remember Robert Louis Stevenson,* she described Louis as "beloved of all who knew him," and added, "Later on, when it came to a parting of our ways, it helped to bear many injustices which nearly broke my heart." Possibly the glee wasn't mutual at all, and the subtext may be that although Louis was lovable, Fanny wasn't.[5]

Louis found Honolulu bustling and modern, a disappointment after the remote islands they had been visiting. He took particular offense at the ubiquity of telephones, and if he needed to place a call would ask someone else to do it for him. After being awakened in the night he wrote to a newspaper, "The telephone broke out bleating like a deserted infant from the nigh dining room. I dare never, from a variety of prudential considerations, approach this interesting instrument myself; I had no choice but to summon others who should prove more bold. The introduction of the telephone into our bed and board, into our business and bosoms, partakes of the nature of intrusion." His lifelong distrust of technology marked a deep temperamental divide between himself and his family of engineers.[6]

For tranquility they moved four miles down the beach to Waikiki, thinly settled at the time, but it wasn't much of an improvement. Louis wrote to Adelaide Boodle, "The Sandwich Islands [the old name for Hawaii] do not interest us very much; we live here oppressed with civilization." He described the Waikiki house as "a grim little wooden shanty; cobwebs bedeck it; friendly mice inhabit its recesses; the mailed cockroach walks upon the wall, so also, I regret to say, the scorpion. Herein are two pallet beds, two mosquito curtains, strung to the pitchboards of the roof; two tables laden with books and manuscripts, three chairs, and (in one of the beds) one Squire busy writing to yourself, as it chances, and just at this moment somewhat bitten by mosquitos."[7]

Working was necessary because, as Louis told Baxter, "We stay here impignorated." That sounds like one of his made-up words, but it was a legal term for being in debt. He drove himself to finish *The Master of Ballantrae,* already appearing in installments in *Scribner's Magazine,* and threw himself into research for the book on the Pacific that S. S. McClure had commissioned, which would begin as serialized installments in the magazine.[8]

The publisher was expecting a travelogue full of personal anecdotes, but to Fanny's horror Louis got fixated on something more soberly factual. She wrote to Colvin ("Best of Friends"), imploring him to intervene:

> Louis has the most enchanting material that anyone ever had in the whole world for his book, and I am afraid he is going to spoil it all. He has taken into his Scotch Stevenson head that a stern duty lies before him, and that his book must be a sort of scientific and historical impersonal thing, comparing the different languages (of which he knows nothing, really) and the different peoples, the object being to settle the question as to whether they are of common Malay origin or not. In fact to bring to the front all the prejudices, and all the mistakes, and all the ignorance concerning the subject that he can get together.... Think of a small treatise on the Polynesian races being offered to people who are dying to hear about Ori a Ori, the making of brothers with cannibals, the strange stories they told, and the extraordinary adventures that befell us. What a thing it is to have a "man of genius" to deal with. It is like managing an overbred horse.

By "Scotch Stevenson head" Fanny seems to have meant a combination of Louis's pragmatic engineering forebears and their earnest Calvinism. "Louis says it is a stern sense of duty that is at the bottom of it, which is more alarming than anything else."[9]

Louis, meanwhile, declared hopefully in his own letter to Colvin, "I shall have the material for a very singular book of travels: masses of strange stories and characters, cannibals, pirates, ancient legends, old Polynesian poetry; never was so generous a farrago." When he did complete *In the South Seas,* however, it would turn out to be much as Fanny feared, which was nothing like what *Scribner's* wanted—or readers either. In 1891 McClure arranged for it to appear in serial form in the *New York Sun* and the London *Black and White,* but it was never published in book form until the posthumous Edinburgh Edition in 1896—and then heavily abridged by Colvin.[10]

During their time in Hawaii the family became friends with Kalakaua, king of the islands (they wouldn't be annexed to the United States until 1898). Louis told Baxter that he was "a very fine, intelligent fellow, but O, Charles! what a crop for the drink! He carries it too [i.e., holds his liquor], like a mountain with a sparrow on its shoulders. We calculated five bottles of champagne in three hours and a half (afternoon) and the sovereign quite presentable, although perceptibly more dignified, at the end." Lloyd said later that accounts of the king as a drunken savage were grossly unfair. "He was, on the contrary, a highly educated man, with an air of extreme distinction in spite of his very dark skin, and had a most winning graciousness and charm. He would have been at ease in any court in Europe. He was the greatest gentleman I have ever known."[11]

Belle remembered an engaging moment with the monarch:

> He would occasionally pick up a ukulele or a guitar and sing his favorite Hawaiian song, *Sweet Lei-lei-hua,* and once he electrified us by bursting into
>
> > Hoky poky winky wum
> > How do you like your taters done?
> > Boiled or with their jackets on?
> > Said the King of the Sandwich Islands.

That was a takeoff on a music hall song whose refrain was "The King of the Cannibal Islands."[12]

A group portrait at this time (fig. 67) makes an interesting character study. The king, looking distinguished, gazes thoughtfully off to the side, as does Margaret in her Queen Victoria mode. Louis looks into the camera with the intensity that struck everyone who met him, while Fanny is more reserved, resting her chin on her hand as she often did when being photographed. Lloyd, sitting on the floor, appears to be gazing quizzically at the monarch, but more likely is just peering nearsightedly through his glasses.

The king had a charming niece named Princess Kaiulani, whose father was a Scot from Edinburgh. She was about to depart for schooling in Britain, and Louis gave her a poem of farewell—"Light of heart and bright of face, / The daughter of a double race"—with a note in prose: "Written in April to Kaiulani in the April of her age; and at Waikiki, within easy walk of Kaiulani's banyan. When she comes to my land and her father's, and the rain beats upon the window (as I fear it will) let her look at this page. It will be like a weed gathered and pressed at home; and she will remember her own islands, and the shadow of the mighty tree, and she will hear the peacocks screaming in the dusk and the wind blowing in the palms; and she will think of her father sitting there alone."[13]

67. The Stevensons with King Kalakaua

THE LEPER SETTLEMENT ON MOLOKAI

Louis's most memorable experience in Hawaii was a visit to Kalawao on the island of Molokai, where anyone with symptoms of leprosy was permanently quarantined. Kalawao has precipitous cliffs on one side and heavy surf on the other. He had been inspired to go there by his San Francisco friend Charles Warren Stoddard, who described his own visit in *The Lepers of Molokai.*

A Catholic convert, Stoddard was profoundly impressed by the self-sacrificing priest who lived with the people and after twelve years developed leprosy himself. He was called Father Damien, and Stoddard represented him as a reincarnation of St. Francis of Assisi. "He brought from his cottage into the churchyard a handful of corn, and scattering a little of it on the ground, he gave a peculiar cry. In a moment his fowls flocked from all quarters; they seemed to descend out of the air in clouds; they lit upon his arms and fed out of his hands; they fought for footing upon his shoulders and even upon his head; they covered him with caresses and with feathers."[14]

Known today as Hansen's disease, leprosy is a bacterial infection treatable with antibiotics, and in any case far less contagious than used to be thought. It can take years of exposure for someone to become infected, and ordinary cleanliness may protect the minority of individuals who carry genetic susceptibility. But back then total isolation was believed to be the only way to arrest the spread of the disease, especially in a population that had no inherited immunity to it, or to the many other diseases that arrived from the outside world.

In addition to considerations of public health, Protestant missionaries invoked the Book of Leviticus: "The priest shall look on the plague in the skin of the flesh: and when the hair in the plague is turned white, and the plague in sight be deeper than the skin of his flesh, it is a plague of leprosy: and the priest shall look on him, and pronounce him unclean." The biblical passage goes on to describe a long series of diagnostic signs, and concludes that if the disease continues to progress, "his clothes shall be rent, and his head bare, and he shall put a covering upon his upper lip, and shall cry, Unclean, unclean. All the days wherein the plague shall be in him he shall be defiled; he is unclean: he shall dwell alone; without the camp shall his habitation be." Molokai was definitely outside the camp.[15]

Born Joseph De Veuster on a Belgian farm in 1840, the priest experienced a strong religious calling and at ordination he chose the name Damien, after an ancient physician-saint, and was sent to Hawaii. In 1873 he went to Molokai, the only clergyman of any denomination who was willing to reside there. A skilled carpenter, Damien built his house, as well as a church that still stands, and no fewer than six thousand coffins during sixteen years, at a rate of just over one coffin per day.[16]

In May 1889 Louis was set ashore at Molokai, together with several nuns. Father Damien, whom he had looked forward to meeting, had died just one month previously. Despite his shock at the residents' deformed bodies and faces, Louis mingled with them freely and won their respect. He especially enjoyed teaching children to play croquet with equipment he had sent ahead for them. One of the nuns recorded a response: "Sister he only one *haole* [European] not scart of us all the other white man too much fraid he our good friend we like he stay with us he not fraid us leper." After returning to Honolulu he purchased a piano and had that sent too.[17]

Damien was already being celebrated as a saint who had given his life for his flock. A Congregationalist clergyman, Charles McEwan Hyde, was more skeptical, and in a letter that he may not have intended to publish called Damien "a coarse, dirty man, headstrong and bigoted. . . . He was not a pure man in his relations with women, and the leprosy of which he died should be attributed to his vices and carelessness. Others have done much for the lepers, our own ministers, the government physicians, and so forth, but never with the Catholic idea of meriting eternal life."[18]

Louis was in Sydney by the time he saw this, and wrote a furious denunciation. In Belle's account,

> His deep voice vibrant with emotion, with heightened color and blazing eyes he read aloud the *Father Damien Letter*. Never in all my life have I ever heard anything so dramatic, so magnificent. There was deep feeling in every sentence—scorn, indignation, biting irony, infinite pity—and invective that fairly scorched and sizzled. The tears were in his eyes when he finished. Throwing the manuscript on the table he turned to his wife. She, who never failed him, rose to her feet, and holding out both hands to him in a gesture of enthusiasm, cried, "Print it! Publish it!"

Belle added that the pamphlet was sent to a long list of people, including the pope, Queen Victoria, and the president of the United States, as well as to newspapers in Hawaii, the United States, and Britain. One copy went to Hyde himself.[19]

Louis's diatribe was intemperate to say the least, and based on little actual information. He reproached the Protestant missionaries for living too comfortably, and for never imagining that the lepers deserved their attention. He agreed with Hyde that Damien was "a man of the peasant class, certainly of the peasant type: shrewd, ignorant and bigoted," but argued that that only made his sacrifice more admirable. As for the rumors about his sexual behavior, Louis had been told that they were untrue, confusing Damien with a different priest with a similar name. That was important because it was widely believed that leprosy was a final stage of syphilis, and people would assume that Damien's leprosy was the wages of sin. Anyway, Louis would never have agreed that sexual misbehavior, even if it did occur, was relevant.

With a copy of the pamphlet that went to Baxter, Louis added this comment: "Enclosed please find a libel; you perceive I am quite frank with my legal adviser; and I will also add it is *conceivable* an action might be brought, and in that event *probable* I should be ruined. If you had been through my experience, you would understand how little I care, for upon this topic my zeal is complete and, probably enough, without discretion." He enjoyed risks, especially when they involved taking a moral stand.[20]

When Hyde saw this attack he was horrified, and told friends, "I am being crucified by the most widely read author of our day, and on the charges of telling the truth about that sanctimonious bigot on Molokai." But he seems never to have considered suing for libel, and was impressively charitable about the controversy.[21]

TO SEA ONCE AGAIN

By now Louis was obliged to support a large ménage, which included Fanny, the cheerful but feckless Lloyd, Belle and her even more feckless husband Joe, and little Austin. It was, he told Baxter, a "Skimpolian household." In Dickens's *Bleak House,* Harold Skimpole is a charming freeloader who sponges unrepentantly off his friends, claiming that he is "but a child" with no understanding of money. There was a further problem with Joe: much of the time he was drunk.[22]

Fanny and Louis decided the best thing would be to separate Belle from her husband, and after what Belle remembered later as "a stormy interview" she was ordered to go with Austin to Australia, leaving Joe behind in Hawaii. Steamship tickets had already been bought. "I loved Honolulu," she said in her memoir; "I had many friends there, and I could earn my own living as I had proved in the past. They did not believe that at all, and thought I'd be safer in Sydney living on a weekly allowance. Then, when their voyage was ended, we would meet there and make further plans." By "safer" she meant financially, not physically; Joe was not abusive in that way.[23]

At this point Louis was still expecting to return to Europe soon. "I shall be home in May or June," he wrote to a French translator of his work, "and not improbably shall come to Paris in the summer." But a yearning developed to voyage further west. Fanny wrote to Frances Sitwell, "Louis has improved so wonderfully in the delicious islands of the South Seas that we think of trying yet one more voyage. You could hardly believe it if you could see Louis now. He looks as well as he ever did in his life, and has had no sign of cough or hemorrhage (begging pardon of Nemesis) for many months."[24]

One possibility was to take passage on the *Morning Star,* a steamer operated by the American Board of Missions that was going to visit islands where missionaries were in place. The Stevensons had made friends with a local missionary who wrote to his superiors in Boston that there should be no objection to accommodating the writer and his family: "He is not a religious man himself, nor is his wife a pious woman. Very far from it; but his mother is a godly woman, now with him here, the daughter of a Scotch minister. So he knows how religious people view things." Lloyd recalled that the projected itinerary was attractive, visiting "the wildest and least-known islands of the western Pacific." On the other hand, "its drawbacks were frightful—no smoking, not a drink, no profanity; church, nightly prayer-meetings, and an enforced intimacy with the most uncongenial of people." It's hard to imagine Louis living without a drink or a cigarette. The godly Margaret left them at this time, returning to Edinburgh to wind up her affairs.[25]

Fortunately a more attractive mode of transport appeared. A trading schooner called the *Equator* was about to set off for a six-month cruise to the Gilbert Islands. Its owners agreed to a contract by which the Stevensons would pay a fixed price to go ashore at any island that lay along the planned route, and be permitted a three-day stay at any of its scheduled stops.

Lloyd recalled the moment when Louis announced the news:

Everybody talked at once amid an unimaginable hilarity, for were we not to sail away in a vessel of our own, and freed from the nightmare of the *Morning Star*?

"And we can smoke on that blessed ship!" cried Stevenson, with uplifted glass.

"And drink!" cried I. "Hurrah for the *Equator!*"

"And swear!" exclaimed my mother delightfully—she who had never said "damn" in her life.

The cook Ah Fu gave a yell and opened the blinds to reveal "the *Equator* herself, under a towering spread of canvas, and as close as her captain dared to put her, parting the blue water in flashes of spray." The captain, a young Scot named Denis Reid who liked to appear in the national bonnet, turned out to be convivial and an expert seaman.[26]

Joe Strong was supposed to go along as expedition artist, but at the last moment was nearly rejected after squandering money that the family badly needed. Fanny described what happened in a letter to Colvin and Frances Sitwell: Joe returned to say goodbye "before destroying himself," and begged forgiveness so earnestly that he was permitted to travel with them after all. "No one can help loving the creature," Fanny concluded, "yet I would push him on to his death sooner than he should harm Louis." A comment by Philip Callow is convincing: "Joe put on his best performance to date, employing a degree of restraint and submission cleverly aimed at a side of Louis he knew only too well."[27]

A week later Louis, Fanny, Lloyd, and Joe were at sea on the *Equator*.

CHAPTER 28

The Cruise of the Equator

DEPARTURE FROM HAWAII

When the *Equator* set sail in June 1889, Louis expected it to be his final voyage before returning to Britain; he wrote to Colvin, "I am glad to say I shall be home by June next for the summer, or we shall know the reason why." There would always be a reason why.[1]

It was common for Britons who could afford it to take holidays on the Continent, less common to venture far away, and rare indeed to live like vagabonds. Louis had enjoyed that during his excursion with the donkey in the Cévennes, and now he could do it for months on end, accompanied by people he loved. He especially adored being at sea, and when they encountered rough weather, he rejoiced in it. Toward the end of this six-month cruise he wrote to Colvin, "Rain, calms, squalls, bang—there's the foretopmast gone; rain, calms, squalls, away with the staysail; more rain, more calms, more squalls; a prodigious heavy sea all the time, and the *Equator* staggering and hovering like a swallow in a storm; and the cabin, nine feet square, crowded with wet human beings, and the rain avalanching on the deck, and the leaks dripping everywhere. Fanny, in the midst of fifteen males, bearing up wonderfully."[2]

A picture Lloyd took aboard the *Equator* (fig. 68) captures a moment of action. Several crew members are on the bowsprit preparing to spear a fish, while Louis, dressed in black, has turned to look at the camera.

68. Spearing fish on the *Equator*

BUTARITARI AND APEMAMA

As shown on Balfour's map (color plate 15), from Hawaii the *Equator* sailed twenty-four hundred miles southwestward to the Gilbert Islands, known today as the Republic of Kiribati. There it made numerous stops, trading goods of various kinds for copra—dried coconut meat that played a major role in commerce. The first extended stay was on the atoll of Butaritari, which had a big lagoon in the middle and only five square miles of land.

Louis and Fanny were moved by the emotional power of the dancing on Butaritari. "The *hula*," he wrote, "as it may be viewed by the speedy globe-trotter in Honolulu, is surely the most dull of man's inventions, and the spectator yawns under its length as at a college lecture or a parliamentary debate. But the Gilbert Island dance leads on the mind; it thrills, rouses, subjugates; it has the essence of all art, an unexplored imminent significance."

Fanny was even more overwhelmed. "The leading man, in an impassioned ecstasy which possessed him from head to foot, seemed transfigured; once it was as though a strong wind had swept over the stage—their arms, their feathered fingers thrilling with an emotion that shook my nerves as well: heads and bodies followed like a field of grain before a gust. My blood came hot and cold, tears pricked my eyes, my head whirled, I felt an almost irresistible impulse to join the dancers."[3]

Married women wore a short skirt called the *ridi,* which looked provocative but was also a warning signal: on one island fourteen whites had been killed in recent years for improper advances. The skirt, Louis learned, "was the badge not of the woman but the wife, the mark not of her sex but of her station." In his opinion that made it "the collar on the slave's neck, the brand on merchandise." Unlike many travelers, he never imagined a Polynesian utopia of free love.[4]

On Butaritari they formed warm friendships, much as they had with Ori a Ori in Tahiti. A photograph by Lloyd (fig. 69) shows them with Nan Tok, at the left, and his wife Nei Takauti between Fanny and Louis. Louis's posture echoes Nan Tok's, as Fanny's does Nei Takauti's; there was never anything stiff about them. In his book he made the couple the subject of a chapter called "Husband and Wife" and described an unexpected balance of power:

> Nan Tok, the husband, was young, extremely handsome, of the most approved good humour, and suffering in his precarious station from suppressed high spirits. Nei Takauti, the wife, was getting old; her grown son by a former marriage had just hanged himself before his mother's eyes in despair at a well-merited rebuke. Perhaps she had never been beautiful, but her face was full of character, her eye of sombre fire. Whatever pretty thing my wife might have given to Nei Takauti—a string of beads, a ribbon, a piece of bright fabric—appeared the next evening on the person of Nan Tok. It was plain he was a clothes-horse; that he wore livery; that, in a word, he was his wife's wife. They reversed the parts indeed, down to the least particular; it was the husband who showed himself the ministering angel in the hour of pain, while the wife displayed the apathy and heartlessness of the proverbial man.

Another extended stay was on the island of Apemama (also spelled Abemama), where they lived for two months while the *Equator* visited less interesting places. There they formed a fast friendship with Tembinok, the chief or "king," whom J. C. Furnas describes as ruling "with vindictive terror, crack marksmanship, and an armed bodyguard of wives of all ages." Fanny wrote to Colvin, "All the South Sea books speak, by hearsay only, of the terrible Tembinoka, but we threw ourselves into his arms, and went and lived with him for months, and learned to love him almost as much as we admired him."[5]

69. Fanny, Louis, and friends at Butaritari

Tembinok had the massive girth considered appropriate for a monarch, as well as a startling overbite (fig. 70). Louis heard that he had been even bigger in the past. "Not long ago he was overgrown with fat, obscured to view, and a burthen to himself. Captains visiting the island advised him to walk; and though it broke the habits of a life and the traditions of his rank, he practised the remedy with benefit. His corpulence is now portable; you would call him lusty rather than fat; but his gait is still dull, stumbling, and elephantine."

For this photograph Tembinok chose Western military attire, but that was only one of his many costumes. "Now he wears a woman's frock, now a naval uniform; now (and more usually) figures in a masquerade costume of his own design: trousers and a singular jacket with shirt tails, the cut and fit wonderful for island workmanship, the material always handsome, sometimes green velvet, sometimes cardinal red silk. This masquerade becomes him admirably. In the woman's frock he looks ominous and weird beyond belief."

The rather bemused-looking boy is his adopted son Tem Bauro. Since Tembinok was childless, he ensured the succession by adopting a nephew.[6]

Louis was charmed by Tembinok's singing. "His description of one of his

70. Tembinok and son

own songs, which he sang to me himself, as 'about sweethearts, and trees, and the sea—and no true, all-the-same lie,' seems about as compendious a definition of lyric poetry as a man could ask."

Their parting, when the time came, was moving. For a time Tembinok sat silently smoking a pipe.

> "I very sorry you go," he said at last. "Miss Stlevens he good man, woman he good man, boy he good man; all good man. Woman he smart all the same man. My woman" (glancing towards his wives) "he good woman, no very smart. I think Miss Stlevens he big chiep all the same cap'n man-o-wa'. I think Miss Stlevens he rich man all the same me. All go schoona. I very sorry. My patha [father] he go, my uncle he go, my cutcheons [cous-

ins] he go, Miss Stlevens he go: all go. You no see king cry before. King all the same man: feel bad, he cry. I very sorry."[7]

When Colvin eventually assembled Louis's travel notes as *In the South Seas,* he didn't think much of the narrative but noted that "a far better qualified judge, Mr. Joseph Conrad, differs from me in this, and even prefers *In the South Seas* to *Treasure Island,* principally for the sake of what he regards as a very masterpiece of native portraiture in the character of Tembinok, King of Apemama." Conrad and Louis would have had much to talk about if Louis had lived long enough, but he died a year before Conrad's first novel was published.[8]

Tembinok organized his people to set up a dwelling for the visitors, described by Lloyd as "a sort of giant clothes basket of much the same color and wattle, with a peaked roof and standing on stilts about a yard high." When it was ready "he walked in a big circle around the settlement, and declared it tabooed during our stay."[9]

Louis enjoyed knowing Polynesian islanders, but many of the whites he encountered were unsavory drifters or even criminals. He wrote to Colvin,

> The whites are a strange lot, many of them good kind pleasant fellows, others quite the lowest I have ever seen even in the slums of cities. I wish I had time to narrate to you the doings and character of three white murderers (more or less proven) I have met; one, the only undoubted assassin of the lot, quite gained my affection in his big home [made] out of a wreck, with his New Hebrides wife in her savage turban of hair and yet a perfect lady, and his three adorable little girls in Rob Roy Macgregor dresses, dancing to the hand organ, performing circus on the floor with startling effects of nudity, and curling up together on a mat to sleep, three sizes, three attitudes, three Rob Roy dresses, and six little clenched fists: the murderer meanwhile brooding and gloating over his chicks till your whole heart went out to him. And yet his crime on the face of it was dark: disemboweling, in his own house, an old man of seventy and him drunk."[10]

Inveterate voyager though Louis was, he had frequent attacks of what Browning called, in a well-known poem, home thoughts from abroad. "A Voice from Home," written at Apemama, begins with an evocation of Edinburgh:

> The tropics vanish, and meseems that I,
> From Halkerside, from topmost Allermuir,
> Or steep Caerketton, dreaming gaze again.

> Far set in fields and woods, the town I see
> Spring gallant from the shallows of her smoke.

He deleted a more personal passage:

> There, in the silence of remembered time
> Sounds yet the innocent laughter of a child,
> Sounds yet the unresting footsteps of a youth
> Now dead forever, and whose grave I am.[11]

The final stage of the voyage was another seventeen hundred miles southeast to Samoa—a grand total of eleven thousand miles on the *Equator,* covered under sail. In December, shortly before making landfall in Samoa, Louis wrote to Colvin that he was still intending to be back in Britain by the following summer. It wasn't yet decided whether that would be for a visit only, or to stay.

> I am growing impatient to see yourself, and I do not want to be later than June of coming to England. We shall return, God willing, by Sydney, Ceylon, Suez and (I guess) Marseilles the many-masted: copyright epithet. I shall likely pause a day or two in Paris, but all that is too far ahead—although now it begins to look near—so near; and I can hear the rattle of the hansom up Endell Street, and see the gates swing back, and feel myself jump out upon the Monument steps—Hosanna!—home again.

Louis ended this letter with a poem he had written at Apemama, describing a stroll on the beach during which he recalled visiting Colvin at his British Museum residence, which it amused him to call "the Monument":

> To other lands and nights my fancy turned—
> To London first, and chiefly to your house,
> The many-pillared and the well-beloved.
> There yearning fancy lighted; there again
> In the upper room I lay, and heard far off
> The unsleeping city murmur like a shell;
> The muffled tramp of the Museum guard
> Once more went by me.[12]

By now the romance of the sea was fading. Louis wrote to another correspondent, "Six months on tinned meats, without any vegetables, is a thing to be remembered; most hardships become easy with continuance, not hardship of diet; towards the end I think we could all have wept at sight of an onion." It was a relief when they landed at Apia, the principal town on the Samoan island of Upolu, and watched the *Equator* sail away.[13]

UPOLU

A missionary named William Clarke, who would become a good friend, left a description of Fanny, Lloyd, and Louis when he encountered them making their way along the beach.

> The woman was wearing a print gown, large gold crescent earrings, a Gilbert Island hat of pleated straw encircled with a wreath of small shells, a scarlet silk scarf around her neck, and a brilliant plaid shawl across her shoulders; her bare feet were encased in white canvas shoes, and across her back was slung a guitar. The younger of her two companions was dressed in a striped pyjama suit—the undress costume of most European traders in these seas—a slouch hat of native make, dark blue sun spectacles, and over his shoulder a banjo. The other man was dressed in a shabby suit of white flannels that had seen many better days, a white drill [cotton] yachting cap with prominent peak, a cigarette in his mouth, and a photographic camera in his hand. Both the men were barefooted.

Clarke thought that they were probably "wandering players en route to New Zealand, compelled by their poverty to take the cheap conveyance of a trading vessel."[14]

Upolu was different from the islands they had visited previously. Although it lacked the spectacular peaks of Tahiti and the Marquesas, it was a shield volcano like the big island of Hawaii, with densely forested hills. Black-and-white photographs from those days don't do justice to its beauty (color plate 16). It was also an unusually large island, 47 miles in length and encompassing 430 square miles.

Louis had had romantic feelings about Samoa, or the Navigator Islands as the archipelago used to be called, for many years. When he was twenty-five he was entranced by a visitor who had come to Scotland to learn about lighthouses. He wrote to Frances Sitwell, "Awfully nice man here tonight. Public servant—New Zealand. Telling us all about the South Sea Islands till I was sick with desire to go there; beautiful places, green forever; perfect climate; perfect shapes of men and women, with red flowers in their hair; nothing to do but to study

71. Wrecked warships at Apia

oratory and etiquette, sit in the sun, and pick up the fruits as they fall. Navigator's Island is the place; absolute balm for the weary."[15]

Apia (pronounced Ah-PEE-a) lay on the north shore, at a point determined by a gap in the coral reef, created by fresh water from a river that empties into the sea. Three hundred Europeans lived in Apia, two-thirds of them British and the rest Germans. Some were drifters, some were traders, and some were professional bureaucrats. At this time foreign powers were competing for control of territories all over the Pacific islands; Fiji had become a British colony in 1874 and Tahiti a French colony in 1880. Britain, Germany, and the United States all had representatives in Apia.

Less than a year before the Stevensons' arrival a bizarre international incident had left the harbor clogged with sunken ships. When a typhoon was approaching in March 1889, the captains of German, British, and American ships delayed steaming to safety for fear of seeming to abandon their stake in Samoa. A picture taken soon afterward (fig. 71) shows the vessels *Trenton* and *Vandalia* (United States) and *Olga* (Germany), which were driven onto a reef and extensively damaged. Three other ships were wrecked altogether. International rivalries in Samoa would concern Louis greatly in the years to come.

In Apia they made a new friend, a shopkeeper named Harry Moors, originally from Detroit, who gave them lodging. At his first sight of Louis, Moors remembered, "I needed not to be told that he was in indifferent health, for it was stamped on his face. He appeared to be intensely nervous, highly strung, easily excited." After they got to know each other Moors saw Louis at his most genial and relaxed. "We exchanged endless yarns, generally in the evenings, as we sat in our pajamas on the balcony. When anything good came his way, he used to tell, it was 'better than a dig in the eye with a sharp stick.'"[16]

Moors was married to a half-Samoan known as Nimo who had spent several years in her father's native Scotland. Since most of the whites in Samoa were men, marriage with Samoan women was common, and seems to have been regarded without prejudice. Fanny described Nimo as "a very stout, very masterful old lady" and their daughter as "a very stout, very masterful young lady." Moors had a thriving business and knew everybody. A recent writer says that "his general store carried garden tools, canned goods, vegetables and fruits from his gardens, and clothing. He bought copra from the traders on Savaii [the largest Samoan island], a rough lot known in those days as the Savaii Squires which included such notables as Crooked-Neck Bill (so-called because he had survived a hanging in England and looked as if he had), Spanish Mike, Monkey Jack Stowers and Petelo Dick." Characters like these were generally referred to as "the beach," and would feature often in Louis's South Seas stories.[17]

Unexpectedly, an opportunity to buy land materialized. Large tracts of forest were available for sale on Upolu, as had not been true on any of the islands visited previously. Louis and Fanny were inspired by a sudden dream of establishing a plantation—what they might produce wasn't clear—and returning to live there after visiting Britain and America.

Moors seized the opportunity and sold them 314 acres of forested land, at a total cost in British money of £450. In February 1890 Louis wrote enthusiastically to Baxter, "We range from 600 to 1,500 feet, have five streams, waterfalls, precipices, profound ravines, rich table lands, fifty head of cattle on the ground (if anyone could catch them), a great view of forest, sea, mountains, the warships in the haven: really a noble place." Actually there were four streams, but they named the place Vailima, Samoan for "five streams," because they liked the sound of the word.[18]

Fanny, with her love of gardening, was thrilled with this prospect of gardening on an epic scale, with the hope that it might produce enough income to support them. She wrote to Colvin,

> This tract consists of between three and four hundred acres, part of it tableland of the richest deep virgin soil: more than enough for a large

> plantation. The rest is wild and picturesque—great cliffs, deep ravines, waterfalls, one some two hundred feet deep, and everywhere gigantic trees of different species. The whole lying some four hundred feet above the sea level, and commanding magnificent views of the harbour, the sea outside, and the surrounding country. We shall be two miles and a quarter from the town, not too near nor yet too far. Think of having three beautiful rivers of one's own, and a waterfall shaded by gnarled orange trees within five minutes' walk of one's door—not that we have a door as yet, but we have chosen the site for our house.

There was no road between Vailima and Apia suitable for wheeled vehicles, so the journey was always made on horseback.[19]

At this time their cook Ah Fu departed. It was agreed that he should make a trip home to China, find his aged mother, and astound her with a bulging money belt. Belle described his plan (leaving out "sailor slang and profanity"):

> "Come in, my son," she would say. "I am a poor widow woman, but what I have I will divide with my dear boy who gladdens my heart by his return." Then, taking off his belt and filling her hands with gold pieces, "It is all for you," he would cry. "I have worked and I have saved and now you will be rich and comfortable for the rest of your life."

Ah Fu left promising to return and work for the Stevensons for the remainder of his own life. He was never heard of again.[20]

While trees were being felled and ground cleared, the Stevenson party took passage to Sydney, intending to wait there until it was time to move in at Vailima. Louis wrote a letter to Baxter that was dated from "the *Dampfer Lübeck zwischen Apia und Sydney*"—the steamer *Lübeck* between Apia and Sydney. In the letter he included "To My Old Comrades," a poem that is far from nostalgic about Edinburgh.

> Do you remember—can we e'er forget?
> How, in the coiled perplexities of youth,
> In our wild climate, in our scowling town,
> We gloomed and shivered, sorrowed, sobbed and feared?
> The belching winter wind, the missile rain,
> The rare and welcome silence of the snows,
> The laggard morn, the haggard day, the night,
> The grimy spell of the nocturnal town,
> Do you remember?—Ah, could one forget!

Gone were the fantasies of brilliant achievements that delighted them during their university days: "Through the breach of the revolving doors / What dreams of splendour blinded us and fled!"

At the side of the page Louis added a further note.

> I take this blank corner to add a warmer expression of my thanks for your friendship; so much has fallen away, death and the worse horror of estrangement have so cut me down and rammed me in, that you and Colvin remain now all in all to me; and Colvin I cannot but fear is sore stricken [he was suffering a breakdown at the time]. I beg of you, dear old friend, to take care of your health physical and moral; you do not know what you become to me, how big you bulk; you must not measure it by my mean letters, nor by anything that I shall ever say: you remain alone of my early past, truer now than ever, and I cling to the thought of you. Hard thoughts, I sometimes have of others, God forgive me; I cannot get farther yet than that half ugly word of pardon, and even so, said with a grimace; I prefer to think of two that have stood by me: you and Colvin, with a warmth that grows ever greater.[21]

Back in 1883 Louis had told Henley that he was grateful to have seven close friends, and he named them in sequence. First came his cousin Bob, whom "I had by nature," joined at the university by Ferrier and Baxter and Simpson. Next he became close to Jenkin and Colvin, older friends who were mentors as well, and finally, "one black winter afternoon," he met Henley at the Edinburgh Infirmary. Now, in 1890, Ferrier and Jenkin were dead, Simpson had drifted away, and Henley and Bob were estranged. That made the unfailing loyalty of Baxter and Colvin especially precious. Fanny told Baxter so in a note she added to Louis's letter: "I think it is something to be proud of that Louis has arrived at nearly forty years and still keeps one friend of his youth, and another of his early manhood. It is *not* a scant allowance."[22]

It should be added that although Louis and Henley would never feel really close again, they both tried to mend fences. Louis sent him the poem "A Voice from Home" and suggested he might want to publish it in the *Scots Observer* that he was editing. The Henleys had recently had a daughter, and since they were living in Edinburgh Louis concluded his letter, "Your little girl will have some common stuff with me; some strings tuned to mine, in harmony at least, perhaps unison: I hope not, or she will flee that neighbourhood when she is forty as if it were the ruins of the eternal city of God. Almost nothing saddens me, but to recall such places." He ended with "Love to your wife. Ever yours affectionately, R.L.S." Two months later Henley did publish the poem. As for little Margaret, their only child, she became the inspiration for Wendy Darling in J. M. Barrie's *Peter Pan,* and was one of the many girls photographed by Lewis Carroll, but died of meningitis in 1894 at the age of five.[23]

Still, the friendship was effectively over. A year later Louis wrote to Henry James, "I had the painful misfortune of breaking off relations with my old friend Henley: a wretched milestone on the wayside of life, which leaves me in the state of a fish with a hook in his throat, any little odd movement of thought catching me with a pang or at least a prick."[24]

CHAPTER 29

Interlude

SYDNEY

Sydney is twenty-seven hundred miles from Apia, slightly further than the distance from New York to San Francisco. There they reunited with Belle, whom Joe had gone ahead to join, and Louis's feelings warmed toward both of them. He wrote to his mother, who was still in Edinburgh,

> Joe is, I think, *very ill* and (in your private ear) not wholly sane. But very, very good and kind and patient; Belle has done wonders, she has been a kind and patient nurse to her husband, has made no bad acquaintances, has made not a halfpenny of debt—and you know what a miracle that is—and has the doctor's praise for her attention and good sense. We are all much pleased and touched with her goodness—that I should be writing such words, even with emotion! For in truth, if ever I despaired of a human creature, it was Belle.

"Very ill" most likely referred to Joe's alcoholism. It's not clear why Louis had previously developed such a low opinion of Belle, but from this time on their relationship improved.[1]

Joe's improvident ways, however, were unchanged. He had managed to sell some paintings, concealed the fact, and squandered the proceeds on drink and other indulgences. After Louis found out he complained to Baxter, "This money that was stolen from me—for he owes me his body his soul and his boots, and the soup that he wipes from his moustache—was spent in pleasures and presents from which his wife and child were excluded altogether."[2]

Apart from their irritation with Joe, Louis and Fanny enjoyed Sydney, a bustling city with modern amenities, and they would visit there several times in the coming years. During this first visit, Louis found that, just as in New York, he was a celebrity. "The morning after his arrival," Belle recalled, "the name Robert Louis Stevenson blazed across the front page of every newspaper. There were pictures of him, editorials about him, articles describing his personal appearance, his history, his books, and in all of them a cordial rejoicing over his arrival."[3]

Louis and Fanny were still expecting that they would make a return visit to Britain. In March 1890, he wrote to tell both Margaret and Colvin that they would be on their way soon, and they actually booked passage by way of Ceylon and the Suez Canal. Soon afterward he cabled to Baxter, "Home September," and told his *Scribner's* editor that he would be in New York in the fall "unless the unforeseen occur." It did. He began hemorrhaging again; in fact, illness would strike every time they visited Sydney. The climate, if not as balmy as Samoa's, is benign enough, so the attacks may have been brought on by stress and by the viruses circulating in a busy port.[4]

Fanny felt sure that a restful sea voyage would be better for Louis at this time than an exhausting journey to Europe, and when he agreed, she made it her mission to find a suitable vessel.

THE *JANET NICHOLL*

Unfortunately, due to a sailors' strike hardly any ships were leaving Sydney. Indefatigable as always, Fanny searched the docks until she located the *Janet Nicholl*, a scruffy vessel crewed by native "kanakas" who were not part of the strike. The captain was skeptical about taking them, but as Graham Balfour heard the story, she brought all of her forcefulness to bear. "Mrs. Stevenson heard of a trading steamer about to start for 'the Islands,' applied for three passages [the third was for Lloyd] and was refused, went to the owners and was again refused; but stating inflexibly that it was a matter of life or death to her husband, she carried her point and extorted their unwilling consent."[5]

The *Janet Nicholl* sailed from Sydney on April 11, 1890, and visited thirty-five islands during the next four months. Louis was no longer "Ona" as he had been on the *Casco*, just a passenger with no say as to where they would stop. The purpose of the voyage was to pick up copra, and that determined the itinerary. He did retain the right to request a longer stay at any island that seemed especially interesting.

The *Casco* had been a yacht chartered for pleasure. The *Janet Nicholl* was engaged in trade, and that served Louis well as a writer. He became familiar with the subculture of grifters and con men in the ports they visited, and many people he encountered would be reincarnated in his fiction. As they were boarding the *Janet Nicholl* one fellow passenger was so drunk that he fell off the gangway and had to be pulled out of the sea. This turned out to be an engaging fellow named Jack Buckland, known as "Tin Jack," who received an annual allowance from England, spent it immediately, and got through the rest of the year as an island trader. In Louis's novel *The Wrecker* he would reappear as Tommy Hadden.

The ship was hot and smelly, and Louis wrote to his mother that even he was seasick, because it was "rolling and wallowing like a drunken tub." He told Baxter, "This *Janet Nicholl* is rolling past belief and I only write in tranquil moments so as to try to be legible. You never saw such a bitch to roll."[6]

Fanny, despite her inevitable seasickness, enjoyed herself thoroughly. Half a century later her grandson Austin related a story he had heard about the trip:

> I can see her now—a small woman in a blue dress, sitting barefoot on the roof of the after-cabin of a trading schooner in the South Seas. Her Panama hat, set at a rakish angle, shades a face of breathtaking beauty. She is holding a large silvered revolver in each hand, shooting sharks with deadly accuracy as they are caught and hauled to the taffrail by excited sailors.[7]

The first stop was at Auckland in New Zealand. Shortly after they left, a shipment of fireworks the *Janet Nicholl* was carrying exploded in flames and choking fumes. "By singular good fortune," Louis wrote to Colvin, "we got the hose down in time and saved the ship, but Lloyd lost most of his clothes and a great part of our photographs was destroyed. Fanny saw the native sailors tossing overboard a blazing trunk; she stopped them in time, and behold! it contained my manuscripts." It's not clear what those were, but it's true that he never stopped writing, even at times when it wasn't easy to manage it.[8]

When they arrived at Niue (also known as Savage Island) there was an engaging encounter, as Louis told Colvin.

> The path up the cliffs was crowded with gay islandresses (I like that feminine plural) who wrapped me in their embraces, and picked my pockets of all my tobacco, with a manner something between a whore and a

child, which a touch would have made revolting; but as it was, was simply charming like the Golden Age. One pretty little stalwart minx, with a red flower behind her ear, had gone through me with extraordinary zeal; and when, soon after, I missed my matches, I accused her (she still following us) of being the thief. After some delay, and with a subtle smile, she produced the box and gave me *one match,* and put the rest away again.

When Colvin printed this letter after Louis's death, he omitted "between a whore and a child" and changed "gone through me" to "searched me."[9]

During the voyage Fanny kept a diary, which was published much later as *The Cruise of the Janet Nichol* (she dropped the second "L" in the name). She recorded her entries "sometimes on the damp, upturned bottom of a canoe or whaleboat, sometimes when lying face down on the burning sands of the tropic beach, often in copra sheds in the midst of a pandemonium of noise and confusion, but oftener on board the rolling *Janet,* whose pet name was the *Jumping Jenny.*" It was mainly a factual account, but with deft descriptive touches: a trader was "a thin, pallid man, with a large hooked nose and soft, frightened brown eyes," and an island girl "was as neat as a little statue, as tight as india rubber." In her preface in 1914 she added, "The little book, however dull it may seem to others, can boast of at least one reader, for I have gone over this record of perhaps the happiest period of my life with thrilling interest."[10]

Most of the islanders they met had been converted by missionaries, but as Fanny noted, "'Being missionary'—religious—goes by waves of fashion. In Penrhyn, at any moment, the congregation may turn on the pastor and tell him he must leave instantly, as they are tired of being missionary. They have the week of jubilee, which means the whole island goes on a gigantic spree."[11]

She was impatient with the missionaries' obsession with clothing the islanders. "Natives have said that the first sight of white people is dreadful, as they look like corpses walking. I have myself been startled by the sight of a crowd of whites after seeing only brown-skinned people for a long time. Louis has a theory that we whites were originally albinos. Certainly we are not a nice color. I remember as a child the words 'flesh color' were sickening to me, and I could not bear to see them in my paint box." On one island Fanny gave a present of cloth to a girl named Fani, whose name so resembled her own. It was much appreciated, "but all the same a pity, for the less Fani covered her pretty brown body the better she looked."[12]

Fanny was always careful to protect her own modesty, and was embarrassed when an islander picked her up from knee-deep water, "my legs waving frantically in the air; I tried to shield them from the view of the ship with my umbrella, which I was unable to open, but I fear my means were inadequate." She was trying to shield herself from the white men on the boat, not from the islanders.[13]

A recurring theme in the diary was Fanny's education in the nuances of trading. She had brought with her a stock of goods for that purpose, including tobacco, cotton dresses, combs, and rings. Perhaps surprisingly, wreaths of artificial flowers were especially desired; as Roslyn Jolly explains, they were valued for festive occasions on atolls where few flowers grew naturally. Fanny needed to learn when an exchange should be regarded as a bestowing of gifts, and when it was a purchase.[14]

At one point she reported, "For a florin [2 shillings] I got an immense necklace of human teeth. A little while ago, in some of the islands, especially Maraki, a good set of teeth was a dangerous possession, as many people were murdered for them. I trust mine were honestly come by—at least taken in open warfare."[15]

In the Marshall Islands they were shown a native sailing chart and heard an explanation of how it was used, a testimony to the seafaring genius of the Polynesians. "These charts are very curious things indeed, made of sticks, some curved, some straight, caught here and there by a small yellow cowrie. The cowries represent islands, the sticks both currents and winds and day's sailing. The distances between the islands have nothing to do with miles, but with hours only." Fanny added that the charts had to be memorized in detail, since they were never taken to sea, where they could easily be lost.[16]

At Natau in the Ellice Islands, two young women in a canoe became terrified when they were brought aboard. The captain only wanted them to meet the Stevenson party, but they were all too familiar with the kidnapping of islanders for forced labor far from their homes. As Fanny described it in her diary,

> I met on the companion stairs [leading to the lower deck] the captain, half dragging, half persuading one of the young women I had seen in the canoe to come down to the saloon. Naturally she did not understand that he was only trying to bring her to me. At the sight of me she gave a cry and, breaking loose from the captain, flung herself upon me and clung to me like a frightened child. I could feel her heart beating against my breast and she was trembling from head to foot. As she held me she bent down, for she was taller than I, and smiled in my face. Plainer than words her smile said: "You are a woman, too; I can trust you; you will protect me, will you not?" I put my arm round her and talked to her in

English and tried to soothe her fears. She understood my English as well as I her smiles.[17]

The voyage ended back at Sydney on August 4. By this time Louis was beginning to suspect that a return to Britain might never happen; he wrote to Henry James,

> I must tell you plainly—I *can't* tell Colvin—I do not think I shall come to England more than once, and then it'll be to die. Health I enjoy in the tropics; even here [in Sydney], which they call sub or semi-tropical, I come only to catch cold.... I was never fond of towns, houses, society or (it seems) civilization. Nor yet it seems was I ever very fond of (what is technically called) God's green earth. The sea, islands, the islanders, the island life and climate, make and keep me truly happier. These last two years I have been much at sea, and I have *never wearied*. Sometimes I have grown indeed impatient for some destination; more often I was sorry that the voyage drew so early to an end; and never once did I lose my fidelity to blue water and a ship.

James was the only one of Louis's friends who fully sympathized with that.[18]

Lloyd was now dispatched to England to sell Skerryvore and to ship the furniture and family possessions to Samoa. Before he left Louis wrote to Baxter, "Please guide Lloyd all you can. We see him go, Fanny and I, with sinkings. He is not—well—not a man of business."[19]

CREATING THE VAILIMA ESTATE

Back on the Samoan island of Upolu, the ground had been cleared where the house was to be built, and a small cottage was put up as temporary quarters. In October 1890, Louis and Fanny moved in. A couple of weeks later, writing to his editor at *Scribner's,* he expressed his delight at the sounds that filled the air.

> You should hear the birds on the hill now! The day has just wound up with a shower; it is still light without, though I write within here at the cheek of a lamp; my wife and an invaluable German are wrestling about bread on the back verandah; and how the birds and the frogs are rattling, and piping, and hailing from the woods! Here and there a throaty chuckle; here and there, cries like those of jolly children who have lost their way; here and there, the ringing sleighbell of the tree frog. Out and away down below me on the sea it is still raining; it will be wet underfoot

on schooners, and the house will leak; how well I know that! Here the showers only patter on the iron roof, and sometimes roar; and within, the lamp burns steady on tapa covered walls, with their dusky tartan patterns, and the bookshelves with their thin array of books; and no squall can cant [overturn] my house or bring my heart into my mouth. The well-pleased South Sea Islander, RLS.

Sheets of galvanized iron—coated with zinc to resist rusting—were favored for tropical roofs. Tapa was a cloth made from tree bark cut into strips, soaked, pounded, and bleached in the sun, after which it would be dyed and painted with designs. Fine examples were considered highly valuable, and the Stevensons would acquire a number of pieces as gifts.[20]

Virtually all of the building materials had to be imported. J. C. Furnas notes that "sawmills are scarce and rolling mills [for shaping metal] nonexistent in the Islands; every nail, sheet of iron, pane of glass, and sliver of wood in Vailima came from the Colonies or the States." Heavy loads were hauled up from Apia by a pair of horses named Donald and Eddie, remembered by a visiting journalist as "the biggest and handsomest horses on the island," which had begun life pulling a tramcar in Auckland.[21]

The finished house (fig. 72) had two stories, with a veranda ninety feet long on the second floor; at its far end the enclosed section was Louis's study. The house was blue, the window and door frames were dark green, and the roof was bright red. Louis wrote to Colvin during a rainstorm, "I scarce know what I write, so hideous a Niagara of rain roars, shouts, and demonises on the iron roof." The runoff was collected in storage tanks; drinking water was carried from a nearby stream, and later on supplied in pipes from further up on the mountain.[22]

As it happens, violent rain was a particular dread of Louis's. Christmas Eve in 1890 was marked by a ferocious typhoon. As he described it to Colvin, "My wife near crazy with earache; the rain descending in white crystal rods and playing hell's tattoo, like a *tutti* of battering rams, on our sheet iron roof; the wind passing high overhead with a strange dumb wuther [blustery sound], or striking us full, so that all the huge trees in the paddock cried aloud, and wrung their hands, and brandished their vast arms." He added, "I have always feared the sound of wind beyond everything: in my hell it would always blow a gale."[23]

That had been the theme of "Windy Nights" in *A Child's Garden of Verses,* in which he imagined a horseman galloping endlessly past. In a late autobiographical note he recalled, "I think even now that I hear the terrible howl of his passage, and the clinking that I used to attribute to his bit and stirrups. On

72. Vailima

such nights I would lie awake and pray and cry, until I prayed and cried myself asleep."[24]

The interior appointments at Vailima were extravagant. Dominating the first floor was the "Great Hall," sixty feet by forty, paneled with California redwood and flooded with light from large windows. In a photograph (fig. 73) Fanny is seated at far left (almost as recessive as in the Sargent painting at Skerryvore), Louis is at the center, and Belle stands on the grand staircase at the right. All of them have bare feet. Graham Balfour mentioned in his biography that a pair of Burmese gilded idols, formerly at Skerryvore, guarded the posts of the big staircase, and that when a Samoan chief was leaving after a visit "he asked indifferently, 'Are they alive?'" The banjo leaning against one of them was Lloyd's.

Years later, when the Heriot Row house was sold, its furniture—including a piano, which would be played by Belle—arrived in thirty-eight huge crates, weighing seventy-two tons in all. Twelve carts were needed to bring them up from Apia, each pulled by two bullocks.[25]

Harry Moors, the shopkeeper who had sold them the property, was scandalized by the Stevensons' extravagance in building what in Upolu was virtually a

73. The Great Hall

palace. Since there was no bank in Apia, he handled their finances and knew that the whole project cost more than $20,000, a huge sum in those days, including $1,000 to construct a massive fireplace. When he remarked that there wasn't much need of that in the tropics, Louis replied, "A fireplace makes a house look home-like." During all of Moors's visits to Vailima he never once saw a fire in it.[26]

Regular upkeep, along with the elaborate parties that the Stevensons began to give, amounted to another $6,500 a year. "We call these our marble halls," Lloyd wryly told a visitor, "because they cost so much."[27]

In a photograph (fig. 74), in front of the fireplace a girl named Fanua is looking up at Fanny, who is seated in the armchair from Skerryvore that Henry James had used; it also appears in the Sargent portrait (color plate 13). The rug was probably a California puma skin. In Samoa the only native mammal is a bat.

Decorating the house brought out Fanny's sensitivity to color. She wrote in her diary, "The dining room we have hung with a yellowish terra-cotta tapa, the window casings and door being a strong peacock blue, and the ceiling a sort of cream color. With the chairs and pictures, the colors make a most delightful harmony. My own room is beginning to have the softly jeweled look that I am so

74. Fanny and Fanua

fond of. Louis's room is still in a state of ferment, the last books having arrived [from Britain] only two days ago. I find it more difficult to manage with his colors, the room being two shades of pale blue, not colors I am on any degree of intimacy with."[28]

A NEW LIFE OF FREEDOM

What Vailima meant for the family, above all, was liberation from conventional constraints. And there was an unforeseen blessing: after decades of terrible health, Louis was stronger and more vigorous than he had been for many years, taking long rides on horseback and working outside for hours at a time. Back when he was alone in the Cévennes and didn't know if he would ever see Fanny again, he had written, "To live out of doors with the woman a man loves is of all lives the most complete and free." At that time it was something he had never experienced. Now, on the other side of the world, it was becoming a way of life.[29]

White people in Apia made a point of dressing "respectably," and visitors to Vailima were shocked by the Stevensons' informality. That was still more the case when the Boston patrician Henry Adams, touring the Pacific with his artist friend John La Farge, paid a call just after Louis and Fanny had moved into their temporary lodging while the big house was under construction. Apparently taking this for their permanent home, Adams described it contemptuously as "a two-story Irish shanty" with "an atmosphere of dirt" about it. As Belle explained later, at the moment he arrived—unannounced—they were struggling to set up a cooking stove "and getting rather moist and blackened in the process."[30]

Adams was deeply offended that Louis had no idea who he was, and wrote to a friend, "He had evidently not the faintest associations with my name, but he knew all about LaFarge and became at once very chummy with him." That was true; a couple of weeks later Louis mentioned to his New York publisher, "I saw Mr. LaFarge here, and another gentleman who knew you: name forgotten." La Farge was best known for murals and stained glass; in another letter Louis referred to him as "the American decorator."[31]

Louis struck Adams as "so thin and emaciated that he looked like a bundle of sticks in a bag, with a head and eyes morbidly intelligent and restless. He was costumed in very dirty striped cotton pajamas, the baggy legs tucked into coarse knit woolen stockings, one of which was bright brown in color, the other a purplish dark tone." As for Fanny, "She wore the usual missionary nightgown which was no cleaner than her husband's shirt and drawers, but she omitted the stockings. Her complexion and eyes were dark and strong, like a half-breed Mexican." Henry James's sister Alice had said something similar—she too was a Boston Brahmin.

Louis favored a loose jacket over striped flannel trousers, and people did often refer to his costume as pajamas, which they took as symptomatic of going native. Similarly, Fanny, Belle, and Margaret wore loose muumuus and holokus, and rejoiced in their freedom from Victorian tight-lacing.[32]

It should be added that Adams's opinion of Louis improved on further acquaintance. "When conversation fairly began, though I could not forget the dirt and discomfort, I found Stevenson extremely entertaining. He has the nervous restlessness of his disease, and although he said he was unusually well, I half expected to see him drop with a hemorrhage at any moment, for he cannot be quiet, but sits down, jumps up, darts off and flies back, at every sentence he utters, and his eyes and features gleam with a hectic glow." Adams didn't know that whether sick or well, Louis had done that all his life.[33]

Adams added, incidentally, that a century from that time John La Farge would be world-famous and Robert Louis Stevenson forgotten.

CHAPTER 30

Life at Vailima

SA TUSITALA

At first Louis and Fanny were the only members of the family at Vailima, but in early 1891 Margaret and Lloyd arrived from Edinburgh, and soon afterward Belle and Joe came from Sydney with their son Austin.

There was a large staff of servants, in due course nineteen of them, not all full-time. A few white workers were tried but found wanting, and by the end of 1891 the entire staff was Samoan, with the exception of three men from other islands, including a Melanesian who had been kidnapped from the Solomons and forced to labor on a German plantation. A runaway, he showed up at Vailima with scars of brutal whipping on his back; Louis bought his indenture to secure his freedom.

Among the regular staff were "my native overseer, the great Henry Simele"; Lafaele, who tended the livestock and was known as "the cowboy"; Simi the steward and Louis's personal attendant; and Talolo the cook. For a formal portrait (fig. 75) Talolo appeared with a lethal-looking knife and a challengingly intense expression—though perhaps he used the knife as a butcher's cleaver. Lafaele (fig. 76) preferred a garland of flowers.[1]

On festive occasions everybody dressed up. Samoan men were accustomed to wear kilt-like garments called lava-lavas around their waists, and at these times they wore actual kilts in Royal Stewart tartan. They also wore striped jackets, as shown on the houseboy Mitaele (fig. 77).

In her biography of Louis, Rosaline Masson (who never saw Samoa) described

75. Talolo

76. Lafaele

his new role as that of a clan chieftain: "The careless bohemian of Fontainebleau, the half-starving pariah of San Francisco, the indomitable invalid of Davos and Nice and Bournemouth—woke in exile to find himself lord and master and priest of a patriarchal home, chieftain of a devoted clan of feudal retainers, friend and adviser of Samoan dignitaries."[2]

This was self-dramatization, with Louis playing the role of great white father, but it also fell into a pattern familiar to Samoans. As the biographer J. C. Furnas explains, missionary friends told Louis that Samoans were loyal to their

77. Mitaele

chiefs, and would cooperate more willingly if he assumed a version of that status. Naturally they were paid wages, but since they were perfectly capable of being self-sufficient, they needed a stronger motive than that to keep them engaged. What worked well at Vailima, Furnas says, was establishing a sort of adoptive family, "all owing services to the head of the family as expressions of the family."[3]

A remarkable group portrait (fig. 78) was taken on the veranda by John Davis, the Apia postmaster and a professional photographer. There is no way to know whether the composition was arranged entirely by Davis or if some of the subjects made suggestions. This picture appears in most biographies with little comment, but as Leonard Bell has shown in a subtle analysis, it repays attention.[4]

All fifteen people can be identified. Eight are whites and seven are natives of

78. Vailima group

Samoa or other islands. Louis is at the center, but seems strangely recessive. Bell comments, "He looks introverted, closed in, withdrawn, elsewhere." Fanny has her chin on her hand, possibly bored with waiting for the photographer to be ready.

Seen in profile is the matriarch Margaret, wearing her customary widow's cap. Her favorite pose might evoke Queen Victoria, but it's also almost identical to the iconic image of Whistler's mother, first exhibited in 1872. Bell suggests, "This resemblance can be seen as a mimetic invocation of that painting and the raft of social and emotional connotations that it carried." It might even have been intentional. "Maybe the Stevenson entourage was performing a kind of charade for the camera."

Two family members are standing. Lloyd, with arms sternly crossed, impersonates a masterful overseer of the estate, but that's only a pose. His unreliability was notorious. Harry Moors commented, "Lloyd Osbourne just liked to sit down and 'watch things grow'; and if they didn't grow, they didn't." At far left,

Joe Strong lounges against a pillar with Cocky the cockatoo on his shoulder. Quite possibly he is drunk—he generally was. He is wearing a lava-lava, the only member of the family in any form of native dress, but for some reason has on thick socks. Relations between Joe and the family were strained, and it wouldn't be long before his marriage with Belle would end.[5]

At far right a third standing figure is the household steward Simi. In the middle row is Margaret's maid Mary Carter, described by Claire Harman as "scowling and utterly encased in whalebone"; she hated Vailima and was about to go home to New Zealand. Between Lloyd and Louis is Talolo the cook, then Belle with a bored-looking Austin leaning against her, then Lafaele the "cowboy," and at far right the assistant cook Tomasi with an ax. In the front row are three low-ranking members of the staff, a worker named Auvea, Tomasi's wife Elena, who did the laundry, and the pantry boy Arrick (he was the one whose back had been lashed). The overseer Simele wasn't present at the time.[6]

Though Margaret liked to appear formal in photographs, she was relaxed in daily life. She preferred to go barefoot, which most Westerners refused to do, and cheerfully partook of the kava drink that was an important part of every Samoan feast. Dictionaries describe it as sedative, anesthetic, and euphoriant. A photograph (fig. 79) shows kava being made, in a process that Margaret explained in a letter to her sister:

> The proper native way of preparing kava is to have the root chewed by young girls chosen for their beauty; then it is steeped in water (but not fermented) and after many strainings it is handed around. But a great many people now grate the root instead of having it chewed. We always have it grated, and when it is given to me elsewhere I just devoutly *hope* it has been grated, and think it safer to ask no questions. You see one cannot refuse it without giving offense.

Margaret did draw the line at palolo, "a very peculiar and highly thought of Samoan delicacy which I confess I have not had the courage to taste. It consists of *long thin green worms.*" However, she had a tolerant attitude regarding other customs. When Fanny remarked that one of their friends must have eaten hundreds of his enemies, she answered, "Now, Fanny, you must really not exaggerate. You know quite well it was only eleven!" Margaret had a playful sense of humor, and there is no reason to take this literally. Ritual cannibalism may have been practiced in the past, but certainly not recently. Missionaries throughout the Pacific had successfully promoted its abolition.[7]

Samoans found English names hard to pronounce and soon bestowed their

79. Girls making kava

own. Louis was Tusitala (also written Tusi Tala), generally translated "Storyteller" or "Teller of Tales"; he himself referred to it less romantically as "Write-tale—really perhaps Write-information." It's not clear whether it was an existing Samoan word or was coined for him. At any rate it was soon applied to any professional writer. Half a century later Furnas "was startled to hear myself called 'tusitala' in Samoan villages."[8]

Fanny was Aolele, "Flying Cloud," and also Tamaitai, "Lady of the House." Margaret was Tamaitai Meuta, "Old Lady of the House"; Belle was Teuila, "Beautifier of the Ugly," because she was fond of decorating the house and giving people flowers to wear (the Samoan name for the vivid red national flower is *teuila*). Others were called by versions of their actual names: Lloyd was Loia and Austin was Ositini.

The Stevensons didn't put on airs, and welcomed playful teasing. Louis described a performance in which Lafaele's wife Faauma sang a comic song about each member of the family. Lloyd was "the dancing man (practically the Chief's handsome son) of Vailima." Belle was thanked for having given rings and thimbles to everyone, "very much in character with her native name Teuila, the adorner of the ugly." As for Fanny, her characterization "was less intelligible, but it was accompanied in the dance with a pantomime of terror well-fitted to call up her haunting, indefatigable and diminutive presence in a blue gown." Louis doesn't mention whether the impersonations included himself.[9]

Faauma, Louis wrote, was "a little creature in native dress and beautiful as a bronze candlestick, so fine, clean and dainty in every limb: her arms and her little hips in particular masterpieces." Six months later she was "now in full flower—or half flower—and grows buxom." Unfortunately she got sexually involved with Joe Strong and had to be dismissed, "poor dear Faauma, the unchaste, the extruded Eve of our Paradise."[10]

In 1892 another relative arrived, Graham Balfour, who would make three extended stays while touring the Pacific and would write a valuable biography. This was apparently the first time he and Louis had met. Graham was a second cousin, not one of Louis's many first cousins; his father, Dr. Thomas Balfour, was a first cousin of Margaret Stevenson. Graham soon acquired the name Palema.

COMMUNAL PRAYERS

On Sundays at Vailima the family and staff gathered to hear a chapter of the Bible read in Samoan (by Lloyd, the most fluent in the language) and a prayer in English composed by Louis. When these were published after his death as "Vailima Prayers," they were hailed by some as evidence that he had returned to his faith. However, they were not in the least doctrinal, emphasizing instead ethical conduct, and it's clear that the sessions were a social ritual. They meant a great deal to Louis in that way, but not as conventional piety. As Lloyd described it,

> Stevenson had an illogical sort of inherited love for religious forms and ceremonies. He could roll out the word "God" with an indescribable conviction, and nothing pleased him more than to read his own prayers aloud and endow them with the glamour of his extraordinarily affecting voice. He liked too—best of all, I think—the beautiful and touchingly patriarchal aspect of family devotions; the gathering of the big, hushed household preparatory to the work of the day, and the feeling of unity and fellowship thus engendered. It was certainly a picturesque assembly— Stevenson in imposing state at the head of the table, I at his right with the Samoan Bible before me, ready to follow him with a chapter in the native language, the rest of the family about us, and in front the long row of half-naked Samoans, with their proud free air and glistening bodies. We were the Sa Tusitala, the Clan of Stevenson.[11]

For Margaret, these Sunday ceremonies were the very least that she would expect. For Louis once a week was plenty. He commented in 1893, "We have prayers on Sunday night. I am a perfect pariah in the island not to have them oftener, but the spirit is unwilling and the flesh proud, and I cannot go it more." He was recalling the Gospel of Matthew, "The spirit is willing, but the flesh is weak."[12]

As for Louis's private beliefs, they can be surmised from an 1893 poem entitled "If This Were Faith":

> God, if this were enough,
> That I see things bare to the buff
> And up to the buttocks in mire;
> That I ask nor hope nor hire,
> Nut in the husk,
> Nor dawn beyond the dusk,
> Nor life beyond death:
> God, if this were faith?[13]

THE "PLANTATION"

Louis referred playfully to Vailima as "my ancestral acres, which I purchased six months ago," and took to calling the place "Subpriorsford." Early in the nineteenth century Walter Scott had sunk the income from his novels and investments into an estate he named Abbotsford, with a faux-medieval mansion and a thousand acres of land. "Subpriorsford" was a clerical joke: an abbot's subordinate was a prior, and a subprior was lower still. Still, this was the first property Louis had ever bought—Skerryvore was a gift—and he got intense pleasure from building something from scratch. He was turning forty, and perhaps felt that becoming a builder marked his maturity. In a small way, it was carrying on the tradition of the lighthouse Stevensons. The allusion to Abbotsford was inauspicious, however. Scott's estate was a money sink, and when he died in 1832 he was deeply in debt, though planning to pay back his creditors with income from future writing.

Fanny, who had always loved gardening, aspired to turn their property into a plantation, but the only profitable plantations in Samoa were run by commercial firms with forced labor. Also, they were in the easily cultivated lowlands. Soon after arriving in Apia Louis mentioned in a letter "the great German plantations with their countless regular avenues of palm," and at another time said that they occupied ten thousand acres. Nothing like that was conceivable on the slopes of Mount Vaea, where Vailima was located.[14]

After he got to know Upolu better, Louis learned how the plantations were managed. It was the overseers, not the workers, whom he called "barbaric."

> You ride in a German plantation and see no bush, no soul stirring; only acres of empty sward, miles of cocoa-nut alley: a desert of food. For the Samoan besides, there is something barbaric, unhandsome, and absurd in the idea of thus growing food only to send it from the land and sell it. And the firm which does these things is quite extraneous, a wen that might be excised tomorrow without loss but to itself; few natives drawing from it so much as a day's wages, and the rest beholding in it only the occupier of their acres. The nearest villages have suffered most; they see over the hedge the lands of their ancestors waving with useless cocoa palms. The sales were often questionable, and must still more often appear so to regretful natives.

This means that Samoans weren't employed there at all, since the owners preferred to import cheap forced labor. And "questionable" sales means that the plantations had been dishonestly acquired.[15]

Nevertheless, Fanny had high hopes at first for their own plantation, and threw herself into planning. Some plantings survived on the site from an earlier settlement, including bananas, papayas, and lemons. To these she added seeds acquired in Sydney—melons, tomatoes, mangoes, pineapples—and began corresponding with botanical collections abroad that might help her to expand her crops. A visitor a few years later listed some of the plants she tried: "breadfruit, pineapples, bananas, cocoa, rubber, sugar cane, ginger, kava, taro, grenadillas, oranges, limes, citrons, coconuts, mangoes, vanilla, coffee, cinnamon, and guava." In 1892 Margaret reported, "There are now 7766 cacao plants out, which is pretty well for a single season's work." However, that crop would have to be sent away from the island to be processed into cocoa, and no planter in Samoa had made a success of cacao.[16]

Fanny was the only family member who actually applied herself to working on the plantation, giving directions to the "outdoor" staff—most of whom had little experience of farming—and taking part energetically herself. Belle looked after arrangements within the household. Lloyd, as Moors commented, was nearly useless, and so was Joe. Louis enjoyed hacking at the "bush" from time to time, and when his *Scribner's* editor complained in 1890 of a delay in receiving material, he replied, "I am a mere farmer.... My hands are covered with blisters and full of thorns. Letters are doubtless a fine thing, so are beer and skittles, but give me farming in the tropics for real interest." In truth, however, for him the outdoor work was recreational.[17]

Besides, he formed an idea of nature as a tormented Darwinian struggle and himself as an abusive invader. He wrote to Colvin, "My long silent contests in the forest have had a strange effect on me. The unconcealed vitality of these vegetables, their exuberant number and strength, the attempts—I can use no other word—of lianas to enwrap and capture the intruder, the awful silence; the knowledge that all my efforts are only like the performance of an actor, the thing of a moment, and the wood will silently and swiftly heal them up. The whole silent battle, murder and slow death of the contending forest—weighs upon the imagination." A few months later he said, "The life of the plants comes through my fingertips, their struggles go to my heart like supplications."[18]

For day-to-day living, the produce grown at Vailima was a success, and the family ate well, supplementing it with supplies from Moors's store in town. Fanny recalled years later, "A fortnightly service of steamships brought us ice, fresh oysters, and other supplies from the colonies [i.e., Australia and New Zealand] or San Francisco. There was a good baker and butcher in Apia, and fish to be bought on the beach. Eels and fresh-water prawns abounded in our streams, wild pigeons could be shot from our back door, and the chickens and eggs of our own raising were excellent."

They kept a number of domestic animals in addition to the chickens, all of which had to be ordered from abroad. Fanny commented on one arrival, "My pig from Sydney is at Apia, but as she cost only thirty-seven shillings, I feel doubts as to her quality. Still, in Samoa a pig's a pig." It was also important to keep a cow. The first one they had was "a pretty little thing that gives very good milk, but with an eye filled with hellfire and the temper of a fiend." Subsequently they sent to Sydney "for a cow warranted of a lamblike disposition, choosing the Jersey breed as the most likely to be amiable."[19]

Cocky the cockatoo, incidentally, was devoted to Belle and regarded Louis with hostility. Louis described what happened when he knocked on Belle's door at breakfast time:

> It was a mighty pretty dawn; the birds were singing extraordinary strong, all was peace, and there was the damned parrot hanging to the knob of Belle's door. Courage, my heart! On I went, and Cocky buried his bill in the joint of my thumb. I believe that Job would have killed that bird; but I was more happily inspired—I caught it up and flung it over the veranda as far as I could throw. I must say it was violently done, and I looked with

some anxiety to see in what state of preservation it would alight. Down it came however on its two feet, uttered a few oaths in a very modified tone of voice, and set forth on the return journey to the mansion. Its wings being cut and its gait in walking having been a circumstance apparently not thoroughly calculated by its maker, it took about twenty-five minutes to get home again. Now here is the remarkable point—that bird has never bitten me since.

Male parrots are fiercely possessive of the person they bond with, and it's true that they waddle rather ridiculously.[20]

SOCIALIZING

Once a week or so Louis would ride his horse Jack down to Apia, have lunch with Moors or a missionary friend or one of the bureaucrats, go on board a visiting warship if one was in port, and perhaps dine in the evening with a Samoan chief before riding home. A photograph in Belle's memoir *This Life I've Loved*, entitled *Packing Provisions for Vailima* (fig. 80), shows him just outside Apia standing by Jack, with Lloyd at the horse's head. The provisions would be all sorts of household goods, usually from Harry Moors's store, that had arrived from abroad. Belle must have known who the other two men in the picture were, but they are identified only as "natives." Though Jack was relatively small, people remarked that it didn't matter since Louis weighed no more than a jockey.[21]

Guests from Apia came up regularly to Vailima, and wine flowed freely. Bordeaux and Burgundy were ordered from the French colony of New Caledonia, fifteen hundred miles to the west, and after the sale of Heriot Row the contents of its ample wine cellar were added to Vailima's. Someone who attended a party there as a girl remembered that she was allowed a glass of 1840 Madeira—it had aged for fully half a century. The "Great Hall" would be cleared for dancing, and another visitor remembered playing Scottish and Irish melodies on the out-of-tune piano while Louis and Belle "danced on the polished floor with a vigor seldom matched and a delight splendid to see." Sailors from visiting ships were often invited, and one of them exclaimed, "Mrs. Strong is a very fine dancer, sir!"[22]

Louis took seriously his role as an honorary chieftain, and gave colossal banquets on special occasions. Belle described the feast for his forty-third birthday, at which all of the guests were Samoans—at least a hundred of them. "We had sixteen pigs roasted whole underground, three enormous fish (small whales, Lloyd called them), 400 pounds of salt beef, ditto of pork, 200 heads of taro,

80. Packing Provisions for Vailima

great bunches of bananas, native delicacies done up in bundles of *ti* leaves, 800 pineapples, many weighing 15 pounds, oranges, tinned salmon, sugarcane, and ships' biscuit in proportion." Guests would be encouraged to take the leftovers home with them.[23]

In 1892 there was a visit from a young Italian painter, Girolamo Ballatti Nerli, who made a striking portrait of Louis looking quizzical or perhaps skeptical (color plate 17). Afterward Louis presented him with some playful verses:

> Did ever mortal man hear tell of sae singular a ferlie
> As the coming to Apia here of the painter, Mr. Nerli?
> He cam; and O, for a hunner pound, of a' he was the pearlie,
> The pearl o' all the painter folk was surely Mr. Nerli.
> He took a thraw to paint mysel, he painted late and early:
> O wow! the mony a yawn I've yawned in the beard of Mr. Nerli!

A "ferlie" is a wonder or marvel.[24]

When uninvited visitors found their way to Vailima, Fanny knew how to deflect them. One group took her for a native, due to her casual dress and dark complexion, and called out, "Is this Vailima? Are Mr. and Mrs. Stevenson at home?" "With great presence of mind," Belle remembered, "my mother answered, 'No spik English.'" When Louis began studying the Samoan language he was delighted to learn that the verb *alovao* "is used in the sense of 'to avoid visitors,' but it means literally 'hide in the wood.'"[25]

CORRESPONDENCE

Much of Louis's spare time was taken up with correspondence. On a single day he dictated six letters to Belle that fill nine pages in the closely printed modern edition. She grew accustomed to inserting comments of her own in parentheses. When he mentioned to Colvin that he was dictating to his amanuensis she added, "Such an amanuensis!!" In a letter to J. M. Barrie, a newly acquired correspondent, Louis claimed that Belle was "believed on the beach to be my illegitimate daughter by a Morocco woman. When we wish to please her we say she is slender. Rich dark color; taken in Sydney for an islander. Eyes enormous and particoloured, one three-fifths brown, the other two-fifths golden." Belle, taking dictation, wrote this down herself. At another time she said, "When he talks about old days in Morocco he is magnificent. He tells me long tales about my mother which invariably wind up with 'She was a damned fine woman!'"[26]

When Belle wasn't available, Louis admitted that his own handwriting wasn't very legible—"I shall probably regret tomorrow having written you with my own hand like the Apostle Paul." One of the epistles ends, "The salutation of me Paul with mine own hand."[27]

There was fan mail to answer, which Louis did dutifully except when his name was misspelled. Belle noted, "Letters that come spelling his name with a ph, or 'Step Henson' as he calls it, are torn up in wrath." As for friends, there was a steady stream of letters to Colvin, but usually not very personal since they were intended to be the basis of his projected book on the Pacific. On one occasion Louis told Colvin, "I breakfasted and read (with indescribable sinkings) the whole of yesterday's work, before the sun had risen. Then I sat and thought, and sat and better thought. It was not good enough, nor good; it was as slack as journalism, but not so inspired; it was excellent stuff misused, and the defects stood gross on it like humps upon a camel." After Louis's death Colvin would stitch together excerpts from these letters as *In the South Seas*.[28]

There were regular letters to Baxter about the finances for which he was the faithful custodian. Louis also expressed concern for a depression into which Baxter was sliding. In 1892 Baxter told him,

> My dear Louis, you may remember this accursed abode of sin and misery; think of me still wandering about it. Alas I am indeed a Wearywald: I care for nobody and nobody cares for me. Edinburgh does me harm; I am never well in it; the one earthly happiness I can think of is to look for the last time upon its walls. As a memory it would be charming; as a reality it leads, I am afraid, only to drink or the Private Asylum or both.

Baxter was recalling a truculent little poem by Burns that concludes "Naebody cares for me, I care for naebody." The implications of "Wearywald" seem clear enough, but the word does not appear in the *OED*. Perhaps that was a character in a story they knew, or an invented term shared by themselves. As for drink, Baxter was becoming an alcoholic. Gosse encountered him at the Savile Club in London "bestially drunk.[29]

In the next year Baxter's wife died, and the best Louis could offer was clichés: "My dear fellow, you have my most earnest sympathy in your bereavement. I never really knew, but always heartily respected and admired your wife, as a handsome gallant honest woman of whom anyone might be proud." Fanny wrote more feelingly,

> My dear Charles, any form of words that I could use seem to me no more than a mockery. I know in my heart that there is no consolation for such a loss; it is the tearing up of the roots of life. I find that I can say nothing. Only this, dear friend, come to us if you can. At least it would be a break and a change. You and Colvin are the last of Louis's old friends, all that is left of his youth. I cannot think that you know how dear you are to us and how we long to have you here. Do try and come.

A year and a half later Baxter would indeed set out for Samoa, but too late. While he was on the way, the roots of Fanny's life would be torn up by Louis's death.[30]

Henry James, as always, was the most sympathetic of Louis's correspondents. As early as 1890 he grasped that there was never going to be a return to Britain, and was disgusted when other members of Louis's old circle claimed that the only place for him was Britain. He wrote to Colvin, "How can one grudge his really *living*—with such an apparent plenitude of physical life, no matter how literature suffers?" To Louis himself James wrote,

Until a few days ago I hugged the soft illusion that by the time anything else would reach you, you would already have started for England. This fondest of the hopes of all of us has been shattered in a manner to which history furnishes a parallel only in the behaviour of its most famous coquettes and courtesans. You are indeed the male Cleopatra or buccaneering Pompadour of the Deep—the wandering Wanton of the Pacific.

James thanked Louis for "the beautiful strange things you sent me which make for ever in my sky-parlour [garret] a sort of dim rumble as of the Pacific surf. My heart beats over them—my imagination throbs—my eyes fill."[31]

James and Louis regularly sent each other their latest writing, and exchanged generous comments. Louis especially enjoyed a story entitled "The Marriages," which relates the experiences of an extremely self-centered young woman named Adela Chart, and sent James "A Sublime Poem":

> Adela, Adela, Adela Chart,
> What have you done to my elderly heart?
> Of all the ladies of paper and ink
> I count you the paragon, call you the pink....
> I pore on you, dote on you, clasp you to heart,
> I laud, love, and laugh at you, Adela Chart;
> But to read of, depicted by exquisite James,
> O, sure you're the flower and quintessence of dames.

As is usual with James, no one in the story ever says what he or she really means, let alone thinks. Everything is indirect and subtle in a way that's totally different from Louis's own style, and it's impressive that he could appreciate "The Marriages" as wholeheartedly as James appreciated *Treasure Island*.[32]

J. M. Barrie, later to be famous for *Peter Pan,* was a fellow Scot ten years younger than Louis. Barrie's letters were recently discovered in the Stevenson collection at Yale where they had been somehow misplaced. When Barrie sent a fan letter in 1892 Louis replied, "Two men who had used the dreadful lavatory at Edinburgh University, though they never met, could never quite be strangers." They found that they shared a sense of humor, and Barrie imagined what would happen if he were to visit Samoa. The family would be shocked to discover what a boring guest they had on their hands:

> RLS.   He has arrived. I have put him into a bedroom. I advised him to rest for a bit—for as long as he could.

MRS. RLS. What did he say?

RLS. He said "H'm." He has been saying that all the way up from the boat.

MRS. RLS. How did he strike you on the whole?

RLS. (glumly) Perhaps he will improve after he has rested a bit. I told him he would have to be tattooed before dinner.

MRS. RLS. What did he say?

RLS. H'm.[33]

THE WRITER AT WORK

For Louis the most important thing was protecting blocks of time for his real work. Every morning he put in four hours, starting before the rest of the family was up, and in the afternoon two hours more. For years he had suffered from painful writer's cramp, and Belle continued to write from dictation (she was paid in an account kept by Baxter in Edinburgh, with instructions to invest the money for her). "He usually walked up and down," she recalled, "talking very slowly. Occasionally when he would begin a sentence, and then pause before going on, I would finish it in my mind, even going so far as to write a few words. I never by any chance got it right, for he never said the obvious thing." Since he had always struggled to write legibly, even before the onset of cramp, he seems to have found the process of dictation freeing.[34]

Sometimes he made comments on his method of composition, as Belle recalled.

> I asked Louis, in the course of the conversation this evening, how he defined the word literature. "It is capable of explanation, I think," he said, "when you see words used to the best purpose—no waste, going tight around a subject. . . . I am wrong to liken literature to painting. It is more like music—which is time; painting is space. In music you wind in and out, but always keep in the key; that is, you carry the hearer to the end without letting him drop by the way. It winds around and keeps on. So must words wind around. Organized and packed in a mass as it were, tight with words. Not too short—phrases rather—no word to spare."[35]

Music was in fact very important to Louis, and for relaxation he played his beloved flageolet, a simple instrument related to the recorder and the tin whistle. A photograph (fig. 81) shows him in bed with a musical score on his knees and a mosquito net pulled back above him. His playing was generally deplored.

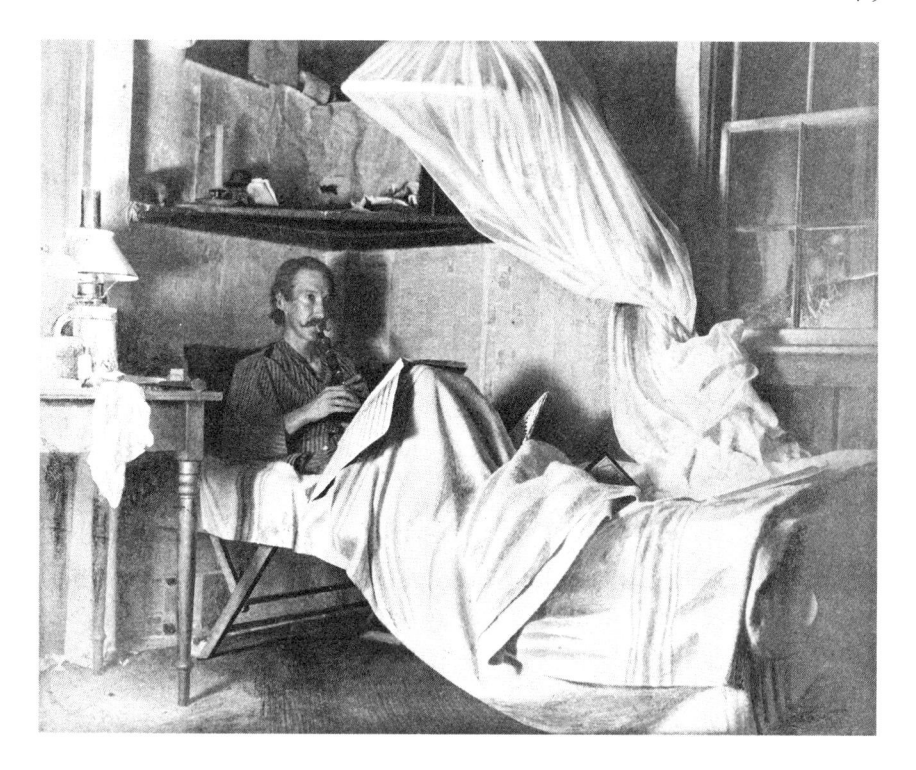

81. Louis with his flageolet

At one point he commented, "I have found my music better qualified to scatter than to collect an audience." Harry Moors said that "he played so dolefully upon the instrument as to be a menace to one's enjoyment of life"; and Lloyd's reminiscence, though affectionate, was pitying:

> There is an unconscious pathos in Stevenson's fondness for his flageolet. He played it so badly, so haltingly, and, as his letters show, he was always poking fun at himself in regard to it. It was amazing the amount of pleasure he got out of the effort. The doleful, whining little instrument was one of his most precious relaxations. The most familiar sound in Vailima was that strange wailing and squeaking that floated down to us from his study.

Though he had little musical talent, Louis sent for printed scores by Chopin, Beethoven, and many others, and "would pore over them for hours at a time, trying here and there, and with endless repetitions, to elucidate them with his flageolet."[36]

Up until this time, Belle acknowledged, "there had always been a hidden antagonism between us. Perhaps because I had adored my father I was unconsciously critical of him." Now, however, "I felt myself to be truly his loving daughter." She was amused by Louis's habit of acting out as he dictated. When he was beginning a novel (never finished) entitled *St. Ives*,

> He quite unconsciously acted the part of his characters. He slouched as the drover, giving even the punctuation marks in a broad Highland accent. He tossed his head as the old lady, and when he was [the Frenchman] St. Ives he put on a gallant swagger, twirled his mustache, and bowed as he dictated a florid compliment. Once, seeing me try to suppress a smile, he pulled up short and laughed. He lived his characters, he explained, and if he once discovered they were only ink on paper he would be unable to go on with them.

At another time Belle did burst into laughter, as she was transcribing a letter in which he commented, "She has a growing conviction that she is the author of my works."[37]

A print (fig. 82) shows Louis in his study, the enclosed room on the second floor of the veranda, dictating to Belle. He is wearing the bright red sash with which he liked to appear in public, and custom-made boots from Sydney which, as Lloyd remembered, "fitted his long, slender, aristocratic feet to perfection." The print was adapted from a (rather blurry) photograph, and no doubt the sash and boots were worn for the occasion of having his portrait taken. Normally he would have dressed more informally, and with no shoes at all.[38]

He had always been partial to red sashes, mentioning in *An Inland Voyage* that French children "could not make enough of my red sash," and in Polynesia was delighted to find that it was a sign of special distinction. A missionary who sent one to a museum in England explained that it denoted "the most honourable appellation which a king could receive, *Arii maro Ura,* King of the Red Sash."[39]

Bookcases, only partly visible here, lined three sides of the room. They contained the Skelt's Juvenile Drama series that Louis had adored as a child, classic and recent English poets, a large number of miscellaneous histories and novels, books on the Pacific, and the complete works of Balzac, Hugo, Scott, and Dickens. He ordered books constantly, mentioning in 1891 titles that included Plato, Montaigne (an old favorite), Flaubert, Meredith, Taine, and Kipling, whose career was just beginning. He also read books by both James brothers, Henry's *The Tragic Muse* and William's *Principles of Psychology,* as well as his friend Gosse's *Father and Son.*[40]

82. Belle taking dictation

Fanny remained the sternest critic of Louis's writing. A sketch by Belle (fig. 83) shows "the critic on the hearth listening to the reading of *St. Ives.*"

Unfortunately, Louis felt intense pressure to turn out material for income, which had not been the case in earlier years when his expenses were moderate and parental assistance adequate. Most of his inheritance had been sunk into the Pacific cruises and Vailima, and since its crops wouldn't be profitable for years, if ever, solvency depended on the sale of his writing. Years later Moors told an inquirer that Louis, "a sick man, was the work horse supporting with difficulty, and in a trembling way, the whole expense of a large household of idling adults—Human Sponges." What Louis didn't discover until much later was that Moors systematically overcharged him for the supplies he provided, no doubt as the normal way of doing business in the South Seas.[41]

Baxter, faithfully managing Louis's affairs, wrote in 1892, "My trouble is that there will require to be a very large production to keep up present expenditure, and that is of course a matter of health. It cannot be imprudent to overhaul all unnecessary expense and get the place as soon as possible into a source of profit. This is not Preaching. It is only the Prudent Forelock of the Painful Doer." A "doer" was the normal Scottish term for a business agent; Baxter was using "painful" playfully in its old sense of painstaking, laborious.[42]

83. Fanny, sketched by Belle

The financial pressure had serious consequences for Louis's writing. The need to maximize income forced him to write fast, which he always hated, and to calculate what he wrote for sales. His best work had always come in moments of inspiration—*Treasure Island, Jekyll and Hyde, Kidnapped,* and stories like "Thrawn Janet" and "The Merry Men." But in striving to appeal to the market he had already produced a number of inferior books—*The Black Arrow, Prince Otto, New Arabian Nights,* and *More New Arabian Nights.* He had had higher hopes for *The Master of Ballantrae,* begun in Saranac Lake and finished in Tahiti, but freely admitted that the second half, written hastily, was not very good.

TALES OF THE SOUTH SEAS

Soon after settling at Vailima Louis began working on a series of stories set in the Pacific. After publication in serial form they were collected in 1893 as *Island Nights' Entertainments,* a nod to the earlier *New Arabian Nights.*

Two were brief fables, "The Isle of Voices" and "The Bottle Imp." A third, "The Beach of Falesá," is altogether realistic, and reflects a deepening grasp of the relations between native islanders and the white men who had arrived to exploit them.

"The Isle of Voices" draws upon Polynesian tales of the supernatural. A young Hawaiian marries the daughter of a sorcerer, and discovers that her father's wealth comes from traveling by magic to an island whose beach is covered with shells that turn into silver dollars after he burns certain leaves. When he goes there he is alarmed by invisible devils: "All about him as he went the voices talked and whispered, and the little fires sprang up and burned down. All tongues of the earth were spoken there; the French, the Dutch, the Russian, the Tamil, the Chinese." He and his wife grab some money and return to Hawaii, where they enjoy their magically obtained wealth. It has been suggested that this tale can be read as an allegory of the commercialized Pacific, with a cacophony of alien voices and foreign wizards who transform leaves into dollars.[43]

In "The Bottle Imp," an uncanny bottle has a spirit inside, and whoever buys it can have as many wishes as he likes, but there's a catch. If he should happen to die before selling the bottle to someone else, he will be tortured forever in hell; also, he must sell it for less than he originally paid. A young Hawaiian couple fall in love, manage to get rid of the bottle in time, and live happily ever after.

A missionary friend of Louis's asked permission to translate "The Bottle Imp" into Samoan, and Louis was surprised to discover that readers thought the story was true. He complained, "I get such a lot of Samoan visitors who stay a long time, keeping me from my work, and when I am obliged to excuse myself they shyly ask if they might just have a peep at the Imp himself before they go away. They think I keep him in my safe." Graham Balfour noted that Samoans couldn't understand where Louis's money came from, since writing on sheets of paper seemed unproductive, and they believed that the magic bottle must be the source of his wealth.[44]

As late as the 1930s these stories were sufficiently well known that P. G. Wodehouse could drop an allusion into one of his Blandings Castle novels: "He took his departure with feelings resembling those of the man who got rid of the Bottle Imp."[45]

"The Beach of Falesá" is a more ambitious tale, almost a novella in length. The idea for it came to Louis while he was hacking at vines in the forest—"a new story which just shot through me like a bullet in one of my moments of awe, alone in that tragic jungle." An English trader named Wiltshire marries an island woman, survives a murderous attack by a rival, and settles down to raise a family in the fictional island of Falesá.

Louis's intention was to show that despite genuinely loving his wife and children, Wiltshire can't escape the racist assumptions of his class and time. He told Colvin, who disapproved of the character, "I think you seem scarcely fair to Wiltshire, who had surely, under his beastly ignorant ways, right noble qualities. And I think perhaps you scarce do justice to the fact that this is a piece of realism *à outrance* [to the limit], nothing extenuated or adorned." Realism of that kind was just what Louis had always deplored in the past, but experience had taught him to deromanticize the South Seas.[46]

One other novel from this period, written on and off with Lloyd between 1889 and 1891, was called *The Wrecker*. A powerful experiment but uneven and episodic, it's the story of sailors who murder the crew of a shipwrecked vessel in order to get the treasure it's carrying, in an appalling bloodbath with which the story ends. Reviewers were shocked. Margaret Oliphant said that the episode leaves the reader "with the scent of sickening blood and disgust in his nostrils rather than a sublime horror in his mind." That was undoubtedly the intention. *The Wrecker* exposes atavistic cruelty that may lurk in apparently ordinary people, and also the provocations for cruelty in the colonial hinterland from which "civilized" European countries got their wealth.[47]

Writing to Will Low (who was the model for one of the characters), Louis said that his goal was to dramatize the modern ethos of "barbaric manners and unstable morals, full of the need and the lust of money, so that there is scarce a page in which the dollars do not jingle; full of the unrest and movement of our century, so that the reader is hurried from place to place and sea to sea, and the book is less a romance than a panorama—in the end, as blood-bespattered as an epic." The ending of the story, he told James with satisfaction, was "one of the most genuine butcheries in literature."[48]

The Wrecker turned out to be immensely profitable, which is why it was written in the first place. *Scribner's* paid the munificent sum of $15,000 to serialize it in twelve parts, beginning in August 1891; they also brought it out in book form, as did Cassell in England. Readers loved it at the time, but not many have since then.

BALLADS

During his cruises Louis became fascinated with Polynesian legends, and based two long poems on them, "The Song of Rahéro: A Legend of Tahiti" and "The Feast of Famine: Marquesan Manners." Together they fill forty-five pages in *Collected Poems*. He thought highly of these poems and was chagrined, when they were published in 1890, to find that he was the only one who did.

At the time there was a fad for ballads that invoked old traditions from a modern perspective, or highlighted aspects of life that "high" poetry had tended to ignore—Kipling's *Barrack-Room Ballads,* for example, published in 1892. What turned out to be problematic was the relaxed, long-line style that Louis chose, entirely different from the tautness of traditional British ballads.

> It fell in the days of old, as the men of Taiárapu tell,
> A youth went forth to the fishing, and fortune favored him well.
> Támatéa his name: gullible, simple, and kind. . . .
> Alone from the sea and the fishing came Támatéa the fair,
> Urging his boat to the beach, and the mother awaited him there.[49]

After reading reviews of the ballads Louis wrote to Gosse, "By the by, my *Ballads* seem to have been dam bad; all the crickets sing so in their crickety papers; and I have no ghost of an idea on the point myself. Verse is always to me the unknowable." Gosse himself was one of the crickets, writing to a friend, "The effort to become a Polynesian Walter Scott is a little too obvious, the inspiration a little too mechanical. And—between you and me and Lake Michigan—the versification is atrocious." Actually the verse is reminiscent not so much of Scott's style as of Longfellow's in *Evangeline* and *Hiawatha.*[50]

To another correspondent Louis said gloomily, "Glad the ballads amused you. They failed to entertain a coy public, at which I wondered. Not that I set much account by my verses, which are the verses of a Prosator; but I do know how to tell a yarn, and two of the yarns were great." Not in verse they weren't. The poet Edwin Morgan explains why: "He writes in a long rough lolloping rhyming couplet which quickly becomes tedious in a lengthy narrative poem. It is obvious that his wonderful command of narrative movement in prose fiction misled him into thinking that poetry presented no special problem if you wanted to tell a story in verse; but of course it does, as even a minor cricket could have told him." So, one might have thought, could the poet who wrote *A Child's Garden of Verses.*[51]

Henry James, tactful but candid, urged Louis to stick to the genres that best suited his gifts. The ballads, he said, "show your 'cleverness,' but they don't show your genius. Behold I *am* launching across the black seas a page that may turn nasty—but my dear Louis, it's only because I love so your divine prose and want the comfort of it. Things are various because we do 'em. We mustn't do 'em because they're various."[52]

From now on Louis would indeed concentrate on prose fiction. He would produce another major novel, *Catriona,* and at the time of his death would be well embarked on *Weir of Hermiston,* which promised to be his finest novel of all.

CHAPTER 31

Missionaries, Chiefs, and Bureaucrats

RELIGION

Westerners took pride in bringing faith to the heathen in the Pacific; that was often invoked as their principal justification for being there. By the Stevensons' time, missionaries were ubiquitous, distributed variously by denomination depending on the region. Maps were published that indicated the predominant territories of Catholics, Congregationalists, United Presbyterians, Free Church of Scotland, Wesleyans, Baptists, and Mormons. In Samoa a minority were Catholics, but the dominant group was the "L.M.S," the interdenominational London Missionary Society.[1]

During the cruises on the *Casco, Equator,* and *Janet Nicholl,* Louis had formed a negative view of missionaries as moralistic bullies, but in Samoa he got to know a number of them well and gained great respect. They were less dogmatic theologically than he had been led to expect, and in fact took a deep interest in native beliefs and did pioneering work in ethnography. They knew and understood the people much better than foreign bureaucrats did, who didn't bother to learn the language and were regularly rotated in and out of Samoa.

In 1892 Louis told a journalist, "Missions in the South Seas generally are far the most pleasing result of the presence of white men; and those in Samoa are the best I have ever seen." He especially admired William Clarke, who had mistaken the family for traveling entertainers when he first saw them on the Apia beach. Louis wrote to Colvin, "The excellent Clarke was up here almost all day yesterday, a man I esteem and like to the soles of his boots; indeed, I prefer him to any man in Samoa and to most people in the world."[2]

Many of the missionaries were fluent in Samoan, and one of them, who gave Louis regular lessons, recalled that Louis "thought the language was wonderful. The extent of the vocabulary, the delicate differences of form and expressive shades of meaning, the wonderful varieties of the pronouns and particles astonished him." The point is striking: he liked language to be complex.[3]

The division between Catholics and Protestants was evident but not hostile, and there were adherents of both at Vailima (the Catholics were known as Popies). Louis's closest missionary friends were Protestants, but he was fond of Catholic priests as well. "He had a special admiration," Graham Balfour said, "for the way in which they identified themselves with the natives and encouraged all native habits and traditions at all compatible with Christianity." Also, he enjoyed speaking French with them.[4]

At one point Louis's friend Adelaide Boodle wrote from Bournemouth to say that she was considering a trip to Samoa but had been urged to avoid places that had no Anglican clergy, presumably because she wouldn't be able to take Communion in the authorized way. Louis replied, "Christ himself and the twelve apostles seem to me to have gone through this rough world without the support of the Anglican communion. I am pained that a friend of mine should conceive life so smally as to think she leaves the hand of her God because she leaves a certain clique of clergymen and a certain scattered handful of stone buildings, some of them with pointed windows, most with belfries, and a few with an illumination of the Ten Commandments on the wall."[5]

As Louis had discovered in Tahiti, islanders might embrace conversion but continue to hold on quietly to their old beliefs. "We may see the difficulty in its highest terms," he wrote in his notebook, "when a missionary asks a savage if he believes it is the virtuous who are to be happiest in a future state, and receives an affirmative reply. The good man is much pleased with such incipient orthodoxy, while all the time they have been juggling with each other with misunderstood symbols. The missionary had Christian virtue in his mind, while the Tupinamba [an Amazon tribe] means by the virtuous 'those who have well revenged themselves and eaten many of their enemies.'"[6]

One of Louis's unpublished fables, "Something in It," explores the mutual incomprehension of belief systems. A missionary violates a native taboo and is carried off by a spirit to be baked and devoured. As a preliminary step he is required to drink ritual kava, which he refuses on the grounds that it is intoxicating and therefore forbidden. He is asked, "Are you going to respect a taboo at a time like this? And you were always so opposed to taboos when you were alive!" He replies, "To other people's. Never to my own." He is thereupon sent back to the world of the living, as unqualified to enter the spirit world. "'I seem to have been misinformed upon some points,' said he. 'Perhaps there is not much in it, as I supposed; but there is something in it after all. Let me be glad of that.'" The taboo and the missionary's rules, Roslyn Jolly says, "are utterly alien to each other, equally valid, with neither able to command universal authority."[7]

Well-meaning and sympathetic though individual missionaries might be, they were still complicit in the deployment of Christianity as an agent of imperialism. Louis would probably have appreciated Jomo Kenyatta's comment in twentieth-century Kenya: "When the missionaries arrived, the Africans had the land and the missionaries had the Bible. They taught us how to pray with our eyes closed. When we opened them, they had the land and we had the Bible."

GEOPOLITICS IN MINIATURE

Before he traveled in the Pacific Louis had never taken much interest in politics. After his youthful flirtation with socialism he regarded himself as a conservative, though with unusual sympathy for the poor and downtrodden, and believed that schemes for social change were likely to make things worse instead of better. He also approved heartily of Britain's imperial role. When a book on the subject was published in 1883 he had called it "a gem," and agreed with the author's claim that he was "divining the destiny which is reserved for us." Now, however, he became sensitized to the exploitation of established cultures by imperialism, whether overt or covert.[8]

In 1890 Samoa was nominally independent, but three so-called "Great Powers" were competing for commercial control; it was their warships that had been wrecked in the recent typhoon and still clogged the harbor when the Stevensons arrived. These powers have been well described as "newly imperialistic Germany, sluggishly imperialistic Britain, and sporadically imperialistic America." In 1889 the Treaty of Berlin attempted to stabilize the situation by creating a chief justice jointly appointed by the foreign powers, who would somehow cooperate with the consuls of all three, as well as with a native king whose authority was dependent on their support. Such an unwieldly system was almost certain to be unworkable.[9]

Louis found it fascinating to see political struggle playing out on a miniature scale, and he began to fantasize about getting involved himself. Many Samoan

84. Louis with Tuimale Alifono

chiefs regarded him as a valuable adviser; Italo Calvino suggests that he became their *consigliere*. An attractive picture shows Louis posing with a chief named Tuimale Alifono (fig. 84), who is wearing a ceremonial jacket and lava-lava. Louis is dressed in his usual costume as laird of Vailima: white shirt, red necktie and sash, tailored cord riding breeches, and leather riding boots. Gosse remembered that when he met Louis for the first time in the Hebrides, he already had "the little tricks with which we were later on to grow familiar—the advance with hand on hip, the sidewise bending of the head to listen."[10]

Ten years previously Louis had said, with no particular cause in mind, that a writer should strive "in some small measure to protect the oppressed and to defend the truth." Now he believed he had a chance to do it. He wrote excitedly to his New York publisher, who was still expecting a travelogue about the South Seas, "Here is for the first time since the Greeks (that I remember) the history of a handful of men, where all know each other in the eyes and live close in a few acres, narrated at length and with the seriousness of history. Talk of the modern novel; here is a modern history." As Homer made the Trojan War come alive by focusing on individuals, so Louis aspired to do with Samoa.[11]

He supported the cause of Samoan independence by exploiting his celebrity to publish lengthy analyses in the *London Times,* eight in all from 1891 to 1894. On these the *Times* commented editorially, "Mr. Stevenson has been only too completely justified by the story of bureaucratic blindness, pompous inefficiency, and financial disaster told in the official record." A few weeks before that the foreign secretary, Lord Rosebery, remarked in a speech that when he was following international events, "I can transfer myself to the Southern Pacific, where three of the greatest States in the world are endeavouring, not always with apparent success, to administer one of the smallest islands—the island of Samoa—in close conjunction and alliance with one of our most brilliant men of letters."[12]

In 1892 Louis also published a book, *A Footnote to History,* using documents and personal interviews to trace the course of recent events. "The material for this," Harry Moors said, "was largely supplied by myself, and for the most part the book was written in my house." All the same, Louis soon found out, as every historian must, that eyewitness testimony may not be reliable, and that motives may remain concealed forever. At one point he wrote, "The history of the month of August [1888] is unknown to whites; it passed altogether in the covert of the woods or in the stealthy councils of Samoans." And even though he was trusted much more than most foreigners by the Samoans, he had to admit that he was still one of them: "Foreigners in these islands know little of the course of native intrigue. Partly the Samoans cannot explain, partly they will not tell." A reviewer in the *Athenaeum* described his book as "the spectacle of a master of fiction struggling, on the whole successfully, with the trammels of fact."[13]

What comes through most clearly in Louis's book is a traditional culture infested and exploited by foreigners. His Pacific travels had inspired warm appreciation of Polynesians and their culture, and now he wrote that in Apia, "the handful of whites have everything; the natives walk in a foreign town. Here, then, is a singular state of affairs: all the money, luxury, and business of the kingdom [are] centred in one place; that place excepted from the native government and administered by whites for whites; and the whites themselves holding it not in common but in hostile camps, so that it lies between them like a bone between two dogs, each growling, each clutching his own end."[14]

The modest title of *A Footnote to History* acknowledged that these remote islands might seem trivial on the world stage, but Louis believed that their story illuminated what was happening all over the globe as Europeans competed for territorial control if not outright colonization. The United States would soon follow the Europeans, acquiring Hawaii, Puerto Rico, and the Philippines before the end of the decade; in 1904 the eastern Samoan islands would become (as they still are) American Samoa.

The twenty Samoan islands—half of which are small and have never been inhabited—had no central government, and there were nearly fifty chiefs scattered through them in a system somewhat similar to the clans of the Scotland. One chief at a given time would be accorded honorary status as the Malietoa, or "highest name," but the title was not hereditary, and he was nothing like a king in a European sense. Louis wrote, "I cannot find but what the president of a college debating society is a far more formidable officer." It suited the "Great Powers," however, to describe their chosen candidate as king, while controlling him through the system of overlapping judges and administrators.[15]

When Louis settled at Vailima there were three principal rivals for the title of Malietoa, and he chose to side with Mata'afa (fig. 85), whom he described as "a beautiful, sweet old fellow." Mata'afa had led a failed armed uprising against Western interference in 1888, and was now living quietly in his village of Malie to the west of Apia. "He sits nightly at home before a semicircle of talking men from many quarters of the islands, delivering and hearing those ornate and elegant orations in which the Samoan heart delights. About himself and all his surroundings there breathes a striking sense of order, tranquility, and native plenty. He is of a tall and powerful person, sixty years of age, white-haired and with a white moustache; his eyes bright and quiet." It was beneath a chief's dignity to speak in public, so a "talking man" did that on his behalf.[16]

Louis's friends in Britain found it hard to sympathize with his enthusiasm for what they regarded as mere local politics. Colvin complained that his letters were too full of "your beloved blacks—or chocolates—confound them. Please let us have a letter or two with something besides native politics, prisons, kava feasts, and such things as our Cockney stomachs can ill assimilate." Louis replied,

85. Mata'afa

"If I were to do as you propose, in a bit of a tiff, it would cut you entirely off from my life. You must try to exercise a trifle of imagination, and put yourself, perhaps with an effort, into some sort of sympathy with these people, or how am I to write to you? I think you are truly a little too Cockney with me." Colvin apologized.[17]

Colvin was no Cockney, but as Roslyn Jolly notes, the term was a pointed reproach. "Which is more parochial, the Cockney or the Samoan? Stevenson's point is that parochialism is not born of any particular place, but of an unwillingness to move imaginatively beyond that place." Also, in Britain politics had seemed abstract and remote; here he could see it play out among individuals whom he knew personally.[18]

In any case his real concern was not with politics as such, but with the economic and cultural imperialism it fronted for. His goal, he told an interviewer, was to depict "the unjust (yet I can see the inevitable) extinction of the Polynesian islanders by our shabby civilization." And for a while it was exhilarating to be immersed in intrigue. A friend of his exclaimed, "I never saw so good a place as this Apia; you can be in a new conspiracy every day!" In 1892 he wrote to Henry James, "Say what you please, it has been a deeply interesting time. You don't know what news is, nor what politics, nor what the life of man, till you see it on so small a scale and with your own liberty on the board for stake. I would not have missed it for much. And anxious friends beg me to stay at home and study human nature in Brompton drawing rooms!"[19]

One feature of world politics on this tiny scale was that everybody knew everybody, and Louis often mixed socially with the very people he was campaigning against. For example, he was sharply critical of Conrad Cedercrantz, an ineffectual young Swede who had recently been installed as chief justice, yet when they ran into each other at a ball, "We exchanged a glance, and then a grin; the rogue took me in his confidence; and through the remainder of that prance, we pranced for each other. Hard to imagine any position more ridiculous: a week before he had been trying to rake up evidence against me by browbeating and threatening a half-white interpreter; that very morning I had been writing most villainous attacks upon him for the *Times;* and we meet and smile, and— damn it! like each other."[20]

The most powerful entity in Samoa was the German Firm, as it was generally known—the Deutsche Handels und Plantagen Gesellschaft für Sud-See Inseln zu Hamburg, which inspired the nickname "the Long Handle firm" (*Handel* means "trade"). Louis described it as "the head of the boil of which Samoa languishes." It played an active role in Germany's campaign to control trade all over the Pacific, with an emphasis in Samoa on coffee and copra. There it exploited the forced labor of eight hundred workers who had been kidnapped from their native Melanesia. Melanesians were much darker-skinned than Samoans; the practice of kidnapping them from their home islands was known as "blackbirding."[21]

Increasingly, Louis had to acknowledge that anything he could do was useless. As early as 1891 he was telling Colvin, "The sense of my helplessness here has been rather bitter; I feel it wretched to see this dance of folly and injustice and unconscious rapacity go forward from day to day, and to be impotent." It's not clear what he meant by "unconscious" rapacity—perhaps that exploitation was taken so much for granted that the foreigners regarded it as simply their right. A year and a half later he called politics "the dirtiest, the most foolish, and the most random of human employments." He was no longer invoking Homeric Greeks.[22]

In 1893 fighting broke out among the rival chiefs; one of them was Mata'afa. Louis was predictably excited, stockpiling weapons for the defense of his family; in the picture that shows him dictating to Belle (fig. 82 in chapter 30 above), six pistols are mounted on the wall. It was an opportunity to play at war games in reality. Only later did he learn that the rival chiefs had placed a mutual taboo on Vailima that would preserve it from attack.

Margaret wrote reassuringly to her sister Jane, "You must not be alarmed; war is very different here to what we are accustomed to think it, or to what I fear it still is in the remoter and more savage islands. Here it is more like a sort of tournament, and very few lives are ever lost. If a band of fighting men should come to Vailima, all that they would expect of us would be that we should kill some pigs and give them a good meal."[23]

Still, it's startling to find Louis declaring, "We have been so long used in Europe to that dreary business of war on the great scale, trailing epidemics and leaving pestilential corpses in its train, that we have almost forgotten its original, the most healthful, if not the most humane, of all field sports—hedge-warfare." How could human beings killing each other, on however small a scale, be a healthful field sport?[24]

As it turned out, Mata'afa's warriors were beaten, and the heads of fifteen men were delivered to his victorious rival. When Louis heard about that he reacted with a bizarre statement, as if murderous fighting was still the fantasy play of Skelt's Juvenile Drama and the toy soldiers at Davos. He wrote to Colvin, "A man brought in a head to [the village of] Mulinuu in great glory; they washed the black paint off, and behold! it was his brother [i.e., the brother of the messenger who brought it]. When I last heard he was sitting in his house, with the head upon his lap, and weeping. Barbarous war is an ugly business, but I believe the civilized is fully uglier; but Lord! what fun!"[25]

What made war worse was that the fighters on both sides were pawns in the foreign powers' game. One day the family on the veranda listened to British warships shelling an inland village:

> The hills and my house, at less than (boom) a minute's interval, quake with thunder; and although I cannot hear that part of it, shells are falling thick into the fort of Latuanuu (it is my friends of the *Curaçao,* the *Adler,*

and the *Bussard* bombarding (after all these—boom—months) the rebels of Atua. (Boom-boom.) It is most distracting in itself, and the thought of the poor devils in their fort (boom) with their bits of rifles far from pleasant. (Boom-boom.)

The Stevensons often mingled with the sailors from HMS *Curaçao*, "a very nice ship." Louis had recently traveled in it to some nearby islands.[26]

The shelling brings to mind Conrad's *Heart of Darkness*, published five years after Louis's death: "Once, I remember, we came upon a man-of-war anchored off the coast. There wasn't even a shed there, and she was shelling the bush. . . . There was a touch of insanity in the proceeding, a sense of lugubrious drollery in the sight; and it was not dissipated by somebody on board assuring me earnestly there was a camp of natives—he called them enemies!—hidden out of sight somewhere."[27]

After Mata'afa's defeat he was deported to Jaluit, a German-controlled island in the Marshalls twenty-three hundred miles away. For Samoans, banishment to a strange place was felt as a disaster. A number of chiefs who had been allied with him were locked up in the Apia jail. That was humiliating, but not as onerous as might be supposed. The prisoners were frequently allowed out to visit their families, and on one occasion Louis was thanked for his help by a feast in his honor—held in the jail. J. C. Furnas commented sixty years later, "This sounds bizarre only to those unacquainted with Polynesia."[28]

In September 1894 the imprisoned chiefs were released, due at least in part to Louis's appeal to the authorities on their behalf. He told Colvin that nine of them came up to Vailima and declared that they would express their thanks by improving the road from Apia. Belle added in a parenthesis in this letter that when their "talking man," after the usual formal preliminaries, "came on the object of their visit—on their love and gratitude to Tusitala, how his name was always in their prayers, and his goodness to them when they had no other friend was their most cherished memory—he warmed up to real burning genuine feeling. I had never seen the Samoan mask of reserve laid aside before, and it touched me more than anything else."

Louis resumed the letter to Colvin and said that what was extraordinary was their volunteering "to execute a thing that was never before heard of in Samoa. Think of it! It is road-making—the most fruitful cause (after taxes) of all rebellions in Samoa, a thing to which they could not be wiled with money nor driven by punishment. It does give one a sense of having done something in Samoa after all."[29]

The chiefs set to work on improving the road, only a crude trail until then, and as a further sign of gratitude and respect did it with their own hands; they asked only for the loan of tools. They gave the road the Samoan name Alo Loto Alofa, usually translated as the Road of the Loving Hearts, but sometimes with "heart" in the singular, which would then refer to Louis rather than to the chiefs. Actually it could mean either: a literal translation would be "the Road of Love."[30]

CHAPTER 32

The End of Paradise

FAMILY FRICTION

By the time the family had lived at Vailima for a year, temperamental differences as well as financial anxiety were dispelling the dream of tropical paradise. Visitors at Braemar in the Highlands, where Louis began *Treasure Island,* had commented on the constantly raised voices in the household, and now there were more people doing the shouting. Louis wrote to James in 1891, "I am writing—trying to write—in a Babel fit for the bottomless pit; my wife, her daughter, her grandson, and my mother, all shrieking at each other around the house—not in war, thank God! but the din is ultra martial, and the note of Lloyd joins in occasionally, and the cause of this to-do is simply cacao, whereof chocolate comes."[1]

Two years later, to Colvin: "Person number one takes a tiff against person number two; person number two takes the day out crying; and then person number one, with characteristic generosity, comes to me (whom she has been routing out half an hour before) and is in a dreadful state about person number two, whose condition is entirely of her own making. And my head and heart are totally distraught between the pair of them." The biographer Pope Hennessy suggests that between Fanny's emotional storms and her daughter's growing role as Louis's affectionate amanuensis, "Belle was now really closer to Louis than was her mother." Belle was young and pretty, Fanny was exhausted with overwork as de facto head of the plantation, and although she wouldn't have wanted to take dictation herself, she may have resented Belle's involvement in Louis's writing.[2]

Belle's son Austin was ten when he arrived at Vailima, and Louis undertook

86. "History Lesson," sketched by Belle

to tutor him. A sketch by Belle (fig. 86) shows Louis in full histrionic mode with the boy looking up at him wonderingly. Describing a typical day to Colvin, Louis mentioned that in the morning "Austin comes for his history lecture. This is rather dispiriting because he ain't a bright child."³

Happily his opinion of the boy improved as they spent more time together, and they developed a companionable style of playful teasing. After Austin had been sent to live with Fanny's sister Nellie in California, where he could go to a proper school, Louis sent a letter addressed to "dear General Hoskyns," the name Austin assumed when they were playing war games. He described to Austin how one of his Samoan playmates had behaved when he caught influenza. "'It is all very well,' [the boy] thought, 'to let these childish white people doctor a sore foot or a toothache; but this is serious—I might die of this—for goodness sake, let me get away into a draughty native house, where I can lie in cold gravel, eat green bananas, and have a real, grown-up, tattooed man to raise devils and say charms over me.'" However, when Austin contributed much later to the *Reader's Digest* series "The Most Unforgettable Character I've Met," the subject was not Louis but Fanny.[4]

As for Austin's father Joe, he had always been a parasite, and in 1892 was exposed as a thief. In her journal Fanny recounted what happened:

> We found Joe Strong out in various misdeeds: robbing the cellar and storerooms at night with false keys. In revenge, when he found that he was discovered, he went round to all our friends in Apia and spread slanders about Belle. We turned him away and applied for a divorce for Belle, which was got with no difficulty, as he had been living with a native woman of Apia as his wife ever since he came here. Louis was made sole guardian of the child [Austin], who has been sent to Nellie for school.

Much to the disappointment of the family, in spite of the divorce Joe didn't leave Samoa but stayed on, drinking with the layabouts in Apia. Still worse, there were rumors that he was continuing to tell lies. Louis had been giving him a modest allowance, but this was the last straw, since further payments might look like a response to blackmail. He wrote to the lawyer who was handling the money, "The willingness to continue to help a beaten man is one thing; the slightest appearance of stopping the mouth of a slanderer another." Joe must have deteriorated physically, too. A couple of months later the Stevenson party passed him when they were riding down to a ball at Apia, and Louis commented, "Neither Belle nor I recognized him until he was actually up to us. It is strange, I never recognize him now."[5]

Lloyd, though not a thief, likewise got into trouble with a woman. Louis wrote in guarded terms to Graham Balfour, who was away on his travels at the time, "I think you will scarce have forgotten that there was present in the establishment a young lady, usually attired in orange, whose position had yet to be decided." That was a young Samoan named Sosifina. "Time passed, the young lady was more than ever present with us, and her position was as vague as ever." Louis and Fanny grew concerned about Lloyd's intimacy with her, and after they talked it over, "[Fanny] wrote him a letter, and I a series of queries—both pointing to the idea that if he was not going to marry she couldn't stay here, and if he was going to marry, the sooner the better."[6]

Lloyd declined, and Sosifina was ordered to leave. Years later an American named Katharine Durham married Lloyd, visited Vailima with him, and discovered that Sosifina still regarded herself as his wife. "The poor girl died, after he took me unknowing to Samoa, of her humiliation and grief." Katharine too had been unknowing.[7]

Since Louis and Fanny had lived together before they were married, their ultimatum may seem a hypocritical double standard, but it reflected a clear understanding of Samoan attitudes about sex. Some years ago there was ferocious controversy among anthropologists, prompted by a claim that in her immensely popular *Coming of Age in Samoa* Margaret Mead had been conned by her informants into imagining that the island culture enjoyed free and guiltless sex. Careful studies of the evidence have established that she was never as naïve as that, but she definitely intended a lesson for repressed Americans. Premarital and extramarital sex certainly occurred, but they weren't condoned. After living on a series of islands in the Pacific, Louis wrote, "Samoans are the most chaste of Polynesians." In *The Trashing of Margaret Mead* Paul Shankman reviews the evidence on both sides of the controversy, showing that even the best informed observers bring expectations and biases with them.[8]

Louis was not an anthropologist and never claimed to be. What he did have was deep and genuine sympathy with the people he lived among. After three years in Samoa he commented that what people in Europe called human nature was really a legacy of the Roman Empire, which "made our European human nature what it is." He had learned that human nature could manifest itself very differently in other cultures, and was thinking about what French historians would later call *mentalités*—deeply shared foundational assumptions.[9]

The one resolutely cheerful member of the household was Margaret, but a hint of friction does emerge in a letter Louis wrote to Baxter in 1892. The building program at Vailima showed no signs of slowing down, and vague though he generally was about money, he got alarmed. "Now I seem to be let in for the addition to my house. It is no choice of mine—I dislike it. But Lloyd has no room [i.e., private bedroom], and my mother objected vigorously to any partial improvement."

With her personal inheritance Margaret was the only member of the family who could have contributed financially, but Louis had to push her to do it. Soon afterward he told Baxter,

> At this stage I went out to suggest to my mother that she should write to you about her £500 and found her ungenially vague. It is particularly she

who wants the house [for Lloyd], and I immediately brought her to a more compliant temper by refusing to go on with it unless the £500 was definitely promised for January or February. This she has done, and I hope she can keep her word. The new house is a damn folly and (to me) a damn annoyance, for I wanted a rest and a holiday, which was all planned and has just had to be given up.

It is a reminder of the slowness of communication between Samoa and Britain that Baxter noted receipt of this letter one month later.[10]

At this time there was a flu epidemic. Margaret got alarmed and returned to Edinburgh, ostensibly to get Heriot Row ready to be sold, and was gone for an entire year. She may well have been homesick, and also ready to get away from the tensions at Vailima.

During this period Louis drafted a number of descriptions of family members, with whom he shared them. The most memorable was "My Wife," honoring the qualities for which he loved and admired Fanny:

> Trusty, dusky, vivid, true,
> With eyes of gold and bramble-dew,
> Steel-true and blade-straight,
> The great artificer
> Made my mate.
>
> Honour, anger, valour, fire;
> A love that life could never tire,
> Death quench or evil stir,
> The mighty master
> Gave to her.
>
> Teacher, tender comrade, wife,
> A fellow-farer true through life,
> Heart-whole and soul-free
> The august father
> Gave to me.

When Colvin was preparing to print this poem in *Songs of Travel* a year after Louis's death, he told Gosse that he liked "its strong personal note, but feared it might strike you as ill-written, and even a little ridiculous in its first line."[11]

At a banquet in Apia hosted by their friend Bazzet Haggard, the British land commissioner in Samoa (and brother of the novelist Ryder Haggard), the Stevensons and a visitor from England named Lady Jersey compiled a playful volume entitled *An Object of Pity: or, The Man Haggard* that contained self-portraits by each of the group. This was Louis's, which has already been quoted in part:

> He had earned fame only to despise it, luxury only to discard it—who had fled from the splendours of a suburban residence to toss in the rude trading schooner among uncharted reefs—who had left the saturnalian pleasures of the Athenaeum [Club] to become a dweller in the bush and the counselor of rebel sovereigns, who loved but three things, women, adventure, art—and art the least of these three, and, as men whispered, adventure the most—was he, even he, at ease? His slender fingers plucked at his long mustache; his dark eyes glittered in his narrow, sanguine face; in his mind—the mind of a poet—the oaths of stevedores and coal-porters hurtled.

As Lady Jersey remembered, a garland of flowers was hung around Haggard's neck, a tankard of ale was placed before him, and Belle lay on the ground holding up an apple "while the rest of us knelt or bent in various attitudes of adoration around the erect form and smiling countenance of Haggard."[12]

Fanny's self-portrait is even more striking than Louis's.

> Insolent, arrogant, generous and unjust, this woman was a compound of extremes. One never knew where to have her; she never knew where to have herself. Her mind was a tangle of broken threads that nowhere joined, and not even those who knew her best could guess into what quagmire she next might drag them; for obedience she exacted as a right, and none could stay her hand. Some said she had the evil eye: a suspicion fostered by her keen, direct glance, like one sighting a pistol, and whose aim is deadly. And the island people in her service believed she kept an evil spirit within call, and could read their thoughts like an open book.

She was never a conventional woman, and many men found her alarming. Of course those were the very qualities that Louis loved.

Fanny's portrait of Louis follows.

> A close inspection revealed silver threads in the thinning brown locks, fine lines in the forehead, traced by the inexorable hand of time, deepened, perchance, by the follies of his dissolute early life. And behind the eyes, so velvet soft, burned the fires of hell. Let no one, in fancied security, make the mistake of touching this creature on a sensitive nerve. The

drooping figure springs erect with a tigerish activity; from the lips, apparently formed to sing the praises of fair dames, leaps a torrent of blasphemy and imprecation that might well appall a fishwife, his terrible voice ringing out like the trump of doom, till strong men crawl shuddering from his presence to lie for days on their beds sick and prone, while women, shrieking and laughing in delirium, flee until they fall in their tracks. The name of this singular being was Tusitala, the Writer of Tales.

Two points are especially striking here: Fanny felt free to highlight Louis's mercurial temperament, and both of them were willing to share these trenchant analyses with their fellow guests.[13]

A BREAKDOWN

Though active and energetic, Fanny had always been subject to illnesses that Louis suspected were psychosomatic. "Fanny has been very ill, or I would say so if she were anybody else. But somehow she is such a hand getting diseases and not seeming to be so much the worse for them after all, that whatever she springs upon me, I cannot feel as anxious as I ought."[14]

Still, there is no question that some of the illnesses were very real, and they certainly took a toll on her spirits. During a trip to Hawaii in 1893 Fanny obtained a diagnosis from a prominent physician named George Trousseau. Louis reported to Colvin, "Fanny has Bright's disease; no doubt about it, says Trousseau; and it explains all the symptoms that have perturbed and puzzled us so much. It is not yet bad; and he says she may last twenty years and get no worse; though of course she can never be better. If this is true, I cannot say it is otherwise than a relief; I feared so much worse, and seemed to have cause for it." Bright's disease, today called nephritis, attacks the kidneys; it may indeed be chronic but in acute cases can be fatal.[15]

The medications prescribed in those days often did more harm than good. In 1891 Fanny noted in her diary, "I am in a horrid state from the drug given me by Uncle George [Balfour]'s advice for what is supposed to be an aneurysm inside my head. The beating in my head is already much less distressing, but my eyes and nose are swollen and I have a continual brow ache and not much sleep. Uncle George recommended chlorodyne. Louis gave me a dose, as he thought, night before last, but it turned out to be something else, tasting like an embrocation of some sort unless possibly the stuff had gone bad." That actually seems to have been the explanation. "Here has just been a fine alert," Louis wrote to Colvin.

"I gave my wife a dose of chlorodyne. 'Something wrong,' says she. 'Nonsense,' said I. 'Embrocation,' said she. I smelt it and—it smelt very funny. I think it's just gone bad, and tomorrow will tell. Proved to be so."[16]

Originally concocted to treat cholera, chlorodyne did relieve pain, as well it might, containing as it did opium, cannabis, and chloroform, but the side effects were often unfortunate or even dangerous. It might have been just as well if she had swallowed a skin ointment by mistake.

Fanny had always experienced mood swings, and these grew increasingly intense. Writing to Barrie in April 1893, Louis presented her as "The Weird Woman":

> Infinitely little, extraordinary wig of gray curls, handsome waxen face like Napoleon's, insane black eyes, boy's hands, tiny bare feet, a cigarette, native dress usually spotted with garden mould. In company manners presents the appearance of a little timid and precise old maid of the days of prunes and prism; you look for the reticule. [But wouldn't be surprised to find a dagger in her garter—Amanuensis.] Hellish energy, relieved by fortnights of entire hibernation.... The Living Partizan: a violent friend, a brimstone enemy.... Is always either loathed or slavishly adored; indifference impossible. The natives think her uncanny and that devils serve her. Dreams dreams, and sees visions.

As so often, Louis was recalling the Bible: "I will pour out my spirit upon all flesh; and your sons and your daughters shall prophesy, your old men shall dream dreams, your young men shall see visions."[17]

Fanny tended to brood when her feelings were hurt, as happened when Louis carelessly said she had "the soul of a peasant" and then tried to explain that he admired peasants. In her opinion he too could hold a grudge. Belle quoted her: "Louis thinks he forgives, but he only lays the bundle on the shelf and long after takes it down and quarrels with it."[18]

There is little mention of Fanny's deeper troubles in Louis's letters, until in the same month as the "Weird Woman" letter to Barrie, he opened up more frankly to Colvin.

> Well, there is no disguise possible. Fanny is not well, and we are miserably anxious. I may as well say that for nearly eighteen months there has been something wrong. I could not write of it, but it was very trying and painful—and mostly fell on me. Now we are face to face with the question: what next? The doctor has given her a medicine; we think it too

strong, yet dare not stop it, and she passes from death-bed scenes to states of stupor. Ross, doctor in Sydney, warned me to expect trouble, so I'm not surprised; and happily Lloyd and Belle and I work together very smoothly, and none of us get excited. But it's anxious.

Later that day a doctor from Apia examined Fanny. "'There is no danger to life,' he said twice. 'Is there any danger to mind?' I asked. 'That is not excluded,' said he."

There had been occasional trips to Sydney, just for a change of scene and to enjoy a big city, but Louis now revealed that they had made a trip to seek medical help for Fanny. There had been a series of crises:

> The last was a hell of a scene which lasted all night—I will never tell anyone what about, it could not be believed, and was so unlike herself or any of us—in which Belle and I held her for about two hours; she wanted to run away. Then we took her to Sydney, and the first few weeks were delightful: her voice quiet again—no more of that anxious shrillness about nothing that had so long echoed in my ears. And then she got bad again. Since she has been back, also she has been kind—querulously so, but kind. And today's fit (which was the most insane she has yet had) was still only gentle and melancholy. I am broken on the wheel, or feel like it. Belle and Lloyd are both as good as gold. Belle has her faults and plenty of them, but she has been a blessed friend to me.

Richard Holmes comments, "The way his stepchildren, Belle and Lloyd, rally to him in this crisis suggests family loyalties far deeper than some biographers have implied."[19]

At this distance in time, and with so little evidence to go on, it's impossible to be sure what was going on. The psychobiographer Jefferson Singer calls it "outright paranoia and psychosis," and suggests that Fanny may have suffered from bipolar illness. It seems that she experienced what would now be called a temporary psychotic break, and in those days simply a breakdown.[20]

Whatever the medicine may have been, it was surprisingly effective. The very next day Louis was able to add,

> I am thankful to say the new medicine relieved her at once. A crape has been removed from the day for all of us. To make things better, the morning is ah! such a morning as you have never seen; heaven upon earth for sweetness, freshness, depth upon depth of unimaginable colour, and a huge silence broken at this moment only by the far-away murmur of the Pacific and the rich piping of a single bird. We have got her back to her

own room where Belle sleeps with her. Belle and I are to take watches all day, off and on, to be with her. You can't conceive what a relief this is. It seems a new world. She has such extraordinary recuperative power that I do hope for the best. I am as tired as man can be. This is a great trial to a family, and I thank God it seems as if ours was going to bear it well. And O! If it only lets up, it will be but a pleasant memory.

Two weeks later Louis reported, "A general, steady advance; Fanny really quite chipper and jolly."[21]

There continue to be hints of further ups and downs, but also confidence that the worst was over. At the end of May Louis wrote to Margaret, who was still in Edinburgh, "I do believe she is all right now; seems as sensible as possible, only with some old illusions not yet—probably never to be—eradicated." He doesn't indicate what the illusions were.[22]

Biographers have tended to be severely judgmental about Fanny, with little sympathy for the stresses that may have contributed to this crisis. Ian Bell is an admirable exception. "She might have cracked after years of strain, the continuous pressure traceable to her disastrous marriage to Sam, to the death of little Hervey, to Louis's repeated flirtations with death, to money worries, to endless upheavals, to the enmity of the London set, to the backbreaking toil of the early days on Samoa, to the ebbing away of eroticism from her marriage."[23]

GROWING DEPRESSION

Throughout 1894, despite Fanny's recovery, Louis's correspondence was increasingly filled with a sense that at forty-three he had already lived too long. His own depression must have been developing for some time, but he concealed it well, and only now did he begin to acknowledge it frankly. He told Frances Sitwell in April, "I have no taste for old age, and my nose is to be rubbed in it in spite of my face. I was meant to die young, and the gods do not love me. This is very like an epitaph, bar the handwriting, which is anything but monumental, and I daresay I had better stop. Many are the annoyances of the sons of man, but mine surely is unusual; that I cannot *get died*." The letter ends, "I cannot make out to be anything but raspingly, harrowingly sad; so I will close and not affect levity which I cannot feel. Do not altogether forget me. Keep a corner of your memory for the exile, Louis." Frances replied affectionately, "In spite of what you say about old age (with which I deeply sympathise) *we* cannot but rejoice that the gods did not love you selfishly, but have left you to us poor humans who can ill spare the like of you my dear." They were remembering the ancient Greek saying, "Those whom the gods love die young."[24]

A couple of months later Louis was telling Henry James, "I am going to try and dictate to you a letter or a note, and begin the same without any spark of hope, my mind being entirely in abeyance. This malady is very bitter on the literary man. I have had it now coming on for a month and it seems to get worse instead of better. . . . I am in one of the humours when a man wonders how anyone can be such an ass as to embrace the profession of letters, and not get apprenticed to a barber or keep a baked potato stall." This letter was dictated to Belle.[25]

To another correspondent Louis wrote on the same day, "I beg of you to write for my sake if for nobody else's. I count it a considerable part of the 'wages of going on' in this perturbed and on the whole unsatisfactory business—life." He added, "My amanuensis protests against the ill name I have given to life in the last sentence. She declares that it comes ungracefully from me, and I dare say it does." The next day he told his editor at *Scribner's Magazine,* "I doubt if I could write essays now. I doubt, even if I tried, whether I should find I wanted to."[26]

A year previously Louis had written to Baxter, "It is strange; I must seem to you to blaze in a Birmingham prosperity and happiness; and to myself, I seem a failure. *No rest but the grave for Sir Walter!* O, how the words ring in a man's head." Louis was recalling the account of Scott's last days in the biography written by his son-in-law. Scott had fallen asleep in his wheelchair, and as he was waking up his attendant said, "Sir Walter has had a little repose." Scott retorted, "No, Willie—no repose for Sir Walter but in the grave."[27]

Birmingham was the center of the Industrial Revolution and the place where big fortunes were being made. But prosperity and happiness had continued to elude Louis. Although his writing brought in more money than he had ever dreamed possible, it was never enough, as Vailima went on swallowing it all. To make all that money he had stooped to publishing potboilers that he knew very well were inferior work. His earnest attempts to reinvent himself as a realist, exposing colonialist corruption, had largely failed. And as always, he was haunted by a feeling that writing was recreational, not "real" work.

At this time Baxter decided to leave Edinburgh and move his own legal work to London, on which Louis commented,

> Strange that you should be beginning a new life when I, who am a little your junior, am thinking of the end of mine. But I have had hard lines; I have been so long waiting for death; I have unwrapped my thoughts

from about life [sic] so long that I have not a filament left to hold by; I have done my fiddling so long under Vesuvius that I have almost forgotten to play, and can only wait for the eruption and think it long of coming. Literally no man has more wholly outlived life than I. And still it's good fun.[28]

In November Andrew Lang received a letter from Louis which he described later to an interviewer: "He displayed (for the first time in his correspondent's long friendship with him) a certain anxiety about himself. He said that he was haunted by a dread of paralysis, of a lingering mental malady, of living on no longer himself like Swift." Swift suffered from extreme dementia in his final years.[29]

The most striking of these gloomy letters was one to Louis's cousin Bob:

> As I go on in life, day by day, I become more of a bewildered child. I cannot get used to this world, to procreation, to heredity, to sight, to hearing; the commonest things are a burthen; the sight of Belle and her twelve-year-old boy, already taller than herself, is enough to turn my hair grey; as for Fanny and her brood, it is insane to think of. The prim obliterated polite face of life, and the broad, bawdy, and orgiastic—or maenadic—foundations, form a spectacle to which no habit reconciles me; and "I could wish my days to be bound each to each" by the same open-mouthed wonder.

The allusion to Wordsworth's "Intimations of Immortality" sharpens the point of Louis's comment. Where Wordsworth lamented that a child's perception of "the glory and the freshness of a dream" fades away in adulthood, Louis is saying almost the opposite. As he gets older, life becomes ever more defamiliarized, astonishing, and overwhelming.[30]

THE CALL OF SCOTLAND

During this time Louis's thoughts were haunted by the homeland he would never see again—the stony hills of his youth, and the religious rebels who lived there long before. Writing to a Scottish poet he admired, he enclosed a poem of his own:

> Blows the wind today, and the sun and the rain are flying,
> Blows the wind on the moors today and now,

> Where about the graves of the martyrs the whaups are crying,
> My heart remembers how!
>
> Grey recumbent tombs of the dead in desert places,
> Standing stones on the vacant, wine-red moor,
> Hills of sheep, and the howes of the silent vanished races,
> And winds, austere and pure!
>
> Be it granted me to behold you again in dying,
> Hills of home! and to hear again the call—
> Hear about the graves of the martyrs the peewees crying,
> And hear no more at all.

"Whaups" are curlews and "howes" are hollows.[31]

The Scottish poet Edwin Morgan says, "It wouldn't be a poem without the wind and the moors and the sheep and the whaups crying, but a steady look at it convinces you that its centre is not these things. Its centre is blood, as its subject is death, the poet's own tiny nineteenth-century death merging into the blood of the martyrs of Scotland's hideous religious history, and even that merging in turn into the far more distant prehistoric blood of the sacrifices at the standing stones." Those are mysterious Neolithic monuments, scattered widely in Scotland and Ireland, that were thought to have been sites of human sacrifice.[32]

At this time Louis jotted down an autobiographical note that was yet another expression of discouragement with his writing career—and of unresolved guilt for refusing the career expected of a Stevenson. "Born 1850 at Edinburgh. Pure Scotch blood; descended from the Scotch Lighthouse Engineers, three generations. Himself educated for the family profession. But the marrow of the family was worked out, and he declined into the man of letters."[33]

CHAPTER 33

The Last Novels

THE RETURN OF DAVID BALFOUR

Louis had always intended to create a sequel to *Kidnapped,* carrying the story forward from the moment when David Balfour entered an Edinburgh bank to withdraw the first installment of his inheritance. Back in 1887 he had signed a contract with Cassell to deliver "as soon as possible" a novel of similar length to *Kidnapped,* to be called *David Balfour* "or some similar title." The Cassell editors were concerned that readers would assume it was just a reissue of *Kidnapped,* so they suggested *Catriona,* as it is generally known today.[1]

A chapter or so may have been written while Louis was still in Bournemouth, but the move to America and other obligations put *Catriona* on hold for several years. At Vailima in 1892 he returned to it and found himself energized, as he had not been with most of his recent writing. "Why did I take up *David Balfour?*" he asked himself in a letter to Colvin. "I don't know. A sudden passion." In three weeks the first twelve chapters were finished, and even with pauses to finish *A Footnote to History,* his account of politics in Samoa, the rapid pace continued. "In spite of endless interruptions," Graham Balfour recalled, "it was actually finished by the end of September [of 1892]. It was the first of his works that was completed while I was at Vailima, and I well remember the agitation and stress with which it was brought to a close."[2]

When *Catriona* begins, no time at all has elapsed since the conclusion of *Kidnapped.* Louis wrote to Colvin, "Is it not characteristic of my broken tenacity of mind, that I should have left Davie Balfour some five years in the British Linen Company's office, and then fall on him at last with such vivacity?" However, this sequel is a deeper and darker exploration of the cultural moment. Its theme has been well described by a modern critic as "the bloody, dirty domain of national and tribal politics, of disappointment, betrayal, and compromise." In *Kidnapped* David was an outsider in the feudal, romantic Highlands; in *Catriona*, as a native of the rural west, he's an outsider in a city he doesn't like or understand. As David describes Edinburgh, "Here I was in this old, black city, which was for all the world like a rabbit warren, not only by the number of its indwellers, but the complication of its passages and holes."[3]

Not just the setting but the political situation is labyrinthine. As a trained lawyer, Louis was well placed to expose the ways a legal system can be misused, especially in light of his recent experiences in Samoa. Just as the foreign powers claimed to be bringing civilized law to the Pacific but constantly abused it, the law is used in *Catriona* to bring about injustice. "It was forced home upon my mind," David says, "how this, that had the externals of a sober process of law, was in its essence a clan battle between savage clans."[4]

The infighting is far too complicated to summarize here, and that's very much the point. David had acquired some experience of life in his journey with Alan Breck, but no experience of sophisticated political scheming. Knowing that he still needs to clear himself and Alan from suspicion concerning the murder of Colin Campbell, the rent collector who was shot dead while David was talking with him, he goes to explain his position to the Lord Advocate Prestongrange, the head of criminal prosecutions in all of Scotland.

Prestongrange is convinced that David is telling the truth, but unwilling to permit him to testify in court. That's because if David did give his evidence at the trial, it would exculpate a Stewart known as James of the Glens whom the government has already selected as the scapegoat for the murder. It doesn't take long for David to grasp that Prestongrange is full of "dissimulation" and "as false as a cracked bell." But David's naïve pursuit of justice has endangered him. Prestongrange wants him out of the way, and he finds himself imprisoned on the offshore Bass Rock (which Louis used to see in boyhood from the North Berwick shore), to be detained there until the trial is over.[5]

David's frustration in the labyrinth of politics is skillfully evoked. However, the heart of the story is a love relationship—the first that Louis had seriously attempted to dramatize, though still with limitations that he believed publishers would require. Another member of the Stewart clan, James More, is suspected of complicity in the murky affair and is imprisoned in Edinburgh Castle. One day David encounters More's daughter in the street without knowing who she is.

> It chanced the girl turned suddenly about, so that I saw her face for the first time. There is no greater wonder than the way the face of a young woman fits in a man's mind, and stays there, and he could never tell you why; it just seems it was the thing he wanted. She had wonderful bright eyes like stars, and I daresay the eyes had a part in it; but what I remember the most clearly was the way her lips were a trifle open as she turned. And, whatever was the cause, I stood there staring like a fool. On her side, as she had not known there was anyone so near, she looked at me a little longer, and perhaps with more surprise, than was entirely civil.

They talk briefly, and David learns that her name is Catriona (the Gaelic version of Katharine) and that she is More's daughter; he wins her confidence by revealing that he has been with people she trusts "across the Highland line." She is brave and independent, but just as inexperienced as he is, and equally out of her element in Edinburgh.[6]

There is another very different young woman in the story, the witty and sophisticated Barbara Grant, whose father is none other than the Lord Advocate Prestongrange. In an essay on the eighteenth-century painter Henry Raeburn, Louis complained that Raeburn's portraits of women lacked flesh and blood. "In all these pretty faces, you miss character, you miss fire, you miss that spice of the devil which is worth all the prettiness in the world; and what is worst of all, you miss sex. His young ladies are not womanly to nearly the same degree as his men are masculine; they are so in a negative sense; in short, they are the typical young ladies of the male novelist." Barbara Grant does have the spice of the devil. Fanny remembered that "from Catriona, who was meant to be the conventional heroine of the book, my husband gradually transferred his affection to Miss Grant, and it was with the greatest difficulty that he was able to keep her in her secondary position in the story."[7]

While he was working on the novel Louis told Colvin, "In season and out of season, night and day, David and his innocent harem—let me be just, he never has more than the two—are on my mind. I am very curious to see what you will think of my two girls. My own opinion is quite clear; I am in love with both. I foresee a few pleasant years of spiritual flirtations. The creator (if I may name myself for the sake of argument by such a name) is essentially unfaithful. For the duration of the two chapters in which I dealt with Miss Grant, I totally forgot my heroine, and even—but this is a flat secret—tried to win away David."[8]

Someone who knew Louis left a striking comment: "He had a sort of coyness and archness which reminds me of nothing so much as Miss Grant in his own *Catriona*. Indeed, I seem to see more of the real Stevenson in that lady than in any male character in his books. He had just that quality of wit, that fine manner and great gentleness under a surface of polished raillery."[9]

As the story develops, Barbara enjoys flirting with David, but only for fun, and she respects his feelings for Catriona. Soon afterward Catriona helps her father to escape from prison by entering disguised as a cobbler and exchanging clothes with him. That actually happened in history, though the daughter's name wasn't Catriona, which Louis made up. It was generally suspected that the "escape" was actually arranged by the authorities to get More conveniently out of the country.

David now boards a ship for Holland with the intention of studying law there, and by coincidence Catriona is a passenger on the same ship, on her way to rejoin her father. When they reach Holland, however, More is nowhere to be found. David and Catriona are compelled to survive as best they can—passing themselves off as brother and sister. Even when alone they resist temptation, for as Catriona frequently remarks, she is a "maid."

David's restraint is touching, however, since in her innocence Catriona doesn't understand why he's forcing himself to behave coolly. She suspects him of being in love with Barbara Grant, and they have repeated quarrels. At last comes the resolution, when she accuses David of not caring for her and then is reassured. "With a small, sudden motion, she clung near to me. I raised her face to mine, I kissed it, and she bowed her brow upon my bosom, clasping me tight. I saw in a mere whirl like a man drunken."[10]

Catriona's father finally shows up at Dunkirk, and startlingly, so does Alan Breck, whom David expected never to see again. An English ship appears, with an evident mission to capture Alan, and soon Alan discovers that he has been betrayed by none other than James More. A fierce sword fight erupts; David tries to intervene and is knocked back against a wall. To save her father Catriona thrusts herself in between, but after that she turns on James in fury: "Begone! take your shame out of my sight; leave me with clean folk. I am a daughter of Alpin! Shame of the sons of Alpin, begone!"[11]

The ending of the story, though happy, is strangely anticlimactic. David's uncle Ebenezer has died and the estate of Shaws is now his own. He and Catriona marry, and we learn that he has written down the story for their children, as Louis originally wanted him to do with *Kidnapped* until Fanny intervened. The children have a nurse named Alison Hastie, and Louis told Cummy that that was in her honor—Alison was her first name and Hastie her mother's maiden name. He dedicated *Catriona* to Charles Baxter "in the venerable city which I must always think of as my home."

In this low-key ending, the romantic adventuring of *Kidnapped* is long gone, and so is the thrill of politics that had grown so sour for Louis in Samoa. "I had had my view of that detestable business they call politics," David says. "I had seen it from behind, when it is all bones and blackness, and I was cured for life of any temptations to take part in it again.... Upon a retrospect, it appeared I had not done so grandly, after all; but with the greatest possible amount of big speech and preparation, had accomplished nothing."[12]

Louis told Colvin that this novel and "The Beach of Falesá" were "nearer what I mean than anything I have ever done—nearer what I mean by fiction; the nearest thing before was *Kidnapped*. I am not forgetting *The Master of Ballantrae*, but that lacked all pleasurableness, and hence was imperfect in essence.... Vital, that's what I aim at first: wholly vital, with a buoyancy of life." Two years later he wrote to Frances Sitwell, "I shall never do a better book than *Catriona*; that is my high water mark."[13]

More than any of Louis's other writing at this time, *Catriona* generated a lot of income. McClure paid £1,600 for serial rights ($8,000 in U.S. money at the time, and $250,000 today), and *Scribner's* another £1,200 to publish it (as *David Balfour*) in book form in 1893. In Britain Cassell brought it out as *Catriona*, and three years later in a two-volume set together with *Kidnapped* as *The Adventures of David Balfour*.

Louis's friends wrote to say how much they loved the book. J. M. Barrie told him, "I think there can be no question that the love story of Catriona and David is the best thing you have ever done. And it is just about the only thing I thought you could never do. All through the book I wanted to take Catriona aside and kiss her." Henry James was likewise complimentary, but he did have an interesting criticism. "The one thing I miss in the book is the note of *visibility*—it subjects my visual sense, my *seeing* imagination, to an almost painful underfeeding." Louis agreed that he had a point.

> 'Tis true, and unless I make the greater effort—and am, as a step to that, convinced of its necessity—it will be more true I fear in the future. I *hear* people talking, and I *feel* them acting, and that seems to me to be fiction. My two aims may be described as—
> *1st.* War to the adjective.
> *2nd.* Death to the optic nerve.
> Admitted, we live in an age of the optic nerve in literature.

As always in Louis's writing, there are brilliant evocations of what experience feels like, but all we know of Catriona's appearance is that she has gray eyes and long legs.[14]

FOUR DISAPPOINTING YARNS

Welcome though the success of *Catriona* was, financial pressure never let up, and Louis continued to drive himself to produce salable fiction. Three other projects were begun at Vailima but not finished. The fourth was a rewriting of an earlier draft; Louis managed to complete it, but neither he nor his readers thought much of it.

In May 1892 Louis made a start on a novel called *The Young Chevalier*. The title evoked Bonnie Prince Charlie, living in exile in France; Alan Breck was to join him there, and later on dig up a buried treasure in Scotland. For a while Louis mentioned *The Young Chevalier* in his letters as a work in progress, but it never did progress. A second project was *Heathercat,* begun in 1893 and likewise set in Scotland. That one went nowhere at all. A third was *St. Ives,* about a French prisoner in Edinburgh during the Napoleonic Wars. Louis freely admitted that it was a potboiler. It was left unfinished at the time of his death, and since the first chapters were already being serialized, a young novelist (and later well-known critic) named Arthur Quiller-Couch was engaged to provide an ending. A reviewer in the *Athenaeum* said accurately, "This is a rattling, touch-and-go tale of adventure of a somewhat ordinary type. This book bears the mark of a fagged mind on almost every page of it. It is largely reminiscent of other works of the same writer. Altogether the book, regarded from the point of view of plot, is a panorama of impossibilities."[15]

The fourth of these efforts, and the only one to be completed, was *The Ebb-Tide,* a dark tale of treachery and brutality in the Pacific. Like *The Wrecker,* it was begun in collaboration with Lloyd in 1889, and eventually finished by Louis in 1893. Most readers have found it disappointing or even repellent, and in a way that was Louis's intention. He had seen enough grifters and con men to lose any romantic idealism about the Pacific, and after a lifetime of rejecting gritty realism he was determined to try his hand at it.

The story begins with three drifters in Tahiti who have "made a long apprenticeship in going downward." They are a sea captain in disgrace because he wrecked his ship while drunk and drowned its passengers, a Dickensian Cockney who has been repeatedly fired for being "wholly vile," and an Oxford graduate who has failed at everything he ever tried: "I am broken crockery; I am a burst drum; the whole of my life is gone to water; I have nothing left that I believe in, except my living horror of myself."[16]

The three of them pick up a job sailing a cargo vessel, and they touch at a little atoll that they realize is the site of a clandestine pearl-fishing operation; they see a chance to kill the owner of the fishery and carry off a fortune in pearls. The owner, whose name is Attwater, is an extraordinary character, a cultivated aesthete with a Cambridge degree. A composite of types Louis had become familiar with, he has been well described as "the spiritual tyrant, the rigid Calvinist, the selfish sybaritic aesthete, all subsumed under the colonialist racist despot."[17]

When the Cockney approaches Attwater with a bottle of sulfuric acid hidden in his hand, Attwater gets suspicious, orders him to open his hands, and points a rifle at him.

> At almost the same moment, the indomitable Huish [the Cockney] decided to throw, and Attwater pulled the trigger. There was scarce the difference of a second between the two resolves, but it was in favour of the man with the rifle; and the jar had not yet left the clerk's hand before the ball shattered both. For the twinkling of an eye the wretch was in Hell's agonies, bathed in liquid flames, a screaming bedlamite; and then a second and more merciful bullet stretched him dead.

Astonishingly, the failed sea captain, witnessing his companion's fate, experiences a religious epiphany: "O! isn't there no mercy? O! what must I do to be saved?" "Ah!" thought Attwater, "here's the true penitent."[18]

The story ends with the third member of the trio preparing to leave the island on a ship that happens to show up, while the born-again sea captain urges him to stay. "O! why not be one of us? Why not come to Jesus right away, and let's meet in yon beautiful land? That's just the one thing wanted; just say, Lord, I believe, help thou mine unbelief! And He'll fold you in His arms. You see, I know! I've been a sinner myself!"[19]

The ending left reviewers baffled, but Louis believed that the sea captain's conversion made psychological sense. Tormented by guilt for the fatal shipwreck and face-to-face with death, he is converted, a commentator says, by "a terrifying and cult-like evangelism." As for Attwater, he has a lot in common with Kurtz in Conrad's *Heart of Darkness*.[20]

Louis suspected, however, that the pessimism of *The Ebb-Tide* might offend readers. He wrote to Colvin that it ought to be titled *Stevenson's Blooming Error*, and to James, "My dear man, the grimness of that story is not to be depicted in words. There are only four characters to be sure, but they are such a troop of swine! And their behaviour is really so deeply beneath any possible standard, that on a retrospect I wonder I have been able to endure them myself until the yarn was finished."[21]

Just as Louis had anticipated, reviewers were horrified. One of them wrote, "Of grace, virtue, beauty, we get no glimpse. All we have in exchange is a picture of the fag-end of certain useless and degraded lives." "It will be an eternal pity," another said, "if a writer like Stevenson passes away without having once applied his marvelous gifts of vision and sympathy to the reproduction and transfiguration of everyday human life; if he is content to play perpetually with wrecks and treasures and islands, and to be remembered as an exquisite artist in the abnormal."[22]

FATHER AND SON

At this stage in his life, Louis was increasingly discouraged about literature and about himself. Fame had failed to gratify him, and now he was driving himself to produce commercially lucrative work. Even when the result was good, the achievement seemed somehow hollow. Early in 1894 he wrote to Will Low,

> I think of the Renaissance fellows, and their all-round human sufficiency, and compare it with the ineffable smallness of the field in which we labour and in which we do so little. I think *David Balfour* a nice little book, and very artistic, and just the thing to occupy the leisure of a busy man; but for the top flower of a man's life it seems to me inadequate. Small is the word. It is a small age, and I am of it. I ought to have been able to build lighthouses and write *David Balfours* too. *Hinc illae lacrymae.*

The phrase from Horace means "Hence those tears."[23]

A couple of weeks later Louis wrote to thank a former classmate for dedicating a book of poems to him. Quoting from one of them, he said,

> "Call not blessed"—yes, if I could die just now, or say in half a year, I should have had a splendid time of it on the whole. Had I been an engineer and literature my amusement, it would have been better perhaps. I pulled it off, of course, I won the wager, and it is pleasant while it lasts; but how long will it last? I don't know, say the Bells of Old Bow. All of which goes to show that nobody is quite sane in judging himself. Truly, had I given way and gone in for engineering, I should be dead by now.

In wondering "how long will it last," he was remembering the nursery rhyme that begins "Oranges and lemons, say the bells of Saint Clement's":

> When will that be?
> Say the bells of Stepney.
> I do not know,
> Say the great bells of Bow.

The answer would turn out to be: in ten months.[24]

Catriona wasn't the only tale that carried Louis back to Scotland. Immediately after finishing *The Ebb-Tide* he experienced a Proustian moment.

> I am exulting to do nothing. It pours with rain from the westward, very unusual kind of weather; I was standing out on the little verandah in front of my room this morning, and there went through me or over me a heave of extraordinary and apparently baseless emotion. I literally staggered. And then the explanation came, and I knew I had found a frame of mind and body that belonged to Scotland, and particularly to the neighborhood of Callander. Very odd these identities of sensation, and the world of connotations implied: Highland huts, and peat smoke, and the brown swirling rivers, and wet clothes, and whisky, and the romance of the past, and that indescribable bite of the whole thing at a man's heart, which is—or rather lies at the bottom of—a story.

Twenty-seven years previously, when he was in his mid-teens, his family had vacationed at Callander, fifty miles northwest of Edinburgh and a traditional gateway to the Highlands.[25]

At this point Louis returned briefly to *St. Ives,* which was set in Scotland, but got discouraged again. Finally, in September 1894, he found the right subject and his imagination caught fire. Belle noted in her journal, "Louis and I have been writing, working away every morning like steam engines on [*Weir of*] *Hermiston.* . . . He never falters for a word, giving me the sentences, with capital letters and all the stops [punctuation], as clearly and steadily as though he were reading from an unseen book. 'Belle,' he said, 'I see it all so clearly! The story unfolds itself before me to the least detail—there is nothing left in doubt. I never felt so before in anything I ever wrote. It will be my best work; I feel myself so sure in every word!'"[26]

An Irish writer named Sidney Lysaght happened to visit Vailima just then and described Louis reading the first chapters aloud.

I can hear the tone of his voice and see the changing expression of his face as he read, for he was in love with the work, happier in it, perhaps, than in anything he had ever done, and his reading showed his interest. He had no more false modesty in praising his own work when it pleased him than contempt in condemning it when he disapproved. "Now, isn't that confoundedly good?" he said.[27]

The story is set in the early years of the nineteenth century, and the setting is the Pentland Hills just south of Edinburgh that Louis knew so well. "All beyond and about is the great field of the hills; the plover, the curlew, and the lark cry there; the wind blows as it blows in a ship's rigging, hard and cold and pure." This is no adventure yarn, however, but a tale of people trapped in the selves they can't help being, which leads to tragedy.[28]

At the center of the novel is Archie Weir, only son of a domineering chief justice (based on the notorious eighteenth-century "hanging judge" Lord Braxfield). In Louis's novel, Judge Weir's wife has inherited a small estate at Hermiston, a hamlet now part of greater Edinburgh, and by convention her husband is known as Lord Hermiston. Unusually, in this story Louis employed an omniscient narrator, which gave him freedom to enter the minds of all of his characters. It also made possible a new crispness of description. Archie's mother "came to her maturity depressed, and, as it were, defaced; no blood of life in her, no grasp or gaiety; pious, anxious, tender, tearful, and incompetent."[29]

As in Louis's childhood, the piety takes the form of rigid Calvinism, though Mrs. Weir is nothing like the affectionate Margaret Stevenson. Her mind is "lighted up with a glow out of the doors of hell." Never physically strong, she dies at her fireside of an apparent stroke. Her husband's reaction is characteristic as he gazes at the body.

> Dressed as she was for her last walk, they had laid the dead lady on her bed. She was never interesting in life; in death she was not impressive; and as her husband stood before her, with his hands crossed behind his powerful back, that which he looked upon was the very image of the insignificant.
>
> "Her and me were never cut out for one another," he remarked at last. "It was a daft-like marriage." And then, with a most unusual gentleness of tone, "Puir bitch," said he, "puir bitch!" Then suddenly: "Where's Erchie?"[30]

Unlike Louis and Thomas Stevenson, Archie and his father have virtually no relationship. When they do talk, which isn't often, Lord Hermiston is wounding and sarcastic. Still, a judge who knows them both assures Archie that his father truly loves him, but is simply unable to express his feelings. The narrator concludes, "Sympathy is not due to these steadfast iron natures. If he failed to gain his son's friendship, or even his son's toleration, on he went up the great, bare staircase of his duty, uncheered and undepressed."

Eventually a crisis erupts. Archie is studying law, and at the age of nineteen attends a trial at which Judge Weir brutally mocks a cringing defendant "with a monstrous, relishing gaiety, horrible to be conceived, a trait for nightmares." The judge condemns the defendant to death, and on the day of execution Archie goes to see the hanging. What he witnesses is "the paltry dangling of the remains like a broken jumping-jack. He had been prepared for something terrible, not for this tragic meanness. He stood a moment silent, and then—'I denounce this God-defying murder,' he shouted."

What Archie does next throws more fuel on the fire. We have been told that "he shone in the Speculative Society," the debating club in which Louis had been prominent in his university days. There Archie rises to speak "by the chimney-piece, the shine of many wax tapers from above illuminating his pale face, the glow of the great red fire relieving from behind his slim figure." He even looks like Louis. He then vehemently denounces capital punishment, and that too is autobiographical. When Louis was nineteen the "Spec" debated the question "Is the Abolition of Capital Punishment Desirable?" and he argued for the affirmative.[31]

This leads to a confrontation between father and son during which Lord Hermiston declares Archie unworthy for the law, orders him to drop his studies, and dismisses him to supervise the estate at Hermiston.

"I will do my best," said Archie.

"Well, then, I'll send Kirstie word the morn, and ye can go yourself the day after," said Hermiston. "And just try to be less of an eediot!" he concluded with a freezing smile, and turned immediately to the papers on his desk.[32]

Kirstie (short for Christina) is the middle-aged housekeeper at the estate. She turns out to be a goddess, and a frustrated one.

Kirstie was now over fifty, and might have sat to a sculptor. Long of limb, and still light of foot, deep-breasted, robust-loined, her golden hair not yet mingled with any trace of silver, the years had but caressed and embellished her. By the lines of a rich and vigorous maternity, she seemed destined to be the bride of heroes and the mother of their children; and behold, by the iniquity of fate, she had passed through her youth alone, and drew near to the confines of age, a childless woman. The tender ambitions that she had received at birth had been, by time and disappointment, diverted into a certain barren zeal of industry and fury of interference. She carried her thwarted ardours into housework, she washed floors with her empty heart.

Physically she resembles Frances Sitwell, and Fanny too. In the comment about childlessness, Louis may have been thinking also of Cummy. Nicholas Rankin says, "He saw how being a professional substitute mother could blight a woman's emotional life."[33]

There is not just one Kirstie Elliott, but two. The younger is the housekeeper's niece, who appears at Hermiston for a visit. Young Kirstie is sexual in a different way, consciously deploying her youthful charms. "The girl had been taught to behave: to look up, to look down, to look unconscious, to look seriously impressed in church, and in every conjuncture to look her best. That was the game of female life, and she played it frankly."

It is in church that Archie first sees young Kirstie.

According to the pretty fashion in which our grandmothers did not hesitate to appear, and our great-aunts went forth armed for the pursuit and capture of our great-uncles, the dress was drawn up so as to mould the contour of both breasts, and in the nook between, a cairngorm brooch maintained it. Here, too, surely in a very enviable position, trembled the nosegay of primroses.... Archie continued to drink her in with his eyes, even as a wayfarer comes to a well-head on a mountain, and stoops his face, and drinks with thirst unassuageable. In the cleft of her little breasts the fiery eye of the topaz and the pale florets of primrose fascinated him. He saw the breasts heave, and the flowers shake with the heaving, and marveled what should so much discompose the girl. And Christina was conscious of his gaze—saw it, perhaps, with the dainty plaything of an ear that peeped among her ringlets; she was conscious of changing colour, conscious of her unsteady breath.

In Louis's earlier writing there would never have been heaving breasts.[34]

These words were written down by Belle, who noted in her journal, "The story is all the more thrilling as he says he has taken me for young Kirstie." She has "tawny skin," as Belle and Fanny both did.[35]

Young Kirstie imagines that she might be falling in love with Archie; her aunt simply is in love with him. "This perpetual hunger and thirst of his presence kept her all day on the alert. When he went forth at morning, she would stand and follow him with admiring looks. As it grew late and drew to the time of his return, she would steal forth to a corner of the policy wall [the estate boundary] and be seen standing there sometimes by the hour together, gazing with shaded eyes, waiting the exquisite and barren pleasure of his view a mile off on the mountains."[36]

In a memorable scene, "She stood before the looking-glass, carried her shapely arms above her head, and gathered up the treasures of her tresses." When the fragmentary *Weir of Hermiston* was published, a reviewer wrote, "Here, for the first time in Stevenson, you really have the atmosphere of woman, the glamour of sex, not only in the younger Kirstie, but in her elder of the same name—a far more wonderful and difficult piece of portraiture—who pours out to Archie a heart that has not known how to grow old."[37]

Soon a college acquaintance shows up at Hermiston, begins flirting with young Kirstie, and persuades Archie to leave her alone. She reacts with grief so intense that Archie calls it "a willful convulsion of brute nature." As it would turn out, that's where the story breaks off, though Belle wrote down part of a further draft that Louis died before revising. He had talked with her and Fanny about how the story might continue: Archie would kill his rival, who had gotten young Kirstie pregnant, and at his trial be condemned to death by none other than Lord Hermiston. In Scottish law it was forbidden for a judge to preside in the trial of a family member. Louis knew that, but hadn't figured out how he was going to deal with it.[38]

In any case, execution was going to be averted. Aided by Kirstie's brothers, Archie would break out of prison and escape with her to America. That would be a surprisingly happy ending for what seemed certain to be a tragedy, and many critics have thought that the surviving fragment is more effective as a self-contained piece of writing than it would have been as prologue to a melodrama. Louis often admitted that he was better at beginning stories than ending them, but in a letter to Barrie he was defiant about his plan.

> Braxfield—only his name is Hermiston—has a son who is condemned to death. Plainly there is a fine and tempting fitness about this, and I meant he was to hang. But now on considering my minor characters, I saw there were five people who would—in a sense who must—break prison and attempt his rescue. They were capable hardy folks too, who

might very well succeed. Why should they not then? Why should not young Hermiston escape clear out of the country? and be happy, if he could?[39]

When *Weir of Hermiston* was published, Fanny asked Colvin to be sure to include the intended dedication: "Please put it in as he meant it to be. He pinned it to my bed curtains when I was asleep, with other explanatory verses. Please do not leave it out."[40]

The poem was duly printed, under the title "To My Wife." It reads in part:

> Take thou the writing: thine it is. For who
> Burnished the sword, blew on the drowsy coal,
> Held still the target higher, chary of praise
> And prodigal of censure—who but thou?

"Chary of praise and prodigal of censure"—Fanny was happy to let it be known that she was Louis's severest critic, and that he was grateful for it.[41]

Lloyd left an account of a conversation he had with Louis after the family listened to him read some of the early chapters aloud. "I knew I should have spoken, but I could not. The others praised it; lauded it to the skies; but I was in a dream from which I could not awake." The group was breaking up when Louis rushed at Lloyd, breathless and trembling. "'My God, you shall not go like that!' he cried out, seizing me by the arm, and his thin fingers closing on it like a vice. 'What! Not a single note, not a single word, not even the courtesy of a lie!' The bitterness and passion he put into these words are beyond any power of mine to describe."

After Louis calmed down, Lloyd explained that he had simply been overwhelmed, and was sure that it would be the greatest novel in the English language. "In the all-pervading darkness we were for once free to be ourselves, unashamed. Thus we sat, with our arms about each other, talking far into the night. Even after thirty years I should not care to divulge anything so sacred as those confidences; the revelation of that tortured soul; the falterings of its Calvary." Perhaps the anguish had to do with the tensions in the family, particularly with respect to Fanny. Possibly, too, Louis sensed that his high hopes for *Weir* would not be realized.[42]

However this novel might have been completed, its unfinished state at the time of his death has given it special significance, as Claire Harman comments: "What his friends really valued was *Weir*'s potential, and perhaps an end to having to worry about the meaning of Stevenson's oeuvre. The line had been drawn, the author had died young, and his last work naturally acquired a symbolic status beyond all the others."[43]

Considered autobiographically, *Weir* builds on the complex relationship between Louis and his own father, and twists it to the breaking point. While the inflexible Judge Weir is not a portrait of Thomas Stevenson, Louis is exploring the complexity of any father-son relationship. Frank McLynn puts it well: "He portrays in Archie a man who, by not understanding his father, does not understand himself, and the implicit reproach is directed as much at himself as at his fictional creation." The novel also reflects Louis's dislike of a career in the law, accompanied by shame that he had found himself unable to endure it.[44]

Beyond that, the story embodies sexual and romantic tensions in Louis's life. If Belle was the model for one Kirstie, the passionate Fanny had much in common with the other. No one knows what would have become of the older Kirstie if the novel was finished; perhaps at this stage Louis himself didn't know. At any rate it would be with the younger Kirstie, not the older, that Archie would escape to America and freedom.

Still more largely, the conflict is between irreconcilable cultural worlds. One is the conventional, legalistic Edinburgh of rigor and rules that Louis had chafed against. The other is the world of openness, action, nature, and adventure that he had successfully attained. In the ending he envisioned for *Weir of Hermiston*, Archie would enjoy the same liberation that had been so transforming for Louis himself.

CHAPTER 34

"I Was Not Born for Age"

At the end of October in 1894 Margaret wrote to her sister Jane, "In a few short years, what a lovely place this will be, and what a delight to us, if we are still here to enjoy it." And on November 11, again to Jane, "Dear Lou, what cause for thankfulness it is that he has been spared to see his forty-fourth birthday in so much health and comfort." Two days later that birthday was celebrated with a lavish feast attended by a host of Samoan friends. Belle remembered that a whole heifer and twenty pigs were roasted, in addition to fifty chickens, seventeen pigeons, and great quantities of fruit and vegetables. "After the feast there were dances and songs by various groups of Samoans, all especially composed for the occasion. These went on until dark, and when our guests finally departed, an exhausted family was very glad to retire early."[1]

On Thanksgiving there was another, more modest dinner for the family and a few guests. Fifty years later Fanny's grandson Austin recalled her joy during the occasion. "Dressed in black velvet and point lace, the sparkle from her jewels vying with the happiness in her eyes, she made a radiant figure at the foot of the long table ablaze with silver candelabra, cut crystal and flowers. Her dream had come true; she saw her husband brown with health, tall and distinguished in the evening dress of the tropics, white mess jacket, red sash and black trousers—a gay and brilliant host."[2]

Louis's letters, however, continued to reflect the discouragement he had been feeling, and on December 1 he wrote to Gosse ("my dear Weg"),

> I was not born for age. And curiously enough I seem to see a contrary drift in my work from that which is so remarkable in yours. You are going on sedately traveling through your ages, decently changing with the years to the proper tune. And here am I, quite out of my true course, and with nothing in my foolish elderly head but love stories.... Come to think of it, Gosse, I believe the main distinction is that you have a family growing up around you, and I am a childless, rather bitter, very clear-eyed, blighted youth. I have in fact lost the path that makes it easy and natural for you to descend the hill. I am going at it straight. And where I have to go down, it is a precipice.

In earlier days he would never have described himself as bitter (childlessness is another matter, since he and Fanny seem not to have wanted a child of their own). When Henry James read Colvin's edition of the letters six years later, he quoted this one appreciatively and added, "Two days later he met his end in the happiest form, by the straight, swift bolt of the gods." Gosse himself told his daughter, "I feel as if it was almost the very most precious thing I possess, this goodbye from the great genius that I loved so much."[3]

December 3 began as an altogether normal day, during which, Margaret wrote to a friend, her son was "in the best of health and spirits, full of interest in his new novel." He worked on *Weir* in the morning, after that rode to Apia and back, and then went for a swim in their little pool in the forest. As evening approached he poured glasses of wine for Fanny and himself, and they were making a salad together when the blow struck.

Several members of the family described afterward what happened; Belle's account, written down just a day later, is the fullest. "It seems he had been looking on watching my mother making a salad, and was dropping the oil for her with a perfectly steady hand. He suddenly said, 'What is that?' or 'What a pain!' and put both hands to his head. 'Do I look strange?' he asked, and then he reeled and fell backwards. His favourite boy Sosimo caught him and carried him into the big room, and he never was conscious after."

Louis was set down, breathing in gasps, in the armchair that had belonged to his grandfather—the one Henry James used at Skerryvore. Lloyd leapt on horseback and galloped down to Apia, returning with a doctor as soon as he could. It seemed clear that Louis had experienced a catastrophic stroke. Five years earlier, in Honolulu, he had probably experienced a transient stroke without realizing it. He wrote to Baxter at that time, "Overwork brought on a very distressing attack of blood to the head, so that I could scarcely see, scarcely understand what was said to me, and presented by way of face a purple expanse only enlivened by a pair of white lips."[4]

Belle's account continues:

> When [the doctor] arrived he ordered the little brass bedstead from the guestroom and it was placed in the middle of the great hall. Four boys carefully carried Louis and laid him upon it, and then the missionary Mr. Clarke came. We were all about the bed then, and Mr. Clarke knelt beside Aunt Maggie [i.e., Margaret] and prayed. Lloyd supported Louis with his arm; he was still unconscious and only breathed fainter and at longer intervals until at last he died at ten minutes past eight. . . . Lloyd and I and Sosimo and Talolo dressed him and laid him out; the two brown boys that he loved kissed his hands and clasped them together upon his breast, interlacing the fingers with tender care. He did not look at all ill, but lay with his eyes closed and his hair slightly curling on his forehead as though he were asleep. Lloyd sent for the English flag, the one he flew on the *Casco,* and laid it over the bed. He looked so tall and slender lying there, and very handsome, the light shining on his clear profile. It was very quiet. There were no terrible outbursts of grief—we seemed dazed and numbed, hardly drawing breath as we sat and looked at him lying so still and peaceful.[5]

Margaret, however, remembered an exclamation of her own before he expired: "Fanny and I were rubbing his arms with brandy, and his shirtsleeves were pushed up and showed their thinness. Someone made a remark about his writing, and the doctor said, 'How can anybody write books with arms like these?' I turned around indignantly and burst out with, 'He has written *all* his books with arms like these!'"[6]

"Late that night," Lloyd recalled, "we washed his body and dressed it in a soft white linen shirt and black evening trousers girded with a dark blue silk sash. A white tie, dark blue silk socks, and patent leather shoes completed the costume." In Honolulu Louis had given a talk at the Scottish Thistle Club—the thistle is emblematic of Scotland—and when he was presented with the club's badge he pinned it to his lapel and said, "I will never part with it; it is near enough to my heart now to be buried with me." That now came to pass. The Union Jack that had covered his body was afterward sent to Charles Baxter, who had it hung at the Speculative Society in Edinburgh.[7]

Fanny, always good at letters of consolation, included a kind of self-consolation in a letter to Anne Jenkin:

> I try to remember how he had longed and prayed to go like this. That very day he had said to me, "The thought of dying in a bed is horrible to me; I want to die like a clean human being on my feet. I want to die in my clothes, to fall just as I stand." His life had been one long romance, and he hoped to have a romantic end; the artist in him demanded that completeness, and to grow old he could not bear. He has had all his wish, and for that I try to be thankful, though all the rest of my life will be empty and lonely. True I have my children, but I have not Louis. No one knows what that means but me.

They had been in Samoa for just over four years—the longest Louis ever lived in one place during his entire adult life. Only a year and a half had passed since Fanny herself emerged from her frightening breakdown.[8]

Afterward Lloyd collected tributes by Clarke and others in *A Letter to Mr. Stevenson's Friends,* printed "for private circulation." A copy that has survived at the University of California at Berkeley is inscribed "To Robert Louis Stevenson's dear friend Jules Simoneau, from Fanny V. de G. Stevenson." In this pamphlet Lloyd quoted—translating from Samoan, with biblical cadences—a eulogy delivered by an elderly chief on the morning of the burial: "When Mata'afa was taken, who was our support but Tusitala? We were in prison, and he cared for us. We were sick, and he made us well. We were hungry, and he fed us. The day was no longer than his kindness. You are great people and full of love. Yet who among you is so great as Tusitala? What is your love to his love?"

Throughout that day of the burial, Lloyd continued, "No stranger's hand touched him. It was his body-servant that interlocked his fingers and arranged his hands in the attitude of prayer. Those who loved him carried him to his last home; even the coffin was the work of an old friend. The grave was dug by his own men."[9]

Louis had made it clear that he wanted to be buried at the summit of Mount Vaea and not "shipped back to Scotland in a box." He had recently declared to the chiefs who made the Road of the Loving Hearts, "I love the land, I have chosen it to be my home while I live, and my grave after I am dead; and I love the people, and have chosen them to be my people to live and die with." He was recalling the Bible, in which Ruth says to her Moabite mother-in-law, "Thy people shall be my people; where thou diest will I die, and there will I be buried."[10]

A solemn procession, composed mostly of Samoans, carried Louis's coffin up

Mount Vaea through the dense forest and interred him 700 feet above Vailima and 1,350 feet above the sea. Plans were soon made for a permanent tomb, on which were inscribed a Scottish thistle and Samoan hibiscus, and also (in Samoan) the text from the Book of Ruth. Fanny told Colvin later that Margaret had to be dissuaded from including some pious texts of her own choosing. "I know what she really wants, poor soul. She was always doubtful of Louis's belief in what are called the truths of religion, and being doubtful, wishes to convince the world at the sacrifice of her own sincerity. I said to her that he had been in his life a true follower of Christ, and that should be enough. She knows that as well as we. How many of the rest of us can say half as much?"[11]

Also inscribed on the tomb was Louis's poem "Requiem," which he had written when gravely ill in San Francisco a decade and a half previously.

> Under the wide and starry sky,
> Dig the grave and let me lie.
> Glad did I live and gladly die,
> And I laid me down with a will.
>
> This be the verse you grave for me:
> Here he lies where he longed to be;
> Home is the sailor, home from sea,
> And the hunter home from the hill.[12]

As the Samoans laid flowers on the tomb, they sang a song that Belle translated eloquently:

> Groan and weep, O my heart in its sorrow!
> Alas for Tusitala, who rests in the forest!
> Aimlessly we wait, and sorrowing; will he again return?
> Lament, O Vailima! Waiting and ever waiting!

Graham Balfour mentioned that the chiefs tabooed the use of firearms at the top of Mount Vaea, "so that the birds may live there undisturbed, and raise about his grave the songs he loved so well."[13]

At Grez in his twenties Louis had written:

The changes wrought by death are in themselves so sharp and final, and so terrible and melancholy in their consequences, that the thing stands alone in man's experience, and has no parallel upon earth. It outdoes all other accidents because it is the last of them. Sometimes it leaps suddenly upon its victims, like a Thug; sometimes it lays a regular siege and creeps upon their citadel during a score of years. And when the business is done, there is sore havoc made in other people's lives.

"Thug" was capitalized because it was originally the name of robbers in India who strangled their victims. Louis had endured the siege for the whole of his life. When the thug did strike there was indeed sore havoc in the lives he left behind.[14]

Margaret wrote to Colvin in February 1895, "It is just two months today since that sad procession up Vaea mountain took place, and the blank seems as fresh as ever and as impossible to realise. My own life is plucked up by the roots a second time." Louis's friends in Britain could hardly believe the news when it reached them. They were aware that his health had seemed much improved, and in any case they never expected an instantaneous death. Barrie was mystified by a telegram reporting that Louis had died of "asalad," as if that were some kind of malady. Only later did he learn that it meant he had been making a salad.[15]

Henry James wrote to Gosse,

> I meant to write to you tonight on another matter—but of what can one think, or utter or dream, save of this ghastly extinction of the beloved R.L.S.? It is too miserable for cold words—it's an absolute desolation. It makes me cold and sick—and with the absolute, almost alarmed sense, of the visible material quenching of an indispensable light. That he's silent forever will be a fact hard, for a long time, to live with. Today, at any rate, it's a cruel, wringing emotion. One feels how one cared for him— what a place he took; and as if suddenly *into* that place there had descended a great avalanche of ice. I'm not sure that it's not for *him* a great and happy fate; but for us the loss of charm, of suspense, of "fun" is unutterable. And how confusedly and pityingly one's thought turns to those far-away stricken women, with their whole principle of existence suddenly quenched, and yet all the monstrosity of the rest of their situation left on their hands. I saw poor Colvin today—he is overwhelmed, he is touching.[16]

To "my dear Fanny Stevenson" James sent a long and tender letter of sympathy, beginning with "What can I say to you that will not seem cruelly irrelevant and vain?" After praising her "courage and patience and fortitude," which would be much needed, he went on to say, "To have lived in the light of that splendid life, that beautiful, bountiful being—only to see it, from one moment to the other, converted into a fable as strange and romantic as one of his own, a thing that *has* been and has ended, is an anguish into which no one can enter with you fully, and of which no one can drain the cup *for* you. You are nearest to the pain, because you were nearest the joy and the pride."

Without minimizing her loss, James encouraged Fanny to feel that Louis's life had at least a symbolic completeness.

> He has gone in time not to be old—early enough to have been so generously young and late enough to have drunk deep of the cup. There have been—I think—for men of letters few deaths more romantically right. Forgive me, I beg you, what may sound cold-blooded in such words—and as if I imagined there could be anything for *you* "right" in the rupture of such an affection and the loss of such a presence. I have in my mind, in that view, only the rounded career and the consecrated work. When I think of your own situation I fall into a mere confusion of pity and wonder—with the sole sense of your being as brave a spirit as he was (all of whose bravery you endlessly shared) to hold on by.[17]

It had been an extraordinary life. Fanny was right when she said, "There have been few lives of such absorbing interest as Louis's—even leaving literature out of the question." By force of imagination and will he made himself into a great writer. And the better we know him, the more we understand that the life he lived was a great achievement in its entirety. Oppressed by poor health from childhood onward, frequently close to death, he never lost the energy and enthusiasm that inspired everyone who came into contact with him. As Sidney Colvin said, "The most robust of ordinary men seemed to turn dim and null in the presence of his vitality." Seven years after his death G. K. Chesterton wrote, "He realized this great paradox: that life becomes more fascinating the darker it grows, that life is worth living only so far as it is difficult to live."[18]

In writing as in life, Louis cut his own path. Defying the artistic conventions of the time, he recovered the narrative power of storytelling and romance with a skill that would win the admiration of such masters as Calvino, Borges, and Nabokov. His essays, too, are fresh and alive with what Chesterton described as "a perfect mental athleticism, which enabled him to leap from crag to crag, and to trust himself anywhere and upon any question."[19]

Born to privilege, destined for a comfortable life and a respected profession, Louis rebelled against conventions of every kind. During his intermittent schooling and his university years he never fit in, and his teachers regarded him as unpromising. Meanwhile he was learning to think and imagine for himself, developing the skills that would create "Thrawn Janet," "The Merry Men," "The Beach of Falesá," *Treasure Island, Dr. Jekyll and Mr. Hyde, Kidnapped,* and *Catriona.* If he had been granted a normal life span there would have been far more.

Although an outsider by choice, throughout his life he attracted devoted friends, and he married an extraordinary woman altogether unlike the eligible young women of his early milieu. Theirs was a lasting love affair, and his stepson and stepdaughter loved him too. At his father's death he might have been expected to move into the family home in Edinburgh; instead he departed for America and then for the Pacific, ending his days on the other side of the world; he didn't just write about adventure, he lived it, with a fearlessness that impressed all who knew him. Henry James was right: his death was the quenching of an indispensable light. In this biography I have sought to re-illuminate his unique qualities in their full range and depth.

Over the years Stevenson's writing has lived on, loved by readers even when critics sometimes dismissed it. More than most novelists, he was able to achieve his declared goal, tales that are "wholly vital, with a buoyancy of life." He knew how to immerse readers in the action, experiencing each knife-edge moment of danger and suspense as fully real. The stories have a driving energy—he called it "kinetic"—that is sustained by a tactile experience of time and place, not as description but as re-creation of how it *felt.* His tales of the Scottish past make it as real as the present, as it was for the people who lived then. He created unforgettable characters—Alan Breck, Long John Silver—whose complexity and charisma we experience through the consciousness of young narrators during their personal quests for self-discovery. Underlying it all is the art that conceals art, with the "marvelous lightness" that Calvino admired.

Stevenson's novels have always found readers around the world, and they deserve to find still more. If this biography encourages that, it will have achieved its goal.

Epilogue

Toward the end of 1893, Baxter and Colvin had begun working on an Edinburgh Edition of Louis's complete works, which they and he hoped would be lucrative. When the first two volumes were ready in November 1894, Baxter set out for Samoa to present them to his friend, but received news of his death while at Port Said on the Suez Canal. One month before Louis died he had objected vehemently to Colvin's plan to include a note stating that "all additions, omissions, and corrections had the sanction and approval of the author." The slowness of communication between Samoa and Britain made such approval unfeasible, and Louis had demanded that Colvin state clearly "that you are the editor, and that I *did not* make all excisions, alterations and additions. I'm afraid, dear fellow, that you cannot thus play fast and loose." Once Louis was gone, however, Colvin revised whole passages of text to suit his own notions of propriety—a high-handed practice that he would continue when it came time to edit Louis's letters.[1]

In addition to the Edinburgh Edition, no fewer than five other editions of Louis's writings were published during the next thirty years. As explained in the introduction to this book, they resulted from multiple publishers wanting a piece of the action. All of them brought handsome royalties to Louis's heirs for decades to come. In addition there was ample provision for the heirs in his will, notwithstanding the financial drain of Vailima. One quarter of his father's estate, to be held by Margaret during her lifetime, was to be shared by Bob Stevenson, who got £3,136, and his sisters Katharine and Dora (£1,568 each)—this in spite of the rupture with Katharine during the quarrel with Henley. A sum of £4,704 was to be invested for Belle's benefit, and £14,112 went to Fanny at once, with anything remaining at her death to be passed on to Lloyd.[2]

An encounter with Fanny at this time was recorded by Joshua Slocum in his classic memoir *Sailing Alone around the World.* During his forty-six-thousand-mile journey in a small sailboat Slocum paused at Samoa. "I was of course thrilled when I found myself, after so many days of adventure, face to face with this bright woman, so lately the companion of the author [whose books] had delighted me on the voyage. The kindly eyes, that looked me through and through, sparkled when we compared notes of adventure. I marveled at some of her experiences and escapes. She told me that, along with her husband, she had voyaged in all manner of rickety craft among the islands of the Pacific, reflectively adding, 'Our tastes were similar.'"

Fanny gave Slocum Louis's sailing directories for voyagers, writing on the flyleaf of the first, "To CAPTAIN SLOCUM. These volumes have been read and re-read many times by my husband, and I am very sure that he would be pleased that they should be passed on to the sort of seafaring man that he liked above all others. FANNY V. DE G. STEVENSON."[3]

With Louis's death, Vailima's reason for being ceased. After hanging on there for two years Fanny gave it up and left, selling the estate to a German businessman for the modest price of £1,750. After housing various governmental occupants over the years, today it is a Stevenson museum.

Back in Edinburgh, Margaret added a note to the family Bible in which she had previously recorded Louis's birth and marriage: "Died suddenly of apoplexy at Vailima, Samoa, and I am left alone and desolate." She herself died in 1897, outliving her son by just three years.[4]

Fanny went to San Francisco and had a huge house built after her own design on a hilltop lot at the corner of Hyde and Lombard Streets, the famous "crooked street," with a superb view of the bay. She said it was like a fort on a cliff. "The creation of a new thing," her sister Nellie observed, "whether it might be a dress, a surprise dish for the table, a garden or a house, always appealed strongly to her. As she remarked, 'It is awfully exciting to build a house.'" Summers were spent on a little ranch Fanny acquired in the Santa Cruz Mountains, to which she gave the Samoan name Vanumanutagi, "Vale of the Singing Birds."

Numerous testimonies confirm that she lost none of her compelling power. Nellie quoted this from a San Francisco newspaper: "Once a man told me that Mrs. Robert Louis Stevenson was the one woman in the world he could imagine being willing to die for. Every man I asked—every single man, rich or poor, young or old, clever or stupid—all agreed that Mrs. Stevenson was the most fascinating woman he had ever seen." A young English writer who met her at this time had the same impression. "To know Mrs. Stevenson, with her splendid leonine head, her hypnotic eyes, and her overwhelming magnetism was easily to understand her lover's devotion."[5]

After living in San Francisco Fanny moved to Montecito near Santa Barbara. She never remarried, but became involved there with her new secretary, a newsman and film writer named Edward Field who was thirty-eight years younger than herself—dwarfing the age difference with Louis. In 1914 she died of a cerebral aneurysm at the age of seventy-four. Her grandson Austin wrote, "To say that I miss her means nothing. Why, it is as if an era had passed into oblivion. She was so much the Chief of us all, the Ruling Power. God rest her soul!"[6]

Early the next year Belle made a final pilgrimage to Samoa and buried her mother's ashes next to Louis on Mount Vaea. An old friend told her that the Samoans were saying, "This is a day of rejoicing and not of sorrow. Tusitala has lain there alone so many years. Now his true love has come back to him." A photograph (fig. 87) shows the funeral procession up the mountain. At left front is Belle, holding a drape; Edward Field carries the small casket of ashes at the head of the procession. The tall man behind him is a British administrator, Colonel Logan; the other woman at the front is Laulii Willis, the wife of an Englishman and described by Nellie Sanchez as "a charming Samoan lady of rank, and a warm and attached friend of the Stevenson family." White clothing was standard formal attire in the tropics.[7]

Lloyd, as might have been predicted, went on to lead a very miscellaneous existence. He served briefly as United States vice-consul in Samoa, moved back to the States, and published more than a dozen novels and short story collections, all forgotten today. The most interesting titles reflect his passion as a pioneer motorist, much like Kenneth Grahame's Toad of Toad Hall; they included *Baby Bullet: The Motor of Destiny* (1905) and *Three Speeds Forward: An Automobile Love Story with One Reverse* (1907). Lloyd had a comfortable income not from his own work but from his share of the Stevenson estate, which he inherited at Fanny's death. He married twice, had three children, and died in 1947 at the age of seventy-nine.

At the age of fifty-six Belle remarried—and her choice was none other than Fanny's companion Edward Field. He began speculating in real estate, and when oil was discovered under one of their properties they became millionaires, after which Belle established an artist's studio in Santa Barbara. Though twenty years

87. Fanny's funeral procession

her junior, Field died in 1936, while she lived on until 1953, dying at the age of ninety-five. Lloyd had died six years before that.

Belle even outlived her son Austin, who had become a successful playwright in the 1920s; his *Seventh Heaven* ran on Broadway for 704 performances. The Nantucket Historical Association remembers Austin on its website as "one of the great Nantucket personalities of the twentieth century, a stage designer, theatrical producer, author, landscape architect, Mason, clairvoyant, commodore of the Nantucket Yacht Club, and founder of the Wharf Rat Club." He died in 1952 at the age of seventy-one.

As for friends who had been important in Louis's life, Bob Stevenson's attempts as a painter were unsuccessful, but he published a series of articles on art, was a professor of fine art in Liverpool for several years, and became a prolific critic. In 1895 his well-regarded book on Velázquez appeared, followed by others on Rubens and Raeburn—an admirable career, but not the dazzling one that had been anticipated when he and Louis were young.

The old quarrel with Henley provoked a posthumous explosion, when he published a scathing review of Graham Balfour's biography for presenting an utterly false image of "a barley sugar effigy of a real man." In Henley's opinion Louis's marriage to Fanny, and subsequent departure from Britain, were fatal steps. "For me there were two Stevensons: the Stevenson who went to America in '87, and the Stevenson who never came back. The first I knew, and loved; the other I lost touch with." After that, "his books began to sell and his personality was a marketable thing," and from then on he was an intolerable moralist and pontificator. Worst of all, "He was incessantly and passionately interested in Stevenson. He could not be in the same room with a mirror but he must invite its confidences every time he passed it. He was never so much in earnest, never so well pleased (this were he happy or wretched), never so irresistible, as when he wrote about himself." As for the writings, they were elegant but shallow. "If I crave the enchantment of romance, I ask it of bigger men than he, and of bigger books than his."[8]

Henley's diatribe was widely deplored; Andrew Lang said, "A more loathsome exhibition I never saw." The best that can be said is that Henley felt abandoned by the friend of his youth whom he knew and loved. Beyond that, he was highly egotistical himself, and jealous of Louis's brilliant success that put his own work in the shade. He died two years later, as a result of injuries incurred when he fell from a railway carriage.[9]

Charles Baxter, always so dependable during Louis's lifetime, faded rapidly from view. After the loss of his wife in 1893 he encountered serious financial trouble, suffered a breakdown, and became a confirmed alcoholic. He remarried, and after retiring from the law lived in Paris and Siena.

Sidney Colvin finally married Frances Sitwell in 1903, and eight years later was knighted as Sir Sidney. However, he never got to be the head of the British Museum as he always hoped. His 1900 edition of Louis's letters contributed to the sanitized image that infuriated Henley. A writer on Victorian families says that in the opinion of Louis's executors, "candor in such matters inflicted grave harm, not only upon Stevenson's family and his public reputation, but upon society itself. Certain veils were essential if social values were to persist." Louis's early days of roistering in the Edinburgh underworld could not be acknowledged, let alone comments like the one in a late letter about the supremacy of the lingam and the yoni. An early reader of the Colvin edition thought it obvious that Louis "had a chivalrous regard for good women that would prevent him trespassing into that domain of over-familiarity which is apt to bring us too close to the fiery springs of passion."[10]

In 1898 contributions were invited for a memorial in Louis's native city. As it turned out, there wasn't enough money for a big outdoor monument, so a plaque was decided on instead, to be mounted in St Giles' Cathedral, built in the Middle Ages but known now as "the mother church of Presbyterianism." Thanks to the success of Saint-Gaudens's often-reproduced medallion of Louis (fig. 57 in chapter 25 above), he was commissioned for this task. The result was a bronze relief, rectangular this time and not circular, that showed Louis sitting up with his legs stretched out in front of him under a blanket. Scottish heather and Samoan hibiscus symbolized his places of birth and death. As previously mentioned, there was one significant change from the medallion: instead of holding a cigarette, he now held a pen.

It would not have surprised Louis that the dignitaries of Edinburgh, including some of his former professors, were reluctant to promote the project, no doubt remembering his disreputable student days. It achieved success when the former prime minister Lord Rosebery took charge, and contributions were obtained from many admirers, including Hardy, Kipling, Meredith, Barrie, and Conan Doyle. However, it would have struck Louis as ironic at best to be memorialized in the mother church of Presbyterianism.

Meanwhile Cummy lived on; a photograph (fig. 88) shows her gazing contemplatively at Louis's portrait. Fanny regularly sent money to supplement the pension Thomas Stevenson had bequeathed her. When she heard that Cummy had fallen in 1913 and broken a leg Fanny wrote, "Please, dear Cummy, always let me know instantly if there is anything in the world I can do to add to your com-

88. Cummy in later life

fort, or your happiness, or your pleasure. The merry days are all past now. But we must try to be cheerful instead, and make others happy. You and I are the very last, and we must help each other all we can till we too follow." Soon afterward Cummy died, at the age of ninety-two; Fanny sent money for the funeral and a tombstone.[11]

Chronology

Note: Major publications are listed here, but only a few of the most significant essays and stories.

1850   November 13, Robert Louis Balfour Stevenson born at 8 Howard Place, Edinburgh to Thomas Stevenson and Margaret Balfour Stevenson.

1852   In January the family moves to 1 (now 9) Inverleith Terrace. Alison Cunningham ("Cummy") becomes Louis's nurse, and will remain in the family until he is twenty. His uncle Alan Stevenson suffers a breakdown and retires from the engineering firm, which is managed thereafter by his father Thomas and his uncle David.

1856   Receives a toy theater as a birthday present; dictates "The History of Moses" to his mother.

1857   The family moves to its permanent home, 17 Heriot Row. First meeting with Louis's cousin R.A.M. ("Bob") Stevenson, Alan's son. Brief attendance, until withdrawn for ill health, at Mr. Henderson's Preparatory School, India Street. Various illnesses, including the beginning of lifelong pulmonary troubles, afflict Louis at this time.

1859   Summer stay at Bridge of Allan, Perth, and Dundee, Louis's first encounter with the Scottish Highlands, which would figure in much of his fiction. Return to Mr. Henderson's school.

1860 Death of his grandfather, the Reverend Lewis Balfour, putting an end to the stays at Colinton Manse in the Pentland Hills just south of Edinburgh.

1861 Begins fifteen months at Edinburgh Academy.

1862 Summer trip with parents in Germany.

1863 In the spring, two months with parents and Cummy at Menton on the French Riviera, followed by rapid tour through Genoa, Naples, Rome, Florence, Venice, and Innsbruck. In the fall, a single unhappy term at Burlington Lodge Academy in Isleworth west of London (part of greater London today in Hounslow). Just before Christmas, return with Thomas Stevenson to Menton to rejoin Margaret, who was staying there for her health.

1864 Enrolls at Robert Thomson's private school in Frederick Street, where he will stay until 1867.

1865 In May, stays with his mother at Torquay, Devon, on the English south coast.

1866 First publication, privately printed by his father, a brief account of the Pentland Rising of 1666, the Covenanting rebellion that would fascinate him from then on.

1867 In November enters Edinburgh University to study engineering. The family leases Swanston Cottage in the Pentlands.

1868 In the summer, stays with his father at Anstruther in the northeast and at Wick still further north, as preparation for joining the family firm of lighthouse building.

1869 Election to the Speculative Society at the university; accompanies his father on a tour of the Orkney and Shetland Islands.

1870 At another lighthouse construction site, stays on the island of Erraid off Mull in the Hebrides, which will play a memorable role in *Kidnapped*. Probable brief affairs with young Edinburgh women who are not now identifiable; spends much time in howffs (semi-legal drinking establishments) and with prostitutes.

1871 After delivering a successful paper on lighthouse design to the Royal Scottish Society of Arts, gives up engineering. To please his parents by choosing an alternative profession, begins studying law, but is chiefly interested in the amateur theatricals mounted by the engineering professor Fleeming Jenkin and his wife Anne, who become close friends.

1872 Passes preliminary examinations for the Scottish bar. With his cousin Bob and a few others, founds a short-lived club called the L.J.R. (Liberty, Justice, Reverence). Summer in Germany with Walter Simpson.

1873 Reveals to parents that he no longer believes in the Christian religion. His father is horrified; blames Bob Stevenson and bans him from their home. Sent in

July to stay with cousin Maud (Balfour) Babington at Cockfield Rectory, Sussex. There he is smitten with an older woman named Frances Sitwell, and forms a lifelong friendship with her partner Sidney Colvin, Slade Professor of Fine Art and director of the Fitzwilliam Museum at Cambridge (they don't marry until her estranged husband dies years later). After a breakdown, travels under doctor's orders in November to stay alone in Menton. In December, first paid publication, an essay entitled "Roads."

1874 Returning from Menton in April, stays with Colvin in London and is elected to the recently founded Savile Club, where he meets prominent writers. In the summer, a cruise in the Inner Hebrides. Publishes more essays, and resumes legal studies.

1875 Meets the writer William Ernest Henley, who is seriously ill at the Royal Infirmary in Edinburgh; they will be close friends for many years. In the spring, visits Paris, and also the artists' colony at Barbizon where Bob is staying. In July, passes final examination and is admitted as an advocate to the Scottish bar, but immediately gives up the law. Two-month walking tour in France with Simpson.

1876 Walking tour in Scotland, and in late summer a canoe trip in France with Simpson that will be described in *An Inland Voyage*. Stays with artists at Grez-sur-Loing and meets the American Fanny Osbourne, there with her daughter Isobel ("Belle") and son Lloyd; they fall in love, but will not be able to marry until she obtains a divorce from her husband four years later.

1877 Stays in Paris with Fanny during this year and the next. Among other short publications, "On Falling in Love" in the *Cornhill Magazine,* whose editor, Leslie Stephen, will regularly encourage his writing. Publication of his first short story, "A Lodging for the Night."

1878 Publication of his first books, *An Inland Voyage* and *Edinburgh: Picturesque Notes*. In June, acts as nominal secretary in Paris (the only paid job he would ever hold) to Fleeming Jenkin at the exposition there. In August, Fanny returns to California with her children to try to work things out with her husband Sam Osbourne. In the fall, solitary walking tour in the Cévennes mountains in south-central France.

1879 With Henley, begins collaboration on a play, *Deacon Brodie,* that they hope will make money but that will lead to dissension between them. Stays in London and France. *Travels with a Donkey in the Cévennes* published. In August, summoned by an urgent telegram from Fanny, sails secretly from Glasgow to New York and then travels westward by rail. Writes *The Amateur Emigrant,* which will remain unpublished until 1895. Stays in Monterey where Fanny and her children are, but she is undecided about making the break from her husband. Goes by himself into the Santa Lucia Mountains and nearly dies of illness and exposure. Moves to Bush Street in San Francisco to be near Fanny, who obtains a divorce in December. This period is described in the second part of the book *Across the Plains* (published in 1892).

1880   Suffers a dangerous hemorrhage and gradually recovers, moving in with Fanny at her house in Oakland. Thomas Stevenson, finally made aware of Louis's alarming condition, promises £250 a year, which means financial security at last. On May 19, marries Fanny; they honeymoon (accompanied by Lloyd) in an abandoned mining cabin in the Sierras, as described in *The Silverado Squatters* (published in 1884). In July they travel with Lloyd to New York (Belle has eloped with the artist Joseph Strong and remains behind) and then sail to Liverpool, where they are met by Louis's parents. In November, begins a six-month stay with Fanny and Lloyd at Davos in Switzerland, a favored resort for patients with lung troubles.

1881   Publication of essay collection *Virginibus Puerisque* ("For Girls and Boys"); returning to Scotland in the summer, they stay in Perthshire and Aberdeenshire. At Braemar in the Highlands, inspired partly by Lloyd, Louis starts to work on *The Sea Cook,* which begins serial publication in October in *Young Folks Magazine* (under the pseudonym of Captain George North) with the revised title *Treasure Island.* In October, returns with Fanny to Davos for another six-month stay and completes *Treasure Island.* One of Louis's best short stories, "Thrawn Janet," is published in *Cornhill Magazine.*

1882   Summer in Scotland; spends the fall near Marseille. Suffers a bout of dangerous hemorrhages. Publication of essay collection *Familiar Studies of Men and Books,* and also stories collected as *New Arabian Nights,* and the impressive tale "The Merry Men."

1883   In March, settles with Fanny in the little Chalet La Solitude in Hyères on the Riviera. Works on *Prince Otto* and *The Black Arrow* (again as Captain George North). *Treasure Island* published in book form.

1884   Winter in Nice and Hyères, punctuated by bouts of terrible illness. Fleeing an outbreak of cholera, the family goes to London and then in late summer to Bournemouth in the south of England, first in rented lodgings and later in a house bought for them by Louis's parents. They name it Skerryvore after one of the Stevenson family's lighthouses. Publication of *The Silverado Squatters.*

1885   Publication of *A Child's Garden of Verses* and *Prince Otto;* writes *Strange Case of Dr. Jekyll and Mr. Hyde.*

1886   In January, publication of *Strange Case of Dr. Jekyll and Mr. Hyde,* which quickly becomes a bestseller. *Kidnapped* begins serial publication in *Young Folks* and is issued in book form in July. Then a stay with Colvin in London, now Keeper of prints and drawings at the British Museum. Also published (in collaboration with Fanny) *More New Arabian Nights*.

1887 Publication of *The Merry Men and Other Tales and Fables;* also *Memories and Portraits,* and a second volume of poems, *Underwoods*. On May 8 Thomas Stevenson dies; Louis is too ill to attend his funeral, but soon publishes a memoir of his father, "Thomas Stevenson: Civil Engineer." Leaves Edinburgh for the last time and returns to Bournemouth. On August 22, sails for New York with Fanny, Lloyd, and the newly widowed Margaret Stevenson. After a stay in New York they settle at Saranac Lake near the Canadian border, bitterly cold but like Davos well reputed for lung troubles. Signs a generous contract with *Scribner's Magazine* for a monthly series of articles. Begins writing *The Master of Ballantrae*.

1888 *The Black Arrow* finally published, five years after it was written; also a *Memoir of Fleeming Jenkin*. Painful break with Henley, who has accused Fanny of plagiarizing a story from Louis's cousin Katharine de Mattos (Bob's sister). Signs a contract with the publisher S. S. McClure to write travel articles from the South Pacific. In March, Fanny leaves for California to find a suitable vessel. After a couple of months in New York, Louis and his mother go by train to San Francisco, and on June 27 they set sail on the rented schooner *Casco,* visiting successively the Marquesas, Puamotos, Society Islands (Tahiti), and Sandwich Islands (Hawaii), where Belle and her husband Joe have been living for five years.

1889 Publication of *The Master of Ballantrae,* and (in collaboration with Lloyd) *The Wrong Box*. In June they leave Hawaii on the trading vessel *Equator,* and after an extended cruise arrive in December at Upolu, the largest island in Samoa. They decide to settle there.

1890 Purchase of 314 hilly and wooded acres that they name the Vailima Estate. During this year there is further cruising, this time on the *Janet Nicholl,* as well as stays in New Zealand and Australia, but Louis's health is bad again and he realizes that life in Samoa suits him best. In October they settle permanently at Vailima, where a house has been built for them while they were away. Publication of a third volume of poems, *Ballads*.

1891 Margaret Stevenson, who had returned to Scotland, joins them at Vailima, as do Belle, her husband Joe, and their young son Austin. With ample Samoan help, the family works hard at attempting to develop an income-producing plantation. Publication of *In the South Seas,* a descriptive account of the history and cultures of the islands.

1892 Increasing involvement in Samoan politics, and strong opposition to exploitation by Western powers; publishes *A Footnote to History: Eight Years of Trouble* in Samoa, and *The Wrecker* (in collaboration with Lloyd). Louis's best Pacific story, "The Beach of Falesá," begins serialization in the *Illustrated London News*. *Across the Plains,* a collection of essays written a decade previously, is finally published. Cousin Graham Balfour, Louis's future biographer, arrives and stays at Vailima off and on during the next two years. Belle is divorced from Joe Strong.

1893 Final stay in Sydney. Publication of a sequel to *Kidnapped, Catriona* (also known as *David Balfour*) and *Island Nights' Entertainments,* stories set in the Pacific. Supports the Samoan chief Mata'afa in a brief civil war against his rival Laupepa, who, however, is victorious. Final stay in Honolulu.

1894 Publication of *The Ebb-Tide,* in collaboration with Lloyd. A feast at Vailima in October marks completion of the "Road of the Loving Hearts" in gratitude for Louis's support during the late war, and a second feast on November 13 celebrates his forty-fourth birthday. On December 3 he dies from a cerebral hemorrhage, and is buried on the summit of Mount Vaea. Left unfinished is the promising *Weir of Hermiston.*

1895 Publication by Colvin of *The Amateur Emigrant,* the account of the voyage to America in 1879, and a selection from Louis's correspondence (with many omissions from the originals) as *Vailima Letters.*

1896 Under Colvin's editorship, the Edinburgh Edition of Stevenson's works begins to appear; also publication of *Weir of Hermiston, In the South Seas, Fables,* and *Songs of Travel and Other Verses.*

1897 Margaret Stevenson dies in Edinburgh; the unfinished novel *St. Ives* is published.

1900 Publication of *Letters of Robert Louis Stevenson to His Family and Friends,* heavily altered and bowdlerized by Colvin.

1914 Fanny dies in Santa Barbara, California; Belle takes her ashes to be buried with Louis on Mount Vaea.

1947 Lloyd Osbourne dies in Glendale, California.

1953 Belle (now Isobel Field) dies in Santa Barbara.

Notes

LIST OF SHORT TITLES

Note: For a number of these titles, the American and British editions have different pagination.

Balfour: Graham Balfour, *The Life of Robert Louis Stevenson* (New York: Scribner, 1901).
Baxter *Letters: RLS: Stevenson's Letters to Charles Baxter,* ed. Delancey Ferguson and Marshall Waingrow (New Haven: Yale University Press, 1956).
Beinecke: Edwin J. Beinecke Collection of Robert Louis Stevenson, Beinecke Rare Book and Manuscript Library, Yale University, New Haven.
Bell: Ian Bell, *Dreams of Exile: Robert Louis Stevenson, A Biography* (New York: Henry Holt, 1992).
Calder: Jenni Calder, *Robert Louis Stevenson: A Life Study* (New York: Oxford University Press, 1980).
Callow: Philip Callow, *Louis: A Life of Robert Louis Stevenson* (Chicago: Ivan Dee, 2001).
Chesterton: G. K. Chesterton, *Robert Louis Stevenson* (London: Hodder & Stoughton, 1927).
Collected Poems: Robert Louis Stevenson, *Collected Poems,* ed. Janet Adam Smith (London: Rupert Hart-Davis, 1950). [*Note:* When poems are quoted from the identically titled *Collected Poems* edited by Roger C. Lewis, that is specifically indicated to avoid confusion.]
Complete Stories: The Complete Stories of Robert Louis Stevenson, ed. Barry Menikoff (New York: Modern Library, 2002).
Critical Heritage: Robert Louis Stevenson: The Critical Heritage, ed. Paul Maixner (London: Routledge & Kegan Paul, 1981).

Furnas: J. C. Furnas, *Voyage to Windward: The Life of Robert Louis Stevenson* (New York: William Sloane, 1951).

Harman: Claire Harman, *Myself and the Other Fellow: A Life of Robert Louis Stevenson* (New York: HarperCollins, 2005).

Henley *Letters: The Letters of William Ernest Henley to Robert Louis Stevenson,* ed. Damian Atkinson (High Wycombe, UK: Rivendell, 2008).

I Can Remember: I Can Remember Robert Louis Stevenson, ed. Rosaline Masson (New York: Frederick Stokes, 1922).

Interviews and Recollections: Robert Louis Stevenson: Interviews and Recollections, ed. R. C. Terry (Iowa City: University of Iowa Press, 1996).

Intimate Portrait: Lloyd Osbourne, *An Intimate Portrait of R.L.S.* (New York: Scribner, 1924).

Lantern-Bearers: Robert Louis Stevenson, *The Lantern-Bearers and Other Essays,* ed. Jeremy Treglown (New York: Farrar Straus Giroux, 1988).

Letters: The Letters of Robert Louis Stevenson, ed. Bradford A. Booth and Ernest Mehew, 8 vols. (New Haven: Yale University Press, 1995).

Mackay: Margaret Mackay, *The Violent Friend: The Story of Mrs. Robert Louis Stevenson* (New York: Doubleday, 1968).

Masson: Rosaline Masson, *The Life of Robert Louis Stevenson* (Edinburgh: W. & R. Chambers, 1923).

McLynn: Frank McLynn, *Robert Louis Stevenson: A Biography* (New York: Random House, 1993).

Pope Hennessy: James Pope Hennessy, *Robert Louis Stevenson* (New York: Simon & Schuster, 1974).

Rankin: Nicholas Rankin, *Dead Man's Chest: Travels After Robert Louis Stevenson* (London: Phoenix, 1987).

Sanchez: Nellie Van de Grift Sanchez, *The Life of Mrs. Robert Louis Stevenson* (New York: Scribner, 1921).

Singer: Jefferson A. Singer, *The Proper Pirate: Robert Louis Stevenson's Quest for Identity* (Oxford: Oxford University Press, 2017).

Stevensoniana: Stevensoniana: An Anecdotal Life and Appreciation, ed. J. A. Hammerton (Edinburgh: John Grant, 1910).

Swearingen: Roger G. Swearingen, *The Prose Writings of Robert Louis Stevenson: A Guide* (Hamden, CT, Archon Books, 1980).

This Life I've Loved: Isabel Field, *This Life I've Loved* (New York: Longman's, Green, 1937).

INTRODUCTION

1. Andrew Lang, "Recollections of Robert Louis Stevenson," in *Adventures among Books* (London: Longman's, Green, 1905), ch. 2; Sidney Colvin, *Memories and Notes of Persons and Places* (London: Edward Arnold, 1921), 99–102; William Ernest Henley, "Apparition."
2. RLS to his parents, Sept. 23, 1868, *Letters* 1:160.
3. Henry Bellyse Baildon, *Robert Louis Stevenson: A Life Study in Criticism* (London: Chatto & Windus, 1901), 21; Bernard Jenkin in *I Can Remember,* 182.

4. Mark Twain, "Chapters from My Autobiography," *North American Review* 183 (1906), 457.
5. Fanny Stevenson to Sidney Colvin, March 20, 1896, quoted by E. V. Lucas, *The Colvins and Their Friends* (New York: Scribner, 1928), 264; Stevenson is quoted from Lady Jersey's *Fifty-One Years of Victorian Life* by Swearingen, 173.
6. Richard Holmes, "On the Enchanted Hill," *New York Review of Books,* June 8, 1995.
7. David Daiches, *Robert Louis Stevenson* (Norfolk, CT: New Directions, 1947), 1; Furnas, 437.
8. Marcel Proust, *Le temps retrouvé* (Paris: Gallimard, 1954), 716; Vladimir Nabokov, *Lectures on Literature,* ed. Fredson Bowers (New York: Harcourt Brace Jovanovich, 1980), ch. 4; Italo Calvino, "Riposte a 9 domande sul romanzo," quoted by Richard Ambrosini and Richard Drury, *Robert Louis Stevenson: Writer of Boundaries* (Madison: University of Wisconsin Press, 2006), xix.
9. Italo Calvino, *The Written World and the Unwritten World,* trans. Ann Goldstein (New York: HarperCollins, 2023), 119.
10. *Borges y Yo, El hacedor* (Buenos Aires: Emecé, 1960), and preface by Borges to "The Isle of Voices," *L'isola delle voci* (Parma: Ricci, 1979).
11. Hopkins to Robert Bridges, Oct. 28, 1886, *The Letters of G. M. Hopkins to Robert Bridges,* ed. Claude C. Abbott (Oxford University Press, 1935), 239; Chesterton, 13.
12. RLS to Bob Stevenson, Sept. 30, 1883, *Letters* 4:169; George Saunders, *A Swim in a Pond in the Rain: In Which Four Russians Give a Master Class on Writing, Reading, and Life* (New York: Random House, 2021), 379.
13. Unsigned review, *Graphic,* Dec. 1, 1883, *Critical Heritage,* 141; Conan Doyle, "Mr. Stevenson's Methods in Fiction," *National Review,* Jan. 1890.
14. "A Gossip on a Novel of Dumas's," first published in *Memories and Portraits* (1887); "A Gossip on Romance," *Longman's Magazine,* Nov. 1882, reprinted in *Memories and Portraits* and in *Lantern-Bearers,* 172–82.
15. E. M. Forster, *Aspects of the Novel* (New York: Harcourt, Brace, 1927), 47.
16. Unsigned review in the *Graphic,* Dec. 1, 1883, *Critical Heritage,* 141.
17. RLS to Sidney Colvin, Sept. 6, 1891, *Letters* 7:154.
18. RLS to *Scribner's,* March 14, 1886, *Letters* 5:230.
19. RLS to Alfred Dowson, Oct. 1875, and to Maud Babington, summer 1871, *Letters* 2:160, 1:214; Lloyd Osbourne, introduction to the South Seas Edition of Stevenson's *Works* (New York: Scribner, 1925), 1:xx.
20. *The Letters of Robert Louis Stevenson to His Family and Friends, Selected and Edited with Notes and Introduction by Sidney Colvin* (London: Methuen, 1899), introduction; Henry James, "The Letters of Robert Louis Stevenson," *North American Review* (Jan. 1900), 61ff.
21. RLS to Sidney Colvin, Jan. 19, 1874, to Horatio Brown, April 1, 1881, and to Charles Baxter, Nov. 1893, *Letters* 1:454, 3:166.
22. Robert Kiely, "Robert Louis Stevenson," *Victorian Fiction: A Second Guide to Research* (New York: Modern Language Association of America, 1978), 336.
23. Roger G. Swearingen, "Recent Studies in Robert Louis Stevenson: Letters, Reference

Works, Texts 1970–2005," *Dickens Studies Annual: Essays on Victorian Fiction* 37 (2006), 345–46.
24. Holmes, "On the Enchanted Hill."
25. RLS to William Archer, Oct. 1887, *Letters* 6:32.
26. Hermione Lee, *Biography: A Very Short Introduction* (Oxford: Oxford University Press, 2009), 18; John Pemble, *The Mediterranean Passion: Victorians and Edwardians in the South* (Oxford: Oxford University Press, 1988), v.
27. Baildon, *Robert Louis Stevenson,* 45.
28. Camille Peri, *A Wilder Shore: The Romantic Odyssey of Fanny and Robert Louis Stevenson* (New York: Viking, 2024).
29. The story of the successive editions is told by Andrew Nash, "'The Dead Should Be Protected from Their Own Carelessness': The Collected Editions of Robert Louis Stevenson," *The Culture of Collected Editions,* ed. Nash (Basingstoke, UK: Palgrave Macmillan, 2003), 112. See also Glenda Norquay, *Robert Louis Stevenson, Literary Networks and Transatlantic Publishing in the 1890s: The Author Incorporated* (London: Anthem, 2020), 111–14.
30. *The Collected Poems of Robert Louis Stevenson,* ed. Roger C. Lewis (Edinburgh: Edinburgh University Press, 2003), has numerous drawbacks, as trenchantly described by Roger G. Swearingen, "Recent Studies in Robert Louis Stevenson," *Dickens Studies Annual* 38 (2007), 371–79.

CHAPTER 1. THE EARLY YEARS

1. *Edinburgh: Picturesque Notes* (1878), ch. 9.
2. *Records of a Family of Engineers,* written 1891–94, never completed and not published until posthumous editions of Stevenson's works.
3. "Some Aspects of Robert Burns," *Cornhill Magazine,* May–Aug. 1879; *Familiar Studies of Men and Books* (1882) and *Lantern-Bearers,* 106.
4. "A Penny Plain and Twopence Coloured," *Memories and Portraits* (1887); Edmund Gosse, *Critical Kit-Cats* (New York: Dodd, Mead, 1903), 287.
5. Pope Hennessy, 26; Bell, 35; W. E. Clarke, "Robert Louis Stevenson in Samoa," in *Interviews and Recollections,* 166.
6. Mrs. Dale in *I Can Remember,* 14; Balfour, 1:30.
7. Mehew's introduction, *Letters* 1:31; Will H. Low, *A Chronicle of Friendships* (New York: Scribner, 1908), 378.
8. Mrs. Douglas MacLagan and Flora Masson in *I Can Remember,* 57, 161.
9. "Thomas Stevenson, Civil Engineer," *Contemporary Review,* June 1887; *Memories and Portraits* and *Lantern-Bearers,* 211–14; *Records of a Family of Engineers.*
10. *Stevenson's Baby Book,* ed. John Howell (San Francisco: John Henry Nash, 1922).
11. Charles Guthrie in *Interviews and Recollections,* 11; Balfour, 135.
12. Masson, 32.
13. Quoted by Marie Clothilde Balfour in her introduction to Margaret Stevenson, *From Saranac to the Marquesas and Beyond* (New York: Scribner, 1903), xvii.
14. Eve Blantyre Simpson, *Robert Louis Stevenson's Edinburgh Days* (London: Hodder & Stoughton, 1914), 6.

15. RLS to Frances Sitwell, Jan. 11, 1875, *Letters* 2:103.
16. Charles John Guthrie, *Robert Louis Stevenson: Some Personal Recollections* (Edinburgh: W. Green, 1924), 25–27.
17. Simpson, *Robert Louis Stevenson's Edinburgh Days,* 78.
18. "Memoirs of Himself," first published in posthumous editions.
19. *Westminster Shorter Catechism* (1748), no. 84.
20. Andrew Bonar, *The Biography of Robert Murray McCheyne* (1844), chs. 1, 6. Cummy reading the book is mentioned by Patrick W. Campbell in *I Can Remember,* 18.
21. Andrew Lang, introduction to vol. 1 of the Swanston Edition (London: Chatto & Windus, 1911).
22. "Memoirs of Himself."
23. "A Chapter on Dreams," *Scribner's Magazine,* Jan. 1888, reprinted in *Across the Plains* (1892) and in *Lantern-Bearers,* 217; Revelation 20:11–12.
24. "Memoirs of Himself."
25. "Selections from His Notebook," Tusitala Edition (London: Heinemann, 1924), 29:192; Clayton Hamilton, *On the Trail of Stevenson* (New York: Doubleday, Page, 1916), 72.
26. Balfour, 1:43–44.
27. Simpson, *Robert Louis Stevenson's Edinburgh Days,* 107; Margaret is quoted in *Letters* 1:87.
28. "Memoirs of Himself"; "Stormy Nights," *Collected Poems,* 86–87.
29. "Rosa Quo Locorum," drafted in 1893 on the stationery of the Union Club of Sydney and then set aside; first published in the Edinburgh Edition (1896). The title alludes to an ode of Horace: "Stop searching places where the last rose may linger."
30. Stevenson wrote fables at various times in his life; they were first printed in posthumous editions of his works. Sidney Colvin dated this one around 1874.
31. "Sketches: Nurses: A Character," first published in the Edinburgh Edition (1896).
32. RLS to Alison Cunningham, 1873, *Letters* 1:279–80.
33. Charles Guthrie in *Interviews and Recollections,* 13.
34. Masson, 223; Henry James, "Robert Louis Stevenson," *Partial Portraits* (New York: Macmillan, 1888), 146.
35. RLS to J. M. Barrie, Dec. 7, 1893, *Letters* 8:204; "A Retrospect," written in the early 1870s, first published in the Edinburgh Edition. On this theme, see Ann C. Colley, "Robert Louis Stevenson and the Idea of Recollection," *Victorian Literature and Culture* 25 (1997), 203–23.
36. The complete *Child's Garden of Verses* is in *Collected Poems,* 361–411.
37. "Child's Play," *Cornhill Magazine,* Sept. 1878, reprinted in *Virginibus Puerisque* (1881).
38. RLS to Jane Balfour, 1887, *Letters* 6:96.
39. "A Plea for Gas Lamps," London, April 1878, *Virginibus Puerisque.*
40. Balfour, 1:40.
41. RLS to Alison Cunningham, Feb. 16, 1883, *Letters* 4:76.
42. William Archer, *Pall Mall Gazette,* March 1885, *Critical Heritage,* 157; Stevenson to Archer, March 29, 1885, *Letters* 5:97.
43. Hamilton, *On the Trail of Stevenson,* 20–21; Hamilton met Cummy in 1910.
44. An 1873 manuscript quoted by Balfour, 1:37; "Memoirs of Himself"; "My First Book:

Treasure Island," a contribution to *My First Book,* ed. Jerome K. Jerome (London: Chatto & Windus, 1894).
45. RLS to Cosmo Monkhouse, March 16, 1884, *Letters* 4:259.
46. "A Humble Remonstrance," *Longman's Magazine,* Dec. 1884, *Memories and Portraits* and *Lantern-Bearers,* 196.
47. "A Penny Plain and Twopence Coloured," *Magazine of Art,* April 1884, *Memories and Portraits.*
48. "A Gossip on Romance," *Longman's Magazine,* Nov. 1882, *Memories and Portraits* and *Lantern-Bearers,* 180.

CHAPTER 2. SCHOOLING AND TRAVELS

1. George Lisle in *I Can Remember,* 192.
2. William G. Boss in *I Can Remember,* 4; William Butler Yeats, "Among School Children."
3. James Milne in *I Can Remember,* 6.
4. RLS to his father, Nov. 12, 1863, *Letters* 1:98.
5. "The Foreigner at Home," *Cornhill Magazine,* May 1882, *Memories and Portraits* (1887) and in *Lantern-Bearers,* 164–67.
6. Notes quoted by Mehew, *Letters* 1:28; Eve Blantyre Simpson, *Robert Louis Stevenson's Edinburgh Days* (London: Hodder & Stoughton, 1914), 31.
7. Balfour, 1:64; Francis Watt, *R.L.S.* (London: Methuen, 1913), 30.
8. Henry Bellyse Baildon, *Robert Louis Stevenson: A Life Study in Criticism* (London: Chatto & Windus, 1901), 17.
9. Baildon, dedication to *The Rescue and Other Poems* (1893); RLS to Baildon, Jan. 15, 1894, *Letters* 8:236.
10. The stories are quoted by Balfour, 1:78–79.
11. "Popular Authors," *Scribner's Magazine,* July 1888, not reprinted in Stevenson's lifetime. *Black Bess* is quoted by Jeremy Hodges, *Mrs. Jekyll and Cousin Hyde* (Edinburgh: Luath, 2017), 14.
12. David M. Lewis in *I Can Remember,* 27.
13. Manuscript examples quoted by Menikoff in the notes to "The Misadventures of John Nicholson," *Complete Stories,* 784; *The Letters of Robert Louis Stevenson to His Family and Friends,* ed. Sidney Colvin (London: Methuen, 1906), introduction, 1:xliv.
14. RLS to Thomas Stevenson, March–April 1865, March 1866, *Letters* 1:108–10. On the name "Robert" at school, see *Letters* 1:155n.
15. RLS to his mother, Nov. 19, 1864, *Letters* 1:99.
16. Francis Lacassin, introduction to Stevenson, *La France que j'aime* (Paris: Union Générale d'Éditions, 1978), 7.
17. *Cummy's Diary: A Diary Kept by R. L. Stevenson's Nurse Alison Cunningham while Traveling with Him on the Continent during 1863* (London: Chatto & Windus, 1926).

CHAPTER 3. HAPPINESS IN THE COUNTRYSIDE

1. "Memoirs of Himself," first published in posthumous editions of Stevenson's works.
2. "The Manse: A Fragment," *Scribner's Magazine,* May 1887, reprinted in *Memories and Portraits* in that year.

3. "Memoirs of Himself."
4. "Memoirs of Himself"; "Mrs. Dale" in *I Can Remember*, 10.
5. "Keepsake Mill," *Collected Poems*, 376–77; Margaret Armour, *The Home and Early Haunts of Robert Louis Stevenson* (Edinburgh: W. H. White, 1895), 55.
6. "Child's Play," *Cornhill Magazine*, Sept. 1878, reprinted in *Virginibus Puerisque* (1881).
7. *Stevensoniana*, 5–6.
8. Quoted respectively by Craig Mair, *A Star for Seamen: The Stevenson Family of Engineers* (London: John Murray, 1978), 172, and Jeremy Hodges, *Mrs. Jekyll and Cousin Hyde* (Edinburgh: Luath, 2017), 11.
9. "To Minnie," *Collected Poems*, 409.
10. Calder, 21; *Edinburgh: Picturesque Notes* (1879), ch. 10.
11. S. R. Crockett, "The Apprenticeship of Robert Louis Stevenson," *Robert Louis Stevenson: The Man and His Work*, extra number of the *Bookman* (London: Hodder & Stoughton, 1913), 68.
12. "The Lantern-Bearers," *Scribner's Magazine*, Feb. 1888, in *Lantern-Bearers*, 228–34.
13. "A Gossip on Romance," *Longman's Magazine*, Nov. 1882, reprinted in *Memories and Portraits* and in *Lantern-Bearers*, 174–75.
14. Robert Burns, "Epistle to J. Lapraik, An Old Scottish Bard."
15. "Ille Terrarum," *Collected Poems*, 147–49; Horace, *Odes* II.6.
16. RLS to Frances Sitwell, May 14, 1874, *Letters* 2:8; "Pastoral," *Longman's Magazine*, April 1887, reprinted in *Memories and Portraits*.
17. "The Foreigner at Home," written in 1882, published in *Memories and Portraits*.
18. John A. Ross, *Good Words*, March 1895; *Edinburgh Evening Dispatch*, Aug. 30, 1902, both in *Stevensoniana*, 19, 22.
19. Francis Watt, *R.L.S.* (London: Methuen, 1913), 90.
20. James Milne in *I Can Remember*, 7. The story was first published in *Robert Louis Stevenson: The Scottish Stories and Essays*, ed. Kenneth Gelder (Edinburgh: Edinburgh University Press, 1989), 16–21.
21. RLS to Margaret (who was in Edinburgh at the time), July 18, 1893, *Letters* 8:137.
22. Balfour, 1:77.
23. "A College Magazine," first published in *Memories and Portraits*.
24. RLS to W. Leslie Curnow, Feb. 1891, *Letters* 7:82.
25. "A Gossip on a Novel of Dumas's," *Memories and Portraits*.
26. David Coward, *The Vicomte de Bragelonne*, ed. David Coward (Oxford: Oxford University Press, 1995), xi, xix; this edition is an adaptation of the 1857 translation.
27. Eve Blantyre Simpson, *Robert Louis Stevenson's Edinburgh Days* (London: Hodder & Stoughton, 1914), 160.
28. Balfour, 1:42; James Hyslop, "Cameronian Dream," first published in the *Edinburgh Magazine and Literary Miscellany* (1821); Mary Lascelles, *The Story-Teller Retrieves the Past* (Oxford: Clarendon, 1980), 23.
29. *The Pentland Rising: A Page of History* (Edinburgh: Andrew Elliot, 1866).
30. Balfour, 1:80.
31. RLS to Sidney Colvin, May 18, 1893, and Charles Baxter, June 18, 1894, *Letters* 8:288, 308; "My First Book: *Treasure Island*," *Idler*, Aug. 1894, reprinted in *My First Book*, ed. Jerome K. Jerome (London: Chatto & Windus, 1894).

CHAPTER 4. THE MASTER BUILDERS

1. Robert Southey, "The Inchcape Rock" (1802).
2. *Records of a Family of Engineers,* written 1891–94, never completed and first published in posthumous editions of Stevenson's works.
3. *Records of a Family of Engineers.*
4. RLS to Margaret, Sept. 5, 1868, *Letters* 1:142.
5. RLS to Margaret, Sept. 7–8, 1868, *Letters* 1:144–45 and note.
6. "On the Enjoyment of Unpleasant Places," *The Portfolio,* Nov. 1874, not reprinted in Stevenson's lifetime; Swearingen (p. 15) says it was based on the time at Wick.
7. RLS to Margaret, July 28, 1868, *Letters* 1:136.
8. Anonymous reminiscence signed "Lantern-Bearer" in *I Can Remember,* 32–33.
9. Rankin, 45; "The Education of an Engineer," *Scribner's Magazine,* Nov. 1888, reprinted in *Across the Plains* (1892); Florence MacCunn in *I Can Remember,* 24.
10. RLS to Thomas, Sept. 2, 1868, *Letters* 1:139.
11. "The Education of an Engineer."
12. "The Light-Keeper," *Collected Poems,* 79–81.
13. Craig Mair, *A Star for Seamen: The Stevenson Family of Engineers* (London: John Murray, 1978), 207; Bella Bathurst, *The Lighthouse Stevensons* (London: HarperCollins, 1999), 233.

CHAPTER 5. A NEW LIFE AT THE UNIVERSITY

1. The evidence is persuasively reviewed by Harman, 332–33, citing Alan E. Guttmacher and J. R. Callahan, "Did Robert Louis Stevenson Have Hereditary Hemorrhagic Telangiectasia?" *American Journal of Medical Genetics* 91 (2000). The condition is also known as Osler-Rendu-Weber disease.
2. "The Foreigner at Home," *Cornhill Magazine,* May 1882, *Memories and Portraits* (1887) and in *Lantern-Bearers,* 168–69.
3. "Some College Memories," contributed to *The New Amphion: Being the Book of the Edinburgh University Union Fancy Fair* (1886), reprinted in *Memories and Portraits.*
4. Untitled, *Collected Poems,* 329. It's not certain which professor is meant.
5. Balfour, 1:126.
6. RLS to Aeneas MacKay, June 1881, *Letters* 3:200–201.
7. Etta Younger (née Henrietta Balfour) in *I Can Remember,* 79–80.
8. Masson, 57, 60.
9. Patrick Campbell in *I Can Remember,* 20.
10. William Ernest Henley, "R.L.S.," *Pall Mall Magazine,* Dec. 1901.
11. "An Apology for Idlers," *Cornhill Magazine,* July 1877, reprinted in *Virginibus Puerisque* (1881) and *Lantern-Bearers,* 35, 39.
12. "Some Aspects of Robert Burns," *Cornhill Magazine,* May–Aug. 187, *Familiar Studies of Men and Books* (1882) and *Lantern-Bearers,* 102. *Leaves of Grass* is recalled in "Books Which Have Influenced Me," included with essays by eleven other writers in *British Weekly Extras,* no. 1, *Books Which Have Influenced Me* (1887), 3–16.
13. Isobel Strong, quoted by Elsie Noble Caldwell, *Last Witness for Robert Louis Stevenson* (Norman: University of Oklahoma Press, 1960), 310–11.

14. "A College Magazine," *Memories and Portraits*; Chesterton, 141.
15. "The Modern Student Considered Generally," *Edinburgh University Magazine,* Jan.–April 1871, first reprinted in the Edinburgh Edition (1896).
16. RLS to Charles Baxter, May 18, 1894, *Letters* 8:290.
17. *Weir of Hermiston,* ch. 2; Shakespeare, *A Winter's Tale,* IV.iv.
18. Quoted from 1880 manuscript notes by Balfour, 1:103.
19. "Talk and Talkers," *Cornhill Magazine,* April 1882, *Memories and Portraits.*
20. Quoted by Balfour, 1:107.
21. RLS to Bob Stevenson, fall 1868, *Letters* 1:143, 169.
22. Richard Le Gallienne, *The Romantic '90's* (London: Putnam, 1926), 82.
23. Preface to *Familiar Studies of Men and Books* (1882).
24. Richard Holmes, "On the Enchanted Hill," *New York Review of Books,* June 8, 1995.
25. RLS to Baxter, Jan. 1874 and March 4, 1881, *Letters* 1:144, 2: 86. "Do you twig?" means "Do you get it?"
26. John Geddie in *I Can Remember,* 126–27; Masson, 90.
27. Rankin, 55.
28. Furnas, 498; *A Book of R.L.S.*, ed. George E. Brown (New York: Scribner's, 1919), 166.
29. RLS to Baxter, March or April 1872, *Letters* 1:217–18; Acts 2:13.
30. *The Collected Poems of Robert Louis Stevenson,* ed. Roger Lewis (Edinburgh: Edinburgh University Press, 2003), 312.
31. RLS to Bob, Jan. 7 and March 29, 1870, *Letters* 1:192–94.
32. "Old Mortality," *Memories and Portraits* (1887), ch. 3.
33. Charles John Guthrie, *Robert Louis Stevenson: Some Personal Recollections* (Edinburgh: W. Green, 1924), 34.
34. RLS to Baxter, March 25, 1873, *Letters* 1:275.
35. RLS to Baxter, Nov. 10, 1891, *Letters* 7:192; "Walt Whitman," *Familiar Studies* (1882) and *Lantern-Bearers,* 87.
36. "Crabbed Age and Youth," *Cornhill Magazine,* March 1878; *Virginibus Puerisque* (1881) and *Lantern-Bearers,* 61–62; "Victor Hugo's Romances," *Familiar Studies of Men and Books.*
37. RLS to Sidney Colvin, Nov. 1875, *Letters* 2:165; Archibald Bisset in *I Can Remember,* 60.
38. Henry James, "Robert Louis Stevenson," *Century Magazine,* April 1888.
39. Balfour, 1:102.
40. Barry Menikoff, *Narrating Scotland: The Imagination of Robert Louis Stevenson* (Columbia: University of South Carolina Press, 2005), 13–14.
41. Guthrie, *Robert Louis Stevenson,* 40, 31, 12–13.
42. Thomas Barclay in *I Can Remember,* 124.

CHAPTER 6. "I WANT PLEASURE"

1. RLS to Frances Sitwell, Oct. 25, 1874, *Letters* 2:69.
2. *Edinburgh: Picturesque Notes,* ch. 9; Walter Scott, *Waverley,* ch. 44; Flora Masson in *I Can Remember,* 159.
3. George Crabbie in *I Can Remember,* 44–45; William Henry Duncan, "Stevenson's Second Visit to America," *Bookman,* Jan. 1900, 460.

4. "The Modern Student Considered Generally," *Edinburgh University Magazine* (1871), not reprinted until the posthumous editions of Stevenson's works.
5. "My First Book: *Treasure Island*," contribution to *My First Book*, ed. Jerome K. Jerome (London: Chatto & Windus, 1894).
6. David M. Lewis, *I Can Remember*, 26–27; Eve Blantyre Simpson, *Robert Louis Stevenson's Edinburgh Days* (London: Hodder & Stoughton, 1914), 248.
7. Walter Grindlay Simpson, *The Art of Golf* (Edinburgh: David Douglas, 1892), 135.
8. John Howell, *Stevenson's Baby Book* (San Francisco: John Henry Nash, 1922), facsimile page 19.
9. "Duddingston," *Collected Poems*, 62; Calder, 55–56. Eve Simpson herself left no mention of this.
10. *Collected Poems of Robert Louis Stevenson*, ed. Roger Lewis (Edinburgh: Edinburgh University Press, 2003), 243–44.
11. "A College Magazine," *Memories and Portraits* (1887).
12. RLS to Henley (writing from San Francisco), Jan. 26, 1880, *Letters* 3:55.
13. See *Letters* 3:55n; and Furnas, 399.
14. J. A. Steuart, *Robert Louis Stevenson: Man and Writer* (London: Samson, Low, Marston, 1924).
15. Furnas (457–63) decisively rejects the "Claire" hypothesis, showing that it was one of the pet names Louis used years later for Frances Sitwell, and possibly a character in a projected story as well. But when he thereby dismisses "Claire-Kate," he is assuming more than anyone can know.
16. *Collected Poems*, 332–33 and 59; Horace, *Odes* II.4.
17. "My brain swims empty and light," *Collected Poems*, 82.
18. Walt Whitman, *Leaves of Grass*, "I Sing the Body Electric," section 5.
19. Masson, 78; see E. H. Hunt, "Industrialization and Regional Inequality: Wages in Britain, 1769–1914," *Journal of Economic History* 46 (1986), 935–66.
20. Balfour, 1:99; Henry Bellyse Baildon, *Robert Louis Stevenson: A Life Study in Criticism* (London: Chatto & Windus, 1901), 29; Colvin in the *Empire Review* (1924), quoted by E. V. Lucas, *The Colvins and Their Friends* (New York: Scribner, 1928), 269.
21. *Edinburgh: Picturesque Notes* (1879), chs. 1–2.
22. Isabella Bird, *Notes on Old Edinburgh* (Edinburgh: Edmonston & Douglas, 1869), 10, 14, 30.
23. T. C. Smout, *A Century of the Scottish People, 1830–1950* (London: Fontana, 1987), 2.
24. "Samuel Pepys," *Cornhill Magazine*, July 1881, *Familiar Studies of Men and Books* (1882) and *Lantern-Bearers*, 155.
25. *Collected Poems*, ed. Lewis, 319 (not included in Janet Adam Smith's *Collected Poems*); Matthew 21:31.
26. Balfour is quoted in *Letters* 1:210–11.
27. "Selections from His Notebook," *Works*, Tusitala Edition (London: Heinemann, 1924), 29: 172.
28. Quoted from the Balfour papers by Harman, 56–57.
29. Balfour, 1:99–100; Wilson McLaren in *I Can Remember*, 256.
30. Lloyd Osbourne, introduction to South Seas Edition (New York: Scribner, 1925), 1:x–xvi.

31. Calder, 54.
32. RLS to Colvin, March 9, 1884, *Letters* 4:246; Augustine, *Confessions* I.ix and II.ii, trans. Henry Chadwick (Oxford: Oxford University Press, 1991), 12, 24. In the original Louis's text reads: "See his splendid passage about the *luminosus limes amicitiae* and the *nebulae de limosa concupiscentia carnis,* going on *utrumque in confuso aestuabat et rapiebat inbecillam aetatem per abrupta cupiditatum.*"
33. Masson, 67.
34. "Talk and Talkers," *Cornhill Magazine,* April 1882, *Memories and Portraits* (1887).
35. Eve Blantyre Simpson, *Robert Louis Stevenson's Edinburgh Days* (London: Hodder & Stoughton, 1914), 205, 214, 268.
36. David Daiches, *Robert Louis Stevenson* (New York: New Directions, 1947), 20; Rosaline Masson in *Interviews and Recollections* (Iowa City: University of Iowa Press, 1996), 30.
37. Moray McLaren, *Stevenson and Edinburgh: A Centenary Study* (London: Chapman & Hall, 1950), 117; Flora Masson in *I Can Remember,* 159. Stevenson's *Memoir* was printed as preface to a two-volume edition of Jenkin's *Papers Literary, Scientific, Etc.* (London: Longman's, Green, 1887), quoted here from 1:lxv.
38. Sidney Colvin, *Memories and Notes of Persons and Places* (London: Edward Arnold, 1921), 160–61.
39. J. Alfred Ewing in *I Can Remember,* 133–50.
40. Flora Masson in *I Can Remember,* 165.
41. *Edinburgh: Picturesque Notes,* ch. 1.

CHAPTER 7. A "HORRIBLE ATHEIST"

1. RLS to Walter Ferrier, Nov. 23, 1872, and to Baxter, Dec. 1890, *Letters* 1:259 and 7:55.
2. *Collected Poems of Robert Louis Stevenson,* ed. Roger Lewis (Edinburgh: Edinburgh University Press, 2003), 319.
3. *British Weekly Extras,* no. 1, *Books Which Have Influenced Me* (1887).
4. Rev. Archibald Bisset in *I Can Remember,* 66–67.
5. RLS to Baxter, Jan. 16, 1873, *Letters* 1:270–71; Shakespeare, *Hamlet,* I.ii.
6. RLS to Baxter, Feb. 1, 1873, *Letters* 1:273–74.
7. RLS to Baxter, Dec. 15, 1881, and to Katharine de Mattos, Oct. 1874, *Letters* 3:264, 2:63.
8. RLS to Frances Sitwell, Sept. 9, 1873, *Letters* 1:294–95.
9. RLS to Frances, Sept. 12, 1873, *Letters* 1:298.
10. RLS to Frances, Sept. 17 and 22, 1873, *Letters* 1:302, 312.
11. Colvin to Margaret Stevenson, March 21, 1896, Beinecke 4386.
12. Luisa Villa, "Quarreling with the Father," *Robert Louis Stevenson: Writer of Boundaries,* ed. Richard Ambrosini and Richard Dury (Madison: University of Wisconsin Press, 2006), 112–13, 118–19.
13. Masson, 99.
14. RLS to Frances Sitwell, Sept. 22, 1874, *Letters* 2:56; Henry James, review of Stevenson's Letters, *North American Review,* 1900, reprinted in *Notes on Novelists* (1914).
15. Samuel Butler, *The Way of All Flesh* (1903), ch. 67.
16. Steven Mintz, *A Prison of Expectations: The Family in Victorian Culture* (New York: New York University Press, 1983), 78.

17. "Truth of Intercourse," *Cornhill Magazine,* May 1879, reprinted in *Virginibus Puerisque* (1881) and *Lantern-Bearers,* 98.
18. "Selections from His Notebook," Tusitala Edition (London: Heinemann, 1924), 29: 180, 174; Genesis 22:7.
19. "A Chapter on Dreams," *Scribner's Magazine,* Jan. 1888, reprinted in *Across the Plains* (1892) and in *Lantern-Bearers,* 221–22.
20. Kay Redfield Jamison, *Exuberance: The Passion for Life* (New York: Knopf, 2004), 278–86. Though she doesn't identify sources, the quotation comes from Edmund Gosse, *Critical Kit-Cats* (New York: Dodd, Mead, 1903), 279.
21. RLS to F. W. H. Myers, July 14, 1882, *Letters* 7:331–34.
22. Romans 7:23; Masson, 95.
23. "A Christmas Sermon," *Scribner's Magazine,* Dec. 1888, 764–68.

CHAPTER 8. A MENTOR AND A MADONNA

1. RLS to Margaret, Oct. 6, 1870, *Letters* 1:207.
2. Lady Colvin (Frances Sitwell) in *I Can Remember,* 111; Calder, 70.
3. E. V. Lucas, *The Colvins and Their Friends* (New York: Scribner, 1928), 64; Pope Hennessy, 7.
4. Quoted by Ann Thwaite, *Edmund Gosse: A Literary Landscape, 1849–1928* (Chicago: University of Chicago Press, 1984), 500, and by Lucas, *The Colvins and Their Friends,* 184.
5. Colvin's introduction to *Vailima Letters* (London: Stone & Kimball, 1895), 11–12; Leslie Stephen, *Studies of a Biographer,* second series (London: Duckworth, 1902), 4:207.
6. RLS to Frances Sitwell, Sept. 1 and 8, 1873, *Letters* 1:288–93.
7. RLS to Frances, Oct. 8, 1873, *Letters* 1:335.
8. RLS to Frances, Sept. 29, 1873, *Letters* 1:322.
9. RLS to Frances, Dec. 2, 1873, *Letters* 1:385; Katherine Ashley, *Robert Louis Stevenson and Nineteenth-Century French Literature* (Edinburgh: Edinburgh University Press, 2022), 8.
10. RLS to Frances, late June and Aug. 19, 1874, *Letters* 2:25, 40.
11. RLS to Frances, Dec. 25 and 28, 1874, *Letters* 1:322 and 2:94, 96.
12. RLS to Frances, Oct. 22 and 29 and Nov. 1, 1874, *Letters* 2:68–72, 76–77.
13. RLS to Frances, Jan. 9, 1875, *Letters* 2:100–101.
14. *When the Devil Was Well,* ed. William P. Trent (Boston: Bibliophile Society, 1921), 29–30, 90.
15. McLynn, 71.
16. E. V. Lucas, ed., *Her Infinite Variety: A Feminine Portrait Gallery* (London: Methuen, 1908), 71–72.
17. RLS to Frances, May 8, 1875, *Letters* 2:135.
18. "To Sidney Colvin," *Collected Poems,* 258–59.
19. *The Letters of Robert Louis Stevenson to His Family and Friends,* ed. Sidney Colvin (London: Methuen, 1906), 1:xx, xxix; "Crabbed Age and Youth," *Cornhill Magazine,* March 1878, *Virginibus Puerisque* (1881).
20. Sidney Colvin, *Memories and Notes of Persons and Places* (London: Edward Arnold, 1921), 104–5; RLS to Colvin, March 1879, *Letters* 2:307.

21. RLS to Colvin, April 1879, *Letters* 2:315.
22. "Memoirs of Himself," in posthumous editions of Stevenson's works.
23. Colvin, *Memories and Notes,* 119–20; Clayton Hamilton, *On the Trail of Stevenson* (New York: Doubleday, Page, 1916), 59–60.
24. Colvin, *Memories and Notes,* 121; "A Portrait," *Collected Poems,* 140 (Gosse is quoted on 484); RLS to Gosse, April 27, 1881, *Letters* 3:173.
25. Colvin, *Memories and Notes,* 109, 125.

CHAPTER 9. "ORDERED SOUTH"

1. RLS to Elizabeth Crosby, July and Oct. 7, 1873, *Letters* 1:277, 340.
2. RLS to Frances, Nov. 4, 1873, *Letters* 1:354–55.
3. Margaret's diary entry is quoted in *Letters* 1:350.
4. James Henry Bennett, quoted in John Pemble, *The Mediterranean Passion: Victorians and Edwardians in the South* (Oxford: Oxford University Press, 1988), 26; RLS to Margaret, Nov. 18, 1873, and to Frances, Nov. 13, *Letters* 1:363–65.
5. RLS to Frances, Nov. 13; Bob's letter is quoted in a note on p. 364.
6. RLS to Baxter, Nov. 15, *Letters* 1:369.
7. RLS to Frances, Nov. 18, 1873, *Letters* 1:373.
8. RLS to Frances Sitwell, Nov. 16–22, 1873, *Letters* 1:371–75; these entries are dated but were all sent as a single letter. On Louis's diagnosis, see Julia Reid, *Robert Louis Stevenson, Science, and the Fin de Siècle* (London: Palgrave Macmillan, 2006), 64.
9. Pemble, *The Mediterranean Passion,* 84.
10. Pemble, *The Mediterranean Passion,* 84; "Ordered South," *Macmillan's Magazine,* May 1874, *Virginibus Puerisque* (1881); Kay Redfield Jamison, *Exuberance: The Passion for Life* (New York: Knopf, 2004), 283.
11. RLS to Frances, Dec. 7–8, 1873, and to Margaret, Dec. 9, 1873, *Letters* 1:401–2, 407.
12. RLS to Frances, Dec. 11 and 19, *Letters* 1:403, 414.
13. For example, in a letter to Colvin, Jan. 10, 1874, *Letters* 1:430.
14. RLS to Frances, Dec. 15 and 18, 1873, *Letters* 1:411–13.
15. RLS to his mother, Dec. 19, 1873, *Letters* 1:417.
16. Sidney Colvin, *Memories and Notes of Persons and Places* (London: Edward Arnold, 1921), 113.
17. *The Letters of Robert Louis Stevenson to His Family and Friends,* ed. Sidney Colvin (London: Methuen, 1906), introduction, 1:xxxii. The mock advertisement is quoted by E. V. Lucas, *The Colvins and Their Friends* (New York: Scribner, 1928), 84.
18. Andrew Lang, "Recollections of Robert Louis Stevenson," *Adventures among Books* (London: Longman's, Green, 1905), 43.
19. Clayton Hamilton, *On the Trail of Stevenson* (New York: Doubleday, Page, 1916), 82–83.
20. Lang, "Recollections of Robert Louis Stevenson," 51.
21. "To Andrew Lang," *Collected Poems,* 123–24. Louis sent this poem to Lang on March 10, 1886, *Letters* 5:227; Colvin's introduction to *Works by R. L. Stevenson* (London: Chatto & Windus, 1911); RLS to William Ernest Henley, Oct. 10, 1881, *Letters* 3:241.
22. Colvin, *Memories and Notes,* 118.
23. Sheriff Maconochie in *I Can Remember,* 101.

24. RLS to his mother, Feb. 5, 1874, and to Frances, Jan. 26, *Letters* 1:379, 465.
25. RLS to his mother, Jan. 11, 1874, *Letters* 1:432.
26. RLS to Frances, Jan. 13, 1874, *Letters* 1:437–38.
27. RLS to his mother, March 9 and 20, 1874, *Letters* 1:488, 496; Edmund Gosse, *Critical Kit-Cats* (New York: Dodd, Mead, 1903), 283.
28. Bob Stevenson to RLS, Feb. 4, 1874, quoted in *Letters* 1:477n.

CHAPTER 10. FIRST STEPS AS A WRITER

1. "John Knox and His Relations to Women: Private Life," *Macmillan's Magazine,* Sept. 1874, reprinted in *Familiar Studies of Men and Books* (1882) and in *Lantern-Bearers,* 7–24.
2. "A Gossip on a Novel of Dumas's," *Memories and Portraits* (1887); RLS to George Saintsbury, March 4, 1886, *Letters* 5:217; Ralph Waldo Emerson, "Montaigne, or, the Skeptic."
3. *Familiar Studies of Men and Books,* preface.
4. RLS to Colvin, July 15, 1874, and to W. Craibe Angus, Nov. 1891, *Letters* 2:32, 7:208.
5. *The Academy,* Aug. 8 and 15, 1874.
6. RLS to Frances Sitwell and Colvin, May 28–June 8, 1875, *Letters* 2:138–42.
7. *Letters* 4:332–34 (appendix).
8. RLS to Frances, Feb. 13, 1875, *Letters* 2:117.
9. Lang's introduction to vol. 1, *The Works of Robert Louis Stevenson,* Swanston Edition (London: Chatto & Windus, 1911); RLS to Henley, May 1883, *Letters* 4:129.
10. Henley to RLS, May 1876 and July 31, 1879, Henley *Letters,* 38, 72.
11. Henley, *In Hospital,* first published in *Verses* (1888), nos. 24, 5, 27; RLS to Bob Stevenson, March 10, 1875, and to A. Trevor Haddon, April 24, 1884, *Letters* 2:124 and 4:276.
12. Margaret Stevenson to Henley, Feb. 1876, quoted by Edward H. Cohen, *The Henley-Stevenson Quarrel* (Gainesville: University Press of Florida, 1974), 13; the "Ballade" is quoted on p. 18.
13. "Talk and Talkers," *Cornhill Magazine,* April 1882, *Memories and Portraits*; RLS to Henley, Nov. 1883, *Letters* 4:202.
14. John Connell, *W. E. Henley* (London: Constable, 1949), 62.
15. Henley to RLS, Dec. 14, 1877, Henley *Letters,* 47.
16. Etta [Henrietta] Younger in *I Can Remember,* 65.
17. Charles John Guthrie, *Robert Louis Stevenson: Some Personal Recollections* (Edinburgh: W. Green, 1924), 59.
18. George Moody Stuart in *I Can Remember,* 23.
19. RLS to Bob, Oct. 1872, *Letters* 1:254. Swearingen (p. 39) dates "On the Choice of a Profession" to January 1879. Stevenson's stepson Lloyd found it among his papers and published it as a pamphlet (London: Chatto & Windus, 1926).

CHAPTER 11. ARTISTS AND BOATS

1. Lloyd Osbourne, introduction to the South Seas Edition of Stevenson's *Works* (New York: Scribner, 1925), 1:xxi.

2. Bob Stevenson to RLS, March 1875, Beinecke 5694.
3. Andrew Lang, "Recollections of Robert Louis Stevenson," *Adventures among Books* (London: Longman's, Green, 1905), 49.
4. Will H. Low, quoted in *Stevensoniana,* 37.
5. "Fontainebleau: Village Communities of Painters," *Magazine of Art,* May 1884, reprinted in *Across the Plains with Other Memories and Essays* (1892).
6. Will H. Low, *A Chronicle of Friendships* (New York: Scribner, 1908), ix.
7. "Fontainebleau: Village Communities of Painters"; Low, *A Chronicle of Friendships,* 174, 176.
8. "Envoy" to *Underwoods, Collected Poems,* 111.
9. "Forest Notes," *Cornhill Magazine,* May 1876, *Lantern-Bearers,* 26; RLS to Colvin, June 1876, *Letters* 2:174.
10. Low, *A Chronicle of Friendships,* 426.
11. RLS to Bob, Oct. 20, 1874, and to Henley, May 1883, *Letters* 2:64 and 4:122.
12. "Samuel Pepys," *Cornhill Magazine,* July 1881, reprinted the next year in *Familiar Studies of Men and Books* and in *Lantern-Bearers,* 146, 142.
13. *The Diary of Samuel Pepys,* ed. Robert Latham and William Matthews (Berkeley: University of California Press, 1974), 7:2.
14. RLS to his mother, Aug. 5, 1872, *Letters* 1:243.
15. "Talk and Talkers," *Cornhill Magazine,* April 1882, *Memories and Portraits* (1887).
16. Margaret Bertha Wright, "Bohemian Days," *Scribner's Monthly,* May 1878.
17. McLynn, 106; Harman, 143.
18. RLS to Frances Sitwell, July 9, 1876, *Letters* 2:176.
19. *An Inland Voyage,* "The Royal Sport Nautique"; "At Maubeuge," "Sambre and the Oise Canal." The brief chapters have titles but are not numbered.
20. "La Fère of Cursed Memory."
21. "On the Sambre Canalised: To Landrecies."
22. RLS to Bob Stevenson, April 1884, *Letters* 4:269; Henley to Baxter, April 19, 1884, *Letters* 4:269n; see the note in *Collected Poems,* 527.
23. E. M. Forster, "The Story of a Panic."
24. Kenneth Grahame, *The Wind in the Willows,* ch. 7.
25. "Pan's Pipes," *London,* May 1878, reprinted in *Virginibus Puerisque* (1881).
26. Sydney Low, "Some Memories and Impressions: William Ernest Henley," *The Living Age* (1903), 150; Low, *A Chronicle of Friendships,* 53.
27. *An Inland Voyage,* "Changed Times."
28. Michel de Montaigne, *Essais,* III.13, "De l'expérience."
29. Anonymous review in *London,* May 25, 1878; George Meredith to RLS, June 4, 1878; both in *Critical Heritage,* 48–54.
30. RLS to his mother, June (or early July) and Sept. 19, 1878, *Letters* 2:258, 276.
31. "Epilogue to *An Inland Voyage,*" *Scribner's Magazine,* July–Dec. 1888, 250.
32. McLynn, 106.
33. *An Inland Voyage,* "At Landrecies."

CHAPTER 12. ENTER FANNY

1. RLS to Margaret, Aug. 1875, *Letters* 2:156.
2. "Fontainebleau," *Magazine of Art,* May 1884, reprinted in *Across the Plains* (1892).
3. *This Life I've Loved,* 104.
4. "On Falling in Love," written Nov. 1876, *Virginibus Puerisque* (1881) and *Lantern-Bearers,* 43–46; RLS to Fanny, May 15, 1888, *Letters* 6:186.
5. "Story of the House with the Green Blinds," *London* (1878), reprinted in *New Arabian Nights* (1882); *Complete Stories,* 113; "The Story of a Lie," *New Quarterly Magazine,* Oct. 1879, *Complete Stories,* 671.
6. Richard Holmes, *Footsteps: Adventures of a Romantic Biographer* (New York: Vintage Books, 1985), 41–42.
7. *The Autobiography of S. S. McClure* (New York: Frederick A. Stokes, 1914), 197; "Dark Women," *Collected Poems of Robert Louis Stevenson,* ed. Roger C. Lewis (Edinburgh: Edinburgh University Press, 2003), 175.
8. Birge Harrison, "With Stevenson at Grez" (1916), in *Interviews and Recollections,* 80; Eve Blantyre Simpson, *Robert Louis Stevenson's Edinburgh Days* (London: Hodder & Stoughton, 1914), 287.
9. Gosse as recalled by Edward Marsh in a letter to Neville Lytton, June 1, 1898, and by Fanny to her friend Dora Williams in 1885; both quoted in *Letters* 1:66 and 4:28n.
10. *The Autobiography of S. S. McClure,* 197–98.
11. Austin Strong, "The Most Unforgettable Character I've Met," *Reader's Digest,* March 1946.
12. Singer, 64.
13. Bruce Porter, quoted by Sanchez, vii.
14. Margaret Mackay, *The Violent Friend: The Story of Mrs. Robert Louis Stevenson* (New York: Doubleday, 1968), 3. This valuable study is thoroughly researched, but gives no page references to her sources.
15. Sanchez, 3, 7.
16. Sanchez, 10–19.
17. Sanchez, 23–24.
18. *This Life I've Loved,* 7.
19. Mark Twain, *Roughing It,* chs. 29, 43.
20. Sanchez, 32, 41.
21. McLynn, 111.
22. Fanny to Timothy Reardon, quoted by Pope Hennessy, 111.
23. Lloyd Osbourne, introduction to the Tusitala Edition (London: Heinemann, 1924), 1:ix.
24. Fanny's postscript to Louis's letter to Baxter, Sept. 1881, *Letters* 3:234.
25. Will H. Low, *A Chronicle of Friendships* (New York: Scribner, 1908), 185.
26. Bohemian Days," *Scribner's Monthly,* May 1878.
27. *This Life I've Loved,* 105–6; in *King Lear* V.iii, "Her voice was ever soft, / Gentle, and low, an excellent thing in woman." Eve Blantyre Simpson, *Robert Louis Stevenson's Edinburgh Days* (London: Hodder & Stoughton, 1914), 289.

28. Sanchez, 48.
29. Fanny to Rearden, quoted by Mackay, 58.
30. RLS to Will H. Low, March 1883, *Letters* 4:88.
31. Fanny to Rearden, Nov. 27, 1877, quoted in *Letters* 2:222n; Simpson, *Robert Louis Stevenson's Edinburgh Days,* 290–91.
32. Birge Harrison, "With Stevenson at Grez," *Century Magazine,* Dec. 1919, reprinted in *I Can Remember,* 234.
33. Low, *A Chronicle of Friendships,* 290, 343.
34. Henry Bellyse Baildon, *Robert Louis Stevenson: A Life Study in Criticism* (London: Chatto & Windus, 1901), 45; "The Family," *Collected Poems,* 311.
35. Osbourne, introduction to the Tusitala Edition, 1:xx.
36. Thomas to Louis, Oct. 4, 1877, and Louis's reply, Oct. 10, *Letters* 2:223 and note.
37. Fanny to Timothy Rearden, quoted by Pope Hennessy, 122; RLS to Frances, Nov. 1877, *Letters* 2:225; Fanny is quoted in a note.
38. RLS to Henley, Dec. 1877, *Letters* 2:227.
39. RLS to Colvin, Jan. 1878, and to Frances, Feb. 7, *Letters* 2:237–38.
40. McLynn, 127–28.
41. RLS to his parents, summer 1878, *Letters* 2:260–61.
42. RLS to Baxter, March or April 1877, *Letters* 2:205. On this episode, see Roger G. Swearingen, "Recent Studies in Robert Louis Stevenson: Survey of Biographical Works and Checklist of Criticism, 1970–2005," *Dickens Studies Annual: Essays on Victorian Fiction* 38 (2007), 254.
43. Sanchez, 29.
44. *From Scotland to Silverado,* ed. James D. Hart (Cambridge, MA: Harvard University Press, 1966), introduction, xv.
45. *Intimate Portrait,* 12–13.
46. *This Life I've Loved,* 113.
47. Singer, 48; "Truth of Intercourse," written in Jan. 1879, *Cornhill Magazine,* May 1879, reprinted in *Virginibus Puerisque* (1881) and in *Lantern-Bearers,* 97–99; Rankin, 118.

CHAPTER 13. THE DONKEY BOOK

1. "Walking Tours," *Cornhill Magazine,* June 1876, *Lantern-Bearers,* 28–32.
2. "Walt Whitman," *Familiar Studies of Men and Books* (1882) and *Lantern-Bearers,* 76.
3. RLS to Baxter, Sept. 8, 1878, *Letters* 2:268; Psalm 137:4–5.
4. As with *An Inland Voyage,* the chapters in *Travels with a Donkey* have names but not numbers. However, there is an excellent modern edition, and I give page references to it as well as chapter titles: *Travels with a Donkey in the Cévennes and The Amateur Emigrant,* ed. Christopher MacLachlan (London: Penguin, 2004). This quotation comes from "Upper Gévaudan: Cheylard and Luc," 35.
5. William Wordsworth, "At the Feast of Brougham Castle" (the allusion is to "The silence that is in the starry sky, / The sleep that is among the lonely hills"). "Books Which Have Influenced Me" was published in *British Weekly Extras,* no. 1, *Books Which Have Influenced Me* (1887), and reprinted in posthumous editions of Stevenson's works. The point about "art for art's sake" is made by Alex Clunas in "'Out of My Country and Myself I

Go': Identity and Writing in Stevenson's Early Travel Books," *Nineteenth Century Prose* 23 (1996), 55.
6. Richard Holmes, "On the Enchanted Hill," *New York Review of Books*, June 8, 1995.
7. *Travels with a Donkey*, "Upper Gévaudan: A Camp in the Dark," 32; Richard Holmes, *Footsteps: Adventures of a Romantic Biographer* (New York: Vintage Books, 1985), 29.
8. RLS to Henley, Sept. 14, 1878, *Letters* 2:274.
9. For example, RLS to Henley, May 1883, *Letters* 4:113.
10. "Velay: The Donkey, the Pack, and the Pack Saddle," 9–10.
11. "Velay: The Green Donkey-Driver," 15.
12. Quoted in the notes, 232.
13. "Velay: I Have a Goad," 9, 21–22, and note on 235.
14. "Velay: I Have a Goad," 19, 22.
15. "Velay: The Green Donkey-Driver," 14.
16. "Velay: I Have a Goad," 21; "Upper Gévaudan: A Camp in the Dark," 25.
17. "Velay: I Have a Goad," 20; journal quoted on 233.
18. RLS to Bob, April 1879, *Letters* 2:313; "Upper Gévaudan: A Night among the Pines," 58; journal version in the notes, 243; Holmes, *Footsteps*, 54.
19. "The Country of the Camisards: The Heart of the Country," 89; Milton, *Paradise Lost* I.65; Holmes, *Footsteps*, 62.
20. *Travels with a Donkey*, "Our Lady of the Snows," 37–49.
21. The notebook version is quoted in the notes, 236; the revised version, "Our Lady of the Snows," is in *Collected Poems*, 131–32.
22. "The Country of the Camisards: Pont de Montvert," 67, 69.
23. "The Country of the Camisards: Farewell, Modestine," 95–96.
24. *Spectator*, Sept. 27, 1879, *Critical Heritage*, 71–74; RLS to Colvin, Aug. 27, 1880, *Letters* 3:96.
25. Unsigned review in *Fraser's Magazine*, Sept. 1879, *Critical Heritage*, 67.
26. *Collected Poems*, 536; the book was presented in 1888 to Dr. Edward Livingston Trudeau in Saranac Lake, New York. The ambiguities in the account of Modestine and her treatment are persuasively explored by Lesley Lawton, "Brutality and Sentimentality in the Cévennes: Doubleness in Robert Louis Stevenson's *Travels with a Donkey*," *Caliban: French Journal of English Studies* 59 (2018), 119–38.
27. Thomas Stevenson to RLS, June 8, 1879, quoted in *Critical Heritage*, 64.
28. Harold Orel, *The Victorian Short Story* (Cambridge: Cambridge University Press, 1986), 1–2.
29. RLS to Colvin, Sept. 6, 1891, *Letters* 7:155. On the origins of the modern short story, see Peter Keating, *The Haunted Study: A Social History of the English Novel, 1875–1914* (London: Secker & Warburg, 1989).
30. George Saintsbury, unsigned review, *Pall Mall Gazette*, Aug. 1882, *Critical Heritage*, 107–8.
31. H. C. Bunner, unsigned review, *Century Magazine*, Feb. 1883, *Critical Heritage*, 120.

CHAPTER 14. FROM GLASGOW TO SAN FRANCISCO

1. Furnas, 127.
2. RLS to Baxter, early Dec. 1878, *Letters* 2:292.

3. Colvin to Gosse, Feb. 6, 1879, quoted by McLynn, 144–45; Pope Hennessy, 137.
4. RLS to Baxter, May 1879, *Letters* 2:318.
5. RLS to Gosse, July 28, 1879, *Letters* 2:330; Gosse's letter is quoted in a footnote.
6. "Some Aspects of Robert Burns," *Cornhill Magazine,* Oct. 1879, reprinted in *Familiar Studies of Men and Books* (1882) and in *Lantern Bearers,* 108, 121.
7. Quoted by Ann Thwaite, *Edmund Gosse: A Literary Landscape* (Oxford: Oxford University Press, 1985), 179.
8. The details are reviewed by Mehew in *Letters* 2:251–52n.
9. RLS to Baxter and to Colvin, Aug. 6, 1879, *Letters* 3:2–3.
10. Henley to Baxter, Aug. 16, 1879, *Letters* 3:4–5.
11. Thomas Stevenson to Colvin, Beinecke.
12. *The Amateur Emigrant,* in *From Scotland to Silverado,* ed. James D. Hart (Cambridge, MA: Harvard University Press, 1966), 5, "The Second Cabin."
13. Rankin, 123.
14. *Amateur Emigrant,* "Steerage Scenes," 27–28, 73.
15. Furnas, 156–57.
16. *Amateur Emigrant,* "Early Impressions," 11–12.
17. "The Sick Man," 54.
18. "Personal Experience and Review," 72; William Hazlitt, "On Going a Journey."
19. Pope Hennessy, 147; "Personal Experience and Review," 84.
20. "Popular Authors," *Scribner's Magazine,* July 1888, not reprinted in Stevenson's lifetime.
21. RLS to Edward Burlingame, April 12, 1888, *Letters* 6:162.
22. "Personal Experience and Review," 79.
23. *Amateur Emigrant,* "New York," 96–98.
24. Thomas to RLS, Sept. 7, 1881, quoted by George L. McKay, *Some Notes on Robert Louis Stevenson: His Finances and His Agents and Publishers* (New Haven: Yale University Library, 1958), 16.
25. "The Sick Man," 49, 52. The history of the successive versions of *The Amateur Emigrant* is reviewed by Swearingen, 42–45; he has also published an accurate transcription of the original manuscript, rather than interpolating changes as Hart did: *The Amateur Emigrant,* 2 vols., ed. Roger D. Swearingen (Ashland, OR: Lewis Osborne, 1976).
26. "The Story of a Lie," *New Quarterly Magazine,* Oct. 1879; *Complete Stories,* 661–709.
27. *From Scotland to Silverado,* 106, "Notes by the Way to Council Bluffs."
28. RLS to Colvin, Aug. 20, 1879, to Baxter, Aug. 22, and to Henley, *Letters* 3:7–10.
29. RLS to Colvin, Aug. 20, 1879, *Letters* 3:8, also *Collected Poems,* 100.
30. Robert Louis Stevenson, *New Poems and Variant Readings* (London: Chatto & Windus, 1918), 106. This poem is not included in either of the modern editions of *Collected Poems.*
31. "Notes by the Way to Council Bluffs," 110.
32. "To the Golden Gates," 146–47; Edmund Spenser, *The Faerie Queene,* I.ii.7.

CHAPTER 15. A YEAR IN CALIFORNIA

1. Sanchez, 53.
2. *This Life I've Loved,* 117.

3. Quoted by Elsie Noble Caldwell, *Last Witness for Robert Louis Stevenson* (Norman: University of Oklahoma Press, 1960), 10.
4. *This Life I've Loved*, 34, 36, 40–41.
5. *This Life I've Loved*, 41.
6. RLS to Baxter, Sept. 9, 1879, *Letters* 3:12.
7. RLS to Gosse, Oct. 8, 1879, *Letters* 3:15–16.
8. RLS to Baxter, Oct. 15, 1879, *Letters* 3:17–18.
9. Anne Roller Issler, *Happier for His Presence: San Francisco and Robert Louis Stevenson* (Stanford: Stanford University Press, 1949), 115.
10. Mackay, 84.
11. *This Life I've Loved*, 116–18.
12. *This Life I've Loved*, 121.
13. Bob to RLS, quoted by Jeremy Hodges, *Mrs. Jekyll and Cousin Hyde* (Edinburgh: Luath, 2017), 45–46.
14. *Intimate Portrait*, 20–22.
15. RLS to Colvin and to Henley, Oct.–Nov. 1879, *Letters* 3:19, 21; Sanchez, 59.
16. Masson, 185–86, quoting Frank Holman's address at a 1907 meeting of the Stevenson Society of America.
17. "The Old Pacific Capital," *Fraser's Magazine,* Nov. 1880, reprinted in *Across the Plains* (1882).
18. "Henry David Thoreau: His Character and Opinions," *Cornhill Magazine,* June 1880, *Familiar Studies of Men and Books* (1882).
19. See *From Scotland to Silverado,* ed. James D. Hart (Cambridge, MA: Harvard University Press, 1966), xxv.
20. "The Old Pacific Capital"; this section of the essay is reprinted in *Lantern-Bearers,* 126–27.
21. RLS to Henley, Jan. 26, 1880, *Letters* 3:55.
22. RLS to Gosse, Dec. 8, 1879, *Letters* 3:32.
23. RLS to Colvin, Dec., 26, 1879, *Letters* 3:39.
24. Henley *Letters,* Jan. 20, 1880, 77.
25. Issler, *Happier for His Presence,* 6, 11.
26. "A Modern Cosmopolis," *Magazine of Art,* May 1883, reprinted with the essay on Monterey in the Edinburgh Edition (1896) as "The Old and New Pacific Capitals."
27. *The Collected Poems of Robert Louis Stevenson,* ed. Roger C. Lewis (Edinburgh: Edinburgh University Press, 2003), 270 (not included in Adam Smith's *Collected Poems*).
28. *This Life I've Loved,* 128.
29. RLS to Stoddard, Dec. 1880, *Letters* 3:139; the poem became known after Stoddard published it in his memoirs in 1903.
30. Furnas, 307; Stoddard in *Stevensoniana,* 48.
31. Howard Wilford Bell, "An Unpublished Chapter in the Life of Robert Louis Stevenson," *Pall Mall Magazine,* June 1901; *Stevensoniana,* 45.
32. Gosse to RLS, Dec. 29, 1879, quoted by Issler, *Happier for His Presence,* 97; RLS to Gosse, Nov. 15, 1879, *Letters* 3:26.

33. *The Wrecker,* chs. 8, 10.
34. Walter Ferrier to his sister Elizabeth ("Coggie"), June 1, 1880, quoted in *Letters* 3:74n.
35. RLS to Baxter, Jan. 9, 1880, to Colvin, Jan. 18, and to Henley, Jan. 23, *Letters* 3:43–44, 47–49.
36. *This Life I've Loved,* 55.
37. Johnny Wright, quoted by Issler, *Happier for His Presence,* 143.
38. RLS to Gosse, April 16, 1880, *Letters* 3:77.
39. Sanchez, 60, 65.
40. Quoted by Nancy Everett, "Dora Norton Williams: A New England Yankee in San Francisco Bohemia," *The Argonaut* 21 (Spring 2010).
41. RLS to Virgil Williams, July 11, 1881, *Letters* 3:211.
42. Thomas's letter to Louis of Feb. 17 is quoted in a note at *Letters* 3:54n; Calder, 141.
43. RLS to Colvin, April 1880, *Letters* 3:75; Calder, 141.
44. RLS to Baxter, April 1880, and to Margaret, June 1883, *Letters* 3:79, 4:130.
45. Mackay, 113.
46. *Reflections and Remarks on Human Life,* written in spring 1880, first printed posthumously in the Edinburgh Edition. Swearingen dates this piece to Jan.–Feb. 1880 (50).
47. RLS to P. G. Hamerton, July 1881, *Letters* 3:203; Sanchez, 65–66, 77.
48. *This Life I've Loved,* 128.
49. *This Life I've Loved,* 129; Sanchez, 81.
50. Richard Holmes, "On the Enchanted Hill," *New York Review of Books,* June 8, 1995.
51. RLS to Colvin, mid-April 1880, *Letters* 3:76.
52. *From Scotland to Silverado, The Silverado Squatters,* 197–98, "Calistoga."
53. *From Scotland to Silverado,* 232, 215, "The Return," "To Introduce Mr. Kelmar"; RLS to Adelaide Boodle, May 1891, *Letters* 7:111.
54. *From Scotland to Silverado,* 234, "The Act of Squatting."
55. "The Act of Squatting," 233.
56. *From Scotland to Silverado,* 263, "A Starry Drive."
57. *From Scotland to Silverado,* 281–82, "Toils and Pleasures."
58. Sanchez, 74–75.
59. *From Scotland to Silverado,* 246–47, "The Hunter's Family."
60. *From Scotland to Silverado,* 210–11, "The Scot Abroad."
61. Fanny to Margaret, July 16, 1880, *Letters* 3:88–89.
62. Anne Issler, *Stevenson at Silverado* (Fairfield, CA: James Stevenson, 1974), 33, 112, quoting interviews conducted several decades previously.

CHAPTER 16. EDINBURGH AND DAVOS

1. Sidney Colvin, *Memories and Notes of Persons and Places* (London: Edward Arnold, 1921), 129; "Thomas Stevenson, Civil Engineer," *Contemporary Review,* June 1887, *Lantern-Bearers,* 214.
2. Margaret's diary is quoted by Calder, 150.
3. Fanny to Dora Norton Williams, Oct. 1880, *Letters* 3:105.
4. Introduction to the Tusitala Edition (London: Heinemann, 1924), vol. 2.

5. Austin Strong, "The Most Unforgettable Character I've Met," *Reader's Digest,* March 1946.
6. *Collected Poems,* 320.
7. RLS to Frances Sitwell, June 4, 1874, *Letters* 2:14.
8. Masson, 196; RLS to J. M. Barrie, April 3, 1893, *Letters* 8:45.
9. Balfour, 1:212; Colvin, *Memories and Notes,* 137.
10. Henley to RLS, Nov. 3, 1882, Henley *Letters,* 173.
11. Colvin to Baxter, Oct. 19, 1880, and Louis and Fanny to his parents, Oct. 28, *Letters* 3:111–12.
12. Ernest Mehew, "Robert Louis Stevenson," *Dictionary of National Biography,* online version 2014.
13. RLS to Frances Sitwell, June 5, 1875, *Letters* 2:141; "Alcaics to H. F. Brown," *Collected Poems,* 288.
14. RLS to Albert George Dew Smith, Nov. 1880, *Letters* 3:116–18; "To A. G. Dew-Smith," *Collected Poems,* 342.
15. Susan Sontag, *Illness as Metaphor* (New York: Doubleday Anchor Books, 1989), 15.
16. Quoted by W. G. Lockett, *Robert Louis Stevenson at Davos* (London: Hurst & Blackett, 1934), 41.
17. Richard Woodhead, *The Strange Case of R. L. Stevenson* (Edinburgh: Luath, 2001), x.
18. RLS to his parents, Nov. 10, 1880, *Letters* 3:118–19.
19. RLS to Colvin, Jan. 25, 1893, and to Henley, Dec. 13, 1881, *Letters* 8:13 and 3:262.
20. RLS to Henley, Feb.–March 1881, *Letters* 3:159; Chesterton, 19.
21. Sontag, *Illness as Metaphor,* 3.
22. Fanny's postscript to RLS's letter to his mother, Feb. 5, 1881, *Letters* 3:155.
23. RLS to his mother, March 1881, *Letters* 3:164.
24. Harman, 198.
25. Lloyd Osbourne, "Stevenson at Thirty-One," South Seas Edition (New York: Scribner, 1925), introduction to vol. 5.
26. RLS to his mother, Dec. 26, 1880, *Letters* 3:149–51.
27. Edmund Gosse, *Critical Kit-Cats* (New York: Dodd, Mead, 1903), 287.
28. J. A. Symonds to H. F. Brown, Feb. 1881, *Critical Heritage,* 91.
29. "Some College Memories," contributed to *The New Amphion: Being the Book of the Edinburgh University Union Fancy Fair* (1886), reprinted the next year in *Memories and Portraits.*
30. *Intimate Portrait,* 33–34.
31. RLS to his father, Dec. 1880, *Letters* 3:127, 131.
32. "The Misgivings of Convalescence," *Pall Mall Gazette,* March 17, 1881, not reprinted in Stevenson's lifetime; *Lantern-Bearers,* 160–62.
33. RLS to Baxter, March 25, 1881, *Letters* 3:164.
34. RLS to Frances, June 17, 1880, and to his parents, Dec. 20, *Letters* 3:86, 151.
35. RLS to Colvin, March 12, 1881, and to his parents, April 4, *Letters* 3:161–62, 168.
36. RLS to Colvin, March 12, 1881, *Letters* 3:161; RLS and Fanny to his parents, May 5, 1881, and to Jenkin, also in May, *Letters* 3:175–77.

CHAPTER 17. A BREAKTHROUGH IN THE HIGHLANDS

1. Henley to Baxter, May 18, 1881, *Letters* 3:182.
2. Henley to Baxter, May 26, 1881, *Letters* 3:183–84.
3. Gavin Bell, *In Search of Tusitala: Travels in the Pacific After Robert Louis Stevenson* (London: Picador, 1994), 16.
4. RLS to Colvin, July 29, 1881, *Letters* 3:214.
5. "The Body Snatcher," *Pall Mall Christmas Extra* (1884); *Complete Stories*, 710–27.
6. RLS to Colvin, July 3, 1881, *Letters* 3:204, and to Charles Morley, Dec. 3, 1884, *Letters* 5:41; G. K. Chesterton, review of Balfour's biography of Stevenson, *Daily News*, Oct. 18, 1901, reprinted in *Stevensoniana*, 318.
7. His reading is documented by Coleman O. Parsons, "Stevenson's Use of Witchcraft in 'Thrawn Janet,'" *Studies in Philology* 43 (1946), 551–71.
8. Prefatory Note to Vailima Edition (New York: Scribner, 1921–23), 11:4–5.
9. Henry James, "Robert Louis Stevenson," *Partial Portraits* (New York: Macmillan, 1888), 155.
10. "Thrawn Janet," *Cornhill Magazine*, Oct. 1881, *The Merry Men and Other Tales and Fables* (1887); *Complete Stories*, 410–19.
11. Walter Scott, *The Heart of Midlothian*, ch. 15.
12. James, "Robert Louis Stevenson"; Andrew Lang, introduction to vol. 1 of the Swanston Edition (London: Chatto & Windus, 1911).
13. RLS to Colvin, July 3, 1881, *Letters* 3:204.
14. Barry Menikoff, introduction to *Complete Stories*, lii; Balfour 2:169.
15. "The Merry Men," *Cornhill Magazine*, June 1882, *The Merry Men and Other Tales and Fables* (1887); *Complete Stories*, 325–68.
16. Henley to Colvin, quoted by E. V. Lucas, *The Colvins and Their Friends* (New York: Scribner, 1928), 130; Henley to RLS, July 20, 1881, Henley *Letters*, 132–33.
17. RLS to Lady Taylor, Feb. 22, 1887, *Letters* 5:365; her comment is quoted in a note.
18. Isobel Strong and Lloyd Osbourne, *Memories of Vailima* (Westminster: Archibald Constable, 1903), 9–10.
19. Quoted by Mackay, 150.
20. Roslyn Jolly, *Robert Louis Stevenson in the Pacific: Travel, Empire, and the Author's Profession* (Farnham, UK: Ashgate, 2009), 69–74; Barry Menikoff, *Narrating Scotland: The Imagination of Robert Louis Stevenson* (Columbia: University of South Carolina Press, 2005), 22–26.
21. "A Humble Remonstrance," *Longman's Magazine*, Dec. 1884, reprinted in *Memories and Portraits* (1887).
22. Edmund Gosse, *Critical Kit-Cats* (New York: Dodd, Mead, 1903), 289.
23. Prefatory Note to *Treasure Island* (London: Heinemann, 1924), xix; RLS to Gosse, Aug. 1881, *Letters* 3:222.
24. RLS to Frances Sitwell, Aug. 1881, *Letters* 3:221.
25. Fanny to Dora Williams, quoted in *Letters* 3:224n.
26. Edmund Gosse to his wife, Aug. 26, 1881, quoted by Ann Thwaite, *Edmund Gosse: A Literary Landscape, 1849–1928* (Chicago: University of Chicago Press, 1984), 216–17.

27. Alexander H. Japp, *Robert Louis Stevenson: A Record, an Estimate, and a Memorial* (London: Werner Laurie, 1905), 22.
28. "My First Book: *Treasure Island*," Tusitala Edition (London: Heinemann, 1924), 3:xxiii–xxxi; *Lantern-Bearers*, 277–84.
29. *Treasure Island*, ch. 1.
30. *Treasure Island*, ch. 4; Robert Kiely, *Robert Louis Stevenson and the Fiction of Adventure* (Cambridge, MA: Harvard University Press, 1965), 73.
31. *Treasure Island*, ch. 5.
32. *Treasure Island*, ch. 8; RLS to Colvin, Feb. 1, 1892, *Letters* 7:231.
33. *Records of a Family of Engineers*, ch. 2, written 1891–94, never completed and not published until posthumous editions of Stevenson's works.
34. *Treasure Island*, chs. 10–11.
35. Leslie Stephen, *Studies of a Biographer*, 2nd series, vol. 4 (London: Duckworth, 1902), 233.
36. "My First Book"; RLS to Henley, May 1883, *Letters* 4:129.
37. *Treasure Island*, chs. 22, 14.
38. Edmund Gosse to his wife, Sept. 3, 1881, quoted by Thwaite, *Edmund Gosse*, 291.
39. Japp, *Robert Louis Stevenson*, 13–14.
40. "Victor Hugo's Romances," *Cornhill Magazine,* Aug. 1874, *Familiar Studies of Men and Books* (1882).
41. "A Gossip on Romance," *Longman's Magazine,* Nov. 1882, reprinted in *Memories and Portraits* (1887) and in *Lantern-Bearers*, 172–82.
42. C. S. Lewis, *An Experiment in Criticism* (Cambridge: Cambridge University Press, 1965), 8, 36–37, 72.
43. Italo Calvino, "L'isola del Tesoro ha il suo segreto," *Saggi 1945–1985* (Milan: Meridiani, 1995), 1:968.
44. RLS to Henley, Sept. 19, 1881, *Letters* 3:231–32; Fanny is quoted at 233n.
45. "My First Book."

CHAPTER 18. ALPINE COLD, AND TREASURE ISLAND

1. "Talk and Talkers II," *Cornhill Magazine,* Aug. 1882, *Memories and Portraits* (1887).
2. RLS to Henley, early Nov. 1881, *Letters* 3:244–45; Giovanni Gioviano Pontano, *Baiae,* trans. Rodney G. Dennis (Cambridge, MA: Harvard University Press, 2006), 62.
3. RLS to his mother, Dec. 26, 1881, *Letters* 3:270; Fanny in a joint letter with Louis, Feb. 16, *Letters* 3:286.
4. RLS to Henley, Feb. 1882, *Letters* 3:291; Henley to RLS, March 5, 1882, Henley *Letters*, 160.
5. Henley to RLS, Feb. 1882, Henley *Letters*, 157.
6. RLS to Colvin, Feb. 13, 1882, *Letters* 3:283–84; Edmund Spenser, *The Faerie Queene*, II.xii.24.
7. RLS and Fanny to R. D. Blackmore, April 19, 1882, *Letters* 3:329–30.
8. Leslie Fiedler, "R.L.S. Revisited," *No! In Thunder: Essays on Myth and Literature* (Boston: Beacon, 1960), 80.
9. *Stevenson's Baby Book* (San Francisco: John Howell, 1922), 51.

10. "A Martial Elegy for Some Lead Soldiers," *Collected Poems,* 426.
11. *Intimate Portrait,* 38–39; RLS to Bob, Oct. 20, 1874, *Letters* 2:65.
12. Lloyd Osbourne, introduction to the Tusitala Edition (London: Heinemann, 1924), 1:xxi.
13. Mentioned by Alexander H. Japp in *Robert Louis Stevenson: A Record, an Estimate, and a Memorial* (London: Werner Laurie, 1905), 11.
14. *Collected Poems,* 436–43.
15. Lloyd Osbourne, preface to *Moral Emblems and Other Poems Written and Illustrated by Robert Louis Stevenson* (London: Chatto & Windus, 1921).
16. RLS to Henley, March 1882, *Letters* 3:293–94.
17. "My First Book: *Treasure Island,*" *Idler,* Aug. 1894, *Lantern-Bearers,* 277–84.
18. *Treasure Island,* ch. 14.
19. Henry James, "Robert Louis Stevenson," *Partial Portraits* (New York: Macmillan, 1888), 168.
20. *Fables,* I, "The Persons of the Tale" (not published in Louis's lifetime).
21. *Treasure Island,* ch. 30.
22. *Treasure Island,* chs. 26–27; George Saunders, *A Swim in a Pond in the Rain* (New York: Random House, 2021), 60.
23. *Treasure Island,* ch. 34.
24. "The Fine Pacific Islands, Heard in a Public House at Rotherhithe," *Collected Poems,* 355; RLS to Colvin, Jan. 31, 1892, *Letters* 7:231.
25. RLS to Henley, Aug. 25, 1881, *Letters* 3:225; *Treasure Island,* ch. 20; Charles Dickens, *Great Expectations,* ch. 46.
26. RLS to Henley, and to his parents, May 1883, *Letters* 4:128, 119; Henley's exclamation is quoted by Swearingen, 67.
27. See Roger G. Swearingen, "Recent Studies in Robert Louis Stevenson: Letters, Reference Works, Texts, 1970–2005," *Dickens Studies Annual: Essays on Victorian Fiction* 37 (2006), 369.
28. Oscar Wilde, *The Importance of Being Earnest,* act 2.
29. Henley to RLS, April 26, 1881, Henley *Letters,* 114.
30. RLS to Henley, Feb. 8, 1882, *Letters* 3:280.
31. RLS to Baxter and Henley, March 1882, *Letters* 3:292, 295.
32. *Collected Poems,* 131, first published in *Underwoods* (1887); Bishop Francis Paget, *The Spirit of Discipline,* quoted by Balfour, 1:232.
33. RLS to Henley, April 1882, *Letters* 3:322.

CHAPTER 19. TWO YEARS ON THE RIVIERA

1. RLS to Fanny, Aug. 3, 1882, and to A. Trevor Haddon, June 1882, *Letters* 3:343–44, 355.
2. RLS to Henley, Oct. 1882, *Letters* 4:2; Shakespeare, *Hamlet,* I.v.
3. RLS to his parents, Feb. 1, 1883, *Letters* 4:64.
4. Hermione Lee, *Edith Wharton* (New York: Vintage, 2007), 540.
5. RLS to his parents, Feb. 24, 1883, *Letters* 4:80.
6. See *Letters* 4:79n.
7. RLS to Will H. Low, March 1883, *Letters* 4:87.

8. RLS to Jules Simoneau, Nov. 1883, *Letters* 4:196–97.
9. *Treasure Island,* ch. 30.
10. RLS to Colvin, March 1891, *Letters* 7:93; *Hamlet,* V.i.
11. Lloyd Osbourne, "Stevenson at Thirty-Four," South Seas Edition (New York: Scribner, 1925), 7:xi.
12. RLS to his parents, Feb. 15, March 3, and later in March 1883 (the final one with a postscript by Fanny), *Letters* 4:75, 84, 86, 88.
13. Lloyd Osbourne to G. S. Hellman, quoted in *Letters* 1:67–68.
14. Fanny quoted by Mackay, 186; notebook at the Huntington Library quoted by Ann C. Colley, *Robert Louis Stevenson and the Colonial Imagination* (Aldershot, UK: Ashgate, 2004), 201.
15. Isobel Strong, *Robert Louis Stevenson* (New York: Scribner, 1911), 26–27.
16. RLS to Colvin, July 1884, quoted by E. V. Lucas, *The Colvins and Their Friends* (New York: Scribner, 1928), 159.
17. Callow, 181; *The Black Arrow:* prologue; book 1, chs. 1 and 3; book 4, ch. 1.
18. RLS to William Archer, March 27, 1894, *Letters* 8:260.
19. RLS to Henley, Oct. and May 7, 1883, *Letters* 4:194, 120.
20. RLS to Will H. Low, Dec. 1883, *Letters* 4:215–16; to George Iles, Oct. 29, 1887, *Letters* 6:48.
21. *Pall Mall Gazette,* Nov. 6, 1885, *Critical Heritage,* 181; Edmund Purcell in the *Academy,* Feb. 27, 1886, *Critical Heritage,* 197.
22. Henry James, "Robert Louis Stevenson," *Century Magazine,* April 1888, *Critical Heritage,* 294.
23. RLS to Henley, May 1883, *Letters* 4:120.
24. RLS to Henley, May 1883, *Letters* 4:115.
25. RLS to Bob Stevenson, Sept. 9, 1894, *Letters* 8:365.
26. See Jessica R. Feldman, *Gender on the Divide: The Dandy in Modernist Literature* (Ithaca: Cornell University Press, 1993), 262–64.
27. RLS to Henley, Sept. 1883, *Letters* 4:154, 159.
28. RLS to Coggie Ferrier, Sept. 30 and Nov. 22, 1883, *Letters* 4:165, 206.
29. RLS to Bob, April 1884, *Letters* 4:270.
30. RLS to his mother, April 19, 1884, *Letters* 4:272.
31. Fanny to Henley, May 2 and 13, 1884, *Letters* 4:288–89, 292–94.
32. RLS to Baxter and Colvin, late May 1884, *Letters* 4:296, 300; RLS to Bob Stevenson, March 12, 1884, *Letters* 4:24.

CHAPTER 20. A HOME IN ENGLAND

1. Francis Watt, *R.L.S.* (London: Methuen, 1913), 175–76.
2. Balfour, 1:150.
3. RLS to Harriet Monroe, June 30, 1886, *Letters* 5:273.
4. Clayton Hamilton, *On the Trail of Stevenson* (New York: Doubleday, Page, 1916), 64–65.
5. Letter to Dora Williams quoted by Callow, 192; Fanny to Margaret, July 29, 1885, *Letters* 5:123n.
6. RLS to Gosse, March 12, 1885, *Letters* 5:58; *Intimate Portrait,* 59–60.
7. Fanny to Colvin, quoted by Callow, 199.

8. *Underwoods,* I.xxxviii, *Collected Poems,* 144; RLS to Will H. Low, Jan. 15, 1894, *Letters* 8:235.
9. RLS to Will H. Low, March 10, 1885, *Letters* 5:82; Fanny and Louis to Louis's parents, May 25, 1886, *Letters* 5:258; Louis to Henley, Colvin, and Bob Stevenson, July 6 and 10 and August 1, *Letters* 5:258, 277, 281, 298–99.
10. RLS to Bob Stevenson, July 1886, *Letters* 5:293; Lloyd Osbourne, introduction to the Tusitala Edition (London: Heinemann, 1924), 1:xxiii.
11. *I Can Remember,* 265–67.
12. RLS to Trevor Haddon, July 5, 1883, *Letters* 4:141; Darwin is quoted by Philip Prodger, *Darwin's Camera: Art and Photography in the Theory of Evolution* (Oxford: Oxford University Press, 2009), 75–76.
13. Postscript by Fanny to Louis's letter to Harriet Monroe, June 30, 1886, *Letters* 5:274.
14. RLS to his mother, Dec. 15, 1884, and to Henley, Dec. 17, *Letters* 5:49–51.
15. RLS to Will H. Low, Oct. 22, 1885, *Letters* 5:137.
16. S. R. Lysaght in *I Can Remember,* 327; Masson, 237.
17. Sargent is quoted by Stanley Olson, *John Singer Sargent: His Portrait* (New York: St. Martin's, 1986), 114–15.
18. RLS to Will H. Low, Aug. 6, 1884, *Letters* 5:4.
19. RLS to Baxter, Oct. 4, 1884, *Letters* 5:12–13.
20. RLS to Henley, Nov. 6, 1884, *Letters* 5:22.
21. RLS to Colvin, Sept. 10, 1894, *Letters* 8:357; Fanny's letter to Colvin is quoted by Calder, 216.
22. William Archer, *The Critic,* Nov. 5, 1887, reprinted in *Stevensoniana,* 76–78.
23. Quoted by Calder, 155.
24. Letter of May 18, 1884, quoted by Balfour, 1:255; the comment about catching colds was noted by Sanchez, 86–87. On immune deficiency syndrome, see Harman, 76.
25. Sidney Colvin, *Memories and Notes of Persons and Places* (London: Edward Arnold, 1921), 129–30, 142–43.
26. RLS to Colvin, May 9, 1892, *Letters* 7:280.
27. Fanny to Colvin, quoted by Janet Adam Smith, *Henry James and Robert Louis Stevenson: A Record of Friendship and Criticism* (London: Rupert Hart-Davis, 1948), 12–13; Colvin to Henley, Nov. 30, 1884, E. V. Lucas, *The Colvins and Their Friends* (New York: Scribner, 1928), 160.
28. Adelaide A. Boodle, *R.L.S. and His Sine Qua Non: Flashlights from Skerryvore by the Gamekeeper* (London: John Murray, 1926), 104–5.
29. RLS to Bob, Jan. 1887, *Letters* 5:350.
30. Edmund Gosse, *Critical Kit-Cats* (New York: Dodd, Mead, 1903), 275, 302.
31. Henley to RLS, Dec, 21, 1886, Henley *Letters,* 326; see Ann Thwaite, *Edmund Gosse: A Literary Landscape, 1849–1928* (Chicago: University of Chicago Press, 1984), 192–96, 320–22. Strachey is quoted on p. 194.
32. Quoted by Thwaite, *Edmond Gosse,* 320–21.
33. RLS to Will H. Low, undated, 1886, *Letters* 5:177.
34. Fanny to Colvin, July 1885, *Letters* 5:120–21.
35. Boodle, *R.L.S. and His Sine Qua Non,* 9–10, 34, 17, 57–64.
36. Boodle, *R.L S. and His Sine Qua Non,* 10–11, 116–17.

37. Balfour, 2:9.
38. *The Diary of Alice James,* ed. Leon Edel (London: Penguin, 1982), introduction, 7; Fanny to Louis's parents, May 4, 1885, *Letters* 5:104.
39. James to T. S. Perry, Sept. 14, 1879, *Henry James Letters,* ed. Leon Edel (Cambridge, MA: Harvard University Press, 1980), 2:255; RLS to Henley, Feb.–March 1881, *Letters* 3:159; "the weaker vessel" comes from 1 Peter 3:7.
40. Henry James, *The Art of Fiction and Other Essays* (New York: Oxford University Press, 1948), 19.
41. "A Humble Remonstrance," *Longman's Magazine,* Dec. 1884, reprinted in *Memories and Portraits* (1887) and in *Lantern-Bearers,* 194–95.
42. James to RLS, Dec. 5, 1884, *Henry James Letters,* 3:57.
43. RLS to James, Dec. 8, 1884, *Letters* 5:42.
44. "A Gossip on Romance," *Longman's Magazine,* Nov. 1882, reprinted in *Memories and Portraits* and in *Lantern-Bearers,* 172–82; Henry Adams, *The Education of Henry Adams,* ed. Ira B. Nadel (Oxford: Oxford University Press, 1999), ch. 10, p. 139.
45. Fanny to Colvin, July 1885, *Letters* 5:120; James to RLS, Nov. 6, 1885, *Henry James Letters,* 3:495.
46. "The Mirror Speaks," *Collected Poems,* 129; James to Grace Norton, May 9, 1885, *Henry James Letters,* 3:83. James's letter to Wister is quoted by Pope Hennessy, 107.
47. RLS to James, Dec. 23, 1886, *Letters* 5:340.
48. James to RLS, Jan. 21, 1887, *Henry James Letters,* 3:17; James to Colvin, Jan. 5, 1911, quoted by E. V. Lucas, *The Colvins and Their Friends* (New York: Scribner, 1928), 284.
49. *Diary of Alice James,* 92–93 (Feb. 20, 1890). Alice must have been recalling an earlier incident, since by 1890 the Stevensons had left Britain.

CHAPTER 21. A TORRENT OF WRITING

1. RLS to Gosse, March 12, 1885, *Letters* 5:85.
2. Masson, 231–32.
3. George Eliot, *Middlemarch* (1872), ch. 29.
4. William Archer, "Robert Louis Stevenson: His Style and His Thought," *Times,* Nov. 1885, *Critical Heritage,* 16–61; Alan Sandison, *Robert Louis Stevenson and the Appearance of Modernism: A Future Feeling* (London: Macmillan, 1996), 4–6.
5. RLS to Archer, Nov. 1, 1885, *Letters* 5:150.
6. RLS to Henley, Nov. 1885, and to Symonds, March 1886, *Letters* 5:151, 220.
7. Fanny's preface to the Tusitala Edition (London: Heinemann, 1924), 3:xi–xii.
8. Audrey Murfin, *Robert Louis Stevenson and the Art of Collaboration* (Edinburgh: Edinburgh University Press, 2019), ch. 2; Fanny's letter of May 20, 1885 is quoted on p. 63.
9. Edmund Purcell, *Academy,* Feb. 1886, *Critical Heritage,* 194.
10. Chesterton, 167; *The Dynamiter,* "The Superfluous Mansion (Concluded)."
11. On sales of the book, see George L. McKay, *Some Notes on Robert Louis Stevenson: His Finances and His Agents and Publishers* (New Haven: Yale University Library, 1958), 18.
12. William Sharp, *The Academy,* Oct. 1, 1887, *Critical Heritage,* 268–69; RLS to Sharp, Oct. 1887, *Letters* 6:34.
13. *Collected Poems,* 117, 124, 132, 134, 141, 257, 260, 287, 309.

14. "Epitaphium Erotii," *Collected Poems,* 292 (the note on 523 explains why this poem was written at Hyères in 1883–84); "Epitaph on Erotion," *The Poetical Works of Leigh Hunt* (London: Edward Moxon, 1832), 238. Both poets are translating Martial X.61.
15. Henry James to William James, Oct. 1, 1887, *Henry James Letters,* ed. Leon Edel (Cambridge, MA: Harvard University Press, 1980), 3:204.
16. RLS to Colvin, Dec. 14, 1886, *Letters* 5:336.
17. "The Maker to Posterity," *Collected Poems,* 145, and note on 486.
18. "To Charles Baxter," *Collected Poems,* 104.
19. "The Spaewife," *Collected Poems,* 157.
20. *Intimate Portrait,* 53.
21. "Sketches: Nuits Blanches," first published in the Edinburgh Edition of Stevenson's *Works* (1896), 31–48.
22. *Intimate Portrait,* 55.
23. Henley to RLS, Feb. 12 and March 2, 1880, Henley *Letters,* 84, 87.
24. *Deacon Brodie,* act 2, scenes 5 and 9; act 3, scene 5.
25. Henley to Baxter, July 11, 1884, quoted in *Letters* 5:4n; RLS to Colvin, June 1884, *Letters* 4:309.
26. RLS to Henley, April 8, 1885, *Letters* 5:101; an example of "the Barebum" is in a letter of Henley's to RLS, April 9, 1883, Henley *Letters,* 182.

CHAPTER 22. CREATING A MYTH

1. Balfour, 2:15; "North-West Passage," *Collected Poems,* 387.
2. "A Chapter on Dreams," *Scribner's Magazine,* 1888, reprinted in *Across the Plains* (1892), and in *Lantern-Bearers,* 216–25.
3. *Intimate Portrait,* 64–66.
4. RLS to J. R. Vernon, Feb. 15, 1886, *Letters* 5:211.
5. Vladimir Nabokov, *Lectures on Literature,* ed. Fredson Bowers (New York: Harcourt Brace Jovanovich, 1980), vii–viii.
6. *Times,* Jan. 25, 1886, *Critical Heritage,* 206–7.
7. Borges is quoted by Daniel Balderston, "Borges's Frame of Reference: The Strange Case of Robert Louis Stevenson" (PhD diss., Princeton University, 1981).
8. Nabokov, *Lectures on Literature,* 179.
9. *Dr. Jekyll and Mr. Hyde,* "Search for Mr. Hyde"; see Stephen Arata, *Fictions of Loss in the Victorian Fin de Siècle* (Cambridge: Cambridge University Press, 1996), 34, quoting Cesare Lombroso; "Olalla," *Court and Society Review,* Christmas 1885, reprinted in *The Merry Men and Other Tales and Fables* (1887); *Complete Stories,* 420–57.
10. *D. Jekyll and Mr. Hyde,* "Henry Jekyll's Full Statement of the Case" (the chapters are titled but not numbered).
11. *Dr. Jekyll and Mr. Hyde,* "The Carew Murder Case."
12. Furnas, 441; Hopkins to Robert Bridges, Oct. 28, 1886, *The Letters of G. M. Hopkins to Robert Bridges,* ed. Claude C. Abbott (Oxford: Oxford University Press, 1935), 240 (also in *Critical Heritage,* 229).
13. Symonds to RLS, March 3, 1886, *The Letters of John Addington Symonds,* ed. Herbert M. Schueller and Robert L. Peters (Detroit: Wayne State University Press, 1969), 3:120. On

the theme of "homosexual panic," see Elaine Showalter, *Sexual Anarchy: Gender and Culture at the Fin-de-Siècle* (New York: Viking Penguin, 1990), 107.
14. RLS to John Paul Bocock, Nov. 1787, *Letters* 6:56–57.
15. RLS to Symonds, March 1886, *Letters* 5:220; Epistle to the Romans 7:23.
16. *Dr. Jekyll and Mr. Hyde*, "Remarkable Incident of Doctor Lanyon"; 1 Timothy 1:15.
17. *Dr. Jekyll and Mr. Hyde*, "The Last Door."
18. Longman's letter of October 1886 to Graham Balfour is quoted in Richard Dury's edition of the novel (Edinburgh: Edinburgh University Press, 2004), 182.
19. Balfour, 2:17–18; anonymous review in *The Rock*, April 1886, *Critical Heritage*, 224–27.
20. "The worst thing" was reported by Charlotte Eaton in R. C. Terry, *Robert Louis Stevenson: Interviews and Recollections* (Iowa City: University of Iowa Press, 1996), 136.
21. Susan E. Cook, *Victorian Negatives: Literary Culture and the Dark Side of Photography in the Nineteenth Century* (Albany: State University of New York Press, 2019), 90.
22. *Pall Mall Gazette*, Sept. 1888.

CHAPTER 23. KIDNAPPED

1. RLS to Theodore Watts-Dunton, Sept. 1886, *Letters* 5:313; "Some Gentlemen in Fiction," *Scribner's Magazine*, June 1888, not reprinted in Stevenson's lifetime; Balfour, 2:19–20.
2. *Kidnapped*, ch. 26.
3. Linda Colley, *Britons: Forging the Nation, 1707–1837* (New Haven: Yale University Press, 1992), 15.
4. "The Foreigner at Home," *Cornhill Magazine*, May 1882, reprinted in *Memories and Portraits* (1887) and in *Lantern-Bearers*, 171.
5. T. C. Smout, *A History of the Scottish People, 1560–1830* (London: Fontana, 1969), 313.
6. Fernand Braudel, *The Mediterranean and the Mediterranean World in the Age of Philip II*, trans. Sian Reynolds (New York: Harper & Row, 1972); *Kidnapped*, ch. 16.
7. Samuel Johnson, *A Journey to the Western Islands of Scotland*, ed. Mary Lascelles, *Yale Edition of the Works of Samuel Johnson* (New Haven: Yale University Press, 1971), 9:51.
8. Balfour, 1:12, 16–17 (using the traditional spelling "Mohr").
9. *Kidnapped*, ch. 4; Chesterton, 119.
10. *Kidnapped*, ch. 10; Graham Greene, *A Sort of Life* (New York: Simon & Schuster, 1971), 20.
11. *Kidnapped*, ch. 10.
12. Leslie Fiedler, "R.L.S. Revisited," *No! In Thunder: Essays on Myth and Literature* (Boston: Beacon, 1960), 81.
13. Singer, 142; *Intimate Portrait*, 72.
14. *Kidnapped*, ch. 9.
15. *The Letters of Robert Louis Stevenson to His Family and Friends*, ed. Sidney Colvin (London: Methuen, 1906), introduction, 1:xxviii.
16. *Kidnapped*, ch. 20; Graham Good, "Rereading Robert Louis Stevenson," *Dalhousie Review* 62 (1982), 52; Jenni Calder, "Figures in a Landscape: Scott, Stevenson, and Routes to the Past," *Robert Louis Stevenson, Writer of Boundaries*, ed. Richard Ambrosini and Richard Dury (Madison: University of Wisconsin Press, 2006), 128–29.
17. *Kidnapped*, ch. 20.

18. Andrew Wyeth in *An American Vision: Three Generations of Wyeth Art* (Boston: Little, Brown, 1987), 80; Susan R. Gannon, "The Illustrator as Interpreter: N. C. Wyatt's Illustrations for the Adventure Novels of Robert Louis Stevenson," *Children's Literature* 19 (1991), 93.
19. *Kidnapped,* ch. 24.
20. Henry James, "Robert Louis Stevenson," *Century Magazine,* April 1888, in Janet Adam Smith, *Henry James and Robert Louis Stevenson: A Record of Friendship and Criticism* (London: Rupert Hart-Davis, 1948), 159.
21. James, "Robert Louis Stevenson," 158.
22. *Kidnapped,* ch. 30.
23. Quoted by Mildred Wilsey, "*Kidnapped* in Manuscript," *American Scholar* 17 (1948), 213–20.
24. Unsigned review (by Theodore Watts-Dunton), *Athenaeum,* Aug. 1886; unsigned review, *St. James's Gazette,* July 1886, *Critical Heritage,* 242, 233.
25. James's note is reproduced in Barry Menikoff's edition of *Kidnapped: or, The Lad with the Silver Button* (San Marino: Huntington Library Press, 1999).

CHAPTER 24. FAREWELL TO EUROPE

1. RLS to Colvin, March 17, 1886, and to Anne Jenkin, April 7, 1887, *Letters* 5:236, 384.
2. Margaret quoted by Calder, 224; "The Last Sight," *Collected Poems,* 282.
3. Fanny to Colvin, spring 1887, quoted by E. V. Lucas, *The Colvins and Their Friends* (New York: Scribner, 1928), 174–75.
4. Masson, 245.
5. *Intimate Portrait,* 71–72.
6. RLS to Margaret, July 1, 1887, *Letters* 5:430–31.
7. RLS to Colvin, Aug. 19, 1887, *Letters* 5:443; RLS to Henley, Aug. 2, 1887, *Letters* 5:437; Henley's reply quoted in a note.
8. Fanny to Adelaide Boodle, Aug. 21, 1887, *Letters* 5:445.
9. RLS to Fanny, May 6, 1885, *Letters* 5:107.
10. Evan Charteris, *The Life and Letters of Sir Edmund Gosse* (London: Heinemann, 1931), 217; Colvin's preface to the Tusitala Edition (London: Heinemann, 1924), vol. 33.
11. RLS to Ida Taylor, Oct. 7, 1892, *Letters* 7:394; RLS to his mother, Oct. 16, 1874, *Letters* 2:60.

CHAPTER 25. AN ADIRONDACK WINTER

1. RLS to Colvin and to Bob Stevenson, Sept. 18 and Oct. 1887, *Letters* 6:5, 17.
2. *Sunday World,* Sept. 11, 1887, *Critical Heritage,* 30.
3. Masson, 255, 263.
4. Will H. Low, *A Chronicle of Friendships* (New York: Scribner, 1908), 377; Jeanette L. Gilder, "Stevenson—and After," *Review of Reviews,* Feb. 1895, reprinted in *Stevensoniana,* 90.
5. Saint-Gaudens's letter, now lost, was reproduced by Low in *A Chronicle of Friendships*. On some implications of the episode, see Alexis L. Boylan, "Augustus Saint-Gaudens, Robert Louis Stevenson, and the Erotics of Illness," *American Art* 30 (2016), 14–31.

6. Clayton Hamilton, *On the Trail of Stevenson* (New York: Doubleday, Page, 1916), 72.
7. RLS to Mark Twain, April 12, 1888, *Letters* 6:162 (using the English title of the book, *Innocents at Home*).
8. RLS to Mark Twain, April 16, 1893, *Letters* 8:57.
9. Mark Twain, "Chapters from My Autobiography," *North American Review* 183 (1906), 457.
10. Low, *A Chronicle of Friendships*, 401–2.
11. *The Autobiography of S. S. McClure* (New York: Frederick A. Stokes, 1914), 184.
12. See Robert Thacker's introduction to Willa Cather, *The Autobiography of S. S. McClure* (Lincoln: University of Nebraska Press, 1997).
13. See Glenda Norquay, *Robert Louis Stevenson, Literary Networks and Transatlantic Publishing in the 1890s: The Author Incorporated* (London: Anthem, 2020), 37.
14. *The Autobiography of S. S. McClure*, 190.
15. RLS to James, Oct. 6, 1887, *Letters* 6:15.
16. Details from Sanchez, 129.
17. *Intimate Portrait*, 74–75.
18. Sanchez, 134; Fanny to RLS, April 1888, Beinecke 3744.
19. Edward Livingston Trudeau, *An Autobiography* (New York: Doubleday, 1916), 203, 225.
20. Quoted by Stephen Chalmers, *The Penny Piper of Saranac: An Episode in Stevenson's Life* (Boston: Houghton Mifflin, 1916), 22.
21. Hamilton, *On the Trail of Stevenson*, 139.
22. RLS to Harry Oldfield, Feb. 3, 1888, *Letters* 6:107.
23. *Intimate Portrait*, 79–80, 107–8.
24. Unsigned reviews in the *Athenaeum*, July 1889, and *Pall Mall Gazette*, June 1889, *Critical Heritage*, 334–37.
25. *The Master of Ballantrae*, ch. 6.
26. Barrie to RLS, May 8, 1892, in *A Friendship in Letters: Robert Louis Stevenson and J. M. Barrie*, ed. Michael Shaw (Inverness: Sandstone, 2020), 67.
27. RLS to Edward Burlingame, April 2, 1889, *Letters* 6:277.
28. RLS to Baxter, Dec. 30, 1887, *Letters* 6:93.
29. RLS to Gosse, May 20, 1883, *Letters* 4:125.
30. RLS to Baxter, March 22, 1888, *Letters* 6:132–36.
31. "Popular Authors," *Scribner's Magazine*, July 1888, not reprinted in Stevenson's lifetime.
32. "Popular Authors"; "To K. de M.," *Collected Poems*, 118.
33. RLS to Katharine de Mattos, Jan. 1, 1886, *Letters* 5:168.
34. RLS to Katharine de Mattos, Oct. 1874, *Letters* 2:62.
35. Henley to RLS, March 9, 1888, *Letters* 6:129–30.
36. Baxter to Charles Guthrie, March 25, 1914, quoted in *Letters* 6:147n; John Connell, *W. E. Henley* (London: Constable, 1949), 112.
37. Katharine and Henley to RLS, April 1888, *Letters* 6:169–70.
38. Fanny to Baxter, May 10, 1888, *Letters* 6:181–82.
39. Katharine de Mattos to RLS, June 1888, *Letters* 6:204; Baxter to RLS, June 6, 1888, Baxter *Letters*, 230–31.
40. RLS to Baxter, July 1890, *Letters* 6:398; Charles Lamb, "The Old Familiar Faces."

41. *Intimate Portrait*, 83–84.
42. *The Autobiography of S. S. McClure*, 191.
43. *Intimate Portrait*, 86; RLS to Baxter, May 22, 1888, *Letters* 6:193.

CHAPTER 26. SAILING THE HIGH SEAS

1. Will H. Low, *A Chronicle of Friendships* (New York: Scribner, 1908), 428; RLS to William Archer, May 15, 1888, *Letters* 6:183–84.
2. RLS to Harriet Monroe, Dec. 19, 1887, *Letters* 6:85.
3. Balfour, 2:46–47, and see Anne Roller Issler, *Happier for His Presence: San Francisco and Robert Louis Stevenson* (Stanford: Stanford University Press, 1949), 161.
4. Arthur Johnstone, *Robert Louis Stevenson in the Pacific* (London: Chatto & Windus, 1905), 15–18.
5. Quoted by Elsie Noble Caldwell, *Last Witness for Robert Louis Stevenson* (Norman: University of Oklahoma Press, 1960), 31–32, 359.
6. *This Life I've Loved*, 223.
7. Margaret Stevenson, *From Saranac to the Marquesas and Beyond*, ed. Marie Clothilde Balfour (New York: Scribner, 1903), 63–64, 68.
8. "My Ship and I" and "Foreign Lands," *Collected Poems*, 389, 365.
9. Charles Warren Stoddard, in *Interviews and Recollections*, 90.
10. James to RLS, July 31, 1888, *Henry James Letters*, ed. Leon Edel (Cambridge, MA: Harvard University Press, 1980), 3:239–40.
11. As noted by Christina Thompson, *Sea People: The Puzzle of Polynesia* (New York: HarperCollins, 2019), part 1.
12. Johnstone, *Robert Louis Stevenson in the Pacific*, 19–22, 46; RLS to Baxter, Oct. 9, 1888, *Letters* 6:211.
13. RLS to Colvin, April 2, 1889, *Letters* 6:276; "The Day After Tomorrow," *Contemporary Review*, April 1887, *Lantern-Bearers*, 207.
14. RLS to Baxter, Sept. 6, 1888, *Letters* 6:207; Andrew Lang, "Recollections of Robert Louis Stevenson," *Adventures among Books* (London: Longman's, Green, 1905), 46.
15. RLS to Baxter, Sept. 6, 1888, *Letters* 6:207.
16. Balfour, 2:212; Lloyd Osbourne, preface to Vailima Edition (New York: Scribner, 1921–23), reprinted in *I Can Remember*, 311; Rankin, 239.
17. Stevenson, *From Saranac to the Marquesas and Beyond*, 61. "The Isle of Palms" was by the Edinburgh philosophy professor John Wilson, best known for his contributions to *Blackwood's Magazine* under the pseudonym Christopher North.
18. RLS, *In the South Seas*, ed. Neil Rennie (London: Penguin, 1998), 6–8.
19. RLS, *In the South Seas*, 22; Richard Henry Dana, *Two Years before the Mast* (1840), ch. 19.
20. RLS, *In the South Seas*, 37–38.
21. Stevenson, *From Saranac to the Marquesas and Beyond*, 76, 79, 164.
22. Stevenson, *From Saranac to the Marquesas and Beyond*, 99; on "Ona," see Furnas, 315–16.
23. *This Life I've Loved*, 225, 227.
24. Fanny to Colvin, Dec. 1888, *Letters* 6:228–29.
25. "The Song of Rahéro," *Collected Poems*, 181; RLS to Thomas Archer, Dec. 18, 1888, *Letters* 6:238.

26. Johnstone, *Robert Louis Stevenson in the Pacific,* 41–42.
27. RLS, *In the South Seas,* 141.
28. Fanny to Colvin, *Letters* 6:231.
29. RLS to Colvin, Oct. 18, 1888, *Letters* 6:217.
30. Fanny to Frances Sitwell, late March 1889, *Letters* 6:272–73.

CHAPTER 27. HAWAII

1. RLS to Bob Stevenson, Feb. 1889, *Letters* 6:256–57.
2. RLS to Baxter, Feb. 8, 1889, *Letters* 6:248.
3. Callow, 219.
4. RLS to Baxter, Feb. 8, 1889, *Letters* 6:249.
5. *I Can Remember,* 265–68.
6. RLS to the *Daily Pacific Commercial Advertiser,* Oct. 6, 1893, *Letters* 8:173.
7. RLS to Adelaide Boodle, April 6, 1889, *Letters* 6:279–80.
8. RLS to Baxter, Feb. 8, 1889, *Letters* 6:248.
9. Fanny to Colvin, May 21, 1889, *Letters* 6:303–4.
10. RLS to Colvin, June 1889, *Letters* 6:312.
11. RLS to Baxter, Feb. 8, 1889, *Letters* 6:248–49; Lloyd Osbourne, "Stevenson at Thirty-Nine," South Seas Edition (New York: Scribner, 1925), 24:xi.
12. *This Life I've Loved,* 175.
13. *Collected Poems,* 266, 508.
14. Charles Warren Stoddard, *The Lepers of Molokai,* quoted by Gavan Daws, *Holy Man: Father Damien of Molokai* (Honolulu: University of Hawaii Press, 1973), 114.
15. Leviticus 13:3, 45–46.
16. The number of coffins is recorded at Damien's birthplace in Belgium, as noted by Rankin, 277.
17. Quoted by Rankin, 284.
18. Quoted by Harold Winfield Kent, *Dr. Hyde and Mr. Stevenson* (Rutland, VT: Charles E. Tuttle, 1973), 260–61.
19. *This Life I've Loved,* 271; *Lantern Bearers,* 265–76; the pamphlet was reprinted in posthumous editions of Stevenson's works.
20. RLS to Baxter, March 12, 1890, *Letters* 6:377–78.
21. Kent, *Dr. Hyde and Mr. Stevenson,* 278.
22. RLS to Baxter, April 12, 1889, *Letters* 6:286.
23. *This Life I've Loved,* 240.
24. RLS to Marcel Schwob, Feb. 8, 1889, Fanny to Frances Sitwell, late March, *Letters* 6:250, 271.
25. *Intimate Portrait,* 93–94; the missionary's letter is quoted in *Letters* 6:270.
26. *Intimate Portrait,* 101.
27. Fanny to Colvin and Frances Sitwell, June 18, 1889, *Letters* 6:321; Callow, 263.

CHAPTER 28. THE CRUISE OF THE EQUATOR

1. RLS to Colvin, Aug. 22, 1889, *Letters* 6:327; on the proposed itinerary, see *Letters,* p. 337.
2. RLS to Colvin, Dec. 2, 1889, *Letters* 6:334–35.

3. RLS, *In the South Seas,* ed. Neil Rennie (London: Penguin, 1998), 190–91 (quoting from Fanny's shipboard diary).
4. RLS, *In the South Seas,* 199–204.
5. Furnas, 346; Fanny is quoted by Rennie, introduction to *In the South Seas,* xvii.
6. RLS, *In the South Seas,* 211–12.
7. RLS to Colvin, Sept. 30, 1889, *Letters* 6:329; RLS, *In the South Seas,* 255.
8. Sidney Colvin, *Memories and Notes of Persons and Places* (London: Edward Arnold, 1921), 149.
9. *Intimate Portrait,* 103–4.
10. RLS to Colvin, Aug. 22, 1889, *Letters* 6:327–28.
11. *Collected Poems,* 270, 512.
12. "To S.C.," *Collected Poems,* 271–72, and RLS to Colvin, Dec. 2, 1889, *Letters* 6:337–38.
13. RLS to Elizabeth Fairchild, Jan. 21, 1890, *Letters* 6:356.
14. Quoted by Gavan Daws, *A Dream of Islands: Voyages of Self-Discovery in the South Seas* (New York: Norton, 1980), 172–73.
15. RLS to Frances Sitwell, June 22, 1875, *Letters* 2:145.
16. H. J. Moors, *With Stevenson in Samoa* (Boston: Small, Maynard, 1910), 4, 79–80.
17. Fanny and Robert Louis Stevenson, *Our Samoan Adventure,* ed. Charles Neider (New York: Harper, 1955), 125; Joseph Theroux, "Rediscovering Samoa's 'Unconquerable' Harry Moors," *Pacific Islands Monthly* 52:8 (1981), 51–57.
18. RLS to Baxter, Feb. 3, 1890, *Letters* 6:359–60.
19. Fanny to Colvin, Jan. 20, 1890, quoted by E. V. Lucas, *The Colvins and Their Friends* (New York: Scribner, 1928), 223.
20. *This Life I've Loved,* 270.
21. RLS to Baxter, Feb. 3, 1890, *Letters* 6:361.
22. Baxter *Letters,* 260 (Fanny's addition to Louis's letter is not included in the Yale *Letters*).
23. RLS to Henley, Feb. 1890, *Letters* 6:363–65.
24. RLS to James, Dec. 7, 1891, *Letters* 7:210.

CHAPTER 29. INTERLUDE

1. RLS to Margaret, Aug. 25, 1890, *Letters* 6:410.
2. RLS to Baxter, Sept. 1, 1890, *Letters* 6:418.
3. *This Life I've Loved,* 267.
4. RLS to his mother and to Colvin, March 20, 1890, *Letters* 6:381–82; to Edward Burlingame, March 11, 6:377; to Baxter, April 10, 6:385.
5. Balfour 2:108.
6. RLS to his mother and to Baxter, mid-April 1890, *Letters* 6:386–87.
7. Austin Strong, "The Most Unforgettable Character I've Met," *Reader's Digest,* March 1946, 36.
8. RLS to Colvin, April 30, 1890, *Letters* 6:389.
9. RLS to Colvin, April 30, 1890, *Letters* 6:389–90.
10. *The Cruise of the Janet Nichol among the South Sea Islands* (first published in 1914), ed. Roslyn Jolly (Seattle: University of Washington Press, 2004), 50, 68, 89.
11. *Cruise of the Janet Nichol,* 99.

12. *Cruise of the Janet Nichol,* 84, 91.
13. *Cruise of the Janet Nichol,* 139.
14. Roslyn Jolly, "Women's Trading in Fanny Stevenson's *The Cruise of the Janet Nichol," Economies of Representation, 1790–2000: Colonialism and Commerce,* ed. Leigh Dale and Helen Gilbert (Aldershot, UK: Ashgate, 2007), 143–55.
15. *Cruise of the Janet Nichol,* 188.
16. *Cruise of the Janet Nichol,* 165.
17. *Cruise of the Janet Nichol,* 125–26.
18. RLS to James, Aug. 19, 1890, *Letters* 6:402–3.
19. RLS to Baxter, late July 1890, *Letters* 6:398.
20. RLS to Edward L. Burlingame, Oct. 7, 1890, *Letters* 7:12.
21. Furnas, 376; H. W. Triggs, in R. C. Terry, *Robert Louis Stevenson: Interviews and Recollections* (Iowa City: University of Iowa Press, 1996), 179.
22. RLS to Colvin, Dec. 22, 1890, *Letters* 7:58.
23. RLS to Colvin, Dec. 24, 1890, *Letters* 7:59.
24. "Sketches: Nuits Blanches," first published in the Edinburgh Edition.
25. Balfour, 2:130.
26. H. J. Moors, *With Stevenson in Samoa* (Boston: Small, Maynard, 1910), 43, 46–47, 60–61.
27. "One Who Knows Him," *Woman at Home,* Feb. 1894, *Stevensoniana,* 100.
28. Fanny's diary for July 1, 1891, quoted in *Letters* 7:123–24n.
29. *Travels with a Donkey in the Cévennes and The Amateur Emigrant,* ed. Christopher MacLachlan (London: Penguin, 2004), "Upper Gévaudan," 58.
30. *This Life I've Loved,* 311.
31. Henry Adams to John Hay, Oct. 16, 1890, *The Letters of Henry Adams,* ed. J. C. Levenson (Cambridge, MA: Harvard University Press, 1982), 3:303; RLS to Edward Burlingame and to Colvin, Nov. 4, and 25, 1890, *Letters* 7:33, 42.
32. See Ann C. Colley, "Stevenson's Pyjamas," *Victorian Literature and Culture* (2002), 129–55, reprinted in her *Robert Louis Stevenson and the Colonial Imagination* (Aldershot, UK: Ashgate, 2004).
33. Henry Adams to Elizabeth Cameron, Oct. 17, 1890, *Letters* 3:296–97.

CHAPTER 30. LIFE AT VAILIMA

1. RLS to Colvin, Oct. 7, 1891, *Letters* 7:162.
2. Masson, 307.
3. Furnas, 383.
4. Leonard Bell, "Pictures as History, Settlement as Theatre: John Davis's Photo-Portrait of Robert Louis Stevenson and Family at Vailima, Samoa, 1892," *Journal of New Zealand Literature* 20 (2002), 93–111.
5. H. J. Moors, *With Stevenson in Samoa* (Boston: Small, Maynard, 1910), 11.
6. Harman, 422.
7. *Letters from Samoa, 1891–1895, by Mrs. M. I. Stevenson,* ed. Marie Clothilde Balfour (New York: Scribner, 1906), 186, 245; Charles John Guthrie, *Robert Louis Stevenson: Some Personal Recollections* (Edinburgh: W. Green, 1924), 60.

8. RLS to Anne Jenkin, May 25, 1892, *Letters* 7:295; Furnas, 537.
9. RLS to Colvin, Oct. 8, 1892, *Letters* 7:388.
10. RLS to Colvin, June 25 and Dec. 2, 1891, March 25, 1892, *Letters* 7:140, 202, 248.
11. Lloyd Osbourne, introduction to the Tusitala Edition (London: Heinemann, 1924), 1:xvii.
12. RLS to George Meredith, Sept. 5, 1893, *Letters* 8:163; Matthew 26:41.
13. "If This Were Faith," *Collected Poems*, 261–62. Graham Balfour dated this poem to 1893 (see note in *Collected Poems*, 508).
14. RLS to Edward Burlingame, July 13, 1890, *Letters* 6:393, to George Sainsbury, Feb. 1892, *Letters* 7:236, and to Baxter, Dec. 28, 1889, *Letters* 6:347; *A Footnote to History*, ch. 2. This work was first published as *A Footnote to History: Eight Years of Trouble in Samoa* (London: Cassell, 1892).
15. *A Footnote to History*, ch. 3 (I have somewhat abridged this passage).
16. Marie Fraser, "One Who Knows Him," *Stevensoniana*, 107–8; *Letters from Samoa*, 172.
17. RLS to Edward Burlingame, Nov. 4, 1890, *Letters:* 7:33.
18. RLS to Colvin, Nov. 4, 1890, and March 20, 1891, *Letters* 7:27, 93.
19. Fanny and Robert Louis Stevenson, *Our Samoan Adventure*, ed. Charles Neider (New York: Harper, 1955), xv, 29.
20. RLS to Colvin, Aug. 10, 1892, *Letters* 7:345.
21. James Mulligan, quoted by Furnas, 379.
22. Annie Ide (under her married name Mrs. Bourke Cochran) in *I Can Remember*, 344; RLS to Colvin, July 17, 1894, *Letters* 8:338.
23. Isobel Strong and Lloyd Osbourne, *Memories of Vailima* (Westminster: Archibald Constable, 1903), 65–66.
24. "Impromptu Versus Presented to Girolamo, Count Nerli," *Collected Poems of Robert Louis Stevenson,* ed. Roger Lewis (Edinburgh: Edinburgh University Press, 2003), 281.
25. *This Life I've Loved,* 327; *A Footnote to History*, ch. 1.
26. Six letters on May 18, 1894, *Letters* 8:284–93; RLS to J. M. Barrie, April 3, 1893, *Letters* 8:45; Belle to Charles Stoddard, Feb. 21, 1893, quoted in a note on that page.
27. RLS to Colvin, Aug. 10 and 19, 1892, *Letters* 7:345, 359; 1 Corinthians 16:21.
28. Strong and Osbourne, *Memories of Vailima,* 41; RLS to Colvin, March 20, 1891, *Letters* 7:96.
29. Baxter to RLS, July 1, 1892, *Letters* 7:348; Robert Burns, "I hae a wife of my ain." Gosse is quoted by Ann Thwaite, *Edmund Gosse: A Literary Landscape, 1849–1928* (Chicago: University of Chicago Press, 1984), 376.
30. RLS to Baxter, May 20, 1893, and Fanny to Baxter, May 21, *Letters* 8:77–78.
31. James to Colvin, March 1889, quoted by E. V. Lucas, *The Colvins and Their Friends* (New York: Scribner, 1928), 273; James to RLS, April 28, 1890, and Jan. 12, 1891, *Henry James Letters,* ed. Leon Edel (Cambridge, MA: Harvard University Press, 1980), 3:278, 325.
32. RLS to James, May 25, 1892, *Letters* 7:292–93; *Collected Poems,* 356.
33. *A Friendship in Letters: Robert Louis Stevenson and J. M. Barrie,* ed. Michael Shaw (Inverness: Sandstone, 2020), 8, 102.
34. *This Life I've Loved,* 296.
35. Strong and Osbourne, *Memories of Vailima,* 50–51.

36. RLS, *In the South Seas,* ed. Neil Rennie (London: Penguin, 1998), 231; H. J. Moors, *With Stevenson in Samoa* (Boston: Small, Maynard, 1910), 61; Lloyd Osbourne, preface to the Vailima Edition (New York: Scribner, 1921–23).
37. *This Life I've Loved,* 296, 278, 299–300.
38. *Intimate Portrait,* 148.
39. *Inland Voyage,* "On the Sambre Canalised"; John Williams, *A Narrative of Missionary Enterprises* (1837), quoted by Ann C. Colley, *Robert Louis Stevenson and the Colonial Imagination* (Aldershot, UK: Ashgate, 2004), 58.
40. Lloyd Osbourne, introduction to the Tusitala Edition (London: Heinemann, 1924), 1:xix; see A. E. Day, "The Library at Vailima," *Library Review* 25 (1975), 107–110.
41. Moors to Merritt A. Farren, Dec. 16, 1916, quoted by George L. McKay, *Some Notes on Robert Louis Stevenson: His Finances and His Agents and His Publishers* (New Haven: Yale University Press, 1958), 41.
42. Baxter to RLS, Oct. 1892, quoted in *Letters* 7:397n.
43. *Complete Stories,* 620; see Manfred Malzahn, "Voices of the Scottish Empire," *Robert Louis Stevenson: Writer of Boundaries,* ed. Richard Ambrosini and Richard Dury (Madison: University of Wisconsin Press, 2006), 158.
44. Arthur Claxton in *I Can Remember,* 315; Balfour 2:130.
45. P. G. Wodehouse, *Heavy Weather* (New York: Little, Brown, 1933), ch. 9.
46. RLS to Colvin, May 17, 1892, *Letters* 7:281–82.
47. Margaret Oliphant in *Blackwood's,* Oct. 1892, *Critical Heritage,* 397.
48. RLS to Will H. Low, Jan. 15, 1894, *Letters* 8:345, and to James, May 25, 1892, *Letters* 7:292.
49. "The Song of Rahéro," *Collected Poems,* 181.
50. RLS to Gosse, April 1891, *Letters* 7:106; a footnote quotes Gosse's letter to George Armour.
51. RLS to H. B. Baildon, fall 1891, *Letters* 7:187; Edwin Morgan, *Crossing the Border: Essays on Scottish Literature* (Oxford: Carcanet, 1990), 143.
52. James to RLS, Jan. 12, 1891, *Henry James Letters,* ed. Leon Edel (Cambridge, MA: Harvard University Press, 1980), 3:327.

CHAPTER 31. MISSIONARIES, CHIEFS, AND BUREAUCRATS

1. See Ann C. Colley, *Robert Louis Stevenson and the Colonial Imagination* (Aldershot, UK: Ashgate, 2004), ch. 1.
2. RLS to G. A. Sala, Sept. 12, 1892, *Letters* 7:377; RLS to Colvin, June 15, 1892, *Letters* 7:307.
3. S. J. Whitmee in *I Can Remember,* 294.
4. Balfour, 2:152.
5. RLS to Adelaide Boodle, Jan. 17, 1890, *Letters* 7:73–74.
6. "Selections from His Notebook," *Works,* Tusitala Edition (London: Heinemann, 1924), 29: 176.
7. *Fables by Robert Louis Stevenson* (London: Longman's, Green, 1902), fable 16, "Something in It"; Roslyn Jolly, *Robert Louis Stevenson in the Pacific: Travel, Empire, and the Author's Profession* (Farnham, UK: Ashgate, 2009), 58.

8. RLS to Colvin, Nov. 1883, *Letters* 4:199, commenting on J. R. Seeley's *The Expansion of England.*
9. Calder, 395.
10. Italo Calvino, "L'isola del Tesoro ha il suo segreto," *Saggi 1945–1985* (Milan: Meridiani, 1995), 1:970; Edmund Gosse, *Critical Kit-Cats* (New York: Dodd, Mead, 1903), 277.
11. "The Morality of the Profession of Letters," *Fortnightly Review,* April 1881, not reprinted in Stevenson's lifetime; RLS to Edward Burlingame, Nov. 1891, *Letters* 7:196.
12. *Times,* May 18, 1893, and Lord Rosebery's address to the Royal Academy on April 29, both quoted in *Letters* 8:87n and 88n.
13. H. J. Moors, *With Stevenson in Samoa* (Boston: Small, Maynard, 1910), 23; *A Footnote to History,* in the South Seas Edition of Stevenson's *Works* (New York: Scribner, 1925), vol. 26; these quotations are from chs. 4 and 11, pp. 205, 296; *Athenaeum,* Sept. 1892.
14. *A Footnote to History,* ch. 2.
15. *A Footnote to History;* ch. 1.
16. RLS to Colvin, May 9, 1892, *Letters* 7:281; *A Footnote to History,* ch. 11.
17. RLS to Colvin, April 25, 1894, *Letters* 8:281–82; Colvin's letter is quoted on 279n.
18. Jolly, *Robert Louis Stevenson in the Pacific,* 104.
19. RLS to the editor of the *Pacific Commercial Advertiser,* quoted by Swearingen, 176; *A Footnote to History,* ch. 2; RLS to James, Dec. 5, 1892, *Letters* 7:449.
20. RLS to Colvin, Sept. 12, 1893, *Letters* 7:368.
21. *A Footnote to History,* ch. 2.
22. RLS to Colvin, Sept. 6, 1891, and to James, June 17, 1892, *Letters* 7:153, 8:107.
23. *Letters from Samoa, 1891–1895 by Mrs. M. I. Stevenson,* ed. Marie Clothilde Balfour (New York: Scribner, 1906), 62–63.
24. RLS, *In the South Seas,* ed. Neil Rennie (London: Penguin, 1998), 33.
25. RLS to Colvin, July 12, 1893, *Letters* 8:127.
26. RLS to James Payn, Aug. 1, 1894, *Letters* 8:347.
27. Joseph Conrad, *Heart of Darkness* (1899), ch. 1.
28. Furnas, 404.
29. RLS to Colvin, Sept. 8, 1894, *Letters* 8:358–59.
30. See Joseph Theroux, "Some Misconceptions about RLS," *Journal of Pacific History* 16 (1981), 164.

CHAPTER 32. THE END OF PARADISE

1. RLS to James, Dec. 7, 1891, *Letters* 7:210.
2. RLS to Colvin, Aug. 24, 1893, *Letters* 8:157; Pope Hennessy, 279.
3. RLS to Colvin, Oct. 26, 1891, *Letters* 7:179.
4. RLS to Austin Strong, Jan. 27, 1893, *Letters* 8:17–18.
5. Fanny and Robert Louis Stevenson, *Our Samoan Adventure,* ed. Charles Neider (New York: Harper, 1955), 185; RLS to Richard Carruthers, July 17, 1892, and to Colvin, Sept. 13, *Letters* 7:355, 367.
6. RLS to Graham Balfour, Jan. 8, 1893, *Letters* 8:8–9.
7. RLS to Graham Balfour, Jan. 8, 1893, *Letters* note on 8:9.

8. RLS, *In the South Seas,* ed. Neil Rennie (London: Penguin, 1998), 32; Paul Shankman, *The Trashing of Margaret Mead* (Madison: University of Wisconsin Press, 2009).
9. RLS to Elizabeth Fairchild, Sept. 1892, *Letters* 7:374.
10. RLS to Baxter, Aug. 11 and Sept. 12, 1892, *Letters* 7:352, 377.
11. "My Wife," *Collected Poems,* 262–63, see note in *Collected Poems,* 508, quoting Colvin's letter to Gosse, Nov. 14, 1895.
12. Lady Jersey's *Fifty-One Years of Victorian Life* is quoted by Swearingen, 173.
13. Robert Louis Stevenson and Five of His Friends, *An Object of Pity: or, The Man Haggard* (New York: Dodd, Mead, 1900).
14. RLS to Colvin, Aug. 10, 1892, *Letters* 7:344.
15. RLS to Colvin, Nov. 5, 1893, *Letters* 8:179–80.
16. RLS to Colvin, Oct. 24, 1891, *Letters* 7:179; Fanny's diary is quoted in a note.
17. RLS to J. M. Barrie, April 3, 1893, *Letters* 8:45; Joel 3:28, repeated in Acts 2:17.
18. Isobel Strong and Lloyd Osbourne, *Memories of Vailima* (Westminster: Archibald Constable, 1903), 37.
19. RLS to Colvin, April 6, 1893, *Letters* 8:39–40; Richard Holmes, "On the Enchanted Hill," *New York Review of Books,* June 8, 1995.
20. Singer, 167.
21. Continuation of RLS to Colvin, April 6, 1893: April 7 and 20, 8:40–43.
22. RLS to his mother, May 22, 1893, *Letters* 8:80.
23. Bell, 254.
24. RLS to Frances Sitwell, April 25, 1894, *Letters* 8:82–83; her reply is quoted on 283n.
25. RLS to James, July 7, 1894, *Letters* 8:312–13.
26. RLS to Stanley J. Weyman, July 7, 1894, and to Edward L. Burlingame, July 8, *Letters* 8:316, 317.
27. RLS to Baxter, July 18, 1893, *Letters* 8:141, recalling John Gibson Lockhart's *Memoirs of the Life of Sir Walter Scott.*
28. RLS to Baxter, Aug. 12, 1894, *Letters* 8:353.
29. *Daily News,* Dec. 18, 1894, quoted in *Letters* 8:388.
30. RLS to Bob, Sept. 9, 1894, *Letters* 8:362; William Wordsworth, "Ode: Intimations of Immortality from Recollections of Early Childhood."
31. "To S. R. Crockett, on Receiving a Dedication," *Collected Poems,* 283–84, and letter of Aug. 15, 1893, *Letters* 8:153–54 (I follow the punctuation in this manuscript version).
32. Edwin Morgan, *Crossing the Border: Essays on Scottish Literature* (Oxford: Carcanet, 1990), 144.
33. Undated "Autobiographical Note," Beinecke 5998.

CHAPTER 33. THE LAST NOVELS

1. See Swearingen, 166–70.
2. RLS to Colvin, March 2, 1892, *Letters* 7:243; Balfour 2:167.
3. RLS to Colvin, March 12, 1892, *Letters* 7:246; Ian Duncan, "Stevenson's Scotland," *Approaches to Teaching the Works of Robert Louis Stevenson,* ed. Caroline McCracken-Flesher (New York: Modern Language Association, 2013), 129; *Catriona,* ch. 1.

4. *Catriona,* ch. 17.
5. *Catriona,* ch. 18.
6. *Catriona,* ch. 1.
7. "Some Portraits by Raeburn," written in 1876, published in *Virginibus Puerisque* (1881); Fanny's prefatory note to the Vailima Edition (New York: Scribner, 1921–23), 10:4.
8. RLS to Colvin, June 8, 1892, *Letters* 7:305–6.
9. Anonymous writer in the *Westminster Budget,* quoted by Eve Blantyre Simpson, *The Robert Louis Stevenson Originals* (New York: Scribner, 1913), 145.
10. *Catriona,* ch. 24.
11. *Catriona,* ch. 30.
12. *Catriona,* ch. 20.
13. RLS to Colvin, Sept. 30, 1892, and to Frances Sitwell, April 24, 1894, *Letters* 7:384, 8:282.
14. Barrie to RLS, Feb. 4, 1894, *A Friendship in Letters: Robert Louis Stevenson and J. M. Barrie,* ed. Michael Shaw (Inverness: Sandstone, 2020), 140; James to RLS, Oct. 21, 1893, *Henry James Letters,* ed. Leon Edel (Cambridge, MA: Harvard University Press, 1980), 3:438; RLS to James, Dec. 5, 1893, *Letters* 8:193.
15. Joseph Jacobs, writing anonymously in the *Athenaeum,* Oct. 1897, *Critical Heritage,* 485–86.
16. *The Ebb-Tide,* ch. 10.
17. Frances R. Hart, "Robert Louis Stevenson in Prose," *The History of Scottish Literature,* vol. 3 (Aberdeen: Aberdeen University Press, 1987), 303.
18. *The Ebb-Tide,* ch. 11.
19. *The Ebb-Tide,* ch. 12.
20. Audrey Murfin, *Robert Louis Stevenson and the Art of Collaboration* (Edinburgh: Edinburgh University Press, 2019), 173.
21. RLS to Colvin, June 18, 1893, and to James, June 17; *Letters* 8:94, 107.
22. *The Speaker,* Sept. 1894, and Israel Zangwill, *New York Critic,* Nov. 24, 1894; *Critical Heritage,* 450, 462.
23. RLS to Will H. Low, Jan. 15, 1894, *Letters* 8:235; Horace, *Epistles* I.xix.
24. RLS to H. B. Baildon, Jan. 30, 1894, *Letters* 8:243.
25. RLS to Colvin, June 5–6, 1893, *Letters* 8:90–91.
26. Isobel Strong and Lloyd Osbourne, *Memories of Vailima* (Westminster: Archibald Constable, 1903), 69–71.
27. Sidney Royce Lysaght in *I Can Remember,* 332.
28. *Weir of Hermiston,* ch. 5.
29. *Weir of Hermiston,* ch. 1.
30. *Weir of Hermiston,* ch. 1.
31. Masson, 73–74.
32. *Weir of Hermiston,* ch. 3.
33. *Weir of Hermiston,* ch. 5; Rankin, 20.
34. *Weir of Hermiston,* ch. 6.
35. Strong and Osbourne, *Memories of Vailima,* 70.

36. *Weir of Hermiston,* ch. 5.
37. *Weir of Hermiston,* ch. 8; Stephen Gwynn, "The Posthumous Works of Robert Louis Stevenson," *Fortnightly Review,* April 1898, *Stevensoniana,* 194.
38. *Weir of Hermiston,* ch. 9.
39. RLS to Barrie, Nov. 1, 1892, *Letters* 7:414.
40. Fanny to Colvin, July 17, 1895, quoted by E. V. Lucas, *The Colvins and Their Friends* (New York: Scribner, 1928), 258.
41. *Collected Poems,* 326.
42. *Intimate Portrait,* 138–39.
43. Harman, 453.
44. McLynn, 490.

CHAPTER 34. "I WAS NOT BORN FOR AGE"

1. *Letters from Samoa, 1891–1895 by Mrs. M. I. Stevenson,* ed. Marie Clotilde Balfour (New York: Scribner, 1906), 303, 312; *This Life I've Loved,* 340.
2. Austin Strong, "The Most Unforgettable Character I've Met," *Reader's Digest,* March 1946, 37.
3. RLS to Gosse, Dec. 1, 1894, *Letters* 8:399; Henry James, review of "The Letters of Robert Louis Stevenson," *North American Review,* Jan. 1900, 61ff.; Gosse to his daughter Tessa, quoted by Ann Thwaite, *Edmund Gosse: A Literary Landscape, 1849–1928* (Chicago: University of Chicago Press, 1984), 303.
4. RLS to Baxter, May 9, 1889, *Letters* 6:294.
5. Belle's journal in *Letters* 8:402–3.
6. *Letters from Samoa, 1891–1895,* 327.
7. *Intimate Portrait,* 147; Arthur Johnstone, *Robert Louis Stevenson in the Pacific* (London: Chatto & Windus, 1905), 143; Clayton Hamilton, *On the Trail of Stevenson* (New York: Doubleday, Page, 1916), 16–17.
8. Fanny to Anne Jenkin, Dec. 4 or 5, 1894, in *Letters* 8:409.
9. *A Letter to Mr. Stevenson's Friends* (1894), 4, 6, 32.
10. Elsie Noble Caldwell, *Last Witness for Robert Louis Stevenson* (Norman: University of Oklahoma Press, 1960), 339, quoting Belle's recollection; "Stevenson's Speech to the Chiefs," *Robert Louis Stevenson: His Best Pacific Writings,* ed. Roger Robinson (Brisbane: University of Queensland Press, 2004), 148; Ruth 1:16–17.
11. Fanny to Colvin, 1896, quoted by E. V. Lucas, *The Colvins and Their Friends* (New York: Scribner, 1928), 262.
12. "Requiem," *Collected Poems,* 130.
13. Isobel Strong and Lloyd Osbourne, *Memories of Vailima* (Westminster: Archibald Constable, 1903), 151; Balfour 2:188.
14. "Aes Triplex," *Cornhill Magazine,* April 1878; *Virginibus Puerisque* (1881).
15. Margaret to Colvin, Feb. 4, 1895, quoted by Lucas, *The Colvins and Their Friends,* 240; *Letters of J. M. Barrie,* ed. Viola Meynell (London: Peter Davies, 1942), 231.
16. James to Gosse, Dec. 17, 1894, *Henry James Letters,* ed. Leon Edel (Cambridge, MA: Harvard University Press, 1980) 3:495.
17. James to Fanny, also Dec. 17, *Henry James Letters,* 3:495–97.

18. Fanny to Colvin, March 20, 1896, quoted by Lucas, *The Colvins and Their Friends,* 264; Sidney Colvin, *Memories and Notes of Persons and Places* (London: Edward Arnold, 1921), 99; G. K. Chesterton, "Robert Louis Stevenson," *Bookman,* Oct. 1901, *Critical Heritage,* 504.
19. Chesterton, "Robert Louis Stevenson," 501.

EPILOGUE

1. RLS to Colvin, Oct. 1, 1894, *Letters* 8:383–84.
2. See the note in *Letters* 8:110.
3. Joshua Slocum, *Sailing Alone around the World* (New York: Century, 1900), ch. 12.
4. Quoted by Mackay, 466.
5. Sanchez, 265, 319; Richard Le Gallienne, *The Romantic '90's* (London: Putnam's, 1926), 83–84.
6. Quoted by Sanchez, 311.
7. *This Life I've Loved,* 329; the people in the procession are identified by Sanchez, 330.
8. W. E. Henley, "R.L.S.," *Pall Mall Magazine,* Dec. 1901, *Critical Heritage,* 494–500.
9. Andrew Lang to J. Brander Matthews, Dec. 28, 1901, *Friends over the Ocean: Andrew Lang's American Correspondents, 1881–1912,* ed. M. Demoor (Ghent: Rijksuniversitet Gent, 1989), 146.
10. Steven Mintz, *A Prison of Expectations: The Family in Victorian Culture* (New York: New York University Press, 1983), 65; Henry Bellyse Baildon, *Robert Louis Stevenson: A Life Study in Criticism* (London: Chatto & Windus, 1901), 200.
11. Quoted by Charles John Guthrie, *Robert Louis Stevenson: Some Personal Recollections* (Edinburgh: W. Green, 1920), 62.

Illustration Credits

FIGURES

1. Margaret Stevenson in 1848. Margaret Stevenson, *Letters from Samoa, 1891–1895,* ed. Marie C. Balfour (New York: Scribner, 1906).
2. Thomas Stevenson, 1880. Capital Collections, Edinburgh.
3. First page of the "Baby Book." John Howell, *Stevenson's Baby Book* (San Francisco: John Henry Nash, 1922).
4. Margaret Stevenson and Louis. Margaret Stevenson, *From Saranac to the Marquesas and Beyond,* ed. Marie C. Balfour (New York: Scribner, 1903)
5. Louis at the age of four. Stevenson, *From Saranac to the Marquesas and Beyond.*
6. 17 Heriot Row. *A Book of R.L.S.*, ed. George E. Brown (New York: Scribner, 1919).
7. Thomas Stevenson and Louis, 1860. Capital Collections, Edinburgh.
8. Alison Cunningham ("Cummy"). Beinecke Rare Book and Manuscript Library, Yale University, New Haven.
9. Stevenson family group. Beinecke Rare Book and Manuscript Library, Yale University, New Haven.
10. "Auntie's Skirts," by Jesse Wilcox Smith. *A Child's Garden of Verses* (New York: Scribner, 1905).
11. "The Child Alone," by Jesse Wilcox Smith. *A Child's Garden of Verses.*
12. The shop in Leith Walk. Eve Blantyre Simpson, *The Robert Louis Stevenson Originals* (New York: Scribner, 1913).
13. The Reverend Lewis Balfour. Stevenson, *From Saranac to the Marquesas and Beyond.*
14. Colinton Manse. Simpson, *The Robert Louis Stevenson Originals.*
15. The Pentland Hills from Fairmilehead. Simpson, *The Robert Louis Stevenson Originals.*
16. Swanston Cottage. Capital Collections, Edinburgh.

17. Bell Rock Lighthouse. Robert Stevenson, *An Account of Bell Rock Lighthouse* (Edinburgh: Archibald Constable, 1823).
18. John Horsburgh after Joseph Mallord William Turner, *Bell Rock Lighthouse.* Yale Center for British Art, Paul Mellon collection.
19. Charles Baxter. Beinecke Rare Book and Manuscript Library, Yale University, New Haven.
20. Inner hall of the Speculative Society. Charles John Guthrie, *Robert Louis Stevenson: Some Personal Recollections* (Edinburgh: W. Green & Son, 1920).
21. R. Kent Thomas, Planestones Close. RLS, *Edinburgh: Picturesque Notes* (London: Seeley, Jackson, & Halliday, 1879).
22. Fleeming Jenkin. Beinecke Rare Book and Manuscript Library, Yale University, New Haven.
23. "Desiderata." *Robert Louis Stevenson: The Man and His Work,* extra number of the *Bookman* (London: Hodder & Stoughton, 1913).
24. Frances Sitwell by Edward Burne-Jones. © The Trustees of the British Museum, London.
25. Sir Sidney Colvin. © National Portrait Gallery, London.
26. Andrew Lang. E. V. Lucas, *The Colvins and Their Friends* (New York: Scribner, 1928).
27. Stevenson as advocate. Charles John Guthrie, *Robert Louis Stevenson: Some Personal Recollections* (Edinburgh: W. Green & Son, 1920).
28. Stevenson to Frances Sitwell. Guthrie, *Robert Louis Stevenson.*
29. Will H. Low, self-portrait at Montigny. Low, *A Chronicle of Friendships* (New York: Scribner, 1908).
30. Walter Simpson. Simpson, *The Robert Louis Stevenson Originals.*
31. Walter Crane, frontispiece for *An Inland Voyage* (London: Keegan Paul, 1878).
32. A group at Grez. Low, *A Chronicle of Friendships.*
33. Bob Stevenson, self-portrait. Elizabeth Robins Pennell, *Nights: Rome, Venice, in the Aesthetic Eighties; London, Paris, in the Fighting Nineties* (Philadelphia: Lippincott, 1916).
34. Fanny Stevenson. Isobel Strong and Lloyd Osbourne, *Memories of Vailima* (Westminster: Archibald Constable, 1903).
35. John Singer Sargent, Frank O'Meara. Low, *A Chronicle of Friendships.*
36. Frontispiece by Walter Crane, Robert Louis Stevenson, *Travels with a Donkey in the Cévennes* (London: Kegan Paul, 1879).
37. Sketch by Stevenson, "Château Beaufort from Goudet sur Loire." Sidney Colvin et al., *Robert Louis Stevenson: His Work and His Personality* (London: Hodder & Stoughton, 1924).
38. Alfred Stieglitz, *The Steerage.* Library of Congress, Washington, DC.
39. Monterey rooming house. Katharine D. Osbourne, *Robert Louis Stevenson in California* (Chicago: A. C. McClurg, 1911).
40. Jules Simoneau. Osbourne, *Robert Louis Stevenson in California.*
41. 608 Bush Street, San Francisco. Osbourne, *Robert Louis Stevenson in California.*
42. Fanny's cottage in Oakland. Beinecke Rare Book and Manuscript Library, Yale University, New Haven.
43. Fanny by Dora Norton Williams (1880). Anne Roller Issler, *Happier for His Presence: San Francisco and Robert Louis Stevenson* (Stanford: Stanford University Press, 1949).

44. Fanny at the time of her marriage. Nellie Van de Grift Sanchez, *The Life of Mrs. Robert Louis Stevenson* (New York: Scribner, 1921).
45. Joe Strong, frontispiece to Robert Louis Stevenson, *The Silverado Squatters* (London: Chatto & Windus, 1883).
46. Davos, Dorfli and Seehorn, 1890–1900. Library of Congress, Washington, DC.
47. Veranda of the Hotel Buol, Davos-Platz, 1900. Library of Congress, Washington, DC.
48. The cottage at Braemar. Beinecke Rare Book and Manuscript Library, Yale University, New Haven.
49. Lloyd Osbourne, *Moral Emblems and Other Poems Written and Illustrated by Robert Louis Stevenson* (London: Chatto & Windus, 1921).
50. The Chalet La Solitude, Hyères. Beinecke Rare Book and Manuscript Library, Yale University, New Haven.
51. Leslie M. Ward, Skerryvore. *Robert Louis Stevenson: The Man and His Work.*
52. Fanny in Bournemouth. Beinecke Rare Book and Manuscript Library, Yale University, New Haven.
53. Sir Percy Shelley, Louis in Bournemouth. *Stevensoniana: An Anecdotal Life and Appreciation,* ed. J. A. Hammerton (Edinburgh: John Grant, 1910).
54. John Singer Sargent, Henry James. *The Yellow Book* 2 (July 1893).
55. Henry Van der Weyde, Richard Mansfield as Jekyll and Hyde. Library of Congress, Washington, DC.
56. The Lowlands and Highlands. (Map by Bill Nelson.)
57. Augustus Saint-Gaudens, Robert Louis Stevenson, bronze relief. Metropolitan Museum of Art, New York.
58. S. S. McClure. Lilly Library, University of Indiana, Bloomington.
59. The Saranac Lake sanatorium. Edward Livingston Trudeau, *An Autobiography* (New York: Doubleday, 1916).
60. The Baker cottage in Saranac Lake. Library of Congress, Washington, DC.
61. Lloyd, Fanny, and Louis at Saranac Lake. *Robert Louis Stevenson: His Work and His Personality.*
62. Dr. Trudeau. Trudeau, *An Autobiography.*
63. The *Casco.* Rosaline Masson, *The Life of Robert Louis Stevenson* (Edinburgh: W. & R. Chambers, 1923).
64. Lloyd Osbourne as a young man. Robert Louis Stevenson Silverado Museum, St. Helena, CA.
65. Map of the Pacific, by C. Scott Walker. Harvard University Map Collection and Geospatial Library, Cambridge.
66. Ori a Ori. Beinecke Rare Book and Manuscript Library, Yale University, New Haven.
67. The Stevensons with King Kalakaua. Beinecke Rare Book and Manuscript Library, Yale University, New Haven.
68. Lloyd Osbourne, Spearing fish on the *Equator.* Capital Collections, Edinburgh.
69. Butaritari group. Robert Louis Stevenson Silverado Museum, St. Helena, CA.
70. Tembinok and son. Capital Collections, Edinburgh.
71. Wrecked warships at Apia. H. J. Moors, *With Stevenson in Samoa* (Boston: Small, Maynard, 1910).

72. Vailima. Capital Collections, Edinburgh.
73. The Great Hall at Vailima. Capital Collections, Edinburgh.
74. Fanny and Fanua. Strong and Osbourne, *Memories of Vailima*.
75. Talolo. Strong and Osbourne, *Memories of Vailima*.
76. Lafaele. Moors, *With Stevenson in Samoa*.
77. Mitaele. Strong and Osbourne, *Memories of Vailima*.
78. Vailima group. *Robert Louis Stevenson: His Work and His Personality*.
79. Girls making kava. Moors, *With Stevenson in Samoa*.
80. *Packing Provisions for Vailima*. Beinecke Rare Book and Manuscript Library, Yale University, New Haven.
81. Louis with his flageolet. Capital Collections, Edinburgh.
82. Belle taking dictation. Alamy.
83. Fanny, by Belle. Beinecke Rare Book and Manuscript Library, Yale University, New Haven.
84. Louis with Tuimale Alifono. Strong and Osbourne, *Memories of Vailima*.
85. Mata'afa. Stevenson, *Letters from Samoa, 1891–1895*.
86. "History Lesson," by Belle. Robert Louis Stevenson Silverado Museum, St. Helena, CA.
87. Fanny's funeral procession. Sanchez, *The Life of Mrs. Robert Louis Stevenson*.
88. Cummy in later life. *R.L.S. Memories* (London: Foulis, 1926).

COLOR PLATES

1. Portrait of Stevenson in Sydney, Australia, by Henry Walter Barnett. A copy of the original is held by the Robert Louis Stevenson Silverado Museum, St. Helena, CA; colorized version by kind permission of Grant Kemp.
2. Locks of Robert Louis Stevenson's hair. Beinecke Rare Book and Manuscript Library, Yale University, New Haven.
3. Norman Wilkinson, "The Lamplighter." Robert Louis Stevenson, *Virginibus Puerisque and Other Papers* (London: Chatto & Windus, 1921).
4. A Skelt illustration. Metropolitan Museum of Art, New York.
5. Skerryvore Lighthouse. Ian Cowe / Alamy Stock Photo.
6. Samuel Bough, *Snowballing outside Edinburgh University*. Alamy.
7. Albert Marquet, "Harbor of Menton" (1905). VTR / Alamy Stock Photo.
8. William Ernest Henley by "Spy" (Leslie Ward). *Vanity Fair*, Nov. 26, 1892.
9. John Hayls, "Samuel Pepys." National Portrait Gallery, London.
10. Louis at Grez by Fanny. Beinecke Rare Book and Manuscript Library, Yale University, New Haven.
11. N. C. Wyeth, Blind Pew. RLS, *Treasure Island* (New York: Scribner, 1919).
12. Map of Treasure Island. RLS, *Treasure Island* (New York: Scribner, 1911).
13. John Singer Sargent, Robert Louis Stevenson and His Wife. Private collection, Metropolitan Museum of Art, New York.
14. N. C. Wyeth, David Balfour and Alan Breck. RLS, *Kidnapped* (New York: Scribner, 1913).
15. Map of Pacific voyages. Graham Balfour, *The Life of Robert Louis Stevenson* (New York: Scribner, 1901).

16. Upolu, Samoa. Image Professionals GmbH / Alamy Stock Photo.
17. Stevenson by Girolamo Ballatti Nerli. Beinecke Rare Book and Manuscript Library, Yale University, New Haven.

Compass ornament credit: iStock.com/duncan1890

Index

Note: Titles of works by Stevenson appear as separate entries throughout the index. The genre (e.g., novel, poem, essay) is indicated in parentheses following the title. Titles of works by other authors appear as subentries under the name of the author.

Across the Plains (memoir of RLS's railway journey to California), 198–200; publication of, 200
Adams, Henry: impressions of RLS and Fanny during his stop on Upolu, 397
Admiral Guinea (play by Henley and RLS), 304
"Adventures in the South Seas" (short story), 41
Ah Fu (Chinese cook), 361, 373; departure of, 384
Albert, Prince, 248
Alifono, Tuimale, 425
Amateur Emigrant, The (memoir of RLS's journey to California), 190, 192–93, 207, 215; publication of, 196, 200; sequel to, 198
Americanisms: RLS's use of, 211–12, 222, 243

Apemama (Gilbert Islands): RLS's poem written at, 380; Tembinok as chief of, 376–79
Apia, Upolu: Stevenson family's arrival in, 382–83; whites' predominance in, 426–27; wrecked warships at, 382
"Apology for Idlers, An" (essay), 71
Archer, William, 298, 330, 351
Arrick (pantry boy at Vailima), 403
Athenaeum: review of *The Wrong Box* in, 343
Augustine: *Confessions*, 92–93
"Auntie's Skirts" (poem), 31
Auvea (worker at Vailima), 403

Babington, Churchill, 107
Babington, Maud: RLS's visit with, 107, 109
Baildon, Bellyse: as RLS's collaborator on the *Jack o'Lantern*, 40

Bain, Bob, 64–65
Baker, Andrew, 337
Balfour, David (fictional character). See *Catriona*; *Kidnapped*
Balfour, George (uncle), 18, 52, 227; and concerns about RLS's health, 255, 328
Balfour, Graham (cousin), 12, 59, 70, 81, 91, 227, 243, 291, 305, 365, 388, 435; biography of RLS by, 362, 394; and Henley's review of Balfour's biography of RLS, 473; on *Jekyll and Hyde*, 312; on *Kidnapped*, 315; on RLS's connection to the Scottish Highlands, 319; on RLS's death, 465; at Vailima, 405
Balfour, Henrietta (cousin), 55, 56, 139
Balfour, Jane ("Auntie"), 46, 94, 358
Balfour, Lewis (cousin), 52
Balfour, Lewis (grandfather), 12, 46, 47
Balfour, Thomas (Margaret Stevenson's cousin), 405
Ballads and Songs of Scotland, The: RLS's review of, 134
Balmoral Castle, 247
Balzac, Honoré de: RLS on, 4
Baneful Potato, The (opera libretto), 56
Barbizon School, 144
Barker, Lucy Sayle: *Kate Greenaway's Birthday Book for Children*, 29–30, 246
Barrie, J. M., 474; on *Catriona*, 450; on *The Master of Ballantrae*, 344; *Peter Pan*, 386, 413; RLS's correspondence with, 411, 413–14; and RLS's description of the ending to *Weir of Hermiston*, 458–59
Bass Rock, 52
Baudelaire, Charles, 78
Baxter, Charles, 73, 79, 80, 136, 139, 142, 147, 189; as alcoholic, 412; and the breach between Henley and RLS, 345, 348, 349; and the death of his wife, 412; depression experienced by, 412; difficulties encountered after RLS's death, 473–74; and Edinburgh Edition of RLS's complete works (with Colvin), 469; and Fanny Osbourne, 165, 236; photograph of, 76; as RLS's business agent, 75, 236, 336, 411–12, 417; RLS's correspondence with, 75, 76–78, 98, 99–100, 123, 171, 173, 187, 188, 189, 199, 202–3, 212, 214, 215, 234, 278, 350, 357, 366–67, 411, 443; RLS's friendship with, 292, 384–85; RLS's poem to, 302; and RLS's request that he assist Lloyd in handling RLS's business matters, 392
"Beach of Falesá, The" (story), 418–19, 450, 467–68; plot of, 419–20
Beau Austin (play by Henley and RLS), 304
Beecher, Henry Ward, 162
Beerbohm, Max, 110
Bell Rock Lighthouse, 60–61, 62
Bell, Ian, 8; on stresses experienced by Fanny Stevenson, 442
Bell, Leonard, 401
Benson, A. C., 110
biographers of RLS, 3, 7–9. See also Balfour, Graham; Calder, Jenni; Daiches, David; Furnas, J. C.; Harman, Claire; Holmes, Richard; Masson, Rosaline; McLynn, Frank; Pope Hennessy, James; Rankin, Nicholas; Singer, Jefferson; Steuart, J. A.
Bird, Isabella, 89–90
Black Arrow, The: A Tale of Two Roses (novel), 273–74, 418; Scribner as publisher of, 336; serialization of, 273–74; RLS's opinion of, 274
Blake, William: "The Garden of Love," 106; *Songs of Experience*, 106
"Body Snatcher, The" (short story), 238–39; publication of, 239–40
Bogies: as described by RLS's nanny Cummy, 305
Boodle, Adelaide, 289–91, 329, 366, 423;

R.L.S. and His Sine Qua Non, 290; RLS as her writing instructor, 290–91; on Sargent's painting of RLS and Fanny, 291
"Books Which Have Influenced Me" (essay), 99, 174
Booth, Bradford, 7
Borch, Valentine, 354
Borges, Jorge Luis, 4; on *Jekyll and Hyde*, 308
Boswell, James, 319
"Bottle Imp, The" (story), 418, 419
Bough, Samuel: *Snowballing outside Edinburgh University*, 84
Bournemouth, England: RLS and Fanny in, 279–96. *See also* Skerryvore
Boyle, Anna, 139
Braemar cottage: Gosse's visit to, 248; rainy weather at, 247; Stevenson family's stay at, 246–48
Brash, Peter, 78
Brasheana (series of sonnets), 78
Braudel, Fernand, 318
Bridge of Allan, Scotland, 321; as setting for *Kidnapped*, 315–16
British Museum: Colvin as keeper of prints and drawings at, 109
Brodie, William (Deacon Brodie): as subject of play by RLS and Henley, 303–4
Brown, John, 247–48
Browne, Thomas, 72
Browning, Robert: *Pippa Passes*, 181
Buckland, Jack: as basis for character in *The Wrecker*, 389
Bunyan, John, 174; *Grace Abounding to the Chief of Sinners*, 311; *Pilgrim's Progress*, 175, 271
Burke, William, 238
Burlington Lodge Academy: RLS as student at, 39
Burne-Jones, Edward: *The Annunciation*, 110; drawing of Frances Sitwell by, 109–10

Burns, Robert, 11–12, 52, 71, 73, 86, 302; as a Don Juan, 188; RLS's essay on, 188
Butaritari (Gilbert Islands): friendships formed there, 376; photograph of, 377; powerful dancing displayed on, 375–76
Butler, Samuel: *The Way of All Flesh*, 103

Calder, Jenni, 8, 50, 85, 92, 109, 215, 323
California, RLS's journey to, 189–96; arrival in, 195–96; concerns of friends and family regarding, 190; on the *Devonia* (steamship), 189–95; financing of, 189; poems inspired by, 199; by railroad, 198–200
Calistoga, CA: RLS and Fanny's honeymoon in, 218–24
Callow, Philip, 8; on Joe Strong, 373
Calvinism: as instilled in RLS, 105–6
Calvino, Italo: on RLS, 3, 425; on *Treasure Island*, 254
"Cameronian Dream," 57–58
Cameron, Richard, 57
Camisards: uprising by, 182–83
"Canoe Speaks, The" (poem), 150
Carolus-Duran, 143
Carroll, Lewis, 386
Carson, Mary, 208
Carson, William, 208
Carter, Mary, 403
Casco (RLS's yacht), 79
Casco: captain of, 353, 354, 355–56; crew of, 354; and the incident with the decayed wood of the mast, 361–63; photograph of, 352; repairs needed for, 336; as yacht secured by Fanny for their Pacific sailing adventure, 350, 351–54. *See also* Pacific sailing adventure
Cassell: as publisher of *Kidnapped*, 326
Cather, Willa: *My Ántonia*, 335
Catriona (novel), 29, 52, 59, 81, 233, 266, 319, 421, 468; J. M. Barrie on, 450; Barbara Grant as character in,

Catriona (novel) (*continued*)
448–49; income generated by, 450; Henry James on, 450; plot of, 446–51; as sequel to *Kidnapped*, 446–47
Cedercrantz, Conrad, 429
"Celestial Surgeon, The" (poem), 268
Century Magazine: review of *New Arabian Nights* in, 185
Cézanne, Paul, 144
"Chapter on Dreams, A" (essay), 24–25, 104–5, 306
"Château Beaufort from Goudet sur Loire" (sketch from Louis's walking journey), 178–79
Chekhov, Anton, 4
Chemin de Stevenson, 178
Chesterton, G. K., 4, 72, 230, 239; on *More New Arabian Nights*, 300; on RLS's death, 467
"Child Alone, The" (poem), 33
Child's Garden of Verses, A (collection of poems), 29–35, 48–49, 50, 94, 246, 279, 354–55, 421; composition of, 273; and dedication to Cummy, 34–35, 116; publication of, 300. *See also names of individual poems*
"Child's Play" (essay), 49
"Christmas Sermon, A" (essay), 106
City of Chester (ocean liner): RLS's departure for England on (along with Fanny and Lloyd), 224
Clark, Andrew: and diagnosis of RLS's mental state, 122; and RLS's hemorrhaging, 270
Clarke, William: as missionary, 422–23; and Stevenson family on Upolu, 381
Coleridge, Samuel Taylor: "Kubla Khan," 100
Colinton Manse: description of, 47–49; as favorite place for RLS, 46–47
"College Magazine, A" (essay), 73
Colley, Linda, 316
Colvin, Sidney, 1–2, 42, 89, 93, 95, 102, 114, 187–88, 189, 227, 330; book dedicated to, 174; collection of RLS's letters published by, 6–7, 109, 389–90; and communication with RLS's parents, 214–15; on *Deacon Brodie*, 304; and Edinburgh Edition of RLS's complete works (with Baxter), 469; on Fanny as RLS's caregiver, 287; and Fanny Osbourne, 170; on Fanny's meeting with RLS's parents, 225; as friend and mentor to RLS, 111–12, 116–20, 122, 131, 132, 133–34, 146, 174, 184, 385; impressions of, 110–12; knighted as Sir Sidney, 474; on lack of female characters in RLS's books, 266; and Andrew Lang, 129; and marriage to Frances Sitwell, 474; photograph of, 111; and RLS's ambivalence about traveling to California, 189–90; on RLS's appearance at Skerryvore, 287–88; and RLS's complaints about Victorian taboos' effect on his writing, 266; and RLS's comment on *The Ebb-Tide*, 452; RLS's correspondence with, 199, 205, 208, 212, 214, 234, 235, 238, 258, 272, 282, 331, 357, 374, 408, 411, 433; on RLS's death, 467; and RLS's description of Woggs, 258; RLS's friendship with, 1–2, 116–18, 126, 292, 385; and RLS on his father's illness, 327; and RLS's Lallan poems, 301; on RLS's parents, 288; on RLS's sympathy for the native Samoans, 427–28; and Frances Sitwell, 109–10, 115, 118, 120, 122, 131, 169; *Travels with a Donkey* dedicated to, 174; and trip to see RLS in France, 126–27; on Woggs, 227
Comstock Lode, 163
Conan Doyle, Arthur, 4, 307, 335, 474
Conrad, Joseph: *Heart of Darkness*, 431, 452; on *In the South Seas*, 379
Cook, Captain James, 355
Cornhill Magazine: RLS's publications in, 118, 132, 146, 173, 188, 212, 267

Cousina, Antone, 354
Cramond, Scotland: Stevenson family vacations in, 52
Crane, Walter, 130, 175, 176
Crosby, Elizabeth, 121
Cruise of the Janet Nichol, The (Fanny Stevenson's diary entries), 390, 391–92
Cummy. *See* Cunningham, Alison
Cunningham, Alison (Cummy), 330, 474–75; *A Child's Garden of Verses* dedicated to, 34–35, 116; death of, 475; description of, 21; diary entries by, 43–45; Fanny's ongoing concern for, 474–75; on Gosse's reading from the Bible, 248; impressions of Europe, 43–45; in Italy, 45; photographs of, 22, 23, 475; as RLS's nanny, 20–29; and stories of sin and damnation, 23–28, 44, 45

Daiches, David, 3, 94
Damien, Father (Joseph De Veuster): as priest serving the leper settlement, 369, 370–71
Dana, Richard Henry: *Two Years before the Mast*, 359
"Dark Women" (poem), 159
Darwin, Charles: on photographs of himself, 283–84
Davis, John: group photograph of staff and family at Vailima taken by, 401–3
Davos, Switzerland: money worries in, 260–61; recommended for RLS's health, 227, 256–57; RLS's letters to Henley from, 256–58; RLS's departure from, 268; RLS's diagnosis and treatment in, 229–32, 233–34; RLS's feelings about, 228; RLS's outdoor recreation in, 233–34; RLS's reading in, 233; RLS with Fanny and Lloyd in, 256–61; the weather in, 257; Woggs in, 258

Deacon Brodie, or, The Double Life (play by Henley and RLS), 303–4
De Quincey, Thomas: *Confessions of an English Opium Eater*, 125
Devonia (steamship): and arrival in California, 195; demographics of passengers on, 191–92; description of, 190–91; RLS's description of passengers on, 193–94; RLS's journey to California on, 190–95, 196
Dhu Heartache lighthouse, 64, 67, 243
Dickens, Charles, 332; *Bleak House*, 372; *The Cricket on the Hearth*, 291; *Pickwick Papers*, 234
Dobson, Austin, 110
Don Quixote (Cervantes): RLS's reflections on, 358
doppelgänger: as theme in literature, 305. See also *Strange Case of Dr. Jekyll and Mr. Hyde*
Dostoevsky, Fyodor: *Crime and Punishment*, 298–99
Dr. Jekyll and Mr. Hyde. See *Strange Case of Dr. Jekyll and Mr. Hyde*
Drummond, Kate, 86
Dumas, Alexandre, 5; *Le Vicomte de Bragelonne*, 56–57
Durand, Charles, 143
Durham, Katharine: and marriage to Lloyd, 436

Earraid (island): in RLS's fiction, 64
Ebb-Tide, The (novel), 336; plot of, 451–53; reviews of, 452–53
Eddystone Light, 61
"Edifying Letters of the Rutherford Family" (short story), 196–98; as reflection of his feelings for Fanny, 198; as suggestive of his relationship with his father, 197
Edinburgh Napier University: RLS's letters at, 7
Edinburgh: Picturesque Notes (memoir), 83, 89, 96–97

Edinburgh, Scotland: urban squalor in, 89–91; universities in, 68. *See also* University of Edinburgh
Edinburgh University magazine, 73
"Education of an Engineer, The" (essay), 64
Elena (laundry worker at Vailima), 403
Eliot, George, 298
Eliot, T. S.: *The Waste Land*, 92–93
Elizabeth I, Queen, 318
Emerson, Ralph Waldo, 133
Equator, the (trading schooner): spear fishermen on, 374, 375; the Stevenson family's cruise on, 373, 374–81. *See also* Apemama; Butaritari
Erikson, Erik, 82
Euripides: *The Bacchae*, 77–78
evolution: as controversial among believers, 99; RLS's interest in, 308
Ewing, Alfred: on Anne Jenkin, 95; on RLS as entertainer, 96

Faauma: RLS's description of, 405; and song about members of the Stevenson family, 404; and Joe Strong, 405
Familiar Studies of Men and Books (collection of essays), 133, 267
"Feast of Famine, The: Marquesan Manners" (poem), 420
Fergusson, Robert, 73
Ferrier, Elisabeth Anne ("Coggie"), 277, 288, 330
Ferrier, Walter, 73, 77, 80, 136, 212, 385; death of, 276–77
Fiedler, Leslie, 258; on David and Alan's relationship in *Kidnapped*, 322
Field, Edward: death of, 473; and Fanny Stevenson, 471; and Belle Strong, 471
Fitzgerald, F. Scott: *The Great Gatsby*, 248
Fitzgerald, Moira, 9
Fitzwilliam Museum: Colvin as director of, 109

Flaubert, Gustav: on RLS, 4
"Fontainebleau: Village Communities of Painters" (essay), 144
Footnote to History, A: as RLS's perspective on the Great Powers' ambitions in the Pacific, 426–27, 446; review of, 426
"Foreign Lands" (poem), 355
"Forest Notes: Idle Hours" (essay), 145–46
Forster, E. M., 150, 152; on "story" in fiction, 5
Foss, Clark, 218–19
France: RLS's travels in, 143–46, 149, 154–55, 156–57
Freeman, Morgan, 136
French language: RLS's fluency in, 70, 71, 143
Freud, Sigmund, 105
Friedberg, Morris (Kelmar), 219
Furnas, J. C., 3, 77, 376, 404, 431; on advice to RLS as "chief" of Vailima, 400–401; on the building of the Vailima estate, 393; on the "Long Depression," 192; *Voyage to Windward: The Life of Robert Louis Stevenson*, 8; on Fanny's situation in California, 187

Gaelic: as the language of the Highlands, 63, 316
Galton, Francis: *Record of Family Faculties*, 12–13
Genesis, Book of, 104
George I, King, 318
George IV, King, 60
germ theory: as explanation for disease, 228–29
German Firm, the: and campaign to control trade in the Pacific, 429
Gilbert and Sullivan: *The Pirates of Penzance*, 303
Gilbert Islands: the *Equator*'s journey

to, 373, 375–79; friendships formed during their stops there, 376–79
Goethe, Johann Wolfgang von, 107; *Faust*, 200
Goldsmith, Oliver, 54
Goltz, Baron von der, 363
Goncourt, Edmond de: *Chérie*, 292
Gosse, Edmund, 119, 187–88, 203, 412, 425–26; on the death of RLS, 462; on Fanny Osbourne, 160–61; *Father and Son*, 103, 105, 416; as homosexual, 289; on RLS's consideration as history professor, 246; RLS's correspondence with, 207, 211, 213, 462; on RLS's reading aloud from *Treasure Island*, 253; on saying goodbye to RLS, 330
"Gossip on Romance, A" (essay), 37, 254, 267, 294
Grahame, Kenneth, 471; *The Wind in the Willows*, 152
Greene, Graham: on *Kidnapped*, 321
Grez-sur-Loing, France: RLS's stay in, 156–57
Guthrie, Charles, 21, 139–40, 142, 348; on RLS, 81–82

Haggard, Bazzet, 437–38
Haggard, Ryder, 437
Hales, Samuel, 146
Hansen's disease. *See* leper settlement
Hanson, Rufe, 223
"Happy Thought" (poem), 33
Hardy, Thomas, 474
Hare, William, 238
Harman, Claire, 8, 149, 231, 403, 459–60; *Myself and the Other Fellow*, 105
Hawaii/Hawaiian islands: Kalakaua as king of, 367–68; leper settlement on Molokai, 369–71; Stevenson family's arrival in, 365, 367–68
Hawthorne, Nathaniel, 72
Hayes, Bully (pirate), 361

Hayward, Stephen, 194
Hazlitt, William, 72, 133, 193
Heathercat (unfinished novel), 451
Henderson's school: RLS as student at, 38–39
Henley, Anthony, 156
Henley, Margaret, 386
Henley, Teddy, 288; as actor in *Deacon Brodie*, 345
Henley, William Ernest, 2, 71, 172, 330; "Apparition," 138; "Ballade R.L.S.," 138; and breach with RLS, 344–49; as "Burley" in "Talk and Talkers," 267; on Colvin, 257; and concerns about RLS's well-being, 236–37, 278; and Katharine de Mattos, 345–49; description of, 303; and diatribe against RLS after his death, 473; and efforts to mend the breach with RLS, 385–86; and Fanny, 237; on Gosse's sexual orientation, 289; *In Hospital* (poem sequence), 136–38; as inspiration for Long John Silver, 136; "Invictus," 136, 252–53; marriage of, 139; "Nocturne," 137–38; "Operation," 137–38; as Pan, 152; playwriting venture proposed by, 303–4; poem sequence by, 136–38; as RLS's agent, 236, 266, 345; and RLS's complaints about others' expectations of him, 261–62; RLS's correspondence with, 86, 170, 175, 199, 205, 230, 256–58, 270, 274, 275, 282, 329, 385–86; and RLS's description of Henry James, 292; and RLS on Ferrier's death, 276–77; RLS's friendship with, 136–39; on RLS's marriage to Fanny, 208; on RLS's "The Merry Men," 245; and RLS's payment for *Treasure Island*, 266; RLS's poem written to, 255; at Skerryvore, 288; and surgery to save his leg, 135–36
Hoffmann, E.T.A., 305

Hogg, James: *Confessions of a Justified Sinner*, 305
Hokusai, 146
Holmes, Richard, 3; on family loyalties, 441; on Fanny Osbourne's photograph, 159; *Footsteps: Adventures of a Romantic Biographer*, 174–75, 180–81; on RLS's letters, 7, 75; on RLS's marriage to Fanny, 218
Hopkins, Gerard Manley, 4, 310
Horace, 87, 123, 453
"House of Eld, The" (fable), 27–28
Huckleberry Finn (Twain): RLS's admiration for, 334
Hugo, Victor: *Les Miserables*, 80–81
Huguenots: uprising by, 182–83
"Humble Remonstrance, A" (essay), 292–94; Henry James's response to, 293–94
Hunt, Leigh, 301
Hyde, Charles McEwan: as critic of Father Damien, 370–71; RLS's critique of, 371–72
Hyères, France: RLS's stay in, 270–72, 274–75

I Can Remember Robert Louis Stevenson: Valentine's contribution to, 282, 366
"If This Were Faith" (poem), 406
Impressionism: early examples of, 146
In the South Seas (travel narrative), 359, 379, 411; Fanny's concerns about RLS's approach to, 367
Inland Voyage, An (memoir), 149–50, 153, 157, 173, 196, 416; "Epilogue to," 154; frontispiece of, 151, 220; reviews of, 153–54
Invictus (film), 136
Island Nights' Entertainments (story collection), 418–20
"Isle of Voices, The" (story), 418, 419
Italy: the Stevenson family's travels in, 45

Jack o'Lantern: magazine published by RLS and Bellyse Baildon, 40
Jack the Ripper, 314
Jacobites, 318
James I, King, 318
James III, King (the Pretender), 318
James, Alice, 292; on Fanny Stevenson, 296, 397
James, Henry, 81, 103, 330, 337; Henry Adams on, 294; on *A Child's Garden of Verses*, 29; "The Art of Fiction," 292; and Fanny, 292, 295–96; initial impression of RLS, 292; on *Kidnapped*, 324, 326; on Andrew Lang, 355; on Long John Silver, 263; "The Marriages," 413; plays by, 303; portraits of, 292, 293; on *Prince Otto*, 275–76; on RLS and Fanny's disagreement, 295–96; RLS on the breach with Henley, 386; RLS on the politics of imperialism, 429; on RLS's ballads, 421; and RLS's comment on *The Ebb-Tide*, 452–53; RLS's correspondence with, 412–13, 433; on RLS's death, 466–67; and RLS's description of his depression, 443; RLS's friendship with, 291–96; RLS's initial impression of, 292; and RLS's letter on island life, 392; RLS's observation regarding, 36; on RLS's letters, 6; on RLS's writing, 242; Sargent's portrait of, 292, 293; on "Thrawn Janet," 240, 467; *The Tragic Muse*, 416; on *Treasure Island*, 36, 292, 295; on *Underwoods*, 301; as visitor to Skerryvore, 291–92, 294; *Washington Square*, 334
James, William, 301; *Principles of Psychology*, 416
Jamison, Kay Redfield: on depression, 105, 125; *Exuberance: The Passion for Life*, 105
Janet Nicholl (trading vessel): Fanny's diary entries relating to, 390, 391–92;

and Fanny's trading with the native people, 390; in the Marshall Islands, 391; RLS and Fanny's experiences on, 388–92

Japanese prints: as appealing to RLS, 146

Japp, Alexander, 253; and serial publication of *Treasure Island*, 255, 261; and Thomas Stevenson, 248

Jeffrey, Francis, 79

Jekyll and Hyde. See *Strange Case of Dr. Jekyll and Mr. Hyde*

Jenkin, Anne, 86, 136, 139, 327; and Fanny's news that RLS had died, 464; RLS's friendship with, 93, 95

Jenkin, Fleeming, 86, 94, 168, 235, 270, 297; plays performed at the home of, 95–96; RLS's friendship with, 93–95, 118, 385

Jersey, Lady: *An Object of Pity, or the Man Haggard*, 437–39

"John Knox and His Relation to Women" (essay), 133

Johnson, Samuel, 54, 294; in the Scottish Highlands, 319

Jolly, Roslyn, 246, 391, 424

Jonson, Ben, 300

Joyce, James, 11

"justified sinner": as Calvinist doctrine, 305

Kaiser Wilhelm II (steamship): Stieglitz's photo of, 190, 191

Kaiulani, Princess: RLS's poem written to, 368

Kalakaua (king of the Hawaiian islands), 367–68; diverse characterizations of, 368; photograph of, 369

Kate Greenaway's Birthday Book for Children (Barker), 29–30

kava (Samoan beverage), 403

Kegan Paul, Charles: as RLS's publisher, 196

Kemp, Grant: and colorized photograph of, RLS, 2

Kenyatta, Jomo, 424

Kidnapped (novel), 29, 52, 59, 64, 161, 233, 297, 418, 468; David and Alan's relationship in, 321–25; David Balfour as narrator of, 319–22; Fanny's comments on, 325–26; historical characters in, 318–19; manuscript of, 325–26; plot of, 319–25; publication of, 314; reviews of, 326; Scottish Highlands as the setting for and inspiration for, 315–16; serialization of, 326

Kiely, Robert, 7

King James Bible: as influence on RLS, 26–27

Kinnaird Cottage: the Stevenson family's stay at, 238, 240

Kipling, Rudyard, 335, 474; *Barrack-Room Ballads*, 421

Kiribati, Republic of. See Gilbert Islands

Knox, Robert, 238

Kooamua (chief of Nukuhiva), 359–60

Lafaele (livestock manager at Vailima), 398, 403; photograph of, 400

La Farge, John: and visit to RLS on Upolu, 397

Lamb, Charles, 133, 349

"Lamplighter, The" (poem), 32–33

"Land of Counterpane, The" (poem), 30

Landrecies, France, 155

Lang, Andrew, 1, 139, 473; Colvin's description of, 129; and concerns about RLS's state of mind, 444; on Henley, 136; Henry James on, 355; on Julius Caesar, 357; "Recollections of Robert Louis Stevenson," 127–28; RLS as described by, 128–29; RLS's friendship with, 127–29; RLS's poem about, 129; on *Prince Otto*, 275; on "Thrawn Janet," 242

"Lantern-Bearers, The" (essay), 51

Lascelles, Mary, 58

La Solitude (chalet in Hyères), 270, 271

Lassen, John, 354

"Last Sight, The" (poem), 328
Lawrence, D. H., 218
Lawrence, Frieda, 218
Lecocq, Charles: *Giroflé-Girofla*, 182
Lee, Hermione, 8
Le Gallienne, Richard, 75
Le Monastier-sur-Gazeille: as the starting point for RLS's journey on foot, 173, 175
leper settlement: on Molokai, 369–72
Letter to Mr. Stevenson's Friends, A (collection of tributes after his death), 464
Leviticus, Book of: leprosy as described in, 370
Lewis, C. S.: on adventure stories, 254
Lewis, Robert C., 10
Liberty, Justice, and Reverence society, 80, 276
lighthouse building: as the Stevenson family business, 60–63, 81
lighthouse keeper: RLS's poem about, 66
Lister, Joseph: as physician to Henley, 135–36
"Little Land" (poem), 31
L.J.R., the (club), 80
London, Jack, 335
London Missionary Society (L.M.S.), 422
Long John Silver, 248, 251, 262–63; Henley as inspiration for, 136, 252–53; parrot belonging to, 263. See also *Treasure Island*
Longman, Charles: as publisher of *Jekyll and Hyde*, 312
Longman's Magazine, 200
Loquitur Puella Fuscula (Renaissance poem), 256–57
Low, Berthe, 332
Low, Will H., 144–45; on Fanny and Belle Osbourne, 165; in France with RLS, 156; on *Kidnapped*, 146; in New York City with RLS, 332–33; on RLS's appearance, 152–53; RLS's correspondence with, 270–71, 275, 280–82; and RLS's comment on his own work, 453
Lowland "Lallans" dialect: RLS's interest in, 52–54, 316; RLS's poems written in, 301–2
Lübeck (steamer): as the Stevensons' transport to Sydney, Australia, 384–85
Lucas, E. V.: *The Colvins and Their Friends*, 109; *Her Infinite Variety*, 115
Ludgate Hill (cargo ship): the Stevensons' journey to America on, 330, 331
Lysaught, Sidney: on RLS's reading aloud of *The Weir of Hermiston*, 454–55

Macaire: A Melodramatic Farce (play by Henley and RLS), 304
Macbeth (Shakespeare), 121
Macgregor, Rob Roy, 319
Mackay, Aeneas, 70
Mackay, Margaret, 162, 216
Macmillan's Magazine: RLS's essay published in, 124–25, 132
"Maker to Posterity, The" (poem), 302
Mallock, W. H.: RLS's grudge against, 119
Mandela, Nelson, 136
Mann, Thomas: *The Magic Mountain*, 228
Mansfield, Richard: as Jekyll and Hyde, 313, 314
Marquesas Islands: as controlled by France, 359
Marryat, Frederick: *Newton Foster*, 37
Marshall Islands: RLS and Fanny's experience in, 391
Martial: RLS's translation of, 301
Masson, David, 70
Masson, Flora, 83, 95, 96
Masson, Rosaline, 70, 77, 88, 93–94, 95, 102, 105–6, 285, 328; on RLS's role as clan chieftain in Samoa, 399; on RLS's serious health problems, 297–98; on Thomas's affection for Fanny, 227
Master of Ballantrae, The (novel), 59, 77, 233, 308, 363, 418; J. M. Barrie on,

344; plot of, 343–44; serialized in *Scribner's Magazine*, 343, 367
Mata'afa: defeat of, 430, 431; as Samoan chief, 427, 428; and tribute to RLS (Tusitala), 464
Matthew, Gospel of, 91, 406
Mattos, Katharine Stevenson de, 330; and apology to RLS, 348–49; as beneficiary of RLS's estate, 470; and Fanny, 347; *Jekyll and Hyde* dedicated to, 346–47; and tensions between Henley and RLS, 345–49
McCheyne, Robert Murray, 23–24
McClure, S. S.: *Autobiography of S. S. McClure, The*, 335; background of, 335; on Fanny Osbourne, 161; on meeting RLS, 335; and RLS's sailing adventure, 350, 367
McClure's Magazine, 335; RLS's work published in, 336
McLynn, Frank, 8, 115, 149, 154, 164, 170–71, 460
Mead, Margaret: *Coming of Age in Samoa*, 436
medical knowledge (in RLS's lifetime): limitations of, 18–19, 207–8, 227, 228–29, 272–73, 287, 340–41
Mehew, Ernest, 7, 100
Mehew, Joyce, 7
Melville, Herman, 357; *Omoo*, 210, 359; *Typee*, 210, 358–59
Memoir of Fleeming Jenkin, 297
Memories and Portraits (essay collection), 297, 331–32; and dedication to his mother, 331
Menikoff, Barry, 81, 246; *Complete Stories of Robert Louis Stevenson* (ed.), 20
Mennell, Dr.: engaged to treat RLS, 278
Menton, France: RLS's stay in, 43, 122–27, 131
Meredith, George, 474; on *An Inland Voyage*, 154
Merritt, Samuel, 352–53
"Merry Men, The" (short story), 64, 186,

243–45, 309, 467; Henley's praise for, 245
Merry Men and Other Tales and Fables, The (short story collection), 297
Michelangelo: love sonnets, 233
Millais, John Everett: on RLS as "artist," 323
Milton, John, 181
Mintz, Steven: *A Prison of Expectations: The Family in Victorian Culture*, 103
"Mirror Speaks, The" (poem), 294–95, 301
"Misgivings of Convalescence, The" (essay), 233–34
missionaries: and Christianity as agent of imperialism, 424; RLS's changing view of, 422–23
Mitaele (houseboy at Vailima), 398; photograph of, 401
"Modern Cosmopolis, A" (essay), 208–9
modernism: RLS as emblematic of transition to, 298
Modestine (RLS's donkey), 175–78, 183–84; RLS's treatment of, 177–78
Moë, 361
Molokai, Hawaii: leper settlement on, 369–72
Monaco: RLS's visit to, 126
Montaigne, Michel de, 72, 133; *Essais*, 153
Monterey, California: Belle Osbourne in, 203–4; Fanny Osbourne in, 201; RLS's impressions of, 205–7
Montigny, France: RLS's visit there, 144–45
Moors, Harry, 426; on the extravagance of Vailima estate, 394–95, 417; on Lloyd Osbourne, 402; on RLS's appearance upon arriving in Samoa, 382–83; on RLS's musical talent, 415
More New Arabian Nights: The Dynamiter (short story collection, with Fanny Stevenson), 297, 299–300, 418; reviews of, 300
More, James, 319

Morgan, Edwin: on RLS's ballads, 421; on RLS's poem about Scotland, 445
Morning Star (steamer): as possibility for further sea travel, 372–73
Morris, William, 80
Murfin, Audrey, 299
Murray, William Bazett, 277
"My Ship and I" (poem), 354–55
"My Wife" (poem), 437

Nabokov, Vladimir: on *Jekyll and Hyde*, 307, 308; *Pale Fire*, 276; on RLS, 3
Nan Tok, 376
Navigator Islands. *See* Samoa
Nei Takauti, 376
Nerli, Girolamo Ballatti: portrait of RLS by, 410; RLS's poem honoring, 410
"Ne Sit Ancillae Tibi Amor Pudori" (poem), 87
New Arabian Nights (short story collection), 185, 186, 267, 299, 418
Newton, Isaac, 69
New York City: RLS as celebrity in, 332; RLS's time in, 332–36
Nimo (Harry Moors's wife), 383
North Berwick, Scotland: RLS's vacations at, 51–52
North, Captain George: as pseudonym for RLS, 261, 274
"Notes on the Movements of Young Children" (essay), 132–33
Nukuhiva: the *Casco*'s landfall at, 358–59
"Nurses" (unpublished essay), 28

Oakland, California: Fanny's life in, 212, 213; RLS in, 212
"Ode by Ben Jonson, Edgar Allan Poem, and a Bungler" (poem), 78
Oedipus complex, 105
"Olalla" (short story), 308
Oldfield, Harry, 342
"Old Pacific Capital, The: Monterey" (memoir), 206–7
Oliphant, Margaret, 420

Olsen, Charles, 354
O'Meara, Frank: and Belle Osbourne, 167–68, 172
"On Falling in Love" (essay), 158–59
"On the Choice of a Profession" (essay), 142
"On the Enjoyment of Unpleasant Places" (essay), 64, 132
opium: as therapeutic for RLS, 125
"Ordered South" (essay), 124–25, 132
Ori a Ori (RLS's Tahitian friend), 361–64; letter to RLS from, 363–64; photograph of, 362; RLS's poem to, 361
Orwell, George, 89; *Down and Out in Paris and London*, 192–93
Osbourne, Belle, 163, 164, 273, 353; and affection for her father, 201–2, 204; descriptions of, 165, 166; on Fanny's decision to return to California, 172; on Fanny's marriage to RLS, 217–18; in Grez, 157–58, 166; in Hawaii, 280; and marriage to Joe Strong, 204; on meeting RLS, 166; in Monterey, 203–4; and Frank O'Meara, 167–68; on RLS's arrival in Monterey, 201; on RLS's "The Merry Men," 245–46; at Saranac Lake, 339. *See also* Strong, Belle
Osbourne, Fanny. *See* Stevenson, Fanny Osbourne
Osbourne, Hervey: birth of, 164; illness and death of, 164–65, 237
Osbourne, Lloyd, 6, 157, 164, 220; and affection for his father, 204; Belle's description of, 353; as beneficiary of RLS's estate, 470, 471; and collaboration on poems with RLS, 259–60; and departure for America, 327; dispatched from Sydney to England to handle business on RLS's behalf, 392; on Fanny's decision to return to California, 171–72; on William Ernest Henley, 303; on the king of the

Hawaiian islands, 268; on life in Davos, 232, 260–61; and marriage to Katharine Durham, 436; photograph of, 354; printing press operated by, 259–60; as published author, 471; on RLS's concerns regarding women, 92; RLS's dedication of *Treasure Island* to, 266; on RLS's kinship with Alan Breck Stewart (in *Kidnapped*), 322; on RLS's last day, 463; and RLS's marriage to his mother, 204–5; on RLS's playing the flageolet, 415; and RLS's reading of *Jekyll and Hyde*, 306; on RLS's religious views, 405–6; at Saranac Lake, 337, 338–39; at Skerryvore, 280; and Sosifina, 435–36; at Vailima, 398, 402; and war games with RLS, 258–59

Osbourne, Paulie, 340

Osbourne, Sam, 163, 171, 212; disappearance of, 340; and divorce from Fanny, 203; Fanny's mixed feelings for, 171–72, 187, 201

Otis, Albert: as captain of the *Casco*, 353, 354, 355–56, 357; and the decayed wood of the mast, 361–63; and his impressions of RLS, 353

Our Lady of the Snows (Trappist monastery): RLS's visit to, 181–82

Pacific islands: foreign powers competing for control of, 382, 426–31; map of, 356. See also Polynesian islands; Samoa

Pacific sailing adventure: on the *Casco*, 350, 351–52; diverse experiences among the family members, 365; hardships experienced during, 380–81; hazards encountered during, 356–57; and landfall at Nukuhiva, 358–59; RLS on his love of the sea, 357. See also *Casco*; Hawaii/Hawaiian islands; Nukuhiva; Tahiti and Tautira; Upolu

Pall Mall Gazette: publication of "The Body Snatcher" in, 239–40

"Pan's Pipes" (essay), 152–53

Paris, France: Louis's experiences in, 143–44

"Pastoral" (essay), 54

Paul, Saint, 105, 106; on dualism, 311, 312–13

"Pavilion on the Links, The" (short story), 207, 212, 238

Pentland Rising (Scottish rebellion), 57, 58

Pentland Rising, The: A Page of History, 1666 (nonfiction), 58–59

Pepys, Samuel: RLS's essay about a portrait of, 146–47

Peri, Camille: *A Wilder Shore: The Romantic Odyssey of Fanny and Robert Louis Stevenson*, 9

"Plague Cellar, The" (fiction fragment), 56

Planestones Close, 89–90

"Plea for Gas Lamps, A" (essay), 33

Poe, Edgar Allan, 72

Polynesian islands: unsavory whites encountered on, 379. See also Apemama; Butaritari; Gilbert Islands; Hawaii/Hawaiian Islands; Samoa

Pope Hennessy, James, 8, 188; on Louis's voyage to California, 194; on tensions between Fanny and Belle, 433

"Popular Authors" (essay), 194–95

Prince Otto (novel), 297, 418; dedication to Nellie Sanchez, 275; Henry James on, 275–76; reviews of, 275–76; and serialization in *Longman's Magazine*, 274–75

Proust, Marcel: *Combray*, 36; *Le temps retrouvé*, 3; on RLS, 3

Psalm 23, 27, 135

Psalm 47, 26

Psalm 121, 218

"Quiet Waters By, The" (prose poem), 135

Quiller-Couch, Arthur, 451

Raeburn, Henry: RLS's essay on, 448
Rankin, Nicholas, 8, 64, 172, 191, 358, 457
Rearden, Timothy: Fanny Osbourne's correspondence with, 166–67, 170, 171
Reid, Denis: as captain of the *Equator*, 373
religion: RLS's struggles relating to, 98–102, 121. *See also* King James Bible
"Requiem" (poem): inscribed on RLS's tomb, 465
Revelation, Book of: RLS's early exposure to, 25
Richter, Jean Paul, 305
ritual cannibalism: as no longer practiced in Samoa, 403
Robert Louis Stevenson Silverado Museum, 9
Robert Louis Stevenson State Park (California), 224
Robertson, William, 243
"Robin and Ben: or, The Pirate and the Apothecary" (poem, in collaboration with Lloyd), 259–60; RLS's woodcuts as illustration for, 260, 261
Roch, Valentine, 272, 282, 327: RLS on her departure, 338
Rosebery, Lord, 426, 474
Rossetti, Dante Gabriel: *The House of Life*, 299
Roughing It (Twain), 334
Rousseau, Jean-Jacques, 153, 173
Ruedi, Karl, 337; as RLS's physician in Davos, 229–30, 268, 328

sailing adventures. *See* Pacific sailing adventure
Saint-Gaudens, Augustus: medallion of Stevenson created by, 333–34, 474
St. Giles Church (Edinburgh): bas-relief of Stevenson displayed in, 334, 474
St. Ives (unfinished novel), 336, 416, 451, 454
Saintsbury, George, 185

Samoa: Fanny and RLS in, 227, 272; RLS as "clan chieftain" in, 398–401, 409–10; and fighting among rival chiefs, 430–32; "Great Powers" competing for control of, 424–25, 428–29; language of, 423; missionaries in, 422–23; RLS as "Storyteller" in, 5, 404; RLS as supporter of Samoan independence, 424–29; RLS's insights regarding the people of, 436; Samoan names given to members of the Stevenson family, 404; and the Treaty of Berlin, 424. *See also* Apia, Upolu; Upolu; Vailima estate
Sanchez, Adulfo: Nellie Van de Grift's marriage to, 204
Sanchez, Louis, 204
Sanchez, Nellie Van de Grift, 471; *Prince Otto* dedicated to, 275
Sand, George: *Consuelo*, 112–13; *Le Marquis de Villemer*, 175
Sandison, Alan: *Robert Louis Stevenson and the Appearance of Modernism*, 296
Sandwich Islands (Hawaii): RLS's opinion of, 366
San Francisco, California: earthquake in, 209; Fanny's move to, 470; RLS's description of, 200, 208–9; RLS's move to, 208–10; RLS's poem about, 210; Stock Exchange in, 210
Saranac Lake, New York: frigid weather in, 338–39; Stevenson family's home there, 337–38; RLS's memories of, 338; RLS's novels written at, 342
Sargent, John Singer: portrait of Henry James by, 292, 293; portrait of Frank O'Meara by, 167–68; portrait of RLS and Fanny by, 284–86, 291
Satan's Invisible World Discovered, 240
Saunders, George, 4, 264
Savile Club: RLS as member of, 118, 119, 128

Schröder, Fred, 354
Scots Observer: RLS's poem published in, 384–85
Scott, Walter, 59, 79, 248, 318; and Abbotsford estate, 406; *The Heart of Midlothian*, 241; and RLS's description of Scott's last days, 443; *Rob Roy*, 319; *Waverley*, 83
Scott, William Anderson, 216
Scottish Highlands/Highlanders: clans of, 316–18; as distinguished from the Lowlands, 316–18; RLS's identification with, 319; as the setting for *Kidnapped*, 315–16
Scottish Thistle Club (Honolulu): RLS's talk at, 463
Scribner's Magazine: Fanny's short story published in, 347; RLS's essay published in, 332
Sénancourt, Étienne de: *Obermann*, 72
Shakespeare, William: *Hamlet*, 100, 272; *Macbeth*, 65, 121; *Twelfth Night*, 96; *A Winter's Tale*, 73, 130
Shankman, Paul: *The Trashing of Margaret Mead*, 436
Sharpe-Weseman, Adrienne, 9
Shelley, Jane, 289
Shelley, Sir Percy, 283, 289
Shelley, Percy Bysshe, 289
Sherman, William Tecumseh: RLS's impression of, 335
Silver, Long John. *See* Long John Silver
Silverado Squatters, The (memoir), 218–24, 267, 297; frontispiece for, 220, 221
Silverado, California: RLS and Fanny in, 218–24
Simele, Henry, 398
Simi (household steward at Vailima), 403
Simoneau, Jules, 205–7, 210, 271, 464
Simoneau, Martina, 205
Simpson, Eve, 57, 84, 85, 168; on Fanny Osbourne, 159–60, 166; on RLS's appearance and mannerisms, 93–94

Simpson, Habbie, 302
Simpson, James Young, 77
Simpson, Walter, 73, 75, 77, 166, 227, 385; *Art of Golf*, 84–85; portrait of, 147–48; as RLS's traveling companion, 147–50, 154–55
Simpson, Willie, 156
Sinclair, Upton, 335
Singer, Jefferson, 8, 172; on David and Alan (in *Kidnapped*) representing aspects of Stevenson, 322; on Fanny and Louis's relationship, 161
Sitwell, Albert, 109
Sitwell, Bertie, 109, 234–35
Sitwell, Frances, 7, 161; as Colvin's companion, 109–10, 115, 118, 120, 122, 131, 169; and concerns about RLS's health, 122; and Fanny Osbourne, 170; and her son's treatment in Davos, 234–35; and marriage to Colvin, 474; RLS's admiration and affection for, 112–18, 120; on RLS's apology to a servant, 227; RLS's correspondence with, 109, 122, 123–24, 125, 129–30, 139–41, 149, 247, 381–82, 442–43
Skelt's Juvenile Drama: RLS's essay on, 36–37
Skerryvore (the Stevensons' home in Bournemouth): description of, 279–80; drawing of, 281; destruction of, 330; Fanny and RLS's stay there, 280–82; RLS's health while there, 280, 286; RLS's parents at, 288; selling of, 392; the Stevensons' final departure from, 329–30; servants at, 329–30; visitors to, 287, 288–91
Skerryvore Lighthouse, 62, 279
Slocum, Joshua: and encounter with Fanny, 470; *Sailing Alone around the World*, 470
Smith, Janet Adam, ed.: *Collected Poems* (of RLS), 10, 78
Smith, Jessie Wilcox: as illustrator of *A Child's Garden of Verses*, 31–32, 33

Smout, T. C., 316–18
socialism: RLS's interest in, 80, 91
"Something in It" (unpublished fable), 423–24
"Song of Rahéro, The: A Legend of Tahiti" (poem), 420
Songs of Travel (collection of poems), 437
Sontag, Susan: *Illness as Metaphor*, 228–29, 230
Southey, Robert, 60
"Spaewife, The" (poem), 302
Speculative Society, 456; RLS as member of, 78–80, 463
Spencer, Herbert, 99, 190
Spenser, Edmund: *The Faerie Queene*, 200, 258
Sport (dog), 338
Stephen, Leslie, 114, 118, 135, 142; as publisher of RLS's essays and stories, 132, 188, 212, 242–43
Steuart, J. A.: *Robert Louis Stevenson: Man and Writer*, 86
Stevenson, Alan (uncle), 230; breakdown experienced by, 49, 105; as lighthouse builder, 61, 62, 279; at Skerryvore, 288
Stevenson, David (uncle), 43, 61
Stevenson, Fanny Osbourne, 1, 62, 255; as art student, 157, 164, 165; as beneficiary of RLS's estate, 470; and the breach between Henley and RLS, 345–49; as co-author of *More New Arabian Nights* with RLS, 299–300; in Davos with RLS, 230; death of, 471; and departure for America, 327; descriptions of, 159–60, 161, 165, 166, 287, 438; and divorce from Sam Osbourne, 203, 208; family background of, 161–62, 163; and Edward Field, 471; and first husband's infidelities, 164, 171; and first meeting with Thomas Stevenson, 170–71; funeral procession for, 472; health concerns experienced by, 230–31, 272–73; independence of, 163; and Henry James, 292, 295–96; on the *Janet Nicholl*, 389, 390, 391–92; literary acumen of, 161; and land purchased on Samoa, 383–84; and love of gardening, 162; and Margaret Stevenson, 223–24, 226; and marriage to RLS, 8–9, 168–69, 203, 214, 216–18, 340; and marriage to Sam Osbourne, 163–64; in Monterey, 201; "The Nixie" (short story), 347; and the origin of *Jekyll and Hyde*, 305–7; in Paris with RLS, 169; photographs of, 159, 160, 217, 283; and portrait of RLS, 168; on Queen Victoria, 247; reflections on RLS, 2, 166; on RLS's appearance, 284; as RLS's caregiver, 273, 278, 287; as RLS's "critic," 218, 291, 306–7, 417; RLS's description of, 440; RLS's feelings for, 117, 168–69, 174, 180–81, 437; RLS's first encounter with, 158–59, 165; on RLS's improving health, 372; at Saranac Lake, 338, 339; and seagoing adventure, 350; sense of humor of, 161; serious illness experienced by, 439–42; in Silverado, 220; sketch of, 214, 215; and tensions with Belle, 433; as torn between RLS and Sam, 187–88; and visits to Skerryvore, 288; and warm reception by RLS's parents, 225–26
Stevenson, Katharine (cousin), 41–42, 101. *See also* Mattos, Katharine Stevenson de
Stevenson, Margaret Balfour (mother), 12, 63, 102; *The Amateur Emigrant* dedicated to, 196; "Baby Book" kept by, 15, 85, 140–41, 258–59; Cummy's opinion of, 29; death of, 470; and departure for America, 329; and disagreements with RLS, 122; Fanny's note to, 280; health problems of, 18, 42, 44, 68; and her husband's illness, 327–28; on meeting Fanny, 225; on the native people of the Pacific, 360;

on her son's appearance, 94–95; photographs of, 13, 17; on poem by Henley, 138; and return to Edinburgh, 436–37; and RLS's crisis of faith, 101; RLS's description of, 12–13; on RLS's last day, 462; and the Stevensons' seagoing adventures, 350, 353–54, 365; on St. Swithin's day, 240; at Vailima, 398, 402, 403; and visits to Skerryvore, 288

Stevenson, Robert (grandfather), 12, 61

Stevenson, Robert Alan Mowbray (Bob) (cousin), 49–50, 73, 81, 115, 131, 278, 385; and Belle Osbourne, 167, 204; as beneficiary of RLS's estate, 469–70; and the breach between Henley and RLS, 349; as conversationalist, 74; foretelling RLS's future, 168; in Grez with RLS, 156, 157, 166, 167; in Paris, 143, 144; portrait of, 157, 158; RLS's bond with, 74–75, 122–23; and RLS's comment on J. S. Bach, 282; and RLS's crisis of faith, 101; and RLS's depair as expressed in a letter, 444; and RLS's sailing to America, 331; as scholar and professor, 473; at Skerryvore, 288–89; and war games with RLS, 288–89

Stevenson, Robert Louis: on Abraham and Isaac, 103–4; as actor, 95–96; admirers of, 3–4; allowance allotted to, 88–89, 141; appearance of, 15, 19–20, 211, 332; and awareness of death, 272, 273; ballads attempted by, 420–21; on being a writer, 5–6; on the benefits of walking, 173–74; biographers of, 3, 7–9; birth certificate of, 16; birthday celebration for, 461; birth of, 11; as book reviewer, 134; in Bournemouth, England, 279–96; and breach with Henley, 344–49; breakdown experienced by, 123–25; breathing problems experienced by, 1, 122, 207–8, 227, 229, 278, 286, 328; in California, 201; on cannibalism as practiced by Pacific islanders, 359–60; as celebrity in New York City, 332; childhood home of, 15, 19; on Christianity and sex, 276; and collaboration on poems with Lloyd, 259–60; collected letters of, 6–7; *Collected Poems*, 10, 420; and Sidney Colvin, 111–12, 116–20, 122, 131, 132, 133–34, 146, 174, 184, 385; and concerns about Fanny's illness, 440–41; on conversation, 74; as craftsman and narrator, 4; crisis of faith experienced by, 98–102; and Cummy's stories of sin and damnation, 23–28, 98; in Davos, for medical treatment, 228, 229–32, 233–34, 256, 257; death and burial of, 1, 68, 462–66; death as preoccupation of, 453–54; and decision to go to California, 189; dental problems experienced by, 215–16; and departure for America, 327, 329–30; depression experienced by, 78, 99–100, 105, 124–25, 286, 288, 442–44, 462; as described by Fanny, 438–39; "Desiderata" as expressed by, 107, 108; and difficulty with spelling, 42; and dislike of engineering, 81; diving experience of, 64–65; early education of, 38–40; early fiction by, 41, 184–86; early publications of, 132–34; early travels of, 42–45; editions of works by, 9–10; and efforts to mend the breach with Henley, 385–86; on evolution, 99, 308; eye infection suffered by, 169–70; and Fanny's departure for California (1878), 171–72; Fanny's description of, 438–39; female characters created by, 266; on fiction, 37; and financial challenges in Samoa, 436–37; as financial support for his extended family, 372, 418; and first meeting with Fanny, 157–59, 166; and

Stevenson, Robert Louis (*continued*)
the flageolet (musical instrument), 414–15; friends gathered for goodbyes as the family left for America (1887), 330; Gosse's impressions of, 289; in Grez-sur-Loing, 156–57, 171; health problems experienced by, 1–2, 18–19, 107, 117, 201, 203, 207–8, 211, 212–13, 227, 228, 236–37, 238, 255, 270–72, 278, 280, 286, 297–98, 328–29, 340–41; honeymooning in California, 218–24; imaginative life of, at an early age, 35–37; impressions of, in Edinburgh, 93–95; improving financial circumstances of, 332; influences on, 11–12, 25, 26–27; as instructor of other writers, 290–91; and interest in soldiers and warfare, 258–59; and Henry James, 291–96; journey on foot in France, 178–81; known as "Storyteller" by the Samoans, 5, 404; as a law student, 81, 82, 83; as a lawyer, 139–42; as letter writer, 6–7; and lifelong friendships formed at university, 73–81; on lighthouses as the family business, 6, 81, 280–82, 445; on marriage, 256; and marriage to Fanny, 8–9, 168–69, 203, 214, 216–18, 256–57, 277; on the meditative state, 153; as member of the Savile Club, 118; in Menton, France, 43, 122–27, 131; and money problems in London, 228, 236–37; in Monterey, 205–7; multiple editions of his writings published after his death, 469–70; in New York City, 332–36; nightmares experienced by, 21; and nostalgia for Scotland, 444–45, 454; parasite affecting, 286; periods of slumps in his work, 268; on the pessimism of his family, 15; photographs of, 2, 9, 17, 20, 23, 140, 284, 339, 369, 377, 415, 425; and playwriting venture proposed by Henley, 303–4; pleasures enjoyed by, 83, 84, 282; on the pleasures of the piano, 282; poem for Fanny by, 269–70; poem about one of his professors, 69; popularity of, 5–6; prose poems by, 134–35; on prostitution, 91–92; and provision for his heirs in his will, 469–70; recollections and reflections on, 466–68; and reflections on death, 465–66; reflections on friendships enjoyed by, 385–86; and the religious indoctrination he received as a child, 23–28; reminiscences of, 91–92, 357; on the rocky coast of Scotland, 64; romantic interests of, 85–88; sailing adventure proposed by, 349–50; Samoan chiefs' gratitude to, 431–32; at Saranac Lake, 337–42; Sargent's portrait of, 284–86; on the "sedulous ape," 72; serious illness experienced by, 212–13; as self-critical, 194–95; self-education of, 71–72; short stories by, 185–86; and Frances Sitwell, 109–10, 112–18, 120, 123–24, 125, 129–30; as a skater, 83–84; as a smoker, 78, 286, 342; state park named for, 224; as a storyteller, 2–6; telephones as regarded by, 366; and tensions with his father, 102–6; in Torquay, 42–43; and uncertainty about Fanny's situation in California, 187–88; as voracious reader, 56–58, 71–73; and war games with Lloyd, 258–59; on working men, 194; writers admired by, 72–73; on writing, 3–4. *See also* Pacific sailing adventure; Samoa; Vailima estate; *and titles of specific works by Stevenson*

Stevenson, Thomas (father), 12, 59, 182; and concerns about RLS's future, 81, 190, 196; death of, 327–28; dementia evidenced by, 327–28; descriptions of, 13–15; Fanny's affection for, 225–26; financial support provided by, 215–16,

227; and first meeting with Fanny Osbourne, 170–71; as inspiration for episode in *Treasure Island*, 251–52; as lighthouse builder, 61, 62–63, 65–66, 279; moodiness of, 14–15; and ongoing tensions with RLS, 102–6; response of, to news of RLS's marriage to Fanny, 214–15; and tensions relating to RLS's crisis of faith, 99–102, 121; photographs of, 14, 20, 23; as storyteller, 35–36; on *Travels with a Donkey*, 184; and *Treasure Island*, 249, 251–52; views of, on conventional education, 39–40

Stevenson family: as characterized by the Samoan staff, 404; Samoan names bestowed upon, 403–5; tensions among the members of, 433–36. *See also names of individual family members*

Stevenson family business, 6, 81. *See also* Wick, Scotland

Stevenson's letters: Mehew's annotation of, 7; publication of, 6–7

Stewart, Alan Breck (character in *Kidnapped*): description of, 322–23

Stieglitz, Alfred, 190

Stirling Castle, 315

Stoddard, Charles Warren, 210, 233; *The Lepers of Molokai*, 369; on RLS's Pacific sailing adventure, 355; *Summer Cruising in the South Seas*, 211

"Story of a Lie, The" (short story), 196, 198

Strachey, Lytton, 289

Strange Case of Dr. Jekyll and Mr. Hyde (novel), 3, 34, 104, 161, 297, 315, 418, 468; dedicated to Katharine de Mattos, 346–47; duality as theme in, 311, 312–13; Fanny's suggestion regarding, 306–7; movie versions of, 310; narrators of, 308; origin of, 306; plot of, 307–12; publication of, 312; popularity of, 312–13; RLS's assessment of, 313; sexuality as aspect of, 311; as stage play, 314

streptomycin, 340

Strong, Austin, 161, 339, 365; accomplishments of, 473; on Fanny's joy at RLS's birthday celebration, 461; death of, 473; on the first dinner with Fanny and RLS at Heriot Row, 226; on his grandmother, Fanny, 471; as playwright, 473; RLS's relationship with, 433–35; *Seventh Heaven*, 473

Strong, Belle: as beneficiary of RLS's estate, 470; and burial of her mother's ashes next to RLS, 471; and Cocky the cockatoo, 408–9; death of, 473; and divorce from Joe, 433; Fanny's jealousy of, 433; and growing affection for RLS, 416; and marriage to Edward Field, 471; *Packing Provisions for Vailima* (photo), 409–10; RLS's impressions of, in Sydney, 387–88; on RLS's last moments, 462–63; RLS's writing and correspondence as dictated to, 411, 417, 433; and separation from Joe, 372; and tensions with Fanny, 433; *This Life I've Loved* (memoir), 409; at Vailima, 398, 403, 408–9; welcoming her family to Honolulu, 365–66. *See also* Osbourne, Belle

Strong, Hervey, 366

Strong, Joe, 210, 280, 339, 373; as alcoholic, 372, 373, 387; as artist, 365–66; Belle's divorce from, 435; and Faauma, 405; and frontispiece for *The Silverado Squatters*, 220; and marriage to Belle, 204, 220; RLS's impressions of, in Sydney, 387–88; RLS's view of, 220; at Vailima, 398, 403; welcoming the Stevenson family to Honolulu, 365–66

Stuart, Charles Edward: rebellion led by, 318

"Summer Night, A" (prose poem), 135

Swanston Cottage, 68, 134; RLS's vacations at, 52–55, 56–57
Swearingen, Roger, 7; *Prose Writings of Robert Louis Stevenson*, 5
Swift, Jonathan, 444
Sydney, Australia: RLS and Fanny in, 387–88; RLS as a celebrity in, 388; RLS's health problems recurring in, 388
Symonds, John Addington: in Davos, 232; on *Jekyll and Hyde*, 310–11; *A Problem in Greek Ethics*, 233; *Renaissance in Italy*, 232; and RLS, 232–33; and RLS's remarks on Dostoevsky, 298–99; sonnets by, 289

Tahiti and Tautira (village): the Stevenson family's stay in, 360–64; RLS's illness in, 361
"Talk and Talkers" (essay), 74, 93, 138–39, 147, 232; Henley as "Burley" in, 267
Talolo (cook at Vailima), 398, 403; photograph of, 399
Taylor, Ida, 330
telephones: invention of, 218–19; RLS's distaste for, 366
Tem Bauro, 377
Tembinok (king of Apemama), 376–79; RLS's friendship with, 378–79
Tennyson, Alfred, Lord: "Ode on the Death of the Duke of Wellington," 259
Thackeray, William Makepeace: *Vanity Fair*, 202
Thomson, Robert, 40, 42
Thomson's school: RLS as student at, 40–41, 42
Thoreau, Henry David: RLS's essay on, 207
Thorneycroft, Hamo, 289
"Thrawn Janet" (short story), 186, 240–43, 267, 309; publication of, 243
"To Any Reader" (poem), 33–34

"To Charles Baxter" (poem), 302
Todd, John, 54–55
Tomasi (assistant cook at Vailima), 403
"To My Name Child" (poem), 204
"To My Old Comrades" (poem), 384–85
"To the Stormy Petrel" (poem for Fanny), 227
Trappist Monastery: RLS's visit to, 181–82
Travels with a Donkey in the Cévennes (memoir), 173–78, 183–84, 196, 242; and the Camisards' uprising, 182–83; and dedication to Colvin, 174; descriptions of weather in, 179–80; feelings for Fanny expressed in, 180–81; frontispiece of, 176; "A Night among the Pines," 180; reviews of, 183–84
Treasure Island (novel), 3, 4, 29, 36, 55, 84, 186, 233, 245, 315, 319, 418, 468; as adventure story, 254; as Bildungsroman, 262; characters in, 299; critics' comments regarding, 253; and dedication to Lloyd, 266; Henry James on, 36; Jim as narrator of, 249–52, 262–65; Long John Silver character in, 136, 248, 251, 252–53, 262–63; map of, 267; narrative tension in, 263–64; "The Persons of the Tale," 263; plot of, 262–66; review of, 5; RLS's account of beginning the writing of, 336; RLS's payment for, 266; RLS's reading aloud from the manuscript of, 253; serialization of, 255, 261–62; Thomas Stevenson's enthusiasm for, 249; the writing of, 35, 235, 248–54, 255
Treaty of Berlin: and imperialistic ambitions, 424
Treglown, Jeremy, ed.: *The Lantern-Bearers* (RLS's essays), 10
Trousseau, George, 439
Trudeau, Edward Livingston: as head of the sanatorium at Saranac Lake, 337, 340; photograph of, 341; and research

on tuberculosis, 340–41; as RLS's physician, 340
"Truth of Intercourse" (essay), 103, 172
tuberculosis: diagnosis of, 340; RLS affected by, 340–41
Turner, J. M. W., 52, 61
Tusitala ("Storyteller"): as RLS's name in Samoa, 5, 404
Twain, Mark: on RLS, 2; RLS as described by, 334–35; RLS's meeting with, 334; *Roughing It*, 163; on Virginia City, 163–64

Underwoods (collection of poems), 273, 297, 300–301, 346; Henry James on, 301
United States: RLS's growing popularity in, 270
University of Edinburgh: friendships formed at, 73; RLS's essay on, 68–69; RLS as student at, 68–70
Upolu (Samoan island): Henry Adams's visit to, 397; description of, 381; land purchased on, 383–84; and RLS as honorary chieftain on, 409–10; Stevenson family's arrival on, 381–82; plantations on, 407; Vailima estate built on, 392–96. *See also* Vailima estate

Vailima estate: book collection at, 416; building of, 393–96; Cocky the cockatoo at, 408–9; colors used in design of, 395–96; and communal prayers on Sundays, 405–6; description of the interior of, 393; domestic animals on, 408; extended family at, 398, 404–5; and Fanny's hopes of turning it into a plantation, 406–8; Fanny's management of, 407–8; financial pressure on RLS at, 417–18; impact of, on RLS's well-being, 396; photographs of, 394, 395, 396; as protected from local fighting, 430–31;

and road built by grateful chiefs, 431–32; RLS's correspondence from, 411–14; RLS's description of the sounds heard at, 392–93; RLS's outdoor work at, 407–8; RLS's writing habits at, 414; sale of, 470; socializing at, 409–11; staff at, 398–403; as Stevenson museum, 470; uninvited visitors at, 410–11
Van Amburg, Gabrielle, 9
Van de Grift, Esther, 162
Van de Grift, Jacob, 162, 188
Van de Grift, Nellie, 162, 166, 201, 338, 339; on Fanny's life before marriage to RLS, 218; and marriage to Adulfo Sanchez, 204; and nephew Austin's joining her household, 434, 435; *Prince Otto* dedicated to, 275; on RLS's reading aloud, 214
Van Gogh, Vincent, 144
Velázquez, Diego: cousin Bob as admirer of, 143
"Victor Hugo's Romances" (essay), 133
Victoria, Queen, 22, 247–48
Viles, Edward: *Black Bess*, 41–42
Virginia City, Nevada, 163–64
Virginibus Puerisque (collection of essays), 242, 267
"Voice from Home, A" (poem), 379–80, 385–86

Wallin, Charles, 354
Weir of Hermiston (unfinished novel), 5, 73, 81, 86, 233, 421, 454–55; Belle's comment on, 457; dedication to Fanny in, 459; the father-son relationship in, 560; plot of, 455–59; as RLS's last work, 460
Wharton, Edith, 270
"When the Devil Was Well" (novella), 114–15
Whitman, Walt, 80, 173; "I Sing the Body Electric," 88; *Leaves of Grass*, 72, 88; "Song of the Open Road," 72

Wick, Scotland: breakwater project at, 63, 67, 102
Wilde, Oscar, 110, 332; *The Importance of Being Earnest*, 267
Wilkinson, Norman, 33
Williams, Dora, 214, 218, 353; as beneficiary of RLS's estate, 470; and Fanny's account of meeting RLS's parents, 226; Fanny's correspondence with, 247, 280; sketch of Fanny by, 215
Williams, Virgil, 214, 218, 353
Willis, Laulii, 471
Wilson, John: "Isle of Palms," 358
"Windy Nights" (poem), 393–94
Wister, Owen: *The Virginian*, 295
Wodehouse, P. G., 419
Woggs (Skye terrier), 227, 258; death of, 291
Wolseley, Viscount, 259
Woolf, Virginia: *To the Lighthouse*, 132
Wordsworth, William, 153, 183; as influence on other writers, 174; "Intimations of Immortality," 444

World Economic Forum, 228
Wrecker, The (novella), 210, 389, 420, 451; reviews of, 420
"Wrecker, The" (short story), 41
Wright, Martha Bertha: "Bohemian Days," 165–66
Wrong Box, The (novel, with Lloyd Osbourne), 342–43; reviews of, 343
Wyeth, Andrew, 324
Wyeth, N. C., 251, 324

Yeats, William Butler, 302
Young Chevalier, The (unfinished novel), 451
Young Folks: *The Black Arrow* serialized in, 273–74; *Kidnapped* serialized in, 326; *Treasure Island* serialized in, 261, 266

Zechariah, Book of, 44
"Zero's Tale of the Explosive Bomb" (short story), 300